THE COMMON LAW
TRADITION

THE COMMON LAW TRADITION

Deciding Appeals

BY

KARL N. LLEWELLYN

Professor of Law, University of Chicago

LEGAL LEGENDS SERIES

QUID PRO BOOKS

New Orleans, Louisiana

Previously published in 1960 by Little, Brown and Company, Boston and Toronto.

Published in 2016 by Quid Pro Books. This is an unabridged republication of the original work, part of the *Legal Legends Series*, in a new library-quality hardcover printing.

ISBN 978-1-61027-792-1 (hbk.)
ISBN 978-1-61027-301-5 (pbk.)

QUID PRO BOOKS
5860 Citrus Blvd.
Suite D-101
New Orleans, Louisiana 70123
www.quidprobooks.com

qp

Publisher's Cataloging in Publication

Llewellyn, Karl N. (Karl Nickerson), 1893-1962.
    The common law tradition : deciding appeals / Karl N. Llewellyn.
        p.   cm. — (Legal legends)
    Reprint. Originally published: Boston and Toronto: Little, Brown and Company, 1960.
    Includes bibliographical references and index.
    Includes 2015 Foreword.
    ISBN 978-1-61027-792-1 (hbk., 2016); 978-1-61027-301-5 (pbk., 2015)
1. Appellate procedure — United States. 2. Stare decisis — United States. 3. Judicial process — United States. 4. Appellate courts — United States. I. Title. II. Series.
KF9050 .L58 2016

Also available in high-quality eBook formats, 2015, from Quid Pro Books.

To
the undying succession of the
Great Commercial Judges
whose work across the centuries has given
living body, toughness and inspiration
to the Grand Tradition of the Common Law

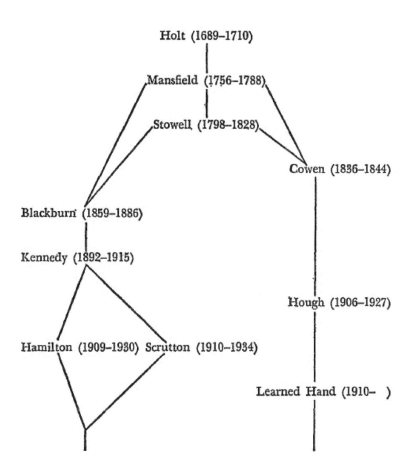

Holt (1689–1710)

Mansfield (1756–1788)

Stowell (1798–1828)

Cowen (1836–1844)

Blackburn (1859–1886)

Kennedy (1892–1915)

Hough (1906–1927)

Hamilton (1909–1930) Scrutton (1910–1934)

Learned Hand (1910–)

CONTENTS

[Page numbers in brackets above reference the original pagination of the previous printed editions, retained in this republication for continuity in citations and the convenience of the reader. The original page numbers are embedded into the text by the use of brackets. See "Detailed Contents," to follow, for breakdown on sections and further use of the original pagination. (Cross-references in notes also refer to the original page numbers.) Numbers to the right, above, refer to *new* pagination found at the bottom of pages in this *Legal Legends* edition.]

DETAILED CONTENTS
FROM THE ORIGINAL BOOK

Page numbers shown below are of the original pagination from earlier printings, retained here for continuity and citation purposes. Internal cross-references also use this pagination. These numbers are embedded into text in brackets. Footnotes appear as section endnotes, but otherwise the original structure is retained. For current pagination, see the Contents page.

PART II
The Style of Reason at Work

FOREWORD

Karl Nickerson Llewellyn was a legal legend in every way. This book was in many ways the culmination of his famous and sometimes controversial jurisprudential inquiries into the nature of law and judicial decision-making. It was a subject that he explored for decades as a leader of legal realism, as a contracts professor and scholar, as a law-making drafter of universal commercial codes, and as an influential professor of law at Columbia University and, in his later years, at the University of Chicago. His influences continue today, not the least in how he framed the judicial inquiry throughout the pages of this book.

New students of law have, through generation after generation, been introduced to the precision and mastery of the law and judicial thinking through the classic primer *The Bramble Bush*.[1] Like this book, Llewellyn's *The Bramble Bush* also contains the author's musings in poetry and verse (found here in song, at pp. 399-400). And he lectured like a poet, as reflected in his majestic and sometimes difficult writing style. The effort it may take to understand his challenging thoughts is, as with good poetry, worth the expenditure. The reader is rewarded with an understanding and depth of analysis that simply does not exist from reading more simplified prose. Yet the ultimate thoughts he shares are not obscured by any false pretenses about law and the way judges think. Llewellyn's goal seems to be to strip it of the obscuration offered in legal formalism, the pretense of judicial magical thinking. Ultimately the project Llewellyn proposed was a straightforward one, if not a simple one. It explored the very nature of law and rules.[2]

When he published this book in 1960, Llewellyn was apparently offering it to the broader audience of judicial thinking and not some cloistered specialists. It was a grand and pervasive common law tradition he described, not a secret society of legal masons. The book was accessible in every way. So it is a strange reality today that access to this book is limited to rare and pricey used copies or to finding old library copies. It really is a foundational text of American legal thought which ought to be accessible again to any reader who wants it. And so we determined to make it available in ebook and a paperback version in a way that did not exist before. We hope that project helps the modern reader rediscover this classic work and find it easily available the world over. With that goal in mind, it is presented to the modern reader in this format and with this modern presentation. Nonetheless, to promote continuity of referencing and citation, we have retained the original printing's pagination by inserting the page numbers into the text by the use of brackets; the index and all cross-references, too, use this original pagination. Every effort was made to allow it to be presented in this modern form, and particularly in standard and searchable digital formats, yet all while respecting its tradition of law and judicial decision-making — a tradition highlighted in the title itself. This book and edition is located, then, within the new tradition of modern print and ebook formats, while maintaining a call back to the past reflected in this enduring work.

STEVEN ALAN CHILDRESS
Conrad Meyer III Professor of Law
Tulane University Law School

New Orleans, Louisiana
May, 2015

Notes to the Foreword

1 Karl Llewellyn, *The Bramble Bush: On Our Law and Its Study* (2d ed. 1960), reprinted with new foreword by Stewart Macaulay in 2012, by Quid Pro Books.

2 See also Karl Llewellyn, *The Theory of Rules* (2011), edited and with new foreword by Frederick Schauer in 2011, by the University of Chicago Press.

THE COMMON LAW
TRADITION

THE WHY AND WHAT OF THIS BOOK

{page 3 in original}

This book starts with the fact that the bar is bothered about our appellate courts — not the much discussed Supreme Court alone, but our appellate courts in general. The bar is so much bothered about these courts that we face a crisis in confidence which packs danger. Of course, ever since lawyers began to lawyer, there have been losing counsel aplenty who have so believed in their causes that they have bitterly blamed the court. And, of course, ever since issues in court have had political flavor, i.e., roughly since before Genesis, each new crucial decision has been, for some vocal citizens, the brink of perdition. And of course ever since men began to generalize, the particular decisions of the day or week have been enough to make many see the whole system as in decay. And of course and as usual, "never in history" has there been a crisis to match today's crisis. Despite all this, the bar *is* bothered these days with a bother which has a new corrosiveness. For all the old worries centered on things which at least left to a man his pride in himself and his craftsmanship, and his skill to fight and fight back with, though he might be overpowered. The evil used to lie in results basically political: the ravening demagogues were taking over, or the vested exploiters were too deeply entrenched; or else the ring or the syndicate or the racketeers had spread their tentacles; or, perhaps, some particular court (contrary to the manner of our courts at large) was corrupt. And a man equipped with the skills of craftsmanship and a high heart may suffer, and may have to suffer it out, but he can fight; and a healthy body will in time cast out corruption; and in this country political monsters, however gruesome, seem to have a limited span of life.

But today the worry has a novel corrosiveness. In most it no longer inspires healthy fighting reaction to effect its cure; for most it has come to lay a pall and palsy on heart and hand because it goes to whether there is any reckonability in the work of our appellate courts, any real stability of footing for the lawyer, be it in appellate litigation or in counseling, whether therefore there is any effective craftsmanship for him to bring to bear to *{page 4}* serve his client and to justify his being. A right man cannot be a man and feel himself a trickster or a charlatan. It is the appellate court, it is particularly the highest court in any given hierarchy, which is the organ and even more importantly the symbol of reckonable recognition and reward for decent careful craftsmanship in law. It is that court — those courts — in whom as persons, but also and no less importantly in whose ways of work, and finally further and again no less vitally, in whose general run of results, the man at the bar must have *confidence* on pain of feeling his own sustaining faith in his craft, in his craftsmanship, in his very office and utility as a lawyer, to ooze and seep away from him until he stands naked and hollow, helpless and worthless, a nithing, or a medicine man who has discovered his medicine to be a cheat.

You cannot listen to the dirges of lawyers about the death of *stare decisis* (of the nature of which lovely institution the dirge-chanters have little inkling) without realizing that one great group at the bar are close to losing their faith. You cannot listen to the cynicism about the appellate courts that is stock conversation of the semi- or moderately successful lawyer in his middle years without

3

realizing that his success transmutes into gall even as it comes to him. You cannot watch generations of law students assume, two thirds of them, as of course and despite all your effort, that *if* the outcome of an appeal is not fore-doomed in logic it *therefore* is the product of uncontrolled will which is as good as wayward, without realizing that our machinery for communicating the facts of life about the work of our central and vital symbol of The Law: the appellate courts, has become frighteningly deficient.

For the fact is that the work of our appellate courts all over the country is reckonable. It is reckonable first, and on a relative scale, far beyond what any sane man has any business expecting from a machinery devoted to settling disputes self-selected for their toughness. It is reckonable second, and on an absolute scale, quite sufficiently for skilled craftsmen to make usable and valuable judgments about likelihoods, and quite sufficiently to render the handling of an appeal a fitting subject for effective and satisfying craftsmanship.

It is in the contrast between these joyous facts and the therefore needless but truly perilous crisis in confidence that the book takes its start.

We shall set a background by examining fourteen clusters of factors which have grown or been built into our system in an effort {5} to render the deciding done by our appellate courts more reckonable and stable than is the deciding done in most other phases of American life on most other types of fighting issue. Only after the horse-sense assurance, thus gained, that we ought to expect some reckonability to flow from such machinery, shall we settle down to detail.

We shall then examine the technical tools for prediction and stability which are commonly discussed or assumed in talk about precedent, or about *stare decisis,* or about courts' use and application of authorities in general, and we shall see that the range for *different* kinds of action which is open to an appellate court while it "stands" on "the things decided" is a vast range, and that the most careful "standing" is therefore not only over the long haul, but continuously, daily, a process of creative choice and of reshaping doctrine and result.

We shall observe, however, that the huge unnoticed or forgotten or ignored *correct* range for action *which our American system has afforded to our appellate courts from the beginnings of the nation* in no way produces an undue unreckonability of results. We shall see that the most vital element in reckona-bility and stability is the courts' constant use, in application of doctrine, and also in choosing among the branching doctrinal possibilities, of the best sense and wisdom it can muster — but always in terms of those same traditions of the work which we have seen as "steadying factors." We shall demonstrate that sense is thus used not occasionally but constantly, not in great cases only but in the mine-run of cases as well; and we shall demonstrate also that sense and wisdom are thus used daily not only in application of doctrine or in choice among competing rules but in an area by no means so frequently observed, to wit, in the on-going, careful readjustment of doctrine to needs by way of overt recourse to the sense which ought to control in the given type-situation. We shall show that this is not novel, but is old, is not occasional, but is standard, is not unsettling, but is stabilizing.

It is, in fact, the manner of appellate judicial work which prevailed in this country from Jefferson's administration up roughly until Grant's. Pound has called it the manner of "our classic period"; I call it our Grand Style. Its very existence has been obscured and buried by the incursion later of a way of work in which the appellate judges *sought* to do their deciding without reference to much except the rules, *sought* to eliminate the impact of sense, as an intrusion, and *sought* to write their opinions as if wisdom (in contrast to logic) were hardly a decent attribute {6} of a responsible appellate court. I call that way of work the Formal Style; its image is with us still, distorting the common perception both of what our appellate courts are doing and of what they ought to do. The prevalence still of that unhappy image is indeed the major cause of the crisis in confidence.

But we shall demonstrate that that image is a false picture of what our appellate courts are doing today. We shall demonstrate also that today's opinions, on their face, give excellent indication of what kinds of sense and views of sense are at work, when any particular court sets about its high task of so applying and so reshaping doctrine as to marry its duty to justice with its duty to the rules of law as it has received them. And the argument will be that there results both an ongoing and vitally needed improvement of our law and a way of reckoning the forthcoming results which is not only that now used by the ablest and most successful appellate and drafting counsel, but is also available to any lawyer of ordinary intelligence, and which offers to any lawyer who will open his eyes an understanding of what *stare decisis* in our system really is and a resulting solid comfort and confidence as he turns again to his responsible and needed work.

A feature of the book which is unique and which goes to the essence is that demonstrations will be undertaken not on cases carefully selected to convenience, nor yet on cases of high importance, nor on cases of particular subject matter, but on mine-run stuff as it comes unselected from the mine: the cases in sequence as they stand in the reports, often enough the cases of a single opinion-day. *Illustrations* are indeed selected, for discussion; sometimes from sequences, sometimes from my general reading, again and again from the samplings of the current work in fifteen supreme courts. But the *demonstrations* which clinch the vital points are done on stuff from the daily grist which is like your tomorrow's case and mine.

A further unique feature is that the book is addressed, throughout, not to the long and the large, the comforting sweep of the decades, but to the *individual* case, such as you or I will be handling on Thursday next. Reckonabilities *there,* not "statistical" or "historical" reckonabilities, are in question. For it is a significant degree of reckonability *in the individual case* which the bar demands, and which the lay public expects, as a condition of its confidence. This is an inhuman demand to make on human machinery. The very reason that appellate courts exist is that there is doubt, that skilled men do not agree about the outcome. To require reckonability is therefore to require the absurdly impossible. {7} Nevertheless, let it be repeated: this amazing institution, our Law, answers in significant degree to the demand. That fact is vital. It needs knowing. It also needs use.

It has seemed appropriate, in consequence, to put into words a few of the more elementary conclusions about the sound handling of appellate argument which flow from this way of seeing the work of the appellate courts; the lesson of our law is that the general gains bite from the particular application.

The discussion turns then, at some length, to the work of the appellate courts themselves, with some canvass of suggestions which the manner of their best and most effective doing offers for articulate and standard guidance at all times, if they are to complete their recapture of our Grand Style.

Finally, from this perspective, the present debate about the Supreme Court of the United States takes on a useful cross-lighting. And a few other applications of the general thesis are explored — for instance, to the mean problem of form-contracts.

The general lines of the study are thus as simple as the main proportions of, say, a Greek temple or an early Gothic cathedral, and are as easy to take in without sweat. I have endeavored, however, to write carefully and with attention to detail; and I suggest that for all the simplicity and pervasiveness of the general scheme, the book's significance is far from exhausted when that scheme is seen. I have long been an admirer of Gothic sculpture and of Gothic glass — of the subpart that, within a whole, must yet have its independent lesser but whole unity and beauty. Such is, in my belief, the proper way of work in jurisprudence, too; and to that end also the book has been devoted.

PART I

Deciding Appeals

THE PROBLEM AND THE WORRY

When the psychologists began to look into how people go about reaching decisions, the question they were concerned with was: how do people get to a decision at all, to any decision, when faced with a problem-situation out of life? Roughly, they arrived at the conclusion that if it was a true problem-situation, i.e., if it was really a puzzler, then it was seldom that the actual deciding was done by way of formal and accurate deduction in the manner of formal logic. The common process was rather one either of sudden intuition — a leap to some result that eased the tension; or else it was one of successive mental experiments as imagination developed and passed in review various possibilities until one or more turned up which had appeal. In any ordinary case a reasoned justification for the result represented a subsequent job, testing the decision against experience and against acceptability, buttressing it and making it persuasive to self and others.

*   *   *

Today all of this is so familiar and obvious as to bore, but there were reasons why, four or five decades ago, it shocked our legal world. The ingrained practice of that time was to write an appellate opinion as if the conclusion had followed of necessity from the authorities at hand and as if it had been the only possible correct conclusion. Accept those premises, and a "well-reasoned" opinion not only shows why the decision is wise and right, but would also show the *process* by which the decision was arrived at. Men liked that. A "well-reasoned decision" had meant a reasoned and rational deciding. Now these psychologists were insisting that that was not so at all — except of course by accident or on very occasional occasion. It is not hard to see why they, along with those men of law who adopted and adapted their insight, looked challenging, seemed like attackers and destroyers.

Then the logicians moved in to the support of these iconoclasts. The logicians pointed out that to deduce anything you needed a {12} major premise, single and solid; but they or their legal pupils pointed out that in our legal system we have large numbers of mutually inconsistent major premises available for choice: "competing" rules, "competing" principles, "competing" analogies; and they pointed out that cases which raise true problems are likely to lie in those open areas which are the very arenas of such competition. Not content with this, they went on to insist that before a rule or principle can be used for deduction about any case in the border zone, it must be given a clean-staked outside edge; and that insofar as the rule has not taken on a frozen verbal form, the way the court happens to catch it into words may make all the difference in the case in hand; whereas even when the verbal form is already frozen, there still remains the problem of classifying the facts of the case, and wherever the problem is a real life-problem, that classification is in turn a job of fresh creation which has to be done before a true deduction becomes possible. Thus in any ordinary case worth both appealing and defending — i.e., in any case presenting an honest arguable issue — the opinion, however well reasoned, must either express the doubt, the choice, and the creation, or else fail to show the actual process of deciding.

Worse and more terrifying, all of this seemed to force to the fore the fact that a certain cherished principle did not, does not, and cannot hold true in life: "This is a government of laws *and not* of men"; "It is the law, not the court, the judge, that decides the case."[1]

These things were enough to jolt a tradition-oriented profession many of whose leaders were still caught in the belief that law did not change, unless by legislation. Three further matters were added by accident.

(1) In 1920, as a result of James Harvey Robinson's *Mind in the Making,* a Freudian interpretation of judicial opinions broke upon the little world of legal scholarship: an opinion was seen as not at all a reasoned justification; it was instead a "mere rationalization," a term which for fifteen years or more meant (i) false, (ii) tricky, and (iii) a cover for the nastiest imaginable hidden motives, with carte blanche to anybody to fill in without evidence.

(2) As a second matter, the truth was that much of our law, and our Constitutional law most importantly, had gotten pretty {13} badly out of touch with an industrial age and with the almost frenzied financial exploitation of such an age during the roaring '20's. This meant that the "forward-looking" scholar (who was most likely to be abreast of the thinking in the neighboring disciplines) found grist aplenty in the current product of the appellate courts to disapprove and to "show up" as being by no means inherent in the scheme of our law. There thus began to develop in several law schools a baleful line of reading, thinking, and teaching in terms of "They can decide any way they want to, and they do, and then they write it up to suit; and the opinion tells you nothing." The exciting thing in this connection is that in spite of all such talk a powerful current of sound inquiry also set in, which fell into no such error, which, though in full recognition of leeways for decision and of the importance of the man in office, yet felt and took careful account of the fact that there was heavy reckonability of and for decision, and moved then in sustained, though groping, fashion into analysis and study of various possible factors which might be at work to produce that reckonability. Cardozo's path-breaking lectures of 1921 (with three follow-ups through 1931);[2] Pound's admirable series of papers in 1923;[3] Nelles' stirring individual case studies;[4] Dickinson's series in 1930-1931;[5] my own sustained studies of case law and of Sales doctrine, its growth and its use, from 1928 on;[6] Hamilton's beautiful mimeographed material which traced the growth of industrial and public utility accident law in Pennsylvania, his essays on the {14} appellate judicial craft, and his general paper on The Judicial Process;[7] Powell's studies of the Supreme Court;[8] John R. Commons' powerful study of steadiness, *Legal Foundations of Capitalism* (1924) — these and the like were building into a rounded body of theory buttressed here and there by test-studies of theoretical significance.[9] Indeed, packed into Hamilton's sensitive and rounded general paper — which, far transcending any other presentation before or since, has not to my knowledge been cited a single time in the literature, much less used — packed into that is a whole working theory, expressed with a beauty even Hamilton never elsewhere equaled.

(3) Unhappily, Bentley's publication of 1908, *The Process of Government,* had set the example of going unheeded. The entire body of writers passed it by.[10] With Bentley as a foundation, the development ought by 1932 to have achieved at least the level of the present study. Instead, a third accident threw the whole emerging line of inquiry off-center. That accident was the advent of the New Deal. Jurisprudence promptly became a football of politics, study of the courts' processes of deciding was suddenly taken as an attack on decency of the court's

operation, issues were distorted, energies were wasted, continuity was destroyed.[11] {15}

One looks around, after war and foreign danger have sweated some of this
silliness out of us, and sees a vastly different scene. No longer does the Supreme
Court sit in a holy of holies which no respectable lawyer may profane by criticism or even honest inquiry. No longer is the established bar convinced that laws
"*and not*" judges are doing the deciding of cases. No longer is "certainty" in the
outcome of appellate cases an idol too sacred for binoculars. The danger lies now
in altogether different quarters. "You never can tell on what peg an appellate
court will hang its hat." "The Supreme Court is going to hell." "What has become
of the doctrine of precedent?" "What we need is to get back to *stare decisis*." The
danger today is that an older generation of the bar may be losing all confidence
in the steadiness of the courts in their work. That is bad. The danger today is
that the middle and younger generation of the bar may have already lost all
confidence in the steadiness of both the courts in their work and in the law in its.
That is worse. The danger today is indeed that the courts themselves may by
tomorrow have lost their own feeling for and responsibility to continuity. That
would be worst.

* * *

Meantime, the logicians have helped us further almost exactly not at all.
What they gave us in the first quarter of the century has been mildly supple-
mented by semantics — which has in the main been of small aid in this area. For
the rest, they have left us on our own. The psychologists, during this last decade,
have made advances in learning and communication theory and in motivation
research which seem to me to have real promise for our problem, but the
applications to our work do not seem to me, as yet, to carry beyond what can be
reached out of our own materials and experience by way of skilled horse sense.

Neither is this to be wondered at. For the inquiry across the border is still
primarily into how men find *some* answer to a problem-situation, followed then
by inquiry into what are lines of wise procedure in approaching a problem-
situation (especially one involving policy); and more recently moving into
questions of how *groups* arrive at some decision ("small-group behavior"
studies). Whereas our problem is vastly harder, so much harder as to belong
almost to a different universe of thought. The lawyer does not ask: How does an
appellate tribunal arrive at *a* decision, *some* decision, *any* decision — in general,
as an approximative pattern, in perhaps three, even four or seven, cases out of
{16} ten? The lawyer asks, instead: How does *this* appellate tribunal arrive at *the
particular and concrete answer* which it reaches *in the particular and concrete*
case?

I know of no man in the social disciplines who would dare to ask such a question. But the lawyer wants to know in order that he *may apply the knowledge in
advance to a particular concrete tribunal in the next* SPECIFIC *appeal* with which
he will be concerned. In the present state of the other social disciplines or of
behavioral science at large — so far as published work goes — this would be a
dream-inquiry. It would be fantastic.

The astounding thing is that in our own discipline, all unnoticed, very real
progress has been made toward not only intuiting, but documenting, some very
useful leads indeed.

* * *

One begins by observation of the really extraordinary body of institutions
and techniques we have built and which we use daily to focus the deciding and

then to guide it. It pays to set out some of these with a bit more care than is customary, and it pays to set out beside them some of the deficiencies or counterdrives which we are not always mindful to consider when we do get to talk or to serious thought about the situation. I shall run through fourteen factors, or better, clusters of factors, which bear with much regularity on the way in which appellate cases get decided, and which combine to produce a significant steadiness in the work of a court; a steadiness amounting, I shall argue, to a significant *and most neglected* degree of predictability of outcome *case by case*. It is of course vital that the factual impact of these clusters of factors be discussed as a factual matter, undisturbed by any question of whether you or I ought to be approving or indorsing or applauding whatever it may be that is going on. I shall therefore attempt to limit text — all through this immediate discussion — to simple observation and description. But these are matters which involve value-judgments as well, value-judgments both about objectives and, when one approves one or another objective, value-judgments about measures; and I wish neither to disregard those aspects nor to leave undisclosed any biases which may, despite precautions, be slithering in to slant either the observation or the presentation. The text will therefore be accompanied from time to time by a footnote devoted to the value side.

Excursus on "Certainty," "Predictability," "Reckonability"

There has been so much cross-purposing in discussion of "certainty in the law" that any writer needs to clarify his use of the term or idea. First, then, I am dealing throughout *this particular study* with predictability of the outcome in life of one particular phase of litigation, to wit, *appeals*. Second, in dealing with any aspect of life which is relevant to the great-institution of Law-Government, I reject as useless and misleading the dichotomy which infected so much writing of the '20's and '30's: absolute or 100 per cent certainty versus anything else at all as being "*un*certainty." I see no absolute certainty of outcome in any aspect of legal life, and think that no man should ever have imagined that any such thing could be, or could be worth serious consideration. Instead I see degrees of lessening uncertainty of outcome ranging from what to the observer or participant seems pure chance, into a situation where a skilled, experienced guess (though only a guess) is yet a better bet than the guess of the ignorant, through a situation where the odds run plainly a little one way, through one where skilled counsel can be expected to materially increase the odds, and on through the situation which is a business gamble or better into the one which is for human living "safe." The lines or clusters of factors here under discussion are lines which, properly taken into consideration, push reckonability, including reckonability of the outcome of a *particular appeal,* materially further than is available without such consideration.

The next thing which needs note is that certainty of outcome means different things according to the base line of judgment. Here is a counseling situation, with existing "law" phrased somewhat unfavorably, although malleable; with the flavor good, the operating personnel informed and careful, clear written records feasible to make, the prospective favorable witnesses capable and dignified, and trends of the times mobilizable to serve the flavor; and the operation is on a sufficient scale to permit settlement of badly unfavorable cases, should they occur. Nevertheless, if the reckoning is from original *lay action* to the legal result on eventual appeal in an eventual lawsuit arising out of such action, that whole picture must be discounted as still subject to skewing or scuttling by the uncontrollable possible early appearance in some unhappy forum of a parallel situation botched by some other outfit in the doing and by ninnies in the litigating. If the base line of reckoning {18} is, in contrast, from a dispute already ripening for litigation, then documents, witnesses, prospective testimony, prospective forum, counsel, and even opposing counsel are all growing definite; yet even so, who is not familiar with the accidents of trial and the vagaries of the trier or triers of fact?[11a] Our institution of law-government would be highly satisfactory, as a human device, if at this stage it could commonly offer, on the scale of "certainty" of outcome, a reckonability equivalent to that of a good business risk. Surely, however, we should be able to hope for that level of reckonability by the time one reaches the stage under primary discussion in this study, where, with the trial over, with the record and the technical points for possible appeal frozen, a lawyer turns to sizing up the advisability, as a legal venture, of pressing an appeal.

MAJOR STEADYING FACTORS IN OUR
APPELLATE COURTS

{19}
In appellate judicial deciding we have, materially steadying the activity and its results, at least those lines of factor which follow. The most important one I shall at this stage merely mention, leaving it then for fuller discussion to the last: All the persons who do the deciding do so as officers holding office in a tradition long known, clearly felt, and proud: the American appellate judicial tradition. But consider this whole sequence of other relatively stable and strongly stabilizing factors:

(1) Law-conditioned Officials

(2) Legal Doctrine

(3) Known Doctrinal Techniques

(4) Responsibility for Justice

(5) The Tradition of One Single Right Answer

(6) An Opinion of the Court

(7) A Frozen Record from Below

(8) Issues Limited, Sharpened, Phrased

(9) Adversary Argument by Counsel

(10) Group Decision

(11) Judicial Security and Honesty

(12) A Known Bench

(13) The General Period-Style and Its Promise

(14) Professional Judicial Office

These we shall look over one by one.

1. Law-conditioned Officials

(a) The personnel are all trained and in the main rather experienced lawyers. Few judges "make" the American appellate bench without twenty and more years of active work in some aspect of the law, in addition to their schooling. The judges are therefore not mere Americans. They have been law-conditioned. They *see* things, they see *significances,* both through law-spectacles, in terms of torts and trusts and corporations and due process and motions {20} to dismiss; and this is the way they sort and size up any welter of facts. Moreover, they *think* like lawyers, not like laymen; and more particularly like *American* lawyers, not like German lawyers or Brazilian lawyers. Cases have authority, dictum can be and is to be marked off from holding, strict "system" is unfamiliar and uncomfortable, "freedom" is an underlying drumbeat and slogan that informs not merely life but law.

(b) *Per contra,* the American schooling or training for the law varies from apprenticeship or even in occasional cases correspondence school on through to leading universities; the active "work" can have varied from that of the rounded small-town man to tight specialization in the metropolis, it can be primarily that of trial lawyer, office lawyer, government official, law teacher, or what have you. It can be that of the civic leader, that of the political hack, that of the lion of justice or that of designing Maginot lines for vested privilege, that of a prophet, of a crusader, of a pussy-footer, or of a purblind routineer. Mostly, it has been a bit-better-than-average work, done with a bit-better-than-average conscience, done with at least some contact with at least some one variety of ordinary guy; but there are so many and so divergent varieties of ordinary guy. Moreover, and particularly, in this country any preliminary work or training of the appellate judge has no need at all to be in any aspect of office as a *judge*.[12]

2. Legal Doctrine

(a) It is understood and accepted that the context for seeing and discussing the question to be decided is to be set by and in a body of legal doctrine; and that where there is no real room for doubt, that body is to control the deciding; that where there is real room for doubt, that body of doctrine is nonetheless to guide the deciding; and that even when there is deep trouble, the deciding should strive to remain moderately consonant with the language and also with the spirit of some part of that body of doctrine.

That body, of course, includes not merely the very elaborate body of recorded directions which we know as rules of law, whether gathered and phrased in unchanging rigor (e.g., statutes) or scattered and loosely phrased in case law style. The body includes also the accepted lines of organizing and seeing these materials: concepts, "fields" of law with their differential importance, pervading principles, living ideals, tendencies, constellations, tone. {21}

(b) *Per contra,* in any case at all decently handled below and also worth appealing, either interpretation of language or the sizing up of the facts, or the choice open as among available divergent premises or tendencies in our multi-wayed legal scheme, or the like, will allow a fair technical case to be made either way or a third or fourth other way, *if one looks at the authorities taken alone.*

3. Known Doctrinal Techniques

(a) It is understood and accepted that the doctrinal materials are properly to be worked with only by way of a limited number of recognized correct techniques. Among these techniques many are phrased, taught, and conscious; many are rarely phrased or *taught,* but are still to be viewed as known and conscious and *learned;* many are felt and are used in standard fashion, but are learned and indeed used almost without consciousness of the users as they use them. There can hardly be a better illustration of this "almost without consciousness" phase than the course I took in Constitutional Law under the then ex-President Taft. He used Wambaugh's *Cases.* He had said to the Dean (T. W. Swan) that he had never in his life worked so hard as, the first time he taught it, the preparation of that casebook made him work. In my year he used his handwritten series of hard-board covered student-type notebooks.

He knew nothing of case teaching. Someone would be asked to state the case. Taft would correct the statement as needed — which closed the "discussion." Then — and he sold the class (including me, may the Lord forgive me) the idea that this was only for interest, for anecdote — there would be five to fifteen minutes from Taft, the man of politics; Taft, the student of governmental history; Taft, the student of life and man; Taft, who both from inside and from out had seen political arena, the bench, and all varieties of executive office.

Whether this came out of the notebook,[13] we never knew; but Taft imparted to us by his manner his own clear feeling that it was no part of "the law" or, really, of "the course." Thus — almost the only piece which is still with me — "And I said to Holmes: 'But do you think it was right or fair to leave *that* fact out of consideration?' And," continued Taft with the mountainous chuckle, "he said, 'I'm sorry; I didn't read that far in the record.'" {22}

Such phenomena spell a man who *felt* the bearing of all the "background" and "human" and "situation" factors, and felt also deep value in communicating them, but whose conscious and doctrinal thinking saw them nevertheless as "outside" — "collateral," like a pre-Sales Act "express warranty" to the "sale."

The matter is clinched by Taft's treatment of doctrine itself. From time to time, instead of just giving an illustration or two of what the court's *announced* rule covered, he would produce an intellectual scalpel and slice the court's phrased ruling down into an almost nothing. You then got, with another half-ton chuckle: "Mr. Justice Zilch sometimes let enthusiasm run away with him!"

Now I had a good brain and no sense, and this scalpel technique was as exciting to the one as it was uninhibited by the other. I started volunteering applications of it to opinions *which Taft had never had professional reason to distinguish*. Such admiring misuse of his technique — its use not in a situation already crammed with intuitive search for the needed and "right" answer, but in a bald wondering, exploratory way — such use, which to me was that of a disciple, seemed to him that of a boor and a blasphemer. He complained to the Dean: he did not want to be subjected to half-grown children in the law "*criticizing* the Supreme Court of the United States." Note the term. *Un-called-for* analysis, *mere* analysis, however accurate, meant *adverse* criticism. It verged on the indecent.

That accidental phrasing voiced the attitude of two or three generations of careful legal craftsmen. For when, *for a pressing professional reason,* you search in the formal tradition for "the true rule," the stuff simply lines up, and *you* have almost nothing to do with lining it up except "to make it clear." On that, all your industry, intellect, and skill may indeed be needed. But you do not need to be conscious at all of how you are dealing with, shaping, and selecting among, the many pre-existing doctrinal *possibilities*.

(b) *Per contra,* the known and felt correct techniques for use of the authoritative materials contain huge correct leeways to produce variant results, and contain almost no explicit guidance for work with or within the leeways. But of course we must not get the idea that an absence of explicit guidance means an absence of guidance, or that the actual use of the leeways can be at all depicted by a canvass of the huge range of the leeways which are available. Appellate judges feel and work within what I like to call *The Law of Leeways,* which we shall examine in some detail below (pp. 219 ff.). In essence, in regard to the use or treatment of authorities, that law is that the degree of need dictates the degree and {23} manner in which it is really correct and proper to exploit the formally available correct and proper techniques for handling authorities. Overruling, sharp shift in direction, striking extension, for instance — these demand a truly pressing need. And disregard of the law of leeways is felt as unjudicial.[14]

4. *Responsibility for Justice*

(a) There exists, and guides and shapes the deciding, an ingrained deep-felt need, duty, and responsibility for bringing out a result which is just. It is not to the point that this is only semi-articulate {24} in the "legal" phase of the tradition. One sees it unmistakably in the net behavior of the men.

(b) *Per contra,* re the matter of steadiness,

(i) the drive for justice may run somewhat or utterly at odds with the pressures set up by legal doctrine; with results which diverge by tempera-ment, by occasion, by epoch, and which vary frequently because of the relative skill of counsel, and sometimes (I believe) because of matters which so far as our present powers of analysis reach are accident; and also

(ii) the meaning of "justice" either for the particular case or for the rele-vant type of problem-situation is commonly both intangible and language-baffling and can also vary vastly from judge to judge or court to court. But common accepted phrasings of principle, common accepted spectacles of concept to see with, to arrange with, and to judge by, common attitudes toward those goals present more in intuition or tradition or battle-stir than in phrased clarity — these can lessen variances.[15]

5. One Single Right Answer

The deciding is done under an ideology which in older days amounted to a faith that there is and can be only one single right answer. This underlies such ideas as "finding the law" and "the true" rule, and "the" just decision. I refer not merely to a manner of writing the opinion but to a frame of thought and to an emotional attitude in the labor of bringing forth a decision. Even judges who know with their minds that varying answers would be legally permissible will be found with a strong urge to feel that one alone among them must be *the* right one.

There is here no suggestion that there cannot be found in fact one answer or several answers which are better, much better, in contrast to others which are worse. Commonly, even under the straitness imposed by pleadings and by the points of appeal, I think one can dig out a number of answers any one of which has some worth and would be better than its contrary; it is precisely for that {25} reason, and because "the better is the enemy of the good," that an atmosphere or climate of thinking that *the* right answer must be single can acquire its effect on the process of deciding.

That climate seems to me to be still a fact and a condition of much current American appellate judging. Whether it adds to over-all reckonability of the results, I can form no clear opinion. My suspicion is that in the less troubling case it does (but at too high a price), by discouraging inquiry into available alternatives. It tends, along with pressure of work and human avoidance of sweat, to encourage taking the first seemingly workable road which offers, thus giving the more familiar an edge up on the more wise. But where the case is really puzzling (which most un-"foredoomed" cases[16] are) my suspicion is that this approach throws the ultimate decision into materially greater chanciness than does the tougher inquiry into which of the known permissible possibilities seems the probable best, and why.[17] {26}

6. An Opinion of the Court

(a) The deciding is, in the main, done under felt pressure or even compulsion to follow up with a published "opinion" which tells any interested person what the cause is and why the decision — under the authorities — is right, and perhaps why it is wise.

This opinion is addressed also to the losing party and counsel in an effort to make them feel at least that they have had a fair break — a matter of importance to the polity and the law, and often enough (as is suggested by long Per Curiams in some touchy cases) of political importance also re a judge's re-election. The "single *right* answer" idea still has some tendency to dominate the form of the opinion, and the need for an opinion, often enough the opinion itself, often casts its shadow before, into the process of the actual deciding.

In our law the opinion has in addition a central forward-looking function which reaches far beyond the cause in hand: the opinion has as one if not its major office to show how like cases are properly to be decided in the future. This also frequently casts its shadow before, and affects the deciding of the cause in hand. (If I cannot give a reason I should be willing to stand to, I must shrink from the very result which otherwise seems good.) Thus the opinion serves as a steadying factor which aids reckonability. Its preparation affords not only back-check and cross-check on any contemplated decision by way of continuity with the law to date but provides also a due measure of caution by way of contemplation of effects ahead.

More: the effort is to make this opinion an opinion of the court, a group expression, at the worst one which will command adherence of the group. This, like the process of consultation and vote, goes some distance to smooth the unevenness of individual temper and training into a moving average more predictable than the decisions of diverse single judges.

In another fashion the dissent and its possibility press toward reckonability of result. Mention has been made of "the law of leeways"; but it is a law without immediate sanction for breach. In real measure, if breach threatens, the dissent, by forcing or suggesting full publicity, rides herd on the majority, and helps to keep constant the due observance of that law. {27}

(b) *Per contra,* the very fact that the opinion has varied functions makes it possible to play up one to the neglect of another. In particular even the legitimate leeways[18] available in the use of authority are so great as to make it possible for an opinion to obscure or completely cover from any but the few experts in a field the doctrinal novelty of a decision which *on the pure doctrine* as it has stood to date would be surprising. Save in the very rare case of dishonesty, however, my feeling is that such surprise affects chiefly persons who have not yet awakened to the power — and value — of the quest-for-justice factor discussed above under 4.

Much more important is the growing tendency of our busiest courts to substitute in many cases memoranda or mere announcements of result for the old-style full opinion. However sound this approach to an overloaded calendar, it does remove from the particular case one of the most compelling pressures toward steadiness. Nevertheless, when wisely administered, such removal can prove immaterial. For today's misunderstanding by most of the bar of the actual (and useful) nature of our precedent-system and of the way in which our appellate courts in fact go about their work — that misunderstanding leads to a plethora of footless appeals whose outcome is so predictable as to need no steadying effect of an opinion.[19] {28}

7. A Frozen Record from Below

The fact material which the appellate judicial tribunal has official liberty to consider in making its decision is largely walled in. It includes the transcript of what happened at the trial, and it includes common knowledge about things in general. It includes also (as if it were common knowledge) a sometimes startling selection from what the court sees in the kaleidoscope of life outside. But no new facts about the particular case are supposed to disturb, distract, or change the picture. More: if the jury or the judge at trial has decided on conflicting evidence, the court on appeal is supposed to abdicate its own judgment on the matter if any man could in reason reach the result the trial tribunal did reach.

(b) *Per contra*, this rule, though it regularly controls official discussion and also enlists sustained effort on the part of appellate judges, is yet colored in operation by the appellate court's duty to justice and by its experienced "feel" for what may lie, unspoken, underneath the record.[20] {29}

8. Issues Limited, Sharpened, and Phrased in Advance

(a) The ultimate matter (Do we affirm? Do we reverse? Do we modify?) and the mediate matters (What do we do about Assignments of Error Numbers 1, 2, 3, etc.?) which come before the appellate judicial court to be decided are each an issue already drawn, drawn by lawyers, drawn against the background of legal doctrine and procedure, and drawn largely in frozen, printed words. This tends powerfully both to focus and to limit discussion, thinking, and lines of deciding. And a choice between two alternatives is vastly more predictable than one among a welter. Betting on a football game is risky, but not as risky as betting on a steeplechase.

(b) *Per contra*, an appellate court in quest of justice can do (and often has done) more reformulating of ill-drawn issues than is generally realized even by lawyers, and in most jurisdictions modern procedure furthers operation along this line. Nevertheless, such action, on the large scale (like any such severe revamping of the authorities as has been discussed under 3(b), p. 22), is both relatively rare and a function of peculiarly sharp pressure from felt need. A law of leeways operates here not as a compulsion of tradition, decency, and wisdom, but as a compulsion of inertia from the pressure of work and from the effort needed to redo a job from the ground up. Moreover, especially in jurisdictions not addicted to rehearings, the bench is likely to share the feeling of the bar that there is something unfair in putting a decision on a ground which losing counsel has had no opportunity to meet.[21]

9. Adversary Argument by Counsel

(a) The American appellate judicial tribunal moves into its deciding only after argument by trained counsel — argument always written and mostly oral as well. If the explicit issue-drawing directs, narrows, sharpens the deciding process; if limitation of available {30} "fact"-material by the trial record renders the deciding an operation bounded and semitraceable, and insofar more reckonable and testable, by way of its fact-foundation; then the regime of argument renders the deciding also a process oriented partly from without by analysis, by arrangement of data, and by persuasion: oriented, however, not by judicially-minded helpful consultants but by adversaries to each of whom the tribunal serves either as an obstacle or as a tool, or, more commonly, as both at once. If counsel are skillful and reasonably in balance, I see argument as greatly furthering predictability by finding and pointing the significant issues, by gathering and focusing the crucial authorities, making the fact-picture clear and vivid, illumining the probable consequences of the divergent decisions contended for, and by phrasing with power the most appealing of the divers possible solving rules.

Moreover, and not to be forgotten, the *adversary* bar goes far to insure that the court shall be confronted with and pressed by the authorities, reinforcing that factor of continuity and reckonability which legal doctrine affords. Maitland — than whom our law has never had a shrewder observer — urged that our system of precedent itself drives far less from the bench than, once the courts had taken up a fixed site at Westminster, from the sergeants who would not let the bench forget what they had done before. Seldom indeed does it not pay at least one adversary to marshal and deploy "established law."

(b) Nevertheless, my guess is that under current American conditions argument by counsel cuts reckonability down much more often than not, if you figure in terms of the formed record, the given authorities, and the court, without yet seeing the respective briefs or even knowing who the respective counsel will be. There are two main reasons for this guess. First, every one of the many law professor friends who have mounted the bench tells me that the general run of briefs which has come before his court — with of course many gratifying exceptions — seems to him barely and scrapingly passable, or else inadequate or worse. And running through records from various other courts, in an effort to find good moot court material, has led me over the years to amazement and some dismay at the frequency with which the relevant briefs miss or obscure telling points, choose foreseeably losing ground, or mismanage promising positions. But any poor handling of argument sets up roadblocks for the court as they read and feel their way into the record, and chanciness of outcome is of necessity increased by any increased difficulty in seeing and setting things straight — whether on the "law" side or on the side of what the {31} essential fact-picture is or on the side of what is a fair and wise result to strive for in either the general situation or the particular case. Secondly, skill of counsel, where found on one side only, terrifyingly weights the scales of judgment. We have some sections of the country and some lines of practice in which skills tend to be mostly pretty much in balance; but in the appellate field my belief is that imbalance shows, over the country, a materially higher percentage than in the trial court. In any event, unequal skill throws off all prediction which has as its base line merely the completed trial, and be it remembered that the American bar, especially in the larger cities, is uneven beyond easy visualization.[22]

10. Group Decision

(a) It is trite that a group all of whom take full part is likely to produce a net view with wider perspective and fewer extremes than can an individual; and it is a fair proposition also that continuity is likely to be greater with a group: prior action, attitudes, and unrecorded doubts or reservations which an individual can later easily overlook are likely to be recalled and revived by some other group member. The American appellate court, moreover, is guarded against one price too commonly attending the commitment of deciding to a group: the price of total inaction or indefinite postponement. The medieval day is gone in which decision could be refused; and even in the rather rare cases when the potato is hot or the court can find no answer which at all satisfies, {32} a group decision does finally emerge. One recalls also that the drive for a written group opinion — with some members intent upon the past and typically some members concerned about the future — tends also to stabilization and to a consequent rise in reckonability in the deciding process itself.

(b) *Per contra*, there have been courts in which one man completely dominated the whole group. One thinks of Mansfield, or of the years during which Hughes' "dead-list" determined without more which certioraris would not be heard. And there have been courts whose way of work so heavily stresses the judge to whom the case has been assigned that case after case goes by without real participation by most of the group. Add to this a possible discretionary assignment by the chief, and a five-to-nine-man court can function in spots as if it had only one or two judges. One thinks also of courts whose practice has been to be so delicate about pride of authorship that drafts of opinions are almost regularly approved without comment. Put all of these possibilities together and the reckonability-effects of having a bench would pale. But vanish they would not.[23]

11. Judicial Security and Honesty

(a) Not only can the decision of the highest appellate tribunal in any case not be upset, but appellate judge and appellate court are given institutional guaranty against repercussions or retaliations because some person or persons may dislike the decision or find it wrong. It will not do, because we are used to this, to take it for granted, or to overlook the degree to which it makes for reckonability by eliminating the incidence of fear or hope or secret favor. If (as in medieval times) a tribunal can be penalized for "wrong judgment," a factor of fear enters which increases chanciness of outcome. If a boss will fine, fire, exile, or kill for a vote or judgment which annoys him, but may reward the willing, then in any case in which his interest is not obvious, one big weight in the scales may drop blind until one knows the whether and the which-way of the fix. England's lesson under the Stuarts, and then under the Hanovers, ran indeed less to such uncertainty in lesser cases than to altogether too much certainty when the Crown was openly {33} on one side, but we have seen enough in modern Europe to know that judicial servility produces not only injustice but a day-to-day unreckonability.

The immunity of court and judge from attack because of their judgments has the by-product of greater reckonability of those judgments chiefly, I think, because it presses the major factors which motivate decision so largely into the open, paralleling in this our institutional discouragement of presents, loans, and extra-mural solicitations from persons who do not happen to be in disciplinary position. I speak of a "by-product" because judicial independence, tenure for life or the term, the law and tradition against turning away after lucre and taking bribes or favors, are of course all aimed in first instance not against unreckonability but against the sin of the sons of Samuel: the perversion of judgment. But the very fact that not every threat, gift, or promise "works" (one remembers Pepys' pride in *not* being influenced in his award of contracts by the expected gift) points up the way in which a regime of offerings or hopes peppers the pot with extra *uncertainty.*

(b) Enough has been said to dispose of any idea that political control might add to reckonability *in general* because in one single and obvious class of cases a bossed court can be pretty well counted on to lickspittle the boss. Such lesser influences as our own current conditions sometimes show, say, of re-elections ahead, or of intermediate judges' ambitions, or of yen in the occasional notorious case for popularity or prestige, or of felt need to over-steel oneself against such a yen, and all such matters more, are too minor in quantitative incidence to affect seriously our general picture; indeed, where present at all, they tend to be plain enough in the situation and in the known character of the man to be somewhat taken into account in advance. The contrast would be to a regime of recall of judges by election, or to their removal by the dictator, or to the "displeasure" of a ramrod commanding officer when the subordinate member of his military tribunal has no hope at all of getting out from under. It is a contrast.[24] {34}

12. A Known Bench

(a) The court before which the cause is to come has issued opinions which do more than lay down "law" on particular points; they also and especially cumulate to show ways of looking at things, ways of sizing things up, ways of handling authorities, attitudes in one area of life-conflict and another. Over a five-year, indeed over a one-year, stretch these facets of the opinions furnish a revealing and appealing study which no appellate lawyer can afford to do without. For one must not forget that a particular bench tends strongly to develop a characteristic going tradition not only of ways of work but of outlook, and of working attitudes of one judge toward another. New judges get broken in to all of this; each normally adjusts largely to the harness which the going tradition seeks to fit upon him. Of course the tradition changes. Occasionally, it can change with relative speed. Thus a Cardozo joining the New York Court of Appeals, a Schaefer joining the Illinois Supreme Court, can be felt within a year or two,[25] and though with strong men beside them can within a few years have strong impact upon the tradition; but even this is a process which leaves its marks upon the published record, so that the going tradition of the moment, {35} though in transition, can be somewhat known and to a greater degree felt.

This is not all: those strange and beautiful institutions, the signed opinion and the recorded vote,[26] allow particular study of the judges one by one — a fact long familiar and practiced on with regard to the Supreme Court of the United States but neglected in disheartening fashion by all but the best of our appellate bar in regard to most other courts.[27]

(b) *Per contra*, there are situations (some suggested above at p. 32) where part of the bench's personnel dominate the deciding and where it may be impossible to know in advance which of the personnel will move into the driver's seat. Some courts commonly sit in divisions whose personnel, tone, and tendencies are far from identical; some, like the Circuit Courts of Appeal, sit in benches not even permanent, but reshuffled continually. There are new arrivals on the bench, sometimes completely unknowable; at long intervals, a whole batch at a time. And in some States short terms and a practice of rotating the office among the bar cuts down on the bar's experience with the man-as-a-judge as contrasted with the man-as-a-man; the two are related, but they are not the same, nor are the differences the same from judge to judge. Again, however, such things mean dilution, not elimination, of the gain in reckonability which can be had by knowing the nature of the official personnel.[28]

13. The General Period-Style and Its Promise

(a) and (b) There is a further cluster of conditioning and steadying factors in the work of the appellate courts (and commonly at {36} the same time of other branches of legal work) which has been curiously disregarded. It is the general and pervasive manner over the country at large, at any given time, of going about the job, the general outlook, the ways of professional knowhow, the kind of thing the men of law are sensitive to and strive for, the tone and flavor of the working and of the results. It is well described as a "period-style"; it corresponds to what we have long known as period-style in architecture or the graphic arts or furniture or music or drama. Its slowish movement but striking presence remind me also of shifting "types" of economy ("agricultural," "industrial," e.g.) and of the cycles or spirals many sociologists and historians discover in the history of political aggregations or of whole cultures.

Thus, for instance, the outlook and manner of Mansfield, or of Marshall, Kent, Cowen, Parker, Tilghman, Gibson, are in no wise peculiar to these giants; both are shared unmistakably by most of the lesser men of the period. The *type*-thinking of the time is to view precedents as welcome and *very* persuasive, but it is to test a precedent almost always against three types of reason before it is accepted. The reputation of the opinion-writing judge counts heavily (and it is right reason to listen carefully to the wise). Secondly, "principle" is consulted to check up on precedent, and at this period and in this way of work "principle" means no mere verbal tool for bringing large-scale order into the rules, it means a broad generalization which must yield patent sense as well as order, if it is to be "principle." Finally, "policy," in terms of prospective consequences of the rule under consideration, comes in for explicit examination by reason in a further test of both the rule in question and its application. The tone and mark consist in an as-of-courseness in the constant questing for better and best law to guide the future, but the better and best law is to be built on and out of what the past can offer; the quest consists in a constant re-examination and reworking of a heritage, that the heritage may yield not only solidity but comfort for the new day and for the morrow.

This is the Grand Style of the Common Law. I am referring to a way of thought and work, not to a way of writing. It is a way of on-going renovation of doctrine, but touch with the past is too close, the mood is too craft-conscious, the need for the clean line is too great, for the renovation to smell of revolution or, indeed, of campaigning reform. Of the judges named above, Mansfield and Gibson stand out from the others in that in each an impatience to built *fast* sometimes stirs strongly enough to permit breaks with {37} the past that jar the rhythm of the law and of the work. To that degree and on those occasions they are out of key with the Grand Style at its peak. There will of course always be an opposition, and some of it will be factious and fractious; and contemporary criticism and abuse are inherent in the controversy which produces law. But some of the sparks caused by Mansfield and Gibson, great judges though both were, were struck by a brusqueness of manner and language toward men and toward tradition which is no part of that grace in work which is the Grand Style at its best. For let me repeat: "style" refers in this connection not to literary quality or tone, but to the manner of doing the job, to the way of craftsmanship in office, to a functioning harmonization of vision with tradition, of continuity with growth, of machinery with purpose, of measure with need. This can conceivably work out into florid words or into ponderous Elizabethan euphuism; if so, I am prepared to be laden with the language if I may have the thing. But it is worthy of note (and it is perhaps some evidence that style grips in one fist more phases of man and culture than we always realize) that work in the Grand Style has, historically, tended into simplicity of verbal form and of sentence and paragraph structure, in combination with a certain pungency.[29]

It will also be obvious that in this reference to the early nineteenth-century work in this country I have in mind something greater, deeper, and of more far-reaching implication than the "formative" character of the early American era as discussed by Roscoe Pound. His other phrasing, "our classic period," comes much closer to what is here in mind. With "formative" his eye was on the effective creation of needed doctrine — by selection, by modification, by invention. That was indeed in process, in say 1820-1860, and the Grand Style is peculiarly apt to such a task. But the matter goes much further: the Grand Style is *always* the best style, even though the cabin of doctrine may seem for the moment complete, with only chinks and leaks left to attend to.

On reckonability of result, three points cry for attention: first, the Grand Style is the best device ever invented by man for drying up that free-flowing spring of uncertainty, conflict between the {38} seeming commands of the authorities and the felt demands of justice. Second, when a frozen text happens to be the crux, to insist that an acceptable answer shall satisfy the reason *as well as* the language is not only to escape much occasion for divergence, but to radically reduce the degree thereof. (Compare the Laws of Compatibility and Incompatibility, discussed below at page 180.) Third, the future-directed quest for ever better formulations for guidance, which is inherent in the Grand Style, means the on-going production and improvement of rules which make sense on their face, and which can be understood and reasonably well applied even by mediocre men. *Such* rules have a fair chance to get the same results out of very different judges, and so in truth to hit close to the ancient target of "laws and not men." Of the results of such rules, handled in such a manner, one can rightly say what Carter pungently but most wrongly said of the common law of his own day: "forefelt, if not foreseen."[30]

That was not true in Carter's day because the Formal Style which was coming into dominance when he began his writing and froze his views in the early '80's can yield reckonable results only when the rules of law are clear; and whatever one may say in praise of Our Lady of the Common Law (to whom I do bow), clarity and precise outline of her rules of law are not the chief jewel in her crown. Moreover, to thicken the obscurity, the statutes of Carter's day had come to approach the involuted sloppiness of drafting which is too familiar still, and the courts had also opened that war of guerrilla raids on statutes by way of "strict construction" in unforeseeable spots which made a faro game of every statutory case.

The Formal Style is of peculiar interest to us because it set the picture against which all modern thinking has played — call it, as of the last eighty or ninety years, "the orthodox ideology." That picture is clean and clear: the rules of law are to decide the cases; policy is for the legislature, not for the courts, and so is change even in pure common law. Opinions run in deductive form with an air or expression of single-line inevitability. "Principle" is a generalization producing order which can and should be used to prune away those "anomalous" cases or rules which do not fit, such cases or rules having no function except, in places where the supposed "principle" does not work well, to accomplish sense — but sense is no official concern of a formal-style court.

Langdell's dazzling contract-construct is the American archetype of such a set of principles: without consideration, no legal obligation on a promise; consideration is *only* a bargained-for detriment {39} (this planes off, for example, all enforcement via reliance, and all matters already past when a promise is made); the detriment can move *only* from the promisee (this chops off all enforcement by beneficiaries); an offer requires communication in order to be capable of acceptance (this prunes away the old sensible "unknown reward" cases); acceptance must be by *either* a promise *or* "an act," the very promise *or* the very act "called for" by the "master of the offer" — a jealous master, who has no desire to close a deal (this puts the ax to any expectation of alternative or even reasonable modes of acceptance, glorifies last-minute revocation in the continuing performance cases, and crowns verbal ribbon-matching between communications with a kind of ponderous dignity). Sense, the ways of men with words, the ways of businessmen in dealing, these are irrelevant and literally inadmissible: they do not get into the hall, to be heard or considered. Generations of law students were introduced to their profession by way of these strange ideas, and courts have in consequence made actual decisions in their image, sometimes with a touch of patent Parkeian pleasure as the pretty little puzzle-pieces lock together to leave for hundreds of good business promises no legal container but the garbage can. But in the ideal of the Formal Style, as has been said, thus to prune away anomaly is to vindicate Principle: large-scale Order. And it is a good judge's business to steel himself against emotion, and against deflection by sense or sense of justice which may run counter to "the law," lest such should lead him to neglect of his stem duty; in the titans of the style there develops a perverse drive for the "strong" opinion dear to Parke.[31] Finally, even as the common law is thus moved with sweat toward a simpler and more peacefully life-remote structural system, the disturbing statute (inconsistently with "Policy for the Legislature") is dealt with as an enemy invader.

This deeply etched and revered picture or idea-pattern did not, as the labor injunction cases[32] and the familiar Constitutional cases remind us, in fact bar out innovations of doctrine as far-reaching as they could be sudden; far less did it bar out those more gradual and less noticed cumulative changes which have {40} been with us throughout our history. But it did, in its devotees (and that means by say 1885 practically the bar and bench entire) drive *conscious* creation all but underground, make change and growth things to be ignored in opinions, and to be concealed not only from a public but from a self. Meanwhile, the available doctrinal material (then even more grievously afflicted than today with preindustrial concepts and flavor, while major reformatory statutes were being knocked out again and again) — that material lagged further and further behind conditions which were remodeling with increasing speed, and the urge for felt right which no judge of conscience can ever wholly escape tended more and more into clash with prevailing doctrine and with the death's-head duties of the prevailing pattern of judicial ideal. It is true that a widespread public revolt put on the bench a great body of State court judges to replace many whose feeling for justice had merged in peace with obsolete or otherwise unhappy doctrine. But note: whatever their political or economic or social outlook, these new appellate judges, too, had grown up in and into the formal-style picture of how to go about their work. Pound's famous American Bar Association speech of 1906 had sounded warnings and blown the charge, but it had died out on the inert re-sistant air.[33] What was left in the State courts at large was an astounding decrease in reckonability of result: judges who wanted to go right, and did not know how to; other judges who more often than not, though felt justice cried loud, could yet deafen their ears as they remembered duty to "the law," but who nevertheless with frequent, persistent, and almost random irregularity jumped "legal" traces and coursed to fulfillment of their other duty by way of bad logic, or by distortion of authority or fact, or by main strength. The effects not only on reckonability but on "the law," during the early decades of the twentieth century, were devastating.

Such generalizations as the foregoing can offer light and perspective; they cannot offer basis for conclusion to any particular, re either jurisdiction or era. What, for example, is true in general of Massachusetts, New York, Ohio, and Pennsylvania in the first half of the nineteenth century holds much less for Illinois until {41} the advent of Breese in 1857; and in New York the Supreme Court can show the Grand Style in perfection in the same volume in which the Court for the Correction of Errors is bogged in wordy senators. Similarly, the Formal Style, which had begun to lose control of the New York Court of Appeals before 1920, continued to dominate the Supreme Court of Maryland (both in manner of writing and manner of deciding) for more than a generation thereaf-ter; and while the Supreme Court of Massachusetts were in 1939 still writing largely in the strict Formal Style, there can be no question that their process of actual deciding had already materially departed therefrom; indeed, even in 1939 Chief Justice Field was casting the Opinions of the Justices in a manner strongly reminiscent of the Grand Style,[34] and within a few years thereafter the Formal Style had completely lost control of the law opinions, too. No, a "prevailing" style does not mean a uniformity. Indeed, just as some judges can become almost an ideal embodiment of the prevailing style, others can and do stand out in powerful idiosyncratic contrast to their surroundings: for instance, Doe.

It is of course when this type of contrast ceases to seem idiosyncratic that "change of style" has begun. This showed in the New York Court of Appeals and in the Second Circuit before 1920; the work of Burch and Mason showed clearly in Kansas by 1905. Long before the movement became characteristic of the Supreme Court of the United States its mark had become clear upon the State courts in general; the Supreme Court — save for some dissenters — was indeed amazingly slow in responding to the tide.[35]During the last three decades it has become clear that the Formal Style, though still of influence and moment, has yet lost its grip. It offers still one of the standard styles for the writing of opinions, but I do not believe that it anywhere wholly dominates opinion-writing style today, nor do I believe that in any of our appellate courts it retains its ancient aspect of a deep, unquestioned, and powerful faith. Today's typical appellate judge is interested first of all in getting the case decided *right* — within the authorities; and however he writes, it is the goal of rightness which gives the main drive and direction to his labors. The danger, as has been said above, has become one of giving too little attention to continuity and to guidesomeness of legal doctrine. {42}

What now of the effects of this shift on reckonability of outcome?

(i) *Re statutes,* the gain has been great. Today's appellate courts have long made their peace with the legislatures. Today, nine times out of ten, or better, legislative policy is not resisted, but is accepted cheerfully, and the court works with it. This obviously aids prediction of result.

Not yet, however, has the Grand Style of statutory treatment been recaptured. The courts do not yet regularly and as of course face up to their job of integrating the particular statute into the doctrinal whole; and while the sound principle "where the reason stops, there stops even the enacted rule (*lex*)" is receiving attention half the time or more, often even when the statutory language makes it difficult, yet the courts at large are still caught in the theories of the '90's on the equally important matter of implementing the clear purposes of a statute with the full resources of a court or the matter of recognizing a clear and broad statutory policy in an apt area even though that area is not embraced by the literal language.[36]

(ii) *Re the bar:* To the degree that the appellate courts have — as they have — resorted to conscious consideration of right and wisdom in order to guide choice between or among the permissible doctrinal possibilities, a tool for producing much more reckonable regularity has been added to their actual working kit. But to the degree that such consideration fails to be unmistakable on the face of the opinion, most of the bar remains in the dark about what is happening, and accordingly is troubled in prediction. Moreover, *occasional* display of process and reason in *occasional* opinions does not do the necessary work for the bar in general, as contrasted with the really good appellate lawyer. For the bar in general, in the first place, does not read the current local reports, as such. Most of the bar *read* (I am not saying "note" {43} or "skim") almost exclusively the cases whose *subject matter* is of interest to the individual reading lawyer, and so will never see most of such indications as have been referred to. In the second place, the bar in general reads to discover what the last authoritative statement or decision is about "the law" of a point; it does *not* read to get light on how the court is, in general, going about its perplexing job of deciding tough cases. And in the third place, the bulk of the bar reads still with the spectacles of "orthodox ideology," so that a court's remarks about the reason and wisdom of the decision just do not come through. At best: "*mere* dicta."

It is of first importance to observe that any such general ignorance and confusion of the bar does more than yield worry and distress, does more than undermine that confidence in the law and in the appellate bench which every lawyer needs for his soul's health. It also drives into a vicious circle. For it produces appeals based not on sound judgment but on wild speculation, therefore vastly too many appeals, half or more of them those footless, "foredoomed" ones of which Cardozo wrote. These proceed to heap waste-work on the appellate court until that court's time gives out and the full job which is the court's function must, in most instances, be scanted or passed over. Meantime, an American advocate's nature being to acquire belief in his cause, the appealing lawyer finds himself once again kicked in the teeth "without ground"; the slow bleeding of his faith *and* of his judgment continues — fertilizing a new crop of footless appeals.

(iii) *Re the judges themselves:* Meantime the inarticulateness of the vast body of appellate judges about how they do their work and why — their inarticulateness even to themselves — leaves them man by man somewhat soul-troubled, albeit their consciences are clear. This tells against reckonability of result; case by case, a troubled man is less certain in his action than a man who, like James Stephens' salmon, "is all one piece from his head to his tail." There obviously results some waste of effort, some waste of energy in internal friction, and especially an unevenness in operation which lessens predictability for the most skilled observer, whether at the bar or outside.

But the biggest single effect of the inarticulateness is that it tends to focus the court's known duty to justice — to what is right and fair — on the particular case and on the particular parties who happen to be in hand. This is a better way {44} of going at decision than to discard the earthy concreteness of the case and to ignore the starry-eyed or knave-fool equities; but it is for all that a half-baked technique and one which strains toward both discontinuity and unwisdom. The wise place to search thoroughly for what is a right and fair solution is *the recurrent problem-situation* of which the instant case is *typical.* For in the first place this presses, this drives, toward formulating a solving *and guiding rule;* and to address oneself to the rule side of the puzzle is of necessity both to look back upon the heritage of doctrine and also to look forward into prospective consequences and prospective further problems — and to account to each. In that work, the tang of the case at bar gives feel and flavor, and stimulates the imagination; but the immediate equities fall into a wider, paler frame which renders it much easier both to feel and to see how much and what parts of them are typical and so are proper shapers of policy, how much and what part on the other hand is too individual for legal cognizance or appeals rather to sentimentality than to the sensitivity and sense proper to a legal-governmental scheme. It is not to appellate courts that our polity commits the pardoning power, nor yet the dispensing power, to be exercised along any lines which cannot be put into a form significantly general.

It seems to me obvious at sight that this order of approach to the problem of deciding an appellate case *must* materially raise the level of reckonability, make results more even, make the operating factors easier to foresee and forefeel, make the ways of handling prior doctrine stand forth, make the new formulations so reached increase in adequacy both of content and of phrasing. It seems to me no less obvious at sight that this same order of approach *must* at the same time raise the level of wisdom of result.[37] At the moment it is a procedure employed from time to time by every court, employed consistently by none that I have studied.

Some of what has just been said may suggest heavy uncertainty of result to be today's condition. I mean no such suggestion. I hold that from the beginning of this century to say 1950, there occurred in the State supreme courts a rise in reckonability of result (and, let me add, of wisdom of result as well) which resembles the percentage rise in national production. It was, as I see it, an outgrowth of groping, not of plan; it was uncoordinated; {45} it just happened, over fifty years of cumulative drift, with many men worried and independently at work. In process, as in impact on the particular case, such a change is irregular and unreckonable; but its net can and slowly has thrust the whole of operation up into a higher and much more even plateau of forecastability. I do not spot heavy influence of any particular leading figures unless it be Cardozo.[38] I incline to believe, moreover, that until rather recently the ferment among the intellectuals which was discussed at the outset of this paper has been of minor moment. Today, taking the close of the trial as a base line, my judgment (this is much more than a guess or a "guesstimate") is that a skilled man careful of the lines of factor here discussed ought even in the present state of our knowledge to average correct prediction of outcome eight times out of ten, and better than that if he knows the appeal counsel on both sides or sees the briefs. This, of course, presupposes the existence of that half or so of the cases which really are foredoomed.[39]

Meantime the position is one to put to shame the ancient friendly cynic: the leopard of the appellate court *can* change his spots, and the courts *can* by taking thought add more than a cubit to their stature.[40]

14. Professional Judicial Office

(a) Finally[41] we recur to the most important among all the lines of factor which make for reckonability in American appellate {46} judicial deciding: the office. The men who do the deciding hold office; they hold judicial office as full-time professionals. This is not a simple matter to be just glanced at or indeed assumed without a glance. Neither is it to be casually dismissed as a mere illustration, say, of role theory,[42] or with such a vague concept and label as "impartiality." In one aspect everything treated above enters into this line of factor as part or element; but there is enough extra to be worth scrutiny as a separate topic.

In our tradition *judicial* office is with peculiar intensity *office*, and is perhaps unmatched in the doggedness with which it presses upon the officeholder a demand to be selfless. Time, place, architecture and interior arrangement, supporting officials, garb, ritual combine to drive these matters home. The pressures are unremitting, time gives them further power; I hold this shaping force to be as important as the skill-values of bench-experience in making the case against unnecessary replacement of appellate personnel.

Various aspects of the role have indeed rooted deep in the folkways and moral judgments even of childhood: an umpire is *not* to "take sides"; "wait a minute, we gotta see what *he* has to say." And a deep and rich as-of-course grasp of the idea and ideal of this office is revealed when our language to describe it has no need to strike close to the mark. The typical word, used as a sufficient word, is "impartial," which describes a condition: "not on either side, and without personal interest or desire re the outcome" is about as far as that word really takes you, though the dictionaries tend to add "just." But we mean when we use the word about a man in judicial *office* a great deal more. We mean, and definitely in addition, "upright." We also mean — and if we stop to think we know that we mean — not a passive but a positive and active attitude: the judge must be *seeking,* as best he can, to see the matter fairly, and with an eye not to the litigants merely, but to All-of-Us as well. We mean further, and importantly, still {47} another attitude: "Open, truly open, to listen, to get informed, to be persuaded, to respond to good reason." Nay, more; we gather into this one weak, bleak word "impartial" a drive: an idea of effort, of self-denying labor, toward patience, toward understanding sympathy, toward quest for wisdom in the result.

It is very queer that our fraternity of appellate judges, whose professional skill is centered on sharp verbal definition of the duty and breach of duty of any other citizen, should remain more inadequate than the man in the street when it comes to fixing in words the limits of permissible judicial behavior. The man in the street cuts straight to the heart on this one: "Hell, is that any way for a *judge* to act?!" But the judges themselves have not progressed even to adapting from the military such a phrase as "conduct materially unbecoming a judge and a gentleman," or from the bar such a phrase as "flagrantly unjudicial."[43] Thus Thacher, ex-name-partner in a major Wall Street firm, ex-solicitor-general, ex-district-judge, ex-president of the Association of the Bar, when chosen to frame charges against Capshaw, a judge whose conduct in office skunk-stank, came up with — as a crux — "*He has decided cases on considerations outside the record*" — a procedure which, used rightly and wisely, had made the glory of a Mansfield, a Marshall, a Cardozo. — However, if we can push ahead in cutting removal of judges loose from impeachment procedure, entrusting that sad task instead to an appropriately craft-skilled and craft-responsible commission, this present lack will tend both into unimportance and into disappearance as the infrequent but successive cases cumulate.

What is thus a gap on the extreme penal side, though tragic when the need bites, is yet too rare in incidence to affect (except as a possible vagary) our problem of the daily grist. And in contrast, there is a whole gamut of lesser informal corrective pressures to steady an appellate judge's work and channel it into greater reckonability; in these, the whip and carrot come, if one may scramble a figure, intertwined. The intermediate court of appeal is subject to the pat or slap of affirmance or reversal. And on any appellate court there sit beside a man, as already mentioned, his brethren of the particular bench, with their example, their warmth or aloofness, their praise or even remonstrance. Also to be felt are the bar and the vocal portion of the public; one recalls the {48} impact of recorded vote and signed opinion. These days, the law reviews, too, manage to smooth or ruffle pride — or vanity. Even those judges who make and file notes and write letters for posterity with the care and hope which Pliny lavished on his "letters" — even they are steadied into greater predictability by their conscious need to seem to themselves consistent, and duly noble.[44]

In the net, our appellate bench has been strikingly self-corrective in morale as well as manner. Despite all mistakes and despite all passions of the day, they have either maintained or speedily regained a standing with the lay public hardly rivaled by any scattered, unorganized aggregation of equivalent size in all recorded history. I think of only one period when the supreme courts at large (in contrast to the Supreme Court of the United States) have come under general and continuous attack — the period which culminated in Theodore Roosevelt's onslaught on "government by injunction" and in that movement for recall of judges which captured seven States before it ebbed. But we have with us today two legal generations for whom that story no longer has a meaning, while despite ups and downs of particular persons and particular benches, honesty, reasonable effort, and reasonable dignity remain, along with position, prestige-attributes of the appellate bench. Odd, individual delinquencies fade out like the ripples from a flung stone: for instance, even the continued self-will and corruption and final public disgrace of a Manton left the Second Circuit still for decades with the most distinguished and admired bench in these United States. All of which means that the *office* waits and then moves with majestic power to shape the man. An image so poignantly perceived, so imperiously held up for imitation, is not to be escaped. It sorts and lifts out of a man the best he has to offer, with a degree of consistency foreign to the past of all but a few; it builds that initial best up to levels which were not in him when he first became a judge; with every robing he renews a silent covenant with self and office. This is not merely a matter of squeezing or cutting away the idiosyncratic and so shaping the man more nearly to an average; it is a matter, no less, of so dealing with idiosyncratic might or vision that, without loss of character, it is yet channeled into service of the whole, no longer of the part, and channeled into teamwork; channeled therefore into a new reckonability. There is in this last phenomenon at once a mystic and no mystic quality. You can "explain" it, if you will, in relative comfort by a dozen or so of {49} such things as I have been discussing, and come closish to understanding the result. But for myself, I feel more to be there than the sum of such factors, taken even in dynamic interaction, will explain. I think of how a second injection of judicial office and responsibility transformed the rhinoceros-hided and -tempered McReynolds, so resistant to the normal shaping forces that his mannerlessness in the robing or consulting room and on the bench had become a by-word; so "judicial" that he would stalk out of court when a lawyer rose at the bar who was a Jew or was a Negro or was a woman. Yet when the chief was sick and McReynolds came to preside, he was decorous to a woman advocate and even gave her extra time, and we have it from Stone that there had not in his time been fairer or more courteous conduct of the consultation.

(b) It is true — to put a semi-contra, and as the stage itself reminds us — that neither role, costume, setting, nor training means uniformity, nor do the four together. Add ritual, add ingrained felt tradition and ideal and what have you more, still men will differ in temper, background, eyes to see, wit to judge, tongue to say, persuasiveness with their brethren. As a matter of horse sense it is thus clear that the factor of person is still important, even when we limit observation to that overwhelming bulk of the appellate judges to whom improper conduct in office would be unthinkable: Else how could you by their work tell a Brandeis from a Butler, a Hough or Hand or Swan from a Rogers, a Mansfield from an Ellenborough, a Coke from a Jeffreys,[44a] a Cardozo or Cuthbert Pound from an O'Brien or McLaughlin? How, indeed, could you justify allowing an appeal from any honest and diligent trial judge to any appellate court; or, especially, from any immediate appellate bench to any other court; or permit dissent save at penalty of impeachment? So that any conception of appellate deciding done "by laws *and not* by men" is patent error.

But this does not mean lack of effect in those factors which work like a fly-wheel for stability. I am minded of Kinsey-Pomeroy-Martin on "un"-chastity among American husbands: for at least half of those husbands, during the lifetime, at least one extramarital orgasm! K-P-M were here wringing their evidence dry; but has anyone ever offered more powerful testimony on the degree to which men — many or most of this 50 per cent and all of the other half — *can* be shaped in conduct by the channeling {50} pressures of a culture? We must expect with the appellate judges a materially greater effect from the molding factors because in the main those influences are accepted by them, not resisted, are welcome, are to only a slight degree a source of trouble or conflict with individual or even queerish aspects of the person, call for no release of re-sistance-tensions — as sex-control does in so many persons and cultures — by way of break-over or carnival or convention or binge. Let me say this again: over the vast bulk of persons and of occasions for each person, appellate judges labor to be judicial, appellate judges learn to be judicial, appellate judges like to be judicial. It seems to me obvious that this is much more nearly universal among them than among the judges who sit at trial or as magistrates; certainly the working team, the bench of which each appellate judge is but one working part, goes far to elicit these attitudes and to restrain or root out any contrarying tendency. Where, as occasionally, this fails to work out, the matter is largely one of individual insensitivity: an anteater-hide stuffed with either egotism or naïve bigotry or both.

In sum, re reckonability under this head, there is no suggestion here of any slot-machine or conveyor-belt complete predictability; I refer instead, let me repeat, only to a case-by-case reckonability that can be brought to the level of a reasonable, sometimes a very good, business risk. The question here goes thus not to some queer calamitous corruption, or to some occasional breakthrough of personal ill will, or to any other accident or volcanic intrusion. The question goes instead to the daily grist. It will be *Jones v. Smith,* say an automobile collision; and the next case, *McDuffy v. O'Fallon,* perhaps a feud over surface water; and the next case, *Cohen v. Levine,* say a textile sale; and the other arguments of the same day: *Angelotti's Estate,* say on the meaning of the fourteenth paragraph of a badly drawn will; the *Newton School Board* case; the alleged railroading for a particular burglary of a certain professional burglar whose name no man can spot among his aliases; and a point or two of appellate procedure. And the argument here is that what remains significantly singular and individual among the personnel of a given bench at a given time is precisely what the good advo-cate and the skilled observer should and can study and merge into his reckoning. Such was Hughes' practice when preparing an appeal to the Supreme Court, while Davis, a block away, was marshaling parallel thinking for a contrary result.

* * *

{51} In regard to this matter of the office, I have found it not only difficult but unwise to keep description unmixed with my value-judgments and desires. Let me repeat that I have no wish to allow even a casual reader to get any idea that I am interested only in facts, "*and not*" in goals and ideals; nor yet that I see predictability of appellate decision as a uniquely valuable goal. The steady stress on reckonability is indeed necessary to this job here in hand; as is the making of that case on a basis of straight fact-observation. But these things having been done, here and elsewhere in this volume, there is health in letting one or another portion of the discussion come from the whole man and go to the whole scene.

* * *

Here then are ten to fifteen clusters of what we may see as flywheel factors making for steadiness and reckonability in American appellate judicial deciding in contrast with any general type of group-deciding, factors which if they have any power should be expected to produce a degree of depersonizing in the deciding far beyond that when such flywheel factors are not present. With such clusters at work one can, as has been repeatedly indicated, hope to get further down in than merely into the large and the long. "Steadiness" of our appellate judicial decision *over the decades,* as it has been so often praised,[45] is good for historians of culture or of government, but it affords to the person with pending litigation comfort as chilly as that which an economist's secular trend offers to a businessman contemplating a particular venture. Our factor-clusters whisper hope of something vastly different: a wherewithal, perhaps, of wrestling *in prospect* with the outcome *of the concrete appeal in hand.* We thus set ourselves against the wail of bar and public which has been waxing steadily stronger, in anger or in anguish, over forty years.

THE FURTHER COURSE OF THE ARGUMENT

To say is one thing, to show is another, and despite the soaring cost of living, unbuttressed assertion remains a five-and-dime ware: {52} a full old-fashioned package for a nickel. Moreover, the skeptics are with us; verily they have been fruitful and multiplied. And they are vocal: How, to rehearse the trade-cant, is the presence of our body of so-called authoritative doctrine plus the pressure to write an opinion and all the rest to be flywheel and depersonizing stuff when "everybody knows" that appellate judges typically first decide any way they want, and write opinions afterward, to suit? How, the tale continues, can results be other than vagrant when psychology shows that prettifying the results of deciding as you want to is a major sport of man (and one which flourishes peculiarly in the hothouse of any specialist in words)? How even suggest any reckonability from doctrine and office when dissenting opinions demonstrate in many cases what adversary briefs come close to demonstrating in all, to wit, that in any case worth discussion an opinion can be built either way on and out of the authorities, while special concurrences and separate dissents demonstrate for some times and suggest for all times that the possibilities available to skilled craftsmen from the prior authorities are many more than two? Plainly, to repeat the shiny shallow "observation" of the cynic, the judges just decide any way they please, certainty of decision is an illusion, steadiness is a myth, opinions are a ritual that ranges from the absurd to the vicious, and the law is in truth "*la volonté des juges*";[46] the cynic meaning thereby their will, uncontrolled, and reckonable only as you may be able to reckon the habit, attitude, prejudice, passion, or whim of F. X. Quinlan, Silas Quincy, or Thorgard Olsen, JJ., in 1960 or in 1978.

In dealing with such skeptics let us move first in terms of the self-evident and sense about the same. Let us thereafter make the case for the court's published opinion not indeed as a description of how the court went about its work, but as being nevertheless if rightly read, a deposit of rich ore little worked but available in prodigal profusion. Let us next look into some of the things to be learned from opinions in comparisons or in sequence, with or without reference to various outside factors which may be within {53} reach. Let us look finally into the daily mine-run of the cases, unsorted, unselected, and so reach for true typicality, for light on the ordinary case.

HORSE SENSE ON STEADYING AND DEPERSONIZING

The place to begin is with the fact that the men of our appellate bench are human beings. I have never understood why the cynics talk and think as if this were not so. For it is so. And one of the more obvious and obstinate facts about human beings is that they operate in and respond to traditions, and especially to such traditions as are offered to them by the crafts they follow. Tradition grips them, shapes them, limits them, guides them; not for nothing do we speak of *ingrained* ways of work or thought, of men *experienced* or case-hardened, of *habits* of mind. Tradition, moreover, wreaks these things upon human beings notwithstanding that in a real degree men also make use of the tradition, reshape it in the very use, sometimes manipulate it to the point of artifice or actual evasion if need, duty, or both, seem so to require. To a man of sociology or psychology or government this needs no argument, it needs not even statement, with regard to human beings at large. But the laws of human beings at large and of human institutions in general apply as of course to the men and institution of Law-Government as well. Is it not then queer, because some of the looser thinkers from the law-field (thinkers who have *not* been *good* sociologists or psychologists) have been giving some currency to this kind of quarter-truth about "any way that seems good to them," that such nightmares should spread to members of the academic fraternity whose very home-disciplines deny the possibility that the nightmares could be truth? Is Law-Government so esoteric that one must forego his own judgment and simply believe the "confidential dope" peddled by any disillusioned but highhearted "insider" who seems to be a fellow-crusader against obscurantism? I do not know. But I call upon any university teacher's experience to unmask the pretenders; and I call particularly upon law school men to check against their own firsthand and truly "inside" knowledge certain horse-sense probabilities about the workings of appellate courts.

A CHALLENGE TO THE LAW SCHOOL SKEPTIC

Take, you law professor, the case of some semipromising student who comes to you as a teacher for some deeply needed {54} non-routine advice. The student himself normally bothers you as much as does his problem, though it may not be easy to put into words either why or how. You can say clearly that you will of course use and weigh the particular facts you get and the general experience you think you have. You can say clearly that you will have an eye both on what you know or discover of his past (which is so far as it goes limiting, controlling, guiding) and on what you can see of his future (which you are about to try to partly control). The important thing thus far is that while the answer is as yet wholly unknown, and will take work, and will bear the imprint of your individual self as the particular answerer, nevertheless the answer is plainly and materially conditioned and influenced in advance both by a given past and by an impending future — not only his past and future, but your own as well. And do not overlook that you are going to scan all of these matters not alone for knowledge, nor alone to find keys to prudence, but also to uncover leads to an answer which will in comfort fit with what is — in your view — right. This applies strikingly to the rightness of your own conduct. For instance, I suggest that whether or not you think about it, you will be moving with a "feel" that what you do for this one should not run too far below or indeed too far above what you have been doing or will try to do for "like" cases; and I suggest that whether or not you so plan, what you do in fact must move toward fixing, reinforcing, or resetting a standard of effort and care to be called on "in like case." What "like" may mean may never be analyzed at all, or even grow conscious, and whether or not analyzed may still be in considerable flux. But the "feel" is there, and the flux is not *free*. And the "feel" is neither merely you nor merely human, it reflects also a felt tradition of office; at the least, however unverbalized: "How *I* treat students in *my* office." You may indeed cut Bob very short because you are irritated or worried at the moment or because he or his problem is personally distasteful, or whatever; you may go all out for Charlie because he has special promise or because of his engaging twinkle or because of his father or because he is disadvantaged; but my suggestion is that unless the boy classifies rather easily and "rightly" for the kind of treatment he gets, you run into internal friction. And I am not asking you to consider crux-cases here, only the normal run of those which ask for a bit of thought.

Now suppose that on each such case in addition to deciding you had also to write a justifying "opinion," conforming

> (a) to University or School rules phrased in words, *and* {55}
>
> (b) to University, School, or Committee past decisions, and present attitudes, etc., *and*
>
> (c) to your own prior practice, "recorded."

Of course, at need, you would still be able to beat the book. You could, you can, build some road around or between rules and precedents or by way of some lucky phrase designed years back to wholly different purpose. But does this mean that that will be your practice, your daily procedure, your standard cynical disregard of the regime in which you hold office?[47]

If, now, in addition, you (like appellate judges) see the whole regime as a pretty good one, as a going whole worthy of support and even reverence, is it not going to call for a case where the particular regime-result is meanly at odds with sense before you go in for the more highfalutin varieties of finagling? Suppose further that your decision and opinion must win their way past a whole and fully-informed committee (as must those of an appellate judge). Suppose still further (as with the appellate judge) that the opinion will be *published for use* as a controlling or guiding precedent. Concede that when the hot one comes up it can be wrapped or smothered in words ambiguous or misleading. Concede that on occasion skilled phrases can smooth and hide the trail of work that loveth not noonday. Do such facts alter the deeper fact that dogmatic authorities (written or remembered, "rules" or precedent-making decisions and/or opinions) serve as powerful flywheel forces in the deciding which gets done? In the appellate courts authorities of this type are joined by all the other clusters of factors canvassed above. Horse sense can give but one answer as to the consequent channeling and heightened reckonability-of-outcome in the activity we know as deciding.

But the more sophisticated skeptic now shifts his ground. "I overstated a bit," says he. "Not '*any* way they *want* to.' And so what? '*Either* way they think fitting will do me. And I mean '*they*': the three or five or seven particular individuals. I concede that they have consciences, mostly, and use them. But I mean *them*, not any 'The Law' you may conjure up."

This more sophisticated skeptic is not so easy to deal with. I think informed horse sense plus a touch of imagination goes far to take care of him, as well; but he is unlikely to come along without a goad. Let us turn therefore to what right reading can dig {56} out of the opinions. We can smelt that ore to make an ankus even for an elephant.

ORE IN THE PUBLISHED OPINION

Of course, only by happenstance will an opinion accurately report the process of deciding. Indeed, I urge flatly that such report is not really a function of the opinion at all, though if the court so chooses there is no impropriety in recording such significant portions of the work as doubt, long pondering, independent research, any published source of illumination, division within the college, and the like. And one has ever to bear in mind as among the possibilities of deflection the type of thing which infatuated the cynics of the '20's and '30's: If the opinion is a justification, nay, a "mere rationalization" of a decision already reached, a justification intended "only" for public consumption, its "light" can be contrived delusion. Vital factors may go unmentioned; pseudo factors may be put forward; emphasis and weighing of factors may be hugely skewed; any statements of policy may be not for revelation but merely for consumption; the very alleged statement of "the facts" may be only a lawyer's argumentative arranged selection, omission, emphasis, distortion, all flavored to make the result tolerable or toothsome. That something of this does occur is demonstrated by that occasional dissenting opinion which, for instance, pounds home facts or authorities the majority has found it convenient to ignore. In such a maze, to reach for signs of actual motivation and process by watching say tone of language or manner of stress and arrangement or the like is surely, urges the skeptic, to do blind amateur pseudo-psychoanalytical guesswork on data so intangible and scanty as to make a professional lose his lunch — the very kind of guesswork which many (this present writer included) sneer at as lightheaded and unwarranted when it is practiced by jejune or jaundiced jibers at the courts. No, says the skeptic, the only safe course is to follow the lawyers' ancient practice. Confine study of the opinion to what the opinion really offers: official authoritative light not on the birth-pangs of the decision, but on that very different something: what, on the relevant points, is the resultant actually prevailing state of correct legal doctrine — provided always, scoffs our dear skeptic, that *that* means anything, in life.

One can begin an answer with reminders from our friends across the alley, in the work called History. They have learned, not merely as a matter of individual intuition but as a moderately {57} transmissible and moderately reliable craft-skill, to mark off even in a private diary, like that of Pepys, passion or prejudice from reporting, observation of a facet from observation of a whole, interpretation from accurate record of the event. They read letters or pronunciamentos, speeches, or reports, with moderately effective corrections for the twisting of fact by the nature and bias of the writer, by his sources of information, by his known or seeming purpose, and the like. They have learned to test and supplement one piece of evidence by another, and each single piece both by its immediate context, by its inherent probability in the circumstances, and by the shape, color, flavor of the great whole. It is not to the purpose that since the successful raid of the quantity-boys on the ears and imaginations of deans and grant-givers historians may have tended into an unbecoming overmodesty. For the type of knowledge we are after here is not "scientific." It is what is sure enough to be moderately reliable for use in practice and to offer sound leads for further refinement; and I shall follow no historian into thinking that what we have already in this area and can see coming up will be subject to radical revision of meaning or interpretation with every generation.

As has been noted (pp. 13 f.), by the early '30's there had been a fair beginning of what may be called critical study of certain documents known as opinions of the court. Some individual decisions had been subjected to deep and careful study of context, of legal and other background, of argument and personnel, so that the opinion came both to take on and to give new light about its genesis. Some judicial biographers had brought insight into the deciding process by exploring the sequence of a given appellate judge's life, times, and product. Holmes, while still on the Supreme Judicial Court of Massachusetts, had suggested one piece of a large picture, one "outside" factor, "fear of social-ism," as having heavily affected one whole group of untoward decisions. Cardozo had again and again drawn on his own experience in efforts to articulate various processes of conscious shift and conscious refusal to shift doctrine when trouble-some case law problems had come before his court.

But to me much more significant is that by 1925 there had come to be a top bracket of the bar all over the country — not too many by percentage or even by nose count, but enough to be a bracket, not isolated poets, geniuses, or freaks — a top bracket who had begun to read any current case of interest not only for what it had laid down in words as doctrine or principle, nor only further (or in contrast) for what it had actually and narrowly decided, but for {58} the "flavor" that could indicate how far that court, tomorrow, would stand to today's deci-sion, or would expand it.

Now such reading, though addressed in intention to the future, is addressed in fact even more to the past: it reaches into the opinion for light on what has most strongly moved the court into the actual deciding. It presupposes that when taken in conjunction with, say, the times and what is known of the judges concerned, and read with sensitivity, the *opinion* yields such light. More, it presupposes that there are processes of deciding which remain constant enough to be reckoned with, at least by an artist. Still more, nay, most: this approach to opinions proved to work out in the practical life of law. It made for safer counsel-ing. It won cases on appeal. It brought its practitioners into the top bracket and it kept them there. Here was the *best* practice, ready to feed theory. What remained to be done was to turn into a standard and sustained procedure for anybody's practice (and also for observation inquiry) an approach which had already become familiar for particular persons, particular cases, and particular occasions.

But a "procedure" means more than the flashing insights of the master in the craft. To be a "procedure" a way of work and judgment must be communicable. It must be communicable to a wider variety of lesser men. It must be moderately reliable. It must approach objective terms; it must yield moderately "same" or similar results, within a decent range of human scatter, in the hands of any seven or seventeen different competent and careful users.

Two very different aspects of appellate judicial opinions will be here dis-cussed which thus lend themselves to study and which join to lay the foundation for such a "procedure."

First, most complex, and of basic importance, is the manner in which the opinions use and deal with the prior authorities. (I shall deal here primarily with case authorities, but I wish to make and keep unmistakable the proposition that substantially equivalent principles govern the courts' use of statutory authori-ties.)[48] This involves a re-examination and sharp correction of widely current misbeliefs about our standard practices of precedent and about what theories are appropriate thereto; it involves then some consideration of leads given into the processes of deciding by the {59} ways in which the courts operate within those amazing leeways which are afforded by our system of precedent (and afforded *of course,* I repeat, also by our system of handling statutory or other frozen-word material of authority). There will be some separate treatment of the light on processes of deciding which is to be got from precedents-in-batches, together with the constructs built thereon, be it in grand divisions (concepts and "fields" such as Contracts, Trusts, Agency) or in smaller clusters, be it in com-parative gatherings from different jurisdictions on a single "point" or in time-sequences within a single jurisdiction; in conjunction with all of which we shall be reminded of Fuller's neat observation on the importance, again and again, of the happenstance presence or *absence* of a "conceptual bridge" into a good solution of any novel problem.[49]

The second main matter discussed will be the importance in the deciding process of considerations of sense, decency, policy, wisdom, justice, with special attention to the aid in understanding given these days by the courts' stubborn but still purblind groping toward full recapture of our classic Grand Style.

EXCURSUS ON "SENSE," "WISDOM," "JUSTICE"

The effort in this study is to root discussion and observation in the soil of practice, of common knowledge and the common case. I do not want herrings, red or other, confusing a straight-forward simple trail. I want therefore to avoid any intrusion of issues about the nature or content of justice, and I should like to avoid intrusion of any reactions either to that "unruly horse," "public policy," or, for instance, to such matters as the Macdougal-Lasswell sloganizing of "policy" "science."[50]

There is no need for disagreement or obscuration because of any such things. I am dealing here with A.B.C.'s, and I shall try to keep my key terms fittingly blunt and simple. Thus it is ABC stuff that our appellate courts *are* interested in and *do* feel a *duty to* the production of a result which satisfies, placed upon a ground which also satisfies. One can indicate this crudely as the presence of a felt duty to Justice, a felt duty to The Law, and a third felt duty to satisfy both of the first two at once, if that be possible.

But I am persuaded that "Justice" figures in the daily operations of the appellate court so to speak at one or two removes. That {60} general concept is in its actual impact, I believe, almost utterly vague except for some few ideas fairly well gathered for our lawyers under such heads as "due process". And especially I believe that the general idea of justice has most infrequent direct effect on the deciding in any terms which are at all close to any of the verbalizations current among the philosophical theorists except Edmond Cahn:[51] I believe that there is indeed at work, and consciously, a recognition of and a will to avoid some possible results as being *un*just, or, more closely, "unfair."

For my belief is that "unfair" matches the *working* "justice" concept of the appellate courts almost point for point and with an intensity which the word "Justice" does not often entail for them.[52] And on the side of suggesting positive content, my guess is that "fair," and "right," and, to mark the minimum, "only decent" are words which come close to the flavor of the justice-duty as it works and cooks in the men. What is of interest, what is crucial in this regard, is that such words and the idea they carry can hardly reach and register unless they come all impregnated with a *relatively* concrete *going* life-situation seen as a *type*. The next aspect of the crux is that, in a *going* life-situation, fairness, rightness, minimum decency, injustice look not only back but forward as well, and so infuse themselves not only with past practice but with *good* practice, *right* practice, *right guidance* of practice: i.e., with felt net values in and for the type of situation,[52a] and with policy for legal rules. The crux is completed by the obviousness that this drives the whole "justice" idea, inescapably in some part (I think, in prime part) forward, into prospect, not merely retrospect: into what one can perhaps call the quest for wisdom in the decision.

One can get all of this, for the present purpose, pretty much into three phrases. *Situation-Sense* will serve well enough to indicate the type-facts in their context and at the same time in their pressure for a satisfying working result, coupled with whatever the judge or court brings and adds to the evidence, in the way of knowledge and experience and values to see with, and to judge with. *Wisdom* will serve well enough to indicate a goal of right {61} decision weighted heavily with and for the future. *Reason* I use to lap over both of these, and to include as well the conscious use of the court's best powers to be articulate, especially about wisdom and guidance in the result.

Now no one has insisted or will insist more vocally than I on the importance, for sound analysis, of finding words to mark off the do-elements from the ought-elements in some of the terms too loosely used in discussion of legal-governmental institutions: the importance, for instance, of noting that such an inadequate term as "rule *of* decision" connotes a "*practice of* decision" on the one hand, and a "rule *for* decision" on the other, which two may or may not coincide or even coexist, so that for purposes of analysis "rule *of* decision" becomes a clumsy and tricky tool. "Custom" is another fused and confusing concept of the sort.[53] But I am engaged at this point not in analysis but in description, in description of processes *as they work,* of the processes by which our appellate courts in fact arrive at their decisions. If, as observation, conversation, and published evidence combine to suggest, the things which reach or rise in the judicial mind and moil toward a solution — if those things are in fact multielement compounds, then we have need for descriptive terms which moderately match the nature of these compounds of Isness and Oughtness and what have you more; and "situation-sense" and "wisdom" and "reason" do just that. Somewhat similarly, it was a most inadequate analysis which, several centuries back, took water to be one of the elements; but the most modern breakdown of water into further elements and combinations remains largely irrelevant to the grosser facts and problems of flood, rainfall, irrigation, hydraulics, and water as a natural resource. It is in an area like these latter that this study labors.

I do not wholly disregard, either, a pleasant rhetorical effect: an unfriendly person may feel "justice" to be little concern of a court of law, and may know for certain that "policy" is committed solely to the legislature and the executive. But it takes a bold man to assert that an appellate court should work without the use of either sense or wisdom.

THE LEEWAYS OF PRECEDENT

EARLY AND GRAND STYLE

I know of no phase of our law so misunderstood as our system of precedent. The basic false conception is that a precedent or the precedents will in fact (and in "a precedent-system" ought to) simply dictate the decision in the current case — not sometimes, nor often, nor in special lawn-areas long seeded, weeded, and rolled, and well provided with known expert consulting draftsmen of the third or fourteenth generation, but instead always and everywhere save for freak cases "of first impression" or for uncommon cases which involve "competing analogies," or "conflicts of principle," or a hundred years of creaking obsolescence. It is less precedent than this false conception of precedent which in fact does a certain amount of dictation — much more dictation than is realized by many who may think they are not subject to it. For our style of legal argument is cast in its mold, with inevitable effects (partial but potent) on ways of work and ways of thought and ways of attitude, *and on ways of selective observation.* The misimage seduces counsel into judgment and behavior based on the crazy premise that if you have a good case on available doctrine you *therefore* have a winning case; such behavior loses appeals, which is bad for clients, and it clutters the courts, which is bad both for the courts and for All-of-Us. Moreover, as has been suggested earlier, this false conception perverts by indirection even many who recognize that it does not square with life. These are lawyers who see dismally that the precedents stamp out decisions in no such fashion; the misimage of what "a" precedent-system would be, should be, then beguiles those lawyers into thinking that we do not have one "any more"; or else into thinking that some of the most appellate judges are not on their job, and that appellate judicial work is shot through with hypocrisy.

Now the truth is this: only in times of stagnation or decay does an appellate system even faintly resemble such a picture of detailed dictation by the precedents, and even in times of stagnation and deliberated determination to plant feet flat "upon the ancient ways" {63} movement and change still creep up on the blind side of the stagnators. In contrast, one gets a quick glimpse of the range of precedent's meaning and power in the latter eighteenth century in Fifoot's chapter on *Principle and Precedent*.[54] Mansfield's practice played the gamut from "The cases are hard, but they are too strong to be got over," or flat refusal to move where, and allegedly because, no precedent could be adduced, on through to "All the cases in King William's time are founded on mistaken principle," and to overthrow even of general professional practice "founded . . . in mistake," and to "The reason and spirit of cases make law, not the letter of particular precedents," and to the application of natural justice where the reports made complete default. Moreover, I go wholly with Fifoot that "As a craftsman. Lord Mansfield *observed the accepted canons* of judicial dialectic. . . . The charge of iconoclasm under which he labored was the product not of his methods, but of the policy to which they were directed and of the personality with which they were inspired."[55] (My italics.) It will be noted, moreover, that

Mansfield kept steadily in mind and deed the duty of his office not only to set. precedent and rule for the future, but also to align such precedent with explicit principle and to inform both with life-reason.

But lest you should deem such variety of precedent-use and effect to be absent or unsuitable in hands other than those of the most successfully creative of England's chief justices, correct such error by reading in succession 100 pages from each of a few volumes of reports from the 1840's or 1850's which reflect the American {64} Grand Style, or Classic period, or Manner of Reason, which was briefly discussed above (pp. 36 ff.). Meantime, since you will probably do no such thing, I offer samples.

EXCURSUS: THE AMERICAN GRAND STYLE

One concern here is to illustrate and persuade that such a style existed by showing the persistent and overt recourse to situation-reason in the testing, shaping, and reshaping of the deciding rules — a matter of importance throughout this volume. The companion concern is the one of immediate importance: to demonstrate both careful attention to the received authorities and the presence of a wide and diverse range of techniques at work, in this period too, in the following and use of those authorities. History serves indeed in this study only as background, though essential background; we must therefore be content with two illustrations of what I have tested, for instance, carefully from Massachusetts, 1820-1850, New York, 1804-1864, Pennsylvania through Tilghman's time and Gibson's, the early Indiana and Ohio reports, and the like. Here are presented twenty successive cases from New York; then, with a bit more discussion, ten successive cases (the arguments of counsel made the reports bulkier) from Ohio.

The Grand Style in New York, 1842

To test early New York, I turned first to 1 Hill; I had a desire to show Cowen at work.[55a] But 1 Hill, first hundred pages, turned up little but Bronson. 2 Hill (1842), in contrast, yielded a reasonable variety: Bronson, Cowen, Nelson, and Per Curiam. I report through page 94, where a term ends: twenty cases.

Let me first get rid of the four tailenders, pleading and/or practice cases which are treated purely in those terms. *Briggs v. Brown,* p. 87, sustained a demurrer to a plea in trover, a special plea which amounted to the general issue. *Jessel v. Williamsburgh Ins. Co.,* p. 88, knew "no principle upon which an assignee of a policy of insurance [though taking with insurer's consent] can be allowed to sue in his own name." *People v. Jackson,* p. 92, a Per Curiam (nevertheless headnoted to a couple of points "per Cowen") simply runs through history to sustain the propriety of conviction for a lesser offense. *Haywood v. Miller,* p. 90, which {65} (Per Curiam) wrestles with a somewhat complicated farming contract, might not seem to belong here, until one discovers that it is made to turn on the difference between a lease and a contract-farming, and so on the fact that the action was *trespass.* "The mistake lies in the form of action — in bringing trespass, and not assumpsit." I should like to know more than I do about the share-farming situation in the agricultural New York of the time. I should also like to know why these cases appear, in clump, at the end of the term's work: "Unimportant, to the reporter?" (No: Hill worked with Cowen.) "Tailend stuff?" Hard to tell; I personally see nothing from page 79 on that can be seen as at all controversial, except possibly this farm-labor one.

Let us, therefore, come to the operations which have sharper character. Take first the range of the case law techniques, with the due intermixture of explicit reason:

(a) *Fleming v. Griswold,* pp. 85, 86: "The Court ... did not think their opinion could be changed by discussion ... They considered the rule entirely settled, that where the statute has begun to run against the ancestor ... it continues to run against the plaintiff, notwithstanding any disability [she was then married] when the right accrues to the latter." There is no policy discussion, but in the then conditions of land settlement and the then absence of a recording system, a policy against allowing ancient heirs to inch in under must have been too clear to need discussion. More typical is (b) *Winants v. Sherman,* p. 74, where a common sense ruling on evidence is so stated as to display its common sense and is approved with a single simple cite, or (c) *Young v. Miller,* p. 21, where per Bronson, "a rule has been laid down and acted upon in this state, which, although not entirely satisfactory to my mind, I feel bound to follow," The rule that false words charging an indictable crime involving moral turpitude amount to slander per se, is then shown by five cases, the Bible, theological commentators, and the analogy of forgery of a deed to be very reasonable indeed as applied to a charge of removing landmarks. Cowen sees the rule as perhaps a broadening, but thinks the objection that it is unduly uncertain to be somewhat silly, in the light of the general law of slander.

(d) *Pierce v. Schenck,* p. 28, is an action of trover for logs and boards: the logs had been delivered to defendant under an agreement to saw, he to receive half the boards, which agreement he had broken. Cowen handles the case as a matter of applicable concept: bailment, not sale; policy being touched only in viewing a manufacturer's contract as having the same "entire" character {66} as a laborer's. I have a personal blind spot here; Cowen, for once, bores me with this discussion of "sale or bailment," as Holmes bores me with his similar technical discussion of grain in elevators.[55b] The way to deal with a situation is to look at the situation and its needs, and if no appropriate concept is available, then to make one. Perhaps, underneath, that is what Cowen was doing (cf. pp. 31-32); if so, the arrangement of the opinion is backhanded, and Nelson and Bronson felt Cowen to be pressing too far on the damage phase of the plaintiff's right. But there is no backhandedness in (e) *McMurray v. Rawson,* p. 59; forms of action are still making trouble, but this one is the action of account, seen as "one of the most difficult, dilatory and expensive actions that ever existed." Learning from the Year Books on is mustered by Bronson and Cowen to the good end that account may never again be brought in New York, (f) *Taintor v. Prendergast,* p. 72, is similar in basic drive, completely contrary in method; the liability of the disclosed and undisclosed "foreign" principal — central to the then factorage type of market organization — is explained by Cowen with care and skill. Then: "I am still in want of an authority" that the sensible result in the case in hand, suit *by* the undisclosed principal, can*not* be achieved. Finally, in this context, (g) *Orser v. Hoag,* p. 79, recurs to the problem of ancient heirs, this time those of Tories emigrating during the Revolution; the public policy of the country parades with flags; and to fit New York into it a prior New York case is *overruled.*

There are four cases on various aspects of probate or J.P. administration, in each of which overt sense shapes the rule; in three of them statutes, read with a variety of techniques, are either controlling or helpful. *Shaw v. Beveridge,* p. 26, trespass q.c.f. for a church pew, contrasts American with English conditions of church government and rests on cases which recognize "individual right of property" in a pew. "The remedy by ... trespass ... is, therefore, entirely consistent with established principles; and, indeed, seems to be the most appropriate one that can be brought." (pp. 27-28.) A statute on trespassing cattle, *Stafford v. Ingersoll,* p. 38, and one on notaries, *Onondaga v. Bates,* p. 53, are each construed in the light of history, circumstance, and the court's overt use of sense, as well as the exact language, the former not to destroy a prior common law remedy, the latter to require a notary's personal presentment and certificate thereof. My guess is that the {67} commercial conditions of the time made a notary's presentment, even on a domestic note, a meaningful ceremony, and that the court's judgment was good. *Onondaga* also *extends* the action of debt to cover a suit against an indorser.

I have left for the last two cases of peculiar interest on their facts. *Alexander v. Greene,* p. 9, involved a contract to tow a canal boat, for $30, from New York to Albany, "at the risk of the master and owners thereof." By negligence of the steamboat captain the canal boat became a total loss, and plaintiff had a verdict for over $5000. The elaborate arguments, fully reported, cover almost every imaginable phase of public policy relative to a relatively new and utterly vital industry. Bronson's approach to the policy questions is more stilted: the manner of the operation makes clear that loss by fire would not rest on the towing concern; therefore, they are not common carriers, and fall under the same rule as bailees for hire, which means that they could *bind* themselves as insurers, hence, that they can contract *out of* any risk except their own fraud. The terms "are broad enough to embrace every risk arising from a want of ordinary care and skill, and I think we are not at liberty to construe them in a more limited sense." (pp. 20-21.) Here is not only the full free contract philosophy we shall also meet in Ohio, but an approach to policies on new enterprise and to the hazards of life which was reflected in frontier fighting and city nonsanitation, and which Shaw was shortly to introduce into the field of labor. But conscious policy is at plain work upon the rule.

The other case is *Ex parte Heath,* p. 42. The ward inspectors in a New York City election turned in results from three of the districts of the ward, but certified that violence had dissipated the ballots, uncounted, in the fourth district, making it "impossible" to declare, etc. Mandamus was sought to command the mayor to administer the oath to the men prevailing on the incomplete result. Granted. "Once admit the principle that the loss of a part of the votes . . . avoids the whole and it is difficult to conceive how a system of government so entirely elective as ours could be carried on." (p. 46.) Subsidiary rulings make the statutory date for the canvassers' return directory, so that "The public shall not suffer," and mildly but sensibly manhandle statutory language about administering the oath. Then Cowen comes to a provision of the amended charter that "each board shall be the judge of the qualifications of its own members." A prior charter had spoken of the *sole* power of determining and deciding all elections of all corporate officers. "It is quite doubtful whether the word *qualifications* {68} can, by the most liberal construction, be made to comprehend elections." (p. 51.) And Cowen urges that the court's supervisory power can be destroyed only by enactment "in so many words." In any event, until the common council may act to annul an election, the court can take hold by mandamus. The mayor, Robert H. Morris, had appeared in person to oppose the motion for mandamus. On writ of error to the Court for Correction of Errors, unanimously affirmed. Cowen's opinion speaks for itself in regard to his method and manner of reason, and in regard to the technical ingenuity the judges of the day could mobilize when need was felt to press. But it is especially interesting, in contrast to the standard doctrine of strict hands off regarding Congressional elections — e.g., from one of our Ohio samplings, *Smith v. Polk,* 135 Ohio St. 70, 19 N.E.2d 281 (1939) — to realize that identical words in a statute or constitution can with wisdom and legitimacy be given completely different effect according to whether the body concerned is the Congress of the United States, or the coordinate branch of the State government, or on the other hand some lesser board, body, or common council which experience suggests to most desperately require, at times, the supervisory power of the courts.

Ohio, 1844

The Ohio material is pages 1-84 of 13 Ohio, the first volume I pulled off the shelves one morning during the Cincinnati lectures, when it occurred to me to check up, locally, on a possible early Grand Style. Of course, in regard to the Manner of Reason or any other style, we recall that "a *prevailing style*" does not mean a thing of universal incidence. Men differ, occasions differ. A "prevailing style" is what you reasonably come to expect, and recurrently and characteristically find; in cases of importance you ought to find it eight or nine times out of ten.

Thus the first case deals with a company never chartered as a bank but which had immediately and so successfully assumed banking powers that the law passed thirteen years later to charter and regulate banks was explicitly extended to it only on a point of taxation. This company had refused a domestic discount, and had put the discount into the form of a New York draft, at 11 per cent instead of the 6 per cent permitted by the banking act. The majority see no banking *power* except on terms of compliance with the banking act; see the New York draft as a device of pure evasion; and refuse recovery. The dissenting Chief sees an outfit {69} "whose notes constituted the largest portion of what was called money in the west," which the state has deposited with, borrowed from, and taxed, as recognized in the possession of the banking franchise; and then, in the absence of an Ohio statute flatly declaring more than 6 per cent immoral or corrupt, wishes to follow nonbanking cases which allow recovery of principal and lawful interest not on "the security," but on the loan. Each line of reasoning is in the Grand Manner. *Miami Exporting Co. v. Clark,* p. 1.

In the next case, *McClintock v. Inskip,* p. 21, a statute easing the pleadings in trespass q.c.f. is held nevertheless to require notice of all the material alleged facts of defense which the plaintiff will have to meet; thus that stone taken for a road, even from unimproved land, was really needed. *Brown v. Willis,* p. 27, without citation, cuts through misleading argument by both counsel to upset a verdict for a non-bona-fide holder on a note for which the consideration had failed. *Bancroft v. Blizzard,* p. 30, also makes out without citations: a levying constable levies at his peril on goods not the debtor's; and a debtor's fraudulent intent, if unknown to his assignee for creditors, does not infect the sound purpose of equal distribution or the validity of the transfer. In *Keenan v. Saxton's Administrators,* p. 41, a statute on claims against estates is construed in the light of the court's careful views on the operating needs of intelligent administration. In *Bridgmans v. Wells,* p. 43, a statute which might oust justices of the peace from jurisdiction where title to lands "*may* be drawn in question" is confined so as to avoid application to "small suits," and to the same end "contracts for real estate" do not cover leases or the building of a house; while the formal inadequacy of a purported 5-year lease which has been lived out is met by the fact that the document is sufficient to serve as a personal covenant: a rather pretty set of operations.

Lake v. Columbus Ins. Co., p. 48, shows the court less resilient. A stump or rock tore a four-foot hole in a schooner carrying a cargo of wheat; the master attempted to run her on the towpath, but she grounded and was at once found full of water. The suit was for a partial loss. The policy excepted partial loss unless it exceeded 7 per cent "*and* happen by stranding" in place of the usual "*or* the ship be stranded." The court saw the loss as due to the rock, and bilging — a peril of the sea while under way; stranding and unlading had simply reduced the loss. "It may be presumed that if the plaintiff had read and understood the effect of this clause of the policy, he would not have taken it. . . . {70} And it may be that the phrase 'and happen by stranding' was insidiously inserted with an expectation that the alteration would not be noticed. If this be so, we can only regret it, not help it." (p. 66.) But in contrast, *Easton v. Pennsylvania & Ohio Canal Co.,* p. 79, even while it upheld a forfeiture of a canal construction contract for inadequate prosecution, finds half the court forcing the opinion-writer to add "as the opinion of the court" a dictum that under a complete "opinion" clause "the subject is open to inquiry" as to whether the contractor has given any cause which would justify the declaration of forfeiture.

In *Wilson v. Fleming,* p. 68, the argument that a father's covenant to convey to his son and the latter's wife envisaged entireties with survivorship, rather than an estate in common, was rejected as "utterly inconsistent with the genius and spirit of our laws." The two available near-precedents were appropriately extended. Finally, in *Lessee of Neiswanger v. Gwynne,* p. 74, almost as in the opening case, we have two lines of argument, each of which moves in the Manner of Reason; this time the unanimous court brings counsel's two lines together. In those days when land titles were still very troubling things, and recording offices were not yet, a piece of land had been "entered," and even "surveyed," been "assigned" to the *plaintiff-in-ejectment,* and the patent had been issued to him. Meanwhile it had gone into tax delinquency and been forfeited and sold to a purchaser from whom the defendant in possession derived. The one argument was that the only *legal* title in the picture was the plaintiff's; and the action was ejectment. The counterargument is that land must be taxable, and there was a statute giving a tax deed purchaser "a good and valid title"; and there was allegedly a case which had recognized complete alienation of a prospective patentee's interest by a sale under execution against him. The court is brisk and brief. It moves inside an established procedural frame. "This question appears to have been settled" by one case. "Other authorities may be found to sustain this point, but as we are satisfied with this, it is not deemed necessary to cite them." (pp. 79-80.)

"The plaintiff has a *legal title,* and must prevail in *this* action. The defendant has, at best, but an equitable title. If the proceedings in the tax sale were regular, his remedy is a bill in equity. . . .

"The defendant is entitled to his claim for improvements and for the taxes legally assessed and paid by him."

I do not see how any man can doubt the pervasive tone, in this {71} material, of the quest for type-situation-reason as the determining factor in laying down the rule for the situation. Both precedents and statutes are tested by that, even when they are dealt with as controlling. Neither do I see how any man can doubt that the court is moving with clean and honest effort both to attend to the "law" it has received, and to shape and phrase good "law" for future. Nor, finally, do I see how any man can doubt that the net is a decently competent performance. That is the American Grand Style at work, in Ohio, 1844.

Precedent Range in the Ohio Grand Style

So we come to the question on whether we find any range of techniques in the use of the authorities. It is a short sample: ten cases, only twenty-two pages of *opinion* in 13 Ohio (the rest of the report is counsel's argument). Yet in this tiny sampling we turn up (compare the modern varieties illustrated below at pp. 77 ff.).

1. *Following,* in three or four varieties.
2. *Avoidance* clearly seen as a technique available, and *testing* by reason used (though no avoidance or restriction actually occurs *except on statutes,* and though no overruling is suggested).
3. *Expansion* or fresh start constantly in play.

All, I repeat, in the first ten cases taken in sequence, amounting to only twenty-two pages of terse opinions. While authorities infest the many carefully reported arguments of counsel (and are used all the way from "The court will not depart from," through insistence on distinctions, on into the urging of pure principle or policy with no authority in hail), the authorities cited by the opinions are singularly few. Nevertheless:

On page 66 there is a proposition in the court's own language, with a simple cite, followed by a quotation of what is presumably the announced ground of another case. On page 74, as to a prior case: "This decides the case at bar"; but the prior decision against tenancy by the entireties had dealt with a devise, and the case at bar was an *inter vivos* covenant to give a deed. The extension is entirely legitimate; it is also an unmistakable extension and in terms of reason. On pages 78-79 the reason is expressly examined, and then approved: "This question appears to have been settled in this court in . . . where it was held. . . . Other authorities may be found to sustain this point, *but as we are satisfied with this,* it is not deemed necessary to cite them." (My italics.) {72}

Indeed the broad ruling is in this small sample the preferred ruling. Counsel's alleged distinctions are in the main disregarded without comment — and that is out of key with the style. But sharp reading is familiar. Thus, re a statute limiting banks to a 6 per cent interest in advance, the standard medieval device of turning the "loan" into "exchange on New York . . . would make an important distinction where a substantial difference does not exist" (p. 18), while on page 21 the dissenting Chief, who wants, despite the usury, to save the underlying transaction, as contrasted with the bill of exchange itself, distinguishes to the Queen's taste: "The decision in Bank of Chillicothe v. Paddleford, is in no degree inconsistent with this opinion, as that suit was against sureties who were liable on the security only."

Twice language not even suggested to be holding (there "this court say . . .") is used to make the solving rule or rationale; in one of the instances "the reason" is then given. (pp. 25, 46.) Four times (on 29, twice on 40, on 83) the opinion moves in quiet clarity in terms of principles (not so designated) of both law and sense, without bothering to mention an authority; in one of the instances (p. 29), the whole silly argument of both counsel is simply ignored.

Finally, in regard to the statutes, three cases move, each time, in terms of situation and of sense, and do what is required, despite hindrances in statutory language. *McClintock v. Inskip,* p. 21; *Bridgmans v. Wells,* p. 43 (this is a real — and sane — "adjustment" even of an amendment); *Keenan v. Saxton's Administrators,* p. 41.

And I see *Lessee of Neiswanger v. Gwynne,* p. 75, as another such job, in essence, of statutory construction in the reconciling phase. In this aspect, I do not at all like its technique of not wrestling with the text, even though each contrary aspect had already long entered into common practice. But I regard its fundamental approach as of the essence of all sound construction of statutes which have been around, *unattended,* for any number of years. The Ohio Supreme

Court here, in solid wisdom (though we have no proof that it worked its problem out on the text) did have the insight and sense to think in terms not of "What did that ancient Legislature (if it did at all) *intend?*" but of "How can these statutes, in their combination, be made to make going whole-sense today?" {73}

RANGE IN "FORMAL" OR "MATURE" PRECEDENT:
WAMBAUGH AND BLACK

But in regard to the range of precedent thus illustrated from Mansfield and from these samples of our Grand or Classic period you are not to be misled by either the Fifoots or the Roscoe Pounds into thinking that in a so-called "mature" system of law or of precedent these leeways proceed to disappear.

On this, Wambaugh's evidence is, for this country, conclusive. His *Study of Cases* appeared in 1894, his condensation and revision thereof in 1909,[56] dates which could be taken almost as embracing the zenith-run of formalism, pseudo deduction, attempted rigidity, in American appellate judging. The acceptability of the Wambaugh analysis to an experience and intelligence at once critical, strikingly modern in action, and honored by every branch of the profession, was attested when in 1945 Arthur Vanderbilt selected the 1909 job for reprint in his *Studying Law,* a book addressed in plain purpose to the future.

Now, says Wambaugh: "Perhaps an accurate *statement of this common or lawyers' view* [my italics] is that the law consists of principles already recognized, *plus* lawyers' methods of reasoning, *plus,* finally, the requirements of justice. In other words, according to this view law consists of historical reasons (precedents), analogical reasons (lawyers' logic), and moral reasons (justice)."[57] The "analytical jurist's" sharper view is then put forward in contrast, to show that the courts do in fact make law on new questions, or "creeping on slowly." It is typical of the era and of the mode of thought which it has transmitted to us, that the claim re law-*making* is thus stated at, *and is held to,* the outside fringe of appellate work, and that it is chiefly with an eye to palpably novel questions that "justice" dares into the open. But as Wambaugh moves into detail he leaves no doubt of the range of precedent's {74} operation. "Imperative authority" is assigned to an ultimate court's own decisions; but there is also power to overrule prior decisions, and dicta have "quasi-authority." Moreover, his principle that the doctrine of the case depends on what is in the mind of the court allows "imperative authority" to a very broad proposition indeed, if it has been put forward as the expressed basis of a decision; and allows such authority also to any of the all-out rulings in a multiple-point decision.[58]

Though these propositions, coupled with what was quoted above as the "lawyers' view" and with the courts' freedom to build on and with the persuasiveness of dicta, are quite enough to display a roving range of entirely correct possibilities for developing, and for widening, correct possibilities, indeed, for ingesting into the doctrinal scheme quasi-"decisions," or deliberations, or announced theories, or even mere hints recorded and inherited via the reports, yet this outbranching aspect of our precedent system was not the center of Wambaugh's interest. Instead, *The Study of Cases* devotes over thirty sections to over thirty different specific ways of getting free from a precedent: i.e., of *avoiding* any *control* thereby. Fifteen years of experienced wisdom do then indeed tone down this overemphasis with an appeal in essence to the felt law of leeways. Thus from 1909 we read: "There are sound dicta — thousands of them. There are thousands of decisions which are subject to one or another of the comments enumerated, but which, notwithstanding the comments, would be followed by any court, and rightly."[59]

47

Black had an eye as keen as Wambaugh's, a sense of balance which was at work both earlier and more constantly, and a gratifying patience in research and documentation. His dates of publication almost square with Wambaugh's: 1896 and 1912; but Black's later job, instead of condensing, becomes a full book which both widens out and bores in under.[60] I know no work of equal scope, merit, and direct utility which has been so much neglected; I have used Wambaugh in the detail of the text purely for persuasiveness: he comes with Vanderbilt's accolade. But on the point of substance: every point here made from Wambaugh about the precedent techniques of the Formal period is matched and capped from Black. {75}

* * *

Thus through two whole centuries (Mansfield's appointment was in 1756), through "formative" and "mature" periods, if you want to miscall them that, through Grand Style and Formal, the kit of precedent-tools has been and has remained available for reshaping, for building out or fresh creation, for pruning, for avoiding, for overturning, as well as at hand to guide, urge, or even seem to dictate results in each day's cases as they come before the appellate bench. That is, for two whole centuries if this is still the way things are. Is it? Is our precedent-system still what it so long has been: a system of guidance and suggestion and pressure, and only on occasion a system of dictation-"control"?

The Range of Precedent in Our Time

Let us examine some of the techniques for dealing with precedents which are in current, accepted, unchallenged use among our appellate courts of last resort today. The illustrations will be drawn almost entirely from the last twenty years, perhaps a third being from the '50's; but there are occasional jumps back. I have also included, with regret, perhaps four examples which I think unworthy. But there is no other illustration given which will not be recognized at sight as proper to have appeared in an opinion of any respected American court at any date between 1787 and, so far as we can yet see, 1987. To cut down the risk of misattributing any manner of treating an authority, and especially to make sure that the acting court itself views the manner in question as proper and correct, I have wherever feasible presented the manner of treatment in the court's own language. For this purpose of what one may call the authentication or mint-marking of a technique, I also take today's approving description of what the court did yesterday to or with authorities of the day before to be about as good an index as what the court may have been doing as it wrote. Neither have I hesitated to use an occasional illustration from a dissent or special concurrence: accepted and correct methods of work with precedent are evidenced by any normal judge's deliberate official utterance, they are methods he will be using tomorrow when he is writing for the court. But throughout, lest the citation be considered nontypical of the work of any State, the material is drawn from the highest court of the State in question. {76}

The following classification of standard techniques is rough-hewn. It is above all incomplete. The finer shadings are hard to communicate, perhaps hard to agree upon, and the going diversity even of the coarser approaches is too large to warrant the effort needed to exhaust it. It is enough if one can demonstrate a true multiplicity, each aspect in active use, with variation in direction and degree and with different results if the varying procedures should be applied to the same precedent on the same point in any single pending cause.

The multiplicity is real, and it is vital. It disposes of all question of "control" or dictation by precedent. But it does not, of course, as we shall see at length, impair the importance of the rule of law as a tool of law, or the importance of guidance, suggestion, even pressure, which falls short of absolute control; nor, and especially, does it touch the differential effects and the differential values of clean tools as against clumsy or bad tools.

Meanwhile, to the judge or court each individual precedent technique speaks thus: As you search for the right rule of law to govern the case in hand, *I* am *one* of the things which, respectably, honorably, and in full accordance with the common law tradition as inherited and as currently practiced among your brethren of the high bench — I am *one* of the things you are *formally* entitled in and by your office to do to and with any prior relevant judicial language or holding as it comes before you.[61] To the advocate or counselor the technique talks in slightly different terms: *I* am what the court *may* do (and be within its office and tradition) *to* any prior judicial language or holding *you* may bring forward, however relevant, and/or *with or without* any prior relevant judicial language or holding presented by your adversary or discovered by the court itself.[62] {77}

A SELECTION OF AVAILABLE IMPECCABLE PRECEDENT TECHNIQUES

I. FOLLOWING PRECEDENT

A. *Illustrating Some Conscious Controlling or Even Constricting Effects of Standing or Following*

1. The rule is too firmly established to disturb.[63]

2. Even though doubts are felt or policy disapproved, the rule is still too firmly established to disturb.[64]

3. The wide rule on which the court chose to rest bars out what might have been an appealing distinction.[65]

4. The state of precedent overrides a broader principle otherwise applicable.[66] {78}

5. The constellation of prior decisions has frozen the meaning of the rule.[67]

6. The constellation of prior decisions has frozen the number and nature of legal concepts available to hold new states of fact.[68]

7. The fair implications or tendencies of the cases require stasis.[69]

8. (Anticipatory): Care is taken to defend existing precedent against imputation from the present decision.[70] {79}

B. *Illustrating the Range of Choice Open via Simple "Standing" On or by "Things Decided"*

9. A *rule* previously phrased and held is applied as such and without change.[71]

10. A rule is taken as firmly established — yet movement either occurs or is presaged.[72]

11. The *exact language of the ground* on which the court chose to rest the case is applied without reference to anything more than that language.[73]

12. A *holding* not put by the prior case into rule form or language at all is pulled out, phrased, and followed.[74]

13. The *explicit reason or theory,* rather than either the rule or the holding, is accepted and followed.[75] {80}

14. An established *concept-label* is applied, and some corollary rule follows without more.[76]

15. A *practice of judicial action,* previously unaccompanied by discussion, is noted, stated, and followed.[77]

16. The *hole* in the authorities is followed: no positive precedent, *therefore* no positive right.[78]

C. *Illustrating a Variety of the Simpler Types of Creation, Mostly Conscious, While Following Authority*

17. The prior holding is followed, though it is seen to be distinguishable, because its reason applies.[79] {81}

18. The prior rule is consciously applied or extended to a new fact-situation.[80]

19. The prior rule or distinction is kept from application because its reason does not fit.[81]

20. The authorities are re-examined and their reason and rule approved and applied.[82] (The suspicion being that nonapproval might have led to some different course.)

21. A simple positive rule (or concept) has a negative twin attributed to it which is then duly "applied" as if the negative implication had been considered, announced, and held.[83]

22. *Filling the hole* by the following: there is *no* precedent *against* a remedy; *therefore* a "right" calls one forth.[84]

23. The point which has been explicitly reserved as possibly {82} or probably significant is ruled significant, indeed, and is applied.[85]

24. (Anticipatory): Care is taken in the present opinion to lay out guidance on a point considered but not ruled, and to lay a foundation for a ruling later.[86]

D. *Illustrating Importantly Expansive or Redirected Use of the Precedent-Material*

25. An unnecessarily broad basis for decision is applied to the edge of its language, in uncharted territory.[87]

26. An unnecessarily broad basis for decision is applied via language *and reason* to a bold new area.[88] {83}

27. The whole theory of a complex situation announced in a prior case is accepted, and used beyond the actual holding.[89]

28. A principle theretofore unphrased is extracted from the decisions and applied.[90]

29. "The tendency of the decisions" is stated, consecrated, and founds the ruling.[91]

30. A pure dictum is quoted and consecrated as the authoritative rule, and applied.[92] (How frequent and indeed standard this {84} technique is, the precedent-discussions very rarely suggest. But see Wambaugh, above, p. 74.)

31. An unnecessary ruling is accepted as a principle and applied or even extended.[93] (This seems, today, to account for more than a fifth of the simple citations. See below, p. 103.)

32. A dictum about the reason of a situation is quoted, elevated into the foundation of a principle, and applied.[94]

II. AVOIDANCE OF "THE DECIDED"

A. *Avoidance Without Accepting Responsibility to the Future: Legitimate Techniques*

33. "The rule (or principle) was there recognized, the only difficulty being in its application."[95]

34. "Each case of this kind must be dealt with on its own facts."[96] {85}

35. "This case, in any event, falls outside [or inside] the rule."[97]

36. "Distinguishable," without more.[98]

B. *Avoidance Without Acceptance of Responsibility: Illegitimate Techniques*

37. A distinction is taken, but without a difference (dubiously legitimate, except in a system which will not face up to overruling).[99]

38. The older case, though significantly parallel in real facts, is brushed off because of the "facts" (arti-facts often "constructed") there, while a completely different manner of interpretation and classification is used on the raw facts of the case in hand. (Rarely, barely legitimate.)[100]

39. The older case is knowingly disregarded without mention. (Flatly illegitimate.)[101] {86}

40. The facts in the pending case — or of the "precedent" — are misrepresented or misclassified so as to evade the application of the older case and rule.[102] (Flatly illegitimate in either or any branch.)

C. *Limiting or Narrowing, Explicitly*

41. Kill off a dictum, as such and without more.[103]

42. Distinguish on the facts; especially if the reason is discussed.[104]

43. Undercut and distinguish or disregard via the authorities used in the older case.[105] {87}

44. "We here limit that rule," or other whittling "explanation."[106]

D. *Killing the Precedent*

45. "Must be confined to its exact facts."[107]

46. "Can no longer be regarded as authority, since *Younger v. Older.*"[108] (Means: *Younger v. Older* itself was illegitimate, if consciously silent about its effect on prior authority.)

47. "Involves a misapplication of the true principle" (or rule.)[109]

48. "Is (explicitly) overruled."[110] {88}

III. SOME CORRECT BUT LESS USUAL USES OF MATERIALS OR TECHNIQUES, ESPECIALLY FOR EXPANSION, REDIRECTION, OR FRESH START

A. *Fresh Starts from Old Materials*

49. Capitalization of the mere squint.[111]

50. The spirit of some statute or body of law takes on rule-form.[112]

51. Deliberate and important redirection of a rule.[113] {89}

52. Introducing or establishing a new method of construction of the facts.[114]

53. Material enlargement or subdivision of a concept.[115]

54. Introducing or establishing a new concept.[116]

55. Unchaining a new principle to substitute order for conflict or confusion.[117]

56. (Contrast): Introducing a new pseudo principle to continue conflict or confusion *sub rosa:* Words which do not guide.[118] {90}

B. *Enlarging the Standard Set of Sources or Techniques*

57. Tapping the lower courts, the administrative agency, the attorney general, etc.[119]

58. Resort to the briefs or the record or court's unpublished notes, etc., in regard to the prior case.[120]

59. Enlisting the rule's reason to carry the rule into novel territory.[121]

60. Basing decision and rule on common knowledge and sense.[122]

61. Announcing new principle ex cathedra.[123] {91}

62. Introducing rule or principle from the critical literature.[124]

63. (Anticipatory): The deliberate forward-prophecy.[125]

64. (Anticipatory): The deliberate hedge via an alternative which can, on call, render the main ruling "mere dictum."[126]

ARE SEVEN-WAYED TECHNIQUES IN DAILY USE?

To set up such a workbench of tools as the foregoing — however incomplete — raises the immediate question: Is the range typical? Is such variation common? The so-called "illustrations," it may be argued, are misleading. They are not from any single court and its work; they draw on the whole nation, and at that, they range over a library: the reports from a full score of years. Surely this is akin to the population of the circus freak tent rather than to the general population.

In minor part the answer must be that certain of the tools are indeed for rather infrequent use by any particular court; this, though we and the court may be entirely at home with each of them. Thus Numbers 45 and 48 in my listing — confining to the facts and explicit overruling — are known of old to any lawyer; we have commercial and sometimes semiofficial tables of Cases Overruled. Yet neither the virtual nor the outspoken overrulings can well be a "daily" matter in a regime of "precedent"; indeed such upset must run in very low percentage in any developed legal system. Somewhat similarly, though times and technology be in spate, yet the advent of a new principle can be no affair of every day. *Slade's Case,*[127] *Palsgraf v. Long Island R.R. Co.,*[128] and their ilk can be remembered like decisive battles precisely because they are so few. For all that, the flat overruling and the newly minted principle belong, both, in our array of the known and used. Like a freeze or a hurricane in Florida, they must be reckoned with — perhaps tomorrow. {92}

As to the other Heinz varieties presented, I take my first stand on horse sense: which of them, to any lawyer of experience, seems queer? Which, if met in his home reports in a case not being decided *against him,* would shock him, or bother him, or seem out of the ordinary? Which, if it would serve him, would he feel it improper to urge, or would he, in a good cause, feel to be hopeless? Horse sense reaches further: of what moment is it to the fact of a rich variety and a wide leeway that any one or seven or three dozen of these particular described techniques should not be in play, provided that there is in real use in the particular court at any particular time *some* wide leeway, *some* vitally wide range, and provided that a really multiwayed play of the techniques is to be found in *daily* use: say some form or forms from each of the major divisions proposed above: mere following, creative "following," avoidance, whittling down, branching into new direction, for example,

On this the evidence is as conclusive at it is unfamiliar.

PENNSYLVANIA, MARCH 20, 1944

Thus from the one opinion-day, March 20, 1944, there appear in 349 Pennsylvania 143 pages of opinions delivered by the Supreme Court, speaking through each of the seven justices, with three or more opinions from each of five of them. The subject matter included among other matters a review of action of a state board, a problem on a construction contract, the foreclosure of a conditional sale, four negligence cases — mostly on contributory negligence — control by the court of the handling of a charitable trust, the rights of an informer about an escheat, stockholders' liability, the winding up of a partnership, the Labor Relations Act as applied to a Salvation Army shelter, a suit for recovery of a commission from a political boss, a close corporation's acquisition of a minority holder's pledged stock, and a large number of cases on trusts and estates. But when one goes through those cases that are headed only "Zilch Estate" one finds that the actual legal points are widely varied: There come in question the proper remedy of a contestant of a will, the rights of tenants in common, apportionment between life tenant and remainderman, the book account rule, an attorney's collection, the statute of limitations, allowance of attorney's fees, and so on more. One cannot readily hope to find a batch of material more accidental (so far as concerns {93} range and use of precedent),[129] more varied in scope or in individual writing personnel, while still common to a single jurisdiction, bench, and day, or more definitely mine-run stuff. There were twenty-six cases. What do they show in regard to variety or uniformity of precedent techniques?[130]

> If you had a case or a set of cases which seemed to state the law or to contain it in their holdings, let me show you some of the things that could have happened to you in regard to that case or cases you had relied on if you had hit the Supreme Court of Pennsylvania on March 20, 1944.
>
> You might find that the case cited stood for the whole theory of a whole situation that it laid down, reaching infinitely beyond the exact holding of the case itself. That is what happened on page 30, in *King Estate* (36 A.2d 504). It reads: "In *Buist's Estate,* 297 Pa. 537, 541, 147 A. 608, we decided 'The merger of two or more corporations is neither a sale nor a liquidation of corporate property, but a consolidation of properties, powers, and facilities of the constituent companies.' We specifically held: (542) 'the issuance of the new capital stock is merely the issuance of new evidence of ownership to the shareholders. Accepting shares of stock in the merged company is not tantamount to a distribution or division of assets which calls for an apportionment between a life tenant and remainderman.'" Now comes the wide theory. "Also (543), 'The life tenant is not entitled to any division until (1) the increased value is declared as a cash dividend, or (2) distributed in the form of a stock dividend, or (3) the affairs of the corporation are wound up so that assets are distributed to those entitled to receive them'" (You will notice that one can't *hold* (3) about the same transaction which falls under (1) or (2)) "'or (4) there is a sale of this stock so that the connection of shareholder is entirely severed.'" Now that is the rule re-accepted

and laid down to test all the other Pennsylvania cases, and it isn't a "holding"; it is instead a statement of a theory of the entire situation out of which, one small piece of which, the prior holding had flowed. The Court proceeds to test two later Pennsylvania cases and one Delaware and one English case by that theory, and treats those cases accordingly. {94}

On the other hand you may find that you can't trust the case that you have even for what on its face and its stated facts it held itself out as holding. On the same page the broad theory just quoted proceeds to be applied as follows: "Reliance is placed upon what we stated in *Daily's Estate,* 323 Pa. 42, 186 A. 754, in connection with the respective rights of life tenant and remainderman in a merger and re-organization. But here again if the opinion of the lower court (24 D. & C. 628) be examined, it will be found that the stock was *'being distributed in kind to the parties entitled.'"* That is not in the prior opinion of the Supreme Court. If you had rested on the Supreme Court's opinion in *Daily,* you would have had to think that this was a sharp shift from the rule there laid down, but the Court have decided to quarry in the opinion of the lower court in order to distinguish their own prior case — which, I repeat, might well, on its face, have been thought by you to have modified the *Buist* analysis. These two things occur on a single opinion day, nay, in the same opinion.

Or else you may find with regard to this case on which you are relying that the decisive rule of law will prove to be taken from any language used by the court anywhere, without regard to whether that language represented the holding or a dictum. Thus, for example, on page 10 (*Merchants' Warehouse v. Gelder,* 36 A.2d 444) language from prior cases is cited in the same tone as "We said," and "We held," and is used equally to lay down the rule of Pennsylvania which then governs the reasoning. And on page 127 (*Valera v. Reading Co.,* 36 A.2d 644) we find that the rule is laid down in terms of what "is well established," and again in terms of what "We said," and then in terms of "the tendency of our decisions," (which means that we neither held *nor* said what we now will take as the law of Pennsylvania).

Again, what you find the Court turning to as giving Pennsylvania's law on your case in hand may not be the language nor yet the holding of a case, but something altogether different, and to me very lovely. What it states the law of Pennsylvania to be built on may be not the *rule* laid down anywhere along the line, but the *reason* given for a prior rule or holding or announced in the course of its discussion, which is then developed and applied in terms of the reason and not of the rule, and this occurs on page 46 (*Sgarlat v. Griffith,* 36 A.2d 330), and in *Huffman Estate (No. 3)* (36 A.2d 640), on page 61 and on page 62.

Or else, when you present your authority that you are relying on, you may find that the court instead will seize and develop analogies from other cases as being the law, though those cases are concededly not in point and have no quotable language that is in point. Thus, for example, on page 80 (*Speare Estate,* 36 A.2d 489) {95} they "compare" four cases, give no other authorities, and use the proposition for which the "compare" reference was made. On page 84 (*Danner Estate,* 36 A.2d 328) they do the same. But each time they are stating the law of Pennsylvania, remember, as they go along, *and using it to decide the case*

54

before them. On page 40 (*Rosengarten Estate,* 36 A.2d 310) they "see" three cases and no other authority is given, and on page 71 (*Schmick Estate,* 36 A.2d 305) they "see" no less than nine cases which the court does not feel it safe or decent to cite as flat authority, but from which the proposition is derived on which the Court builds.

On the other hand, the fact that a point was actually held under the stricter tests of holding and dictum is so important to its being authority for the rule that the court finds a real value on pages 39 (the same *Rosengarten Estate*) and 68 (the same *Schmick Estate*) in setting forth the facts and precise issue, so that anyone can see that the particular point was really and exactly decided.

Indeed the Court may distinguish your case if the actual holding is not sharply in point on the facts. So it distinguished away on page 31 (*King Estate*) two prior cases that had language which had been relied on by counsel; and on page 104 (*Scheckter v. Rubin,* 36 A.2d 315), again, it distinguishes and discards because of a difference on the facts. But the court may also — always on the same day — decide that it will *not* distinguish in terms of a distinction which you press upon it and which concededly is present on the facts, as was done on page 110 in the *Salvation Army Case,* 36 A.2d 479.

So that the explicit ground on which the court chose to rest the previous case can either be played up as vital, as it was in the same *King Estate* opinion on page 31, or it can be reformulated as it was on page 117 (*Hand Estate,* 36 A.2d 485). That last is not quite a fair citation because in the original case the point had not been a major ground. What the court did do, however, was to take what had been done in the prior case and reformulate it with a materially different emphasis to produce the rule laid down and used in the case in hand.

Finally, and somewhat charmingly, the court reminds us, again in *King Estate,* at page 31 (my italics) that, "*We have never overruled or modified this decision.*" I have to judge from that that the Court is familiar with the modification and overruling of *some* of its *other* decisions.

To cap this particular exhibit, even when you have finally worked out what the *rule* is, then comes the question of certainty of the *outcome* in your particular case, and on this I want to quote you from page 135 (*Disston Estate,* 36 A.2d 457). "The {96} rule in such cases is, as Judge Gest said in *Williamson's Estate,* 3 D. & C. 1, adopted by the Superior Court, 82 Pa. Superior Ct. 444, 446, that '. . . such a broad interpretation will not be given to the bequest, unless it clearly appears from the context to have been the meaning of the testator, or unless the will would otherwise be inoperative.'" So we now know what the law is, though I may note that that one comes not from this court but from a lower court. "*On the application of that principle to the record before us, the six members of this court who heard argument are evenly divided.*"

I urge that a proposition has been demonstrated: The rule of law which will prevail in Pennsylvania and control the cause you will be arguing tomorrow is not to be determined by the authorities *alone;* neither is it to be determined *alone* by those authorities plus the accepted and correct techniques for using and handling those authorities. Indeed, those accepted and correct techniques point in all directions at once.

NEW YORK, JULY 11, 1939,
AND FURTHER SAMPLINGS

So the high court of Penn's Woodland is a strange, abnormal court? Compare a single opinion-day of another court, the New York Court of Appeals, July 11, 1939, recorded in 281 N.Y. 13-317. There were thirty-nine cases, with six or more opinions from each of the six sitting judges except Loughran (three). The subject matter was almost half governmental: two eminent domain cases, two on liability of schools, a case each on control of milk and of public carters, civil service, the manipulation of an appropriation bill, the sales tax, the utilities tax, the estate tax, four cases on phases of judicial administration. There were three labor dispute cases, torts ranging from malpractice to wrongful death, with one suit by brother "against sister." There were liquidations of a bank and of an insurance company, a criminal case, a surrogate accounting, a charitable trust, a forged indorsement, two cases involving errors by corporate officers, an arbitration, and two contracts cases, one of them (believe it or not) on a pure first-year contracts revocation of an offer. Surely this also amounts to daily grist, and with a richer scatter.

Combing of the material turned up twenty-four or more identifiable different precedent techniques reaching repeatedly into every one of the "legitimate" groups suggested above. A crosscheck of the court's work a year later, 283 N.Y. 1-303, *but with a new Chief and with three new judges* on the bench, matched all {97} but two of the July 11 techniques and added on four which had not been spotted in the earlier material.[131]

To further test the typicality of the 1939 New York picture the study was continued into the first 300 pages of comparable volumes from Massachusetts (presumably in 1939, since Rugg had presided 1911-1938, a court rather conservative in manner), Washington, to check on a court sitting in two divisions, North Carolina, and Ohio. Some dozens of the more briefly quotable gleanings from these inquiries are strewn through the annotations to The Range of Precedent in Our Time, above at pages 77 ff. There were differences in manner. There were differences in frankness: e.g., Massachusetts was then still writing often: "*Betts v. Botts* is distinguishable" as if it meant per se: "The *Betts* case *can* be distinguished, *therefore* and without inquiry into reason it *ought* to be distinguished, and it hereby, again regardless of reason, *is* distinguished and confined." But there was no significant difference among the courts in the basic fact of wide scatter of precedent techniques (or of techniques in use of statutes). Neither was there significant difference in the normality for the court or for the individual judge of reaching for any tool from the workbench in order, as the felt need might be, to "follow," or to avoid or whittle, or to extend or expand, or to redirect. There was even a little straight following which involved no net change at all, unless the deeper graving of an already well-graven line be seen as change.

OHIO AND THE SYLLABUS, 1953

Ohio deserves a special word because at the 1940 University of Cincinnati Conference on Precedent I heard Chief Justice Weygandt announce with conviction that the Ohio lawyer knew that the syllabus stated the law — certainly when screened through the facts — so that though nonsyllabus men might smile, Ohio lawyers had much less trouble than others on the matter of precedent.[132] This did not fit either with general theory or with what {98} I had been finding in the Ohio cases, so I have been on the lookout since.

The general theory of the Ohio syllabus system is that the court-prepared syllabus states the law of the State. I do not know whether the Chief meant, also, that the court's opinion does not state the law of the State. But if the "system" were what it officially purports to be, it would be substituting carefully considered digest-paragraphs for the more loosely written opinion-text as the precedent-material for use, and would therefore, *if* the theory were lived by, greatly cut down on growth or direction-shift by way of dicta or of rule-rationale or of such announced rules or rulings as have not seemed vital to the court which decided the prior case. One might of course fear that the opinion would become surplusage, and would not be felt as available to confine and distinguish a syllabus, or, on the other hand, to underpin a syllabus by showing that some current contention had been carefully taken into account before the syllabus rule was formulated — much less, to build a rule of law not mentioned in the syllabus.

Neither the 1939 study, however, nor a subsequent one in 1953 uncovered any effects of this character. Detail to illustrate this is reported chiefly from the latter.

Thus in the *General Cigar* case, 111 N.E.2d 265, 268, a prior case is distinguished on its facts without mention of the syllabus, though the latter had been so worded as to invite the distinction. In the *Grain Dealers Insurance* case, 111 N.E.2d 256, 260 f., a prior syllabus is quoted, doubted, distinguished, and confined. In *Taylor v. Monroe,* 109 N.E.2d 271, 273: "Plaintiff argues that the recent decision rendered in this court in the Gunderson case necessitates a rejection of those contentions of the defendants. However, since no such contentions were considered *in either the syllabus, the majority opinion or the dissenting opinion,* we believe it appropriate to consider these contentions . . ." (my italics). In the *Elyria Telephone* case, 110 N.E.2d 59, 63, a prior syllabus (like any other ruling) is distinguished in terms of its explicit language. In *Daniel's Estate,* 111 N.E.2d 252, a syllabus {99} was (like any other announced ratio) quoted and used to help decide, an available distinction passing unmentioned. The Hamilton County Court of Appeals used Supreme Court syllabi during this period (sixteen cases) in the same way, e.g., quoting and applying a syllabus as such in one case, in another citing and using two pairs of cases as such without mention of the syllabus in either. The pattern squares with the first sketchy observation. And compare *Welsh v. Ledyard,* 167 Ohio St. 57, 146 N.E.2d 299 (1957), where a suit by a wife based on a purchase of a defective appliance by her husband fell outside of a prior syllabus which spoke only of a subpurchaser and the manufacturers, but the court resorted to the prior opinion to find and then apply "no privity, hence no implied warranty." Compare also *Northwestern Ohio etc. Co. v. Public Utilities Commission,* 135 Ohio St. 85, 19 N.E.2d 648 (1939) (per Weygandt, himself): "The single question here presented is whether the principle announced by this court in the syllabus in the *Norwalk* case, *supra,* is decisive. . . . *The difficulty with the appellant's theory is that in the opinion in the* Norwalk *case, supra, the court indicated its rationale in the following language:*" (my italics). The rationale, plus a fact "the court had in mind," is then made to control the decision. Let me mention, finally, *Jolley v. Martin,* 158 Ohio St. 416, 109 N.E.2d 652 (1952), presented below at page 150, where the stubborn insistence of the dissenter on a pertinent syllabus paragraph in a prior case was quietly ignored by the majority. In the net, while syllabi were used when apt (as a simple straight citation or phrased ground of decision commonly is) their treatment by the court — though Weygandt was still Chief — reflected no recognition at all of their supposedly superior status. The current Ohio sample made for the present study shows no break in this continuity. While the scatter of general precedent techniques and their use was in each study cousin-german to that in the other courts.

I have only checked Ohio, but the nature of the case is clear: not even a "syllabus system" can escape from the flat fact: Divergent, mutually inconsistent precedent techniques are at work in the *daily mine-run* of appellate cases. *The little case, the ordinary case, is a constant occasion and vehicle for creative choice and creative activity, for the shaping and on-going reshaping of our case law.*

That is our system of *precedent*.

(And let me remind again, lest saying one thing should be misread as implying the negation of another, and though statutes and their treatment are not the subject of this study — let me remind {100} again that a significantly similar variety of techniques and creativity in their employment is found in the region of the statutory authorities. There, too, superstition obscures the eye of the profession — and of the judges.)

CHOICE, USE, AND FREQUENCY OF THE
TECHNIQUES: LIGHT ON DECIDING

With such assorted wealth of tools at hand, their choice and use become in part a key to craftsman and to craft. I turn to the latest Northeastern advance sheet to reach my desk as I write, and run through the first eight or nine cases,[133] all from the Illinois Supreme Court. Some half of these are criminal cases, but the count of the precedent techniques employed in the use of prior Illinois cases is entirely typical.

Rules of law used to reach the result on points before the court are rested thirty-nine times on simple citations (twenty-two of these to a single case, twelve to two cases each, five to three or four apiece); sometimes the rule is "established" or "well established," or "we have repeatedly held." Once, to complete the forty "followings," the rule is given as "stated" in one case and as applied in another, and then controls. Perhaps half of these citations go to a routine or incidental type of point.

Against this stand only fifteen instances of any other techniques. Once a "well-established" rule is buttressed by three "see's" and one "cf."; once a mere "cf." supports the rule announced and used; three times the support is a "see" (twice to a pair of cases); twice "we have said" a controlling rule; once a case is used, for an application, whose facts "resemble" the case in hand. One case is cited to show an additional controlling purpose in a statute, once two cases are cited to show a controlling policy. One case is distinguished on its facts. One prior heavy innovation is mentioned and relied on, in which one case had been overruled and a batch of cases carefully distinguished; and there is one mention (and following) of a prior refusal to take a distinction.

All of this is typical enough of the mine-run of appellate opinions. (I am not going to "prove" this. All you have to do is pick up a report.) But before either accepting or challenging the conclusion which seems to shine forth — that the work is largely moving through walled channels to pre-explored familiar goals — skepticism, and horse sense as well, must raise the query: can we {101} trust these simple citations? For it takes no labor to pin a citation on behind a proposition of alleged law, and some demonstrably weird things have at times been attributed to cases cited as if they had been precedents.

CAN THE SIMPLE CITE BE TRUSTED?

One begins with the observation that on the whole the finer type of tool does not appeal to the blunter type of mind; and that the easy citation is the undiscriminating simple cite. Hence, if the work of the court is coarse either in doctrinal perception or in the sorting of authority, one ought to expect straight simple cites and little else, wherever the material is being cited for support.

Instead of this, on one point out of every four, we find here the use of some sharper technique. That ought to mean an appropriately careful use of the blunt one. Moreover, a shading down, on the very face of the opinion, of the degree of support attributed to many of the citations suggests candor as well as care, and suggests in consequence that when the simple cite is used without qualification that use ought to prove justifiable if tested.

To this type of presumption from the workmanship one adds a presumption from the nature of the problems: half or so of the points in question are, as noted, the incidental or routine type of point, where a rough foothold is all that is needed, and where there is no occasion or motive to force the material; and point after point, in addition, is the footless product of misguided or incompetent appeal: it is indeed truly and cleanly settled, and a settling case is at hand.

We can add a further presumption, perhaps, from the body of material used as authority: there were four hundred and more volumes of Illinois Supreme Court reports to draw on; clean, simple, correct citations ought thus to be available on a multitude of points.

And still we are not done with the horse-sense probabilities that simple citations will, on testing, stand up. For even the nastier-tongued among the cavilers will have a tough time showing any normal motivation for distorting many of the authorities. We are dealing here, you recall, with the ordinary day-by-day case, the case which to a caviler is "mere routine." If, now, cases generally are really as ambiguous as such a person is likely to claim with his "decide them any [or either] way they find fitting, and then pick the authorities to suit," then there will be straight cites enough at hand, and honest ones, too; but if what is being claimed {102} is some furtive desire on the part of the court to cover-up, what *can* there be, in eleven cases out of twelve, for the court to *want* to cover? Honesty must be conceded; "prejudice" feels little need of secrecy; "bigotry" equals conviction; and politically hot potatoes are infrequent. Unless the charge is to be that our State supreme courts are in general too lazy or too incompetent to read their cited cases accurately, the horse-sense argument for the general trustworthiness of the simple citation is pretty powerful.

That argument is strikingly borne out by a series of sample-checks undertaken for me some years back by Peter Lederer. On two of the volumes discussed above, 281 New York (1939) and 349 Pennsylvania (1944), the first 300 pages were completely canvassed. To get a "current" sample, the same was done with 5 Ill. 2d (1955). A small sample was then checked also from two other of the 1939-1940 studies (218 N.C. and 5 Wash. 2d, both 1940); from 303 N.Y. (1951-1952) (the material of the Buffalo lectures); from 159 Ohio St. (1953) (discussed above); and (since Massachusetts had once been "different") from 331 Mass. (1954). Each of the small samples covered every fifth citation until 100 instances of precedent technique had been located and checked on.

The total simple citations tested were 588 in number. Only 53 (9 per cent) of the instances turned up dicta instead of rulings; in one of the courts the percentage was 13, in two others there was only a single instance out of 30 or so. Except for one of the small samplings, where the court was at the moment faction-ridden, and three-judge fighting dissents were sometimes straining citations, there was a scant one per cent of straight cites which seemed plainly erroneous.

This means a gratifyingly high degree of care in workmanship. It means that on the whole the "we said" tag is being used with discrimination, the simple citation being reserved for rulings as contrasted with mere language.

Lederer picks up a further interesting refinement: in 127 further instances the court, instead of just citing, announced that "we there held" or "we decided." In 116 (91 per cent) of those instances the statement was accurate under the strictest of testings; in only 3 instances (all in a single court) was there merely a dictum to be found; twice the citation went to a ruling which was not, however, in strictness a holding; 5 times, and only 5 times, the proposition allegedly held was expanded enough beyond the narrow actual holding to involve *unmistakable* creation. On this type of expansion of the holding, 4 per cent among the "we held's" compares with 6 per cent among the simple cites. {103}

But what (though I should have foreseen it) came to me from the figures with surprise is that as against the less than 2 per cent of rulings which could not rate strictly as "holdings" among the "we held" citations, *the mere simple cites turned up 172, more than 29 per cent.* There were more than one out of five in every single sample.

It is quite plain what this means, and it is a thing which few people know. It means that whereas there works among the appellate judges a live and careful awareness of the technical difference between a strict holding and a ruling which cannot rate as a holding (as evidenced by the caution in stating "there we *held*"), yet *for the court itself* a ruling no longer needs the credentials of a "holding" in order to be available for unqualified reliance and use. There is nothing new in this, as such; you can for instance cite Wambaugh and Black and Morgan in regard to the respectability of such a ruling. But what I read Lederer's results to mean goes not to doctrine, but to practice. And it is a thing which you will not find suggested in those or any other writers on the subject: to wit, that if you are trying to get away from a "nonholding" ruling today, you would do well to go at it as seriously as if it were the flattest holding; you had better rest your distinction solidly on reason and the facts.[134] The supreme courts are *building*. And they like it.

*   *   *

As human phenomena go, the simple citation has thus proved to be a highly reliable and little abused manner of marshaling authority in an opinion; and we are back to the fact of its overwhelming quantitative predominance, as the opinions actually run, in comparison with any other single precedent technique or indeed with all the others en bloc. Surely the case is made for a high degree of continuity of our appellate deciding with that case law which is the heritage and one main portion of the equipment of our appellate courts. "What has become of our system of precedent" is that that system is in flower. Surely the case is made as well for the fact that the ranging rack of tools upon the wall does not mean the daily exploitation of their more unreckonable possibilities. {104}

*   *   *

Why indeed — if we may get back to horse sense — should we expect other than this overwhelming predominance of the simple cite, with all the continuity which that implies? Few men — including appellate judges — like bootless labor. The books are full of precedents, and one will mostly be in point. And if a simple cite to a clear case will do the work, why not use it? Let us press the point: if a clear precedent (much more so, a clean line of precedents) volunteers to solve the pending problem, and if the solution will strike at least on the target of decency, does this not satisfy without more the felt need of the judicial soul to serve the law and at the same time to serve the right? The relevant authority — called to attention, remember, if counsel has any competence, *before* the court decides — the relevant authority is then *recognized* as showing a way and a light, and its guidance is in deep truth *followed*. Should counsel have proved useless or distracting, and the relevant authority have to be dredged up from memory or by independent research, it still will pack punch in the process of deciding (not merely in relation to a later justification). For the "feel" for the proper outcome which can inform a judge's mind (or inform, indeed, a whole conference room) as an aura of the facts still remains for the normal appellate judge in the normal case in a degree of pendency, of suspension; it remains so to speak in solution until the reagent of some available (and O so welcome) authority precipitates it into visible tangible finality.

True, not every temperament, not every background, effectively maintains — or sustains — such suspension and true suspense. True, again, the inclination "on the facts" to a decision one way or the other may loom strong as well as early; and judge after judge, here and abroad, has spoken or written of it as if it were normally determinative.[135] I am, however, very clear about three things in this regard. The first is that James was right, that for the most part the completed decision wipes off memory's slate most of the process of its attainment;[136] so that I {105} distrust most introspective postevent reports. The second is that such generalizations are almost sure, even when careful and based accurately on instances, to be overgeneralizations of instances selectively remembered and unduly weighted. The third is that the holding of net judgment in suspense is a way of operation which can in material degree be learned, and which is emblazoned before our judges by their office as their duty, to be learned and to be practiced. And while anyone knows of one appellate judge or two or five in history or on the bench today who have lacked either desire or capacity in this regard, I see such as exceptional, so that overearly freezing (as contrasted with inclination) of view about the result of the case seems to me vastly less frequent in incidence on the appellate than on the trial bench — at least partly, I suspect, because of the presence and tradition of the group; at least partly, too, because of the relative speed with which the two sides spread themselves before the appellate court.

In any event, with the whole bright tool kit gleaming before them, the appellate courts do recurrently, persistently, and with commendable accuracy of craftsmanship, "*follow*" single decisions or sequences of decisions, with a simple citation of case to proposition, by a ratio of two to one or three to one or five to one more often than they resort to any other instrument of precedent technique. Neither, where they have available precedents of their own, do most courts, in this, do too much wandering afield.

I am arguing, be it remembered, that this *following* works not merely in the form of the opinion-justification, but also and importantly in the psychological process of reaching the decision.

Justifiable simple citation as the foundation for points, in this relative frequency and in the opinions of a court which is rather careful in indicating its other ways of use of authorities — this seems to me, I repeat, to come close to forcing the conclusion that the court *tends, as a practice,* to follow, or "stand by," "things decided," *and wishes, as a practice,* to follow "things decided."

One might rest on that, in regard to both desire and effect of conscious and careful continuity. Yet there is enough talk abroad about "excuses for doing what they want" to warrant some inquiry into whether we can show this "following" to be more than such an excuse. I think we can make some headway there.

But the moment we have got that done, I want immediate {106} avoidance of any false conclusion: I want to move then promptly into showing how wide the *creative* range is, *even* as a court *follows*, or stands on or by, "things decided."[137]

THE IMPACT OF SHAPED DOCTRINE

That shaped doctrine does shape actual deciding can at times approach demonstration; the argument is then that such phenomena bring out into the occasional sun processes which, although recurrent, almost standard, can in the main be reached only by inference. Let me offer four examples. Two are cases in which given doctrine has fashioned, almost dictated, both form and result of a conclusion recognized both as troublesome to reach and as essentially novel in the law. If doctrine can stamp its signature on such deciding, how much more when an unprickly decision simply "comes to pass"!

(1) The suit was against a city whose waterworks had delivered typhoid-infected water to a householder. The count in question was on sale with implied warranty of fitness for consumption. Retailers had already been held liable; a mere restaurateur who had not made the article he served had been distinguished by dictum. The case now struck seven divergent views from eleven judges in the two appellate instances; three of the opinions elaborately canvassed the policy-problems involved. My interest is in the dissent of Cuthbert Pound, a judge with a consistent record of craftsmanship, forthrightness, and earthy common sense. "If we adopt, as it seems inevitable, the theory that the water supplied by a municipal corporation for domestic purposes is sold as such by it to the consumers, *I fail to comprehend how we can escape the application of the doctrine of implied warranty of wholesomeness.*" (My italics.)[138] What a Pound could here manage in the very midst of hot and vocal clash of policies — a blunt, unreasoned application of a controlling concept, simply {107} as of course — that any lesser judge will be found doing without conscious puzzlement, and again and again, in the less exciting business of the week. If the result had been shocking, a Cuthbert Pound might indeed be expected to rethink and try over, and perhaps find another road. A lesser judge may be more or may be less open to such shock, but he will certainly be harder put to it to engineer his escape from the pressure of the "inevitable" concept (unless "by main strength" in lieu of craftsmanship) and may, along with a Pound's legal ingenuity, lack also his spirit or his industry. But the point is clear: this *given* legal concept can close in, can seem to solve without more, and can assume the air of the inevitable, and it will take much to make a court even *want* to break out of the corral.[139]

(2) In the early days "express warranty" was conceived as a contract "collateral" to the sale of goods. Once title had passed, once, i.e., the "sale" phase of the transaction had "exhausted" itself, nothing was deemed "left" to afford a remedy unless there was this surviving "collateral" contract. Hence an unusable horse, a whole cargo of defective wheat, a steamboat too slow to compete, were not returnable no matter how explicit the words of warranty. But mistake as to the "essence," or fraud: these infected the taking of title, and therefore allowed rescission thereof. During thirty-two years there arose in Massachusetts six successive cases in which mistake, fraud, or total failure of consideration was each time sufficiently present to blend warranty ideas and discussion with the notion of rescission for breach. When the pure warranty question was then presented for the first time, England, New York, and Parsons, C. J. (of the home Commonwealth) were all discarded, and homespun doctrine was followed as controlling law: "the law of this Commonwealth, *as understood and practiced upon for more than forty years.*"[140] (my italics). The flat compulsion which the beliefs and actions of the bar can thus produce in forty years without a holding will be produced by a holding, certainly by a series of holdings, in ten years or five or two.[141]

(3) *Metropolitan Life v. Union Trust*[142] involved alleged liability {108} under title insurance for assessments *not so levied so as to become a lien* till after the date of the policy, though they represented local improvements made before that date with all implementation except the levy. (I omit report citations): "In *Doonan v. Killelea* it was said . . . 'The covenant against incumbrances operates *in praesenti* and is broken the instant it is made if an incumbrance exists, but *unless the assessment is then an actual lien* [*my italics*], *the covenant is not broken'* . . .

"The case of *Mayers v. Van Schaick* . . . is controlling here. It is stronger against plaintiff than is the instant case. . . .

"Plaintiff relies in good part in support of its contention on *De Peyster v. Murphy*. In view of the decisions in *Real Estate Corp. v. Harper, Doonan v. Killelea* and *Mayers v. Van Schaick* it must be considered that *De Peyster v. Murphy* is overruled." I find it hard to conceive that this can represent anything other than an effort simply to apply what is taken as established and controlling doctrine — and to straighten out the rule.

(4) *In Valera v. Reading Co.* the Pennsylvania stop, look, and listen rule was applied to bar recovery by a motorist injured on a dark grade crossing with a 400-foot clear view, despite his testimony that he stopped and looked and listened 25 feet from the crossing. The motorist's passenger, in the same opinion, was allowed his recovery; there can thus be no covert holding that the railroad's negligence had not been made out. No; the court termed the stop, look, listen rule "unbending," and so treated it.[143] Can the decisive impact of established doctrine here be doubted?

MOVEMENT, AS WE "STAND" ON
"THE" THINGS DECIDED

When one has gotten this far, however, it is time to peel the eyes. Too many good men have found themselves talking and indeed thinking as if this following or applying of the established were a simple process, one of no great moment *or responsibility*, in any event one to be played down in a study of the major problems of the appellate court.[144] {109}

Head-on I challenge the soundness of any such approach. For the long haul, for the large-scale reshaping and growth of doctrine and of our legal institutions, I hold the almost unnoticed changes to be more significant than the historic key cases, the cumulations of the one rivaling and then outweighing the crisis-character of the other. If the nature of case law growth and adjustment were the subject of the present study (as it is not), I should even be arguing with detail and persistence that in the main the difference between the great judgments which become leading cases and various equally striking judgments (they are so many!) which have sunk into obscurity lies largely in the massing around the former of these little "insignificant" applications which first built them in and then built them up and thereafter built them out into unsuspected range and into a strength which never was their own.[145] But whatever the long-haul story, the short-haul scene can leave no doubt of how cardinal are these little, these semiautomatic applications and followings. *Each one decides an appellate case.* "There, but for the grace of God, go you!" Those cases which fork off into what will one day be new broad bearing boughs of doctrine are vital indeed; but your litigation and mine, of Tuesday next, or Thursday, plays out among the twigs. "Changes rung upon the familiar" they may be, in Pound's disparaging figure, but they are changes which determine reversal or affirmance; they are vital, to litigants; what we can do with them, or for them, as they come, that we must do.

In presenting a few of the recognized and practiced authority techniques, above at page 77, I tried to group and phrase them in such fashion as to remind of how very many completely distinct aspects of a case or of a doctrine there are, any one of which can be selected to be "followed," each time with the possibility open to the court of preferring to "follow" by way of some other very different aspect. There were set out some twenty-six distinct operations, leading in regard to any ordinary precedent to an impressive divergence in the possible net shaping of the bit of law in question, and *each one of which could be righteously buttressed* {110} *by a simple cite*. And all of this on a level moderately close to the facts, to the exact issue, and to the narrow holding. Let us have that in mind, as we repeat:

"We are back then, with the overwhelming predominance of the simple citation, in the actual building of opinions.

"Why, indeed, should the simple citation not be dominant?"

Why not, indeed! For the smith's hammer still strikes and shapes, notwithstanding that none but the most justifiable of simple citations may stud the shield of the opinion.

*　　*　　*

Let us run through a few illustrations which suggest this type of change, rehammering, reshaping, in two aspects. The first aspect suggests the appellate court as consciously at work, but on a point of application, development, or redirection which appears either so minor or so obvious that it happens as of course. The second aspect suggests that in the absence of a dissident and vocal minority the operation might well have gone by without any active consciousness that what was occurring was other than a routine repetition of the past.

In the New York foreign remittance series, below at pages 208 ff., the Appellate Division first sustained a statute which exempted banks issuing drafts or letters of credit from the requirement of a bond, which the statute imposed upon steamship ticket agents who went into the business of receiving money for transmission abroad. Seven years later, with a cable transfer before it, the same Department relied on the earlier decision with a simple straight citation to a simple proposition, and thereby built out and built up the picture of the *banker's* foreign exchange work as one, indeed the major, significant *type,* with operations not tied to any physical sending of money physically received. Compare, now, the original language with the revised version to which the first case is simple-cited:

Technically speaking, there is a marked distinction between issuing a draft, or traveler's check	Technically speaking, there is a marked distinction between issuing a draft, or traveler's check *or transferring money by cable*
and receiving money for transmission.	and receiving money for *actual* transmission. [My italics.]
[Thus the opinion relied on.]	[Thus the passage which relies.]

The enlargement of scope ("or *transferring money by cable*") and the sharpening of contrast ("*actual* transmission") are both as {111} legitimate as they were deliberate. Yet this apparent "standing" on a point decided has nevertheless launched a whole new judicial enterprise, the intelligent regulation of a vital phase of large-scale international banking — a thing not adumbrated in the earlier case.

Or consider the extension which can come by simple flat "application" of a formula. In *Canton Provision Co. v. Gauder,* 130 Ohio St. 43, 196 N.E. 634 (1935), the plaintiff's mother had bought liver sausage in the original gut-wrapper from a retail butcher. Suit was in tort against the butcher and the manufacturer, and jurisdiction over the latter cause turned on whether the allegations embraced the defendants as joint tort feasors. The court held not; in the process, the opinion adverted to and denied any possible liability based on warranty: "There was no privity of contract between the plaintiff and either of the defendants...." (130 Ohio St. at 48.) In *Wood v. General Electric Co.,* 159 Ohio St. 273, 279, 112 N.E.2d 8 (1953), "no privity and hence no implied warranty" is turned from dictum or rationale into held law, so as to bar suit in warranty by the subpurchaser of a defective appliance against the manufacturer. Only then is the family case cleanly presented, in 1957, in *Welsh v. Ledyard,* 167 Ohio St. 57, 146 N.E.2d 299. The purchaser's wife is now barred in Per Curiam of-courseness by quotation of these two "no privity" passages — this in a day when third-party beneficiary recovery has become normal, and in regard to a domestic cooking appliance bought for the plaintiff's home; this, also, in spite of the fact that two judges drop off the wagon in dissent and that the majority take time out to save a possibility of recovery if the plaintiff will only allege in words what the facts shout without need for words; to wit, that the wife was an intended beneficiary. It is hard to conceive an opinion in which "mere application" is more clearly felt by the applying court to be not "mere" at all — and yet operates.

More frequently such active pseudo "standing" on "the" things decided moves unfretted by such awareness or semi-worry. A good instance is *State ex rel. Oregon-W.R. & N. Co. v. Walla Walla County,* 5 Wash. 2d 95, 104 P.2d 764 (1940). There a coop which owned a grain elevator had induced the county to establish, by regular procedures, 1100 feet of road from the state highway to the elevator, including a 200-foot grade crossing over the relator's track. One vital question went, obviously, to whether the proposed road could qualify as a "public highway." I shall now italicize a succession of significantly shifting words. In *State ex rel. Chicago, Milwaukee & Puget Sound Ry. v. Public* {112} *Service Commission,* 77 Wash. 529, 137 Pac. 1057 (1914), it had been "held that a *railroad spur,* intended primarily for the use of a single shipper, but available upon reasonable terms to the public at large, was a public *use.*" In the course of that opinion, the court had quoted from an Iowa case: "And we think that it makes no difference that the mine owner may be the only member of the public who may have occasion to use *the way* after it has been established.... If all the people have the right to use it, it is a public *way,* although the number of people who have occasion to exercise the right is very small." Later, in a case dealing with establishing a public *necessity,* the court came back to this *Milwaukee Ry.* case as "somewhat analogous to the present situation. Therein it was held that the character of *way,* whether public or private, is not determined by the extent of the use, and if all the people have the right to use it, no matter if but one person asks for its construction, it is a public *way.*" *State ex rel. Northern Pacific R. Co. v. Public Service Commission,* 95 Wash. 376, 163 Pac. 1143 (1917). Thus, with the Iowa mine-road to help in the transition of language and of concept, a railroad's "public *use*" has spread over into a "public *way*," the "but one person" aspect of the case has become central, and — for irony or for evenhanded justice — what was done *for* railroads is now ready to be done *to* one of them: the Walla Walla road *across* the tracks will be a public *highway*. I do not believe that the Iowa case — or others like it — was an essential factor, though it oiled the axles; and while I see the gathering of material in the final *Walla Walla* case as obviously planned and the final expansion from railway to highway as an open-eyed expansion, yet I think the *Northern Pacific* intermediate bridge-interpretation of the original case to be the very type of the unconscious but often prophetic reshaping which is here under discussion.

Such operation in the doing of the daily, none too puzzling chores can sometimes have a surprising get. Thus, in a somewhat earlier Ohio case a mere appropriately "humanitarian" application of an act "humanitarian in its concept" suddenly assumes a life of its own and produces a new phrasing of a rule which if it had been buttressed by following would have been enough to reverse the whole second-stage trend of Workmen's Compensation Act construction on the point of scope.[146] In *Laudato v. Hunkin-Conkey Construction Co.*, 135 Ohio St. 127, 19 N.E.2d 898 (1939), the injured workman was to load wheelbarrows with {113} debris, send them down from the sixth floor, and unload them below. Against instructions, he rode down with his wheelbarrows in the material hoist. "The descent was consistent with a continuance rather than a termination of his work. It cannot be denied that he was at all times in the general performance of the duties he was employed to perform. The injury did not have its cause *outside of and disconnected with the employment*." (135 Ohio St. at 133; *court's italics!!*) Note the knockout wallop packed by "*and*" when the test goes into the negative phrasing; note also the effect of the paraphrase. The statute reads "arising out of and in the course of."

Or an application may be made in the teeth of the reason of the rule applied, the court not noting that effect; which means, once the new application is properly included in a doctrinal synthesis, that the rule has now cut itself loose from the original reason. Cardozo has of course noted this, in general. But I need to drive it home in particular; it is a sharply separate subclass among the many forms of "following." In *Eagles v. General Electric Co.*, 5 Wash. 2d 20, 104 P.2d 912 (1940), one question which required decision was whether the plaintiff cestuis, bringing their action against their trustees and the person in possession of certain disputed realty, were barred because the statute of limitations had run against the trustees as such. The court rested on cases from outside the State, calling attention to the reason those cases stated for the rule which thus bars the cestui: he has failed to do what lay in his own power, to wit, to require the trustee to act. Then that rule is "applied," but thus: "It follows also that the circumstance that the appellants did not learn the facts until May, 1938, is wholly immaterial." (5 Wash. 2d at 31-32.) To me this says that whereas in ordinary limitations cases we make quite a number of qualifications based on opportunity to discover the facts, especially in regard, e.g., to nondisclosures by fiduciaries, yet in this derivative limitations matter, which rests in reason on the cestui's having been improvident in his inaction against his trustee, we are not even interested in whether he ever had any opportunity to be improvident because he never discovered that he needed to move. Surely this is an "application" ("It *follows ... wholly immaterial.*") with new rough-shoeing, an "obviousness" with unacknowledged teeth.

There must be an end to illustrations, but it will never do to leave a misimpression that it is only extension or redirection which slithers in under the guise of solid stance. Under the same guise, one can also find the checking, or the reversal, of movement, {114} of momentum, which has come to be embodied in some "things decided." The New York story on the oddities of seals, told below at pages 206 ff., ought to be enough to make that point.

Meantime there are at least two other processes of redirection of prior rules and holdings which deserve mention here, each of which can often occur in as-of-course nonpuzzlement. The one is the recoloring, by new circumstances, of a word, or what is for the present purpose in the same category, the reassortment or reemphasis, by new circumstances, of the elements of a concept. The latter Levi has followed in illuminating detail in his examination of the cases which led up to and followed *McPherson v. Buick:* the shift of stress from action to article to situation, of idea from imminently to inherently dangerous articles and then to potency for danger, and so on.[147] I cannot doubt that from time to time along the line of those cases counsel managed one or another of these shifts skillfully enough to make the desired result seem obviously "well within" the precedents. Levi also presents cogently the recoloring of particular words, as he traces the sequence of decisions on the Mann Act. A single instance will make my point: against the background of the furor and the debate, the "White Slave Act" in 1910 used the word "debauchery," and what was in mind seems surely to have been young girls and accomplished outrage. Yet by 1913, with the help of a companion case which spotlighted the "purpose" of prostitution, the "purpose" of "debauchery" was satisfied when improper advances were made to a girl on her arrival to join a chorus in a theater. That shift of color and consequent extension seems to me to have been almost automatic.

The second process, which I suspect at least in the stages of transition to force its way into consciousness, and which reaches not one case or one rule at a time, but a whole area of legal thinking, lies in a shift of the manner of seeing and feeling — and in consequence, of reading and classifying — which a court brings to its office and above all to the facts of the cases. This kind of shift can turn results topsy-turvy without disturbing one hair plastered on the balding pate of doctrine. Mansfield's instinct for the jugular showed itself when he sought to construe wills and precedents according to the spirit rather than the letter; and it is not a rigor of rule but a rigor of attitude which closes the iron maiden when a "commercial document is read through the eyes of a convey-ancer." {115}

Look at a couple of offer and acceptance cases. *Neer v. Lang,* 252 Fed. 575 (2d Cir. 1918), laid down a rule that "an acceptance is required to be identical with the offer," and that "Every trade or business has its usages, and persons who make offers relating thereto assume that all the customary incidents of such callings shall be part of the agreement." The case held that where a letter had read: "would sell 20 shares at 400," an answering wire: "We accept twenty Saxon at four hundred *ship with draft attached*" (my italics), "imported a new item into the acceptance and prevented a contract from being made." But the very rules laid down in *Neer* can be *followed* in comfort to produce a reverse result on the same facts. The words I have italicized can be read as a suggestion, not a condition; indeed, offers for spot sale at a distance can more than reasona-bly be seen as including "the customary incident" of a documentary draft for the price presented through normal banking channels.[148]

Again, to bring the matter into a case sequence in a single jurisdiction, in *Wood v. Duff-Gordon,* 222 N.Y. 88, 118 N.E. 214 (1917), an agreement for a minimum of a year gave a plaintiff with an organization the exclusive privilege to market the defendant's style-designs. It was held so to imply an assumption of appropriate duties by the plaintiff as to support his action for breach. The 4-3 decision (in which McLaughlin concurred) represented the third main step in Cardozo's successful campaign to put the reading of a commercial document on a basis dominated neither by conveyancing nor by the Langdell-Williston rigidities of "basic" contract theory. Four years later, however, Cardozo happened to be not sitting when *Oscar Schlegel Manufacturing Co. v. Peter Cooper's Glue Factory,* 231 N.Y. 459, 132 N.E. 148 (1921), presented the problem of a manufacturer's letter "entering . . . your contract for your requirements of 'special BB' glue for the year 1916," with the buyer-jobber's signed "Accepted" at the bottom of the letter. The price had skyrocketed; the buyer had drummed up "requirements"; the manufacturer, after delivering more than double anything in the prior 5-year history, was being sued for nondelivery. McLaughlin wrote to reverse a judgment for the plaintiff. His ground was that the plaintiff had made no enforceable contract because it had made no promise and had incurred no obligation, and that no standard was mentioned by which the quantity to be furnished could be determined. *Duff-Gordon,* 132 N.E. at 150, "is not in conflict." There "this court held that such a promise was {116} fairly to be implied": defendant had there given plaintiff an *exclusive* privilege. The unanimous court plainly sees itself as applying the same little batch of doctrine to a case which falls into the other basket; they can be led by a Cardozo into a commercial reading, but they cannot yet do a commercial reading for themselves. So that in the same year those same judges, all but one (who got converted with a bang two years later),[149] join Cardozo in as strong a statement of the commercial attitude as can be located in the books: "Indefiniteness must reach the point where construction becomes futile."[150] The *Schlegel* case is now shrugged off on its alleged facts: "There the option stood alone." It so stood by force of the court's handiwork of interpretation; it did not so stand by force of the raw facts as they came. Whether all of the court realized this, I do not know; I suspect awareness that the reasoning of *Schlegel* had been a blob. But it is impossible that Cardozo did not know it. His leaving of that case as if it were not out of harmony can be viewed only as a most undesirable precedent technique forced on him, in a good long-range cause, by the necessities of colleagues' face and of amicable relations in the over-all job. — The whole story illustrates how *"following"* a single little batch of rules can lead, *according to the eyes which size up the facts,* in almost any direction, indeed in different directions in succession. Compare page 85, note 100.

The upshot, then, is this: Beneath what looks on the page as "mere" following, beneath what I shall argue to feel and seem, in the main, to the very deciding court itself to be such "mere" following, there swirls a constant current of creation. Kenyon, devoting heart and brain to *standing* on the ancient ways, is nonetheless a subject for any legal Galileo: "And yet it *does* move!" This is the region in which the modern logician revels as he exposes the manipulation of the minor premise and watches the reasoner clamp some concept-label upon a still amorphous mass of problem-facts and thereby haul "the case" in under a major premise which may have no particular need in either history or reason to apply. It is the region of which the psychologist delights to tell how man (including the appellate judge) approaches a new and puzzling mass of data equipped with a very limited number of familiar and possibly suitable gestalts or patterns, absorption into any one of which will tend to reduce or wholly drain off the discomfort of the puzzle. Such gestalts, for the appellate {117} judge, are the legal concepts handed down by his tradition, and even strange things which once get themselves classified under one of them can in the main be dealt with in relative personal peace; and the psychologist joins with the horse-sense observer in insisting that appellate judges are not wholly unlike other men in welcoming peace or surcease after the stress of intellectual toil.

WHY DO WE NOT NOTICE AS WE MOVE?

Cardozo's testimony is interesting on the existence of this creative leeway, also or more so on the dark twilight which shades its use. From *The Nature* on through, his books' picture and emphasis center on the case of *conscious* worry over precedent, on the case where "history" and/or "logic" strive against felt need, and judges wrestle with angels through the night. Those are the queer cases, those are the memorable ones, memorable as much for infrequency as for importance. But all the while both his introspection and his reading were ripening, until he was ready for a richer insight: in 1932 he twice quoted with marked approval: "Every lawyer knows that a prior case may, at the will of the court, 'stand' either for the narrowest point to which its holding may be reduced, or for the widest formulation that its *ratio decidendi* will allow."[151]

"At the will" is an unlucky wording, though beguiling; it means neither "in whimsy" nor "in willfulness" nor "in selfwill"; but the phrase is seductive because it does so neatly sharpen the point of conscious and controlling — even though limited and responsible — *final choice.* Neither by character nor by context does Cardozo leave room for misconstruction; and it is exciting to observe how he opens up the road for heavy reshaping while still "following." On the one hand: "The principle that is invoked *arguendo* may often be whittled down or even rejected altogether," and again (my italics): "*it was not merely what was ruled nor merely what was said* in explanation of the ruling, but at one time the ruling and at another time the explanation, *that has the vitalizing capacity to shape the form of law thereafter.*"[152] More: "I have no doubt that even dicta have been propagating forces and have borne a fruitful progeny."[153] But it is no less {118} exciting that even here each process of which this careful craftsman talks is a conscious process, a matter of full intention, an act verily of "will." To be so keenly aware of the tradition and its compulsions, to have nonetheless become so clear as to the fact, room, and much of the manner of the leeways, yet still to treat the matter (for the fourth time in eleven years, and this time in full and explicit response to realist writing) as if conscious "will" blanketed the ground — this is to demonstrate the almost alarming measure in which remolding while "following" can and does remain obscure or get itself forgotten, so long as the steps taken be either small or easy and "natural."

History and the nature of a lawyer's work have all but formed a conspiracy to dim out what occurs and to sponge away its memory. The fact is that every opinion is in one aspect an argument, an argument prepared by a lawyer. It is an argument to the writer himself, it is an argument to his brethren, it is an argument to bar or public or both. The fact is, moreover, that once a lawyer accepts an outcome, two things happen without need for his perception of their occurrence, and happen even though he may be stewing hard over how to shape the argument. The one of these things is that, without much work or thought, the facts reweigh, realign, recolor themselves, as has been noted above, into a familiar and therefore persuasive pattern or gestalt. The other thing is that every authority the lawyer looks at puts on, within the range of what does not grate or creak, a garb and mien which is favorable to the desired result. These things take place in the very process of his meeting the fact or the authority. The first sniff which warns that an opinion may tend against him puts on the advocate's nose the reading-spectacles of "All that case held was . . ."; whereas any language which may even squint in the desired direction glows on the page, and the eye races forward in hope for what may be a forceful phrasing "of the true principle"; holdings arrange themselves like soldiers at muster call — all, save for the truly tough ones, in the mere process of taking in the print upon the paper. Labor, conscious worry, about such matters begins only when such pseudo-automatic operations have failed to turn up a satisfying result. And in all of this the opinion-writing judge is not only a lawyer but an advocate.

What is thus true of the appellate judge when he turns to the authorities in readying his opinion is true in no less significant degree in the earlier stages of his work. There, too, he is a human being, and there, too, he is a lawyer. He shows one sharp {119} difference from the lawyer in practice. The practicing lawyer's drive is to find and take a side, and at once, to see for, to see with, to see from. This drive the appellate judge must resist, and he does. Nonetheless, as he meets the facts of a fresh case, or, once the facts are semiclear, as he approaches an authority for guidance toward decision, he is engaged in human questing for a diagnosis and an organization of the problem, and in lawyer questing for a *legal* way to see and to pose the issue, and for a *legal* line along which to puzzle. The conclusion is indeed not yet given, but the quest and urge for a satisfying picture, and for a satisfying answer: they are given. The mind therefore sorts, arranges, turns, rearranges the facts in one tryout after another, in search for some firm shape that "fits," that poses and sharpens a problem, perhaps even suggests a solution. The mind thus almost of itself spots and highlights in an authority the available facet which feels as if it may give a lead.

It is true that for the judge as judge and for the judge as lawyer these quick processes will often cross the threshold of consciousness; also, it may take toil to dig out the proper application of an authority or the "proper" or best way to put several authorities together; it may cost time and sweat to work stubborn fact-details into some workable pattern. But two traditions are at the elbow to wipe away all memory of such creative hours or moments, *to prevent the little memories from building into cumulation.* Each of the two traditions is bred in the bone. The first is the old feeling that the answer must be right — which means mostly that the answerer "found" it, "recognized" it, rather than that he made it; even the vain man tends to pride himself in this achievement rather on his sure eye than on his touch upon the clay; the latter is the memory suited rather to the more sustained ventures of the office. The second tradition lies in our mode of argument: its form, as has been mentioned, is deductive, and it, too, speaks the tongue of single correctness; to plan and compose a brief or an opinion in this key is to blur or even erase the recollection of a passing fluidity now long gone. Add that most men by their make-up notice chiefly when at work the peculiar or the bothersome. That also is the stuff a working man recalls. While the notice of the outside observer is attracted by successive records, and these instants of flux are recorded but scantily, if ever, and are never indexed. Finally, I suppose, there is that quirk of selective memory which sets up the remembered as practically the whole: if these seventeen cases are all the cases of {120} significant change I recall from forty years, then they are all the cases of significant change which, in those forty years, I ever saw.

* * *

It was mentioned above that history had played its part in thickening night over what I think of as this tradition-based, hidden, coral-style creation. The reference was to the failure of the Langdell-Williston type of casebook to render the process both patent and trite. Books could hardly have been better designed to such a purpose: each used to contain a long sequence of cases on a single theme, from a single jurisdiction (England), each involving change, each one, moreover, purportedly resting on the very material with which the class itself had just been wrestling. Such case series are hard to find in today's casebooks, though something of the kind is vital to any solid legal education. Yet the conclusions about how appellate courts work which ought to have been drawn from the older casebooks went largely undrawn, the lessons went unlearned or slighted. For the teaching emphasis tended ever more strongly away from how the successive courts had used the slowly changing or expanding body of precedent; it shifted rather to the unfolding and uncovering of some "true" principle assumed to have been in the law all along, or else to the current state of doctrine. The psychological effect was to take the eye off the creative power of the single precedent, or indeed of precedents in series, or of the courts; neither "application" nor "illustration" nor "discovery" nor "net result" points up any shaping by the potter-judge's hand.

SITUATION-SENSE AND REASON

{121}

Noticed or unnoticed, the indications from doctrine are multiwayed, the techniques for handling the authorities are multiform, yet as to most pending cases the prior relevant authority is made to speak with a single, persuasive tongue. The fact that we know the judges assures us that this is owing neither to magic nor to Delphic inspiration. If, on the other hand, it were typically a chance result on the order of roulette or even tossing pennies, the lawyers handling an appellate practice with success would little resemble those who do today, nor could many appellate judges of personal integrity stay out of the asylum.[154] Moreover, plain use of individual personal judgment, good or bad, according to the particular occasion, will not explain such phenomena as the overwhelming ratio of reasonably justifiable simple cites to all the other precedent techniques combined. Nor yet will these three possibilities twine together.

What clue have we then? The answer is found first in that other major duty of the court, unimplemented by much doctrinal or other verbal machinery, but there, live, throbbing like a heart: the felt duty to justice which twins with the duty to the law.

The justice-duty works, as has been noted, through the facts. The thrust of fireside equities may be deplored, but who doubts that an appellate court can be open to it? "Hard cases make bad law" reminds us that the thrust may be enough to twist an otherwise good rule out of shape. The evidence for this draws on more than "common knowledge" (which can so often be unmasked as common superstition); it draws on that most uncommon knowledge which I call horse sense, the balanced shrewdness of the expert in the art. Two legal generations ago the best appellate {122} lawyers were taking pains about their "atmosphere" (though they might blush a trifle in confessing it) and using it to win cases difficult on "the law"; indeed, today, where is the leader of the appellate bar who does not see and preach "the statement of the facts" as the heart of almost any appeal?

Much less frequently phrased is the differential impact of the facts of the individual case and the facts of the situation taken as a type, the distinction on which I have already insisted, and which I shall have to stress throughout. I do not suggest of course that because the two are distinct in nature and in use they need to be separate in life or to be kept separate in argument: one of Davis' greatnesses as an advocate lay in his ability to combine the two and make the particular lend its poignancy and appeal to the more general situation which was in turn to shape the rule. But for purposes of analysis and for purposes of the best appellate judging we need to keep the type-situation-facts clear as a peculiar kind of facts with a peculiar message, nay, mission. I doubt if the matter has ever been better put than by that amazing legal historian and commercial lawyer, Levin Goldschmidt: "Every fact-pattern of common life, so far as the legal order can take it in, carries within itself its appropriate, natural rules, its right law. This is a natural law which is real, not imaginary; it is not a creature of mere

72

reason, but rests on the solid foundation of what reason can recognize in the nature of man and of the life conditions of the time and place; it is thus not eternal nor changeless nor everywhere the same, but is indwelling in the very circumstances of life. The highest task of law-giving consists in uncovering and implementing this immanent law."[155]

When we turn to our own courts, taking cases either in the mass or in time-sequence on a single point, it sometimes becomes possible to document a heavy pressure of the situation-facts.

(a) There was a rule announced in *Littlejohn v. Shaw* about buyers who have rejected their seller's shipment: "By thus *formally* stating their objections, they must be held to have waived all other objections."[156] (My italics.) The rule is fair enough if the buyer at the time of rejection ought to have known or did know of the defect he failed to mention and if his assignment of reason also really deserves the label "formal," meaning "considered and to be acted on," and doubly so if his silence has kept the seller from working a permissible and possible cure of the {123} defective tender, or has led to unwarranted surprise in the litigation. When, in contrast, such qualifications go unobserved and the rule is coarsened into a curt: Any defects unmentioned on rejection are barred, the result can be obnoxious.[157] Disregarding now those courts and opinions in which either the rule is tailored to reason or due reason is manifest in the facts, we find a curious pile of cases in which courts normally sensitive enough to decency announce and apply the rule in its crassest form, without discussion and not infrequently with an air of brusqueness.[158] Though in some of these cases such a ruling is a makeweight, often it appears as an important or main ground.

How is this to be explained? One starts by recalling that in the bulk of business purchases at a distance, the commercial tolerances for deliveries commonly, and especially in respect of standardized types of merchandise bought for resale, run well beyond the legal, and that price adjustment or, more rarely, replacement, is in normal circumstances the expected result of a tender which falls anywhere within reasonable commercial expectation.[159] Against that background, it does not surprise to find in case after case, as Eno shows, the court noting explicitly that the defect in question does not appear to be the true ground of rejection; it is rather that the market has turned sour, and the buyer is seeking a purely legalistic out. But if in those cases the court thus with a touch of relish trumps the sharper's ace, are {124} we not to view it as possible or probable, wherever the market-drop appears in the facts, that the court's reaction, though unelaborated, has been not dissimilar? Especially if it be a court otherwise sensitive to commerce or to decency. Eno pushed his inquiry further, and from facts outside the opinions found cause in a significant number of the "mere" applications of the blunt rule to suspect a contract evasion known to and unwelcome to the court: a rule in its harshest form is applied in a recurring situation *which the harsh form of the rule happens to fit.* Equally important to his conclusion was the infrequency of incidence of the harsh form of the rule in those other recurring situations which the harsh form did not fit.

(b) If this illustration scatters too far over space and time, or shows more exceptions or uncertainties than one could wish, then pick up a couple of time-sequences within single jurisdictions. The common law remedies on conditional sale reward examination. Here is a situation plainly in the nature of security for an earned purchase price. The cases in hand come up "at law," not "in equity," and they rest typically on provisions of the contract. The facts protest that the seller should have a fair remedy, but not an oppressive one. Lo, starting in Massachusetts, the strange and awkward doctrine of election of seller's remedy was first developed, then applied *at law* to whole series of cases in such fashion as, on the particular facts, to yield satisfying results in almost every instance. California followed the Massachusetts trail, with independent grace notes.[160] The test, case by case, and regardless of which clumsy tool may have been called on for make-do, is to weigh the nature of the goods, the price, the amount already paid, the seeming value of the buyer's user to date, the probable depreciation, and then to judge whether the remedy actually granted does not rough-fit into a lay understanding of what an installment-purchase is all about. The work was accomplished at times by qualifying the doctrine — e.g., suit for early install- ments held to constitute no election[161] — but partly the reasonable results were achieved even while the doctrine was being pushed into wording of portentous extravagance — e.g., the mere starting of a suit for the full or remaining price {125} is announced to be an election,[162] or a lease-form requiring surrender after the last "rental" payment is said to allow complete forfeiture of payments plus absolute recapture.[163] With the technical machinery so cumbersome, with an- nounced doctrine getting out of hand in either direction, and with the trade's draftsmen now outraged, now outrageous, a radical retooling of concept and rule was plainly needed. Yet while it lasted each of the two series of decisions demon- strated the unceasing thrust of the situation-facts toward a fair solution and toward application, development, or readaptation of doctrine to decent ends.

(c) The material already mentioned from Levi's book fits here again, alt- hough he was not writing to our purpose. His sequences, it will be recalled, are the English and New York cases up to and after *McPherson v. Buick,* and the history and successive interpretations of the Mann Act.[164] His interest centers more than, at this point, mine does, on the manner of rationalizing the case results and on the manner of their integration into lines for future guidance, but his picture is directly relevant to the processes of actual deciding: the guiding, limiting, and suggestive power of a concept-label or slogan; the incursion of changing or changed community ideas and standards by way of shift in attitudes or in the language-meaning of such a label; the impact of life-conditions and of learned categories and meanings via "reasoning by example" on the legal classification of a novel problem-situation or of a novel variant. Practically all the English cases he so presents as to shed light on how, in the processes of deciding, both the immediate facts and the type-situation played upon the courts, and upon both the use and the shaping of doctrine; so also the *Winches- ter, Litchfield,* and *McPherson* cases from New York and both of the Second Circuit cases. The same is true also with regard to a number of the Mann Act decisions, as the "traffic," "victim," and "coercion" ideas fade away. Neither series leaves room for doubt that, case by case, *one* of the important factors at work as the court decided was the pressure of the facts, with constant reaching for a sound way to fit the facts into some significant pattern or type.

In addition, as to the latter sequence, attention should be called to two fur- ther matters, notwithstanding that the present {126} volume touches only in passing on either statutory material or the Supreme Court. There is first that cornucopia of discrepant techniques for reading statutory language which Levi samples much more freely than is usual, both in quotation and in illustration; there is second the fact that his desire to have any earlier interpretation of statutory language wall in a future court must be recognized as thus far embod- ied in only one of the lines of cases. There are other lines as well. For my money, the matter is not too dissimilar to the case law situation in regard to heavy open departure from or even overruling of a clear case law precedent. There is good doctrine and good sense that either of these is bad to do. There is also good doctrine and good sense that under adequate pressure it is in order. The sound course depends on the vision, tact, and skill of the steersman.

THE SITUATION SPEAKS ONLY THROUGH THE COURT

(d) I have personally never studied in detail any sequence which so eloquently depicts the impact of the situation-facts as do the New York sales warranty cases from 1804 to 1873.[165] They include a tale, stirring even today, on the question of what came to make out a "sample" and to entail responsibility for compliance of the bulk, with the companion question of seller's responsibility for false packing of a bale when the bale was at hand and when nothing got said about the manner of its packing. The insistent facts in question are not those presented in most detail, those of the particular transaction or parties, but instead the background facts, those of mercantile practice, those of the situation-type, which in large measure parties and courts simply assume. The opinion-writers speak with assurance, as if expert in their evaluation of practice and policy. They throw themselves with passion into the production of a *rule* which will do justice to both. We meet a succession of powerful personalities, each of them thus consciously expert and responsible. But the doctrine they lay down is stark seesaw: Savage and Nelson (both prowarranty); then Walworth, *contra;* Cowen (at first anti-warranty, then the greatest creator of them all); Paige (as violently antiwarranty as Gibson of Pennsylvania, and as ruthless in his distortion of prior facts and holdings);[166] Selden and Gardiner swinging {127} back then into the "secular" trend of widening seller's obligation.

What lifts this material out of mercantile and indeed local ancient history — however humanly interesting — into priceless ore for living general theory is that the practices, the situation, the life-needs, to which each of the moiling judges strove to fit the rules: these were identical, though the conclusions gun-fight. The problem was the hurly-burly of the New York factorage market after the Erie Canal had opened, but before the general incursion of contracts for future delivery. A Walworth or Paige had his eye on the seller, the helpless local factor who knew nothing at all of the history or contents of barrels or bales his principal had shipped him, whom it would therefore be shocking to hold responsible when he had made no explicit engagement; doubly so when the goods were there at the dicker, for any careful buyer to look at and to look into before he closed his deal. But before the eyes of Savage, of Nelson, of Cowen within a year of his judgeship, flamed a vastly different scene: a busy market, too busy for the opening of every bale and box, with tacit responsibility an absolute and fair condition of safe informal speed, and with high turnover (plus perhaps remedy over) an adequate protection to any selling factor. The consequent point of general theory goes to the essence: *Only as a judge or court knows* the facts of life, *only as they truly understand* those facts of life, *only as they have it in them to rightly evaluate those facts and to fashion rightly a sound rule* and an apt remedy, *can they lift the burden* Goldschmidt lays upon them: to uncover and to implement the immanent law.[167] Life-circumstances in general, like case-circumstances in particular, work in appellate deciding only on and through definite human beings: the sitting judges.

I make no apology for trumpeting this truth so obvious that it should be shopworn. In the first place, almost everything else thus far "discovered" about appellate judicial deciding which is at all worth knowing has also and all along been so obvious that it ought to have become shopworn. The trouble is that obviousnesses still hang too often hidden like Poe's purloined letter. In the second place, and as has been mentioned above, altogether too much that everybody "knows" just isn't so; there is consequent comfort and cheer in evidence as pungent and persuasive as this chain of cases that one important thing which all good believers believe is really true. In the third place, this particular truth is vital to our instant business. It bears directly on our {128} problem of how appellate courts do their deciding because it throws into ambiguity a basketful of otherwise telling and troubling evidence. For there are decisions whose outcome may turn the observer's stomach, but in which the opinion proceeds as though the matter were flatly settled by the authorities, and may sometimes garnish those authorities with "principle" and even "policy." If read without note of the proposition here in hand, such opinions appear to show a blinding coerciveness in the authorities, coupled often with a survival of the most rigid Formal Style, at times, in addition, with that style's overproneness to perversity. If, however, the court rendering the unhappy decision was ignorant of or insensitive to the life-situation involved, then nothing was present to press at all toward deflection from straight flow down the marked and easy channel, and the holding testifies not to conquest by precedent over judges' impulses, "vagrant" or fine, but merely to the appeal of the normal line of least resistance. Nor is the ambiguity dissipated by the court's recital of what counsel have vainly urged upon it unless one can be reasonably sure that the record or the argument or both were so made as to inform, and register upon, the court. It is astonishing how often the opinion makes unmistakable that that has *not* been done.[168]

FACT AND SENSE IN THE
MODERN APPELLATE COURT

Now the cynic or the perfectionist may chide that what has been adduced above about the pressure of fact and feeling gets nowhere, whether in regard to "fireside equities" or in regard to wise arrangements for the type of problem-situation. Such a mass of cases as those on defects unmentioned at the time of rejection, would run the argument, is typical of too few points of law to be of much daily importance — if indeed the alleged example can itself stand up; and the same holds for such rare and improbable series as those on election in conditional sales, while Levi's cases either share the same defect or else are English or else statutory. {129} As for the New York warranty stuff, this very study — if it be believed — has shown that stuff to be empty of meaning for today, for those opinions derive wholly from the times and manner of a Golden Age as legendary or at least as dead as good King Arthur; they hold no message for this naughty modern world.

Fortunately, our knowledge of what leads to choice among the plethora of correct doctrinal possibilities does not depend upon our earlier history alone, nor yet upon indirect evidence from our Formal period. For decades now, the evidence has been spreading itself weekly upon the printed pages of the current advance sheets.

And let a basic canon of interpretation be well noted: An opinion written in the Formal Style has no need to reflect a deciding done in like cold deductive manner, for in such an opinion no other factor which may have been at work in the deciding rates mention or even hint. Where, however, *despite* the persistent "model" of the Formal Style opinion, and *despite* the continuing idea-picture of the problem-solution as being deductive (the picture being not merely of a deductive form for the justification), and *despite,* in climax, the still green ideal of the One Right Rule — where in the teeth of all of these an opinion does mention doubt, or does canvass the factual situation for light, or does discuss, announce, or make overt appeal to sense or wisdom, then one is up against flat hypocrisy if something of the same sort has not been at work and of weight in the actual deciding which has gone before. The working factor and the opinion factor need not coincide; that is clear; for reasons, like reasoning, can clarify, can alter, as they ripen. But the point remains. Here the opinion tells not the whole story, and yet a goodly piece of it. It is, whenever it so speaks, a mine of paying ore.

I am going to waste little time on those objectors who can be heard growling or sneering that our appellate judges are a bunch of hypocrites, or are dishonest, or lack the sense to sail an even course, or are sacrificing all principle to expedience and to pressure, political or popular, or what have you more. One may, to be sure, pause to recall some of the misconceptions which edge some lawyers over into such lines of thought. If you have not yet grown out of the notion that an opinion's office is to report how the decision was arrived at, then any normal opinion can appear to you as mere pretty-talk. If you still bow to the Calf of the single possible right answer, and also believe in your own cause, then decision against you readily takes on the guise not only of wrongheadedness but of willful wrong as well, and any opinion {130} will then mask as sly manipulation. If you forget that facts show different faces to different folk, you can as mentioned just above see pure pretense in what has been routine; indeed one of the more treacherous slips in any area of passion is the imputation of low motives in action (and so of deceit in the opinion) to persons who happen not to share one's own more fervent faiths. Finally, most lawyers are far from free of those layman's fallacies: the ascription to a court of desiring results which the court itself has seen as just imposed by duty (say by legislation), plus the charge of insincere evasion of some issue which the court has just found absent from the case — or unripe.

However the misguided may come to such general slaverings, the general confutation is twofold and flat. On the one hand, we have the known character of our appellate judges. These men are not sealed off in a citadel or temple, we meet and see them with their robes off, in their daily living. They are normally vain, they have ambitions, party leanings, a decent human share of prejudice, passion, and blindness; most of them have a limited endowment of brains, imagination, and training. But on the whole there is one thing we have learned to size up moderately well in our neighbors' actions and faces, and that is honesty; the secret crook successful from the inside is rare in any walk of life; and these appellate judges insist on seeming to the rest of us to be essentially honest men. I will stand on that platform. To change the figure, if you take the personnel of the appellate bench as an entirety, arranged in the familiar bell-shaped curve re, e.g., brains — knock on that bell, there may be a bit of dullness in the ring, but it rings true.

The second confutation lies in the law of parsimony. Evil character, deliberate hypocrisy — these are devil-aspects in the work of an institution. They are never to be forgotten or ignored, but neither are they without *adequate* evidence to be *assumed*. Certainly they are not to be assumed among the occupants of an office which carries beyond almost any other the combination of an ideal of probity with a machinery for the policing of probity by one's teammates. The inherent probabilities array themselves against the devil-aspects. Meantime, the type of thing we have been looking over is ample and more than ample to explain any large-scale phenomenon at which such growls or sneers have been directed, and to explain those phenomena with no need at all for recourse to any such "higher" cause as devilment among our appellate judicial personnel. {131}

There is, however, much more to the problem of finding solid evidence than any growlers or their confutation. There is the horse-sense doubt about how far the postevent document of justification, of public relations, or of rationalization can be trusted as evidence of what has gone before.

For once again let me stress that in my view the opinion has no function of *describing* the process of deciding. Let me stress again that I do not think that, save on occasions normally impossible to spot, an opinion reflects with any accuracy a third of the variegated great and petty motivating stimuli that have somehow combined to produce the particular decision, or that it shows the weight of such factors as it may happen to mention expressly, nor yet the manner of their interaction.

I hold a much more moderate position, but one quite adequate to the purpose of doing usable forecast.

That moderate position begins with a proposition I wish to signal but shall make no attempt to prove: to wit, that the great bulk of the varying stimuli in question (impossible for us to either spot or trace) can be disregarded in favor of a relatively few variables which we *can* get at. For rough purposes, the unspottables either cancel out or operate rather on the surface than at the root of the deciding, or else hit the crux (in such cumulation as to determine a majority's votes) too rarely to do more than slightly decrease the percentage of available correct forecasts. This includes such very occasionally vital factors as the day's news, insomnia, a secretary's or clerk's sickness or blob, the euphoria from a son's engagement to the right girl, and three hundred unassorted other "irrelevant" but real stirrers of the man. I discard them not as negligible, but as not altering a basic workable reckonability from other and reachable factors alone. As will be seen promptly, my moderate position regards past opinions as being in many aspects significant and useful tools — but by no means in themselves an adequate kit — for getting at these reachable factors.

That moderate position centers then on what was said above in regard to the significance of any sense or policy discussion in an opinion written while the concepts of the Formal Style are still live in the tradition. It moves thence into stress of the point already mentioned that, although in any case there is, of course, an urge to make a result look good, there is in no ordinary case reason to expect or suspect an urge to introduce dishonest justification. If judges are like other human beings, they will omit much {132} as being either trivial or unflattering or open to misunderstanding. They will organize what they do use with weightings which turn more on the job of composition and rhetoric than on any effort to estimate the past, "causative," effects of this item or of that. The work, in view of their office, will also be likely to reflect in important measure what the opinion-writer feels it good for a future court to ponder.

But one matter needs to be very seriously considered, in figuring how far discussion of this type of factor — sense, wisdom — has weight in *reaching* the conclusion, and what kind of weight which kind of factor has. That is the fact, so often overlooked, that *the general run of opinion, these days, is written as much for the opinion-writer's brethren as for any other reader.* It is intended not only to do a right job as such (in the manner of art for art's sake), not only to let losing counsel see they have been fairly heard, not only to persuade the interested public that outcome, underpinning, and workmanship are worthy, not only, either, to provide wise and cleanly guidance for the future. In addition to any or all of these, an opinion is to be an opinion *of the court,* and to that end it must be an opinion which can bring and hold the writer's brethren together. It must persuade them that it is a sound opinion. Crassly put, and with not one whit of change in meaning, its function, among other functions, is to pick up votes, or to hold votes. Its references to sense and wisdom are solid evidence, in any ordinary case, of what the writer, from his inside experience, thinks to be stuff which is likely to influence his brethren, or at least sees as stuff which will not appear to them unseemly or worse.[168a] Let it be granted that there will be an occasional case in which, before the writing, the public eye, or the eye of some portion of the public, is peculiarly felt and thought about; in which, then, one's brothers may be on the lookout more for what will get by than for what will move them into concurrence or conviction. But such cases are the hurricane cases. It is the daily case which sets the pattern by which we must measure in order to spot such occasional deflection.

In sum, again: rich ore, if worked with care. {133}

EXCURSUS: ILLEGITIMATE PRECEDENT TECHNIQUES[168b]

No part of the above is intended as any effort to sanctify the appellate judiciary. There are cowardly appellate judges as well as cautious ones, there are personal prejudices, there are general prejudices which reach the level of besotted bigotry, there are the sly as well as the skillful, not every appellate judge is industrious or steady in attention or careful in his work, politics and "management" can be found inside the court and out, there have even been crooks on the appellate bench. And so what? Taken all together, such things do not materially alter the whole picture: the appellate bench has stood up throughout our history; taken as an institution entire, I should think it the least hypocritical of all our law-governmental institutions; in point of personal responsible conduct in office, it has earned the honor it has enjoyed; and I can see no sign that it has declined, this last quarter century, either in character or in that responsible consciousness of office. True, there are pockmarks on the face and sometimes on the behavior. I will not liken the appellate bench to George Washington, in vision or in steadfastness or in great heart; still it is pertinent that it would not be wisdom to judge Washington by his pockmarks and his occasional lapses.[169]

No. The problem, as indicated, lies elsewhere. And one piece of that problem turns up in one piece of real and evil hypocrisy which has in truth from time to time been indulged in by an appellate court, and which should be gotten out of the way before we settle down generally to the sense or wisdom phases of the modern appellate opinion.

Above, at page 85 f., in the listing of various of our precedent techniques, Numbers 39 and 40 were branded as illegitimate: the disregard of a case in point without mentioning it, and the manhandling of the facts of the pending case, or of the precedent, so as to make it falsely appear that the case in hand falls under a rule which in fact it does not fit, or especially that it falls outside of a rule which would lead in the instant case to a conclusion the court cannot stomach. To this one can add what commonly {134} takes less research to document: the distortion of the case in point beyond all recognition, so as to slip its whole force. And one can include the unvarnished citation of a few alleged authorities which have little or nothing to do with the proposition for which they are cited. In any such situation the court is typically caught between its felt duty to justice and its felt duty to the pre-existing authorities, has as yet found no technique or rationale to reconcile the two, and, like a small boy shoving his plate over spilt soup, is hiding its own inadequacy from immediate pillory. Unlike the small boy, the court's heart in such a situation is, I think, commonly pure enough and its actual holding is commonly at least wiser than the contrary.[169a]

Nonetheless, and conceding the best of intentions, the cost of such procedure is excessive, it is exorbitant. To deliberately leave undealt with, unmentioned, an essentially contrary authority is to inflict upon the bar and the trial and other hierarchically lower bench unresolvable uncertainty where the duty is to give best available guidance. Who can tell whether the omission was intentional? Even if it should be suspected to be intentional, who knows whether the ghost will rise and walk? To duck and deliberately obscure the question is irresponsible judging. That is one point.

The next is this: When the fair — even the strained — meaning of an authority is distorted into nonrecognizability, the immediate effect on the detail of doctrine in question is confusion. For it *may* be an instance of oversight, in which case a recanvass of the matter next time *may* lead to reinstatement of the older authority.

But whether the distortion be planned or sloppy, and regardless of the particular point, such distortion in *any* case opens to every attentive lawyer the peril that in any other case at all the like may be visited upon any authority at all; few situations present more dramatically Bentham's "second order" of harm from an offense: the rush, through a multitude, of insecurity and fear in matters of vital moment.

Not quite so devastating but still very troubling is that rarish {135} form of judicial lying which consists in citing authorities for what simply is not in them. Such action leaves the particular point moderately clear: the court has wanted it badly enough to lie to get it. Neither does it directly undermine the standing of what the authorities have positively ruled. But it does rap at a thing capital: it raises doubts about either competence or candor in judicial craftsmanship, and any such doubt leaks over into worry over wisdom, even over uprightness of the court. Today, with the Formal regime behind us, any practice such as any of the above must be pilloried as flatly and flagrantly illegitimate.

The pseudo gain in stability of the precedent-regime which for the moment at least, and perhaps forever, lies in covering up the particular change is in the current opinion-style no real gain; and, if it were, it would rest still on a mistaken choice of policy. *For the gain sought is a gain in confidence in institutions and in officers;* whereas these vagaries of practice, albeit indulged only on occasion, infect and rot away that very confidence; and whereas we draw from the long years of the Grand Style in our common law tradition abundant evidence that change in case law, when based on reason and accompanied by explicit reason given, not only does not sap but strengthens confidence in the appellate courts and in their work. Any of the *undercover* practices of our regime of precedent, therefore, so far as indulged with deliberation, I indict as evil, more, as illegitimate practice, as true and low abuses of power entrusted for other ends: their cost is too high, their policy is unsound, they are consonant neither with candor nor with courage, they are as unnecessary as they are misleading, they tend to trip up even their practitioners, and they inexcusably undercut clean interaction and understanding between bar and bench.

Be it remembered that not one of these attributes, much less their combination, holds of the sound and legitimate practices of *open* growth-and-change by way of precedent-plus-reason.

EXPLICIT REASON IN THE OPINION,
NEW YORK, 1939

We recur now to our inquiry into what marks the path among the multipossibilities of the case law authorities. We recur to the theory that the main guide is felt sense and decency, the right result on the facts of case and situation (or, more wisely, on the facts first of the situation-type and only then of the particular case) — the something which opinions would openly call Justice {136} if that great word had not so often been made in argument a cover for its opposite, or for mawkishness — or else for counsel's ineptitude or sloth in preparation. Let us recur also to those 304 pages of Court of Appeals opinions handed down July 11, 1939, mentioned above at page 96, and reported, it will be recalled, in 281 New York — the 304 pages with the twenty-four divergent identified techniques of handling precedent-material. We are looking for what guided the court, as it reached to fetch one or another of those techniques from rack to workbench.

This time, let me mix in overt resort to reason in order to make sense out of statutes, too. It makes the recurrence and the importance of this *manner* of deciding stand out as they deserve, when one sees both statutory and case authority being handled by it — each with the same of-courseness.

In *Matter of Porges,* p. 205, 22 N.E.2d 341, the court is consciously choosing: the Appellate Division decisions had divided. "The question is open as to whether, assuming the illegality of an investment made by a prior Chamberlain, a direction to a Chamberlain in office to turn over moneys never received by him is proper, *and the answer to that question is obvious,* namely that such an order is improper and must be reversed." (pp. 210-211; my italics.) It was reversed. Choice rested on the explicit reason of the situation.

In *Rozell v. Rozell,* p. 106, 22 N.E.2d 254, a twelve-year-old boy had a verdict "against" his sixteen-year-old sister for negligently driving him into a collision. Sense was quoted from a prior opinion: "The modern tendency of decided cases is to ignore fictions and deal with things as they are." (p. 110.) Then: "We cannot bury our heads in the sand and ignore the new tendencies and conditions so notorious. Insurance as protection to the sufferer is now a matter of common knowledge. Of course, that fact alone creates no right to sue where one otherwise would not exist. . . . No warrant is found for any prediction that brothers and sisters will flock into the courts on fictitious claims. . . ." (p. 113.) And on page 112 there can be no wrong without a remedy, and the common law "'does expand with reason.'" Judgment affirmed. The whole is explicit horse-sense principle, guided and explicitly restrained by legal principle.

In *Matter of Divisich v. Marshall,* p. 170, 22 N.E.2d 327, the action of the New York City Board of Education abolishing certain kindergarten classes was under attack. "If there be one public policy well-established in this State, it is that public education {137} shall be beyond control by municipalities and politics." (p. 173.) As can be seen by reference to Precedent Technique Number 28, above at page 83, this "well-established" policy with whose announcement the Chief opens the opinion had been nowhere before laid down or expressed. It is a spirit partly sucked out of, partly breathed into, five prior cases from which even a bold responsible scholar would dare draw no more than a possible intimation of what is suddenly to the court a "well-established" principle. The Board of Education's action was, therefore, not subject to control by the city's Board of Estimate. More: ". . . the Board is about $8,000,000 short. In other words, there is a discrepancy between estimated expenditures and revenues receivable of about that amount. No one suggests that any more money can be obtained, so the only possible thing to do, not as a choice but as an absolute necessity, is to reduce expenses." (pp. 175-176.) What is this but the application of reason, first to the type of situation, then to the particular case?

The *Port Chester Wine and Liquor* case, p. 101, 22 N.E.2d 253, had to do with applying a Fair Trade Act which the court had once held unconstitutional, only to be educated by the Supreme Court. The situation had thus acquired new lighting; it is indeed within the legislature's power, the legislature's policy is, therefore, to be made at home in the law, if that may be. The court looks for appropriate sense and law. A pre-Fair Trade Act "principle" is, therefore, located and quoted: "The law endeavors to protect the interest of parties in existing contractual relations from intentional and wrongful interference by strangers. The principle constitutes a limitation upon the doctrine of freedom of contract, which courts have imposed in an attempt to promote justice and fair dealing and to prevent wrongs." (pp. 105-106.) That principle is then made to inform a quite (and quite unnecessarily) expansive reading of the statute.

Alleged "principle," however, acquires by the mere label no credentials: "But it is argued for First National Bank that its judgment against Farmers National Bank is sanctioned by the spirit of the 'rule of reason and practical necessity' connoted by the phrase *res judicata*. . . . This argument can indeed be plausibly stated. We have found it to be unconvincing and indecisive." *Hartford Accident and Indemnity Co. v. First National Bank,* p. 162, 22 N.E.2d 324, at page 168, a problem of "vouching in." So: "[W]e think there is no compelling reason why a procedure so perplexing and inexact should now have operation outside its presently existing limits." (p. 169.) And {138} a statute had opened "a plain and sure track . . . for one complete settlement." (p. 170.) Judgment accordingly.

Matter of Davega-City Radio v. State Labor Relations Board, p. 13, 22 N.E.2d 145, involved a jurisdictional question on control of labor relations. "If an employer, by merely making claim that it was subject to the jurisdiction of the National Labor Relations Board, could oust the State Labor Relations Board from jurisdiction, then, if for any reason the National Labor Relations Board should decline jurisdiction, the employer might be freed from regulation by either agency. This would not seem to be a reasonable construction of section 715." (p. 25.) State Board's order affirmed. (It is no concern of ours here that the Supreme Court later chose to impose just such a no man's land. We are observing a process in the New York Court: the deliberate use of sense to shape the rule — the statutory rule.)

We put on one side as not within the opinion-day *People v. Tremaine,* which opens the volume, 21 N.E.2d 891, where the Constitution's direction on itemizing the budget is dealt with "as it is written, and not as we think it might have been written" (p. 12), but where "We expect in all these matters that the spirit of the Constitution shall be observed and that good sense in its application will govern." (p. 7.) But I may properly include a careful dictum in *Evans v. 2168 Broadway,* p. 34, 22 N.E.2d 152, about a situation which is then duly distinguished: "Respondents urge that a different rule must be applied where an offer has been made in a judicial proceeding [here, a bondholders' foreclosure]. Obviously an offeror cannot play fast and loose in a case where judicial approval is required. If an offeror duly submits an offer for approval to a court, where such judicial approval is required, it would seem that such offer might not be withdrawn pending approval proceedings, provided the latter were not unduly protracted." (p. 40.)

We are not of course, as our skeptic has noted, living in the Golden Age, but even refusal to temper the harsh letter may lack straight-laced primness. *MacKay v. Metropolitan Life,* p. 42, 22 N.E.2d 154, involved a policy with a statutory clause that "affirmative proof of loss must be furnished . . . within ninety days after the date of such loss." "The courts below have construed the provision regarding the giving of notice of injury as also extending the time for giving proof of loss; in other words, if notice of injury may be given as soon as it is reasonably possible, the same extension applies to giving proof of loss. There may be some ground to sustain such reasoning, and, if the company itself {139} had adopted this language, I would be inclined to follow the Appellate Division's conclusion. However, the law of the State requires the standard provisions to be included in such policies. . . . We therefore must hold that the plaintiff has failed to comply. . . ." (p. 47.) On this one, Crane lost two votes, though he got both Lehman and Loughran. I myself see no basis for a court's not reading a statute to make sense in the way it ought to read an agreement, and see reason therefore differently from this majority; but the Grand Style, the Style of Reason, does not, as must always be insisted, guarantee an outcome or the use of a reason or the production of a rule of law which I like or agree with, nor yet one which you like or agree with. What it reaches is the best reason the particular court can manage at the particular time for the particular question.

The next opinion in order, that in *Matter of the City of New York,* p. 48, 22 N.E.2d 157, in eminent domain, denied consequential damages based on a proposed improvement which was still tentative. A "see," a "cf.," and a plain cite are sprinkled in, but the holding rests on the patiently and persuasively expounded reason of the situation. The next is *Hoose v. Drumm,* p. 54, 22 N.E.2d 233, where a boy whose eye had been destroyed by a thrown goldenrod stalk during school recess had had a verdict against the school trustees. "We think the case is outside the statutory direction 'To establish rules for the government and discipline of the schools.' This phrase cannot mean that every detail of school management is the business of the trustees. . . . [T]he Legislature did not thereby intend to cast upon school trustees or boards of education the burden of an attempt to fashion guides for the safe conduct of pupils in the indulgence of their boundless natural instincts for self-amusement." (p. 57.) Dismissal on merits affirmed.

The following case was a suit by an attorney whose client had against his advice and desire abandoned a claim after a referee's adverse decision. "Possibly the plaintiff had justification for his construction of the statute and probably acted in good faith." (p. 63.) But a paragraph from Thornton is quoted and applied, for the client. "The above statement seems to us good law and good sense." (p. 65.) Judgment for defendant affirmed. *Crowley v. Wolf,* p. 60, 22 N.E.2d 234. The reports continue with *People v. Bellows,* p. 67, 22 N.E.2d 238, a picketing case. The first question went to the court's jurisdiction to order a new trial in the circumstances. An elaborate discussion of statutes and practice finds that done in civil cases. "I see no reason why the {140} same rule should not apply in criminal cases, and, although we are obliged to review the evidence to see whether or not there be a substantial question of fact, yet this is not the review on the facts which is prohibited by the Constitution. It is a question of law. . . ." (p. 73.) I stop with the next case in order, a malpractice action, *Bernstein v. Greenfield,* p. 77, 22 N.E.2d 242. Judgment on verdict for the plaintiff was reinstated after a careful analysis of the evidence available to sustain the verdict; but no opportunity for shaping or reshaping any rule or precedent was present.

Let us pause now and consider what we have seen, in regard to overt, explicit, unashamed, and I say proud resort to the reason of the immediate facts or the reason of the life-situation or both as a guide in deciding the appeal, and in shaping the rule of law announced, and therefore and of necessity in selecting from the spread workbench of the precedent and statutory techniques. We began with five fairly succulent instances, concededly selective, from among the thirty-nine cases. But then I turned to page 1and went through the first ten cases. Nine of those ten have been noted, most of them quoted from; not the third one, which contains a solid but merely technical discussion. Of the nine I urge that at least six (I think, myself, at least eight) show the court using the style of reason to guide or test the rule or its application — and this almost wholly without distinction as between case law and statutory authority. The fourteen opinions thus presented derive three each from Chief Judge Crane and Finch and Loughran, two from Hubbs, one from Rippey. O'Brien was in his last illness, and is not represented. If Lehman is not presented in this particular sampling, that is not because he was not a master of the technique.[170] The procedure, then, was common to the whole court.

If measured against the ideal-image of a Formal Style opinion, moreover, the procedure of Reason was striking, almost strident. It was repetitive, it was cumulative, it pounded for attention with the dogged smashes of a pile driver.

HIDDEN IN THE OPEN

How can it be, then, that the phenomenon has not become familiar, a commonplace of all discussion, its understanding and {141} use tools in the kit of every appellate advocate, nay, of every counselor who has to build on, with or against the course of the decisions? That is not an easy one to answer. For one part, and as mentioned above, I suspect that eyes trained to read an opinion not for the how of the deciding but only for the last word of doctrine on a point may well slide over this type of revelation as merely obiter, as almost in the way ("obiter" will stand that rendering), at most as a sort of obligato which may add to the aesthetic quality but hardly to the firm stuff of the decision. For this I suggest it is not even needful that those eyes be still steeped in the belief that it is doctrine alone which handles the deciding.

For another and perhaps greater part, I suspect the answer to lie in the way in which lawyers do *not* read the opinions. The opinions of the Supreme Court of the United States are unique first in that many of the bar of the whole nation follow them, second in that they, and they almost alone, receive much and vocal attention out beyond the range of any specialized line of interest pursued by the particular reader. The Supreme Court's work thus stands to observation somewhat as a *going whole,* each subject matter along with many other subject matters, one or another half-dozen or more aspects of the current work under scrutiny as an aggregate by a plenty of skilled — and sometimes not overfriendly — critics who, however their personal lines of work may diverge, yet find common ground in looking over how that Court is going about its whole field of labor. It is this which led in the late '30's, and has continued since to lead, to awareness that the Supreme Court has recurred to the older practice of using sense in the remodeling of doctrine; and which has led also to the mistaken feeling that in this the Supreme Court, instead of catching up, has been departing from the case law practice of our time. For it is not thus that the advance sheets from a State supreme court were read, or are read yet. (Nor, for that matter, do the State supreme courts cry out for this kind of attention by piling special concurrences on inability to get together even in dissent.) It is the desultory character of each lawyer's attention to any but odd cases and sequences from his own supreme court which seems to me the largest factor blinding him over the past thirty years and more, and in keeping him blinded, to the patent truths about that court's ways of going about deciding; to which one adds that there tends on this matter, within a State bar, to be rather little gathering and cross-stimulation of observations as between the captive slaves of the various specialties — except, of course, possibly, in terms of results; not of process. At most, all {142} join in the dirge: the State supreme court, too, has gone or else is going to the dogs — "who knows where an appellate court will hang its hat?"

Thirdly, the mere "novelty" of the perceptions here recorded hinders them queerly from real denting of the mind. Not that, albeit novel, they are new. Quite the contrary. As has been shown, they are as traditional as our primeval trees. But it can be with truth as it can be with beauty; a table or a sideboard in sweetly balanced Colonial, its grand old pine or walnut painted and flaked, gathering cobwebs in cellar, carriage house, or attic — that is not new. Nor is it looked at, nor if looked at is it seen. Neither does telling of its beauty make that beauty come alive. That takes time, it takes work, *it takes sustained attention* — two things: attention, and sustained. I can serve as a good enough exhibit, for the present context: after a decade and a half of labor in the general area, my manuscript of 1941 on the cases in 281 N.Y. still came nowhere near to bringing out either the pervasiveness or the intensity of the return to the Manner of Reason there displayed. The analysis at that time, and again in 1945 anent the Pennsylvania cases,[171] caught well enough the drive to find sense, as a clue through the maze of authority-possibilities; but although I had already both developed a sound theory of rules and become familiar with our early Grand Style, still, in neither case did the urge of each set of cases toward *improved rules for the situation-types* get, either absolutely or comparatively, anything like the highlight it deserved.

As of 1939 there was a fourth feature at work to keep blind the eyes of the bar in general: over the country as a whole, the formal tradition of opinion-writing had loosened its grip in no such fashion as in the New York Court of Appeals after their eighteen solid years of the Cardozo influence. In my own view the more formal opinion-writing went hand in hand with a relatively stiffer, more formal-style effort of the judges in their actual deciding. In any event, what in the New York court had become almost standard practice was in 1939 or 1940 in the other four courts examined, and in Pennsylvania, 1944, certainly in the opinions and in my judgment not too much less so in the actual deciding, still much more of an occasional phenomenon.

Yet the occasions had already become frequent, and the revealing discussion of reason entered, whenever it did, in dignity and as of right. The Massachusetts opinions were still something of {143} an exception, but at the same time gave ground for believing that the deciding process had shifted materially further than had the style of writing. For while the case opinions retained (with exceptions) an aloofness, a logical form, an aura of compelledness not unakin to 1890, the Opinions of the Justices in the same volume matched in method and manner — and in flavor — the case opinions from New York. This means that in the court's thinking, certainly in the chief's, the finer art of the Grand Style was known, welcome, and at least sometimes practiced. Any doubter will be forced to conviction if he looks into what happened to the Massachusetts opinions within the next five years. The long blight of Rugg had gone, the new sap was rising fast.

During the last twenty years the shift away from formal-style writing and thinking, already unmistakable in 1940, has continued. This will be evidenced forthwith. What does not appear in equal measure is growth of that urgent aspect of a proper replacement of the Formal Style: *stress in first instance on the problem-situation as a type,* with quest for a sound and guidesome form of *rule* to govern, attention addressing itself only in second instance to the "equities" or sense of the particular pending case. In this vital matter the Pennsylvania sampling of 1944 — whose precedent technique scatter was reviewed above[172] —

lags patently behind the Court of Appeals of 1939, both in consistency and in dexterity.

REASON IN PENNSYLVANIA, 1944

Nevertheless, the cases from 349 Pa. join with the New York batch to contrast with any formal way of judging. Let me paraphrase again:[173]

> The first evidence that we are getting back to the style of the grand manner is the recurrence to sense, horse sense, sense outside the law, tested from outside the law and stated quite openly on the face of the opinion as a guide to decision.
>
> Now, does that hold in Pennsylvania? I quote from *Freeman v. Hiznay*, p. 89, 36 A.2d 509, (shareholders' liability after a bank was consolidated with a company which lacked shareholders' liability) at page 94: "The problem is obviously one that does not lend itself to solution by the application of any particular rules of logic, but calls rather for an answer dictated by practical considerations so far as consistent with legal principles." And a rather shrewd discussion produces a type of proration. {144}
>
> On page 81 (*Speare Estate*, p. 76, 36 A.2d 489): "The practical question was," (to which the Court will give the answer) "What was best for all parties in the circumstances?" That was a matter involving the reservation of a certain portion of a trust and putting it aside to pay rent as it might accrue — rent owing by the estate.
>
> In *Huffman Estate* (No. 3), p. 59, 36 A.2d 640, at pages 64 and 65, the Court does not say, "We want to be practical," but just see if you can build a better practical scheme for solving the situation than they quote — not in terms of law am I judging, but in terms of sense: "The things to be taken into consideration in determining the compensation to be recovered by an attorney are the amount and character of the services rendered, the labor, the time, and trouble involved, the character and importance of the litigation, the amount of money or value of the property affected, the professional skill and experience called for, and the standing of the attorney in his profession; to which may be added the general ability of the client to pay and the pecuniary benefit derived from the services." Now that may not have been law until the court first laid it down, but it was sense, before then.
>
> On page 26 (*Brown Estate*, p. 23, 36 A.2d 335, — construing a gift over): "It is a rule of common sense *as well as* law not to attempt to construe that which needs no construction." (My italics.)
>
> I have more illustrations, but on this particular point, which is vital to my argument, I want to know whether I am testing the court or individual judges. I have an opinion with a passage of this kind clean on the nub from Linn, from Hughes, from Drew, from Allen Stearne, from Horace Stern, and from the Chief. I derive the conclusion that it is general to the court. I only had one opinion from Patterson to play with, you remember, so it isn't strange that that single one didn't happen to touch on this particular question. Every other one had, within 143 pages, been handed down on the one day. . . .

Let us look at a few further cases more in detail:

Merchants' Warehouse v. Gelder, p. 1, 36 A.2d 444 was a suit for payment of a claim against the Liquor Board; the claim had been allowed under one set of

86

statutes by a board — the Auditor General and the State Treasurer — to examine and adjust claims on the Commonwealth "according to law and equity"; but the Liquor Board was kept from paying under another set of statutes requiring any board "when any legal difficulty or dispute arises" to consult and be bound by legal advice from the Department of Justice. There was no conveniently quotable passage, but the opinion marshaled horse sense about government together with {145} the available authorities, to reach and apply a distinction between administrative and judicial action by the Auditor General and the Treasurer or their representatives.

Sgarlat v. Griffith, p. 42, 36 A.2d 330, involved a construction contract with a special price agreed for rock "which would require removal by blasting." Such rock was found, but it was deep between two standing structures, so the contractor got the rock out more safely by jack hammer. The owner refused the special high-rate payment. "The result of appellant's claim to date is, the owner has his building, his contract for its construction has been fully carried out, all rock in the excavation was removed by appellant, as certified by the architect, and the consideration for his labor and materials fixed in the contract, now $902.00 and interest for about eight years, is denied him. No wonder the learned judge of the lower court in his opinion admitted that 'greater equity might perhaps be done' if payment were allowed." (p. 45.) The court first construed the contract to mean "that kind of rock which usually requires blasting"; but then drove ahead and also mustered the Restatement and local dicta to justify adoption and application of the New York substantial performance rule.

Under the Uniform Conditional Sales Act, resale after recaption calls for ten days' notice to the buyer, on pain of a penalty of one quarter of the price. A $46,000 machine was retaken by court order after the buyer had applied for an arrangement under the Bankruptcy Act and a creditors' committee had been appointed. The resale was careful and fair. In *Gerety v. Hiller,* p. 49, 36 A.2d 476, the windfall penalty was sought because of alleged technical defects in the notice — for instance, it had not been given to the creditors' committee; and the last known place of buyer's business (to which notice by registered mail had been sent) had come into seller's possession along with the machine. The court found strict compliance with the statute, and used language of severe limitation on the powers of a creditors' committee. Again there is no conveniently quotable passage. The opinion is instinct with repudiation of the attempted perversion of the statute's purpose; but no phrasing was achieved which would keep the situation clear if real damage should follow on some later contrivance of such a "notice," or which might have carried over into a lead for statutory construction generally.[174]

There was a woman, Florence, who as next of kin to one Effie {146} was suing to set aside Effie's will. Effie had been a beneficiary under the will of her sister Elva, who had in turn been sole residuary beneficiary under the will of Elva's husband Harry, whose executor's account was in process of audit. In *Megargel Estate*, p. 14, 36 A.2d 319, Florence was trying to increase Harry's net estate by getting disallowance of allegedly excessive fees and expenses and of the distribution of allegedly void legacies. The court affirmed *on the opinion of the orphans' court* a decree that Florence had no standing under the statute to proceed as she had. Then, in patent deference to the possible equities of the case (p. 16): "There are two practical methods open to appellant to protect her interests" — followed by a full page, free, of the most authoritative legal advice available in Pennsylvania.

These illustrations do not begin to exhaust the material. I close with one more in which one can see reason, regret, authority, and the reason for abiding by the authority, all at work in sunlight. The cafeteria in the Salvation Army Residence, operated not for profit, was held to be outside the Labor Relations Act of 1937, as amended in 1939. *Salvation Army Case,* p. 105, 36 A.2d 479. "If the words of this Act are clear and free from all ambiguity, we cannot disregard its letter under a pretext of pursuing its alleged spirit. . . . On the other hand, if the words of the Act are not explicit, this Court cannot, under the guise of statutory construction, so broaden the operative scope of the Act that our construction of it amounts, in effect, to judicial legislation. . . . Under the guidance of these principles we have reexamined the text . . ." (p. 108.) "Much can be said for the view that a labor relations act should include *all* labor except where specifically excepted. It is to be observed, however, that our decision in the Western Pennsylvania Hospital case, decided on January 6, *1941,* granted charitable institutions an implied exclusion from the operation of the Act and, unless amended by the legislature, this Court's construction of an act has the same effect as if written into the statute at the time of its enactment. . . . It is most significant, therefore, that two legislatures have convened and adjourned since our former decision, and no amendment to the Act, as construed by us, has been enacted. . . ." (p. 110; court's italics.) Personally, I see the two construction principles first announced as untrue re lack of power, as unwise re policy, and re practice as repeatedly departed from in fact by the court in question. (Compare on this last what was done in *Merchants' Warehouse* discussed above at page 144, and, more particularly, {147} immediately below.) But those matters are here beside the point. Even the principle re effect of a first construction (which is also urged by Levi) and which certainly is most at home, and may be wholly wise, in a situation like the one in hand, where the statute is new, the issue is still hot and the court's action therefore very likely to be noticed, and amendment has occurred in other particulars — even that is not directly on the present point. The real pertinence of the quoted passage to our purpose depends on neither its legal soundness nor its wisdom, it depends rather on the fact that the court reopened the whole question in the light of one felt reason and yet refused to disturb the earlier ruling not as merely in duty bound, but also for a reason assigned, which reason the court also saw as apt and compelling in regard to the particular rule and case before it.

We can sum up the 1944 Pennsylvania picture in this matter as showing sense and reason vigorously at work. They are at work not only in terms of the case facts: in guiding application of rules or in the particular outcome or in the semiautomatic singling out of the appropriate authority technique, but they are also repeatedly called on to direct diagnosis of the *type* of problem-situation and in consciously reworking the *rule*-machinery for the general governance thereof. They are at work, though somewhat under wraps, in the statutory area, as well. Discussion of policy is frank, the exploration and assignment of reason is matter-of-course: the Formal Style has *as a style* lost all power. Left, however, is a legacy of crippling doctrine: as, that a statutory procedure can allow of appeal only as provided in explicit detail by the statute (*Merchants' Warehouse* case, p.1; though this is the same case which as of course, and *without* explicit statutory warrant, honors *delegates* of two *named* high executive officials as constituting a "judicial" tribunal!) or the inelastic frame for dealing with statutory authority which the court was still reciting in the *Salvation Army Case* as setting the limits of judicial *power.* Finally, to repeat, it is manifest that we are here still far from any complete recapture of the Grand Style in its full unfolding.

The conscious quest for justice and wisdom is clear, as are the pressures of the office and consciousness of the need for order. Some of the leeway of our case law system is plainly felt; no less felt is the responsibility for discretion in use of leeways. But the language of ordered reason is not yet standard, nor is a re-examination of the sense-base of any authority which pinches badly as it presses. Nor, above all, has a *practice* even budded of trying to {148} grasp and solve *first* the type of problem-situation, coming only then to grips with the specific case. And there is no sign as yet of real grasp of the theory of rules.[175]

THE TIME DIMENSION, AND ON INTO OHIO, 1953

It has seemed useless to elaborate the scatter of precedent techniques in the 1953 sampling from the Ohio Supreme Court. The treatment of the official syllabus, reported above, pp. 97-99, from 159 Ohio St. is enough to suggest the general situation; and Ohio cases from 1939 and from the current decade are conspicuous among the exhibits fished out and mounted above in regard to current precedent techniques. But with regard to the incursion of sense and reason into the opinions and no less into the process of the actual deciding it is as well "to say it very loud and clear." It is important also to document the phenomenon along the time axis. Indeed it is worth a little space to remind of how much of that has been semisystematically gathered here. For New York the job has been pretty thoroughly done. One of the samples of the Grand Style is from that State, page 64; the warranty cases, pages 126 ff., reach over thirty years of the earlier nineteenth century; the *Logan* case, page 230, and the charitable subscription sequence, page 85, note 100, tap the latter half; decisions from the Cardozo period are studded through the book; a full-dress sampling from July 11, 1939, has just been reported in some detail, pages 135 ff.; there were checking studies of 300 pages from 1940 with the heavy shift in personnel, and again in 1951 on the occasion of my Buffalo lectures on the subject, the notes of which are lost but the effect of which was full confirmation of the prior findings. Finally, there is the fullish sampling from current work reported in Appendix A. From Massachusetts my early nineteenth-century warranty studies are tapped at page 107; the turn of the century is sampled in the election cases, pages 124 f.; the 300-page study from 1940 is reported on a thumbnail at page 97; there was a current confirmatory sampling in 1946 on the occasion of an address to the Massachusetts State Bar Association, and report of a contemporary one appears in Appendix A. Pennsylvania also figured in the nineteenth-century warranty studies, and is represented here fully from 1944 and from 1959.

Ohio, at page 68, is more fully presented for the early nineteenth century than any of the above save New York; it was, as {149} has already been noted, one of the cross-check courts for 1939; the use of sense in the handling of statutes at that time is examined below, at page 375. Moreover, in addition to the 1953 material above at pages 97 f. and here, Ohio is of course represented also in the contemporary sampling in Appendix A. The court differs also from the others in that the personnel have held remarkably steady through the times of my more recent Ohio borings. Four of the judges active in the 1939 sampling were still active in that of 1953, and three of them in that of 1957; while from 1953 to 1957 there is a total overlap of five. It is therefore definitely desirable to illustrate the operation of conscious reason rather fully from the 1953 sampling. I want to leave no doubt that the phenomenon is one neither of passage nor of fad, nor one which wears itself out among judges who use it over long periods. It ought by now to have become clear enough that we are dealing here not with queer cases or important cases only, nor with peculiar judges, nor with atypical courts, but instead with what is happening daily, all over the country, with what is palpable in almost every other case. But the time dimension makes clear still another point: the phenomenon is not on the wane, but is waxing steadily.

The 1953 Ohio cases fit this description as if written for the purpose. They are materially more open in their approach to sense and decency than was the 1940 sampling, and I feel clear that the sense-search phase of the work of actual deciding had in the interim become less inhibited, freer in flow, more happily conscious. The cases show of course no slightest slackening of interest in responsibility to the authorities, case law or statutory. One, for instance, simply Per Curiam, quotes a statutory paragraph. The opinion then consists of "The provision is mandatory." The court was stiffer and more awkward in making its adjustments than were the courts which decided the New York cases in 1939, 1940, 1951, or 1959, but as compared with the Ohio work of thirteen years before, that in 1953 has become more easy and graceful, and one is reminded of Ohio, 1844. The evaluations of life-wisdom are of course frequently far from mine, but they run along lines which relatively short study would for any student bring into reasonable reckonability, even while the reforging of Ohio doctrine goes on as openly as if in Longfellow's smithy.

For my Marx lectures in Cincinnati, I used the Ohio Supreme Court in the advance sheets January 14 through April 22, 1953, and thought I had kept my annotated copies; but two of them {150} seem, as the material is checked, to have disappeared. The order of the nineteen cases here discussed runs, therefore, as they appeared January 14, February 4 and 18, March 11 and 25, April 15 and 22. There has been no time, since the gap was discovered, to check the omitted dozen or so cases.

It will be recalled that there were nineteen successive full Ohio Supreme Court cases in these advance sheets.

The first in the series is *Burton v. Durkee,* 158 Ohio St. 313, 109 N.E.2d 265 (1952), where a contractor was making claim on a cost-plus basis for building a residence, despite his statement: "The total cost which we aim to build this house for is approximately $27,000." "It is urged that this court in that case announced the principle that under a cost plus fee contract the builder can only recover the proved reasonable cost of his labor and material. If that theory is applicable then into every cost plus contract will be read a rule of law that the builder is entitled to recover his cost plus fee only if he proves that it is reasonable. The Knott case does not announce that principle." (109 N.E.2d at 271.) And so held. In the second case, *Taylor v. Monroe,* 158 Ohio St. 266, 109 N.E.2d 271 (1952), a suit by a tax-delinquent owner of lands to recover the excess price received at the tax sale: "Plaintiff argues that the recent decision rendered by this court in the Gundersen case necessitates a rejection of those contentions of defendants. However, since no such contentions were considered in either the syllabus, the majority opinion or the dissenting opinion in the Gundersen case, we believe it appropriate to consider these contentions. . . ." (109 N.E.2d at 273.) The relevant statutes, technically, and the sense of the situation, are then held not to subject the plaintiff to an estoppel by judgment, as contended. The next case simply applied the short period of limitation laid down in the same statute which confers a remedy on a tax-delinquent owner where the forfeiture proceeding has been irregular. The next, *Hammer v. Mutual Benefit Health & Accident Assn.,* 158 Ohio St. 394, 109 N.E.2d 649 (1952), extended the coverage of a life and accident policy to cover unexpected sunstroke, a matter of first impression in the state, and by 4-3 made a "departure to some extent" from certain cases "distinguishable . . . on the particular facts." "The apparently better reasoned . . . weight of authority," plus a long quotation of rationale from the court below, guided and pressed toward a changed type of situation-analysis. *Jolley v. Martin,* 158 Ohio St. 416, 109 N.E.2d 652 (1952), follows, untangling a mess of appellate procedure, despite recent statutory changes, {151} according to "the practice generally followed in the Courts of Appeal of this state." (109 N.E.2d at 660.) The dissenting judge saw unfairness: "Having dragged the plaintiff through proceedings before the Court of Appeals and this court on the first appeal, defendant certainly 'caused detriment to' plaintiff. . . ." (ibid. 663.) The dissent also insisted on the exact language of a fairly complex body of statutes, getting no answer from the majority. But the majority, in view of the recent statutory change, did take space off to consider and announce "better practice, if not in fact necessary," on a point "unimportant, however, in the instant case." (ibid. 657.)

The quest for sense now becomes more explicit. ". . . [T]he Company complains that much of the evidence offered at the rehearing could and should have been presented at the original hearing in Columbus, and that its reception and consideration on rehearing contravened Sections 543 and 614-43, General Code. From a theoretical standpoint this contention is not without merit. However, the law should be reasonably interpreted to the end that the commission may have all the relevant facts before it to enable it to reach a just and correct conclusion." *Elyria Telephone* case, 158 Ohio St. 441, 110 N.E.2d 59, 61 (1953). The Public Utilities Commission's order based on the full evidence was partly approved, partly disapproved. The succeeding case, a recovery by a minor under the Workmen's Compensation Act, briefly finds in the record evidence enough to support the award. But the next, *Alliance First National v. Spies,* 158 Ohio St. 499, 110 N.E.2d 483 (1953), revamps the theory under which a power to confess judgment is irrevocable and uses the new theory — implied agreement, with consideration, not to revoke — to keep a part payment from extending the limitations period for exercise of the power. "[P]art payment is significant, in operating to extend the statutory period of limitations, only because such part payment justifies the implication of a new promise." (100 N.E.2d at 486.) Here are two successive "reasons" each of which is at best a legalistic rationalization close to fiction; yet what is sought is not merely order in the law, but decency; and a blindly oppressive prior decision on cognovits is distinguished and, *sub rosa,* curbed. It is true that in *Daiquiri Club v. Feck,* 159 Ohio St. 52, 110 N.E.2d 705 (1953), the sensible emasculation of one statutory section was made somewhat easier by the presence of another passage which, although in truth complementary, was located some four thousand sections away: A provision for "conclusiveness" of an assessment unless the taxpayer took described steps within {152} thirty days was held not to bar the Tax Commissioner from reviewing on his own motion, under another statute. But the latter contained language (unmentioned by the court): "*pursuant to time limitations now provided by law,*" so that there was real need for the basis in reason which the court found for restricting the conclusiveness so as to operate only against the taxpayer (whose "estimates" for the first assessment would have halved its tax). "The legislative purpose in the enactment of statutes — the object sought to be attained thereby — is one of the factors involved in their interpretation and application, and a construction thereof should be avoided, if possible, that would effect a restriction of operation or result in circumventing the evident purpose of the statute. Likewise if a specific provision contained therein has an evident limited purpose its application and effect should not be extended." (110 N.E. 2d at 707.)[176]

The tenth case in order has reference to two statutory sections, but turns wholly on reason. The Fire Department having laid down a requirement of two years' service as lieutenant for admission to examination for captaincy, one lieutenant challenged their power to extend the statutory *minimum* requirement of twelve months, and used temporary restraining orders to prevent the examination for six months, during which he finished out his own two years. The court knocked out the Department's effort to limit eligibility as of the time for which the captaincy examination had been first scheduled (and thereby to bar out the troublemaker). The court saw his suit as not unreasonable and as brought in good faith. *State ex rel. Ritter v. Urban,* 159 Ohio St. 46, 110 N.E.2d 708 (1953). "It thus was the action of the courts, rather than the relators' that prevented the holding of the examination on the appointed day." (110 N.E.2d at 709.) "The respondents cite no authority to support their view of this matter." (ibid. 710.) I do not see that the court did, either, to support their own.

The two next cases, *City of Cambridge,* 159 Ohio St. 88, 111 N.E.2d 1 (1953), and *City of Jackson,* 159 Ohio St. 123, 111 N.E. 2d 7 (1953), sustain the exercise by the Public Utilities Commission of its authority to fix company-wide telephone rates if local circumstances are also reasonably considered. The distinction {153} from gas, electric, and water rates is new to Ohio, and follows the policy generally adopted "in the light of modern requirements and habits," quoting reason from South Dakota. (111 N.E.2d at 6.) In the thirteenth case in order, the last here considered in detail, the plaintiff, employed by one Kendall to assist in a whitewashing job, had a verdict against the operators of the meat market being whitewashed for injuries suffered through collapse of a ladder. The meat market owners had happened to have two ladders around, and when the painting-contractor arrived, had just let him use those ladders. The court applied a tight rule, previously announced, about a bailor who "has no beneficial interest in the bailment." The defendants "received no legal consideration for furnishing the ladder." Reversed: no liability. *Lampe v. Magoulakis,* 159 Ohio St. 72, 111 N.E.2d 207, 210 (1953). "'Such an obligation would unduly restrict the transfer of property, causing persons to refrain from lending chattels to another for the sole benefit of the latter.'" (*ibid.*) The case looks as if no one had been insured.

From the later cases in the sample: "If a bribe has been offered it is impossible to determine at a later time whether the verdict was influenced thereby. It is impossible to analyze the mental processes of the juror. . . ." *Peart v. Jones,* 159 Ohio St. 137, 111 N.E.2d 16, 20 (1953). New trial ordered. From *State v. Anderson,* 159 Ohio St. 159, 111 N.E.2d 248, 251 (1953): "It has long been the practice in this state for legislative bodies of political subdivisions to enact statutes or ordinances appropriating money to pay claims which are by law unenforceable. . . . The city may be just but it may not distribute largess." Remanded, for the rule to be applied. In the *Grain Dealers National Fire Ins.* case, 159 Ohio St. 124, 111 N.E.2d 256, 261 (1953), the situation equities proved disturbing to the rule of a prior decision: "Some of the members of this court are of opinion that if the exact facts of the Pickering case should again come before the court the judgment therein should be re-examined, but we are of the opinion that that judgment must be confined to those facts." A warehouse was held without power to limit its liability by a receipt not delivered till some three weeks after acceptance of three fur coats for storage. In *Reinhard v. Peck,* 159 Ohio St. 116, 111 N.E. 2d 262 (1953), the question went to whether a sale of stock in a close corporation took the proceeds out of the personal property tax, as being a sale in *usual* course of business. "... [T]he conversion resulting from the sale of the securities of the estate was under her administration in the usual course of *her business as* {154} *executrix.*" (111 N.E.2d at 264; court's italics.) The effort to apply reason is patent. Similarly in the *General Cigar Co.* case, 159 Ohio St. 152, 111 N.E.2d 265 (1953), in allowing tax exemption of tobacco picked over, aerated, repacked, and stored under gentle heat in the state, a prior decision which taxed "processed" materials being carefully distinguished on its facts: "In the instant case the tobacco did age and did become dry but the same thing would be true of grain so stored. Some such precaution is required for the *preservation* of various commodities, *e.g.,* the sprinkling of stored apples to prevent drying and consequent wrinkling, correct temperatures are essential for wearing apparel, particularly furs. ..." (111 N.E.2d at 267; my italics.)

Every judge was represented; all but Zimmerman by two or more opinions.

It is, I submit, impossible to escape recognition of this court's overt recourse to its best view of sense not only to guide application or choice among competing rules, but to guide the shaping or restriction or expansion of the rule or holding it sees as apposite. It is impossible to escape recognition that this procedure is applied as well in the use of statutory authorities as in the use of precedents and case law generally. It is impossible to escape recognition that this has in 1953 become the standard manner of the court's deciding.

RECAPITULATION

How far has the foregoing taken us?

The argument has been that we have fourteen or more clusters of factor at work in our appellate courts to hold the processes of deciding steady and to make the work of the group humanly reckonable in result. The argument has been that those aspects or factors which have achieved work-form as rules of law — whether rules of substantive law, or rules of procedure, or rules about how to handle and apply the other rules — that all of these together give in themselves, *in general,* most inadequate guidance about how particular appeals are likely to come out. But, the argument has been, lawyers, and law-consumers, insist on approaching the deciding of appellate courts with a type of demand for reckonability of particular outcome which no lawyer, nor layman, nor social science specialist, would dream of addressing to any other human group ever set up for the making of difficult and responsible decisions. The argument has been that this extraordinary demand, perhaps need, for reckonability in this unique kind of deciding roots so deep that its continuing disappointment {155} is producing, in almost frightening measure has already produced, a crisis in confidence, among the very profession, in regard to the work and workings of the law and of the appellate courts.

The argument has been, however, that whereas about other areas of reaching tough decision the psychologists and sociologists and other experts are still groping for more than indications, or for statistical approaches to mass-phenomena, yet in our area the clustered steadying factors combine with our traditions of craft, craftsmanship, and office to provide the wherewithal to reasonably satisfy even the seemingly unreasonable demands made upon the appellate bench alike by the men of law and by the citizens who are the law-consumers. The argument has been that it is the way in which our profession — lawyers, law teachers, and judges all together — have drifted into mis-seeing and misunderstanding what it is that our appellate judges are doing, into mis-seeing and misunderstanding, no less, what it is that they used to do and ought now to be doing — that it is this drift, and this drift alone, which is today keeping the profession discomfited in work and in spirit, which is raising needless unease even among the appellate judiciary, and which is standing between that judiciary and sure clean satisfying progress toward full recapture of the old fine and effective manner of work rightly called the Grand Style of the Common Law.

The argument has been, moreover, that in fact, though neither in full conscious realization nor in final fulfillment of implication and of promise, the process of such recapture has gone forward so far — in counterdrift — that the results are now there to be seen by any lawyer who can think. If he will only look. The argument has not yet been, but will be, that once a lawyer wakes up to what our appellate courts in fact are doing, he will find that their work *is* humanly and satisfyingly reckonable, so much so that he can at once and with no need for subtle skills or schooling step up the measure of his personal legal competence and — what is more vital still — that he can again find solace to his soul in a living confidence that his law and his appellate bench are on their job. The argument has not yet been, but it will be, further, that the revivifying of a few simple ideas and ideals all ancient in our tradition can also, within the craft of appellate judging itself, step up the level of performance and of the craftsmen's intangible income of satisfaction in their work.

Now what has been offered in the way of fact to buttress all this argument?

There has been a horse-sense canvass of most of the factor-clusters {156} which combine to make American appellate judging a unique activity. Nothing was adduced which is not common knowledge; yet it seems to me that the rather careful gathering and stating of so much pertinent common knowledge, all in order, can hardly fail to rekindle faith, faith that it may be possible to come close to accomplishing this impossibility: the management of moderate reckonability even in the deciding of disputes so serious and contentious as to carry through into the ultimate stages of litigation.

There has then been a presentation (which seems to me conclusive) of the huge and self-inconsistent range of correctnesses with which the materials of received authority can be handled to produce new authority in the pending case; and it has been shown (again, I suggest, conclusively) that this range is nothing new, but goes back to before our Revolution and has remained then in good standing in the 1840's and in the 1890's, and ever since. Daily grist stuff from Pennsylvania (1944) and New York (1939) was then presented to demonstrate that in modern times the range appears in action not, say, in museum pieces which it takes expeditions to collect, but in the everyday work on the everyday case, *your* case tomorrow; and there was informal report on 300-page samplings made in 1939 or 1940 from four other courts.

Meantime enough had been presented from New York in 1842 and Ohio in 1844 (along with the material on warranty in New York at pp. 126 f.) to persuade, I hope, that my picture of a Grand Style of appellate judging before the Civil War is not conjured out of air.

We then went on to do some nose-counts on citations in substantially contemporary opinions, and to sample-check the accuracy of the judicial assertions about what the prior authorities have been. The results confirmed what should have been expected: simple cites far outweigh any other type of use of case-authorities, and in the main prove gratifyingly accurate. Thence we derived a first assurance that continuity with the body of doctrine is felt, is being maintained in action, is a duty and tool in conscious and careful employ — this notwithstanding all hydraheadedness of those correct techniques. We noted then a few illustrations of "mere" following. In some it did seem to be truly "mere," but in some the mereness involved unreasoned but also unmistakable creation by "development," in some the growth "by following" meant not only expansion but new direction. These illustrations were selected to purpose, they were not mine-run stuff; yet their {157} "feel" was mostly normal and typical and, I hope, persuasive that what seems on the surface and often even to the participant or opinion-writer as quiescence is more than likely, in appellate cases, to mean motion which even when small is far from negligible. From this one might derive a first suspicion that the lines of any probable movement on the occasion and for the occasion might be given in, foreshadowed, almost forecast by the *situation* in suit. Argument and illustration then combined, to distinguish *type* or problem-situation and its sense and equity from the peculiar or "fireside" appeal of the individual controversy or parties, and to urge — though again on selected material — that the situation-type could sometimes be seen *by way of the opinion* to be at work in shaping the decision and the rule. But the argument was made and stressed that the situation, however eloquent, could operate only insofar as its eloquence could reach ear and understanding of the particular court or judge.

The question was then explored whether this appeal of the facts — distinguishing the type of situation from the particular case — could be traced by a blunt eye, producing homely and persuasive evidence available to most folk, as a usable tool in spotting what has been influencing certain appellate courts in their actual deciding. This time the cases were not selected, they were taken as they came: from New York, 1939; Pennsylvania, 1944; Ohio, 1953. And I remind that Ohio and New York had also been sampled from a century and more back, to make clear the honorable age of the tradition.[177]

The Contemporary Scene, Nationally

{158}
What then remains, on the matter of evidence? It seems to me that what is called for is a contemporary sampling of appellate judicial work, of sufficient variety to test whether we do indeed have here a nationally prevalent phenomenon — for some of the test-borings put down by students over the years, in regard to period-style, have suggested quite wide variations in the dates and intensities of any such incidence among various of our States. It is desirable also, as has been indicated, to check as of the present the situation in each State previously sampled. Finally, we cannot be satisfied with knowledge that our more interesting phenomena — especially the unmistakable resort to reason and situation-sense as a guide to deciding and as a test of the rule laid down and applied — we cannot be content with knowing *that* these things occur; we need some indication of *how often* they occur, and we need to check the occurrence for whether it characterizes the whole court, rather than perhaps some particular member or two. For a first approach, then, opinions should as heretofore be read in sequence. A promising first lead would be to read until four of them were found which overtly used situation-sense in the testing or shaping of the rule applied, and check how many cases one had to cover in order to turn up the four. That would sample typicality. If, however, those four did not reasonably sample the court's personnel, as well, further reading would be called for. In any event, every opinion examined in the process would have to be accounted for, so that those which proved "positive" for our hypotheses would fall into due perspective with reference to their frequency and typicality.

As for the courts to select, they will be supreme courts, so that there may be no doubt as to their speaking for the respective jurisdictions. On the East Coast the prior studies dictate the choice: Massachusetts, New York, Pennsylvania. North Carolina also needs revisiting; add, to further sample the South, Alabama and Mississippi. For the Middle West, add to Ohio: Indiana and Illinois. For the West Coast, add to Washington: Oregon and {159} California. For Center and Southwest, take Kansas (in piety to the great Burch and Mason) and add Missouri and New Mexico. Surely this is a sampling more than reasonably extensive and fully varied by geography, economic conditions, density of population, manner of court operation, and whatever.

The nature of the sampling of case material of the study, and of the reports, appears in the three jobs which follow in full in the text: that on Mississippi, which ran off largely according to program; that on Alabama, which turned up unexpected problems; and that on Washington, where the sitting of the court in two Departments extended the study, but where the results are peculiarly interesting.

The other twelve are reported in Appendix A, eight in full, four in summary. I do not see how they can leave doubt that what is urged here *on the side of what is going on* is a general phenomenon among our appellate courts, that it not only happens, but happens daily, that it bites, that it is biting everywhere and practically at every session in the consultation room. Nor do I see how there can be doubt that this is new only in the sense that the last twenty or forty years have seen increasing *recurrence* to or toward the Grand Style, which was still in full flower a hundred years ago. Let me add that wherever I have been reading in the State intermediate courts of appeal I seem to find manner, methods, and techniques similar and familiar. And let me add, finally, that with all our judges drawn from the same pools of law schools, lawyers, and communities as the State judges, with *Erie v. Tompkins* to keep even differential subject matter from pressing too greatly toward a differential shaping of techniques or bent of spirit, with, finally, the Hands and Swan conspicuous for more than a legal generation as the country's most distinguished bench, it would be a devil's miracle if the work of the federal Circuit Courts of Appeal should have fallen out along significantly different lines.

* * *

Here, then, are the samplings from current work in three State supreme courts, with an eye to the methods they use in their deciding, to their attention and responsibility to the body of authoritative materials they have inherited, to their incessant reforging of those authoritative materials in the very process of their application, as that process is played upon by their overt resort for guidance to what seems to the court to be sense and wisdom, and with a particular eye out for recourse to situation-sense {160} to guide the choice and shaping of the rule laid down and applied.

MISSISSIPPI, 1958

The advance sheets examined were those of 105 So.2d for November 13 and 20, and the first three cases in 106 So.2d for December 11, all 1958, comprising fourteen cases with opinions, plus two which read simply "Per Curiam: Affirmed." The court was sitting, except in two instances, by fives, but with some shifts in personnel. Six of the cases, though significant in that they had overt recourse to sense-in-the-case, were nonsignificant for our basic inquiry, since such recourse was all but forced by the issues, and the issues gave no occasion to reformulate any rule: *Barber v. Barber,* 105 So.2d 630, sustained the chancellor's exercise of discretion in award of attorney's fees to defend against a husband's cross-bill for divorce, and in failing to impress a lien to secure a separate maintenance award; *Corley v. Mississippi State Oil and Gas Board,* ibid. 633, sustained a Board's rules regulating an oil pool; *Clark v. Magee,* ibid. 753, sustained the chancellor's finding that a deed was vitiated by undue influence; *Calvert Fire Ins. Co. v. Carter,* ibid. 758, sustained a verdict which set the amount of damage to a car. Further, *Heslep v. Millsaps,* 106 So.2d 374, an adverse possession suit which involved a fencing error, where the court sustained the chancellor although they saw the facts differently, and *Mississippi Power etc. Co. v. Town of Coldwater,* ibid. 375, an amazing effort by the Power Company to enjoin a town and two electric co-ops from even more amazing unauthorized activities to "get cheaper power for Coldwater," where a multitude of relevant legal rules all seem clear, and explicit sense is used throughout in threading through the factual maze to a decree.

Of the remaining eight cases, five involved significant overt use of sense; four times such use affected the shape and meaning of the rule. Each of these five opinions was by a different Justice. Thus:

(a) *Koestler v. Dallas Tank Co.,* 105 So.2d 621, involved an appeal from a rezoning of residence property, done as the city administration expired. The outgoing mayor had refused to sign the bill of exceptions; the incoming mayor did sign, and still within the time allowed for filing. The statute provided that the bill "*shall be signed by the person acting as president of the board of supervisors or of the municipal authorities.*" (Court's italics.) "It is {161} patent that the appellees want us to write something into the statute which does not appear there. Under their contention, if a mayor became seriously ill or injured, or mentally incapacitated, or in the event of his death, the offended party would be practically without any remedy whatsoever, and we think that under the plain wording of the statute it means exactly what it says and that is that the person acting at the time the bill of exceptions is presented to the governing authorities is authorized to sign the same." (p. 622.) The statute seems to me to be thus plain only when it is read with the situation-sense which the court thus expounds.

(b) *Green v. Hatcher,* ibid. 624, was an appeal from a $3000 wrongful death verdict. "It is understandable that the jury may have been unwilling to assess punitive damages merely as a deterrent to the said defendant and others from the commission of similar negligent acts in the future, since the jury evidently knew that he was serving a seven-year sentence in the penitentiary under his conviction for the crime of manslaughter in connection with the [same] alleged wrongful killing of Bobby Green." (p. 626.) It might be, in view of Hatcher's sentence and the showing that he had been merely renting his house and the non-showing of leviable assets, that even $3000 would be uncollectible. "But be that as it may, this Court does not feel justified in going on record as upholding as being adequate a verdict for $3,000 for the death of this ten year old boy." (ibid.) I am treating this case, and *Robinson v. State,* below, as, one or the other or both of them, involving the implicit setting up of a subrule.

(c) In *Lenaz v. Conway,* ibid. 762, an action for false arrest, one contention of plaintiffs was that the light fixture they had been chased and arrested for breaking fell within a statute providing that no property rights exist in *fixtures, appliances,* etc., used in violation of the intoxicating liquor laws. The court quoted, applied, and materially extended a prior decision which had read: "It is true that, by the provisions of Section 2618, Code of 1942, there are no property rights in intoxicating liquor, or in motor vehicles used in violation of the chapter on intoxicating liquor. But *the purpose* of this statute is to disqualify any person, unlawfully in possession of *liquor or motor vehicles* used in connection therewith, *from asserting a right to their recovery, or for damages for their seizure.* Undoubtedly, it is not the purpose to abridge the state of its power to punish persons *who steal liquor,* or rob persons and take their liquor." (p. 765; my italics.) {162}

(d) From *Robinson v. State,* ibid. 766, 767 (an appeal from a conviction of murder, sentence for life): "No motion was made for a new trial. Many years ago this court adopted the rule that the contention that the verdict is contrary to the great weight of the evidence is not properly preserved for review by this court on appeal where no motion for a new trial raising the point was filed with and presented to the trial court.... The cases ... are collected ... *However, in view of the gravity of the charge and the severity of the punishment in this case, we have reviewed the testimony....*" (My italics.) Held, that the testimony "amply justified the verdict."

(e) *Goodnite v. Farm Equipment Co.,* 106 So.2d 383, was a case in which the Supreme Court reversed decisions of the circuit court and a commission against the petitioner, and then, pursuant to statute, entered judgment for death benefits. Though there is no statutory provision for interest, precedents gave interest on awards originally made by the commission, if they were affirmed. "There is no sound reason why interest should not be allowed on each such weekly installment ... in a case where the award is made by the commission pursuant to a judgment of the court ..." and "the judgment relates by the force of the statute to the time prescribed by the statute." (pp. 384-385.)

The precedent techniques in this particular series of cases are unexciting, but they range widely: a large number of simple citations, frequent citations which give the substance of the holding, or quote the rationale for application; two instances of expansion and development of one or more prior holdings in full consonance with their reasons; occasional distinguishing on the facts or on the issue, the reason therefore sometimes appearing on the face of the opinion. I have not checked how far the simple citations may involve expansion or redirection of the decisions cited. Repeatedly the controlling authority against the appellant seemed so flat as to make the appeal look almost frivolous. *Koestler* (a), *Lenaz* (c), and *Goodnite* (e) show three strikingly divergent techniques with statutory language used by this court: reading in the light of the situation; whittling language down to fit purpose; insertion of unmentioned provisions, in furtherance of decency and of our normal legal habits of thought.

ALABAMA, 1958

The material examined was 105 So.2d 643-736, the advance sheet of November 13, 1958. All of this was read without turning {163} up more than two overt Supreme Court discussions of sense in the testing or formulation of the rule applied. The opinions of the Supreme Court (fifteen in number: one Per Curiam, the others from seven different judges; no dissents) were indeed so different from the other courts in both tone and method as to make a widish base very welcome before conclusions could feel safe. The unusual aspect was the almost absence of open discussion, in the court's own language, of situation-sense and - reason in or for any rule, as contrasted with sense in the application of the rule to the case in hand. Such discussion of sense for and in the rule applied, so common as to be Standard in the other courts, occurred, I repeat, in only two of the fifteen opinions, with a third in which an application, rested on two simple citations, was phrased in sense-terms and amounted in essence to a subrule: "True, there was some evidence of a timber deed executed in 1946 to one Doc Dearmon. This deed was not introduced into evidence. We do not think this one act constitutes such a possession of wild land sufficient for the purchase of acquiring title by adverse possession." *Reynolds v. Henson*, pp. 679, 680.

There is, however, coupled with this scarcity of personal inquiry by the court into the sense of the rules applied, a striking, almost gnawing, concern with display of some rationale in life or law. In only three of the opinions (including the *Reynolds* case, above) is the controlling rule of law announced in the purer Formal Style simply as being there and being determinative. One finds instead, in twelve cases out of the fifteen, a quotation from some prior opinion which states not only the relevant rule but also some reason therefor, factual or legal. In both aspects (making due allowance for the differences in substantive law, in procedure, and in legal vocabulary), the opinions remind of much of the 1939 work in 303 Mass., mentioned above at page 142, though neither of the characteristics is as strongly present in that material. I read the phenomenon as meaning that the Formal tradition still has power, but has begun to give the judges internal discomfort, and is due to wane soon and fast. (Cf. again Massachusetts, 1939.) That conclusion is strengthened by the fact that the discussions of sense-in-application flow rather easily, and that the two reworkings of rules to fit situation-sense are handled smoothly. One thing seems clear, however: no peculiar condition of Alabama law nor yet its still overtechnical procedure can alone suffice to account for the opinion-style of Alabama's Supreme Court. This is proved by the completely different tone of the twelve cases from the Court of Appeals which are mixed in {164} with the Supreme Court cases. One of those twelve involved only an application of rulings which the Court of Appeals had requested and received from the Supreme Court. But in six out of the remaining eleven the court formulates the situation-sense and the rule in its own language; nor does the Supreme Court show any sign of disapproving this method, for in five of those cases certiorari was applied for and denied; indeed, in the case where the Court of Appeals had certified questions the Supreme Court's answers rested primarily on exact — almost overexact — reading of a long sense-quote from the Court of Appeals itself. (*Speagle v. U.S. Steel Corp.*, pp. 717, 719.)

The "situation-reason" cases, in addition to *Reynolds*, above: *Alabama Farm etc. Ins., Service v. Nixon*, p. 643, involved a policy in the seller's name, paid for by his own funds, on his equity in improved land largely paid for and of which the buyer was in possession when the buildings burned. The seller, paid by the insurer, was nevertheless claiming from the buyer the unpaid portion of the price. The insurer was claiming subrogation to that right of the seller. The buyer was claiming discharge by the insurer's payment. The buyer prevailed, being required, however, to pay seller the amount of the premiums. "No decision in this state has been called to our attention which in our judgment determines the exact question here presented. . . . If Bucklew may collect the proceeds of the insurance and also the full purchase price, he has a windfall and the purchaser is required to pay for that which he does not receive. . . . When there is a loss and the vendor has effected insurance, the proceeds from the insurance come to him in place of his security interest. . . . To allow his claim here would give him $9000, for what he contracted to sell for $7000. Furthermore, to allow such a result would constitute a temptation to vendors to insure and destroy the property . . ." (p. 646.) "Furthermore as we pointed out earlier in the opinion, subrogation is not a matter of right but may be applied only by the court in the interest of justice. . . ." Which takes care of the insurer. Reasoning and decisions from other states were approved.

City of Prichard v. Geary, p. 682, raised a zoning question. Two intersecting streets had been zoned, one for commercial, one for residence use. A corner lot and the adjoining lot abutting on the residence street had been in commercial use as a single parcel, as a restaurant and parking lot. The city was opposing a new use of the combined lots as a filling station. A procedural point is first disposed of on sense ("The only purpose which the {165} law can expect from requiring proof of such matter," etc. — "The rule would seem to derive especial force, when applied to cases like the present . . ." etc. (p. 685.)) On the merits: "We are of opinion that the appellees' property is one unit." (p. 686.) "In the instant case, the disputed property was conveyed to the deceased by one conveyance some eleven years prior to the passage of the zoning ordinance. The deceased and the complainants, trustees under his will, have always regarded and treated the property as a unit, and since 1935 they have leased it for the operation of a restaurant, etc., as stated above . . . At the time of adoption of the ordinances in 1945 and 1946 the neighborhood where this property is located was a commercial location, with a filling station next south and adjoining this property, and all that side of Craft Highway for many years had been commercial. As mentioned, the property does not extend back from Craft as far as most of the commercial property in the same block." (p. 687.) "Although this quoted case dealt with the question, among others, of whether it was permissible for the city authorities to make a municipal improvement assessment singly against property consisting of several lots, *the force of the principle* [that deed description by lot and plot does not bar combination] has been recognized in other cases" — duly illustrated. (p. 686; my italics.)

Typical of the "reason ex quotation" approach in these cases are the following. In *Williams v. Williams,* p. 676, a man in service was seeking an annulment for misrepresentation of age (eighteen for the factual fifteen) and of love (the wife's only true purpose being allegedly to secure an allotment check). The rule, policy, and criterion are quoted at page 678 from a prior case: "Few, if any, kinds of fraud or trickery will warrant a nullity suit, after the marital status is actually entered upon by cohabitation and marital intercourse has intervened.

"But, following the lead of our case of *Raia v. Raia,* supra (214 Ala. 391, 392, 108 So. 11) supported by sound reason and authority, we are of opinion that entering into the marriage covenant by ceremonial marriage is an express declaration of a purpose to fulfill the marriage vows; that, if done with intent not to perform, followed by immediate disavowal and refusal to perform, the party is guilty of fraud which goes to the essence of the marriage relation; and no public policy denies the wronged party relief by a nullity suit." The bill was held insufficient under this test, and the case reversed and remanded.

Again, *Clark v. McGinn,* p. 668, involved overdue advances {166} of some $39,000 by an exclusive factor to one of its lumber company principals. The defendant man and wife who owned the principal part of the stock in the borrower had executed a formal guaranty for present and future indebtedness of the company, containing no explicit request, but with a recital of desire that such indebtedness be secured, and of one dollar in hand paid. No effort appears to have been made to show consideration other than by the instrument. A demurrer to the complaint was overruled. The court quotes the trial court at length, including this subquote from a prior Alabama Supreme Court case:

"It is not material that the expressed consideration is nominal. That point was made, as to a guaranty, substantially the same as this, in the case of *Lawrence v. McCalmont,* 2 How. 426, 452, 11 L. Ed. 326, and was overruled. Mr. Justice Story said: 'The guarantor acknowledged the receipt of the $1, and is now estopped to deny it. If she has not received it, she would now be entitled to recover it. A valuable consideration, however small or nominal, if given or stipulated for in good faith, is, in the absence of fraud, sufficient to support an action on any parol contract; and this is equally true as to contracts of guaranty or as to other contracts. A stipulation in consideration of $1 is just as effectual and valuable a consideration as a larger sum stipulated for or paid.'" "It seems to us," says the present court, "that the trial court's opinion adequately answers the question as to whether the bill sufficiently alleges a consideration for the guaranty agreement." (p. 671.) Overruling of the demurrer affirmed.

This delving into the books rather than into life to find situation-reason or rule-reason must, of course, when the books are narrow, constrict the trove. Thus "while as to liability and the defenses which may be interposed, there is no difference between wanton injury and wilful or intentional injury," pleading the two with an "and" instead of an "or" can trap the plaintiff and cost him his verdict. *Dickey v. Russell,* pp. 649, 651 f. And the court seems, for instance, willing to let failure to specially plead the affirmative defense of payment bar the defense in a foreclosure suit, because there is a vital policy against surprise, but without considering any possibility of amending the pleadings. *Adams v. Baker,* pp. 703, 704.

Reason in the Court of Appeals. Although, to keep its material both single and authoritative, this study centers strictly on the highest state courts, the peculiar Alabama situation warrants presenting two examples of sense as used by the Court of Appeals. In *Smith v. State,* p. 662, 39 Ala. App. 501, jurors had been permitted {167} to separate overnight. "We consider this testimony on cross-examination shows the State failed to overcome the presumption of injury arising from the proof of separation. Particularly, we advert to Mrs. Yates discussing the case in his presence without Mr. Yates admonishing her not to; this was neglect or disregard of the trial judge's instruction . . .

"This court individually prefers, as a matter of workability, the rule laid down by way of dictum by Mr. Justice Bouldin in *Mitchell v. State,* 244 Ala. 503, 14 So.2d 132, which in turn was disapproved by dictum in *Wright v. State,* 262 Ala. 420, 79 So.2d 74. Indeed, it would be far better to do away with all jury separations in felony cases — regardless of consent. Jury tampering or canvassing is not a lost art. See . . ." (p. 665). Conviction reversed; remanded for new trial. Cert. denied, p. 666.

Simmons v. State, p. 691, 39 Ala. App. 477, had to do with a conviction for dynamiting a house. After testimony that on request the appellant had removed his shoes and that the witness had looked at his foot, compared it with barefoot tracks at the scene, and "it looked like the same foot that made the tracks," evidence had been excluded that the defendant had offered to allow a cast to be made of his foot. A Texas case was quoted: there is no telling what effect the testimony would have had in a case wholly of circumstantial evidence. "We think the doctrine of this case sound." (p. 693.) "Further however, additional legal principles we think dictate the propriety of the admission of such evidence. . . . [W]hen in the examination of a witness a party brings out part of a transaction or conversation, the other party may inquire fully into the transaction, bring out the whole conversation on further examination . . .

"Such principle makes admissible self-serving statements which would otherwise be inadmissible . . .

"Particularly is this true in view of the fact that the State's case was based on circumstantial evidence; that no casts or pictures of the prints were made, and further, apparently the prints were not even measured by ruler or otherwise." (p. 694.) Reversed and remanded. Cert. denied, p. 694.

Precedent techniques in the Supreme Court. Along with the constantly recurrent quotation of rule-plus-rationale goes the frequent simple citation, and a variety of minor modifications: definition of a term; "the principle . . . has been followed in later cases," which are then simply cited; the case exactly in point, and typically then set forth in detail; "What was said in . . . is equally applicable here," with the quote following, typically of {168} language which led to the holding in the prior case. "See also" sometimes occurs. Distinctions are sometimes taken, commonly in language which shows the reason for distinguishing. The negative implication of a prior rule is twice made the basis for decision; in one of the instances it definitely blocked off what I read as a prior tendency or thrust toward expansion (in regard to refusal to cross a picket line as disqualifying for unemployment benefits, *Speagle v. United States Steel Corp.,* pp. 717, 720.) New subrules are made, building out an established rule, and a principle which has previously been recognized in passing is made clear and used in novel territory. — There is unusually frequent quotation from and reliance on the court below.

WASHINGTON, 1958

The advance sheets first used were those which had already been used for Oregon: September 5 and December 5, 1958. This netted eight opinions, ranging over four judges, plus two Per Curiams. But the court sits in Departments, and Department 2 was represented only by one of the Per Curiams. The issue of September 26 was therefore drawn on until (with four more cases) three cases were secured from that Department, representing three further judges. (I later discovered that September 12 would have roughly matched the whole of this, with two en banc cases added, and some interesting dissents. But the rules of random sampling do not admit of a switch. Hence I shall say of the September 12 cases only that if they had at all impugned my theses, I should of course have discussed them, anyhow.)

Three of the twelve cases, and one main point in a fourth, are handled on the most technical level, and, on their face, soundly so. When things are clear, and pure technique makes sense, there is no occasion to labor matters. (In two other cases this type of severely technical treatment of a main point or of the whole case occurs, but seems to me unhappy — by which I mean that the problem seems to me, in the one instance, to have called for the court's overt sense-judgment to be added to the formal technique; in the other instance such express judgment, though it was added, seems to me to fly in the face of general sense.) — Three of the opinions turn to overt sense in regard to the application of the relevant rule: good, and sound, but for our main purpose nonsignificant.

But in no less than seven cases out of the nine in which simple technical treatment was not sufficient (the opinions coming from {169} six different members of the court), overt sense is used either to test or to frame or reframe or to redirect the rule, or one of the rules, made to control the result.

In the net, in range and variety of method, in flavor, and in substance, the material comes about as close to the Grand Style as any run-of-the-mill sequence I have seen from this century. Special reference may be made to the first four cases below under the sidehead, *Situation-sense in case law rule and principle*, page 173, but the judgment rests on the whole body of the decisions.

Meantime, it will be recalled that the Washington court's 1940 output had been one of the batches of material originally studied (3 Wash. 2d 1-307). Detail by detail, what is presented in the 1958 material is matchable somewhere among the earlier opinions: e.g., the feeling of responsibility to the authorities, along with willingness to re-examine; the range of precedent techniques; and the open resort to sense as a codeterminant of result. Yet the quantity-relations are altogether different, and tone and flavor have matured amazingly. On the technical side the 1958 work is more deft; sense and basic equities are felt for and used hugely more in terms of *type*-situation and of the testing or reshaping of the *rule*; the *future* bearing of the rule announced is much more palpably a factor in the work; the process of reviewing authorities is much more infused with the quest for coming *ever closer* to the bull's-eye of a sound rule for the whole situation. The very manner of writing has a relative ease that contrasts with the stiffness of a generation back.

Enough of description. Let the stuff speak for itself:

The technical discussions. McClintock v. Rhay, 52 Wash. 2d 615, 328 P.2d 369, an original application *in forma pauperis* for a *habeas corpus,* involved a forgery defendant who after waiver of constitutional guarantees and plea of guilty had nevertheless before the sentencing asked for counsel and for permission to change his plea. Both had been refused. The language of the state constitution was recited and applied, the judgment and sentence vacated, and an order made to afford counsel. *Richert v. Handley,* 330 P.2d 1079, was equally clear. In a partnership dissolution the parties were explicitly found to have made no agreement on certain points covered "in the absence of agreement" by the

Uniform Partnership Act; the Act rules were therefore applied. Where a cross-complaint had joined a possible alternate defendant thereto, *Frank Coluccio Construction Co. v. Kitsap County Sewer District,* 52 Wash. 2d 776, 329 P.2d 189, did little more than quote and find applicable as to venue a rule allowing suit where some {170} one of the defendants (*this time the original plaintiff*) resides. And in one phase of *State v. Kelly,* 52 Wash. 2d 676, 328 P.2d 362 (to which we shall recur), records of the state penitentiary introduced to establish identity under a habitual criminal charge were sustained against a series of hypertechnical attacks by a series of almost purely technical answers.

In contrast stands the meticulous reasoning in two other criminal cases. In *Persinger v. Rhay,* 52 Wash. 762, 329 P.2d 191, the validity of a sentence for grand larceny turned on whether the information was sufficient to allege that the value of the property obtained by a bad check had been more than $25. "The allegation in the present case was that the defendant by uttering a check, calling for the payment of forty dollars, 'did receive money and merchandise therefor.'" (329 P.2d at 195.) A prior case almost flatly in point had held this insufficient: "... criminal statutes, especially those inflicting a penalty of imprisonment in the penitentiary, must be strictly construed." (ibid. 194.) "We can only repeat what we said in the Sorensen case" (ibid. 195) — this though in the case in hand the words "receive *money and* merchandise therefor" (my italics) had surely given in sense the full picture of price plus pocket money to the full face being taken for the check. — I personally consider "not more than fifteen years in the penitentiary" for a $26 bad check to be either legislative inadvertence or commercial savagery or (in this lobby-backed statute) both.[178] Do we have a court here in the tradition of the English courts of a century and a half ago, where a stolen diamond ring or gold watch was gravely admitted or sworn to be "of the value of eleven pence halfpenny" so as to evade the capital penalty for *grand larceny?*

In *Allen v. Rhay,* 52 Wash. 2d 609, 328 P.2d 367, a man convicted on a plea of guilty of taking a motorcar and then placed on *two-year* probation, was *seven* years later, under recital of violation of his probation, sentenced to a twenty-year maximum penitentiary term. In *habeas corpus* he alleged that he had not, as required by statute, been informed of his right to apply to withdraw his plea. "RCW 9.95.200 states that it is within the sound discretion of the sentencing judge as to whether a defendant will be given probation by a deferred sentence. *State v. Williams,* Wash. 1957, 316 P.2d 913. RCW 9.95.240 provides that should a defendant, having been given probation, petition to have his plea of guilty withdrawn, the granting of such petition would also be {171} within the sound discretion of the court; *therefore, we cannot see how the failure* of the sentencing judge, in this case, *to inform petitioner* that he had a right to come into court and ask that his plea of guilty be withdrawn, *could* have prejudiced petitioner *in any way, since,* even if he had been so informed, *there was no assurance* that he would have been permitted to withdraw his plea." (328 P.2d at 368; my italics.) This says, if I can read, that a *chance* at or in a fair hearing (which is about all any lawsuit offers in any ordinary case) can be denied without harm "in any way," merely because the outcome of that chance would not be certain.

Such a rationale, coming Per Curiam from the same court which at about the same time was deciding *Persinger v. Rhay* and the cases which now follow, politely invites disbelief that it either (a) reflects the true grounds for deciding or (b) would be safe to rely on in any other case. As to (a), one notes for the particular decision that "the petitioner nowhere alleges that he has complied with all of the conditions imposed by the order suspending the imposition of sentence ...

which included as conditions, restitution, and the payment of costs. He relies upon the fact that the two years, for which the sentence was deferred, ended five years before he was actually sentenced." (This latter is not further discussed, and one is left with a wonder whether the prosecuting authorities may, over indefinite periods, be using deferred sentences to handle without trial future offenses of any kind of which an ex-probationer may be suspected.) But surely the juice of reason in the case lies elsewhere: "A writ of *habeas corpus is available only . . . to determine whether his constitutional right to due process of law has been violated. . . .*" (ibid.; my italics.) Now consider what would have been the indeterminable possible backward sweep as to any prisoner in the State of a *constitutional* decision to the effect that "The failure of the court to inform petitioner in his probation papers of his 'right'" did in fact "amount to such action as would 'shock the conscience' and thereby violate due process provisions." (ibid.) Nevertheless, the actual decision leaves us with the question of how trial courts can be persuaded to be careful in regard to their statutory duty of informing prisoners of their rights; and of how much difference such knowledge of rights may make.

Sense in application of rule. Throughout the discussion in *State v. Kelly,* 52 Wash. 2d 676, 328 P.2d 362, a distinction between proof of the identity of the prisoner and proof of prior convictions serves to guide a nicely technical discussion of admissibility {172} of various records on the matter of status of habitual criminal. In *Johnson v. Johnson,* 330 P.2d 1075, an application of the sense-rule on child custody, sensible criteria are quoted at length, and the trial court's determination is shown to be permissible and probably wise. In a second point, on application of *res judicata,* technicality and sense are shown to coincide. In *Gerberg v. Crosby,* 52 Wash. 2d 792, 329 P.2d 184, sense was the basis both of a refusal to apply the last clear chance rule and of a conclusion that the widening expert testimony rule approved by the court had failed in the particular case to harm the defendant.

Sense in testing or shaping the statutory rule. Twice sense is made to guide statutory construction. Thus under RCW 72.08.040 it is the duty of the superintendent of the state penitentiary

> "(2) To supervise the government . . . of the penitentiary. . . . He shall keep a *registry* of the convicts, in which shall be entered the *name* of each convict, *the crime of which he was convicted, the period of his sentence, from what county and by what court sentenced . . . to what degree educated, an accurate description of his person, and whether he has been previously confined in a prison. . . .*" [Court's italics; my deletions.]

". . . [W]e hold that in order to carry out the mandate of the statute, it is not only appropriate but necessary for the warden to maintain, as a part of his records and files, a copy of the sentence and judgment and warrant of commitment of the person confined." *State v. Kelly,* 52 Wash. 2d 676, 328 P.2d 362, 365-366. The warden's certificate identifying the appellant from copies of such papers as being the person convicted and committed as described therein was thus admissible on the issue of his being a habitual criminal. Again, in *Bradley v. Department of Labor,* 52 Wash. 2d 780, 329 P.2d 196, an injured workman who had recovered from a third party much more than his allowable compensation, and who was nevertheless seeking medical expenses from the medical aid fund, was denied recovery by virtue of careful and sensible construction. The court had shortly before held the same way, "The decision would seem to be controlling of the question presented in this case; however, the appellant urges that the matter be reconsidered, as he feels that his interpretation of the act was not adequately argued before the court in *State v. Owen, supra.*" (329 P.2d at 197.) It is reconsidered for five full columns. "Had the legislature intended that medical payments {173} should be made in the case of every injured workman, whether or not he elected to take under the act, presumably an exception would have been made in his favor, as it was in the case of the workman who is not entitled to compensation because of the short duration of his disability." (ibid. 198.) It was indeed recognized that "The inequity which may result from this hiatus in the act would present a strong reason for adopting the appellant's theory that such a result was not intended, were it not" for a similar inequity imported by appellant's theory, (ibid. 199.) "Our decision in this matter is fortified by the fact that the attorney general so construed the act a few years after its passage ... the department has consistently followed this interpretation since that date. In the meantime, the workmen's compensation act has been amended in a number of respects ... Where a statute is ambiguous, construction placed upon it by the officer or department charged with its administration is not binding on the courts but is entitled to considerable weight in determining the legislative intention, and the persuasive force of such interpretation is strengthened when the legislature ... silently acquiesces ..." (ibid. 200).

Situation-sense in case law rule and principle. Glaser v. Holdorf, 330 P.2d 1066, was mandamus to compel the trial court to certify a record. The court reporter had claimed to be unable to furnish a transcript and had refused use of his notes. The trial court was furnished by relators with their own narrative statement, to which defendants proposed no amendments within the Rule time. The trial court claimed inability to certify, lacking the stenographer's notes. The Supreme Court gathered four prior cases (which appear only in simple citation) plus general practicality into a horse-sense setup to deal with the difficulty, a setup rather adequate to take care of any squeeze play on either side. "This state has never required a statement of facts on appeal to contain a stenographic transcript...." (p. 1067.) Counsel successful below had lost their chance to propose amendments, but no agreement of counsel, nor yet reporter's notes, can bind the trial court to certify anything it knows to be erroneous; the court may call the litigants or even subpoena third parties to get the statement of facts corrected. But a court's refusal to certify "must indicate the nature of the error or omission upon which it relies so that an appellant, who has filed a proposed statement of facts in good faith, may have an opportunity to correct it." (p. 1067.) But the appellant is not in good faith if he seeks to shift the burden of substantially preparing the statement. Writ of {174} mandate granted. Manner and substance are in the Grand Style.

The next case, *Wenzler etc. Plumbing Co. v. Sellen,* 330 P.2d 1068, has similar flavor. There was a counterclaim against a subcontractor for failure to provide, for maintenance purposes, plans of underground installations. Provision of such plans to cover the delinquency of both the defendant and other subcontractors had been arranged in a single job, and it was necessary to estimate the allocation of the fee, which an engineer testified he could do within 10 per cent. The court drew on a private antitrust case (U.S.), a wrongful death action (Wash.), a case on a construction contract (Cal. App.) to justify, adopt, and apply a principle of full breadth, covering contract as well as tort, and putting this phase of damage law back where it belongs. "'The most elementary conceptions of justice and policy require that the wrongdoer shall bear the *risk of the uncertainty* which his own wrong has created ...'" (Quoted at 1069; my italics.) "... [W]herein we pointed out that while uncertainty as to the *fact of damage* is fatal; nevertheless, uncertainty as to *the amount* or *quantum* of damages is not to be regarded similarly . . ." (Quoted at 1070 from 43 Wash. 2d 36, 259 P.2d 1113; court's italics.) The court's enthusiasm for an excellent idea may even require a bit of tempering later; it quotes what is "most concisely stated in 14 Cal. Jur. 2d 690, §65: '. . . This rule applies both to a *loss of profits by the plaintiff* and to items of expense incurred by him as a result of his wrongful discharge from employment.'" (p. 1070; my italics.) The court also applies overt sense in disallowing a belated claim for extras contrary to the oral contract where the record disclosed no evidence to support the trial court's statement (not "finding") that the contract clause requiring advance notice had been abandoned.

Gerberg v. Crosby, 52 Wash. 2d 792, 329 P.2d 184, is in the same vein. A city policy officer who had for seven years been investigating traffic accidents by the thousand testified as an expert, from skid marks made by a motorcycle, to his opinion about the point of impact of the cycle and the car in question. The court relies on two precedents which had held the testimony of medical and engineering witnesses competent notwithstanding that the questions included "the very fact which was ultimately to be found by the jury," marshals in reasoned support and extension Ladd, the Model Code of Evidence, Morgan, and certain theoretical and practical observations by Learned Hand, and not only supports the trial court in admitting the testimony but gives vigorous {175} encouragement to likeminded trial courts to admit such aid more freely as being "essential to a proper determination of litigated causes." (Quoted in 329 P.2d at 187 from 232 Iowa 328, 5 N.W.2d 655.)

Nor does the fine flow cease here. *Persinger v. Rhay* has been mentioned above anent the reading of the information about what had been taken for the bad check. The ruling to be treated here cuts much deeper. In *habeas corpus* the petitioner was asking the reopening and vacation of a judgment and sentence completely regular on their face because the allegations of the information on which they rested had been insufficient to support the judgment. "Our answer to the petition prior to 1949 would have been a peremptory denial of the writ, because the rule has been that, absent constitutional issues, we would not go behind a judgment regular on its face and a commitment based thereon.

"As recently as 1945, in In re Grieve, 22 Wash. 2d 902, 158 P.2d 73, we expressed our adherence to that rule in a carefully considered opinion in which we quoted at length from the opinion by Marshall, Ch. J. in Ex parte Watkins, 1830 . . . from our own territorial supreme court and from many of our own opinions." (329 P.2d at 192-193.) Cases including *Sorenson v. Smith,* where the judgment had been ambiguous or uncertain as to the offense, are distinguished. "There are, however, two cases. . . . In both of these cases, we examined the information because the petitioner had alleged that he was charged with one offense and sentenced for another. *This is, we recognize, an extension of the holding in the Sorenson case to an entirely different type of case, but we are satisfied that it is a desirable and proper extension. . . .* We make clear . . . that we examine the information not to determine its sufficiency, but for the sole purpose of determining what crime was charged." (ibid. 193; my italics.) The prisoner was discharged.

One cannot expect a court to turn out nothing but cases of such caliber. But reshaping — or refusal to reshape — rules in the process of their "mere" application can occur on a more modest scale and still be significant. Thus in *Kramer v. Zappone,* 330 P.2d 1072, an order for aluminum awning parts had been priced by item, with 20 per cent off the total, but in fact the order made up a specific number of knocked-down awnings. A partial inspection after delivery had led to complaints that some of the materials were damaged by poor packing. Two months later a check for $500 had accompanied a complaint that the paint job {176} was not as represented. Two more months later notice of return of the whole was given, but in so returning the buyers held out randomly chosen material of $500 value. The goods were refused by the seller, who was suing for the balance of the price. "The defendant cross-complained for rescission" (i.e., for a declaration thereof? for the $500? for what?) and had a verdict. Judgment N.O.V. No mention is made of any untimeliness in the rescission or of the effect of any lien by the buyer under Uniform Sales Act §69(5). But the court applies a "single and entire consideration" precedent; it sees the price-term as not making the contract "severable": it was awnings which had been the subject matter, bringing to bear another precedent on bad parts which disable the whole, so as to produce a new and broader phrasing: "In other words, if part of this order did not fulfill the warranty, *the purpose of the order was frustrated.*" (p. 1074; my italics.) Relying, again, upon a precedent which endorsed a *reasonable and equitable application* (court's italics) of the rule requiring restitution to rescind: "The rule . . . has some exceptions; but we are not persuaded to extend these to cover the factual situation which is before us now." (ibid.) N.O.V. affirmed.

The precedent techniques. Present throughout was unmistakable consciousness of the solidity and pressure of the body of existing authorities. This showed not only in the normal frequency of simple citations to establish propositions either in discussion or for application, and in the copious quotation from the relevant statutes, but perhaps especially in the selection, for quotation of rule and rationale, of prior opinions which had in their own time tied in or tidied up the whole prior state of the law. *Per contra,* open willingness to recanvass a situation is present in unusual degree, the result being now confirmation of the old, now the clearing up of divergent leads, now a new direction or position. Capitalization of experience in other jurisdictions, as of the literature, recurs. Refusal to expand or redirect can be overt, after meditation; expansion or redirection in the process of application can either simply occur or be signaled as deliberate. The practice of naming distinguished judges who are relied on is in bud again. Along with all of this goes clean and quiet technical reasoning where that is pertinent and either enough to satisfy, or unavoidable; the care taken in examination of the exact language of statutes, opinions, or documents is evidenced by an uncommonly extensive recourse to italics in the quoted text thereof. The recurrent effort to formulate or reformulate rules or principles for {177} more adequate and more "singing" guidance is the other piece of this same care with the crucial word.

* * *

Such, as is further developed in Appendix A, is the scene in the nation today. It is there for any man to see.

RECKONABILITY OF RESULT:
THEORY OF RULES

{178}
Before we again pick up the forecasting problem, let us make quick audit of this last assertion: Are the lines of inquiry we have been exploring indeed available to ordinary lawyers? Or do these leads or devices go dumb or incoherent in the absence of some peculiar psychological or other technical training, or in the absence of some elaborate and inaccessible data, or in the absence of some intransmissible native knack? I submit that the signs to be looked for, though wholly unstandardized, are nonetheless as gross and unmistakable as road signs, and that there are obvious and valuable procedures of interpretation and use which are well-nigh as simple and communicable as the driving of a nail. Road signs *can* secrete themselves behind hedges, *can* break or fade, *can* be misleading; and nails *can* be hammered on the thumb; but for daily living the signs suffice to guide most folk and the process to rough-carpenter boards into some utility. I submit that the average lawyer has only to shift his focus for a few hours from "*what* was held" in a series of opinions to what those opinions suggest or show about *what was bothering and what was helping the court* as it decided. If he will take that as his subject matter, I submit that the average lawyer can provide himself, and rather speedily, with the kit of coarse tools we have been discussing and with evidence, too, of his own ability to use that kit to immediate advantage.

Is the effort worthwhile? Leave intellectual curiosity on one side, and the fun that comes from sudden novel cross-lighting of scenes otherwise too familiar for notice. Look, if you will, to bald practicality: does this proposed way of reading opinions, this proposed focus on the *How* of the court's deciding, substantially increase the reader's forecasting power, as contrasted with a forecasting based merely on a search for the prevailing doctrine, or with a forecasting based chiefly on feel, hunch, or guess, or with a forecasting based on some unanalyzed cross-play of those two? For the ordinary lawyer I submit that there can be no question as {179} to the gain in predictive power. Spend a single thoughtful weekend with a couple of recent volumes of reports from your own supreme court, read this way, and you can never again, with fervor or despair, make that remark about never knowing where an appellate court will hang its hat. Spend five such weekends, and you will be getting a workable idea of the local geography of hatracks.

Neither can there be question for most of the better appellate lawyers, that these approaches, based as they are on the best practice, make conscious and clear, and thus available even on bad days, values which in the absence of a good day may otherwise fail to come to bear. I speak not, naturally, of the genius or neargenius whose intuition regularly and almost on contact with a case strikes for the jugular, for that point and aspect which will catch and move the court; such a man has little need for these cruder forms of intellectual apparatus.[179] For all except such, however, the point is clinched by certain propositions from the theory of rules:

THE FUNCTION OF RULES IS GUIDANCE

1. Rules Are Not to Control, But to Guide Decision

This is a fundamental truth which is inherent in the duty of a court to intro-duce into its work some touch of reason and some feeling for sense and fairness, in terms of the type-situation. Where the rule rates high in wisdom and is also technically clear and neat, the guidance is indeed so cogent as, in effect, to be almost equivalent to control or dictation; so, also, when the measure is techni-cally well designed and the rule is a legislative product of unmistakable policy and is too fresh off the griddle for modifying circumstance to have supervened. But in such case the near-control is not because those rules are rules of law, but because of the particular kind of rule of law they happen — rather unusually — to be. So that it is of the essence to distinguish among rules of law, both in regard to what may be expected of them and in regard to what should be. This leads into two further companion propositions: {180}

2. The Law of Compatibility

If application of the seemingly apposite rule is compatible with sense, then the use in the deciding of *both* sense and the rule narrows the spread of possible decision and significantly increases the reckonability not only of the upshot but also of the direction which will be taken by the ground on which the decision will be rested. To know this both limits the field of doubt and sharpens the eyes of inquiry.

3. The Law of Incompatibility

If application of the seemingly apposite rule is incompatible with sense, then reckonability of either upshot or direction of the "ground" of decision depends on factors apart from rule, sense, or both. To know this is to escape futile upset and to recognize instead the presence of danger and the need for exploration "outside" the simpler areas of inquiry.

The third of these theorems turns on the court's felt double duty to law and to justice, and is aptly driven home by Fuller's figure:[180] If you pen an animal in an enclosure too close for comfort, you can be sure it will try hard to get out, but to predict whether it will succeed (much more: how it will, if it does) calls for knowledge of more factors than just the "desire" and the "corral."

The second theorem above derives in one part from simple logic. The form of words in which a rule is normally cast is very likely, thanks to the looseness of language, to be subject to a range of readings which not only rove in scope from the perverse literalistic all the way to the semifigurative, but also swing through various compass points according to diverse definitions or flavors of the constit-uent terms. In such a situation an additional requirement that the "application" satisfy sense as well as the rule must materially, even hugely, cut down on both reach and region of the answers which are admissible. Even if sense falls not well within the worded rule (as, *McIntosh* does within *apple*), but in the dubious penumbra (as, *rotting fruit* in regard to *barreled apples*), the employment of the combined criteria will have the narrowing and directive effect propounded by the theorem. This is an outgrowth less of logic than of the curious nature of our case law rules and concepts, which (we keep forgetting) are in essence {181} Platonic; somethings whose reality and essence exist "out there" somewhere, felt more than grasped, indicated rather than bounded or gripped by any form of words at all, so that "the same rule" can be found and recognized in or under

110

seven divergent and only *more or less* coextensive formulations. In our law, "the" rule rephrases of itself, almost, to adjust a notch or three, a compass point or four, to the call of sense, in what even when almost automatic is nonetheless highly *creative* "application."[181] Such readjustments alone, without adding in those which call for heavy puzzling, are enough to lift study of sense as viewed and felt by the particular court into the class of indispensable aids for sound forecasting.

From the combination of these companion theorems it flows almost as a corollary that probability in prediction will vary with the technical excellence of the rule itself — i.e., of its tailoring to purpose — and that ease in such forecast will also increase with any increase in the accessibility of the sense concerned, the simplest access being by way of sense which speaks in and from the rule itself. Thus, for instance, in Mansfield's phrasing of the effects of negotiability, *taking the paper "fairly" and "in current course of trade"* was a major feature of what produced the protection. This criterion, so long as it remained vivid, provided a sane and rather certain guide through troubled circumstance. The disappearance of this "reason" aspect — culminating in the N.I.L. focus not on process, but on form and status: the *holder* in due course — led into a definitional type of discussion and decision which sought to cut doctrine loose from life: What is "Value"? What is "Notice"? What is "Good Faith"? — all without reference, direct or indirect, to function, and so without recurrent check-up by reason. The result was confusion — this on the point of prediction; and much unhappy law — this on the point of sense-in-outcome. The N.I.L. cured neither, and on this point worsened the latter.[182] {182}

Or take the difficult problem of the simultaneous needs for keeping statutes general and for dealing sensibly with a metropolis. Here is an open-eyed formula with its reason on its face: "If the act by its terms was applicable to a class, it did not cease to be general though the fact would appear, if extrinsic evidence were received, that it was local in effect.... Even then there was a point *beyond which evasion was not suffered.* Identifying tokens might be so many and particular that classification would find an end and designation a beginning."[183] (My italics.) The whither, the why, and so the when of application are moderately clear;[184] the deliberately fictional character of the form in question is deliberately exposed, and the form is thereby restricted to the purpose of the fiction. Or take a rule which after fifty years of conflict and weltering lack of theory gathers the better case results into a way for both operation and decision, the reason again being palpable on the very face of the rule: "A term which measures the quantity by the output of the seller or the requirements of the buyer means such actual output or requirements as may occur in good faith, except that no quantity unreasonably disproportionate to any stated estimate or in the absence of a stated estimate to any normal or otherwise comparable prior output or requirements may be tendered or demanded."[185]

Such rules as these not only draw decision into relatively reckonable channels, they also serve as an indexing machinery which leaves reason and purpose fresh and vigorous even while applications are bringing light into some areas of the penumbra.

Note that no explicit purpose clause or preamble is requisite — though one can be useful; it is enough that the phrasing of the rule reveals the reason. Note also that each of the three rules chosen for illustration marks out the sphere of the rule's application with clarity, though elastically. For the marking of scope can be handled without recourse to metes and bounds; a functional category, if both well designed and well labeled, will indicate scope quite as neatly as it does reason. The metes and bounds school of rule theory has sometimes been slow to grasp this fact, a slowness which descends not only from the conveyancer's approach to any legal document but from that individious misreading of statutes which was too common during the Formal period. Yet it must be clear on meditation that given a reasonable judicial attitude toward statutes, given, for instance, {183} today's general attitude of willingness to further any perceptible and reasonable statutory purpose — given that, a functional category can under the law of compatibility count on very reasonable definiteness of application. Especially, if function in both rule and category are clear, the rule draftsman acquires a consoling insurance against those two inevitabilities: the situation overlooked and the unforeseen change of conditions. In a statutory rule intended as most statutes are — and as all rules of case law are — for lasting service, such insurance comes cheap at the price of using a zone rather than a surveyor's line to border the rule. Indeed the metes and bounds boys have a bent for forgetting how commonly the sharp-edged style of rule clashes with cases where it does not make sense, and so backs court and customer up against the law of incompatibility.[186]

Thus we come not only to a general gain in forecasting technique from the lines of opinion-reading here put forward, but to a perception that one particular kind of rule of law, if it be once found and phrased, will have peculiar power, and so to a fourth theorem from the theory of rules:

4. The Law of the Singing Reason

A rule which wears both a right situation-reason and a clear scope-criterion on its face yields regularity, reckonability, and justice all together. We may add that such a rule is a staff and a comfort to any court, as well as to any counselor.

There will be more to say about the rule with a singing reason; here we have to note that in this imperfect day such rules are not the rule. For the most part the courts and the rest of us must still make do with some strain, too often great strain, between authority and sense. This means, of course, that even a full resurgence of the Grand Style of decision would leave us far short of the ideal in either reckonability or satisfaction. For effects must depend in great part upon material. It is true that fine craftsmanship can sometimes work magic with stuff and tools which make the angels weep; but even fine craftsmanship can do this only sometimes {184} — and unpredictably — and the conditional sales sequences[187] remind us that if the work is centered too largely and too long on tolerability or decency merely of the immediate outcome, then the rule- and concept-stuff is likely to get out of hand, losing touch at last with both manageability and reason. It is indeed also true, as will be insisted in due course, that unremitting labor in the Grand Style does mean daily, weekly cumulative output of rules ever sharper in form, ever sounder in substance; but that, measured against the mountained inept or obsolescent stockpile, is still a task for generations. This last is no reason for any court to slacken or put off the effort; but it is good ground for not expecting too much, too often, too soon.

The Juice in the Orthodox Ideology

Meantime, when taken in conjunction with the Style of Reason and with the fact that the rule-stuff of the Grand Style was commonly draped with some canniness upon the needs of life, the law of the singing reason goes a long way to clear up what would else be almost an impasse in intellectual history: How, in contrast to the facts of legal life, could the idea (not the ideal) of decision "by the Law," decision independent of the persons of judges, either spring up or, especially, maintain itself across the centuries? I know that ideals and needs can sometimes and somehow bring forth mirages, mirages embraced with passion, of what "must be" in fact; and I know that man has felt deep need that the Law should in its work be firm and right, all but sacred, unspoiled and unspotted by the meddling or meanness of law's ministers. Yet it seems hard to believe that performance so regularly and openly subject to check-up, so close to daily living, so challenging to scrutiny, could easily become completely misdescribed, or could continue through the generations completely misdescribed, especially when, as with us, the largest segment of the ministers are themselves much more lay than priestly, and are scattered in substantial independence rather than guilded together into any such tight pike-hedge as would permit them to defend a pseudo mystery from exposure and pillory. Horse sense thus seems to urge that we can hardly be faced with a complete misdescription. And pondering goes on to suggest another thing about the standard or orthodox or conventional picture of how it is "the Law" which does — and should do — the deciding of appellate cases. {185} It suggests that that conventional picture was in fact, in the days of the Grand Style, close enough to accuracy to serve as a very respectable description of what was going on.

One must not in these matters chase fireflies into the marshes of absurdity. The essence of the idea that appealed cases are decided "*by* the Law" (and I mean not merely "under law," or "according to law," which, especially when "justice" is used to mean (more or less) "adjudication," I see as a formula almost of issue-evasion)[188] — the essence is not that men, the Voices of the Law, shall play no part in the deciding. Neither is it the essence of the accompanying idea of "certainty" of such decisions that outcomes shall be so manifest beforehand that only fools could litigate and that advocacy must be empty ritual or theatre. Such misreadings or imputations are either the lampoons of adversary dialectic or else the crass thoughtlessness of the silly. In contrast, the ideas themselves include in "the Law," along with the rules of law, all the rest of the doctrinal environment in a fashion which adversary dialectic dares not face and of which the ignoramus is unaware. It is enough to mention here the general conceptual frame, the vibrant though almost unspoken ideals, the force-fields in doctrine and attitude which strain toward or against movement in any contemplated direction, the going techniques and going organization of the work of Law-Government. The ideas thus as of course embrace in "the Law" the skills and the traditions of the crafts of law, the ways of seeing, thinking, feeling, doing, and duty in and into which the craftsmen — the body of craftsmen — have been reared.[189] Implicit, moreover, in the ideas — including that of "certainty" of decision — is a subliminal recognition that "the Law" holds room for men and for desires and for needs and for strivings of many, many kinds; that it holds room, nay rooms, already *partly* bodied forth in urges and tendencies within "the Law" itself — any one of which drives, within the all-pervading leeways, may meet another, clash, join issue, and produce a case in the appellate court. What is then needed is men — a bench — right-minded, learned, careful, wise, to find and voice from among the still fluid materials of the legal sun the answer which will satisfy, and which will render semisolid one more point, as a basis for a further growth. And the *certainty* in question is that certainty *after the event* which makes ordinary men and lawyers *recognize as soon as they see the result* that however hard it has {186} been to reach, it is the right result.[190] Then men feel that it has *therefore* really been close to inevitable. Even most losers, as the strife subsides, may be hoped to look back with something of such understanding. In such a world there is no lack of office for the court, nor for the great creator on the bench; no lack of room, either, for litigants and lawyers. And the consequent "certainty" of outcome is the truest certainty legal work can have, a certainty reached not by deduction but by dynamics, moving in step with human need yet along and out of the lines laid out by history of the Law and of the culture; the certainty, then, not of logical conclusion from a static *universal,* but of that *reasonable regularity* which is law's proper interplay with life.

With such a scene to describe, and with the current legal rules and concepts well enough rough-fitted in the main both to lawyer's use and to the preindustrial layman's need, the orthodox image of decision "by the Law," in high degree decision forecastable and in equal degree independent of the person of the officer, could stand up, I repeat, as a rather true reflection of lawyers' day-to-day experience, and could then merit extra status and prestige by embodying at the same time an ideal valid and cherished: "Thus, it *ought* also to be."

Again, in the heyday of the Formal Style, the phrasing of the image, and no less the ideal of independence of the person, both measurably fit the facts. The meaning has then indeed become very different, what had been life-closeness has drifted away from life, what had been a moving harmony of law and justice builds instead into increasing tension. But the words, just as words, have much accuracy still; nor at any time can the ideal die that the work of an appellate court must somehow reflect and serve a something beyond and above, righter and steadier then, the individuals who happen to be sitting.

One change which occurred was, however, fateful. "The Law," as seen and understood in the Formal period, tended in lawyers' minds more and more to coincide until it substantially coalesced with "the law" as discussed by lawyers in court: the *mere rules* of law. And in action, the whole drive of the Formal Style was toward making sure, so far as might be, that it should be just those phrased rules which did do the deciding.

Hence as the formula traveled down the decades it traveled {187} with its substance thinning and paling like Alice's Cheshire Cat, till what was left by, say, 1909 was a formula which had come to fly in the face of the current facts of work in court. To understand, despite such now flagrant misdescription, the stubborn grip of the formula on men's minds, one must remember not only the lasting validity of the ideal expressed, but the tradition, the long tradition, in which the same words had been a workably accurate depiction, and had acquired a sort of unchallengeable holiness of phrase. Such a tradition makes it easy to center one's noticing, one's attentiveness, at need one's argument, differentially on those cases which do fit the formula; such a tradition smooths the way to acceptance of the justification as if it were a report on the how of the deciding; if one did not look too hard, too closely, or too often, one thus used to be able to live with the illusion that the old "theory" was true — even in that horrible watered-down version of "the law" as meaning chiefly or exclusively the rules of law — except in odd cases or except where particular judges or courts had for some reason slipped off their job.

Yet ineptitudes or deficiencies in Formal description or Formal ideals for work need not at all jibe with equivalent defects in operation. Good work can be and has been done with creaking theory. More, the ideal of order is as valid an ideal as is that of dispassionate judging; when the premise is sound and the case fairly within it, those ideals are hard to rival; indeed, they have their standing even when they cannot claim to dominate, but only to counsel with other ideals as peers. The picture, when the work is in the hands of a good craftsman, is admirably presented by the elder Andrews of New York, or, later, by the elder Sanborn, or by Holmes in most of his non-Constitutional opinions. I do not see how anyone can doubt that Holmes enjoyed the method, the clean line, the finish of a Formal opinion; or that he enjoyed also, when he could come upon it, a premise which carried for the unthinking or untutored a touch of surprise. Job after job moves with a slightly remote, deftly articulated clarity to its seemingly foreordained conclusion.

Whether they are magnificent or maddening depends mainly on the premise. Many of the bailments cases remind of Holmes' own dictum that it is disgusting to have no better reason for a rule than that thus it was in the time of Henry IV. The conflicts cases are nearly as bad, and spread their bane much further afield: consider *Slater v. Mexican National Ry.*,[190a] where a civilized {188} award of tort damages — installments instead of a lump sum — and in the teeth of our familiar alimony procedure, was cast into outer darkness on rigid and unnecessary "logic." On the other hand, the original insights of The Common Law[190b] into the presuppositions of business agreements bloom into quiet, inevitable beauty in *The Kronprinzessin Cacilie*.[190c] The clean lines of private law consideration theory can be drafted, in *Wisconsin etc. Ry. v. Powers*,[190d] and again with simple logic, to keep a statutory tax exemption from becoming a "contract" with an "obligation" to be protected against impairment. In this finest work of Holmes the distance of manner still leaves some pulse of life beneath the logic; and that the Formal Style has always offered, at its best. The bargain-theory of consideration gave just a little at the seams, in a good cause, in *Martin v. Meles*;[190e] the dissent in *Vegelahn v. Guntner*,[190f] notwithstanding its basic conservative resistance to the expanding labor injunction, did involve one item of expansion when it sought to let a labor union into the "competition" protection already recognized for business. So in the criminal law, where Holmes' history, in 1881, had ripened in partnership with keen and deep analysis, the Formal manner of opinion, for all its learning and seeming rigidity, works out in welcome fashion: take *Commonwealth v. Ryan*,[190g] sustaining a conviction for embezzlement against the plea that the offense had by a hair shaded over into larceny — and noting that what force the old spider threads had only served to offer the defendant an opportunity at trial. Or take two cases on attempts, in each of which well-based analysis whips into line both history and folderolish theory: *Peaslee*,[190h] where the would-be arsonist who lost his nerve was saved only by fault in the indictment, and *Kennedy*,[190i] where the arsenic thoughtfully lodged in a mustache cup did not require to be proved to be a lethal dose.

Nevertheless, the Formal Style sets traps, even for its normal masters. Thus in contracts, where Holmes was at his surest, his *Globe Refining* opinion[190j] started out after the mirage of "perfect compensation, not a penny more," and came out with as {189} harsh a result as could a commercial woodenhead; and the glitter of unconditional promises (which in regard to payment in advance of delivery are nonsense to inforce literally against a buyer when repudiation comes before the payment date) misled him, as has been noted above, in the manikin case.[190k]

What held for operation, even sometimes among the best, held more among the lesser, encouraged as it was by the unhappy theory.

But today persistence in the old delusion no longer seems feasible. It is that impossibility which has engendered the crisis of faith to which repeated reference has been made. The fact itself is whiskered like Uncle Sam; it has been available on all hands for more than three score years and ten. By the '90's German-speaking judges of repute had begun to remark on what they thought to be a pattern, in their own work, of "the right solution first, the right reasoning to follow." Holmes published one of his most pungent discussions on the subject in

1897.[191] Seventeen years later World War I broke upon a Europe that had already seen the "free-law" fracas, Ehrlich's *Judicial Logic* and Gény's magnificent *Methode*. Our own discussions of the '20's have been noted.[192] In 1930, Jerome Frank gathered portions of the relevant comment into his queer *Law and the Modern Mind*. The ensuing storm of protest did not really blow itself out; it just in due course vanished, leaving the basic facts clear.

But *what* facts have been left clear? That the *rules of law, alone,* do not, because they cannot, decide any appealed case *which has been worth both an appeal and a response.* Substantially, the mere bare rules of law do today manage alone to decide that obnoxious but persistent body of appeals in which in fact the applicable rules are both firmly and reasonably settled — often enough re-examined, retested, restated, and reaffirmed within the past few years — and in which the facts of the case fall so obviously inside the core of the rule that reasonable judges do not have to ponder. Again, there is that other body of cases which falls outside any firm rule core but yet so plainly within the urge or flavor or force-field of a rule or concept of law that its extension either is obviously imperative or just happens so naturally as to go unnoticed. There a touch of the older, wiser meaning of {190} "The Law" moves into action. Moreover, if what has been said above holds true, then wherever the sense of the situation can be expected to speak clearly to the court and to be understood, there, in these days, another great portion of the older finer meaning of "The Law" will also come to bear, testing, redirecting, reshaping the very rules of law, along forefeelable lines of creation, and with foreseeable results in the particular case. Still more: to the extent that rules with singing reasons emerge and propagate and fight down the less usable and less viable varieties of rule, "The Law"-at-work expands, and we slowly approach complete regeneration of the truth of an orthodoxy always lovely, and whose truth and standing faded only because form and literalism were allowed to dry its pith. The happy day is far ahead; but I count it a signal contribution of that vital method of analysis known as legal realism that its hard-eyed and sustained inquiries could, as they have, come to clean grips with a moribund and misleading orthodoxy and come out then neither with dismay nor with idle defense of emptiness nor yet with shallow cynicism, but with recognition, appreciation, and practical furtherance of a renascence still overlooked but gloriously green and strong.

Hence it is obvious that the factual material here gathered is not set out with any purpose of showing that the rules of our law (those of the singing reason excepted) are only in most restricted measure to be relied on as "in themselves" deciding appellate cases. That fact is manifest. My purposes are very different. I hope, and hope hard, that the present material may make permanently untenable any notion that creativeness — choice or creation of effective policy by appellate judges — is limited to the crucial case, the unusual case, the borderline case, the queer case, the tough and exhausting case, the case that calls for lasting conscious worry. My material aims to put beyond challenge that such creativeness is instead everyday stuff, almost every-case stuff, and need not be conscious at all.

But by the same token, the same material aims to show and then to hammer home that the creation moves in the main with steadiness, that it answers carefully *and regularly* to the body of doctrine as that body has been received and as it is to be handed on; that the creation nevertheless and simultaneously, but in full consonance with that high responsibility to The Law, answers also to the appellate court's duty to justice and adjustment. I should hope to see the material persuade, for example, of a thing like this (which I see no means of *proving*): that in 80 per cent or better of the instances in which a court draws a {191} solving rule from prior (unheld) language, or from a pair of "see's" and a "cf.," or from "the tendency of our cases," the court is not merely reaching for authority or color to justify the decision in hand, but is also seeking and finding comfort in the conviction that the decision and the rule announced fit with the feel of the body of our law — that they go with the grain rather than across or against it, that they fit into the net force-field and relieve instead of tautening the tensions and stresses. I feel something of the same as I watch opinions turn to neighboring jurisdictions for light or for further buttressing — especially when they pick up quotations packed with a combination of authority and situation-sense; even the "weight of authority" can sometimes have a tincture of this. I feel in the advance sheets or the sequence of cases in a current State report an underbeat from the bull fiddle and the drums that tells of courts alive to this feeling of the force-fields and more comfortable when they sense the job in hand to be in touch with that feeling; and I have tried to let that beat come through the sampling reports. This is not such unmistakable stuff as is the resort to overt sense in the deciding; yet I do not think that, once the alert is sounded, its perception calls for too much either of background or of sensitivity. In any event, a report on the matter belongs here for what it is worth; for if I get it right, there could be no more meaningful witness to the continuing dedication of our appellate bench to that one of their twin duties which is to The Law. And, concerned as I am with the crisis of legal faith, I want no stress on the duty to Justice, nor yet on the current use of judges' human situation-sense, vital, powerful, and superb though each is, to lead to any misinference that The Law should be or is being thrust thereby into any second place. I hold, indeed, that in the true Grand Style all of these elements join in a choir like the fabled music of the stars.

IDEAL, MYTH, SYMBOL, SHAM, HYPOCRISY

It is all very well to proclaim that despite much doctrine which is either delusion or myth, or else plain fraud, the appellate courts are still managing somehow to work out some reasonable steadiness of outcome, even some doctrinal steadiness and continuity; that is all very well, but does not the continuance of any such theory-contrary-to-proved-and-known-fact threaten the institution at its very heart? First, in the souls of its key officers; second, in that public faith without which even effective practical work in {192} justice must be and remain empty? Here, surely, is an aspect of the crisis of confidence which can be coped with by no mere reference to "adequate performance" — performance, that is, which even though it may have somehow held up thus far, this long, may yet be termite-eaten.

This is a problem faced by every institution, not merely nor in any special manner by the appellate courts or by Law-Government at large. It is a problem to which there is no easy answer. For in all the work of man one major road to getting needed things done right has always been, it always must be, the building of a faith that the work can be done as it should be done, that almost any right craftsman can indeed come close to adequacy; and in order for such a faith to maintain itself it seems to be well-nigh necessary for the ordinary individual craftsman to believe, as well, that the ideal-picture is in fact approached most of the time by many or most of his brethren, even if not by himself. In this aspect a complete misdescription can have value. It can have value not only as an ideal and a symbol, but as providing stimulus and spur by the very fact of its inaccuracy. The evil, the corrosion "inside" the craft, comes not from misdepiction as such but from a waning of faith in the ideal and in effort toward the ideal; if the explicit or implicit goals come to be seen as worthless or futile, if tools and measures come to be used callously or selfishly (or in cynical routine) without regard to what the institution is for — that is what deadens. Such a waning of faith and effort may of course result in misdepiction of fact by the received theories; it may also itself result from such misdepiction. But it has no need to. For mere knowledge that gears do slip, that theories do need constant help from the skilled hand, that baling wire and chewing gum are often the only means to save "the book" or to save the game itself — this has never meant death, it has instead meant life for any institution whose craftsmen still had sap and feeling for their office. It does not follow that ideals and symbols can with regular impunity kick into loggerheads with life and fact; what does follow is that misdescription by an idealized and dear-held theory-and-symbol can rise even to the obtrusive without need to cause excessive strain. In our particular case, the theory that the Rules of law do decide the appeal, and that they ought to, has come to produce its strain inside the system of the appellate courts; but, inside, that strain is rendered quite tolerable by the understanding that what is essential to the ideal and the symbol and the fact is reasonable consonance not with the letter of the standard misdescription, {193} but with its essential intent: that the judges are not to move on their own, that they are to answer to the Law (which is so much more than the Rules of law) and also, if they can, to sense and justice. A clearer and cleaner descriptive theory would indeed ease the situation, but, inside, its lack has meant not cynicism, only a slowing and slurring of the work.

It is on the outside that the discrepancy of theory has done its ravening. Here, too, the problem is that of every institution. Here, too, there is a defending buffer between misdescription and any quick disaster. Even severely misdescriptive theory can commonly be tolerated by the pure or ordinary lay outsider. Partly, he sees and understands too little, in detail, to take in the full degree of misdepiction; his faith in his institutions is commonly rather tough; he is likely to think what he does take in to be atypical; his normal reaction is to witch-hunt for the evil persons who must be responsible for the distortion: "Throw the rascals out." This, especially, if the times at large are bearable, and if the institution in question is not beating the particular layman's toes into pulp. Hence, since the Depression, laymen at large seem to me to have survived with some comfort the rather patent fact that in the teeth of those laymen's notions about what has been and should be, our supreme courts are doing a good deal of law-making, and are handing down decisions by no means forecastable from the Rules of law alone. Public discussion of such matters seems to me to have had as little direct effect as the blasts of Bentham against the "hypocrisy" of the English courts of his day, or as attacks on waste and occasional corruption in the armed services, or as the successive revelations of gear-slipping and stench in the government of Chicago or New York. Faith in lasting symbols and ideals embodied in basic institutions tends to straighten after the buffets of the wind unless times or toes are pinching beyond endurance.

Thus the infiltration of corrosive cynicism into the appellate scene seems to me to have been by way of a series of processes much more indirect than any mere detection of error and pretense in the orthodox ideology. It starts, as I see it, with politically-minded or incompetent magistrates' or trial courts, and with favoritism, corruption, negligence, or abuse of patronage among policing or administrative personnel. The people who start and spread the gangrene are not the pure or general public, but those of the public (criminals, politicians, businessmen of great, small, or no legitimacy, gamblers, racketeers, mere parasites) who have an "in," and their lawyers, and such official personnel as answer {194} to their whistle or as build political power on the less holy of alliances. The situation reminds a little of an army living in and off a mildly honest country, whose higher officers are on and at the job, but whose company officers, noncoms, and more influential privates are to a third or more sliders, grafters, and fixers dedicated to the main chance, with a point of view and lingo that attribute to the whole and even to the honest craftsmen their own perversities of angle and of action. It is against that general type of situation that the bar at large are led by the orthodox ideology and by their misunderstanding of appellate facts into "seeing" sham, hypocrisy, and irresponsible intrusion of the person even in the solid and healthy work of the solid and healthy core which remains to us despite any main-chancing in our law-governmental system. It is against that general type of situation that the business or union leader — not only uncorrected but actively misguided by his lawyer — measures trial court action, and takes a supreme court or Supreme Court dissent to unmask some covert, highly personalized, general vagary of decision. Over a good half century this "inside" or subpriest or noncom-and-subaltern "knowledge" of "the dirt" has been eating not only inside its own smaller public, but out into the greater public, and also, as indicated above, into the self-confidence of the appellate bench itself. With a typical blind self-inconsistency such a cynicized insider can recognize and respect the personal integrity in office of every individual appellate judge he personally knows, and yet be sure that the appellate bench at large is infected by dereliction which moves through the arbitrary or partisan to the almost corrupt. For when one is not of those high priests who see the formula in terms of its essential intent, and correct it daily, almost automatically, in their daily work, then observation of the discrepancy between the symbol and supposed pattern and the "dirty" fact *must* seem a sign of sham, of hypocrisy deliberate — even of fraud.

The only cure for such misbeliefs and for their evil consequences lies in complete recasting of the orthodox ideology which is their source.

One aspect of such recasting seems to me to offer itself, inside the court or out, rather freely and simply. That is, on the case law side, the open quest for situation-sense and situation-rightness as one main key to wise decision, the other main key being a recurrent accounting at once to the authorities as received and to the need for the ever sounder, ever clearer phrasing of guidance for the future. This is developed at length hereinafter; the concept {195} is simple, and elementary legal education has really supplied all needed illustration; the only difficulty lies in getting a man to realize that what has all along been happening in great and striking cases has been happening (and needs to happen) also from week to week and day to day. Indeed, inside the court, established habits of work already hold enough of give and leeway to keep the most conscious of creative activity in the case law area from taking on any disruptive sense of sham or deceit.

But as things now stand, work with the resistant language of statutory authority seems to me much tougher on the temper of judicial steel, and on that of the bar's understanding and confidence. The problem is suggested below, in the section on Statutes (pp. 371 ff.). Here I wish merely to insist that the art of extracting meaning from fixed language, or of putting meaning into it, can afford almost as wide a range of adjustment to need and situation-sense as do the techniques of case law, and deserves equally careful cultivation. It is to such cultivation that we must turn to keep out of appellate judicial work a feeling of tension, torsion, or hypocrisy when sense is being made out of statutes; for the given language is not to be ignored.

AN APPROACH TO THE CRISIS

What is the utter barebones for viable appellate judicial work is first fourfold and then threefold: (1) Uprightness; (2) a modicum of judgment — neither wild men nor fools must dominate the bench; (3) a modicum of reckonability of result; and (4) that reckonability must in some material degree transcend the persons of the personnel. That is the fourfold aspect, one of objective substance. The threefold is this, one of subjective attitude: not only (1) must these things be there and at work, to the knowledge and in the feelings of the judges, but (2) the general public and, perhaps especially, all but unreasonable litigants, must *feel* their presence, and (3) the bar must *know* them to be there. The present crisis has afflicted in first instance the bar, but it has for at least a decade, perhaps for more than two, been seeping through the bar out into a much wider public which for lack of wherewithal to do constructive or remedial thinking is helpless and a bit pitiable in its trouble.

I am also persuaded, as has been indicated earlier, that there is among our appellate judges themselves an almost tangible unease about their work, that for some years now a certain olden inner sureness of operation and of office has been leaking away. {196} Partly I suspect this to follow directly from the troubles of the bar. If your rooters and only knowledgeable public exude a taint of dissatisfaction and bafflement about your work, *and you can find no reason for it,* you get bothered; and your quondam quiet self-confidence may suffer, too. And indirectly, the troubles of the bar afflict you further. I have spoken earlier of the time-burden imposed by the rank proliferation of footless appeals; but even worse is the slackening of high-class help from brief and oral argument, insofar as either baffled and worried or lightheartedly gambling counsel pile the points high, wide, and hit-or-miss because they have lost understanding of the process and so lack confidence in the simple, the clear, the focused. Finally, I trace the unease to the waning of the conscious, clean-cut traditions of the appellate judges' craft, among the very craftsmen. Next door, by 1910 or 1920, the crutch of the casebook had drained most of conscious working philosophy out of law teaching, and we have been struggling for three decades to get back enough of such to keep curricula from either drying up or coming apart at the seams. Even earlier, the shift away from apprenticeship had, at least in the cities, choked off reliable transmission of most of the old-time conscious working philosophy in the crafts of advocacy and of counseling.[193]

I think the appellate judges have also been feeling such an ebb. I think that as appellate judging began to move out of the Formal Style into that which flourishes around us, with little conscious working philosophy of the craft at hand except the withered pseudo orthodoxy of "It's the rules" — I think the appellate judges, for the most part, did what men were doing in the other crafts of law: they stopped, pretty much, thinking about it, in general, they buckled down instead to doing it, here, now, right, {197} and tomorrow again right, talking and sweating much more over what than over how — and slowly losing all contact whatever with the history of the traditions of their craft. And my guess is — indeed, I think we can show it — that when self-examination did set in — as with a nontypical person like Cardozo — it was substantially from a fresh start. Certainly there has as yet been a failure of the great appellate judges, as also of the articulate appellate judges who are not yet great, to get together into any pooling of their craft-wisdom. It is a failure as striking as that we find among the great advocates or counselors of the past seventy-five years: what has been laid up, phrased, arranged, illustrated, and opened to a rising generation, of the communicable skills and wisdom of John G. Johnson, Rufus Choate, David Dudley Field, Elihu Root, Newton Baker, John W. Davis? Certainly, when one turns to the judges whose writings address themselves to building and communicating a workable working philosophy for the newcomer or the still worried old-timer, their writings, too, during the present century in this country look about like a crop of a couple of dozen alfalfa plants scattered over a ten-acre field — though the last few years have seen a gratifying upturn in hardheaded offerings.[194] It is all right to have a pure {198} heart and to work your head off trying to get the job done as it should be done; but when your rooters stop rooting, your constituents lose ardor, and even the general public begin to mutter — and when the muttering attacks the doing of the very things which your conscience tells you that you *must* do, and which cause you at once your most trying turmoil and your greatest sense of right achievement — then I suggest that if you are to escape unease, you need at hand a working philosophy which for yourself is conscious, which is close and firm in its grasp of the working facts, and which is comforting because it offers a clear target, a craftsman's rifle, and a telescopic sight. That working philosophy needs also to be persuasive to your rooters and aids, the bar, and to the consumer of all law: the general citizen, in his infinite diversity.

Such a working philosophy — though at hand, lies disregarded.

The current crisis of confidence in the appellate courts is thus, as I see it, miles apart from that at the turn of the century, when widespread worry went to the wisdom and judgment of the bench (with the normal backwash into doubts about uprightness; in those days it was "The Interests own 'em!"). Today, for the State courts, neither worry nor attack goes particularly to the content of results, except as losing litigants (and specialized law professors) may grumble. The worry is instead over *reckonability* of results. Results are conceived to be *hopelessly* unpredictable. It is not mere uncertainty that festers, it is the feeling of hopeless helplessness. That hopeless helplessness wars with an old and not unreasonable tradition that it should not be; that it is wrong for such a thing to be. I am not maundering about "certainty" and womb-yearning or about law "the solid" as a father-substitute or similar unnecessary tripe. I am dealing with the sound and right feeling of the American lawyer and the American law-consumer that the work of his appellate tribunals {199} has no business to be hopelessly unreckonable. If it is, then something is wrong; and the easiest thing to see as wrong is that the judges, the court, must be no longer under rein: they have the bit in their teeth and are using their own heads, or they have even slipped the bridle altogether. The reign of law makes a bitter, nasty pun.

As was said at the outset, it is to this crisis that this book and its material are addressed. The material shows, and I assert it shows beyond possibility of refutation, that *the crisis lies wholly in the second, the threefold, the subjective, the attitude area* (above, p. 195). On the objective side of how the work is being done, each one of the elements is open to huge betterment, of course, and needs the same, and needs it plenty; but not a single one of them is absent, and each stands well above the barebones level. Nor do I think that any other craft of our law, *taken as a whole and taken in the light of what is offered the craftsmen to work with,* is coming as close to turning out a proper job as is our appellate bench.[195]

If then the continuity-of-doctrine and the "sense or reason" aspects of our factual material here are to serve their purpose, they must address themselves to reckonability of appellate judicial results in first instance, and in second instance to the depersonizing of appellate judicial work. I have spoken above and shall speak again of the continuity-with-doctrine phase. The material also shows beyond contradiction that the appellate courts are, day by day, drawing on reason and situation-sense to help out, to piece out, to guide, commonly to govern their choice and use of authorities and of authority techniques, with constant impact on the decisions, with a constant consequent reshaping also of the doctrinal materials used. But knowing these things is not in itself enough to allow, generally, of forecast, or of a working approach to forecast, of the outcome of appeals. Forecasting, prediction, reckoning, must for the purpose in hand be doable, it must be done, by the ordinary lawyer. Well, then?

RECKONABILITY OF RESULT:
SENSE AND REASON AGAIN

{200}

The *base line* for discussing forecast which is most serviceable is, I submit, the situation when the judgment below becomes appealable, which can be standardized for our immediate purpose as the situation when the judgment at trial becomes final. We shall further, and not too artificially, standardize in terms of a forecaster who has been defeated below, and who also, in the event of appeal, will be handling the cause himself. In a more exhaustive inquiry this would represent a main type of situation around which most other situations would be grouped, being dealt with in terms of particular variances; here the selected base line appears simply as perhaps the most frequent one in life and as offering a peculiarly critical type of prediction-problem. Thus we are considering a setup in which the particular evidence is in and frozen, with whatever limitation that places upon the picture of the type of problem-situation and of the individual case.

If the clusters of alleged "steadying" factors examined early in this study have actual steadying effect, surely the importance of the court's resort to sense and reason would suggest that resort as being the place where those clusters ought to be spotted most clearly and convincingly at their work; at the very least that should be one main locus for such detection and conviction. But I am afraid that here the direct evidence proves hard to find and harder to marshal. It is simple and easy to display things as rough-hewn as a huge scatter of going precedent techniques or as a constant and overt recourse to sense or reason, even a constant and overt recourse to sense about the chosen situation-type, as influencing the shaping of the rule of law on which decision is grounded. It is a very different problem to set up a demonstrable effect of any single one among ten or fifteen possible causative elements. My belief is that a good deal of rather cogent material is available for gathering, even for this exacting task; but the presentation would call for a refinement and above all for a volume disproportionate to any such rude study as this. Accordingly, {201} what follows runs in terms of simple horse sense; though I do remind that *horse sense* means to me neither the sense of a horse nor ordinary common sense, but that extraordinary and uncommon kind of experience, sense, and intuition which was characteristic of an old-fashioned skilled horse trader in his dealings either with horses or with other horse traders.

One can begin with the fact already mentioned, that the appellate judges are human, all of them. They are, moreover, all American and almost all male, almost all of at least middle age, all readers of news, most of them affected — though with divergence in their "law"-conditioned resistances — by those tides of interest and of opinion which wash over the decades, the years, sometimes shorter periods: for instance, bothers over juvenile delinquency, or the current "crime wave" scare, or the rising and threatening power of the trusts or the enemy or the rackets or corrupt union leaders or subversive organizations, or Russia's technological or educational advances. They are almost all white-collar in background, and raised in Judaeo-Christian morality. State and section by section and State, the particular bench entire also shares its fair portion of the State and section attributes. It is an almost sure bet that there are not two single-taxers, polygamists, anarchists, spies, Moslems, ex-convicts, major poets, first-class trombones, or mining engineers among the lot. As one wanders and ponders among the myriad facts of this nature, it is heartening how much alike these appellate judges come to seem: Strong, J., Gavegan, J., McLeish, J., Bartoletti, J., Olsen, J., Cohen, J., Olinski, J., make up a *bench,* whichever is the Chief.

REASON VIA THE LAW

Let us go on now with the two first of the stabilizing clusters: the judges are *law-conditioned* and they do their judging in an environment of *authoritative legal doctrine.* The stirring thing about these matters is that while they sound like "law" and bear directly on continuity-of-and-with-doctrine, they also bear directly on this sense-and-reason inquiry. For these "law" aspects are factors of might in molding the judges' notions of what sense, reason, and relevance are. They set up in intangible fashion but to a material degree values which play into judgments about sense. "Too remote" is for instance a "law" idea which not only reflects but also directs ideas about what may be needed and wise, what on the other hand may be fraught with doubt and danger. "Consideration" thrusts toward the dubious any claim for enforcement {202} of a promise which falls outside of any *bargain* picture. Any "raw facts" classify themselves, or try to, into familiar *legal* alternatives with familiar *legal* consequences which then come up as a matter of obvious *sense.* This is hard to get into daylight, and I make no apology for risking overrepetition. In another connection I have tried it thus:

> A *problem* becomes known by way of a hitch in operations: something does not go as desired, and one sets about doing something about it. For our purposes we distinguish: easy ones from hard ones; the semi-"automatic" fixing of it from the route over conscious puzzling. Fundamental to all understanding of appellate judging is a vivid awareness of the degree to which semi-"automatic" fixing of minor hitches happens with *no* awareness in the fixer's consciousness, or with none whose memory remains live. (The "easy knot" in the shoe-lace that you handle as you talk or think about something else; the "automatic" complex calculation of the effects of your vehicle's speed and the other's, in relation to something on the road ahead; the "automatic" classification of a law case, even as you hear the facts, as one involving contract and apparent authority with proof of usage of trade as a possible or probable key-question.) If you do not first get this process of semi-"automatic" solution clear with regard to the hundred or thousand tiny problems of every day and hour, there is no use in reading me further on this topic. What we call loosely "habit" (in action *or in judgment*) extends far, far beyond mere repetition; our "habit" apparatus absorbs and handles all the little "problem" unevennesses of the road. This goes so far that even the "Well, I took one quick look . . ." type of adjustment (solution), despite the gratification of success, is unlikely to remain long in live memory unless the stake or the occasion makes other reasons for its importance develop.
>
> *It is at this point more than at* ANY *other that The Law* CONTROLS *the Law-official;* and it controls in good part by moulding in advance his

sense of "what is sense." As with a "good wife," the control happens without the official's knowing that it is happening — and is that much more effective. In regard to the law-consumer, sound legal engineering is well known to reach for lines of regulation whose "observance" is easy because the regulation fits the ways of life, and is willing, because people feel observance to be good. The ideal is observance which "just comes natural." — Well, why should we fail to see the application of this ideal *to the Law-official?* The great Roman jurisconsults appear to have "lived" the curiously clean and systematic character of their thinking about legal problems, deciding in terms of feel for the essential working institution, with "legal tact" {203} in result and legal craftsmanship in method. That means that they got controlled by Law at a deeper level, with greater effectiveness, and with finer results than ever has been achieved by *mere* conscious Rules of Law. — Meantime, *some* of this line of control works into every lawyer: "You are never the same again," once you have met "malice" and "authority" which are neither malice nor authority, or met "confession and avoidance," and a "dying declaration" exception to a rule about "hearsay" (which is "hearsay" only when it isn't "dying declaration" or "*res gestae*").

I repeat, you have to get an understanding of this "automatic" type of control of thought, judgment, action, which just happens as you go. It works, of course, by degrees. The surefooted have more of it than the clumsy. The quick-witted can, but need not, have more of it than the dull. The trained always have more of it than the untrained or the recruits. The experienced always have more of it than the green; but at the end of a wise career an experienced man may be working more free of it, becoming its master rather than its creature.[196]

The vital and final item about this one is that among all persons whom it ought to aid in diagnosing a court's feeling for sense (and so for reason, which is ordered sense), the lawyer stands foremost — our same lawyer who has lost his case below, and who is meditating on his chances in an appeal. That lawyer's own "sense" has been law-conditioned in the same manner, he lives, he works, within the matrix of the same body of authoritative doctrine as his court.

THE OFFICE, AND SENSE

In what has been said above about the fourteenth steadying cluster, professional judicial office, the emphasis was on such office as a subduer of self and self-will, as an engine to promote openness to listen and to understand, to quicken evenhandedness, patience, sustained effort to see and judge for All-of-Us. Such things clear the way for use of sense and reason. But they offer little guidance to the content, better to the net thrust, of sense and reason in this court for this case; and that is our immediate pigeon. However, before we press ahead toward the more specific it will pay to expand a little more on those lines of reckonability that flow straight out of professional judicial office.

In American writing two generations back you will remember that there was some amateur (and often wildish) psychologizing {204} of the judges — treating them more often, to be sure, as overhuman people than as trained and responsible officers. The lines of thinking from psychology most drawn upon, certainly those most resented by the faithful, were the psychoanalytical at the one extreme and at the other the behaviorist approach to the theory of learning, with the conditioned reflex as its then major building-stone. One favorite answering slogan in support of human dignity and responsibility used to be: *"A judge is not Pavlov's dog"* — which is so patently true that it kicked me into a much browner study than had the then rapidly developing theory of learning, much of which was also obviously true. I have come up with the conclusion that the more usable truth about the appellate judges is located closish to a mean at least heavily gold-plated: The sustained and laudable pressures of our law-governmental institutions to condition the appellate judge *as if* he were in Pavlov's laboratory are amazingly effective in regard to his attitudes, his value-judgments, and his very intake of perceptions; yet the judge is so tough that in spite of all we have thus far managed he remains unmistakably *responsible,* a responsible *officer,* a responsible *individual* in office. Nevertheless, the pressures avail, the conditioning proceeds. Hence it pays, anent the issue of forecastability, to review, even to rehearse, some of the achieved conditionings which work toward standardized and so toward semipredictable reactions — including that net thrust of the appellate judge's "sense" and "reason" which most closely concerns us at this point.[197] Consider:

The judge responds to his alarm clock much as Pavlov's dog responded to the food-gong, and it is well for punctuality in judicial labors that he does. The same lines of conditioned responses accompany terms of court, hours of court, the calendar and its handling, the rules of code or court on set periods for appeal or answer or the like. There is *conditioned* by all of this into the slackest, most dilatory, or most wayward human soul a triggerable response to the notion that procedure, orderly and correct procedure, *makes sense* in almost *any* situation; a twenty-day term which is in one real aspect sheer caprice becomes not only a legal {205} command or a legal necessity but a something dictated seemingly by reason.

The judge also, to the degree of our ability to train him, responds to robe, bench, and gavel in the manner of Pavlov's poodle. We set before him a performance to achieve and an ideal (for him to acquire) of how to achieve that performance. With Pavlov, it was, e.g., to spot the difference between a circle and an oval, and to act accordingly. With the judge, it is to spot the difference between being, feeling, thinking, and acting like Arthur Zilch, a man (or a lawyer) in the street, and being, thinking, feeling, and acting like Zilch, J., a (a) responsible, (b) judicial, (c) officer. We give this Zilch a signal for when to "change" from the one into the other (as in a fairy tale): *when he robes, he is to put on also the person of Zilch, J.* While he is new at it, we train him much as Pavlov's dog was trained: by repeated, consistent reward (self-respect, satisfaction of sense of duty, perhaps hope of advancement, certainly admiration of the observers) and by repeated, consistent punishment (appearing ridiculous, sense of failure, self-reproach, reversal) according to his effective handling of this desired role of Zilch, J. — which we tell him, be it noted, *must be much more J. than Zilch.* When he has been trained (of course, in large part by himself) until he has become a "good trouper," a truly conditioned "professional," then he covers up, represses, or even discards, as he robes, such attributes of Arthur Zilch as headache, indigestion, personal worries, cravings for tobacco or sweets, various prejudices, petulancies, and even convictions which depart too largely from "the law" or from the temper and value-judgments of the people at large, whose "representative" he is to be. He does not merely, as he robes, shift his thinking into the gear of "the law" and of Justice as an Official ought to see Justice, and away from the comics, the party (beer, bridge, or political), from getting his score down toward eighty, from the Russian situation, from Dietrich's legs,[198] from whether to serve rye or bourbon on Saturday evening. He also, differentially to be sure, but nonetheless both by conditioning already done and by some degree of *conditioned* conscious exertion, sets himself to see and value — that is, to use his sense and reason — not as Arthur Zilch so much as in his capacity as judge and as a member of his specific court. We read much from the reflective judges about this toning down, this effort to be infused, as being a duty, a job for thought, even struggle, and one which taxes wisdom on where to draw the line. But I am dwelling as much or {206} more, if I may borrow from Holmes, on the necessity: on the fact that most appellate judges have to a real degree become Pavloved not only by and to the law but *in their views* by office and especially by service.[199] Necessity and duty fuse in one further matter: in the readiness of the judge to receive information and real instruction from counsel about what the sense and reason of the problem-situation in hand may be.

SITUATION-SENSE VIA COUNSEL

If one reflects for a minute about how unwilling the mature mere human being normally is to unlearn or unthink what he "knows," one wakes up almost with a start to the degree to which the office has built and shaped in the appellate judge a willingness to be shown where sense may lie, about a problem-situation. The very resentment felt by the bar against the odd imperious stinker who freezes to his crotchets serves in this matter as a citation of honor for the regiment at large. Let me illustrate what can be done; the stuff has value both for counsel and for court.

The law of sealed contracts has come down to us with some queer and seemingly archaic appendages, and the "seal" on a contractual writing (thanks to indulgent construction of the word "seal" in completely different contexts, in order, in the early nineteenth century, to validate such instruments as home-made deeds) has turned from a truly formal "form" which might force true attention and invite serious meditation into a hardly noticeable "[L.S.]" (of which a layman does not even know the meaning) or a scrawl (of which the same layman does not know the legal consequences, or indeed that there are any). When the issue arises as to whether a contractual agreement so "sealed" cannot today be modified by a later signed agreement good in every aspect except for lack of scrawl, it lies close to see the reason of the situation as compelling departure from a senseless rule whose plain effect is to pay off a trickster for his trick. Once such a step is taken, a next, rather foreseeably, would be to excise other even more hoary rules about sealed instruments: say the rule that a seal is needed to empower an agent to make, under scrawl, a contract for his principal, the analogy of stream and source being these days hardly cogent. Again rather foreseeably, one would say, destruction would loom over the anomalous rule {207} which insulates an undisclosed principal from suit if, but only if, the contract in which he is not named is "under seal." It was roughly thus that the law of New York stood in 1925, when *Crowley v. Lewis*[200] presented the undisclosed principal issue. There is in my mind little doubt that if the matter had been left to the sense and reason of the bulk of the judges as that sense and reason stood before the *Crowley* case came up, the pendulum which had begun to swing against the "antiquated and artificial" rules on sealed contracts would have swung further, notwithstanding "precedents of recent date" which Cardozo mentions in his brief discussion.[201] For in *Harris v. Shorall*,[202] only four years before, an unsealed modification followed by performance had been held effective, with powerful indication that the same result was proper even though the modification should be purely executory: "The time to dispose of the rule effectively, if not now, is near at hand. . . . When so much of the old value and high nature of the seal has been lost, the court should not be tenacious to preserve one of its minor incidents for the sake of the rule but should rather strive to give effect to the real agreement of the parties." (230 N.Y. at 348; Cuthbert Pound is writing.) "If reluctance unnecessarily to vary established rules suggests that a final decision be reserved on this point until a case is presented which compels such a decision . . ." etc. (ibid. 348-349.) When the *Crowley* case came up, however, counsel made clear to the court that nondisclosure of the principal in a real estate operation was often of the essence of the enterpriser's success; it was pointed out in addition that this particular method of insulation of the principal from liability was in constant use, relied on. Corporate devices and the like for "limiting liability" (though not for wholly escaping it!) were sold to the court as essentially parallel. Thus, new sense of and for the significant situation was brought home by counsel, and was perceived and acted on by a court even though that court had already been in evident motion in the other direction. I see the shock to the court as having been rude. They had assumed overlightly that all the twists of seal law had become outmoded tortuosities, and then they barked their shins on one which was instead a taut and bearing rope. I think the effects of the shock showed when, the same year, the question of an attempt at executory modification without scrawl {208} was presented squarely, and a majority forsook the dictum of the *Harris* case and held the attempt futile.[203]

FOREIGN REMITTANCES

Even more instructive is one sequence of those foreign remittance cases which still present some bothers. Within less than six years we find that the pressure of facts and the skill of counsel in informing the court carries the legal interpretation of a single transaction-type through three totally disparate concepts.[204]

The first judicial approach to remittance matters is as physical as the "money in a bag" approach to "deposits" with a banker before the nature of deposit banking was understood. As late as *Cutler v. American Exchange National Bank,* 113 N.Y. 593, 21 N.E. 710 (1889), a domestic remittance arrangement (letter of advice, New York bank to Leadville bank: Your account is credited $500.00 received from Cutler for the use of Hall) is seen as a "special" deposit for a particular purpose, and its entirely normal handling by the bank as a matter of credits and their transfer is resented by Gray, J., as a bookkeeping manipulation which cannot be permitted to obscure or change its "nature." The Leadville bank having failed without paying Hall, Cutler was held entitled to recover the money he had paid defendant New York bank.

The remittance to foreign parts now makes its debut in New York's lower courts under circumstances practically designed to perpetuate such an approach. An act of 1907, directed against petty exploitation of confidence inside of foreign language "colonies," had required a bond from any steamship ticket agent who went into the "business of receiving deposits of money for the purpose of transmitting the same or its equivalents to foreign countries." Steamship companies and banks issuing drafts, or letters of credit, were exempted. In sustaining a suit on such a bond the court found the classification and regulation constitutionally reasonable as guarding against a familiar type of imposition *and embezzlement.* And: "Technically speaking, there is a marked distinction between issuing a draft or traveler's check and *receiving money for transmission."* (132 App. Div. at 305; my italics.) *Musco v. United Surety Co.,* 132 App. Div. 300, 117 {209} N.Y. Supp. 21 (1st Dept. 1909). In the same year the same court affirmed a conviction for grand larceny against a steamship ticket agent who had received money and failed to make by mail the agreed arrangements for deposit of the equivalent in an Austrian savings account. "Of course the relation of debtor and creditor existed, but that does not at all affect the question whether under the facts set forth Zotti received the money as a fiduciary." *People ex rel. Zotti v. Flynn,* 135 App. Div. 276, 280-281, 120 N.Y. Supp. 511 (1st Dept. 1909).

The next case, *Strohmeyer & Arpe Co. v. Guaranty Trust Co.,* 172 App. Div. 16, 157 N.Y. Supp. 955 (1st Dept. 1916), has such different background, lighting, and management as to belong to a different world. A private banker doing an international business has "bought" from one of the major international banks more than $14,000 worth of lire for cable transfer. The acceptance note contains an exemption for delay in cable transmission which the court reads into the contract as if that were of course. The action is based on a three weeks' delay which was due wholly to the cable company. "We are relieved from the necessity of undertaking to define a cable transfer, for the parties have stipulated for the purpose of this case ... 'seller engages that he has the balance at the point on which payment is ordered and that on receipt ... his correspondent at such point will make payment ...'" (172 App. Div. at 19). Even so, the old physical approach died hard: the lower court had "decided in favor of the plaintiff upon the theory that what defendant contracted to transmit was the identical money paid to it by the plaintiff, likening the case to one in which a common carrier had received ten trunks for transmission...." (ibid. 20.) The Appellate Division found error. There is a simple cite to the *Musco* case for this proposition (compare with the italicized quote above): "Technically speaking, there is a marked distinction between issuing a draft, or traveler's check, *or transferring money by cable* and receiving money for *actual* transmission.... The very term 'cable transfer' precludes the idea that an actual transmission of money is contemplated." (ibid. 20; my italics.) "What the seller of a cable transfer does is to sell a sum of money, or a credit for a sum of money, payable at the place indicated in the contract." (ibid. 21.) But the exemption clause killed damages except for interest.

The 1907 statute and its background as presented in *Musco,* the grand larceny conviction for misappropriation of a "deposit" with an "agent," the lower court reasoning in *Strohmeyer,* followed then by the facts and decision in that case — these affect {210} the observer like a sequence of fossil deposits which display an evolution followed by a fatal revolution in climate. And one might have thought that *Strohmeyer* would be enough to educate any court, and also enough to awaken banking counsel to the value of such education and to the kind of material which could be drawn on. But the next case loosed old-fashioned fact-pressures which remind one of the *Cutler* picture. *Legniti v. Mechanics and Metals National Bank,* 186 App. Div. 105, 173 N.Y. Supp. 814 (1st Dept. 1919), grew out of a deal in which private bankers, at 6 p.m. on the literal eve of their declared insolvency, had accepted from the plaintiff a certified check on the express oral condition (not found in the written sales note) that the cable would go out that very night to protect plaintiff, who was a smaller private banker, against dishonor of drafts of his which were about to be presented abroad. No cable was sent. The proceeds of the check were in dispute between the plaintiff and the insolvent's bank, which was claiming a banker's lien. The Appellate Division impressed a trust in favor of plaintiff. It distinguished and limited *Strohmeyer* because "there the nature of the transaction and the facts were stipulated" (186 App. Div. at 109). Here, "The case would be one of agency if it involved the purchase of a credit by Bolognesi & Co. [the "selling" banker] from another, and if not and it only involved a transfer of his own credit by cable, it would be analogous thereto, and in either case the proceeds of the check could be used only for the purpose for which it was delivered" (ibid. 108), and *Cutler, Zotti,* and the helpless immigrant laborer set the implicit background scene. The dissent sought to stay this reversion to the primitive picture and, instead, to distinguish the professional exchange market from the petty deals. No one, either here or on the final appeal, seems to have conceived the possibility of urging an implied and deliberate misrepresentation of solvency as given in the peculiar facts, with an insolvent deposit banker's misreceipt of deposits as an analogy. But the degree to which the *particular* equities appealed to the court may be estimated by the fact that the *Equitable* case, only a year later, finds this same court reverting to the *Strohmeyer* interpretation of a cable transfer without one mention of this *Legniti* decision.

Legniti seems to have surprised and alarmed the banking bar, as well it might. When the case reached the Court of Appeals, two sets of distinguished *amici* turned up on behalf of two different branches of the banking fraternity. They contributed importantly to the array of legal authorities, more importantly {211} to the picture of the business, its age, its extent. There was, however, no concentration on a "pure-contract" theory of the banker's cable or other exchange transaction, even though the first decision in the *Equitable* case, to be discussed below, featured in two of the briefs, and had already sounded clear warning that "a transfer of credits between different points by cable" was headed for trouble with the Statute of Frauds as being a "contract to sell goods or choses in action." The Court of Appeals opinion in *Legniti,* 230 N.Y. 415, 130 N.E. 567 (1921), reflects the careful development of the situation by counsel; it spreads over the whole foreign exchange business. "This practice of *selling credit* by means of drafts and checks.... communication by cable and wireless met the insistent demands for haste and dispatch. Thus, the custom has developed of *selling credit* to be established by cable or wireless.... The *thing sold* is the same.... It is the credit of the bank ..." (230 N.Y. at 419; my italics). Counsel's labors bear fruit as the scene expands beyond the narrow cable transfer and beyond any set of stipulated facts and leads to the defendant bank's protection: "All these transactions are matters of purchase and sale and create no trust relationships" (ibid. 420). But the fateful "sale" concept infests the opinion, save for one paragraph: "Whether the transaction be considered a purchase or an executory contract, we need not now determine. So far as this case is concerned, it is a mere matter of nomenclature." (ibid.)

After the argument but before this decision in *Legniti,* the Appellate Division in *Equitable Trust Co. v. Keene,* 195 App. Div. 384, 186 N.Y. Supp. 468 (the same 1st Dept. 1921), held an action on an oral contract to take up within four months a cable transfer for £20,000 sterling to be vulnerable under the Statute of Frauds. The experience in the *Legniti* case had, however, bitten home. Before the Court of Appeals new counsel were introduced on the bankers' side of the case, counsel who had in *Legniti* served as *amicus.* Nor was there this time any diversion or split in the legal theory which the situation-sense was marshaled to support. I wish I might have had that oral argument to make: the almost startling picture of a major international bank's foreign exchange expert at work in an unstable, still free, market, with four assistants and ten or more telephones all busy as offers in the tens or hundreds of thousands are received and held open during a lightninglike shopping around, or are made and held "firm for three minutes" or are "closed" by word of mouth in closings that have to mean binding obligations. It was such a {212} picture of the type-situation which knocked out the Statute of Frauds, such a picture which induced the court to completely recast its so recent, so "modern" and satisfying impression of *sense for that situation.* The necessary shift of concept from "contract to sell an existing credit" to "contract to place to the credit of the person named the amount in question at the time and place specified" — that represents a legal rethinking by the court, one in itself burdensome and unwelcome, one acceptable only because new sense and reason have been shown, *taken in,* made welcome. "The distinction between these two views . . . is narrow and somewhat obscure," writes Hiscock for the court.[204a] How right, for purposes of the Statute of Frauds, since the distinction can be maintained only by ignoring the text of the Statute — which the court does *not* quote — and by cleaving so tightly to the idea of an *existing* credit that the creation of a right to payment against either the "seller" or its correspondent can cease to look like the "contract to sell a chose in action" which it technically just plain is. Surely the nub lies in the information from the briefs that word of mouth is the common method of closing such transactions and that an upset "will be productive of much inconvenience" (p. 292). It is a good nub, and a wise decision; but there is nothing which suggests that the necessary understanding of situation and need was sitting, ready, on the bench; Cardozo's appreciation of banking, for instance, had no at-homeness at all in the hands-and-feet techniques of commercial bank operation.[205] No, what we have is advocacy informing the court *at the appellate stage* about wise choice Of concept and consequent rule, in view of the inherent needs of the type of situation; informing so persuasively that the court turns its back on the plain text of a statute to strong-arm an exception which the legislature has lacked the knowledge and prudence to provide.[205a]

APPELLATE JUDGING AS A CRAFT OF LAW

The third cluster of our stabilizing factors, the accepted techniques for work with the legal authorities, is to be weighed not in terms of verbal description or of the bewildering variety of the techniques as they hang in the rack, for use on call, but in terms rather of their actual use in the active work of the appellate courts, better, of any particular appellate court over any given week or month or year. The two scales yield widely different readings. To the less thoughtful of the realist analysts thirty or forty years ago, and to all but the most thoughtful of the then active Smite-the-Realist clan, a hard-eyed description of all the things which an authority might *correctly* be made to mean, i.e., a laying out of the huge range of doctrine, any single aspect of which could *in posse* prove to be its "true" meaning, this seemed with reference to our appellate judging to be a revelation, an exposure, an unmasking, of vagrant uncertainty; or else, according to the point of view, it seemed to be a destructive and probably vicious effort to produce such uncertainty or at best to denigrate an honest bench and the best law we had. Various persons of either persuasion tended also to find in such a description an aspect or an accusation of irresponsibility: the skeptic because the court answered to nobody, save in a pseudo justification which was a fiat of its own validity; the defender of the faith because the range of techniques, if admitted, seemed to deny control of appellate judges by the law. The whole set of such misconceptions rooted in part in the illusion of dogmatics that there should be, must be, can be only one single right answer,[206] that a multiplicity of answers is wrong, is contra-nature, and as applied to a part of law-government, is practically subversive. They rooted partly, as has also been mentioned, in the notion that deciding properly is and normally can be, even in the tough case, essentially an intellectual process, nay, an intellectualizable process, and essentially {214} one of logical deduction: this for the conserver of tradition; for the iconoclast, on the other hand, the last of these ideas was the idol he was occupied in unmasking as a false god and then in smashing.

But informing all of this, and basic to most of both the misconceptions and the cross-purposings of the realist controversy, was an absence everywhere of the concept of *craft*, of *craft*-tradition, of *craft*-responsibility, and of craftsmanship not as meaning merely the high artistry of God's gifted, but as including the uninspired but reliable work of the plain and ordinary citizen of the craft. The existence of a craft means the existence of some significant body of working knowhow, centered on the doing of some perceptible kind of job. This working knowhow is in some material degree transmissible and transmitted to the incomer, it is in some material degree conscious, it is to some degree articulate in principles and rules of art or of thumb, in practices and dodges or contrivances which can be noticed and learned for the easing and the furtherance of the work. A healthy craft, moreover, elicits ideals, pride, and responsibility in its craftsmen. And every live craft has much more to it than any rules describe; the rules not only fail to tell the full tale, taken literally they tell much of it wrong; and while words can set forth such facts and needs as ideals, craft-conscience, and morale, these things are bodied forth, they live and work, primarily in ways

132

and attitudes which are much more and better felt and done than they are said. Now appellate judging is a distinct and (along with spokesmanship) a central craft of the law side of the great-institution of Law-Government. Every aspect of the work and of the man at work is informed and infiltrated by the craft. It is a tough craft, too; over a whole era it has survived a drift away into formalistic thinking and even believing. More, it has then also survived a degree of neglect of its conscious philosophy which could have choked a less hardy plant, and which remains a peril in the current crisis.

Today the appellate judges are again becoming conscious of their craft as such, conscious of some of its problems, not merely each man for himself but also as general and common problems which merit general and common thought and labor. The advocates are in similar fashion beginning to again become conscious of their craft, the law teachers of theirs.[207] But not one whit {215} of this was live in the thinking — if one can call it that — which fed the Donnybrook of the '30's about realism. Moreover, almost none of it has moved, even today, into the *advocate's* or the *law teacher's* understanding of the work of the appellate courts. And the appellate judges themselves, though conscious and at work today over the problems of the craft in a fashion and on a scale I think unique in our history, are far from being aware as yet, as a group, of what a craft is, or of what knowledge of the nature of a craft, and of their own craft, in particular, can offer toward speed and smoothness in their coping with the problems of appellate judging.

What the fact of the going craft means with regard to our cluster of techniques for handling precedents — or for handling statutes or any other type of legal authority — is that we must view and weigh the steadiness-effect of those techniques as they appear in active use. And others of our factor-clusters play daily into such use, inextricably, potently, decisively: The law-conditioning of each judge; the body of doctrine not only in its detail but in its constellations, its fields sometimes of stress, sometimes of shooting growth, sometimes of cemented solidity; the sense of the peculiar office; the duty imposed by that office to strive after wisdom in the rule and fairness in the result. And when these things are drawn into the account, as the court wrestles with the conflict-puzzles thrown up from a culture churned by technological and international turmoil, I am prepared to argue that the very range of the authority techniques as they hang ready in the rack is a major fighting factor in furthering, often even producing, reckonability in the upshot of the cases.

Not "Certainty," but Reasonable Regularity

Appreciation of this turns in first instance on realization that any single-value deductive scheme of controlling authorities has to be rigid. True, insofar as the categories of scope are phrased in functional terms an important quantum of adjustment and readjustment to shifting circumstance can be achieved by essentially deductive processes, and with results which will satisfy so long as the reason of the rule has been prophetic. But as we all know, the combination of functional category with prophetic reason occurs rarely enough to stand out from the run of our {216} rules. For the mass of those rules a truly deductive application, i.e., "certainty" in the sense of honest logic, means, as new cases arise from moving circumstance, an incessant tension between felt sense and the outcome suggested, even dictated, by the current form of words. The sound goal, amid such tensions, is a yielding of the pattern roughly sufficient to ease the strain. A barebones minimum would be: yielding enough to produce a bearable result, a result which does not produce covert or overt rebellion or even directly shock. A good result will in addition feel moderately satisfactory in the light of life conditions while exuding also a feeling of naturalness, even of-courseness, in terms of the authorities. An excellent result will even reach forward to guide and absorb the next few cases in advance.

All of this means that the ideal is not "certainty" at all, in any of the senses in which that term is commonly applied to matters legal. The true ideal is *reasonable regularity* of decision.[208] If there is *regularity,* there is continuity enough; and be it noted that sharp, sudden upset is almost never needed, *if* there has been no prior piled-up log jam to block the passage of the prior needed small adjustments. The *reasonable* aspect of the regularity, on the other hand, holds out full room to adjust any complex of tension to the hugely variant needs of whatever the relevant type-situations may be: all the way, say, from the sharply defined reliance that underlies validity of a 50-year bond issue[209] through ordinary commercial transactions on into a son's right to sue his insured parent for an automobile injury or into a minor reform in the law of expert testimony.

Now, as each week passes in an appellate court, rules of all varieties of wisdom, modernity, and sharpness or intelligibility of phrasing are brought to bear upon litigated situations and puzzling situation-types also of almost all varieties, with, instance by instance, the hand-me-down fit of relevant rules to the relevant need running all the way from the superb to the Procrustean. And if the court is to do a job *which is reckonable at all,* which is other than the dice-throw gamble appropriate to Fuller's pestered shoat,[210] then, as has been said, the court needs to have as tools at hand not a single one or even three, but well-nigh the whole Croesus-wealth of our American authority techniques to {217} choose from. Neat cabinetmaking is both easier, more likely and more reckonable when the workbench is well stocked. The invitation of the full range, *any one correct,* makes simple, unembarrassed, natural, in many cases half-automatic, the choice and use of some one which is just the one needed to produce reasonable regularity in the particular case.

THE LAW OF LAWFUL DISCRETION

This pattern and ideal of reasonable regularity — in contrast to "certainty" of outcome or "universality" of rule on the one hand and to "free discretion" or "arbitrary" choice or patternlessness and the like on the other — this pattern and ideal of reasonable regularity is marbled through the muscle of a good deal of law-government in the way fat marbles through a steak to make and keep it tender. Reasonable regularity is indeed the principle which comes close to drying up the bubbling flood of words about rule and discretion, whether in the appellate court or in any other activity of law-government. The matter comes to this: *no* discretion has any business to be wholly free; *no* discretion has any business to be truly unique in exercise.

The Law of Lawful Discretion. To be *right* discretion, to be lawful exercise of discretion (though there be neither rule nor precedent nor likelihood of repetition), the action so far as it affects any man or group adversely must be undertaken with a feeling, explicit or implicit, of willingness, of readiness, to do the like again, if, as, and when a like case may arise.

It is not, I repeat, necessary that there be any rule. Neither is it necessary that there be any effort to formulate a rule, nor even that there be effort to phrase a justification. The matter goes instead to an attitude, an attitude in first instance internal to the actor. Indicative often, but again and again nonconclusive, is a willingness to have the action known and looked at; but absence of this is plainly nonconclusive wherever what is deemed by the actor a right exercise of discretion might encounter trouble from misunderstanding or ill will. "Here," I have written elsewhere, "character becomes a part of law." Hence the consciousness of giving undue favor, of being influenced by prejudice or politics or person in a way the actor would not like to stand to before a fair public *in consimile casu* — that consciousness will not square with *lawful* exercise of any entrusted discretion.

This is as sadly neglected a truth as is the nature and central importance of reasonable regularity itself, which has gone substantially {218} begging in the literature ever since John R. Commons' initial development thereof.[211] Let me therefore add an earlier and somewhat more elaborate effort to formulate the same idea, even though it does not sever out the law of leeways:

> These unregularized and so to speak semi- or pre-legal *parts* of the legal regime are complementary and implementary proper working *parts* thereof (even when non-regular, and frequently unwise) whenever the action moves (1) in consonance with the basic objectives of purpose and manner to which the legal system is geared; and (2) in consonance with leeways recognized generally by and within the structure for the play of judgment, to allow of individual action or cumulative experiment in good faith; *and* (3) when individuated or novel "discretionary" operation moves in honest conscious or unconscious *quest* for a *pattern* to guide treatment of what may at the moment seem a unique case. Put from the other side, the unregularized becomes *anti*-legal when it occurs in bad faith; or without quest for a pattern emerging or to emerge; or when it persistently jumps the recognized limits or even persistently pushes daily ordinary action out into limits which exist only to serve the case of pressing need.[212]

A number of things flow at once from observation of this law of lawful discretion — which latter I put forward here without further discussion, as being simply and sweetly self-evident on sight. One is that the discretionary action may be abominably ill-conceived, and yet be lawful. *Inside its range,* and case by case, the leeway for the official to *be* wrong within the discretion entrusted to him is complete; what he has no right leeway for is to *do* wrong. Another immediate consequence is that we outsiders may live out our lives without ever discovering for sure whether many of the acts of discretion which affect us have or have not been lawful. Which is too bad; but it makes no difference to the standard by which it is law for the official to abide and which it is our right to press upon him. Still another thing {219} is that any relevant rule or detailed or even phrased standard may be very slow to grow, and yet action may move into moderately reckonable channels.[213] I seem to recall Herbert Wechsler, after research, reporting that the British Home Office had found no way of phrasing their standards for commutation or pardon after capital convictions, yet that their officials felt a comforting degree of regularity and guidance in and from their practice.

And two further matters seem to me to be clear: the one, that any such search for reasonable regularity, if at all sustained, has its power to shape conduct toward and into the object of the quest; I should link the Home Office experience close with this. The other — as will appear immediately — that even when a man or a court works under explicit rules of law (or of practice, or both) and with such rules and by them, right work must still observe the Law of Lawful Discretion.

For we recur to the fact that choice and use of authorities, like all of an appellate court's deciding, is done within the traditions, the pressures, even the compulsions, of the craft and of the office.

Two broad aspects of this I should like now to develop more explicitly: the Law of Leeways and the Law of Fitness and Flavor.

THE LAW OF LEEWAYS

Wholly apart from all those aspects of the office for which we still use the pallid label "impartial,"[213a] there is a matter of appellate judicial restraint which is at the same time a matter of appellate judicial wisdom. The point is simple: The truly astounding powers over people, groups, even government, *and also over the rules and manner of our law,* which our polity intrusts in formal sovereignty to its highest judiciary — these powers are in deep truth powers in trust, powers for use but not for abuse, and they are so perceived by the appellate judges. That perception is one of prudence as well as one of duty. Judicial security is indeed well-nigh perfect for any one judgment which is honest, however outrageous, or for any six or seven of such judgments. But a sustained course of extravagant judging will transgress limits of toleration which are as inescapable as they are undefined, unphrased. And if the appellate courts should ever take to doing daily what they have absolute and unchallenged power to {220} do sometimes, we should have to get rid of the guilty judges; we might in the process and for a while get rid even of the courts. So that if the appellate judges do without need what Cardozo sees it as their business, office, and duty to do "in hours of stress and strain," then, insofar, their doing is bad.[214] And if their doing is persistently that kind of bad, then, insofar, they are doing wrong. And the leeway which we accord them (though sometimes overgrudgingly) to *be* wrong is not, let it be repeated, at all a leeway to *do* wrong.

But by the same token the daily leeways are there not for neglect but for use; here as elsewhere, official power implies an obligation not only of wise restraint but also of wise employment. It is not to be buried in the earth; the parable of the talents might well have been drawn from and addressed squarely to the leeway-powers of appellate judicial office.

I once sought to phrase the matter in what may be called *The Law of Leeways:*

> [T]he greater the felt need, because of felt sense, the wider is the leeway correctly and properly available in reshaping an authority or the authorities. What is both proper and to be expected in an extreme case would become abuse and judicial usurpation if made daily practice in the mine-run of cases. All courts worthy of their office feel this in their bones, as being inherent in our system of precedent. They show the feeling in their work. Where differences appear is where they should appear: in divergent sizings up of what is sense, and of how great the need may be in any situation [— and, it should be added, in divergent lines and levels of the courts' craftsmanship].[215]

This quoted phrasing errs, let me again insist, as did Cardozo's before it, in stressing only the outside limits and the negative; it needs not only for completeness and accuracy but also for sound implicit counsel an equivalent stress upon the practice and duty in the mine-run of cases: *What sense calls for, in the use of correct leeways, is to be achieved if time permits* — provided, of course, {221} that vision and ingenuity also permit; for a road which later springs to the eye may go undiscovered or unnoticed at the time and long after. Yet in these days of regroping for the Grand Style the duty is unremitting, so far as time and energy extend, to *test* each individual rule and result for sense and reason. For both use of leeway and abdication of a leeway

> correctly available when the sense of the situation and the case call for their use cease to be correctly available *unless used in furtherance of what the court sees as such sense.* There is here in our system of precedent an element of uprightness, of conscience, of judicial responsibility; and motive becomes a factor in determining what techniques are correct and right. Today, in contrast with 1890, it may be fairly stated that even the literal application of a thoroughly established rule is not correct in a case or situation in which that application does not make sense unless the court in honest conscience feels forced by its office to make the application.[216]

Meantime our friend the lawyer who has lost below can get his mead of guidance toward a forecast of his chances. For however any appellate court may be disposed toward the matters of general obligation just propounded, it is only men or moments of aberration which lead any appellate court at any time into conflict with the basic law of leeways. Hence, as the lawyer looks upon the record and the pertinent or competing rules of law, as he sets his detectors for the field-forces and strains of the relevant legal area and of the relevant life-situation, the law of leeways will set his counter clicking hard if heavy change impends, and clicking audibly even in an intermediate case. He must, of course, keep in mind that such warning — or promise — looks to outcome, not to the ground on which the outcome will be rested, which means that the peril cannot be dispelled by the prettiest of cases he may make "on the law." On the other hand, it does not mean safety in appeal, no matter how evident may be the Promised Land, if counsel fail to furnish what Fuller has neatly termed a "doctrinal bridge" over Jordan;[217] doubly not if counsel actually set up barriers {222} by a doctrinal argument so inept as to make a gap and innovation seem bigger, or the urgencies seem less pressing, than they are.

THE LAW OF FITNESS AND FLAVOR

The Law of Leeways is, I suggest, demonstrable; it well-nigh demonstrates itself out of any lawyer's reading; it shines forth from any half dozen or so of my reports on current deciding. The Law of Fitness and Flavor, in contrast, I shall not undertake to demonstrate; I shall merely present it as a fruit of my own study and considered judgment, though I have only reached formulation of it at this stage of the writing of this text. But I believe that except for some wild man or three who may be enlivening the current scene, the appellate judges of the country, State and Federal, will agree that the law is and has been in vigorous operation.

The phenomenon I am seeking to bring to expression is a complex one; in particular, it reaches over beyond the mere deciding into the purpose, manner, and content of the consequent opinion. Let me put it thus; *The work of the job in hand, and even more the work of the job at large, must fit and fit into the body and the flavor of The Law.* In a similar connection, above at pages 190 f., I have tried to reach the idea in terms of working with rather than across or against the grain, of easing rather than increasing the active or latent tensions of the force-fields in the law. I remember the scorn which Konenkov, whose chisel woke in wood the beauty asleep in it, felt for Mestrović, who wreaked his will upon a block of wood as if it had been grainless granite. I recall a great copper disk in an elementary physics experiment, swinging gaily down into an electromagnetic field — and stopped, hot and shuddering, as by a wall. Now as one reads the cases with his nostrils keen for what and why the court is about, discarding as best he can all his own desire for any particular result, it seems to me hard to miss this aura, this atmosphere not only of hesitance to upset the settled or to embark on an uncharted sea, but of a desire to move in accordance with the material as well as within it, to carve with the grain like Konenkov, to reveal the latent rather than to impose new form, much less to obtrude an outside will. Mansfield in Fifoot's admirable telling stands in stark contrast to this normal way of work. He came to the bench without the Law of Fitness and Flavor, nor did he ever learn it. He fitted only when he did not care, or when it served his will, or when fear {223} forced him. But I am hard put to it to find another great judge of whom that can be said, no matter how creative. Gibson, perhaps. Coke may be the closest; his lifetime through, he had more self-will than most, but especially he remained to the end more an advocate, in contrast to a judicial judge, more a user of authority to known ends of statesmanship — or politics. Not so the other notable shaping judges, in Britain or here.

One major feature of this fitting has to do with the use made of the authorities in the opinion: Is it, judged by circumstance and need, and also by the duty of judicial candor with self, bar, and public, a *fair* use? Which includes, where movement is strong, or an authority in the way, an open treatment and a frank one. Side by side goes that other aspect of the opinion: Will the emergent rule guide? Then, does it guide in a way and in a direction which fits not only our law's need but our law's flavor? Mere case-by-case stuff is not enough, however decent each individual result as between the parties; ours is a case *law* system.

Neither can any series of cases pass this muster if they fail to move with care and slowly increasing grasp into a rule which can guide and which so can decrease the flow of litigation or turn it into those other channels natural to new developments out of a point now settled — for a while at least — with moderate clarity. For the cases must build and they must become stones for further building: such is the way, such is the duty of our law. To be sure, the going can be thorny and tricky: consider the short eleven years of the foreign remittance cases above. But there can be, and must be, as happened there, some sense even in such a technical jamboree, some emergent and at least semisatisfying pattern.[218]

Considerable portions of what has just been said will hold true regardless of the prevailing period-style in country or in court. Accounting to The Law as it stood yesterday, guidance in The Law as now laid down for tomorrow, these are demands of and in a case law system always. So also is the demand for moderate consistency, for reasonable regularity, for on-going conscientious effort at integration. So again with the demand for results, in the instant rule, the instant principle, the instant outcome, which fit the flavor of the whole. But what that flavor is will differ radically according to the currently prevailing period-style.

Today the flavor is, and calls for, the further wooing of the Grand Style till there can be announcement of the banns. {224}

THE PARTICULAR COURT

Still, for the lawyer who has lost that case below, while calculations hinge indeed on the nature of appellate judges generally — as of men generally — and on the ways of their deciding, yet it is manifest that they hinge also and sometimes critically on the nature and ways of the particular court before which his appeal will bring him.

On this the eleventh, sixth, and tenth of our clusters join together: the *known bench,* where the strain of the opinion to be a *whole-group opinion* (typically enough with the Chief at work if cleavage should threaten) climaxes the whole process of a *group-deciding.* The leveling effect is patent; in *action* the individuals grow into closer likeness. What is for prediction purposes perhaps still more telling: the quantum of accessible persuasive evidence about the court's views on "sense" widens out. In regard to any particular prospective vote, it includes not only what the man has written but also (though of course with much more dilution) what he has concurred in. What is sure is that a record, rich and varied, lies open for study. It is here especially that the appellate lawyer may and must seek light on how far and wherein the bench in question, and its individual members, may differ from the lawyer's own notions about what is sense and reason: the supplement and complement of that likeness to himself which roots in other factors, passed in review above.

And here one must reaffirm the importance of making study of the court's opinions roam afield. It is a whole variegated volume read in sequence that begins to do the work — read as in the earliest nineteenth century a new volume of those novel and exciting things, reports, used to be read (and reviewed) whenever one might travel in by coach or vessel. This is not to forget that at times single judges, particular majorities, even whole benches may cultivate some rather senseless "sense," some most unreasonable "reason," in odd corners or in special areas: say homicide, or Teal estate brokerage, or some phase of personal civil liberty, or installment selling, or foreign ex parte divorce, or what have you more. Such quirks of man or group, when real, are important, important sometimes (through accidents of triggering and association) out far beyond their immediate area; and when discovered, such a quirk must be explored in theme-sequence as contrasted with simply working through the crazy quilt of a single volume as it stands. So also, and as of course, must the area of the {225} pending case be explored in full theme-sequence — and I mean *sequence,* watching the decisions *develop,* watching each of them *come* to be; I mean no mere illusory time-flat doctrinal "map pattern." Nevertheless, the background for every case, for *any* case, goes first of all to the whole man as he appears in the rounded whole of his work. It goes to the whole man, judge by judge. It goes also and similarly to that "reasonable" whole man, that corporate whole man, who typifies or symbolizes — or embodies — that particular bench-in-action; and it is no more prudent to ignore this not so bodiless corporate person than it would be to fail to wrestle as best one is able with the nature of the constituent individuals one by one. Again one is faced with something that skirts the ineffable. Again intellectual analysis is a powerful and indispensable tool, yet one which plainly proves somewhat wanting when it is *team*-action that must be coped with, and a case as yet unargued whose outcome is to be forecast.

A last point in this connection is as important as it is homely. A court must be measured, for a forecast, in terms not only of average or characteristic output, not only of the persons and constellations of the personnel, but in terms also of its manner of work. Thus in our current sampling we find Washington sitting in Departments, and Mississippi and Massachusetts sitting typically each in groups of five. Thus also, the New York sequence on incompleteness in agreements ran at one point into the period when the Court of Appeals was ten strong, sitting by sevens in order to catch up with a jammed docket, and therefore, if one had been following and forecasting, one hit sudden new hazards of prediction. A case already mentioned shows the problem: The spearhead of the commercial approach to reading a commercial document, Cardozo, was by one chance no member of the seven before whom one possibly crucial case came on to be heard. By another chance, the case equities stood there so strong against the plaintiff that the least commercial-minded of the court joined in using a very blunt instrument to beat that plaintiff on the head;[219] but had the case been more balanced in its surface-fairnesses, the guidance or absence of that one man in the consultation would have been the key to the outcome.[220] The Federal courts of appeal, {226} even when the general results in the particular circuit have a characteristic tone and flavor, present this problem in striking form, not only re forecast but re argument, as does the increasing use in the State courts of divisions or panels. To brief with the tribunal undetermined is to battle in the fog.[221]

And even with the personnel fixed, there remains the manner of work. The scatter, as reported to Wiener,[222] makes the scalp prickle. Conclusions with regard to the hows of advocacy belong below;[223] but the lowering of prediction-accuracy is obvious, to the degree that one cannot forecast the assignment and that the assigned judge (1) is assigned early — e.g., as a reporting judge, even before argument, (2) by practice does especially heavy advance preparation, or (3) is in any manner accorded by the course of operation or the habit of the court more weight than he would have, say, if he were assigned only after the hearing and the conference.

FROZEN FACTS AND ISSUES: DILEMMAS

Three of our clusters of "steadying" factors contribute little further toward reckonability: thus the fourth in the listing, felt responsibility to justice, is what has led to the enlistment of sense to begin with, and of course also plays in one way or another into most or all aspects of the "office." The thirteenth, independence, for all its value as a rampart against deflection, gives no orders and few suggestions inside the rampart; even in the freakish case in which a court feels influence to have been attempted, the net thrust of that feeling baffles guesswork as thoroughly as the courts know attempted bribery does in regard to a jury.[224] The fifth cluster, the near-belief in the singleness of the right answer, may be argued sometimes and in some measure to dampen down the search for best sense. As was said above, such a near-belief does lend first and perhaps sufficient persuasiveness, on first appearance, {227} to any colorable line of possible solution: say to a suggested and semipersuasive "deduction" from or "application" of some nearby rule of law; and this may be enough to halt further inquiry. So, when the initial tries along such lines fall short, the near-belief will tint a bit rosy any other answer which does not too blatantly dissatisfy. But these tendencies can hardly aid a forecast as much as what emerges directly from study of the last half-dozen volumes of reports about how *this* court perceives and classifies and thinks, and what kinds of sense and reason are stirring it and its now members, and how, and how far, and to what.

In contrast, the seventh and eighth of our clusters do promote precision: the frozen record and the formulated issues. Neither of them, as any heedful reader knows, will wholly limit an appellate court; but each does normally hold that court down in regard to what sense and reason the given court can reach for, or can reach. Notwithstanding reforms designed to simplify and speed pleading and procedure or to save clients from incompetent lawyers (or, as I sometimes have suspected, less competent lawyer-legislators from more competent adversaries), notwithstanding the conforming of the pleadings to the proof and the grant of any remedy the court may be able to dig up to fit the evidence, the issues as they have been shaped below and the points of appeal as they are framed by the appellant still insist on shaping, sharpening, or distorting the cause and on narrowing down the choices. And the trite truth is to be noted again that a two-way choice, even a two-way gamble, cannot compete in chanciness with an open field. Hence the joined issue, especially with counsel's argument seeking to confine attention to it, steps up forecast. For the lawyer contemplating appeal — once he has found the sense-phase of his cause to raise no insurmountable barrier — the matter shapes up like any other venture to be planned: he explores and compares in his imagination the various lines of attack which the terrain and his forces render possible. He weighs for each line what he can do with the available legal rules and concepts and weighs what the available appropriate situation-sense can do for him on that peculiar doctrinal foundation or against that peculiar doctrinal background. The likelihoods, though uncomputable, can yet for a man who has soaked himself in the workings of *this* court become comparable enough.

One possibility deserves a more particular word. That is the situation in which the tradition of our doctrine offers no decent answer at all for the situa-tion or the case: the issue frames itself as winner take all, but both parties are fragrant or both parties stink, whether as individual persons or in the roles for which they are cast within the available "legal" situation. Consider a case under the harsh New York usury law: a loan at more than the legal rate is flat forfeit; so also is the security, for amendments have expressly forbidden equity to temper the wind to the shorn wolf. A dubious credit risk now hunts up a professional usurer for a loan on realty. The usurer's "friend" is ready, against a $40,000 note at 6 per cent, to turn over $25,000 in cash; but he insists that the realty be first "incorporated" and that the loan be made to the corporation, because under a later New York statute a business corporation may not plead usury. In due course the honest debtor repudiates completely, and with the $25,000 in his pocket he is suing to have the mortgage declared void and canceled. The battle of counsel is a battle for control of the *background setting* against which the court is to do its judging, from which the court is therefore to derive its reason. Two lower instances saw, each, the very usurer, the very usury, against which the forfeiture statute had been originally aimed, against which it had been fortified later by the amendments explicitly voiding the security; reason was therefore clear, and the court looked through the "form" of incorporation to penalize the illicit "evasion." New counsel appeared for the lender before the Court of Appeals, and persuaded that court to look rather at the loan market when times were bad and at businesses which needed rehabilitation but would be barred from credit by a 6 per cent limit on return; reason was therefore clear, other end to: the legislature had carefully, almost explicitly, made the corporate device available for the very purpose of letting a businessman meet the business cost of a business loan for a prospective business profit.[225]

Compare and contrast a bona fide purchase case of the nastier sort: nobody is really at fault, original owner and purchaser have both acted reasonably enough, as men go, although unwisely in result; but our law has pretty well set its face against any effort to divide the loss, and an "indicia of ownership" concept has been grafted onto the simple initial ownership idea. Again the struggle of counsel in any novel variant will be for capture of the situation out of which sense and reason will draw their meaning. Sufficient normality of what the injured owner did can whittle his "entrusting" to the crooked intermediary down into slivers and {229} can take all substance out of what thus become pseudo "indicia"; sufficient normality of what the injured purchaser did, on the other hand, can give full body to almost anything as being "indicia," and means

141

then that whatever the owner did do, he nevertheless ought — in reason — to have foreseen the possibility, even the likelihood, of the very knavery which occurred and of which he must be held to have "taken the risk" upon himself. The attitude of the court in the aged and well-known *Shaw v. Railroad*[226] is typical enough. A seller's draft, bill of lading for cotton attached, had been presented for acceptance, the understanding being that such acceptance was not of itself to entitle the drawee to the bill of lading and the cotton. The drawee stealthily detached the bill of lading, substituting a copy, and indorsed the original to a third person in pledge to procure advances. The case was made easy in outcome by special verdicts that (1) the bank which had discounted for the seller had not been negligent "in parting with possession of the bill of lading" and also (2) that the pledgee "had reason to believe that the bill of lading was held to secure payment of an outstanding draft." Against a background of modern practice either finding might perhaps have been challenged as unsupported by any evidence; but "The law has most carefully protected the ownership of personal property, other than money, against misappropriation by others than the owner, even when it is out of his possession. This protection would be largely withdrawn if the misappropriation of its symbol or representative could avail to defeat the ownership. . . ." (101 U.S. at 565-566.) Dicta then threw out of the window statutes which had sought to make a bill of lading negotiable "in like manner as bills of exchange." It is not only the flavor of this opinion and the vigor of its reasoning which convinces that the court really meant the *salus domini suprema lex* approach; the commercial policies which had evoked the warehouse receipt and bill of lading statutes of the '70's found no echo in the courts of the seaboard centers: so Massachusetts in 1874 with the *Stollenwerck* case, and New York in 1878 with *Farmers' Bank v. Logan*.[227] {230}

The *Farmers' Bank* case is peculiarly interesting, although here again the actual holding fails to reach squarely a person who purchases by way of "indicia of ownership"; the purchase of a cargo of wheat had been instead by sample, and on the produce exchange, in regular course. The excitement lies in the complete command by Folger, who writes for the court, of the business and financing situation at *each* end of the wheat's voyage. "We doubt not that the [usual course of business on the produce exchange] makes very easy and rapid the transaction of an immense trade in the agricultural products of the country; and that it would tend much to the security and confidence with which it could be done, if the law of market *overt* could be applied to it. But such is not the rule of this State. . ." (74 N.Y. at 586.) Folger matches this from the other end by his clean description and analysis of buying upstate, with the buying factor drawing and discounting his draft on his principal to procure enabling advances from the upstate bank.

All three cases present the same essential conflict, not one born of a single raid by some wandering predator, but one inherent in the working patterns of a metropolitan market. And the sense "of the situation" can be seen in each of two ways: against safety in large-scale purchase on and in the market stands safety in large-scale financing of merchandise into the same market to become available for such purchase. It is no such Mr. Looking-Both-Ways of sense and reason who will overcome or much modify the centuried solidity of farmers' law on sanctity of initial ownership. Two out of the three cases seek even to turn over to the gelder any such "indicium" as a bill of lading drawn to order. One must remember the dilemma to which the court feels shackled: it can serve speed in turnover only by sponging out every right of the so very reasonable original owner.

142

Rights of original ownership are stubborn. As late as 1925, for instance, two cases hit the Oregon Supreme Court together, and came to the same judge for the opinions. In the one an installment contract for a car, together with a note shown on its face to be the price-note, and marked "Paid," had been not torn up but handed back to the buyer in substitution for new papers on slightly different terms. A purchaser taking in reliance on the surrendered papers was held to have acquired good title by estoppel, as against the conditional seller's financer.[228] But in what ought to have been a companion case, the old ghost walks.[229] An {231} installment seller of musical instruments had assigned the contracts batchwise as security. Once a month the contracts were sent back for a day or so to let collected sums be credited and any necessary substitutions be made. At one such opportunity the seller-borrower (like the drawee in *Shaw*) detached the assignment papers, substituted others, and fraudulently delivered the whole to a second assignee as collateral for a new loan. Again, as in *Shaw*, the opinion thunders in favor of the sanctity of "ownership" — this time that of the first assignee of a chose in action; and neither negligence nor estoppel is found in the entrusting, because a "crime" was necessary in order to produce any false appearance. "It is the crime and not the negligent act which is the proximate and effective cause of the injury." Again this all proves to be dictum; the second assignee is made to prevail under the doctrine of redelivered pledge, because while the first assignment was absolute in form, it had been only for security and so "amounted to a mere pledging," which "disposes of any contention that the plaintiff was the absolute owner."

By 1944 new statutes and practice have made a blank-signed certificate of title into a very good "indicium of ownership" when it is in the hands of a salesman trusted to pick up the certificate for a car traded in, and when that salesman has also been reintrusted with possession of the trade-in car itself.[230] "The efficient and proximate cause of the loss was not any criminal act committed by Burke, but the confidence that the defendants placed in Burke, by reason of which he was permitted to have in his possession the certificate of title and the motor vehicle" (145 P.2d at 475). This is the exact reverse of the way the court had read the almost sister-facts in *Schumann*. But the old worry lingers. It took a further case seven years later[231] to validate such "indicia" in the hands of a Sunday swindler who had given a no-funds check and who, according to the original owner's testimony, had been told "no deal on the car until I deposited the check ... and received full payment in cash." "This is a hard case." It is, indeed; and where there is no uniform commercial act or title certificate law to cut the knot, it is a type which will continue to bother court and counsel until some Solomon dares to split the loss.[232] {232}

For prognosticator and for advocate the principle remains: if sense looks in more than one direction, you have to capture the way in which the court will see and judge sense; and even then, if the choice before the court is a hard choice, it continues a chancy one.

THE SITUATION: COUNSEL AND THE COURT

Of course, where the sense and reason of the type-situation must be called upon in order to make the right goal catch the light, then it is counsel's business to get into the pleadings and the proofs material which makes that situation come alive, makes it explain itself, and makes it educate the court into such sympathetic appreciation of that situation that the court will be able, if not to discover, at least to recognize its "immanent law." To this truth it is immaterial that you or I may happen to believe that counsel is in fact clawing the eyes out of the truly immanent law. What is clear is that if counsel's business has been properly done, the very pleadings have in quiet factuality "made the stones speak" and the reason sing — to this court.[232a] Such a foundation, again of course, is a great aid to forecast. Indeed, its absence can also aid forecast; if the pleading and the trial theory have been wrongheaded enough, the issues badly enough mischosen, it may be obvious that an initially promising cause has been turned into garbage.

In between lies such presentation of the situation as, even with the trial record faulty, is manageable on appeal. It is a second best, but in emergency a second best may mean salvation.

This aspect of argument, going as it does to the proper choice, content, and direction of the solving rule or concept, has a standing and efficacy in an appellate argument which are curiously neglected. Its legitimacy is long-attested. "*The briefs make clear*" (my italics), says that meticulously correct Chief Justice, Hiscock, in 1921, "that great inconvenience would result" if the Statute of Frauds were to be applied to foreign exchange transactions; and so sharp has the nature of the whole situation become to him {233} that the cabling (once a necessary bridge out of *thing*-thinking) can become merely one of the various means of notification open to choice, and the court, you remember, follows the reason of the whole situation, so seen, into a "narrow" distinction which "is obscure."[233] In the *Farmers' Bank* case, we have just met essentially similar argument, which had been carefully listened to, in the same court forty-three years before, with regard to the produce exchange and its needs. That was a single year after Brandeis graduated from law school. The later "Brandeis brief" (like so many other good things of our law) was thus no invention or innovation, but instead a sound recurrence to a practice as fine and well-aged as the Grand Tradition itself[234] — one which goes back in fact to Mansfield or beyond. Indeed, any limitation of the idea to constitutional questions, or to statutes, is what would be an innovation, and an innovation most unwise.

There are indeed still to be found in the books some echoes of an aberration which reflects the purer Formal Style conception that law is law "and all alone, and evermore shall be so." Thus, from our Missouri current sample, where briefs had combed the libraries in order to establish the "current" understanding against which the language of certain corporate papers prepared in 1889-1891 ought to be read:

"Counsel have furnished us with a bibliography of approximately 50 texts, treatises and articles, some legal, some financial and some historical. We have read all of these which are available to us. These, we are sure, furnish a comprehensive picture of the group. *Some, being neither legal writings nor properly in evidence* (many not even being offered), *we would not consider anyway.*" (My italics.) *St. Louis S.W. Ry. Co. v. Loeb,* 318 S.W.2d 246, 255-256 (Mo. 1958).

Apart from the fact that there is ample practice (enough has been indicated above) to establish the legitimacy of introducing and of consulting such material as this dictum would reject, there are reasons first of horse sense and second of feasibility to induce even a court heretofore committed to the "pure law book" view to change its mind and its practice. To get rolling, let us remember {234} the utterly parochial background against which the whole scene develops: let us recall the nasty doctrine under which even the law of a sister-State had to be either given in evidence or else presumed identical with the common law of the forum. Our instant case expands happily from this; it opens up the use of the whole *law library,* to build background, in a brief, for the construction of a writing. But surely, in regard to description of fact, or of economic or social conditions or events, or of historical matters, or of the state of current opinion or current use of language at any time, or of business practice, or the like, the literature of the social disciplines is materially more likely to be both pertinent, accurate, and relatively complete than is that to be derived from the "law" books. The same university library offers all. How can one justify, in sense, consulting Webster or Fowler or Oxford about current or older usage in regard to the meaning of a word, and barring out a monograph on the practice or history of the clearinghouse or of marine insurance?

But the matter goes much further. Any effort at limitation to "legal" literature has for now some forty years been growing into something so arbitrary and inept as to verge on farce. Look at today's "legal" literature, the law reviews especially, but the modern good text as well, and you find the footnotes and the argument shot through with social discipline material like double-colored silk. No workable rule can keep such material out of the brief. It therefore becomes a case close to the policy of the best evidence rule: at least *let in* the original, undistorted.

Farmers' Bank, however, lights up another facet of the matter: As has been noted, Folger understood not only the concern of the produce exchange about buyer's safety in speedy turnover but also the concern of upstate bankers about their enabling discounts and their security therefor. He understood this latter so well that he was almost brusque in ruling inadmissible the evidence of "an established course of business in the trade between Buffalo and New York." Instead, he delighted to honor the care with which Buffalo counsel (legal ancestors of the later trust receipt financers) had gotten "the legal title lodged in the plaintiff, not to leave it until the payment by Brown of the draft. . . . The manner in which this transaction was to be carried out was to be determined by the papers which were made between the parties to it. If that manner differed from the established course of business, then that course was overridden by them. If it agreed with them, then evidence of it could neither make nor mar." In this, Folger — and in a case which lies outside the orbit of most {235} men's hotter convictions it is commonly enough to have a single such knowledgeable person on the court — in this, Folger shows the old danger, to counsel, of the judge who knows himself an expert. Such a judge is always a wary bird to snare; and where opinion has divided among the initiate, as in the warranty cases discussed above at pages 126 f., the expert who has already taken sides responds to the clash of battle with the fire — sometimes with the fury — of an ancient war horse; at the best he holds himself in with difficulty and may burst over at what he has come to see as claptrap or as vicious doctrine. I take it that this is one cause of the antipathy which so many great commercial judges have roused among those leading advocates who got their ears pinned back for arguing commercial nonsense.[235] On the other hand, knowledgeability on the bench can smooth the road for a sound — or a persuasive — cause; so Lehman's background in the *Jenkins* usury case, above at page 228, or Cardozo's in the incompleteness cases above at pages 115 f., 86, note 102. And whenever counsel can foresee acceptance by the court of situation-sense and -reason as he shows it, it will be a sad day if ingenuity cannot serve to add the necessary legal-technical support.

ARGUMENT: THE ART OF MAKING
PROPHECY COME TRUE

{236}

In connection with our ninth cluster of factors, adversary argument, suspicion was voiced above at page 30 that that institution may not in our present period of still mixed style and scatter of competence contribute, *for an outside observer,* to reckonability of the result of an appeal. Surely, however, this is not true with respect to estimates made by counsel who has lost below. For he can figure into the equation not only knowledge of who will be shaping and pleading his cause, but if he is to do it himself, then before he fells his final judgment, he can also figure in his own program for the purpose. What is more, if (with an eye to the twelfth, the period-style cluster) he is employing our homely but helpful techniques of prognosis, then he is in a position, no less, to put to use in the planning of his argument the observational bases of those techniques.

Here and there, in the foregoing, suggestions for advocacy have popped out and flapped their wings and loude sung cuckoo; it is time now to look that craft over in a slightly more systematic way. For it is obvious that the light we have gathered on how the appellate courts do their work is instructive on how you can help them do it — on how to help them do it in your favor. I recur indeed to one of the surer tests for whether any of this book makes sense: the fact that the skilled and successful appellate lawyers have been working always in practice and increasingly in conscious theory along just these lines. "Why," said one letter not entirely in fun, "why are you breaking into our monopoly by making our secrets public?" This can be no treatise on appellate advocacy, dear though that craft is to my heart, but a few ABC's do deserve to be set out in words, and in sequence. I quote in substance:[236] {237}

SEVEN ABC'S OF APPELLATE ARGUMENT

First, and negatively, *the Insufficiency of Technical Law: it is plainly not enough to bring in a technically perfect case on "the law"* under the authorities and *some* of the accepted correct techniques for their use and interpretation or "development." Unless the judgment you are appealing from is incompetent, there is an equally perfect technical case to be made on the other side, and if your opponent is any good, he will make it. If you are the appellee, a competently handled appeal confronts you with the same problem. The struggle will then be for *acceptance* by the tribunal of the one technically perfect view of the law as against the other. Acceptance will turn on something beyond "legal correctness." It ought to.

Second, the Trickiness of Classification: a "technically" perfect case is of itself equally unreliable in regard to the interpretation or classification of the facts. For rarely indeed do the raw facts of even a commercial transaction fit cleanly into any legal pattern; or even the "trial facts" as they emerge from conflicting testimony. No matter what the state of the law may be, if the essential pattern of the facts is not seen by the court as fitting *cleanly* under the rule you contend for, your case is still in jeopardy. This is of course the reason for the commercial counsellor's concern with "freezing" the transaction by a well drawn document which does fit cleanly into known and highly certain legal rules. But even documents can have their difficulties (especially in commercial finance). Thus, despite any and every document and the parol evidence rule, the "form" of outright sale will regularly be disregarded if oral testimony and circumstances persuade the tribunal that the "true transaction" was one for security only. Despite any document and the parol evidence rule, moreover, the "form" of legitimacy may even become an adverse factor if the tribunal from oral testimony and circumstance is led to see in that form a "mask" for usury.

Per contra, and *third,* the *Necessity of a Sound Case "in Law":* *Without a technically perfect case on the law,* under the relevant authorities and some one or more of the thoroughly correct procedures of their use and interpretation, *you have no business to expect to win* your case. Occasionally a court may under the utter need for getting a decent result go into deliberate large-scale creative effort; but few courts like to. Such effort may interfere with the court's sense of duty to the law; such effort requires in any event independent skill and labor from a hard-pressed bench. Sound advocacy therefore calls for providing in the brief a job all done to hand; sound advocacy calls as of course for not stirring {238} up any conflict, *conscious* or *unconscious,* between the court's two major duties. . . .

All of this serves only to lead up to the crux:

Fourth, the Twofold Sense and Reason: the real and vital central job is to satisfy the court that sense and decency and justice require (a) the rule which you contend for in this *type* of situation; and (b) the result that you contend for, as between these parties. *You* must make your whole case, on law and facts, make *sense,* appeal as being *obvious* sense, inescapable sense, sense in simple terms of life and justice. If that is done, the technically sound case on the law then gets rid of all further difficulty: it shows the court that its duty to the Law not only does not conflict with its duty to Justice but urges to decision along the exact same line.

. . . It is a question of making the facts talk. For of course it is the facts, not the advocate's expressed opinions, which must do the talking. The court is interested not in listening to any lawyer rant, but in seeing, or better, in discovering, from and in the facts, where sense and justice lie.

This leads to interesting corollaries:

Fifth, the Statement of Facts is the Heart: It is trite that it is in the statement of the facts that the advocate has his first, best, and most precious access to the court's attention. The court does not know the facts, and it wants to. It is trite, among good advocates, that the statement of the facts can, and should, in the very process of statement, frame the legal issue, and can, and should, simultaneously produce the conviction that there is only one sound outcome.

Sixth, Simplicity: It is as yet less generally perceived as a conscious matter that the *pattern of the facts* as stated must be a *simple* pattern, with its lines of simplicity never lost under detail; else attention wanders, or (which is as bad) the effect is drowned in the court's effort to follow the presentation or to organize the material for itself.[237]

Neither is it yet adequately perceived by most that the lines of argument just discussed lead of necessity to *maximum simplicity on the legal side* of a brief, as well. The benighted who, intoning again the pauper's saw about courts and pegs and hats, throw in point after point upon point — such manage only to scatter and waste their fire, to destroy all impact and unity of drive. As with the launching of the foredoomed appeal, this happens because counsel in question have not become clear that it is a vital matter {239} in any normal case to satisfy the court that decision their way is imperative, is at least desirable, as a matter of sense and justice; and they are still thinking and arguing as if "the relevant law" — *before* the decision, were single and clear *and in itself enough*. Whereas in truth three, two, or one good legal points of appeal (i.e., points technically correct and sound) are all that any court needs — or any lawyer — once the court gets satisfied that *this* is the way the case *ought* to, *must* come out. And each unnecessary point sins severally against:

Seventh, The Principle of Concentration of Fire: Even three points, or two, can prove troublesome as dividers of attention unless a way can be found to make them sub-points of a single simple line of attack which gains reinforcement and cumulative power from each sub-point as the latter is developed.[237a]

From this last there follows manifestly, for the respondent, the value, even the necessity, of gathering into a bunch for *joint* treatment as many as possible of such points of appeal as may seem to render a direct answer inescapable. Similarly, in any normal cause, the fourth and fifth principles practically require the respondent to produce both a positive case and his own statement of facts: it is the situation and its reason that are his refuge and his fortress, too.[238] And one may be pardoned annoyance at any seasoned lawyer who can advise the beginner to simply deal with the appellant's points as made: "He chose 'em, and he's stuck with 'em" — as if, quite apart from dispersion into impotence,[239] seven successive denials did not per se take on a flavor of essential confession.

Neither do I see any escape save in extraordinary circumstances from {240}

EIGHTH, THE OBLIGATION TO ARGUE ORALLY

The function of the oral presentation is, if that be do-able, to catch and rivet attention, to focus the issue into a single challenging question, to make the facts create ineluctable conviction as to where right lies, and to fit that conviction into a persuasive, even compelling legal frame. The brief can develop the frame; but the oral argument must get the case set into the desired frame, and for keeps. I do not see how so delicate a task can responsibly be left to paper when an accepted institutional pattern offers a way of dealing with the tribunal face to face. In oral argument lies counsel's one hedge against misdiagnosis and misperformance in the brief, the one last chance of locating a postern missed in the advance survey. In oral argument lies the opportunity to catch attention and rouse interest among men who must be got to read — or to reread — *this* brief not as a routine duty nor under the undiscriminating press of other business, but with the pointed concentration *this* cause merits.

148

Finally, the oral argument is the one chance for *you* (not for some chance-assigned mere judge) to answer any questions you can stir any member of the court into being bothered about and into bothering with, and the one chance to sew up each such question into a remembered point in favor. By the same token, in the measure that this court has the practice of leaning heavily on either the reporting judge, or the chief,[240] or both, or on the court's expert in the field, in that same measure the oral argument gives you your one direct access to the whole team together.

In any but freak situations, oral argument is a must.[240a]

* * *

Three more notes, all long sounding here in overtones, it will be as well to strike directly and singly before we delve into the {241} craft and craftsmanship of those appellate courts whose practices and less standardized behavior we have thus far been observing with an advocate's concern, an advocate's emphasis, perhaps with an advocate's avidity.

The first is what I see as another principle, perhaps not an ABC, but a thing too often grievously slighted:

NINTH, THE PROFFERED, PHRASED, OPINION-KERNEL

If a brief has made the case for what is right, and has made clear the reason of the rightness, and has found and tailored and displayed the garment of law to clothe the right decision fittingly, then it is not only unwise but indecent not to furnish also in that brief a page or two of text which gathers this all together, which clears up its relation to the law to date, which puts into clean words the soundly guiding rule to serve the future, and which shows that rule's happy application to the case in hand. What is wanted is a passage which can be quoted verbatim by the court, a passage which so clearly and rightly states and crystallizes the background and the result that it is *recognized* on sight as doing the needed work and as practically demanding to be lifted into the opinion.[241]

The wisdom, for counsel, of supplying such a passage is obvious. There is the matter of crystallization. An argument can slowly bring a court into a condition like an overchilled windless fjord; such a passage, *recognized,* can firm and fix the whole with the abruptness of the one thrown stone. When the argument has not got quite so far along — or across — then a clean wording of the whole-in-context is a reinforcing stroke which may drive the spike clean home. Finally, if the case is one which concerns the future (as in the foreign remittance cases, or any test case, or any case in a planned series or which is hoped to lay a solid foundation for future counseling), your *own* cleaning up of the authorities to date is the best way toward assurance that they will not rise and haunt, your *own* clean phrasing of the rule for the situation is the best way toward assurance that that rule will take full account of Goldschmidt's immanent law. For it takes more {242} than sap-filled fresh persuadedness to yield seasoned rule-timber that will not warp, and more than the lessons of a single argument to underpin balance in judgment and in the needed measure, and to insure those more cleanly phrasings which avoid misleading suggestion about matters not directly before the court.

This last is a matter which can be demonstrated, and which is worth demonstrating. We have already met two pertinent situations. The one is Cardozo's ten-year campaign, begun in 1914, to render standard in the reading of a commercial document the full use of its commercial background and of general commercial sense. In 1921, as noted earlier,[242] he had lined up the court on a platform along these lines which avoided past error and made goal and method explicit. One judge, Crane, a recent arrival, had held out. But by the time of the *Sun Printing* case in 1923 Crane had become converted in the way an advocate hopes and prays that he may convert his court; Crane's dissent in that case goes into battle with the gusto of the Lionheart and the canny resourcefulness of a Hannibal.[243] Its only trouble is misjudgment about whither to go. The written agreement had provided for "price and length of terms" to be agreed, "in no event to be higher than the contract price for newsprint charged by the Canadian Export Company to the large consumers." It was the buyer who was suing for nondelivery, and what was in issue was the sufficiency of a complaint which gave no light at all on the pricing practices of the Canadian company. Cardozo's opinion for the majority is labored and unsatisfactory; he was working on a corrective angle which was new to his crusade; but what he did rightly feel and convey was that he who wishes to rely on commercial background to fill out an agreement has the job of providing the commercial background which is needed, and that specifics are not for the court to supply. The point for us is that Crane, though blazing with the new faith, missed out on where to point his lance. It was Crane, again, who in the foreign remittance cases accepted with a whole heart counsel's instruction about the nature of the business, but whose still unseasoned learning {243} led him in *Legniti* into stressing almost exclusively a "sale" rather than a "contract" analysis, even though the Statute of Frauds danger was already in the picture for any man whose knowledge had matured.[244]

But the matter is one not of a person, nor of a particular court, but one general to mankind. Below, for instance, at page 317, we ran across Loreburn's blurring and semiblotting of the grand c.i.f. picture which Kennedy had painted and which Loreburn, with enthusiasm, was trying to accept in entirety. In our present context the concurrence of Shaw of Dunfermline is ironically eloquent. Two other Lords have simply agreed with the Chancellor. Shaw now wishes to "express my adherence to the opinion" not of Loreburn, but "of *Kennedy, L.J.* . . . the value of which has not been overstated by the noble Earl on the Woolsack."[245] Your trouble as an advocate, even when you manage to educate the court as successfully as Kennedy did the House of Lords, is that the Loreburns far outnumber the Shaws, and that it is likely to be a Crane or a Loreburn who will write for the court. So put a proper opinion-kernel into your brief, to invite lifting.

This is, let me repeat, not a question of the writing judge's brains, nor of his general vision, nor of his general stature as a judge. It is a question of the extreme rarity, even among great men, of ability to smell out fine but significant distinctions and possibilities in an area in which they are still, technically, freshmen. Let me therefore finish with an illustration in which it is Brandeis himself who juggles and muffs. Before the sugar-bubble of 1920 burst, some of the purveyors to the speculators had had sense enough to get from their buyers banker's letters of credit by which a banker engaged to make due payment, against described shipping documents, of the sales price of described shipments. In *Lamborn v. National Bank of Commerce*, 276 U.S. 469, 48 S. Ct. 378 (1928), the suit was on such a credit, which contained the term "*Shipment . . . from Java by Steamer or Steamers to Philadelphia*" (my italics), though the bills of lading called for were to be f.o.b. *rail* at that city. The steamer on which the tendered sugar arrived had been originally bound for New York; it was diverted to Philadelphia just before arrival, in order that tender might be made within the time. Brandeis now led the majority into holding that the condition of "*shipment*

. . . *to* Philadelphia" was satisfied by this ninth-inning shift, {244} which, though lamentable law, is understandable, for the case had been superbly argued for Lamborn.[246] What makes our point is Brandeis' obtuseness in the opinion to certain facts and expertise before his eyes. For Hough — of all judges! — had written an opinion about another batch of that same sugar, under a contract with the same shipment term. His case, however, had been one between the seller and not the bank but the buyer, and Hough's decision (affirming, incidentally, and explicitly leaning on Learned Hand) had been that certain clauses of the *buyer's* contract *which were not in the letter of credit of the bank* were enough to control the situation and to make the tender good.[247] But it is a basic principle of letter of credit law that the frequent presence of such clauses plus the general unavailability to the bank of the facts about the seller's performance make it utterly unsafe to reason from the sales contract to the letter of credit; indeed, Hough had taken pains to underline that his decision and opinion did not touch the seller's right on the letter of credit, which, said Hough, the master of commercial law, raised very different questions. It is on that strange basis that Brandeis chose to announce his comfort, as against Stone's four-judge dissent, that the Brandeis conclusion was "supported by" the Second Circuit. The example shows the majority captured if not captivated by counsel, and roped into a misviewing of the relevant situation-type. The manner of that goes to our general point about the way in which an appellate argument can inform the court; and the argument had been built with skill and care to seem to rest on essential reason in the situation. But the example is even more directly in point to our immediate and narrower issue: Brandeis thought he was leaning on and resting on Hough, and he must have known Hough's standing in the field. But it was a field in which Brandeis had no background with which to read; so he mistook and misstated a major and vital feature of the Hough position.[248]

The tendered opinion-kernel offers a hope of hedge against this type of slip.

Now it is true that counsel's task in the run of cases is to win this case for this client, not to improve the law. The feature {245} of a truly right rule for the future is thus to be neither demanded nor expected if the client's case will or might be disserved thereby. Let the matter therefore be reformulated thus: insofar as the client's cause admits of including such a rule in the tendered opinion-kernel, the provision thereof is not only an opportunity but a duty which is double; for then no device can more powerfully forward the client's cause.

TENTH, SITUATION-SENSE IS PRIME

The second note to strike is a reminder, brief but sharp, that the sense of the type-situation, where it can be tapped, outranks and outshines any "fireside" stuff. It has been mentioned that situation-reason can normally come with credentials (though of course under handicap) even though no material has been inserted into the record below. It has also been suggested, and should now be stated roundly, that the strain and pull on emotion and on the sense for justice which a type-situation can exert has a flavor and effect like that of a smooth but strong ocean current in contrast to an undertow. Its steady pull may go unnoticed, in any event it is unresented and can readily go unresisted, for it speaks to what is the right rule of law, or the right legal concept, or the right application or a wise extension or limitation or subdivision: these are things traditionally proper for argument, and for pondering, in terms of probable results outside the immediate case; they are flavored with the court's own judicial quest for wisdom, they are familiar, their help is welcome. Against this, the passion or sentimentality of the particular case is as disturbing or upsetting as an undertow, an appellate judge feels moved to, and does, lean and dig in against it, if he can. It may prevail, yes; but it is not an advocate's business to jam resistors into his chosen circuit.

The third "note" is, I fear, a whole melody. It harks back to the theory of rules and to the truth that rules of law are very, very much unlike one another. What is to be said bites two ways at once, but will be treated here only from the side of differential obstruction to the appellate lawyer's cause. It is, however, self-evident that the more trouble an authority makes to him who would avoid it, the more help it promises to his opponent. {246}

ELEVENTH, THE SINGING REASON OR ESTABLISHED RULE AGAINST YOU: CONFESSION AND AVOIDANCE

To begin with, then, a rule with a singing reason (above, pp. 183 f., 186), is by definition both well designed to purpose and unmistakably so. Such a rule gives handhold for direct avoidance only on the matter of application; but the scope clause is also, by definition, drawn with skill, so that the zone of leeway is strait and the line of argument pretty well given. Radical departure from the rule itself, absent cataclysmic change in conditions, is hard to conceive; a radical bulging or constriction for the pending case is also a forlorn hope. But one way does open to invention: if the backdrop can be shifted, if the whole stage can be set against a different background and lighting to gain completely different meaning,[249] then maybe. But that takes genius or inspiration. One instance is enough to show the method. Consider the Workmen's Compensation Acts after the Constitutional uproar was over and the courts, accepting the policy, had begun to interpret the coverage, and "out-of-and-*in-the-course-of*" was mushrooming out to cover any injury which took place within skunk-smell of the factory or the job. Rule and reason were singing a duet — until poetic frenzy touched some defendant's lawyer and he steadied the limelight squarely on "*out-of-and*": words which became dominant forthwith, to shrink the coverage.[250] In a nonstatutory area there can be no such recourse to an accidental and controlling phrase to thus reverse a whole tide; yet a portion of the current can be split off, by fresh insight, to make an eddy that will serve, or the lighting can be shifted.

The case is not greatly different when the rule of the field is unchallengeable not for its beauty but because of its sheer unquestioned thereness. I do not refer to a rule such as that on pre-existing duty and consideration, which is indeed in the main unchallengeable, but which has over much of its scope come into such obloquy that some artifice of evasion is almost expected, and probably welcome. I refer rather to a rule accepted as elementary or too well established for discussion and which has *not* been under overt re-examination and attack, and which the court {247} as thus far advised is quite willing to employ without thinking and in straight routine. Here, too, the approach by way of reasoned distinction and subdivision is as old as good law. *Qui bene distinguit bene decernit.* Thus the rules on the surety's defenses used to be not only rigid, but proverbial: "*strictissimi juris*"; "the chancellor's darling." Then somebody found and sold a slogan — not too apt a one, either — "compensated surety," and opened up a new subdivision; another somebody buttoned that phase up with "really an insurer." Or for a more modern instance one may take the "layaway" plan and its bearing on "seller's retention of possession" in a state which still holds to the rule that such retention is flatly fraudulent against creditors. For the class of layaway buyers, as against a levying creditor, I should see a reasoned subclassification as offering more than a fighting chance, no matter how traditionally iron the past language and attitude of the court. Say thus: "The whole rule rests on fraud, and on a policy against fraud; it standardizes the mere *chance* of fraud by not only presuming fraud but rendering the presumption conclusive. But it would go beyond reason and bearability to give even a fingerhold to the idea of fraud in layaway when, as here, the dealer has for years *advertised* its layaway plan. This is not a secret sale, not a covert mortgage; it is not even a display of inventory, which might conceivably mislead. These goods are not even in the salesroom to be seen; and the books, too, show them to be held as mere security for accounts. And, above all, the whole public has for five years been apprised of every fact. . . ." Whether a court takes this or leaves it, in such a situation it is such an appeal against such a rule which is the kind of indirect attack, the kind of drive toward a complete fresh lighting of the scene, of which I have been speaking.[251]

A related but really different way of dealing with the ingrained rule is by the side step or the back door, a method not open with a true singing rule, because the latter could not sing unless it had been custom-fitted to its proper application. The parol evidence rule — Wigmore's "rule of integration" — will serve as an example. It rests firm on age and on authority, but also on basic sense. But advocates have urged with success that its scope and reason do not extend to terms of a sort which in the circumstances can normally be omitted from the writing; or that words "plain" on their face can yet be set against a background of special usage that fills them out with other than their {248} "plainest" meaning; or that the prior or contemporaneous agreements in hand are not barred by the document from a hearing, but instead show the document never to have become operative or to be vitiated by fraud or mistake. When such arrangements have succeeded often enough to form rules, they result less in subcategories than in limitations on the rule's scope; they offer, for a favorable set of facts, a way to skirt the rule and come in by a "back door" (Patterson's good phrase).

The most amusing instance I know deserves to be sketched because it illustrates, in passing, how nonuniversal are our principles of the crafts — this time, of appellate advocacy. In a cash market involving delivery by rail, the seller has been plagued by the danger that the buyer might repudiate without good cause and then trump up a suit for breach, using the merchandise to obtain jurisdiction and local jury-prejudice to win a verdict, and finally buying in the merchandise on sheriff's sale for the proverbial song. To collect the price, and to retain security-control over the shipment until the price is paid, the seller draws his draft on the buyer, attaching an order bill of lading for the contract-wares. To insulate himself against any attachment (whether of the wares or of the bill of lading or of the proceeds of the draft), the seller has then commonly proceeded to discount the draft with his own banker, who in any such suit against the seller will intervene as "bona fide purchaser" and owner, seeking thus to defeat jurisdiction. Both the earliest cases and the most modern ones honor the seller's banker as such a bona fide purchaser of the documents, commonly dubbing him, at counsel's instigation, a "holder in due course." Seller's counsel has thus been very widely successful, with applause of that result from all and sundry (including me), but by way of a legal argument which, as appears in the margin, holds as little water as a sieve.[252] But I do not believe it would do buyer's counsel one jot of good to expose the technical emptiness of the standard seller's theory. This is one case — almost the only case I know — where I think it predictable that almost any court would bull its way through to {249} the same result, even though the accepted old legal theory should be blown up in its face. For the real issue is wholly different, and is clear enough: Why may not the seller, *when he has carefully so contracted* ("cash against documents"), why may he not, by way of his bank, first get tentative payment ("the sinews of war") in advance of inspection, and then force any controversy about his performance into his home forum? Buyer's counsel have therefore, it seems to me, been well enough advised in trying the side step: granting full rights to any *real* bona fide purchaser, this claimant bank is no such person, but a "*mere* agent for collection," with the bank's own exemptions from liability and its own charge-back clauses as evidence against any "true" and "absolute" "purchase." My interest here is not in the state of the law but in the method of the side step; and above all in how the method was directed not against the seller's vulnerable legal theory, but, by force of the very acceptance of that untenable law-position of the seller, against the guts of his sense-position.[253]

The last item I shall stop to mention here goes perhaps less directly to rules of law than to the concepts which enter into and also generate rules. The item is a warning and a hope rolled into one: again and again the advocate's escape from a threatening concept-label is by way of attention to the *purpose* for which the concept was invoked in the cited case or cases, in juxtaposition and contrast to the unmistakably different demands of the case in hand. One might have hoped, for instance, to persuade even a word-minded court to whom toads are toads and trusts are just trusts that a "trust", had been "impressed" in the *Legniti* case in the Appellate Division (above, p. 210) "not because the transaction in general is at all in the nature of a trust, any more than a general deposit in a bank is, but because — just as with a bank — it is a fraud to accept money on the actual eve of insolvency, knowing the insolvency, and under a promise to execute the transaction that very night. Etc. Whereas in the instant case we have a contract extending over a possible four months, etc." Some such process of thought did occur, for the Appellate Division decided the *Equitable* case before the Court of Appeals had had a chance to reverse the *Legniti* trust impressment; and {250} what was done was, quietly, to recur to the *Strohmeyer* treatment of the cable transfer contract as one for sale without even mentioning *Legniti* (decided less than a year before), much less *Legniti's* explicit confinement of *Strohmeyer* "to its exact facts."

The road can be rough, to escape from either a threatening concept or its bastard negative implication. Some judges rather easily follow Juliet: "A rose by any other name would smell as sweet"; but to some "A rose is a rose is a rose." One recalls Cuthbert Pound in *Canavan:* If the city *sold* the water, he did not see how to escape the warranty of wholesomeness. In the same context court after court has worked with much more woodenness in the reverse direction. "If sale, then warranty" has at least the color of compulsion. But the twin proposition often put forward: "If no sale, then no warranty," springs from no holy wedlock; and here one contrasts sharply a flat formal result of no recovery in warranty because the ice cream with the broken glass was only served, not sold, with the use of the same technical out because to the court recovery seems simply outrageous as against a restaurateur who has in good faith served canned peas of a reputable brand, or with refusal to extend the sales rule by analogy because — as the court sees it — the warranty rule, though made binding by the Sales Act, is harsh against nonmanufacturers and should not be carried beyond the legislature's clear purpose. Indeed it is quite possible, by similar thinking, to find that even in an unmistakable sale there can be no reasonableness in a buyer's reliance on a seller-dealer in regard to the contents of a reputably branded package which is sold in good faith and in good condition. The merits of any of such variations are not the present concern; only the methods: (1) the application of the concept-consequence by "the sound," in Mansfield's term, without reference to the sense; or else the similar application or nonapplication of a bastard twin rule.[254] In contrast, one sees and urges (2) application, extension, distinction, or restriction explicitly because of situation-sense as one may be able to bring the court to reach that sense — a technique which then, because it has been used openly to purpose, will be observed to remain easy of revision as further purpose may appear.

TWELFTH, THE UNDETERMINABLE SELECTION OF JUDGES

Let me turn from all of these more obvious suggestions for appellate advocacy to wrestle with a perplexity presented increasingly {251} by the appellate courts today: the preparation of a brief without knowledge of which selection of judges will come to hear the cause. The combinations of three in a well-staffed Federal Circuit, even when there is no enlargement from the district court or from outside, can result in appallingly different courts. Combinations of four from a bench of seven, as in Oregon, or of five from a bench of nine, as in Mississippi, can yield two courts with only a single common member. Even fives from a seven-man bench, as in Massachusetts, can face an advocate with teasers: consider the fate of the *Peter Cooper's Glue* case, discussed above at pages 115 f., when one certain judge, Cardozo, turned up missing on the panel. Indeed wherever an argument hinges on understanding of some type of situation which lies outside of such experience as, like driving a car or the party system or the Christmas season, comes to most Americans in the sheer process of survival to maturity, the advocate must be alert for the ear which can take the novel in with empathy and for the tongue which can make the fruits of empathy persuasive.

Or there may be on the court some member who already knows the little area or quirk of our culture which is the crux — or thinks he does; and his presence may be as welcome as the flowers in May, or else as a torpedo to a gas tanker. If he has real grasp and has also tact and standing with his colleagues he would, if you knew he would be sitting, represent the bull's-eye for the brief; but if his competence shows less in shrewdly directed persuasion than in arrogant say-so or bluster, he is a peril to navigation; and if his "knowledge" consists in truth of impenetrable misconception, then he mines your channel of approach: remember Paige in the early warranty series (above, p. 126).

To complete the perplexity, even where the personnel of the bench may be known, there is, in quite a number of courts, the assignment of the case before argument, but to a person no brief-writer can foresee. Practice differs, of course, as to how thoroughly the other judges go into cases which they are not reporting; that may also turn more on accident or occasion than on practice. Meanwhile the weight carried by the reporting judge varies of necessity somewhat with his standing on the matter of general judgment and workmanship, and somewhat with his skill in presentation; with any case of reasonably neutral character, for instance, its very statement by a reporting Davis or Hughes ought to be worth at least a couple of votes; in addition, the recommendation of a man known to be sound and careful is not lightly disregarded. {252}

Where the bench which will sit can be determined, it goes without saying that that is the bench to write for. But there is one qualification: if before the opinion becomes final it is circulated also among the members of the court who will not sit, and if the court's practice is for those members to take some active interest in those communications, then the selection and phrasing of positions and especially the proffered opinion-kernel must be wary, even though it may be expected to woo the sitting bench, lest anything in it shock or jolt any other member of the court into participation. For one must remember that the man or judge who is stirred out of being a sleeping dog comes awake with a growl and a mission, and even with some investment of face in establishing that he is not being officious; add that he can seek adherents among men who have neither heard your argument nor read your brief, so that a rehearing en banc may find the fresh personnel already somewhat set in opposition.

Here is, indeed, in principle the whole tactic of approach to the indeterminable panel: on the negative side, to avoid offense, irritation, estrangement, and to reach eyes or ears which may be dull or resistant to the desired point or mistake it, one has to canvass the whole of the bench on the chance that one or all of the most troublesome may get into the act. On the positive side, the substance and manner of the thrust of the cause, one must fall back on the old principles that the quieter form and manner speak as forcefully to the forward-driving man as they do to the holder-backer, and that there are few novel ideas with juice which a good tailor and some pains with manners cannot make acceptable in polite society, and on the old wisdom that he wins double support who wins it in unexpected quarters. The one tactic which becomes prohibitively perilous when one does not know who will hear the cause is that of the discard: the deliberate sacrifice of a couple of votes in order to gain a concentration and drive which are planned to build certain particular votes into a safe majority.

Once these principles are firm in the fist, every other principle of argument remains, and comes to bear, in terms merely of substituting the whole bench for the particular panel as the personnel to be addressed, except that one cannot count on and capitalize the presence (and, one hopes, the consequent aid) of those judges who can most readily be made to see where right and good law lie. It thus needs no saying that oral argument becomes indispensable, so to speak, to the second power. An appellate advocate needs at least one chance to center his fire upon {253} a completely concrete target. It is plain, too, that situation-sense becomes if anything more essential to make utterly unmistakable in the brief. It is plain that the demand rises for simplicity in regard to both the law-picture and that of fact. For it is the least favorable prospect on the court to whom things must be ready to become clear, and to become clear not only with regard to sense but also with regard to the rule which fits that sense.

Let us try to work out an example. Here is a university which has accepted a huge bequest for the purpose of building and carrying on an even more hugely expensive ultraexperimental school, so that with rising prices it finds the experiment running a troublesome deficit, while consolidation into its less expensive (though still expensive) "model modern" school will both increase the latter's capacity and eliminate that deficit, too. The law of the state permits the Attorney General to restrain a charitable corporation from diverting a bequest from its appointed purpose. The embattled experimental parents and alumni are the relators, and you are their counsel. But universities are highly respectable, and their good faith wears epaulettes, and distinguished experts will testify for the substantial identity of purpose and method in the two schools, and on any direct attack the technical morass of their jargon will be enough to bog a charging mastodon. Your one hope is to get the guts across not only in terms a lawyer can understand but also on a terrain where a lawyer feels himself a better expert than any professional "Education" expert: to wit, by way of the analogy of legal education. For "the case system" was once progressive, and is today still "modern and model," and it has rich emotional overtones; but every student did have his personal touch of trouble with it. Which looks good, except that on your court, let us assume, sit also one judge who went to no law school at all, and two who went to night schools that employed practically no cases and mostly practitioner-teachers; and we shall assume further that they are touchy on the subject, or do not view overtheoretical legal education with favor, or have ideas about the social value of poor working boys' access to the profession, or the like. You may draw one, two, or all three of them on your panel of five.

The law side of the cause is not hard; the key concept and slogan are that of significant departure from a purpose appointed by the donor in terms and in those terms accepted by the university. The juice lies then in the type-situation and its meaning: American education in motion, with need for experiment {254} if we are to find progress. Our principle requires that the three non-case-trained judges be not nettled, indeed that they be enlisted in the thrust, if that can be. Maybe this is manageable if "modern and model" education be seen as like "the case system" today, but "experimental" education be something different enough to require a distinct, a separate enterprise, seeking to retain the virtues, for example, of the modern case system while yet (say via much problem-teaching and stress on the theory of the legal crafts) recapturing some of the virtues of those older styles of legal education which "the case system" has too sharply and indeed too completely displaced. I should hope to make a whole court or any panel of it come to see how devastating to needed progress and how significantly gross a "departure" it would be to cancel out such a specifically oriented experiment by merging it into any mere "modern and model" institution; and I should hope that the Educational experts' testimony to the contrary would then sink in its own technical slough, seen by any panel of the court as the meretricious issue-dodging quibble it would be.

Even granting effective practicability in such an argument, however, note how it depends upon the assumption that the law phase of the cause is simple. For if that phase, also, should come wrapped with barbed wire, the odds would be heavy against being able, in a single brief, to surmount the two at once; although counsel could perhaps take heart from an opinion like that in *St. Joseph's Hospital v. Bennett,* 281 N.Y. 115, 22 N.E.2d 305 (1939), where the court (though over a two-judge dissent) seems to me to have worked out, almost without help from argument, a rule pretty much like the one postulated for our example.

* * *

One item remains for meditation regarding our indeterminable panel: how does this condition affect not the mode of any argument but the decision whether to press an appeal at all? For plainly the outcome, as estimated from the date of judgment below, must be taken as less favorable (you *may* get the worst possible grouping) and also as less certain (your argument to undetermined personnel *cannot* be as clean and strong) than would be the case if you knew who was to hear you.

To me the effect seems rather clear. (1) Any appeal is more chancy. This cuts down the class of appeals which can be seen as excellent risks; and as one moves into the region where the prospect is more dubious, the "indeterminable" panel gains extra {255} weight against a recommendation to appeal as the stake at issue dwindles. (2) Any appeal is indeed more chancy. This means that if the stake is high, a recommendation to appeal may be made where one might hesitate to make it if the tribunal were fully designate — for you *may* get the best possible grouping.

CONCLUSIONS FOR COURTS

{256}
It would be strange, and it would be lamentable, if as extensive a study of any law-craft as the present should come out with no suggestions with regard to tightening and sharpening the craft-procedures, certainly so in this day when articulation of working craft philosophies has been so overlong in hibernation. The traceable experience is so rich. So much of it has been informed with wisdom. Some items along this line have surely turned up for gathering into order. There is, for example,

1. The Curse upon Illegitimate Authority Techniques, Whether of Omission or of Commission

Deliberately to turn the back upon a pertinent but uncomfortable authority, leaving it unmentioned and therefore leaving the question open as to how the matter now really stands, this is sin against the nature of our case law. Take again our three Appellate Division cable transfer cases.[255] The first, on agreed facts, talked and ruled "sale." The second, the eve of bankruptcy case, confined the first to its exact facts, and ruled "deposit" and "trust." Within a year the third, a "buyer's" default on a contract to take £20,000 sterling in the future, reverted to "sale" as if neither of the prior cases had been decided. A sophisticated reader could indeed on this basis build a pattern of probability to govern a possible fourth case, and even a counseling chart of legal perils to avoid and the manner of their avoidance; but it is outrage, without need, for the third case to confront any bar with such a mess.[256]

Nor is there need. Today no person feels The Law to wobble when a case that is obsolete is laid to rest, or when one which {257} was a blob is corrected, nor does face require a court to pose as the Voice of Infallibility, nor yet does open overruling *for sufficient shown cause* either shock or dismay. It is not the occasional overt overruling of older doctrine which is cankering the confidence of counselor and advocate, it is the quag-footing of the everyday, the felt par-lousness of any hold at all for hand or foot, since the mere words upon the page, when read just as doctrine, do deceive, and since so many still grope and stumble, blind as yet to the fact and nature of the real reckonabilities in the courts' work. One can almost urge that a frank overruling, when it does crop up, brings with it something of relief: that point, at least, can for a while be counted on as clear. What is certain is that the embarrassment which the Formal Style once caused in regard to facing up to a fractious authority is no longer percepti-ble in the reports. Indeed it is interesting, as one runs through my current samplings, to see how often *recent* explicit overrulings are dealt with as normal — and the new rule then applied — and how any inadvertent inconsistencies, once noticed, are recited, carefully examined, and then cleared up, whether the older[257] or the newer[258] of the inconsistent rulings be preferred. With the currency of this kind of open operation it is plain that the courts no longer feel pressed, as a matter of face, to cover up the authority which is being deliberately readied for the waste bin. It is significant that the cable transfer illustration is already more than two legal generations old, that the intentional *sub silentio* overrulings often enough rehearsed and followed in the samplings date also regularly from an earlier day, and that unintentional inconsistencies, when they come to attention, are so often dealt with openly, in terms of sense, and straightened out.

Yet the picture may not be all as solid as it seems. My brother Meltzer, on reading a goodly portion of the MSS, guided me to a pair of recent Illinois cases which come out on two sides of what seems at least on the surface to be a single issue, the question whether a court's witness must be an eyewitness. Each cites a line of authorities ignored by the other. The two were before the court at the same time, but neither mentions the other, {258} though they were born to be "companion cases" and to clear up an area which has been in confusion for some forty years.[259]

We have here a phenomenon almost as troubling to the bar as deliberate secret overruling. Reliance on authorities is placed in doubt. O.K.; if reason and sense do not square with the authorities in your case, you simply have to learn not to lean too hard on those authorities. But candor of the court is placed in doubt. That is *not* O.K. What becomes of this assurance the opinion is supposed by the learned German and by Chief Justice Simmons[260] to give to losing counsel and his client that the hearing and deliberation have been lawful and fair? It is therefore not only its credit for candor, it is its credit for fairness, which a court throws into jeopardy when it thus suppresses in an opinion all mention of a pertinent authority which has been pointedly called to its attention. Neither is this a matter on which a losing lawyer is nonvocal; he bays the moon, for months. Disturbed by the discovery, I instituted during the last stages of completing the MSS a canvass of the losing briefs in the cases reported in 13 Ill. 2d, to see whether relevant and cogent authorities, insisted on in the brief, had yet been so ignored in the opinion as to leave doctrine in hidden confusion. Fifty consecutive briefs yielded not one instance in which I think losing counsel to have any solid ground to feel his point to have been ignored.[261]

This gives comfort. For we have here a court of power. As is made plain in the sampling presented in Appendix A, the court is in general working entirely in the modern manner of recapture of the grand tradition, and in general with the openness appropriate thereto. Its proportion of straight cites to any other form of citation at all ran in our single sample 2½ to 1: a careful interest in and reliance on the precedents. Out of 163 simple cites checked, only 9 proved to be to dicta and only 2 did not seem to fit: a batting average of .935. When even such a court indulges such a fault as appears in the "court's witness" series below, page 450, one fears it may be turning up elsewhere, too, and one is driven into both inquiry and campaign against its continuance.

A possible key to cause seems to me revealed in the history of this court's witness matter, the one instance which I have followed {259} in detail. It is quite clear in those cases that over the years the court has followed a strikingly consistent implicit pattern, one as cleanly to be *felt* as are, according to repute, the Home Office's unexpressed action-premises on commutation and pardon in capital cases. It is also plain that the court has not yet happened on a satisfying way of putting its felt lines of operation into words. It seems to me obvious that what we have is a simple case of needless embarrassment: this court, like the other courts, has ceased to feel that it must appear godlike or priestlike on the point of infallibility, and feels no impairment of office or loss of face in recognizing old error by an overruling; but it is still caught in a more lowly human type of worry over face. It does not wish to appear technically incompetent by failing to state in clear words the clearly felt basis of its decision. I find most significant the fullness and care with which, throughout this particular long double line of cases, the facts are set forth which persuade of the reasonableness of the various particular rulings; also the fact that one can see the ultimate rationale of discrimination in unmistakable, though dragging, process of shaping up.

But what I cannot understand is why, in any such problem area, with the first case to offer trouble or with any subsequent one, it is not possible to say: "We did indeed hold . . . and we said . . . But the present case is not one to which that policy seems applicable. Here the situation is . . . The line of discrimination may not as yet be clear in general, but it is characteristic of our law, in such a situation, to feel out the way case by case. The instant case falls clearly inside [or outside] the line." Of such an attack, three things can be predicated, two of them certain and one of them likely. First, the mere bringing of such a puzzle to repeatedly open expression will focus the court's own thought, especially the subconscious between-cases fireless-cooker "thought," in such fashion as to materially speed the capture into words of a workable solution. That is certain. In addition, second, it is likely that such expression, especially if repeated, will stir and enlist supplementary labor and suggestion from the scholarly fraternity; which, if it happens, offers hope. Third, and again certain: to substitute this type of frankness for suppression of the uncomfortable authority is to give the bar footing not only for confidence in general, and for more careful work if ever the point recurs, but also for more solid work on any other brief on any other point. We *must* not forget that to have a real authority ignored leaves a lawyer gasping: it goes to care, it goes to competence, it goes to fairness, it goes to responsibility, it leads {260} to rumor. I have said above, and say again, I find it hard to conceive of any more devastating example of Bentham's "second order" of harm from an offense.

What is thus true of willful disregard of authorities holds with bothersome but lesser strength for deliberate fiat misattribution and for perverse fiat evisceration. My own favorite horror-piece is ancient and English. There had been a sale of a certain "ship" for £4200. At the time of the transaction she lay, unbeknownst to either party, helplessly stranded on the other side of the North Atlantic; she sold for salvage "as she lay," after survey, for £10. The jury found she was not, when sold to the buyer in the case, a "ship," and the plaintiff had a verdict for breach of covenant. In *Barr v. Gibson,* 3 M. & W. 390 (Ex. 1838), a new trial was ordered, Parke, B., writing: There was no warranty of condition, seaworthiness, etc., and while the verdict would have sustained the judgment in the amount of the price, "the verdict was wrong." The decision was commercial barbarism, was at odds in tone and substance with the decisions of the Common Pleas and even of the King's Bench, and typified the obtuse perversity of Parke's Exchequer. Thirty years later, in *Jones v. Just,* L.R. 3 Q.B. 197 (1868), Mellor is establishing a seller's obligation for merchantability of hemp sold "expected to arrive," as being supposedly a matter of unchallenged existing law. *Barr v. Gibson* lies across the road like a tree trunk. Mellor removes it this way: "Secondly, where there is a sale of a definite existing chattel *specifically described, the actual condition of which is capable of being ascertained by either party* [!!], there is no implied warranty: *Barr v. Gibson*" (p. 202; my italics). The indecency of such distortion shocks, it is inexcusable. But once again, this has ceased to be a current sin. For instance, it will be recalled that our back-check samplings, some of them from material as early as 1939 and 1940, show almost no trace of such misattribution.

2. Constant Overt Use of Situation-Sense

In lovely contrast, there has been developing the felt need for conscious and reasoned recourse, on each needed occasion, to situation-sense as a guide for testing, for phrasing, for redirecting the applicable rule or principle: the steady and required judicial review of prior judicial decision. This need, with its relatively common fulfillment today, has been hammered in our study until a reader may threaten to rebel. The way of it has been illustrated, too, I hope, almost as Gény illustrated his simple and {261} glorious formula for handling the Code: until the technique moved into the reader's fingers, no longer making call upon the brain. What has not been hammered, however, but what ought to have equal hammering, is that this way of work is not suggested as a cure-all. It is not a cure-all. No technique or method can ever be a cure-all. I have indeed tried again and again to underscore the value of the method *even where the particular job may have been badly muffed,* even where the particular jobs may be muffed frequently. For such instances, singly or in gross, the cure lies in the sixth principle: On-going Recorrection. But no correction, no sound reappraisal, much less a recorrection, can hope to open its possibilities unless the court's recourse to situation-sense, as best the court can see the same, is both conscious and constant *and canny.*

Above, in addressing the advocate, much play was made with the legitimacy and the need for spreading before the court the nature and rightness of the chosen situation-type, for making sure that the court was led to live its way into an understanding and empathy which would enable it to *recognize* the situation's immanent law, and gladly so. I tried, moreover, in the New York usury instance,[261a] to exemplify how even in a single case counsel's skill could paint a picture with an *appeal* that could take on the guise of eternal or at least sound legislative principle. On this a court needs to keep itself awake. Roughly speaking, the best safeguard against counsel's mispainting lies in visualizing the hands-and-feet operations in the picture, seen as a going scheme, a working setup. Such operating aspects are curiously hard to fake; one thinks of the standard advice of the old story-book detective to his junior: forget the impression, look at the *"roots"* of the "beard."[261b] Fake-work has of course peculiar access to the appellate judicial mind because real situation-knowledge and real situation-sense is in this world of specialization at once so hard to come by and so welcome. But when this has been said, it leaves untroubled the deeper solidity: better be fooled on occasion by fake sense than starve by foregoing the manna {262} which only situation-sense can offer. Nor do I find, as I observe and read, that our appellate courts are unduly easy to bamboozle.

I should like, however, at somewhat more length than its current importance in the State courts may deserve, and for reasons which will appear, to explore one special corner of such help from counsel. There is, in this day of organization, public relations, subliminal stimuli, and general pressures, one phenomenon of peculiar concern to the appellate court. I refer to the managed series of educational cases, judiciously selected — even at times arranged — to bring a court or the courts along by gentle stages of understanding and of doctrinal growth until, all unbeknownst to any participant except the managers, a whole new area of law has come into existence, in all its grandeur or lopsided devilry or consolidation of some fighting position, under the hand and to the use and behoof of the aforesaid managers. Of such case series we shall in my judgment see more in the future than we have in the past, and some of them will I think be occupying the State courts. I ran across such a trail first when the Anti-Boycott Association was educating the courts about what could be done with a labor injunction, and instructing management counsel about how to draw an injunction with the tear gas and Tommy guns sandwiched into inconspicuous middle paragraphs between the enjoining of outrages and the forbidding of abominations. The most obvious record of success was the series of decisions in the Supreme Court from the *Danbury Hatters* in 1908 through *Coronado, Tri-City,* and the like. A little later I watched the N.L.R.B. select and put over its succession of extensions of the interstate commerce concept — a line of operation paralleled by a number of government agencies. Indeed, with the far-reaching power and practice of the Solicitor-General in selection and control of appeals, the Government (in its incarnation for the time being as the current administration with its current chief and his current staff) has long become by all odds the most important factor in this planned-sequence business. And that is an aspect which opens equally in any State, in regard to things interesting the State government. Nevertheless, apart from the fact that programs and interests and persons within the labyrinth of "Government" may diverge, compete, or conflict, the problem of Anti-Boycott is with us increasingly as organizations form and turn not to public relations and the legislative lobby alone, but also to the courts; tax-resisters, educators, child-lovers, free-press folk, and what have you more, have been at work, and will be. The National Association for the Advancement of Colored People, {263} for instance, learned long ago direct from Anti-Boycott; their skillfully arranged and still continuing series of cases has had striking effects and repercussions. These are enough to indicate the type of thing I have in mind. And the point is that such series call for their own type of treatment because they are in a real sense out of the usual course.

Be it made clear at once that I offer no objection to such selection and staging of case sequences. For we have a legal system which entrusts its case-law-making to a body who are specialists only in being unspecialized, in being the official depositaries of as much general and balanced but rather uninformed horse sense as can be mustered. Such a body has as its function to be instructed, case by case, by the experts in any specialty, and then, by combination of its very nonexpertness in the particular with its general and widely buttressed expert roundedness in many smatterings, to reach a judgment which adds balance not only, as has been argued so often and so hard, against the passing flurries of public passion, but no less against the often deep but too often jug-handled contributions of any technicians. But our system serves the issues to this law-making body only a tiny slice at a time, and leaves the choice of the particular tiny slice to happenstance, to such accidents as which kind of a dispute happens to break out first, with also at least one party on one side who is obnoxious or a lion or insolvent or else in the hands of a lawyer either signally inept or prematurally able. Such leaping of the lot out of the helmet does mean that in the main the cases cluster in areas of movement, growth, disaster, crosscurrents, or wave-fronts in the economic, social, or political world, the areas either of catastrophe or of burgeoning or of unsettled and unchanneled leeway where people and forces clash. Hence ever novel problems are thrown up at the appellate courts. But, as we know well, the order of the cases can be ill-starred, the bits or slices or splinters which are cast up may be too fragmentary to yield a proper picture or to allow the shaping and joining of complementary hubs and spokes and rims to form a doctrinal wheel. And for my money, in this complicated world, a bit of management in bringing on a related group of cases in a series looks to be much more of a value than an ill. We do not thereby lose the safeguard of the adversary battle; the case must still be real, must still be fought. But the court will see more, learn more from the series; the court will begin to see in the round rather than the flat, and to gain some understanding of the whole in action. For that we should give some thanks to the managers. {264}

Meanwhile the warning is simple, and to my mind so is the parry to the peril. An appellate court's contribution to our law is first, last, and always, I repeat, the element of *balance*. Any series of cases staged from and by one side couples with its offerings of knowledge and of insight a mounting danger not only of partiality but of lopsidedness made seductive. The danger lies in a mis-seeing of the controversial situation-type from a single angle and with a single lighting. The defense is thus given: as soon as a sequence is spotted, the court can depute some member to do enough study in the area to test for balance in the emerging picture, and at need to restore it.

The matter we have just been considering does not now press in the State courts; it may never. But both its nature and the lines of sound dealing with it lead into the deepest and least tangible problem which confronts a working philosophy of the appellate judicial craft.

THE CENTIPEDE AND CONSCIOUS SELF-CRITIQUE

That problem goes to whether a craft like appellate judging can without destruction of its fineness, its sureness, its soul be subjected by its practitioners to self-conscious intellectual analysis. In another aspect, the problem goes to whether articulate principles or rules for doing, phrasings for the inculcation or transmission of knowhow, will not cripple or kill, rather than further and better the doing of the job. There is the old tale of the centipede who, once set to ponder how he managed the coordination of his regiment of legs, discovered in panic that he no longer could. There is the feeling, half-mystic, close akin to those only partly intellectual ideas of the "true" rule and of "finding" the law, that the working processes of a right-minded court have in them something of the ineffable, that they can grasp by a sort of inspiration a result beyond the powers of the members; the feeling that there is some Delphic or Sibylline attribute somehow or at least sometimes at work; and such feelings have more basis than is readily granted by the wiseacre who has once or twice seen judges in a wrangle or "knows" the scuttlebutt about some compromise.

There is an experiment of my own which has its pertinence. In the days when Roosevelt was raiding the law schools to man the circuit courts the summoning hand fell on the shoulders of a good number of close friends of mine. As soon as occasion offered, I tackled each. "You have been looking at the bench {265} and theorizing about its work for years. Now you are going to be there and see how it really does go round. *Make notes on how your cases get decided, how it happens.* Do it this first year; by the second year it will just be happening without your noticing, the way it does with all the others. The notes may not mean anything to you, but they will to me; I am outside. You may not have time to study them, but I will. And if they come from enough of you folks, we are going to find enough patterns to make sense." From seven of such incoming judges, all but two of them rather self-analytical and articulate about their processes of work, from seven, I say, I got an honest well-meant pledge to further their old, still fresh-scented job of helping prospective lawyers understand how and why appellate judges decided as they did. From seven. From not one of the seven came one written note; and my belief is that not one made such notes on more than a case or two. "I tried it. What I could think of to put down seemed so trifling, or so silly, or unworthy."

It is plain enough why good intentions did not pan out. Men who with all their energies are breaking themselves in to a new and responsible job *for which there is no handbook* will only by accident or peculiar temper have time left over to simultaneously occupy a seat on the coach's bench and watch themselves play the game; still rarer is the chance and queer bent which will add a triplet personality to take notes as well as notice and to render those notes intelligible to an outsider. No, it was a brave effort; something might have come of it; but it was not a good bet. So: shall we say that the processes, *as applied to the particular,* as directed to how to go about *this* case, are simply beyond reach? Shall we say that conscious accounting thus addressed to the "trifling" and the "silly" and the "unworthy" can do nothing but deflect from the high task?

I am not ready to file or countenance any such petition of voluntary intellectual bankruptcy. In the first place, what beginners in the craft found neither time nor observation-skill to do may yet have set off in some of them processes which will still fruit in such matured articulate observation and discussion as has been beginning to appear again, these last few years; it is even possible that the initial effort at bird-watching one's own first flutters may have made some significant memories stick which otherwise would have slipped away.[261c] In the second place, even though we should have no such luck, study need not stop merely because self-study does not wholly fill the need. The study of {266} craft-work, the analysis thereof, the reduction of such matters to communicable working principles, is a separate art; there is a place for the side-lines man, if he can use his eyes. True, twenty, thirty, or forty sets of notes apiece, each set about a specific case, and coming from five or seven different judges; matched then after five years by similar sets: this would indeed have been priceless ore. Cardozo's Court of Appeals papers, left by him to Columbia University in connection with his legacy to set up a chair of Jurisprudence — these would have been another treasure. And such materials, if ever they may be forthcoming, will lay the foundation for vastly refining any such lines of working philosophy as this present type of inquiry may develop. But I argue that we need not abide the availability of such happy materials, that we can develop a worth-while number of worth-while leads even in their absence. (Since most of the rest of this study is devoted to that, I shall not explore it further at this point.) I argue, moreover, that intellectual analysis, especially when undertaken in the light of history, can bring out for observation lines of function and method in the craft of appellate judging whose appreciation sharpens the eye for the work, for the detection of deflecting factors, and for the building of procedures which, so far from dispersing or choking off the lovelier and less tangible currents that affect and effect the best judicial craftsmanship, can serve rather to encourage and induce them somewhat as a moving ritual can the contact of a man with God. I argue therefore that hard-eyed analysis has no call to be denied or rejected merely because it cannot hope to compass the whole, and I argue that here — as indeed everywhere when the goals of institutions are rightly kept in mind — the cold intellect can be made an excellent servant to advance a whole which without it risks internal cross-purposing waste or ineffectiveness.

Meantime one aspect of the question has become moot. Like it or leave it, the conscious taking of thought about this thing is with us, and once with us it is little like to leave. "What is new in juristic thought today," was Cardozo's final word almost thirty years ago, "is chiefly the candor of its processes. Much that was once unavowed and kept beneath the surface is now avowed and open. From time immemorial lawyers have felt the impulse to pare down the old rules when in conflict with the present needs. The difference is that even when they yielded to the impulse, it was their habit in greater measure than today to disguise what they were doing, to disguise the innovation even from themselves, and to announce in all sincerity that it was all as it had been {267} before."[262] This is the style of work described early in this study as that of Taft. And you will notice that the juice of Cardozo's observation holds equally of any new turn or development which does not present itself explicitly as "a case of first impression": innovation also moved under cover, "like some Victorian virgin tubbing in her nightgown." The question was not, fifty, sixty, or seventy years ago: "Will the cases, or the principle, stand this extension?" or "Is a new or reframed principle a necessity?" The question was "Does not this novel case fall within the principle?"

That difference in phrasing is a difference in the way of legal life; comforting though it was, the Age of Innocence, in this, is over. It is not that our appellate judges are as a group by any means fully conscious of the manner of their work; much of the most vital part thereof, the part that puts flesh, blood, and nerves upon the bones, tends still to simply happen; some of that most vital part must always do so. But that there is a wide range of available authority which, though *not* compelling, *is* available, and which therefore imposes the responsibility of choice, this has become today a matter perceived throughout the guild, be it welcome or not. To half or more, I do not see it as too welcome a perception. Some, indeed, are still haunted by a restlessness which whispers that such "manipulation" has in it a touch of the obscene. Rare individuals, in contrast, have even found a sense of unshackledness going to their heads. But whatever the variant of effect, the cause will not be rooted out. The appellate bench has eaten of the Tree, and along with or because of the sweat of the brow and the ebb of confidence, and the queer access of shame, has come the need for a conscious working philosophy of the craft. Not just in the large — that has long been done — but, let it be again insisted, for the handling of the daily cases each by each. {268}

And that means, I argue, that intellectual analysis is not merely with us inevitably for the future, but that if its advent be followed by reasonable and careful development, such development can offer a cure for the discomforts of the "awareness" which characterizes today's appellate bench, and can build up as well a wherewithal to elicit even better work than the same personnel could hope to accomplish under the older methods. The staged case sequence illustrates in an extreme situation the way in which craft-awareness and consequent function-awareness can aid diagnosis early, and then find means to insure continued balance, where more purely intuitive techniques have proved less reliable.

No. There is no occasion for downheartedness. We have seen above that, despite all the conditioning we can manage, still "An appellate judge is not Pavlov's dog." One needs to add: "Neither is an appellate judge a centipede."

THE QUEST FOR SITUATION-SENSE IS PRIME

3. *Situation-Sense First; Case Equities only Against that Frame*

Recurring now to the more detailed guide lines which have emerged not for the extraordinary but for the common case, there has been repeated assertion and some discussion of the imperative value that lies in having the court, as a regular procedure, seek and see and weigh first the relevant problem-situation as a type, holding meanwhile so far as may be in suspense its reactions to the fireside equities or to other possibly unique attributes of the case in hand. It is time now for more specific inquiry into such a procedure, and perhaps for some refinement of expression.

In the first place "the" situation-type, while it may frequently be in essence given and evident in the record, is sometimes far from evident, though given, and is often enough not given at all, but requires to be formed or even forged from materials which are raw or rough and can be scanty. In any event — and this holds of the legal concept which is relevant just as it does of the life-situation — the sizing up of "the case" into some pattern is of the essence of getting to the case at all, and the shape it starts to take calls up familiar, more general patterns to fit it into or to piece it out or to set it against for comparison. This much, as we all know, is not a matter of method or of desire, it comes close to being a matter of necessity, it is the way the normal human mind insists on working most of the time. What is not necessity {269} is that the courts should wind up accepting any particular legal category as the controlling pattern unless it proves to be a category with sense-significance as well as doctrinal significance, or without looking around for other possibly more significant ways to type the problem.

Consider *Sleeth v. Sampson,* 237 N.Y. 69, 142 N.E. 355 (1923). A dead man had according to a witness who "overheard" asked plaintiff for a $100 loan; plaintiff said he had already loaned him enough ($1200) without security. The dead man had offered to mortgage his farm. An unknown amount of money had changed hands, and the deceased had handed over the deed and abstract of title: "You look these over, and see what you can do, and we will go down to the lawyer's *in a few days* and draw this up." (My italics.) The death occurred "a few *weeks*" later. Plaintiff sought specific performance of an agreement to mortgage to secure the whole debt. There were two readily available legal situation-patterns, each infused with an appealing policy. The one was "equitable mortgage," where money is advanced only against a promise to mortgage, no mortgage follows, and it seems unfair to let an advance rushed through to aid the borrower be turned by his default, death, or delay from a secured into a naked loan. This situation had already reached a clean conceptual crystallization of the New York cases in the hands of Stone.[263] The other pattern was: agreement "for the sale of any real property, or an interest therein" not in writing and not subscribed by the grantor — which under the New York Statute of Frauds was void; and one remembers not only the care which men commonly bestow on deals involving real estate, and with which they arrange such deals through legal counsel, but also the policy of public record of interests in real estate, for the general benefit. The court chose this second pattern, and affirmed dismissal of the lender's complaint. The case facts which stood out to Cardozo were that such payment as had been made was not "unintelligible or at least extraordinary" in the absence of an agreement to mortgage; and that "the bulk of the indebtedness was antecedent to the promise." Five or six years later he had no recollection of having had at all in mind three other facts which his opinion mentions in passing: the few weeks which had passed without any action to substantiate the making of a promise; the inability of a dead man to testify, and the consequent accidental and unsatisfactory character of the evidence; the fact that the defendants were decedent's mother and two infant nephews. The point {270} to be made is that the office of these last facts or any similar facts was not to decide the case; their office was rather to alert the court to the possibility that the "equitable mortgage" *situation-pattern* might need restudy before it was fitted to this case. Such study then revealed that that situation-pattern had itself been seen and drawn by both the prior cases and the commentator in terms which overlooked certain powerful policies that underlay the Statute of Frauds: To make the required writing unnecessary "The payment of money is not enough, unless followed by other acts, as, for example, possession or improvements . . . A different holding would open wide the door to the entry of the evils against which the statute is directed. . . . The danger is emphasized in this case where the bulk of the indebtedness was antecedent to the promise." (237 N.Y. at 73.) The prior cases were therefore pared down more closely to the facts which had made them reasonable decisions, and so as to exclude the case in hand.

Thus to urge the primacy of the problem-situation as a type, and of the quest for its Goldschmidt immanent law, is not to suggest that the abstract *can* divorce itself from the concrete in which it comes enfolded, or that contrary to the whole bent and beauty of our case law it *should* attempt to do so. It is instead to insist that a court should seek to *channel* the impetus from the concrete, to channel it into a search for a situation-pattern of significance which can be somewhat worked over for its general sense and tendency so as to test the wisdom of letting the equities of the fireside prevail or even count; and, *if* they should be so permitted, *then* to capitalize their poignancy or illustrative power to produce a bit of sounder law for that whole situation. In *Sleeth v. Sampson* the one proffered older category and situation-type was refined and then rejected as inapplicable; an alternative category was re-examined and sharpened and applied. The fireside was disregarded.

A similar whittling and refining process occurred in *Kelley v. Park View Apartments, Inc.*, 330 P.2d 1057 (Ore. 1958). Snow had been cleared off steps onto a sharply sloping lawn of a four-block apartment enterprise in Portland. During the night, meltings ran onto the public sidewalk and made a small ice patch. At 8:30 a.m. the plaintiff tenant slipped and was injured. In a prior case, which had involved slops from window washing which dripped onto a sloping sidewalk, the court had laid down a rule about "placing, or not removing" on the sidewalk "any matter that would cause a slippery or dangerous condition." The court was now bothered about the extent of the obligation which would {271} be imposed in such a large apartment operation if the snow had to be stacked at the curb; it saw no duty to clear the public sidewalk, and no peculiar obligation to tenants. It felt, or was made to feel, that "an imposition of liability in this case would virtually demand that the court employ a rule of strict liability" (p. 1061) (why, I do not personally perceive) — a doctrine not very popular with this court. What this then led to was a careful examination of the sense and the Eastern law of a narrowed situation: snow-covered sidewalks, with a conclusion that normal clearing methods, despite possible melting and freezing, reduce the net danger to walkers and are to be encouraged — making a consequent exception to the prior rule.[264]

Method and meaning are parallel in *Fairweather v. Wiley's, Inc.*, 183 Kan. 579, 331 P.2d 330 (1958), although the technical issues there took sharply different shape and it was the plaintiff who was successful. A department store display window splintered in a high wind, and injured the plaintiff. The defendant argued that the complaint rested on *res ipsa loquitur*, so that the wind, as a supervening cause, would be a defense; but the court found adequate allegations in simple negligence: failure to properly construct and maintain the windows; and saw in the wind no excuse by way of Act of God, a concept as little loved in Kansas as is strict liability in Oregon. One can fairly liken nine-structure garden apartment enterprises to display-filled department store windows as type American situations looking toward beauty, convenience, and gracious living; but surely also the immanent law about where to place the risk in case of breakage could, as it did, with good sense respond to evidence that for twenty-five years the windows had been wind-broken perhaps every two or three years, and that protective padded braces were kept on hand for use at need.

Let me give two more examples, one of which I vigorously disapprove in result; but that will keep sharp the point that it is method, not outcome, which is in question. *Rozell v. Rozell,* 281 N.Y. 106, 22 N.E.2d 254 (1939), was a suit by a twelve-year-old against his sixteen-year-old sister for negligently driving him into a collision. It was a case of first impression, so far as concerned the exact relationship. The court made its choice in terms of significance and sense between two contending situation-types. {272} The one was family disruption with a lawsuit as the lever, plus, where disruption was not happening, family collusion in false claims. The other was the injured family-member's protection by the family liability insurance. Each was thought through. Recovery was sustained. The *Channel Master Corporation* case, 4 N.Y.2d 403, 151 N.E.2d 833 (1958), involved a count in tort alleging that defendant had falsely represented its uncommitted capacity to supply plaintiff with 400,000 pounds of ingot aluminum per month, with the intention and effect of inducing plaintiff to refrain from arranging supplies elsewhere: to which was added another count on false representation of intention to so supply plaintiff for five years. The majority found the significant situation-type to be false representations in, roughly, a business situation, with all five necessary constituent legal elements present; they did see and they inquired into the bearing of the Statute of Frauds on liability for these oral misrepresentations, but their search seemed to them to show the statute pertinent neither technically nor in policy. Hence the law of fraud was sharply extended to sustain the complaint, though this was an oral business negotiation, and one in which the deal had never been closed. (My reasons for thinking the decision dangerous appear in Appendix A, below, p. 473.)

However, it will not do to leave the impression that under sound method the particular case equities simply do and should take a circuitous route through some convenient type-situation, only, at length, having all along been the material motivation, to realize themselves in a happy holding. Neither will it do to create the impression that adopting any type-situation which the case equities may happen to whistle into court will comport with the use of sound method. Thus in the *Channel Master* case the soundness of method lay not in finding the five technical-legal elements of fraud, but in spotting *and then* checking into the possibility that a suit based on oral representations which *looked toward a contract for sale might* be running afoul of the Statute of Frauds. And thus in *Clark v. McGinn,* 105 So.2d 668 (Ala. 1958), where the case equities plainly demanded that the main stock owners of a close corporation be held on their guaranty of corporate borrowings, but the available consideration seems to have been only "one dollar in hand paid," it was sound method to go hunting for a situation-type in which a merely nominal consideration is and ought to be enough to make a $30,000 promise stick; guaranties tend strongly to be such a type, and guaranties in which the guarantor's own interest is sufficiently {273} great to actually match the "main purpose" rule about escaping the Statute of Frauds would be a striking and illuminating type to turn up. Where the *Clark* case slides off sound method is where it is seduced (on the original authority of Story) into resting the guaranty recovery on a nominal consideration theory applicable to *any* contract at all, and into taking that huge generalization without inquiry, on Story's mere say-so. Again, in our friend *Legniti* in the Appellate Division, the "eve of bankruptcy" and "explicit condition" equities shrieked for the plaintiff's recovery of the price out of which he had been virtually defrauded;[265] but it was not sound method to set up a type-situation of *cable transfers* (as contrasted, say, with eve-of-bankruptcy receiving of money) and, against the whole *known* operation-flavor of the *normal* cable transfer, to push an agency or bailment or trust idea into the transaction as such. In contrast, in the Court of Appeals the method was sound. The dominant situation-type is there seen as such, and ruled on as such; and the case equities, though felt and mildly mourned, are relegated to their proper place. This (though short of top-flight achievement of the *Allendorf* variety, below)[266] well displays the way in which the sound method and order of approach and emphasis relight and so revalue and devalue such case equities as remain too individual to properly determine or influence decision.

Two other instances, both in the family field, will further illustrate this sometimes radical revaluation. In the *Dawkins* cases, 183 Kan. 323, 336, 328 P.2d 346, 355 (1958), after twenty-seven years of joint labors, the wife of a revivalist preacher who for substantial purposes constituted in his own person both his tabernacle and all of its finances had persuaded the lower court, in connection with her divorce, to allocate to her the parsonage that had been built "for her." But the majority saw the situation-type, on the financial side, as church-and-schism, and the assets as therefore by the nature of the immanent law trust assets; which — though over a dissent — drowned out the otherwise appealing equities of the wife. In *Loeb v. Loeb*, 4 N.Y.2d 542, 152 N.E.2d 36 (1958), the degree to which the wife's equities registered on the majority is not so clear, but it is certain that any such claims at all were doomed to be smothered by what the court saw and deeply felt as the situation-sense. A Vermont wife had after {274} marrying a New York man lived with him in Vermont, and after his Reno divorce had tried for alimony in the Vermont court, which disclaimed jurisdiction. The wife then moved to live with her mother-in-law in New York, thereafter bought a New York home, and sued for alimony under the New York curative statute — the literal language of which did cover her. The court, like old Holt before the Statute of Anne, "was *totis viribus* against the action." New York was not to bait "emigrant wives" with alimony. The dissent's case for *this* wife thus went unheard.

THE FIRESIDE IN COMMAND:

THE TYPE-SITUATION MISTAKEN

Back, now, for contrast, to examples of the unsound method which lets the fireside "rights" of the case get out of hand, to "make bad law." It has been noted above that an overinterest in reaching justice for *this* case is an error characteristic of a case law court which has lost contact with its tradition of ceaseless minor retooling of the stock of rules. The "hard case" is the case which shows up that stock as in some detail off-design. The hard cases of the proverb have been wise in then doing something about it; the trouble has lain in haste; there has been a kidnaping of the first innocent concept the judicial press gang could corner on the docks, without pause to think over implications; or there has been application of a rule without visualization of what that application will look like when made general, when phrased as a subrule. In a word, the "bad law" flows from the scanting of the effort needed to locate and explore the significant situation-*type*, from thinking of the contemplated measure more as an expedient than as a rule.

One can illustrate by a ruling which so far as my immediate imagining goes looks harmless. *Reinhard v. Peck*, 159 Ohio St. 116, 111 N.E.2d 262 (1953), is thus reported on above at page 153: "the question went to whether a sale of stock in a close corporation took the proceeds out of the personal property tax, as being a sale in the *usual* course of business. ". . . [T]he conversion resulting from the sale of the securities of the estate was under her administration in the usual course of *her business as executrix.'* (111 N.E.2d at 264; court's italics.)" I have no doubt that the result is (1) fair and (2) within the sweep of the general policy underlying the statutory exception. But it would have seemed to me possible to rest the ruling quietly on this latter {275} ground; and without visualizing distinctly any particular warrior as growing from this dragon's tooth, I still, as a commercial lawyer, find goose pimples rising on my back at the thought of the winding up of an estate being the "usual course of business" which I am accustomed to see producing bona fide purchase protection against strong prior claims of lien or ownership.

Statutory language which by accident can be pasted onto the particular case can indeed readily prove a Greek gift. *Gerety v. Hiller,* 349 Pa. 49, 36 A.2d 346 (1944), for instance, discussed above at page 145, which proceeded in a fashion closely parallel to this word-twisting in *Reinhard,* offers an easy picture of trouble ahead. In that case a $46,000 ice-making machine had been retaken by a conditional seller from a buyer who was going through a voluntary arrangement, and the seller had also been put into possession of the premises where the machine was in use. The seller mailed the statutory registered notification of prospective resale to the buyer's last known place of business — but that was those same premises. The sale brought a fair price; nevertheless, the buyer's trustees in bankruptcy were seeking $11,586 of statutory penalty. The court affirmed judgment for defendant. As to the notice: "Notice was sent there in compliance with the statute. There was no responsibility upon appellees to look after the buyer's mail. . ." (349 Pa. at 55.) And the court said: "Had application been made to the court[!!], or appellees awaited the replacement of the buyer's officers and directors, who claimed to have resigned, and as a result the thirty day period after reclamation of the machinery had elapsed, appellees clearly would have become liable in damages to the buyer. *The Uniform Conditional Sales Act makes it mandatory, without exception,* as to the time when the sale must be made following the retaking of possession." (ibid. 54-55; my italics.) Now there is no question that that Act does move *in terrorem.* But neither is there any question that the relevant provisions on notice and time of resale were addressed to furniture, household refrigerators, automobiles, soda fountains, and the like. They never remotely envisaged the Act's application to industrial machinery of great value, possible current earning power, and perhaps quite limited market, defaulted on by a corporate buyer which was under the control of a bankruptcy court. Hence, *in a case where the basic purpose of the provisions has been fully achieved* and a fair price actually realized, to rule that a literal compliance with the provisions is *enough,* and that it protects the conditional seller even when the particular measures make little sense in the {276} particular circumstance: this is judicial wisdom. Whereas to fail to stress such achievement of the basic purpose is to stick in the bark. And to talk statutory literalism in general, as mandatory, is to put a later well-intentioned seller into a distressing box, if no reasonable resale can be drummed up within the thirty days. In a situation like *Gerety,* application to the bankruptcy court for an extension would then be a sane and needed measure; the 30-day limit was designed to keep non-"productive" goods from piling up "storage" charges to wipe out $40 equities, it was not designed to force a working, earning, ice-making machine onto the market for junk.

The Appellate Division treatment of *Legniti* of course belongs here,[267] as does the impressment of Story's "universal" nominal consideration rule to support the main stockholders' guaranty for their corporation.[268] The one led, as we have seen, to a trust theory which the same court found it needful to utterly cast out within a year. The other joins that mass of confusing doctrine which misleads some lawyers into doing contract-drafting as if a nominal consideration were bedrock, without regard to the situation. In contrast with both, from our Indiana sample, stands *Penn v. State*, 237 Ind. 374, 146 N.E.2d 240 (1957), a "three in a bed" rape case in which the testimony of the prosecutrix included lasting cordial relationship with the defendant's wife, but negated any conversation at all with that wife about sex. "It is not necessary that we adopt and employ a special rule regarding corroboration of testimony based on the fact that this is a rape case, *as is urged by appellant.* Rather this case can be and is decided for appellant upon the basis of the well established rule that judgments must be sustained, within the required standard of proof, with evidence sufficiently credible to be of probative value." (146 N.E.2d at 243; my italics.)

Now it can be urged that these last three instances take me wholly out of any discussion of method and squarely into discussion of and measurement by whether I the sparrow, with *my* bow and arrow, like the specific outcome for a target. And apart from the fact that nobody has appointed me or anybody else to be the judge of wisdom, what use is it, anyhow, to say to a court which happens at the moment to lack the knowledge or the insight or the luck to hit upon the most fitting situation-type and the most fitting measure for that type — what use is it to say; "Be wise!" {277}

Talk of this sort can make some pretty good sense appear for a moment to be less than sense. But, I submit, only for a moment. For the standard of wisdom to which appeal is being made (to get that one out of the way first) is not any person's personal standard; it is rather a standard which aims to get idiosyncratic preferences largely hewn off until the standard becomes what the courts also are reaching for: something which can be hoped, on thought, to look reasonable to any thinking man; something that can even be hoped to look reasonable in the light of that uncommon sense, *horse* sense. In the *Legniti* instance, the blob was rejected, both by the deciding court in another case and within a month or so thereafter by the Court of Appeals on the *Legniti* appeal; and no man since has found that rejection other than good. In the consideration matter, a British Parliamentary Commission, a series of reports by the New York Law Revision Commission, a reformatory piece of the Restatement, and almost every serious scholarly discussion of the last forty years have each found troubles flowing from the unconsidered overbreadth of the Story variety of generalization about consideration, whether the universal under the glass be positive or negative in content. Finally, the Indiana court's choice of ground in the rape case seems to me on its face to be not only one of high promise, but one which any appellate court can test in vivid memory and imagination against a true multitude of cases: here truly they are specialists in the varied. Thus each of these evaluations of outcome seems to escape the overly personal.

On the next point, that of method, the advice from our study surely has been no cloud-cuckooland: "Be wise!" It has instead been back-yard homespun stuff: "In trying to be wise, be cautious, *and, and as a regular matter,* consider first things first." Let me test by a sequence of dippings from a brew which still is far from having fully fermented out, that of products liability; and let the material illustrate also the *method* aspect of that on-going recorrection work which is the essence of sound case law.

NEW YORK CONSUMER WARRANTIES

We are dealing with the adoption of warranty as a basis for liability, in regard to food. *Race v. Krum,* 222 N.Y. 410, 118 N.E. 853 (1918), was such a case. It involved a defendant druggist who had himself made the ice cream which the plaintiff had eaten at the store. The court took one hurdle in stride: serving ice cream at the drugstore was classed as a "sale"; but the court {278} stressed that this was a dealer "who makes or prepares the article he is selling"; and a restaurateur or innkeeper was definitely distinguished. This amounts to extending the "sale" concept by but a single step and for the known reason that the liability is thereby pinned on the source of the evil. In the same year, and on the basis of the Uniform Sales Act, *Rinaldi v. Mohican Co., 225* N.Y. 70, 121 N.E. 471 (1918), took a second and much bigger step. Good-looking pork infested with trichinae was held to impose liability on a retail butcher. Still, the court explicitly held back from passing on the resale of an unopened original package. This time the step-by-step caution, sound in method, is dubious in its execution: for trichinae in fair pork from a fair source are as hard for a butcher to spot as if inside any unopened package. But maybe the court did not know that; and in any event step-by-step is safe procedure.

Before these cases, New York had upheld conviction of a hotelkeeper who in violation of the Conservation Law ("not be sold, offered for sale, or possessed for sale for food purposes") had *served* partridges to guests at a meal. "Any other construction" would defeat the purpose of the statute.[269] When serving for hire then came up directly re liability for injury, the prior purpose-construction of the Conservation Law aided in a parallel purpose-extension of the Uniform Sales Act.[270] The *Race* dictum about restaurateurs had in fact rested on a history partly accidental, partly rooted in a policy which, with regard to sales, the Sales Act had flatly rejected. It would have been nonsense to now subdivide the field without reason, and it would have made very dubious sense indeed to drag the feet, because of judicial views of policy, on a line of question so cleanly proper for legislative determination, one, indeed, in which the legislative language of 1910 had moved in prophetic consonance with the whole trend of the times — and, for that matter, with the New York court's own approach to tort claims, in *McPherson v. Buick* (1916). For of course the next discovery had to be that, despite all the noise of so many of the earlier writers,[271] the development has in reality been one not in food, but in consumer-protection generally.[272] {279}

When, then, the defect turned up not in the goods sold, but in the bottle (bailed against a deposit) which allowed a carbonated beverage to explode, it would have been a wise extension of the basic type-situation to see it, say, as "goods put upon the market for use," including in the same class, *unless some reason to the contrary should appear,* not only bailed containers of things sold, but bailments for hire in general. In *Geddling v. Marsh*[273] an English court handled this, however, by enlisting an accident of slovenly draftsmanship: the British Act (ours repeats the language) raises implied warranties with reference not to "the goods" which are the subject matter of a sale but to "goods *supplied under a contract*" of sale. Surely a sounder procedure would have first explored the identity of sane policy with regard to safe use of the contents and of the bottle, and would only then have turned to the lucky phrasing of the Act. And the New York court managed the extension at common law, and without need for the accidental language-bridge of the statute, in regard to hoisting equipment leased for use on an excavating job.[274] Meantime one other piece of language was being discovered which on the point in hand might be misconceived as also an accident, but which in fact represented a policy well-nigh as old as that of the manufacturer's responsibility for fitness: when an exporter contracted with a wholesale grocer for canned milk, and it proved unfit for consumption, the court rested recovery on the statutory implied warranty not of "fitness for a particular purpose," but of "merchantability" generally.[275] This tolls the bell for the *Rinaldi* possibility that sale in the original package might protect a retailer if the food (merchandise) should be asked for by brand; and that consequence Cardozo, in *Ryan,* shortly draws.[276]

In all of this we see as overt, cautious, steady a step-by-step development as one could wish, of what in due course, except for the still not wholly crystallized aspect of allergies, has finally worked out into a rather simple body of law, with the elimination of one after another of the artificial qualifications which in various other courts had produced hesitance or complicating contrary {280} results. The *Canavan* case discussed above[277] in no wise interrupts the sequence. It merely represents a deliberate judgment of the majority that its proper context and type-situation is not the open market in general but rather the large-scale and especially the municipal furnishing of certain general services on which communities depend: in the case, water.

How comes it now that broad across this rather lovely record are smeared, gratuitously, pretended negative corollaries of the "warranty" concept of the very type which the court has with complete consistency rejected in regard to supposed negative corollaries of "sale"? So much of the "privity" idea as aims to keep a defendant from being liable to all outdoors does make sense; but that is all. In New York the misexpansion of "privity" in this series may be partly due to random circumstances in the forking case. The plaintiff there was a waitress in a lunchroom whose meals were part of her wages and had included a nail baked by defendant into a slice of cake. Certainly such facts lack the huge drive toward "finding" third-party beneficiary intent which could have been generated by a housewife's purchase of supplies for her own family table — even though the waitress could have served nobly as a "creditor" beneficiary in the best New York style. Moreover, the opinion[278] came to McLaughlin, whose thinking tended always toward both the formal and the blunt, and who in the original *Race v. Krum* had already marked off *restaurant*-serving as a dubious bet. In any event, the rule laid down was "no privity, no warranty"; and despite the senseless holes thus chopped in the otherwise expanding policy, four years later a child was barred from warranty recovery for injury from broken glass in milk bought by her mother.[279] Indeed, to sustain recovery by the husband in the *Ryan* case (a pin in packaged bread), above at page 279, the pleader and the court both found it necessary to have the plaintiff's wife who had bought the bread do so "as the plaintiff's agent." That can bite back. On just that basis, one lower court in New York actually achieved refusal of remedy to the wife herself; by force of law (being her husband's "agent"), she had been no "party" to the household purchase she herself had made.[280] As of 1959, no one seems to have presented the Court of Appeals {281} with pleadings which would test the availability of a third-party beneficiary warranty inside the family.[281]

The whole sequence gives nice examples of the wisdom and value of moving into any new development with canny caution, of the ease of on-going correction or extension if the possibility thereof be kept constantly in mind, but also of the difficulties, even absurdities, which can grow out of letting a concept's seeming corollaries take over without reference to the sense of the situation. As if our law were not full — and wisely full — of *quoad hoc* use of concepts (such as *apparent* "authority," *indicia* of "ownership," title *inter partes* in a buyer, "partnership" for purposes of liability to a creditor, "acceptance" *as against* the defendant offeree who has remained silent — and so on down the line).

At every stage the lessons from the sequence bear on any work, of any day.

* * *

This is not true of the two procedures now to be mentioned, which, while always welcome, fall perhaps into a class of treats, or bonuses, or services beyond the call of ordinary duty, certainly beyond the reach of the ordinary occasion. The one is what we may call the area clean-up. There will be a region of confusion, perhaps of seeming conflict in the cases, typically with many or most of them not too unpleasing on their facts, but with the threads of rationale a tangle. An issue, an argument, an occasion, a flash of insight or genius, will touch off a realignment which becomes a landmark. *Jones v. Just* and *McPherson v. Buick,* already mentioned, had this caliber; but there are jobs aplenty of equal distinction and high utility which do not happen to achieve international fame. Thus *Slonaker v. P.G. Publishing Co.,* 338 Pa. 292, 13 A.2d 48 (1940), cut into a mass of eleven prior Pennsylvania cases on agreements with an indefinite time term, re-examined them, sorted them, and substituted for the older flat "terminable at will (but maybe not)" approach a discriminating and workable analysis.[282] Not infrequently such a {282} new dispensation is midwived by a pair of companion cases which for the first time focus both aspects of the underlying policies at once and thus produce a new criterion theretofore either only fumbled for or wholly unsuspected: *Atherton v. Atherton,*[283] with its "matrimonial domicile" approach to migra-divorce (which had its merits) was even one of a set of three decisions on the single day. But there is no need for a court to wait until it is thus run down in the bushes. *Glaser v. Holdorf,* presented above at page 173, shows a court in a neat and useful area clean-up. The difficulties which faced the would-be appellant had the external marks of an illicit squeeze by blocking off any certification of a record; but a remedy must not open the door to counterabuse. So, in little over a column, the court puts a whole code of guidance and reason together from the gathered cases. Again, in *Grigsby v. Jenkins,* 184 Kan. 594, 331 P.2d 284 (1958), a general verdict for plaintiff on a snarled question of informal contract-making had been set aside and a judgment *non obstante* then entered for defendant. The court very patiently reviewed the evidence and the law. "This question has been dealt with many times by this court. Some of our most decent decisions are . . . [four cites]." (331 P.2d at 287.) The court's syllabus then digests the lesson into a form hard to mistake:

> "1. A motion for judgment *non obstante veredicto* raises questions of law and is no substitute for a motion for a new trial in testing the sufficiency of evidence. (G.S. 1949, 60-2918).
>
> "2. A general verdict in favor of a party to an action imports a finding in his favor upon all issues in the case.
>
> "3. When dissatisfied with a verdict, it is the duty of the trial court to grant a new trial. [And, adds the opinion, this may be on the court's own motion.]
>
> "4. A trial court may not upon consideration of the evidence substitute its judgment for that of the jury, set aside the general verdict and render judgment in favor of the other party."

The other "luxury" procedure is found in *Allendorf v. Elgin, J. & E. Ry.,* 8 Ill. 2d 164, 133 N.E.2d 288 (1956), a death action under the Federal act. The defendant was complaining that calculations by an actuary of lost earnings had been given in figure totals unduly likely to register on the jury's mind as the figure totals of a proper verdict; and the $127,500 actual verdict might well have been strongly influenced by the $113,000 estimate. {283} The court wrestled its way, modifying an earlier opinion, out of the general situation-type: "expert evidence hypothetical," which would have required or at least permitted use of the concrete figures in evidence. "We are of opinion that the proper method of assisting a jury in making damage calculations is for the actuary to use neutral figures. . . . The actuary . . . is called upon only to describe a mathematical procedure that will simplify the jury's task of determining the present value of the contribution that plaintiffs would have received had decedent not been killed." (8 Ill. 2d at 177-178.) Having thus admirably worked this one out — incidentally, the Key Number System failed to catch it — the court followed plaintiff's counsel into a beautifully persuasive study of the particular record, the particular decedent, and the large number of his possible contributions which had been omitted from the figures actually used. The fireside thereupon receives its full due, *but without disturbing the creative new formulation of the situation-rule.* "Whatever evil might have appeared in the testimony of the actuary, to the prejudice of the defendant, is counterbalanced by the many other advantages as herein outlined." (ibid. 182.) A heartening result.

THE FIRESIDE IN COMMAND:

THE TYPE FORGOTTEN

Far from heartening, and in direct contrast to such whole-case study, is the hingeing of a reversal on one or three narrow points of technical procedure, without serious inquiry into their reasonably possible net effect. What I have in mind goes particularly to matters of procedure at the trial; there is no wish to suggest that it is other than wise for an appellate court to guard lest those technical procedures on appeal which serve clarity and order and which can be attended to in quiet and at leisure, should be allowed to slide into the pigsty. I do note, however, that even in regard to an appellate court's own procedures, disregarded without seeming excuse or shame, the manner which speaks from the reports today has little of the quondam curtness of the martinet and a good deal of a somewhat weary patience which is kin to the spirit of any half-disheartened educator.

In regard to technique at trial, I do not today too often come across brusque, flat reversal. It is my belief that this used to be much more frequent. There can be no doubt, for instance, that a court which feels its justice-duty strongly, but which also, under {284} the spell of the Formal Style, feels that judicial discussion of such matters is tainted with indecency, can often salve both halves of its conscience at once by reversal on a petty procedural point. Nor can one doubt that the more tidy procedural thinking of the Formal period lent to procedural cleanliness a weight and dignity which for good or bad are no longer with us. Moreover, while a very fair proportion of the energy and space in our current samplings is occupied with technical procedure of trial or of appeal, I come away from the study of those cases with a strong net impression that the appellate courts today are feeling and dealing with procedure mainly as a tool and with an eye to its accomplishment of purpose. That is one impression. The next — not quite so clear and sharp — is that the tendency is strong, these days, to reach for the net impact of any procedural errors on the whole case, and to judge in those terms. For of course an affirmance can be as off-target as a reversal, if, for instance, it chops cumulative errors up into many individually, though each one barely, tolerable bits and then disposes of each bit successively as in itself too small to turn the scale.

On whether, two or three legal generations ago, appellate practices were really sinning in these respects as badly as my memory suggests, I must speak with caution. You may recall, for instance, that as late as 1918 all the respectable lawyers of this country "knew" that one of the great defects in the administration of our criminal law was that the appellate courts were "always" reversing convictions on "pure" technicalities. It took just one real study to explode that "knowledge."[284] My "memory" may be of that ilk; and I have neither made nor met a Cleveland Survey of this matter. But I am sure that the urge to reach for the net, in deciding whether error has been really prejudicial, is characteristic of our State supreme courts today. Which is good; for a reversal which on its face looks as if it rests on purely technical grounds, or an affirmance which on its face looks as if it has dealt with matters of juice as if they were purely technical: either one is bad for the bar, unqualifiedly bad.

It is bad for the bar, a little, because the bar is not to be encouraged in any notion that that is how our appellate judges normally think, or act, or want to act or think. But it is bad for the bar much more because the bar knows always with its gizzard and {285} mostly with its brain that the court does not act that way always, or regularly. But that means: sometimes yes, sometimes no, roll the dice, how can you know where you are at, and may the Lord have mercy on us! I know that in my youth it was the seeming unpredictability of whether obvious but minor error would shrink into harmlessness or nondiscussion, or would expand like a djinn issuing from a bottle, which first made me aware of how much open choice there *had* to be in appellate deciding to which the books as they were being written were giving me no clue. I am certain that the appellate bar is crowded with men who feel, still, much of that same bafflement. Of course, not the leaders. But here again a single instance of the evil counts for a hundred, because men notice what they fear, they typify it because they fear it, they make it legion. Therefore let us lay down

4. The Whole Case as the Test

This is a fourth principle from which I see no escape: whether technical errors in procedure are to mean reversal must depend on their bearing on the underlying substance, and, especially, on the case seen as a whole. No matter how a legal system is officially set up, my reading turns up not one in which this feeling and reaching for the *whole* case has not been of the essence of its health. Procedure has purpose, and process is to be seen in terms of goal. The question in regard to *prejudicial* error is not to be settled by form. Indeed, at least partly, this principle (as a principle of action and often of conscious guidance) emerges from our study: for our current samplings are so full of instances of its application, and of instances which demonstrate its value. Consider a handful. *Robinson v. State* (Mississippi, 1958, presented above, p. 162): "However, in view of the gravity of the charge and the severity of the punishment in this case, we have reviewed the testimony." (105 So.2d at 767). *Nellis v. Allen*, 105 So.2d 659, 660 (Ala. 1958) (not presented in my report, though part of the sample): "The principal litigated question in the case was the employment of appellee by the appellant, as a real estate broker, to sell her property. Appellant and Dr. Mosely, the purchaser, testified emphatically that he was not so employed and did not produce the purchaser. Appellee's testimony was in direct conflict. The testimony of appellee's wife, set out above, was clearly hearsay, but carried a strong inference to support the theory that appellee was so employed and did produce the purchaser.

"We cannot say that it was not prejudicial error. . . ." (p. 662). {286}

Or again from the sample, *Jeffrey Manufacturing Co. v. Harsh*, 105 So.2d, 672, 676 (Ala. 1958) (after considering for four columns the main question and two lesser ones); "We have considered the assignments of error which have been treated in brief of appellant. We find no error to reverse presented by any of those assignments." True, one would have wished, in expression as in substance, "in those assignments," or "in any of those assignments or in their combination," rather than just "in *any*"; but the willingness to go to the whole seems clear. Or take *Glaser v. Holdorf,* the Washington problem of getting up a record when the stenographer was holding out, as presented above at page 173; or the ruling in *People v. Flowers,* 14 Ill. 2d. 406, 152 N.E.2d 838, 844 (1958), that a "fatal" variance between the indictment and the evidence had been waived by not being taken at the trial — *and* was also nonexistent; or, in *Farmers State Bank v. Irsik,* 83 Kan. 636, 331 P.2d 292, 296 (1958), after some handsomely technical countering of technical fiddle-faddle: "[I]t is quite apparent that the court was well aware of the maneuver . . ." and the illicit effort to shift venue is blocked. Especially interesting, perhaps, is *Brush Hill Development, Inc. v. Commonwealth,* 155 N.E.2d 170, 172 (Mass. 1958), an eminent domain proceeding: "It was recognized in [a previous case] that the consistent exercise of a trial judge's discretion to exclude testimony bearing on a particular aspect of the value of property may have the effect of denying to the owner the power of proving its real value." And notwithstanding that the petitioner's procedure is found in three particulars to be too loose to sustain objections, and the trial judge's exclusion in a fourth is ruled no abuse of discretion, the court finds one consistent line of exclusion (rapid development of the immediate area and the growing scarcity of land — small residence plots — similarly zoned) to have constituted error. Another exclusion (p. 175) "[S]tanding alone . . . is not prejudicial error in view of the breadth of the discretion given to a trial judge," but as "further action" is added in to make the net case for reversal. One can both contrast and compare *Scofield v. J. W. Jones Construction Co.,* 328 P.2d 389 (N.M. 1958), an auto collision case, where one objection is disposed of (over a dissent) for lack of a proper motion, and two are summed up (p. 393): "We would not be justified in reversing the case *on this point* on the record as made" and "we do not feel we would be justified in overturning the verdict *on this point*." (My italics.) But the treatment, at the end, of the claim that the damages were excessive may well reach back in part to color and interpret this earlier strand-by-strand approach to the appeal: "The trial judge {287} heard all of the evidence, observed the appellee and found the verdict was not the result of passion of prejudice, and left him [after a $10,000 remittitur] with a verdict for $20,000 . . . We will not overturn him in the exercise of his discretion as to damages finally allowed." (p. 395.)

Of a piece with testing of procedural error by probable net effect, of a piece with seeking to focus the significant situation-type and its inherent rightnesses, of a piece with overt accounting to seeming fairness and seeming wisdom is, I do now submit, the regular introduction into an opinion of the only existing craftsmanlike approach to a distinction:

5. No Distinction Without Explicit Reason Addressed to Wisdom of Distinguishing

On this the lore is well-nigh as old as careful conscious work with doctrinal materials. *Good* distinguishing means *good* judging, runs the Latin proverb; "narrow" distinctions — which means distinctions too narrow to make sense — have long been an abomination not only to the loser, but to the bar at large; "technical" distinctions offend the layman — and we cannot wholly shrug him off just because he so often muddies issues, "thinks" with his prejudices, and has no background to understand either technical context or technical necessity. It is his law, too, and more so than it is ours; nay, it is he whom even *our* law is for. So that we come back to the ancient wisdom: "a distinction without a difference" is a stench, and there is no reason why the difference should not be sweetly blazoned on the page.

Again, as in the matter of the illegitimate authority techniques, the writing of our appellate courts has, in general, long responded to this. Again — although this time there is no similar crushing cost of error — one nevertheless finds still, here or there, a hangover of the obsolete manner of smuggish fiat or of that bland — or is it blind? — assumption that distinguishability is itself enough to justify or even to demand distinction. Again, finally, the arbitrary manner has faded with its reason. When modification or at need overruling is respectable, the twisting mazes of distinction by ukase are driven not underground but out; they bring no gain to set against their cost and waste. {288}

THE ROLE OF THE OPINION RE THE BAR

"Well, now," puts in one of these unpleasant carpers, "is this man talking about the deciding of cases or about the writing of opinions? He started out with the deciding, now it's the opinions, it seems he can't tell the two apart." I suppose the truth is that at this stage of our study this man is so much interested in both at once that careful discrimination — never easy — no longer seems to pay. Such discrimination went to the essence so long as the inquiry ran to what we could learn, from the opinions, about the processes which had gone before. But the question now is, what do the best examples suggest about the best ways of getting the whole job done? At no time could any man of careful thought deem the opinion a minor or negligible part of the whole job. At this time of crisis in confidence among the bar, the opinion moves to the fore.[284a] It is the major line of communication to the bar, as it is to the public. Other lines of communication are both awkward and uncertain. Speeches and articles must remain nonrepresentative until they become a flood, and by then they will have moved into the trite, into the colorless commonplace. Communication by demeanor and by the slow solid current of honest and effective work we have had, we have. It is indispensable. It is also not enough. No, it is the opinion which must carry the burden of re-educating the bar; of curing its unease, its disease; of putting iron into its blood and sure quiet into its heart. Of course, little can go into the opinion which has not been thought about before; insofar the opinion reflects the deciding, insofar things urged for the opinion are in the same breath urged for the deciding processes. Again of course, those things which are best done before, and which the bar also needs to know of, should be made to show in the opinion; and insofar things urged for the deciding processes speak in the same words to opinion-composition.

Differences there are aplenty, to be sure. The order of approach to the different kinds of sense looks to the deciding, not to the order of opinion-presentation. Nor is there need, or often wisdom, in revealing in an opinion the work of those major caveats which yet are of the essence as a court weighs and tests counsel's lines and materials of argument. Nor has an opinion any concern with the queer helter-skelter of small but sometimes important stimuli and {289} deflections which have their unpredictable and sometimes indescribable two cents' worth to put into the resolution of a legal puzzler inside a puzzled court. Nevertheless, I think that from here on in there is no need to keep deciding and opinion meticulously apart. It will be just as intelligible and both easier and more interesting to let them swap around a little and get friendly in a Huck Finn stew.

Before so doing it may be as well to recur for a moment to this question of what an opinion is for. Every case lawyer knows somehow of its office as a guide to the future. Though few indeed are the printed discussions of *stare decisis* which show any real understanding either of that office or of that value, or of the manner of its discharge, yet even fewer, I surmise, are those who would deny its existence.[284b] And as we have noted, most, even of the despairing, feel that opinions should and somehow could be made to yield such value. It came then to me with something of a jolt to find in a learned German volume, devoted to the instruction of prospective or less experienced judges, that the prime function of an opinion was portrayed as that of making counsel, especially losing counsel, feel that the case had been dealt with carefully and fairly.[285] {290} Plainly this is one function, and no slight one; but surely at our present juncture an equally, a more, important office is *to let the winner* (and incidentally the loser, and, not at all incidentally, *any* member of the bar) *get some working idea of what did the scoring for the victory*. Our "natural" organization of an opinion does seem to run toward disposition adversely of points of appeal raised, argued and unpersuasive, with some notice of the lines of argument which have failed to persuade. The same naturalness leads, even where the point is successful, to handling more at length, and then dismissing, the objections urged against it. Here, as always, it is the ache or worry which attracts attention.

But I feel deeply that within even three to five years a real measure of the needed re-education of the bar could be accomplished if our appellate courts should as a deliberate and sustained policy attribute, wherever the attribution is fairly earned, to counsel the suggestions both of law *and especially of situation-sense* which the opinion marshals as leading to its conclusion. "Counsel soundly urges that …." "It is difficult to meet defendant's contention that …." — such expressions are not today novel or unusual. Neither, however, are they a thing which crosses an opinion-writer's mind with the casual of-courseness of his canvass of those points which need explicit knocking down.

But we have seen that a main element in the bar's loss of contact with the appellate bench's work today is that the bar at large does not so read enough of the opinions at large that lawyers in general get to perceive — i.e., take in at all — and to *understand* — i.e., make at home in their working equipment — what it is that the appellate bench is actually doing, or what the machinery is for spotting the reckonabilities in that doing, or the measures for effective basic organization of an appellate argument.

Now no exhortation will ever induce the bar to read enough opinions roundedly enough for that, or with enough acumen. Leave the situation alone, moreover, and it is likely, for another legal generation, to worsen — to real and possibly dire misfortune. But each individual opinion composed and published in the manner we have been discussing becomes without more an opinion with a herald, with a trumpeting herald. What the appellate court has put into official print about the insight and the art of winning counsel is not a thing that he or his family, or his friends, or his cohorts, will allow to go unread, even by persons who may shudder at having to read about the subject matter. Nor will the fact that the vanity of many counsel is thus indulged do much to dampen the effect. Allowing ribbons and medals to become moderately common {291} has served little over the past thirty-odd centuries to keep men from wanting them, wearing them, calling attention to them, or shaping conduct with an eye to them. It is humanly impossible that sustained judicial praise of the discovery and urging of sound situation-sense will not within a rather short period sow and cultivate within the bar an insight into how appellate litigation can be handled better and more effectively. It ought simultaneously and by way of the same spread of understanding to somewhat check the present spate of the foredoomed ones. Nor can this be done without, at the bar, an increasing realization of and comfort in that true steadiness of work and result which is already there to see *if a man will read,* and which can be only strengthened by such developments.

One may note as a subsidiary value that so far from introducing a distorting or further competitive element into the already complex mass of opinion functions, this suggestion tends rather to simplify the picture and to reinforce precisely those lines which most need conscious furthering.

6. On-going Correction and Recorrection

If the present study has not yet persuaded of the value, the necessity, of moving the daily corrective function of appellate judging into the forefront of conscious method, no reiteration will help. But it is worthwhile to gather some of the aspects into more of a whole, in a single place, and it will pay to advert to a few items of method.

One begins by recalling that the aim is, by further work with and on the rule-stock — which is the verbal tool-stock — of The Law to develop measures more and more adequate, more and more cleanly of application, until the singing chorus lifts the man-in-office and his work not measurably, as today, but almost immeasurably. One recalls that *good* rules are more than tools, they are also good guides, they almost compel, by their self-apparent wisdom. When the relevant rules are shoddy or clumsy it takes a master craftsman to bring out a fine and satisfying product, but if the rules are good enough they make it hard for even the dull or the duffer to go too far wrong. The power of doctrine is thus negative as well as positive; rules faulty in purpose or in draftsmanship can hinder as much as sound, clean rules can help; and our rules of law, like our legal concepts, we remember, have a frightening range both of technical merit and of goodness of substance, so that on-going daily betterment is of the essence. {292}

The betterment thus has two phases, related always, yet rewarding separate consideration. The one is goal-stuff: to locate and focus for seeing the most significant working situation-types, and then to smell out and shape for seeing and thought the lines along which, in any situation-type, the rightnesses of conduct and solution travel, so as to further the immanent goals of that situation in its relation to the whole of man and culture. In one aspect this is most pedestrian: the cable transfer, or foreign exchange generally, can only to a Ricardian economist seem in direct contact with the cloud-pastures of the Beautiful, the True, the Good; the best rule on consideration in relation to the readjustment of a bilateral contract surely operates at a number of removes from God's determinable will; the "right" balance, in the absence of pre-emptive legislation or within the legislative gaps, in the labor-management struggle or that of competing commodities or brands, presents itself to be worked out in terms so earthy as frequently to require hemidemisemiquavers of subdivision. Let that be granted. But from that very fact will then follow that the patient prosaic search for an ever more significant classification, and within any such for an ever more significant and satisfying line of rightness, must be unceasing.

The other phase of the betterment is that of measures. Rare indeed is the situation in which our legal measures are as well adapted to our goals as we could wish: that fact will not down. Moreover, every slightest shift of goal throws up at once the question whether the measure also may not need immediate appropriate modification. It was a little thing that Kaiser did, to build steel boats keel up, so that an *ordinary* man could do the riveting, and even an expert could do it faster and with less exhaustion; it was a little thing that came from just one fresh look at ancient and hallowed knowhow and "rightnesses" of operation. All over the law-plant such little things in regard to measures are waiting to be fresh-seen and fresh-done; it is a constant, a never-ending job — but so rewarding. Instances clamor: *Wenzler Plumbing v. Sellen* (Washington, presented above, p. 174), where duty and damage are clear, reinstates the early Grand Style approach by thrusting onto the defendant the risk (within reasonable limits) of any misestimate by a merely human tribunal of the damage he has caused. *Gerberg v. Crosby* (Washington, presented above, p. 174) materially and usefully widens the practical utility of expert evidence. *Allendorf* (Illinois, presented above, p. 282) provides a retooling to keep an actuary's testimony on lost earnings available while at the same time freeing it from otherwise probable misuse. {293}

The truth is that whether in matters of goal or in matters of measure most of the little things that we accomplish are unlike Kaiser's; they are only steps, often enough awkward and calling from the outset for redirection; they are typically too short, moreover, in the absence of cumulation, to make much difference to the scheme of the law or even of the field. Legal institutions do not spring mature, like Minerva, from the heads of judges; variation, not mutation, is our habit. This is true not so much because our medium is intractable. In itself the medium is not nearly as resistant as we are prone to believe. It is true rather on the one hand because we lack (or will not use) the more fresh and childlike manner of imagination, so that even in new forgings we tend to cleave close to some familiar model. And it is true on the other hand because of the nature of justice and of our purblind insight into it. There is no place to develop the nature of justice,[286] but it is a place to point out that in application to organization and conflict in a shifting world of mazed complexity the justice ideal must in any given situation-type be very difficult to hit upon with detailed accuracy — doubly so when the problems of goal and measure are cross-conditioned, and when the light and background available to the appellate court is so largely conditioned by, if not confined to, the particular litigation. It has been suggested above that a working solution which is on or even near the felt target tends strongly to seem and feel "right" to a court driven by work, pestered by puzzling, and just plain tired — a court, moreover, already calloused against a finer sensitivity for justice by the coarseness of most legal tools and by the brutal choice between Yes and No so often forced by our legal scheme and our system of legal issues even when the better of the alternative apples offered is unripe, water-cored, worm-eaten, scaled or bruised, or all of these. A man on a bench learns that make-do is the way of an appellate court's quest for justice; and he who has lived long enough with make-do will not too often pine too greatly at giving over the chase when enough is in hand to manage with for tomorrow. The pressure of time and business compels that way of life.

The cure does not lie in chasing far and further. Where it lies is in never failing, *each* time, to take at least one fresh look. The new prodding of the new facts
may bring something better into focus. The queer subconscious may this time be
ready to give up an out which has been cooking down in there since the last time
{294} the court walked through these legal sandburs. In this effort to take a look
each time, the appellate court's job, their duty, to freshen up consciously is as
inescapable as is the law teacher's with a new incoming class — or that of those
neglected heroines who handle primary instruction. It *must not* be what all
habit, all routine, all weariness cry out that it is and has to be: just another of the
shopworn same. The Alabama court has found one standard device to help: to
look for and bring to bear a precedent which gives not only authority but
rationale; an excellent start. Surely, however, only a start: Does the rationale
satisfy? What, if one stops to ponder, does it mean, that rationale? Do the facts
of the cases which have been cited, or located by the court itself, suggest anything about whether the *type* of problem-situation involved may need redefinition? Only when at least a pipeful of time has been spent in this kind of rumina-
tion am I willing to concede that the due effort of an opinion-writer has been put
forth to test his "established" rule of law or his proposed "application." The
demand is for no prohibitive time-outlay, it is for a pittance only. But it is for a
never-failing pittance.

In most instances the inquiry will draw a blank. But our journey through the
current opinions makes it clear indeed that "most" does not mean punishingly,
deadeningly most. It will be a strange clutch of appeals which will not hatch out
at least one cantankerous candidate for improvement of rule, or of measure, or
of situation-diagnosis, whether in substance or in formulation or in both.

Once again, this seems to me to sparkle unmistakably from our samplings as
what the appellate courts today are busy doing, and doing rather well. If you will
read a few current advance sheets from cover to cover, *and* if you still harbor any
lurking misconception either that our appellate courts are unmindful of their
duty to the authorities *or* that their work is following any mindless-quiescence
ideal of *stare decisis,* then you will be amazed and I hope abashed at the frequency of reference to and building on a *recent* case in which a whole set of
cases has been explored, clarified, and put into condition, for a while, to be just
used; and you will be equally amazed, and I hope again abashed, to find the
court nevertheless often looking over such an area again. Normally, the new look
finds the clean-up good. Every once in a while, the new look leads to some
revision, great or small.

7. An Assembly of Procedures

This clean-up procedure — which in contrast to the larger-scale area clean-
up mentioned above we might call *rule*-tidying — can {295} be linked with
certain other procedures to produce a serviceable standard technique for going
at the recorrection job. Neither one by one nor in combination do they offer
anything novel, but the equipment of a craft-workbench consists in making
regularly available good tools — and knowhow — otherwise only occasionally
called on; in proposing vise, chisel, and mallet as an assembly; in the picture of
measuring, cutting, joining, and finishing as a foreseeable sequence of operations in no way dependent on the insight or inspiration of any day or moment.
Though, to be sure, as with the workbench and its knowhow, a warped eye, a
clumsy hand, a dull or slipshod man can botch the job. Nevertheless, let us look
over this serviceable sequence.

The first operation, which is in as good as universal use, is the gathering of the relevant (or if those are too many, the more significant) authorities at home. Not in universal use, by any means, however, is the canvassing of those authorities not only for "the" rule which (in one phrasing or another)[287] may be common to them, but to what they offer of insight and wisdom by way of their rationale and also by way of the nature of their facts. Good men can differ about pertinence and weight in any instance. Thus, in *Gould v. Stelter,* 14 Ill. 2d 376, 152 N.E.2d 869 (1958), we have Schaefer, for the majority, bulldozing out the stump of an old "mutuality of remedy" condition to granting specific performance, a condition which the court finds, on authority, riddled by exceptions and, on policy, untenable in general. Daily, the Chief, concurring in result, sees the broad ruling as uncalled for, and would have simply set up one more exception. The point of interest here is his objection that the majority "disregards the factual situations which led to the decisions" in those two cases which, respectively, had originally adopted Fry's strange general rule and had last revived it. And in truth vital lessons about the most significant location and shaping of a situation-type, as also about the "immanent law" within such a type when significantly defined, are to be learned from such factual situations and their issues, and to be learned both in the exploratory stages and in any retesting; in the instant case it is only that the majority thought those lessons had already been duly learned and that the time had come to act. The case bears here because it suggests so strongly that what a recanvassing court normally has need of is the light from the factual situations *in addition* to the phrasings of the rule. One can add, {296} from the Alabama practice already noted, the need for a regular attention to the lines of rationale recorded in prior opinions; and here (in contrast, for my money, to "weight of authority" nose-counts)[288] is where I see high value in the practice in all three of the old West Coast States: the hunting up — often in addition to quite adequate home *authority* — of outside opinions which carry good indications of good *reasons* for a good position. The old saw is a good saw, that authority may be territorial, but sense and reason have interstate and even international currency.

Now efforts to do, and do thoroughly, what I have just been treating as the first desirable operation of the "law" side of deciding and of composition, have been under considerable criticism, written and especially oral, because of the bulk thereby added to the reports, and because of the inordinate outlay of labor entailed. Wigmore, e.g. — who had a gift for accurate compression of an opinion's essence which I doubt that any other American scholar has equaled — Wigmore was severe about wayward dangling discursiveness in an opinion; and it is evident that it would be a grievous fault if any judge with Wigmore's gift should write at undue length. By most of mankind, however, some space will have to be expended. Yet I do suggest that our study opens up a number of lines of thrift. If the prime job is in truth the better diagnosis and definition of the significant type of problem-situation and the better diagnosis and phrasing of a fair rule and an adequate remedy, all of this with an eye forward, to guide tomorrow — then an opinion acquires a primary focus, and a primary focus is a means to condensation. Today is the occasion and today affords one test; but the job for tomorrow, which *includes* today, remains central.

At this point one perceives a major value in that Syllabus by the Court which, among our samplings, is the practice of the Supreme Courts of Alabama, Kansas, and Ohio. I am not addressing myself to the Ohio superstition[289] that the court's syllabus states the law and their opinion does not. I am addressing myself to what every writer of a brief has learned: that to get his points into concise, clear arrangement and words *before he writes* is both to sharpen his writing and to shorten it. The points may need rephrasing {297} when the text is done — although they should not — but even though they do, they still have served. By the same token, I submit that our study makes persuasive that the *only* sound purpose of publishing a Syllabus by the Court is to make such terse, pondered, *and partly tested* contributions to guidance for the future. A syllabus is to be neither an index nor a summary; it is to be a distillate of ever better doctrine. I should myself always wish for one paragraph to arrange and condense the case, the issues, and the judgment, in the fashion of the headnote to a law review "recent case" of thirty or forty years ago — partly because that shows the testing of the doctrinal extract, partly because it records what facts the court itself has deemed significant; but such a paragraph I conceive as distinct enough to precede, as a "headnote" or as "the facts," any paragraphs or points of *syllabus*.

Do not get impatient with me over these preferences. They are not mere personal vagaries. They are functional in design and they have the balance and edge of a Plumb ax. I will maintain roundly that nine judges out of ten, each one on eight or more occasions out of ten, will write a cleaner and briefer opinion if he arranges and phrases, *before* his opinion, such crowning points or syllabus paragraphs as I have described. That is a simple fact of life about the nature of expository argumentative writing when the writer is neither a genius nor inspired for the occasion. I will maintain therefore that the introduction of a Syllabus by the Court, if rightly handled, promises any court a wherewithal, in large enough degree to count, to sharpen its work, to bring that work home a bit closer to the bar, and also to speed and shorten the work a little in the process.

More, I am prepared to urge that this order of composition (mind you, I am *not* talking about pulling syllabus paragraphs out of an already written opinion) leads much more easily and effectively into the job of rule-tidying mentioned above. We are all conversant with the opinion which gives a clean fresh start. The prior authorities are examined, arranged, so to speak definitely edited, brought into synthesis, and laid away. They are no longer authorities, they have become historical events or museum pieces; the future work can be done and should be done with and from the clean-up job. *Jones v. Just,* mentioned above, was such an opinion; some grandiloquent Britisher gathered it into a book on *Fifteen Decisive Battles of the Law. McPherson v. Buick,* also mentioned, is a more recent example. But the beauty of Cardozo's judging did not consist primarily in production of three dozen transcendent landmarks of *McPherson* stature. He had, like Cassio, {298} "a daily beauty in his life" of judging. As he grew more experienced, the drive grew in him to leave the older authorities *tidied up behind,* to make each litle opinion, in its own little way, a *clean* fresh start. I find in the work of Holmes on the Massachusetts bench no such pervading flavor. But it is a quest and an effort open to any judge on any bench, at any time. And, I repeat, it is a quest which will be measurably furthered by having the points for the guidance of the future in clean words under the eyes before one addresses himself to building, eliciting, or distilling them out of the received doctrinal materials.

Rule-tidying effort saves, moreover, in the long haul, more time of judges than it costs (to say nothing of the tremendous savings in lawyer-hours which are its product when well done). The process is not unlike that of review in the case study of law: The recurrent attempt at synthesis and consolidation does have its values in relation to the specific subject matter, but the major values lie in the building and speeding of the relevant knowhow. That, in turn, when rule-tidying results really begin to click, means an increasing number of those opinions familiar to every court — and beginning slowly to become more familiar to the bar — to which the court looks back as having mustered, examined, and definitively organized some particular body of material: a job put to rest for a generation, and relied on with quiet pride. Courts and bar can do with an increase in those opinions, there is room for a few thousands more of them in the doctrinal scheme of any of our States.

Let me come finally to an intangible value of the rightly fashioned court-syllabus plus rule-tidying which rates with or above the operational merits I have been extolling. That intangibility needs no argument, it needs only a reminder. It lies in this: that he who settles to picking and honing his points for the morrow's guidance and settles then to tidying up the past authorities behind him has lined out for his work a course that will well-nigh assure its consonance with the Law of Fitness and Flavor. Again, there can be no supernal magic in method. Mansfield's arbitrary dismissal of unwanted authorities, the perverse blindness of a Parke, the crookedness of a Manton, the distorting miscraftsmanship of any wrongheaded overastute reformist who as a practice twists the authorities beyond their decencies — these will survive any mere mechanics of operation. But for the plain citizen of the appellate commonwealth, indeed for the leading citizen, simple human truths hold true: Well-designed ways of craft-work develop overtone and rich aroma in the product in the way such simple practices as thinking of others and truthtelling develop unselfishness and tact and honor in the man. {299}

8. Advance Notice of Important Change in Doctrine

Along with the gathering of recorded experience re rules, re rationale, re the fact-problems which have given rise to both and to which either has given rise; along with a sound syllabus-procedure and its promise; along with the daily tidying job — along with these goes, in an age of needed doctrinal change, the rounding out of the judicial workbench by standard equipment to cut down the costs of such change. Again the problem is old; again wisdom has been found and used, but lies largely unnoticed, in good part actively denied; again, even in the middle of unheeding theory, there have been sprouting, all over in odd corners, stalks from good seed which are now ripening to harvest.

One begins with the intimations of the cautious opinion-writer, concurred in by his court, of what is *not* being decided, what is being left open. Thus in *Race v. Krum* (above, p. 277) the court, as it held a manufacturing seller of ice cream for unwholesomeness, carefully reserved the case of a restaurantkeeper. In *Rinaldi v. Mohican Co.* (above, p. 278) the court was holding that "mere purchase by a customer from a retail dealer in foods of an article ordinarily used for human consumption does by implication make known to the vendor the purpose for which the article is required" (225 N.Y. at 73) and "further, that such a purchase, where the buyer may assume that the seller has the opportunity to examine the article sold, unexplained, is also conclusive evidence of reliance on the seller's skill and judgment." It continued, however: "*We here limit the rule. We do not pass upon the question of whether it applies to a sale in the original package bought by the vendor from others.*" (ibid 74; my italics.) Each of these caveats was a warning to lower bench and to bar.

Now I have never, in more than forty years at the law, seen or heard such a warning criticized as improper. This though the warning may have been purest dictum, so far as it might intimate what the court *would* do, when, as, and if. And even though, as in both of these particular cases, the intimation may have proved misleading. Neither have I found criticism when the gratuitous suggestion in an opinion about what the court will do proves prescient, as with *Hogan v. Kirkland*[290] after seventy years. Advance information can indeed go much further in regard to the views of the court or its members on issues raised and avoided, or merely {300} suggested by the case in hand. It is hard, for instance, to believe that the advice about proper procedure given the unhappy Florence in *Megargel Estate* (Pennsylvania 1944, presented at page 146) will be welshed on if Florence follows that procedure. And a plaintiff must tremble for his chances of recovery in Ohio, if he should come to grief because of negligent maintenance of his home town sewer: "It may well be argued that the distinction attempted between sewer maintenance and repair and the collection of garbage is not a persuasive or a valid one. This court has decided that the construction of a sewer by a municipality is a governmental function ... If the matter were one of first impression here, there are members of this court who would place the maintenance and repair of sewers as well as their construction in the category of a governmental activity" — so as to bar suit for negligent injury. *Broughton v. City of Cleveland*, in holding the same for garbage collection.[291] I do not, I say again, recall hearing such remarks as these discussed otherwise than in terms of interest; they have not been disparaged as unseemly. Indeed, such observations can be a very welcome warning; they can lead to remedial action before the actual ax receives its chance to fall. Thus the *Birnbaum* case (New York, 1958, presented in Appendix A, *New York*, p. 478) turned wholly on the fact that the court felt a constitutional amendment, no less, of 1938 to have been "designed to overcome" a dictum of the court's in 1935 that the interest of a member in the teacher's pension fund could before completion of the conditions for retirement "hardly be deemed contractual" and was "subject to change or even to revocation at the will of the legislature."

Now why, against this background, do lawyers or judges go blind, see red, have kittens, stop thinking, gibber, and otherwise engage in scalene behavior at the proposal that it should become a standard tool of the judicial workbench to give explicit warning at a suitable juncture that a particular rotting tree of law is tottering to its fall? The emotional reaction, the rush of blindness to the brain, is quite queer. Such explosions are not set off by even the nastiest of judicial language, just as such, about a given rule, however hoary. No man of law will turn a hair at: "If this were a case of first impression, we should find it difficult to meet appellant's argument," or "The rule is patently obsolete, and causes vastly more injustice than it cures." So, too, my strong guess is that in *Gould v. Stelter* (above, p. 295), the majority would have been a unanimity if the opinion had run along the line: "We have here {301} another case requiring yet another exception to the moribund rule requiring mutuality from the very time of contracting before specific performance can be had by either party. So many holes have been pierced in that so-called rule that there hardly remains anything that one can see as a fabric, and it may well be that the time is near at hand for its official abrogation." But what vote would have resulted if the proposal had been to substitute for this last a flat warning that the time had already arrived, and that when circumstances would permit, the old rule *would* be buried? The case was perfect for the purpose: in any event, it called for no lifting of the old rule from its deathbed. And the case may be perfect even when it is the old rule which practically demands application in the pending cause. Thus in *Fosdick's Trust* (New York, 1958, again from our sample, Appendix A, *New York*, p. 477) "stock dividends" were, under a trust deed of 1918, to go to the residuary legatee. Since before 1918 the court had built and used a particular definition. But a later financial and commercial usage had developed, under which the distribution in question would be a "stock split" rather than a "stock dividend," and would call for radically different allocation between corpus and income. Professional opinion was mobilized, vocal, and persuasive. But a majority dug in, not only on construing the particular deed according to its legal meaning when drawn (which decided the case in hand), but on the startling further position that any redefinition at all of the term "stock dividend" (not in statutes, but in general!) was "properly for the Legislature alone." Here, as in the *Gould* case, I cannot help seeing the unnecessarily broad posing of the issue (Do we here and now just plain overrule?) as having contributed materially both to the disharmony, to the somewhat edged tone of the discussions, and to unyielding insistence of the victors on each last inch of the territory controverted — and, by crickey, conquered!

Here are two courts of reputation facing the kind of difficulty which makes good friends and brothers seem for the moment highly unreasonable. In each of those courts the issue is posed and then joined: Do we overrule here and now, or do we not overrule at all? This is the issue in each court, be it noted, although neither of the litigations demanded any overruling in the case at hand. Neither court even considers the obvious alternative, so clearly suggested by "the tendency of our decisions" in their practice of issuing warnings *in lesser matters.* What is more and much worse, the issue as each of these courts posed and accepted it is the issue which in similar circumstances almost any of our State supreme {302} courts may be expected to pose and accept, *almost as of course,* and almost every time. I hasten to state what I shall shortly demonstrate: this is *not* for lack of precedent to the contrary. Neither do I think it is in many instances a matter of deliberate choice. I think a different choice just does not as yet normally present itself to the mind. It is as if a road led out into glorious open country, but we were so habit-tracked into turning off it at a given corner that we never looked up to see where we should be if for once we did not make the turn.

Certainly as late as 1932 Cardozo himself felt a pronouncement of the kind under discussion, if it led to a judging based on the old rule of law, to stand at the very verge of appellate judicial power:

"'The rule that we are asked to apply is out of tune with the life about us.... We apply it to this case because the repeal might work hardship to those who have trusted to its existence. We give notice, however, that anyone trusting to it hereafter will do so at his peril.' *The effect of such a declaration would be to leave the law uncertain in respect of new transactions* until the court could speak again, though the uncertainty would not be grievous, for litigants could assume with little likelihood of disappointment that the dictum would be followed.... I am not persuaded altogether that competence to proceed along these lines does not belong to the judges even now without the aid of statute." (My italics.)[292] Poetic justice can be a justice of reward as well as retribution: it was bestowed upon Cardozo, with his opinion in the *Sunburst Oil* case,[293] to place beyond doubt, so far as concerns our Federal Constitution, the judges' "competence to proceed along these lines." I do not think many opinions gave him greater pleasure.

But let me nail one thing before proceeding an inch: "The effect of such a declaration would be to leave the law uncertain." Nothing truer. *But the effect of* NOT *making such a declaration is to leave the law* MUCH MORE *uncertain.*[294] Moribund rules have no certainty in them. They are too likely to be overruled *without warning* for any good counselor to build upon them. Careful {303} counselors, when they find a bridge shaky and ready to come down — though no man can foresee precisely when — put no weight on it; they choose another crossing and so run free of upset or disappointment no matter how the point may come to be decided. The trouble is that too many counselors lack the experience of the sensitivity necessary to recognizing that collapse impends. For such, and for their clients, the court's warning is like a danger flag that blocks the bridge and says: Detour! It is an *increase* in the *practical* certainty of legal living.

Much more troubling in regard to any standard policy of deciding the instant case in the old way, even after the court has become convinced that the old rule requires abrogation, is a point I have heard urged by Chief Justices Kenison (N.H.) and Weintraub (N.J.): a court which accepts such a policy cuts itself off from the very opportunity to determine whether it wants to overrule, for where is the lawyer who will spend his own time and his client's money when all that he can hope for is to *lose his client's case?* To me this argues with utter cogency the need for a practice of warning given as soon as the court becomes clear that the time has come to change or kill a rule, and preferably before the exact case forces the issue. We have seen an instance from Cuthbert Pound in *Harris v. Shorall* (above at p. 207) and we have just looked (pp. 300 f.), in *Gould v. Stelter* and *Fosdick's Trust,* at two cases perfect for the purpose. The *Harris v. Shorall* sequence even shows the second think at work, on the basis of new experience, to upset the prophecy. I join Cardozo in thinking that particular upset unwise; but it does show how new experience *can* come to bear. And the astounding expansion of critical legal literature in the last quarter century offers both an avenue and a hope that such a judicial warning-forecast may elicit and marshal material which court and policy may need.

As to the case which forces the issue without advance notice, I would suggest that the difficulty can be met by substituting for any *practice* of deciding the old way because there *may* have been reliance a *possibility* of so deciding if *enough* reliance is *demonstrated* in the case in hand. If the threshold of "enough" is set high as to both quantity and certainty, such an approach would leave an ample carrot for the bar. — Neither, one may observe, are the risks of changing law so different from the risks of a changing technology and market, or of deterioration of a neighborhood, or the like, as to put upon the conscience of a court reliance-losses which are not shown to be both quite direct, and serious.

Whatever the causes of the still current aversion to public {304} announcement — though always on fitting occasion — of the court's intention to weed out a noxious rule of law, it seems manifest that the reasons are overwhelming for seeking to do the job itself in two stages. First, that causes vastly less disturbance, even inside the court, and need cause none at all, outside the court. Second, it is a much safer procedure. As stated above, objectors get a chance to marshal the arguments for Why Not with a freedom and especially with a completeness which the single litigation seldom affords. A clearer case is hard to find.

As to the causes of aversion, the blind spot, or whatever it be, seems to me to derive mainly from a pair of doctrinal images — they are too tenuous to be termed tenets — which have long lost all blood. The one, which haunts the Digests under "Courts, Key 100(1)" is the doctrine that to overrule a decision is to rule "not that it is [or was] bad law, but that it was never law at all"; which joins or is a part of the old slogan (using "law" in a different sense) that "decisions are not the law, but only evidence thereof." The other image is the image of the court which does not, because it cannot, make law, but only searches for it, doing for the most part a successful job of finding it. Above I have paid my respects to the portion of truth and solidity which informs this last idea.[295] I note here merely that subjection of the court to The Law, the Whole of the Law, and the limitations imposed thereby, rather plainly warrant no denial of that creative action which the court cannot escape in its work among the leaves and twigs of the Great Oak. But there has been no opportunity above to pay due disrespects to this still-recited doctrine about "was never law at all."

One recalls first that for more than a century that doctrine has been too much for most courts to stomach in action, in regard to either case law decision or statutory construction, whenever either property or contract rights have been built on the older decision before its overruling.[296] The courts keep stepping in to safeguard particular litigants against backlash. Such action, it will be noted, so far as it fails to occur, means an unnecessary human price imposed for the betterment of rules; so far as it does occur, it still makes the change in a single move instead of two, and so throws away the chance at neater retailoring which the two-stage process {305} affords. But what brings a lover of the law close to disgust or to despair is the assertion, by a craft-conscious supreme tribunal, in the very moment of sharpest creation, that it is not doing and cannot do what it is at that moment proceeding to do because its very office demands of it that action. It may be that in 1840 or 1850 there was some sense in arguing and feeling that the decision about to be reversed was just a mistake, to be corrected. But that is not, four times out of five, why cases or rules are overruled today. Today they are overruled typically because although they were good law once, and in their day have served a decent purpose, conditions have changed around them until their service has run out. Today's overruling does not one time in five uncover the true rule the court should have seen two or three generations back. It consciously declares, instead, a *new* rule for *new* conditions, a rule which in the older days would have been dubious at best.[296a] And in any event, a court conscious of its inevitable function of *daily* creative choice must stultify itself when in the moment of the most responsible of choices it denies its function as a *maker* of that case law, or of that statutory interpretation, on which it is right for people to rely. I am not much for matters of status or of etiquette, but I find it unworthy, I feel queasy, when I come upon courts mouthing doctrine under which a man who has with reason and demonstrably built his house upon the decision of the supreme court of his State is to receive protection — *if* he does — not of right, nor even of due grace, but with a sort of squeamish apology by the legal system to the legal system for bothering to take note of what it is doing to him.

9. The Two-Stage Principle Generally

To sum up, there is the prophecy that we will overrule as soon as opportunity appears, and there is the statement that it really does seem to be time, and doubtless the rule is on its way out, and there are various lesser ways of sawing the dead limb more or less completely through. Speaking as a counselor, I do not find my response to any of these ways of warning to differ by a hair. Any of them is a tocsin; none states a certainty; nothing could be easier in {306} counseling than to shape one's course with safety. Thus, in the seal case: do not let your modification go unsealed; in the trust case, state in the instrument what you want done; etc. People who after the siren sounds do not so deport themselves no court need worry over; they have embarked on no reliance. Either they knew nothing of this old rule, or else they do not care.

Speaking now not as a counselor, however, but as a jurisprude and friend of the court, I see no reason for the opinion not to step up its warning to the point of direct prophecy and expression of intention, in any situation in which the court's view has become that definite; and I see no reason for the opinion to go beyond, or even as far as, Cuthbert Pound's style of phrasing where the court's judgment has not yet wholly clarified; but I see every reason why any doubt or worry which is felt to be really maturing should come in some fashion to expression.

Speaking as an observer of the legal public, judicial and other, I note again that such language as Pound's in the *Harris* case seems to raise no hackles. It appears to be only when the new rule would lead to deciding the instant case itself the other way that lawmen find it strange for courts to be sensible — so that application of the Cardozo procedure in either *Gould* or *Fosdick* (above, pp. 300 f.) would have been entirely decorous. But if the untenability of such a test for what is proper procedure is not manifest by now, no further words of mine can make it so.

Let me therefore move to a related point, to another type of two-step procedure in the building of doctrine. I refer, when a ruling has novelty, or its desirable range is still cloudy, or no means has been found to cut the issue down to tolerable or comfortable scope — I refer to the *deliberate provision of an alternative* ground for the decision. This also amounts to a two-stage operation, though the goal is made plain and though the first step is firm. The main ground is a carefully considered, carefully explored, carefully buttressed ground; no man can doubt its intention. Consider *Simmons v. State*, quoted fully above at page 167. Or consider the old *Shaw* ruling against effective bona fide purchase of a bill of lading, presented above at pages 229 ff., where the whole drive of the court's opinion can be technically parried as having been unnecessary. But there could be no doubt as to what the court wanted there, and what it wanted was what it got; *Shaw* was for a while a leading case. Yet the ease with which that main ruling was discarded after it had outlived its span (as the similar ruling in the related *Farmers' Bank* case, pp. 230, 234, was not) is an ease which would have been open to the court itself on the next occasion, if it had been able to detect its slip that early. {307}

Now I am quite unable to comprehend why the provision, as a practice, of such an out, is not sound judicial policy. In the first place, it has been noted (p. 103) that our courts, these last twenty years, are relying freely (and I urge wisely) on non-"holding" rulings as being authority solid enough for citation without qualification or apology. Provision of an alternative ground, as here suggested, can therefore in no manner undercut the power of the main and meant ruling. More, since it takes a veritable peabrain to mistake a point which a court is seeking to make central, the main ruling must continue to appear and to function as such. The only thing which will lead to discarding it or to a striking shift away from it will have to be such new light on the situation or on the desirable scope and nature of the remedy as shows the ruling to have lacked solid basis; and new light of that kind is what ought to have just that effect. At hand, if needed, is then the alternative ground, to provide a technical distinction — but, both pursuant to principle and by the nature of this situation, never to be conscripted except for reason good and reason given.

It is I trust obvious that by "alternative" I do not mean a mere makeweight; I mean a ground, if one can be found, which can handle the decision *on the facts* in independence of the main chosen ground; and I trust it is if possible even more obvious that I do not refer to one of those general tags of loose incidence (typically twinned with an available matching tag to the contrary) which are alone no sound basis for any decision. The difference is well illustrated by *In re Holder,* 218 N.C. 136, 10 S.E.2d 620 (1940), where a judgment upholding an adoption proceeding was reversed. The unmarried mother, in turning the child over to a Children's Home Society, had signed a general consent to possible adoption by such person as the Society might choose. In the adoption proceedings two and a half years later, this consent was not included. The court held that the statute required the jurisdictional facts, including parents' consent or abandonment, to appear on the face of the record. It also quoted and followed a prior holding that the living parent's consent "must at least be in fair contemplation of the proposed adoption," and must include the identity of the proposed parents. And reasons for these positions were carefully set forth. Furthermore, "The proceeding is in derogation of the common law and must be strictly construed." (10 S.E.2d at 622.) This last, within the meaning of my position, is at best surplusage. But either of the two first rulings, if the court had chosen to load the major weight upon the other, would have been a good alternative to add.[297] {308}

Such was in fact the procedure in *Maxwell v. Saylor,* 359 Pa. 94, 58 A.2d 355 (1948), which I shall use for my last example here, and where the subsequent course shows first the alternative taken seriously, with a portent of a narrowing of the rule, and then the sloughing of it off as a mere makeweight so as to let the novel rule, on second thought, run free. A "common law" husband and wife in a State which did not recognize common law marriage took realty purportedly by the entireties. After a careful canvass of rationale the court decided that the deed effected a conveyance in joint tenancy with the right of survivorship, which "best effectuates their intention to the extent legally permissible." That decision just squeaked by, 4-3. The majority in their last paragraph remarked (seemingly without benefit of a finding below: an alternative indeed!) that the decision was especially just and proper since every dollar invested had been that of the survivor. Only six volumes later, in *Teacher v. Kijurina,* 365 Pa. 480, 76 A.2d 197 (1950), the lower court, on that foundation, gave evidentiary effect to the survivor's having paid the purchase price. The Supreme Court — this time unanimous — pointed out the facts I have just set forth, and continued: "However, this was said after the decision was made on the basis of the language of the deed and uttered merely to show the ruling made accorded with the morals of the particular case" (76 A.2d at 201), thereby avoiding any effect of *Maxwell* on the case in hand. In *Bove v. Bove,* 394 Pa. 627, 149 A.2d 67 (1959), all of this is retailed with a certain gusto, and the rule applied, this time unanimously, in a case in which the survivor seems to have contributed not a cent to either of two purchases.

There is a final reason for such deliberate provision of a solid alternative ground whenever decision moves into an area at all novel or unexplored. We have seen again and again the need, if choice, direction, limitation, phrasing of a solving rule is to be safely wise, for the court to be informed about the scope and nature of the significant type-problem-situation, of how inside that situation life works out, of the implicit values and standards which the situation holds to channel conduct and to guide resolution of conflicts within itself — in a word, about its Goldschmidt's immanent law. {309}

As our economic and social relations grow more complex and differentiated, we know that such necessary information becomes for any unspecialized appellate court less and less likely to be available, on call and at first hand, merely out of the living and maturing of the judges. Increasingly, then, as chance or contrivance or the turbulence of some new area of change throws up those cases which force problems of doctrine into consciousness — increasingly the court is dependent, for provision of such needed knowledge and understanding of background, on the facts of the instant case and on the information and skill of the instant counsel.

Now the chanciness of light from the case is proverbial: beside every "leading case" which has illumined sit five or ten "cases of first impression" which instead of being followed got themselves done over. The chanciness of light from counsel has not achieved proverb-status because its importance is not yet proverb-clear; but it is a chanciness which flickers like a candle in a fitful draft. Look: there are the overskilled counsel who slant the needed knowledge; there are the under-skilled counsel who know not even that background, situation, and immanent law have meanings; and, worse than either, there are the bison who smash up the china in half-suspicion that it might be important.

With these the conditions of their labor and illumination, it becomes for the appellate court a minimum condition of craftsmanship to reach for an alterna-tive ground, and so always for a *second* hope of further needed knowledge and understanding.

FINDING THE TIME

10. The Individual Judge

As is indicated above, that piece of the Grand Style of appellate judging which consists in an order of approach — the situation-type taken as first and prime, the particular case as second and subsidiary — seems to me rather a timesaver than the contrary. But the doing of a right job, even of a right first job, on an unfamiliar situation-type, is time-costly; so is good rule-tidying, when the situation is better known. And few are the courts who are not pressed for time.

Nevertheless, we have here surely the type of embarrassment which faces the overbusy prosecutor's office rather than the type which faces the overburdened post office. The prosecutor cannot reduce deliveries everywhere to one a day, nor even meditate on raising the rates to shake off some of the load. He therefore simply {310} cannot escape the necessity for selection of where to throw in adequate time and energy, relegating what he sees as less vital matters to some lesser form of treatment — adequate if possible, inadequate if need be, but in any event such as not to block off the right doing of what he has selected as the most vital of the jobs in hand.

Such, it seems to me, even though the court may change no whit of its rou-tine, is the obligation and the opportunity of any individual judge to whom the Grand Style opens as his task. His cases for opinions come to him rarely one by one, and even under the dictatorship of a Vanderbilt there is room to pick the most promising of the litter for the most careful raising. The intangible return from the job clean on target and tidied up behind is such that few men can experience it even once without setting up within themselves a hunger like the hunger of a good angler for a trout stream in his favorite weather. The joy of compression of a right job into one even righter, when one can manage it, purrs in the heart over the years. If you have any literary sensitivity at all, you can feel the writer's pleasure from the page whenever the creation was yielding him this sort of satisfaction.

But a judge's, or a court's, satisfaction and craft-pride in a right performance can be brought home without need to rely on a reader's flair for style. Thus, in the *Slonaker* case, mentioned above at page 281, Horace Stern — a craftsman of parts — had done as pretty and at the same time unassuming a job of clarifica-tion as one will often find. There had been eleven prior Pennsylvania cases on agreements for service with an indefinite time term. Eight had followed the old exaggerated quest-for-meta-physical-certainty will-o'-the-wisp rule: "no words of certainty" equals no agreement on the point equals terminable at will equals no obligation. Three of the cases, under the rule quite unpredictably, and without any effective reformulation of the rule, had come out otherwise. Stern examined them all, and sorted them, and substituted for the old general and flat principle with uncharted misapplication or exceptions a rule "in general" of terminability at will, followed by a "but" sentence which invited in any instance attention to circumstances which might require such a sharply different result as a reasonable time or some particular period inferred from the nature of the undertaking. This offered to Pennsylvania the new light Cardozo had spent ten years acclimatizing in New York (pp. 115 ff.; 358 ff.; 368 n.). As for the neatness of the job, in this field which twenty years later is still rank with confusion, I adduce along with my own judgment the observation that rarely have I seen a young man more kindled {311} with admiration than was Lederer when in his citation-check he came upon and examined these particular eleven references. The unpretentiousness lay in the fact that only the net of the analysis was given, the eleven cases being not digested but merely collected.

Still, willingness to soft-pedal all personal display need not spell absence of a due craftsman's pride nor even of a decent human touch of vanity in achievement. And those appointed to signal the birth of this bit of legal beauty had dull eyes. The Pennsylvania reporter headnoted the general terminability at will (which had the originality, but none of the accuracy, of 2 + 2 = 4); then he stopped. The Key Number digester did exactly the same. Horace Stern was willing, for himself, to blush unseen, but he did not feel that way about this gem; and I submit that what next happened is inexplicable except in terms of a craftsman's continuing pleasure in, and feeling of responsibility to salvage from oblivion, a needed job well done. A few years later another opinion came his way which involved not an agreement but a testamentary direction that had no fixed time term about the contemplated employment. But Stern starts with, "It is established *in the law of contract*" (my italics) in regard to agreements for service, and rephrases the complete principle *into a single sentence,* with the "unless" clause built up to force attention and to give full directions for construction. He attributes the new proposition (quite accurately) to the *Slonaker* case, but repeats in two footnotes the citation of each foundation case thus reviewed and clarified. The new tactic, one is glad to report, got at least one piece of good work nailed home: both the Pennsylvania and the Atlantic headnotes, this time, caught and reproduced this growth-vibrant regeneration of the moribund old rule — a matter to which we shall be recurring.

Let another and shorter example clinch the proposition that courts and judges, like other honest craftsmen, have proper pride and pleasure in clean work. I find it charming. The case is *State v. Smith,* 135 Ohio St. 292, 20 N.E.2d 718, decided April 19, 1939. I quote from 135 Ohio St. at 293: "In the leading case of *Hoffman v. Knollman,* ante, 170, appears this apt language: . . ." The "leading case" which is thus recognized, honored, quoted, and duly applied, had been decided twenty-eight days before.

So let it be repeated: This type of pleasure is there, on tap, for any individual appellate judge. He requires, in order to reach it, no change in the manner of operation of his court. And job by job, from any appellate judge, this type of service to the community and to its law is needed. {312}

11. Sieving the Cases

Those courts are wise who make a standard practice of sorting out some proportion of their cases for memorandum opinions, thus mobilizing resources for more solid effort where more solid effort is more needed. I do think that even a memorandum could contribute its touch to the great job, however, if a minor shift in the common phrasing could lead to an equivalent shift, even in the memorandum decision, of angle of judgment. "Affirmed on the authority of *Older v. Younger*" may say the same thing and mean the same thing as "The case *falls within the reason* of *Older v. Younger*. Affirmed." But in from two to six cases out of ten the latter phrasing runs a real chance of inducing a longer and a deeper look at the controlling case, in the way in which controlling cases should be looked at.

Sometimes, of course, the statute "requires" an opinion. On the *power* of a legislature in this, I go with Arkansas;[298] but that is immaterial. Even if the requirement were constitutional, still, for a century and more the practice of this country has allowed opinions to vary in length according to the needs of the case, and where, for instance, the point in dispute has been really covered in a recent prior opinion, good faith compliance with even such a provision can be achieved in brevity. In no event can I escape the conclusion that for the court, as for the individual judge, it ought to become conscious practice to do regularly, and in connection with each consultation, what over the centuries every court has done from time to time under pressure of circumstance, namely, to single out one or a few cases as proper for an effort at clean-up. Somewhere in Holmes, I seem to recall, there is a passage about the rules of law turning over every twenty-five years, and somewhere in Pound there is one as to twenty-five years being the average life of such a rule. Neither accords too well with my experience. But what ought to accord with any man's experience is the virtue of coming as close as we can to a re-examination and tidy-up about that often, throughout our whole scheme of case law rules and statutory interpretations. Only a regular fixing on candidates for such treatment can get and keep such leaven working.

But the easing of the load by way of sifting and nondiscussion comes at a price in care and in responsibility — a price which {313} reminds us of the reason for both the older practice and those statutes which demand opinions. The candor which in a full opinion forbids ignoring an uncomfortable authority must scorn equally its disregard in silence by way of a Per Curiam. The task of smithying discordant materials into some working harmony is not to be ducked by pretense that it is not there; nor does it square with appellate judicial duty to make new law, deliberately, without open accounting not only to the fact of the old but to the reason for the new. Summary Per Curiam is properly the portion only of a case which is in essence clear not only as to outcome but as to adequate ground as well; and no line of worry about our Supreme Court seems to me to compare in solidity with the fear that Per Curiams there *may* be developing some leak in the dike of restraint against unwarranted resort to unauditable secrecy.[298a]

12. Divisions and Panels

To relieve the pressure of the docket, more and more courts have been turning to operation either in fixed divisions or in shifting panels of judges. Except as it bears on the advocate's problem (pp. 251 ff.), such operation is in one sense outside of the immediate focus of this study: the process of deciding, the competing goals of the process, the culmination in an opinion, and the most telling procedures in regard to each of these differ not at all whether the bench be made up of three or of nine, whether it be a panel or a division or a whole court.

Insofar, however, as we are addressing ourselves to the law-building effects of decisions, a regime of either division or panel, as all men know, raises special questions; and there are related, though lesser, questions which have to do with what help is to be gotten from the advocate. Useful general lines of guidance are hard to find. Primarily, it seems to me, this is because the attitude of the judges differs so largely among the courts. The most striking variable here is the degree to which each individual member is imbued with active responsibility for the team-product; almost equally weighty is the working intensity among the membership of a felt need for conscious continuity of the work from year to year, and for keeping the doctrines which are brought to bear harmonious in both their operation and their articulation. {314} We have had courts — we seem still to have some — in which once the conference has come to an accord the opinion-writer is pretty much on his own. We have indeed had courts in which he was assigned the case before the hearing, in which he reported on it at the conference as the sole person present who had read either record or briefs, and in which he found his recommendation normally concurred in without further check. We have had courts — and some are still with us — in which pride of opinion, or bother about offending such pride, or weird views about manners or delicacy, have made any suggested change of wording, thought, even of citation, a thing to worry over or to shrink from as threatening ill-feeling in the college. It is manifest that any of such ways of individual withdrawal from the team-job, or of such resultant overdelegation of the control and shaping of the job as hinders real and firm team cross-check, raises tremendously the likelihood of discontinuity among a court's results over the years. The enlistment of more memories, of more individuals' recalled experience, cannot help but produce more lines of guidance as well as more threads to be tied in; the enlistment of more imaginations and more individuals' projections of possibility and likelihood cannot help but call forth a more serviceable advance exploration of the prospective bearings of the announced reason and rule.

In all of this there is nothing new. But it is worthwhile to gather some of the devices that testify to courts' awareness of the price in continuity which divided operation threatens to exact. The most conspicuous maneuver has been to keep the chief in the chair, regardless of division or panel membership, thus assuring that at least one man is in on every case, and putting on him the consequent responsibility, as occasion requires, for initiating some procedure to preserve or repair continuity. Least conspicuous, perhaps, but surely of the essence, is reliance on the advocates in each pending case to gather and present relevant material from the court's past work. Help is here, but stinted help: in both diligence and skill, counsel remain, as has been noted, alarmingly uneven; and even though counsel should offer peak performance, their tools are faulty: we have in this one study, in passing, come across two of the countless instances in which a valuable point of ruling has completely escaped those indexing techniques which are counsel's almost sole machinery for prospecting.[299] Besides, {315} wherever memorandum decisions are in use, and repeatedly in regard to regular opinions, there are notes and memories of various sitting members of the court which counsel cannot reach, but which shed often enough most worthwhile light on that continuity in results which must not infrequently elude the language of the moment.

A third device is circulation among the whole court of all the prospective opinions. Here, even in a court which has already built club and team feeling, with critique and suggestion both ready and welcome, one is still faced with the inertia of the man whose attention is engaged by his own unending load, and with the time-competition from that same burden. What concerns one in regard to this particular problem of continuity and doctrine-tidying is that under these circumstances special attention to those cases in which the division or panel has split will provide less guaranty of help than one could wish. For division in any court not only goes in first instance to result, and not only turns half or more of the time on the gestalt or pattern into which the diverging voters have arranged the facts, but by sharpening an internal issue it tends to drive the two sides into *ad hoc fighting* positions, as contrasted with long-range *judging* positions. True, it is possible in theory for the more detached colleague from off the panel to spot a line of solution wiser than either line of battle, one which with fitness and flavor will both resolve the tensions and avoid the extremes; but rarely does such insight come without the kind of soaking in the detail of record and authorities for which the nonparticipant has trouble finding time. Unless therefore the matter goes into banc, he tends simply to throw his counsel to one side or the other of an issue which, I repeat, is likely enough to jar in either version. And even where such mishaps are escaped, a major hazard to continuity seems to me to be the recurrent case where the outcome is too clear to bother about; where, therefore, precisely because no worry is involved, the temptation is strong to hang that judicial hat on any convenient peg.

I have said before, and I now say again, that that shoddy way of opinion-writing seems to me to be distinctly *not* the current one among our American appellate courts today. But "not the current one" does not mean "not existent" nor even "really infrequent." And nobody in his senses, on or off the appellate bench, has any idea that even that great institution has screened itself {316} free of all laziness, all slipshod work, all resort to dodges and evasions to gloss over a failure to locate really satisfying grounds of decision. Least of all, when the outcome is so clear as to be laughably easy, and when other and troubling matters are sucking up available time, attention, and resilience, will anybody doubt that an occasional case will fall heir to a rather sad-eyed make-do of a "ground."

Which brings us back to the question of cross-check on the panel or department; for I hold it to be inescapable that, level of participation for level of participation, and on any basis other than a pure one-man delegation which no court would today defend or indulge, the more members are sitting, the greater is the chance of catching and preventing such an easy-case slip as we have been considering. As was said at the outset, general measures tend to have little meaning when circumstances vary like the colors in a bed of portulaca. But I do think it clear that unless the chief rolls into a single extraordinary treble marble-cake the industry of a Cardozo, the memory of a Taft, and the vision of a Mans-field, the court and "The Law" will suffer materially if either relies upon the chief, alone, to carry the burden of playing goalie on cross-check and continuity. I think it clear, second, let me repeat, that it is the cases in which the upshot is most obvious in which (when one cannot simply point to a "tidying" recent case and quote both result and reason) the opinions are mostly likely to raise trouble another time. I have wondered, therefore, where the court sits in fixed divisions, whether one small line of insurance might not be to pass around, week by week, in each division the burden of reporting on the current proposed opinions of the other. From outside, I find myself dubious about the return per man-hour of a procedure in which the full bench "listens" to the reading of all proposed opinions; some courts seem to find that procedure to elicit real and effective improvement, but my own experience with men of law has been that few of them do much to better a text without the use of eye and pencil; and at least one court has found the substitution of circulated copies to step up the effectiveness of corrective "listening" in very gratifying fashion. Most baffling, in regard to possible cross-check machinery, I find the spreading practice of sitting in shifting panels, unless some rough division of check-up responsibility can be arranged by subject matter.

Two other points may merit attention. The one: the more I meditate, the more it seems to me that sitting in panels or divisions is more wisely done by even numbers than by odd. It was {317} the older English experience. Each of the old courts was a four-man court. And today, on the public relations side, a three-to-one vote is immensely easier to stomach than a three-to-two, when there is another batch of judges not sitting on the particular bench. On the side of an easy test for hearing en banc, a four-man bench is automatic on a two-man vote, which would again seem to have some working value. Moreover, when it comes to the shaping of issues on opinions circulated for the views of nonpartic-ipants, while I have made no study and while I have in mind some cases in which with but a single dissenter the issue has been sadly overdrawn, yet I lean to the view that that phenomenon is materially more likely where a sitting court divides into two camps. Finally, of course, as against fives, fours save hearing time.

The other point has to do with a court where by etiquette, practice, or temper of the current bench opinions and their authors are lightly or heavily insulated against "meddling." One rather feasible road toward slow betterment of any such regrettable condition lies open and inviting: few indeed are the men of the law whose craftsmanship and vanity are proof against a request from time to time for critique and suggestion about a drafting job, such as the requester's own proposed opinion. One swallow does not make a summer, but a dribble of such requests judiciously distributed and spaced by even a single judge can hope to change attitudes and even a regime.

13. Extra Manpower: The Lower Courts and Counsel

"[T]he remarkable judgment of Kennedy, L.J., illuminating, as it does, the whole field of controversy, relieves me from the necessity of saying much upon the subject." This is Loreburn, L.C., speaking for the entire House of Lords in an off-beat c.i.f. contract case in which Kennedy's dissent below had handled the c.i.f. situation entire, with the insight, precision, and breadth which once were Mansfield's manner in commercial law, and had then resolved the particular issue against that Goldschmidt background.[300] Loreburn goes on, for a few paragraphs, to make clear that he thinks he has learned the lesson from the expert and also to leave no doubt that he has learned it only in crude line, devoid of all finer shading, and misleading in suggestion. There is, however, {318} and fortunately, not enough from, him to disturb the fact that the reversal is *on the opinion of Kennedy.*

Now contrast this with what happened to Hough of our Second Circuit. Like Kennedy, he rates among the nine greatest of all English-speaking commercial judges;[300a] Learned Hand, for instance, attributes to Hough's teaching and inspiration his own mastery of the field, and it is hard to choose between them. But Hough, after more than twenty years of distinguished service, died substan-tially unknown outside of New York City, and embittered.[301] Practically every great opinion he had written had happened to go up, and had been completely superseded in authority and therefore in notice — often enough by a Loreburnish job upstairs. Indeed to this day that court, though increasingly overburdened, has still not turned to that well-known and deft device: affirming on the opinion, or reversing on the dissent, below, or heavily quoting and adopting valuable passages.[301a]

I say the device is deft. When a fitting occasion offers, it saves obvious time. It runs flat free of cost. It capitalizes what is sometimes superb skill. *It builds morale below as does no other device available to a supreme tribunal* — another point our Supreme Court could afford to note. What was said above in regard to the effect of any earned mention of a winning advocate's contribution is as nothing compared to what adoption of an opinion can build in a junior judge and court. But what is of still more weight is the unchaining over the whole bench below, wherever either craftsmanship *or* ambition *or* vanity has settled in, of a drive to build sometimes or always toward the kind of opinion which ought to get and now may get this type of recognition. Let it be granted that only a smallish percentage may prove borrowable; nevertheless, the whole level of the work goes up. And every job which turns up done really right either prevents an appeal or lifts the law of the State in the same thrust which opens up more room for the relevant supreme court to expand its own best production. {319}

It has never been clear to me why this asset of the appellate bench has remained so spasmodic in employment. Let it be granted that transcendent masters — a Hough in the commercial field, a Surrogate Foley in probate matters — do not grow on bushes. But no man can read the classic opinions which get turned in here and there by some unknown master in chancery in some relatively unexplored or tricky field without awareness that here is a product worth cultivation, nor can he read through the reports from the lower courts without coming again and again on an opinion which well deserves to be singled out and made an official repository of the relevant law of the State; which most vigorously, in the event of appeal, should be preserved from the death-in-life which the mere fact of appeal threatens otherwise to visit upon it. The argument is that such samplings do show the quality of what the less exalted gardener can grow, but yet give no remote suggestion of how great is the yield which would become harvestable if once the idea should get abroad that what is toward is not recognition or adoption as a sport of nature but recognition and honor and use, *by sustained policy*. A puisne judge, too, yearns to leave his mark.

What is both certain and good is that this type of explicit reliance on the work below, with extended quotation even when the whole opinion is not adopted, is not infrequent in our current samplings. I have made no comparative study, but my impression is that one meets more of it than was the case twenty, forty, or sixty years ago. An increase would be natural enough in conjunction with the modern easing of the tone of composition, and in conjunction with what seems to be a marked wane during my professional lifetime of stuffiness of office on the part of our appellate judges. Be that as it may, it is clear that a court program of alertness to and capitalization of Class-A work below would fit into the modern reports without a jar. "If anything be clear," writes Fuld for a three-judge dissent,[302] "it is, as Presiding Justice Nolan wrote in dissent in the Appellate Division, that 'a proceeding in the nature of mandamus will [not] lie to compel a general course of official conduct, as it is impossible for a court to oversee the performance of such duties.'" The quotation continues for one third of the entire short opinion, the rest of which merely introduces and applies the quoted principle. Again, in *Clark v. McGinn*,[303] after presenting the substance of the bill and the grounds of the defendants' demurrer, the court deals with the

{320} merits: "The trial court, in overruling the demurrer, rendered the following opinion giving the reasons for its ruling:" which opinion the Supreme Court then quotes for a column and a half. Then: "It is apparent that the trial court, in overruling the demurrer, considered only those grounds (4 through 7) going to the sufficiency of the bill in alleging a consideration for the guaranty agreement. In this situation, those are the only grounds presented for review on this appeal. [Citation.]

"It seems to us that the trial court's opinion adequately answers the question as to whether the bill sufficiently alleges a consideration for the guarantee agreement. Affirmed."

Or again, on a preliminary branch of the case in *Birnbaum v. New York State Teachers Retirement System*,[304] the Chief quotes half a column from Special Term and proceeds: "The foregoing reasoning is sound and we think that nothing more need be said herein with respect to the plaintiff's right to prosecute this action." Yet again, in *State v. Miclau*,[305] Taft for the majority states on the crucial issue: "We agree with the following statement by Judge Hurd in his concurring opinion in the Court of Appeals," and proceeds to quote half a column and apply it. To cap the exhibits, we turn to the Supreme Court of Pennsylvania on March 16, 1959. In *Ricciardi v. Board of Adjustment*, 149 A.2d 51, the report opens "The opinion of Judge Forrest follows: . . ." and, for four columns, it does. Then: "*Per Curiam.* The judgment is affirmed on the opinion of Judge Forrest for the court below." In *Acchione v. City of Philadelphia*, ibid. 125, the procedure is identical, on the opinion of President Judge Sloan.

So long as such unqualified affixing of a "sterling" stamp is found only amidst a court's own opinions of standard quality, it packs the perfect punch for morale-building and yet runs free even of suspicion of shirking. When used with discretion, it saves time while it improves the law.

Of course, as with all mint-marks, one is faced with the temptation to increase quantity by debasement of the currency. This batch of Pennsylvania cases shows, along with these two complete adoptions, two other instances in which large portions of the opinion below have been adopted. In sixteen of the twenty cases, however, the court prepared its own opinion in the customary fashion. It would be hard to argue that this shows or even suggests less careful work than would the substitution of four Per Curiam memoranda for the four adoptions or semiadoptions. I {321} argue the exact contrary: it takes care to select not only what, but exactly how much, the Supreme Court will make its own.

In all its variants, then, the adoption procedure is nationally familiar. No one has ever doubted its gentility or — excepting, seemingly, the Supreme Court of the United States — its wisdom. Its rarity is thus a function not of distaste but of inattention. The opportunity is not too dissimilar to that of shifting from the gun to the trap and again from the trap to the ranch, in the matter of furs.

As against the adoption of lower court opinions, that saving and profit which lies in the lifting of seductive passages from counsel's briefs is a more delicate business. But I do not see it as a dubious one, once the court has reached its conclusion about the soundness of the passage. Quite the contrary.[306] On the other hand, here I see little or no gain to be had from overt acknowledgment, except by accident. Explicit credit for a course of thought, a line of argument, a body of material, is one thing: such credit is good to give. Counsel's phrasing seems to me another matter. It is offered to the court as a gift, but it may be a Greek gift, it calls for scrutiny. If such a gift, after scrutiny, proves acceptable, the court can properly assume dominion.

14. *Extra Manpower: The Judge's Law Clerk*

Before the present century Gray began a practice of using as a law clerk a fresh graduate, of changing the clerk annually, and of treating the clerk as a responsible participant in the office aspects of the judicial job. Holmes, succeeding Gray, continued the practice. I should be inclined to rate it as Frankfurter's greatest contribution to our law that his vision, energy, and persuasiveness turned this two-judge idiosyncrasy into what shows high possibility of becoming a pervasive American legal institution.

Experience has established that a law clerk of this kind, and of the caliber of those who seek the position, so increases the judge's working capacity as to far outweigh the time-drain of breaking in a novice every year, and has shown, too, that the outgoing clerk can do a good part of the breaking in. A gossip-ridden trade has yet to broach a whisper that any one of these untried cubs has ever been found wanting in discretion in regard to the judicial matters pending. I have also yet to hear of an appellate judge who, having once begun the practice, has discontinued it, unless perhaps to substitute a two-year for an annual employment. {322}

The practice itself, and the high desirability of its becoming universal, are redolent with meaning for our study. First, and directly, there is the manpower and the stimulus provided by an able, well-trained cub of independent spirit. Second, less directly but of importance wherever appellate judges are allowed to ripen on the bench, the recurring and unceasing impact of a *young* junior in the task is the best medicine yet discovered by man against the hardening of a senior's mind and imagination. Third, and directly on our theme: one emphasis of legal education has for thirty years, and especially for the last ten, been ever increasingly on the fact-situations which give rise to problems and to need, nor is there any likelihood that that line of emphasis will wane.[306a] "A new model every year" may have little to commend it in the matter of appliances or motor-cars or appellate judges, but it has a great deal to offer in the matter of appellate judges' clerks: there then arrives yearly in the judge's chambers a reasonable sampling of information and opinion derived from the labors, over the three past years, of an intelligent group of men specializing in the current growth and problems of our law: the faculty which has reared the new apprentice. This is a time-cheap road to stimulus and to useful leads. Fourth, and again directly on our theme, the spread of this institution spills out annually into the bar a batch of young lawyers — future leaders — who *know* from the inside that the appellate courts move with continuity, and move with responsibility, that they answer to their duty to the "law," that they move not as individuals or as persons, but as officers; a batch of young lawyers who have learned to see growth, and yet to feel the stability, the reckonability of the lines of growth — or of growth-resistance. Our trouble in regard to the crisis of confidence is, here, that there are not yet enough of these young men, so informed, to be spilled out. The second trouble is that the young men, like their elders, find difficulty still in phrasing for communication what they feel and know.

Finally, years ahead, to be sure, but perhaps the most important of all, ex-law clerks of the type we are discussing come out equipped far better than most to build a *good* appellate argument, with judgment also far better than most about when they lack a reasonable chance to win. Such judgment spells, over the years {323} ahead, a slackening off of time-consuming futilities; such skill spells not only help in seeing and in judging, but also, to an appellate court, a piece of intangible return as fragrant as phlox: the pleasure of fingering and shaping craftsmanlike materials, and a consequent speeding and smoothing of judicial labors.

15. *Extra Manpower: Outside Experts*

The occasional directly usable material in a brief is far from exhausting the aid to be derived from the bar. The sometimes remarkable master's opinion has been mentioned. One may add the possibility of requesting or inviting, on occasion, an *amicus* brief. This has been little institutionalized, and if institutionalized unwisely it could turn into an abuse; but the idea has much merit, for occasional use, especially when light is needed on situations technical and relatively unfamiliar to the court. Resort has also been had, and frequently, to members of my own branch of the profession, who are taken as having peculiar competence in their areas of specialization.

And there are other trusted friends, some at the bar, some not, with whom puzzled judges may discuss this case or that, sometimes for light on doctrine, sometimes for light on laymen's practice, sometimes to test the general reaction of a man valued for his much more than common judgment, his *horse* sense, sometimes to see whether a person of known ingenuity can turn up some unsuspected lead. The degree to which the details of the pending case show in such a discussion can range all the way from a formalized "question of law" painstakingly abstracted into vapid unreality on through into a depiction of the whole scene which is as mirror-like as a Vermeer.

What I have to say will squander no words on the legitimacy of thus taking counsel with an outside friend or expert, nor yet on the desirability thereof. As have kings and presidents, judges have long found it needful. Mansfield's merchant jurymen were not consulted in court alone; and they were a regular panel, known. At the other end of the period which this study covers stands the signally skillful and successful wholesale enlistment of the Oklahoma bar by the Supreme Court of that State, in the confidential preparation of suggested opinions, until a clogged docket got cleaned up.[307]

Amid the technological cross-complexities of this world with which our appellate tribunals are faced, I find every reason why {324} they should remain free to consult sources of knowledge and wisdom by voice and ear as well as by eye, and on the particular as well as on the general. I am prepared to take as a platform such use of the living reference book. Indeed, believing as I do that situation-sense for rightly diagnosed types of problem-situation is the key to good law and good judging, I find recourse to such knowledge and judgment, where available, to move beyond the desirable and into the urgent, or the necessary. Always, one remembers, it is only knowledge and suggestion which is in question; it is the judge who will be doing the deciding, for himself; it is he and his brethren who will be doing the deciding, for the court.

But problems open, and they are better dealt with when they are spread out.

The first is ideological. Only the appellate judge is supposed to do appellate deciding, only he is elected or appointed to *office*. His deliberations and consultations are to be secret, runs the thought; certainly before the event, probably also after.[308] Even this business of letting a deceased judge's private papers be worked over for use in publication has seemed to some a very dubious business indeed. In this line of feeling the matter can go further, because of the supposed nature not only of an official judiciary but of our own general polity: in a "democracy" there must be no back stairs; all officials should be kept free from any possibility of outside secret influence, but first of all the judges and first and most of all those supreme court judges to whom citizens, officials, and even other judges answer. {325}

One can write some rather appealing music on such themes. Yet the appeal seems to me as shallow as ringing changes on "separation of powers" to try to keep judges from creation. What is needed is to restate the themes in terms not of slogans but of the real needs and also of the real dangers which there are, to restate them in the light of ideals not pillowy or gaseous like "the nature of a democracy" but firm and hard enough to take hold of, such as "a fair break to the losing litigant." Then we can come to grips with the problem: Can we summon the wherewithal to cut costs and risks to the bearable or even to the negligible, and still tap this almost indispensable reservoir? Let me, only, before tackling that task, urge that if outside conference of this sort is to occur at all, it requires normally to be confidential, which means secret at the time and into the immediate future. There is no other way to insulate the consultant against the ingenuity of counsel interested in the case or in the pending ruling; and whether a man is reached, or whether he thinks he has been approached, or whether he fears that he may be failing to spot some line of influence too subtle for his detection, or whether he has vague wonders about any of such matters, the intrusion roils the spring before the bucket dips.

But any confidential consultation or discussion opens at once the problem of fair play. No matter how knowledgeable the consultant, he *may* be overlooking or understressing facts or factors which informed counsel could mobilize to counter the whole effect of the suggestion; no matter how wise the consultant, he *may* be either inattentive to or ignorant of matters which, stressed by counsel, might even realign the consultant's own conclusion. It is manifest, in a system which depends in good part on adversary presentation, that where light on law, situation, or measure derives from outside consultation and plays palpably into the result, the side against which the "new" material tells is in simple fairness entitled to a chance to meet it if they can. It seems to me therefore that a sound hedge, not wholly complete, yet adequate, offers by spreading the nature and effect of such material on the face of a *proposed* opinion, the court remaining open to reargument addressed to that material. Precisely the same holds, of course, for any decision which is placed in part on any basis dug up by the court itself, but which is theretofore new to the case. Reargument is indeed in my view wisely limited to situations where the showing of its probable value is cogent; but the entrance of such a new element surely lays a good foundation for such a showing. {326}

The other dangers go to the new material itself. On the side of the doctrine these are negligible. The building-stones are there for the judge to check. The proposed analysis and application either appeal or they do not. On the whole, when the doctrinal theoreticians get too spiderwebby, the courts smash through the web; on the whole, therefore, when the courts accept a bit of academic analysis, it proves to be a bit which brings not merely order, but useful order. The matter is not different in regard to the unsuspected neat road out which an outside suggestion can turn up; there is again no danger, if only machinery be used to allay the effects of possible surprise. Such a new lighting as the "eve of bankruptcy" idea to solve *Legniti* (above, pp. 210 f.), or as a suggestion, say, that refusal to recognize rescission of the awning sale in *Kramer v. Zappone* (above, pp. 175 f.) could more comfortably be based on lateness of notice of rescission, or that in *Gerety v. Hiller* (above, pp. 143, 275 f.) the actual achievement of the purpose of the resale requirements might better be played up — such matters again will either persuade or they will not. But acceptance of such a suggestion is fraught with no threat to balance: the technical foundation of each such idea is simple for any judge to check, once the idea itself is in the ring.

When, however, we pick up material outside the books of doctrine: What is the wise relevant situation to select as the type? What is the nature of operations within that situation? What are the needs which call to be watched and served? What are the other trouble-possibilities, not in the case at issue, which require to be kept in mind? — here dangers can lurk which demand a different kind of talisman.

There is indeed no occasion to worry over the consultant's having any direct connection with or interest in the case; judges have sense, and so will any person with whom a judge may talk; and we are not dealing with a Byzantine Empire in its least happy days nor with a regime of "What's the Constitution between friends?" nor do five percenters or pleasant "casual" interested inquiries from highly placed persons haunt our appellate bench.[309] And one remembers, from the theory of rules, that whereas men of good will can profit by rules and procedures well designed to avoid trouble, temptation, doubt, or embarrassment {327} (such as the audit of a treasurer's accounts or the separation of a lawyer's personal from his clients' funds) yet the problem of rules and other measures to control men of good will is one wholly different from that of rules and measures addressed to men who care nothing for the measure's purpose, nor for the right doing of the job, but rather and only for what they want, what they can get, and what can or will happen to them. In the particular situation before us, a conscious and effective ethic against any such discussion with a trusted friend or an impartial scholar would have exactly no effect on its true target, the Manton who may be hiding among the multitude, but would deprive five hundred honest judges of access to knowledge which they need in order to get their job done right.

The chance of deflection by direct interest in the litigation can thus be disregarded. But there are other lines of deflection and distortion. There is, to begin with, a possible bias out of expertise itself. Rare is the rounded expert. Arthur Nussbaum, a singularly well-informed and careful observer, was thoroughly dissatisfied with the pre-Hitler German system under which courts could and did call on commercial bodies for expert information regarding usage and practice. His view was that too much "usage" was manufactured or remade by the expert panels in the process of their reporting; and too much of what he saw as such creation he did not approve. What amounts to manufacture of "practice" or "conditions" along some such lines has, moreover, no need to involve bad faith; to a real extent, as will be suggested below, it can occur without the knowledge of the manufacturer. One can gather the trouble-factors for short discussion under the heads of (1) possible lack of balance; (2) the problem presented by the confused, the unsettled or unsettling, or the conflicting; (3) the question of sensitivity to the semijudicial function; and (4) the question of wisdom in suggestion.

Lack of balance in the observer is the basic and most serious source of worry. To take a familiar example, there are in the labor field not only "management" and "union" to be felt for and with, but there are also among others the investor on the one "side," the individual union member or other employee on the other. It is by no means every expert who sees and feels the relevant going situation whole, and in its relation to the greater whole it serves; there are plenty whose honest outlook can be depicted by some relevant version of "What's good for General Motors is good for the country." Given any such slant of outlook or indeed of experience, it is well-nigh inevitable that practice or {328} usage should be seen and remembered selectively, the "good" becoming the typical, the "bad" being forgotten or dispersed in memory or otherwise shunted off, the whole flavored into what may be utter unreality with consequent grievous misimplications about the proper rule — often, be it repeated, with as little consciousness as has a judge when he is classifying, "in law," a relatively "easy" set of facts.[309a]

A striking illustration of such mis-seeing is found in the *Dixon Irmaos* case.[310] The letter of credit with which a bank, on behalf of a buyer, promises to pay the price of a shipment of goods commonly protects the buyer-customer by requiring that an order bill of lading evidencing the shipment shall accompany the seller's draft for the price. Where, as so often, it is an overseas shipment which is contemplated, a complication arises: in overseas shipping, contrary to domestic law and practice, the bill of lading is not single, but is issued in a "set" of two or more separate "parts," each part numbered and expressed to be void if any of the other parts is "accomplished." And the law is that a good faith purchaser of any one such part gets the goods, as against any later purchaser of any other part. In this situation, New York banks issuing letters which envisaged export shipments made their promises call not for "a bill of lading," but for a *"full set of bills of lading"* covering the shipment. This caused neither trouble nor confusion: The seller-beneficiary made his shipment, received his set of bills of lading, took them a few blocks to the bank, and duly collected. But when the shipment is to be made *from* overseas, the picture is very different. For centuries, and still, the practice has been to separate the parts of the bill of lading, hedging against the inconvenience of loss by sending forward only one part at a time — which may, in some locations, mean a severe delay in reassembly of the parts. The practice has therefore been universal, both in mercantile circles as between seller and buyer, and in banking circles as between seller-beneficiary and the banker who is lifting the buyer's obligation of payment, for the payment to be made and collected against the first "part" of the bill of lading which is presented, the other parts either dying on the vine or, more commonly, being delivered casually later, when the second mail runs in. This practice can go to the essence of the seller-beneficiary's protection in those cases in which the shipment, though made properly, is {329} yet not made until close to the time limit set by the credit for getting the documents to the bank. Meantime, the protective condition calling for a "full set of bills of lading" was carried over from the export letters of credit, where the clause makes sense, into the import letters, where in its literal form it makes no sense at all.[310b] Despite having so carried over the language into all their forms, the bankers of course went on, like good bankers, honoring their import credits on the presentation of the customary documents, requiring delivery only of the first part to arrive, but securing themselves against any possible dishonesty in regard to the missing part or parts of the bill of lading by taking a letter of "guaranty" from the presenting bank against any loss due to the absence thereof.

It is against this background, and in regard to a credit which they had opened on behalf of a Belgian bank in favor of a Brazilian shipper and had then confirmed as their own obligation, that the Chase National Bank of New York saw fit to threaten by a dishonor the world reputation of American bankers' credits. The Germans had broken into Belgium on the day the documents were presented. The fascinating thing for our purpose is the expert testimony in the case. One rarely finds such classic documentation of the quirks of *homo expertus*. The Chase's experts had two lines of fact to work with: the one was an unbroken practice of honoring a single part of the bill of lading when it was presented with an appropriate guaranty; the other was the routine of writing "full set" into the import letter of credit. They therefore saw a practice of honoring, *but only as a matter of grace and discretion*. This, although not one witness could, on request, offer as much as one instance of *exercise* of the alleged "discretion" not to honor. Their "but" idea had added to nature's picture an element which simply was not there. Equally interesting is the reaction of one witness to shifting behavior: he saw a "custom" before the date of the invasion to find a proper letter of "guaranty" acceptable, but *not on that date* or thereafter: all import credits had been colored for him by the events in Belgium.

But most illuminating of all is the fact that it was possible for the Chase to rally so much of the New York international banking {330} community behind a view of rightness-and-practice which not only sees the letter of credit situation as if the sole interest involved were that of the bank which issues the credit, but which also measures the interest of that bank itself in the shortest-range terms, those merely of escaping one or another particular possible loss. Whereas what we have in fact is a machinery built for the protection of trade (that means the sellers) and of financing shipments (that means the overseas bankers who discount the papers for the sellers) by providing as the source of payment a written, irrevocable, supposedly unshakable engagement of a "prime" American bank ready to honor in what hitherto has been a "prime" currency, American dollars. To introduce grace and discretion into that kind of engagement, on a point not peculiar to the individual transaction but utterly standard in practice and understanding, is to introduce a feature disruptive of the institution and flatly repugnant to the meaning carried to any merchant or overseas banker by the documentary words "irrevocable" or "confirm." Such introduction, if successful, would have amounted to the court's sanctioning of irresponsible banking. And it would have been banking no less unsound than irresponsible. For the documentary letter of credit service of a bank is not in first instance a department of direct earnings; it is in first instance a department promoting other business, both of the particular bank and of the community. That service rests on the general confidence in bankers' credits, and in the credit of the particular issuing bank, which in turn depends on never repudiating. So that any specific losses which outrun the absorptive capacities of the going department income are properly to be seen either as general promotion expenses or as particular losses due to faulty banker's credit judgment about particular customers: in the *Dixon Irmaos* case, it was faulty credit judgment about a Belgian bank which came to be overrun by war. But such are the very contingencies against which the issuing bank by its letter of credit engages to insure the community of trade and mercantile finance; and the office and function of a bank which is to rate as "prime" is to perform, not welch, on the insurance.

Nor did the court leave any doubt as to that obligation.[311]

The foregoing is enough to exemplify the peril of lack of balance in the expert, and of consequent unwisdom as he may misread a confused scene or read material into the picture when the lighting changes. But one must not conclude from such possibilities {331} that it is the function of an expert consultant to merely reproduce the life outside. If photography done rightly is a matter also of timing, lighting, angle, and interpretation (one thinks of that planting of the flag on Iwo Jima), how much more so is the presentation by a friend of the court of some type of life problem-situation with its going needs and "immanent law." The very fact that conflict has arisen bespeaks the necessity both for pertinent, though congruent, overgeneralization and for the mixing in of interpretation, projection, judgment. As with good photography, or good judging, the goal is true *significance*. The creative action, both in portrayal (where does Cardozo write "a distortion, *but such that the effect is true*"?) and in the milking of the situation for implicit standards perhaps never before perceived or phrased — that creative action is indeed curiously similar to what the appellate court does daily on its own; and mere reproduction would be as unfaithful to the job in hand as would slot-machine-style judging to the job of the appellate bench. No, what the consulting judge must guard against is not selection, patterning, and interpretation as such, but a lack of balance which may induce addition, subtraction, or interpretation that fits neither flavor nor function.

That same lack of balance can be one root of the troubling phenomenon I am terming lack of sensitivity to the semijudicial function of a judge's consultant. But there can be also other roots of that. What is certain is that there are some kinds of activity or job in which it becomes a man, so far as is in him, to think and act for the whole rather than for clan, clique, or client. A bar association legislative committee, work as a Commissioner on Uniform State Laws, membership in the council of an A.B.A. section, and the like, are of this nature. We recognize freely in such connection a man's freedom to advance himself and his career, but we present him with an obligation to do so via sound work for the job and for whatever whole the job is there to serve. And we do not recognize at all the propriety of his using position of this kind to advance separate or separatist or conflicting interests of class or client. As applied to our friend or other consultant of the judge, it is plain that his function, so far as he does anything other than listen, is quasi-judicial,[312] with appropriate public responsibility.

What bothers is that in this century (I have never traced the earlier history) there has grown up among some otherwise sound {332} lawyers, and among some laymen, an obtuseness to the "public and therefore different" obligations of such activities, a slanting and manipulation of issues and opportunities to further special interests with the as-of-courseness one associates rather with the work of some group's "man" on some key committee of the less pleasant sort of political machine. My observation suggests that during the last thirty years the sensitivity I am discussing has increased strikingly in the American Bar Association membership in regard to that Association's public activities. Nevertheless, scattered here and there among the many devoted donors of time and experience with whom I have had the good fortune to work in such matters there have been those who blithely and skillfully ministered to client and special interest under the guise of working and thinking for the larger whole — likable souls, mostly, and the more treacherous because they had no internal wherewithal to realize that they were out of line, and because they labored in an atmosphere in which their expressed judgments on policy and measure were commonly accepted by their colleagues as if flowing not alone from some expertness, but also from the same disinterested and successful effort to judge for the whole which characterized the efforts of the team. And the point to be made is that until we gain — or regain — *throughout* our guild and country, this sensitivity to the informal "office" of semipublic activity, until then the judge who seeks light from the living reference book has this risk, too, to mull over.

Two things, I hope, stand out from our consideration of this topic of significant situation-sense sought informally. The one is, again, the way in which overt recognition of a need, and careful canvass of hazards in filling it, can clarify, for more general use, a device to which occasional recourse has been had over the generations, and can at the same time suggest procedures and caveats in regard to the winnowing of the harvest. The other is the way in which sometimes one simple hedge-device: in this instance the tentative opinion which displays any accepted new material *and* its proposed effect, with opportunity left open for counsel to respond or rebut — the way in which such a device can serve not only to meet the basic need against surprise (in this or any other "new" aspects of an opinion) but also, at the same time, to provide some safeguard against lopsidedness or fallacy in the garnered situation-"sense." {333}

16. The Court's Expert or the Expert Court

If situation-sense and the equities or immanent law of the significant type of situation are a dominant factor in the right shaping of the rule, in the wise determination of principle, and in the outcome of the case, then the question arises as to whether such twigs as are pliable should not be bent toward insuring, inside the appellate judicial institution itself, the development of such knowledge as, to paraphrase Brandeis, is essential to understanding, just as understanding should precede judging. Mansfield informed himself on commercial matters *inter alia* by way of his special jurymen; on certain technical matters of conveyancing, information was stuffed by Fearne down a most unwilling Mansfield gullet. Continental countries specialized out commercial courts, as we (as if on the model of the ancient Court of the Exchequer) have specialized out Courts of Customs Appeals and of Tax Appeals. The old Reichsgericht not only divided off those benches which heard solely criminal cases, but did a good deal of subject matter specialization among the six benches which sat on civil matters. The French have a special judicial system to handle administrative cases. There have been specialized labor courts, military courts, courts dealing with matters of family and inheritance, juvenile courts. There is no end.

In regard to all of this my own view has over the years settled into clarity. In regard to first instance litigation, I see great values in the specialized tribunal. Our Workmen's Compensation schemes appeal to me, for instance, as our Federal Employers' Liability scheme does not; and I see great value to be had from putting traffic accident litigation on some similar basis.[313] And little though I like the probate rackets I have run into, I think a special court for that class of business (as for family matters) so useful when handled moderately well as to outweigh the dangers of politics and patronage. And I expect shortly to be devoting a good deal of personal time to the development of a commercial tribunal to pass on questions of commercial fact with commercial sense in a commercial manner. When all of that has been said, however, and much more, it still seems to me that increasingly as technological complexity piles high, our ancient institution of ultimate review by those complete nonspecialists, the {334} *general* Supreme Court, stands out as one of the wisest institutions man has thus far managed to develop.

The days are gone, we must remember, and tiny is their chance of ever recurring, in which our courts of review either esteemed themselves omnicompetent or viewed with jealousy the regulatory or decisional activities of more specialized governmental bodies. Today the expert technician is handled with a gentle rein, indeed — granted only that he use good faith and a decent modicum of fair procedure. But until our technical kings become philosophers (and I will hope, even then, not Plato's) we surely need, to keep them from unbalanced divagation, an ultimate possibility of review by our sole official voices of noncombatant, residual horse sense: the bench of the *un*specialized appellate court. No gain in expert competence could make good a loss of that grass-roots soil-cover and earth-feel.

Yet much of the value of expertise is available within that framework. Water experts tell me that the elder Sanborn stood majestic in that life-giving field; I have myself measured the sureness in commercial matters of Hough and Learned Hand, and Swan, and Cowen; Lehman's understanding of realty dealings was like a good violinist's of his instrument. True, surpassing intellectual power is by definition rare, not many judges are called to make, or remake, the law of water rights or of realty dealings or overseas contracts or of contracts in general or otherwise to occupy a niche in the judicial hall of fame; nor can we demand or hope from many the prodigious labor of a Brandeis or Cardozo. But an appellate judge is entitled to a few hobbies, like any other man, and it does not take too much sustained reading and observation to build some interest in and understanding of one or another industry or line of activity or problem in this bewildering but bewitching world around us. That is what gives the relevant law-stuff — cases, statutes, briefs — body, depth, meaning. Yet insofar as bent or hobby may make any appellate judge, on and inside his own court, an expert or the expert in any field, he will be still subject to the sound review to which his court subjects all other experts. Traynor's neat phrasing has already been quoted: "Actually the expert in water law or tax law or oil and gas law knows more than most the complex uncertainties of his subject and the risks that would attend insulated study. *What knowledge he has he can share with his colleagues, who are competent to understand him if they are competent to sit on a court.*"[314] (My italics.) {335}

But when the expert (who should be measured by his knowledge and understanding of the facts far more than of the law) has persuaded his colleagues, if he does, then there is real value in having the expert do the writing up of the results. Above (pp. 241 ff.), in addressing the advocate, there was indication of the blurring or misleading implication which lies so close when a writer does not "know the complex uncertainties of his subject." Commonly, difficulties are weathered, and better law is made cleaner and faster, when the phrasing is done by the man most aware of the whole problem-situation. *Per contra,* there is a strong case to be made *against* having that man do any preliminary report on a case in his chosen field. There *are* "risks that would attend insulated study," and the best guaranty against such insulation is the committing of the preliminary study to some person outside the insulation. That raises high probability of effective cross-lighting: for it is a rare expert who can keep from digging, on his own, into his own favorite corner of the legal garden. Any time-cost of having report and opinion by two different men would therefore normally be halved; and it can be argued with some force that even the half would be far from wasted, as knowledge of an expert field would come to spread around the college.

GAMBLES PERSIST

Back in the '20's and the '30's, there was much talk, and some attempted demonstration, to the effect that you could not trust "the" rules of law as guides to what appellate courts would do. And we have seen that if you are attempting to use rules of law *alone* as guides, then most of them, still, are tricky "guides." Notwithstanding that truth we have seen that there is in the main a very workable measure of guidesomeness. But we have also seen that it is spread anything but evenly. And surely it has become evident that one large element in the unevenness consists in the varied degrees to which our relevant rules of law are adequate to their office. The best of them are relatively clear as to whether and when they apply; the best of them are shrewdly tailored to significant types of problem-situation; the best of them carry, also, their reason on their face. Such rules, we have seen, furnish to court and to counsel as much of reasonable regularity, as much of guidance, as is healthy for any living legal system. But in the measure that any of these attributes is lacking, the rule, as such, loses in value. Insofar as not all of them but any of them may fall short we are forced, for guidance, into dependence on supplementary or even substitutional factors: the sense {336} and equity of the type-situation, the sensitivity, steadiness, and vision of the men. We have noted a quantum of steadiness in the latter which is altogether too little appreciated, and a quantum of impact of the former already notable, open, and waxing. Where the rules, though not well made, are at least on target, this yields workable results, and a greater awareness can step up the product. But where the design of the rules is downright poor or even bad, we have seen that the very power that is in them can destroy much of that guidance and predictability that otherwise could be gotten from the other factors.

Now despite all desire, and despite all need, and despite the help, even, of situation-sense and man-conditioning and the resurgence of much of the Grand Tradition — despite all of these we only have to open our eyes to see what a truly disheartening quantity and indeed percentage of our received and prevailing rules of law are, within the meaning of the foregoing, downright poor or bad. So that notwithstanding the current performance and the high hope of our appellate courts there is still an unnecessary quantum of irregularity, unreckonability, gamble about the results of cases on appeal. Notwithstanding all the pleasure in the picture, let me repeat, the quantum of gamble that remains is in one sense shocking. I speak not of healthy uncertainty: the *somehow* adjustment to eventualities which may be as unforeseeable in answer as they are in arrival. I speak of *un*necessary uncertainty, of variances avoidable by human care and human skill. And I assert that the size of that costly and curable gamble-factor in our American legal system of appellate decision is still such that if it had come to us by plan or intention it would have to be termed unconscionable.

Four Fallacies and Four Caveats

But before we turn to this or that which can partly reduce this painful swelling, let me clean up a few lines of misconception whose possibility it is not prudent to ignore.

I have, for example, laid out as manifest that the singing rule may indeed be loved of God, but that it is not for Lincoln's reason about the common man: neither He nor we have as yet "made so many of them." I have also asserted that substantial incompetence is found growing among the American bar like weeds in a half-tended garden, and that even among the most competent and responsible lawyers there is still except among the odd, the lucky, or the gifted a wasting ignorance of what our appellate {337} courts are really doing, and how, and how well. Observations (by which I mean not casual remarks, but careful and thoughtful reporting of facts carefully and thoughtfully observed) — observations of this character, when made by realists two generations back, produced either casual shrug-off[314a] or the type of lampoon which buries merits under mud. I do not want light reading or some flip phrase to damn the present study in any such fashion.

In the first place, then: to see sharply and to feel it needful to say bluntly does *not* mean, equal, or suggest that one likes or approves what one sees and says. For example I despise and hate rules of law which hang on the significant type of problem-situation like gunny sacks or else like one-armed scarecrow coats; I despise and hate such as fumble about whether and when they are to be applied and such as leave their reason and purpose clouded in conjecture. But no man who wishes to see clearly what lawyers or appellate judges are up against — or, for that matter, legislators — can afford to do his seeing as if rules (or, indeed, lawyers) were of one single ilk, nor can he ignore the way in which many of ours hinder as much as they help, or more. What has the existence of any such fact, or its reporting, to do with liking it? True, in a balanced study (as contrasted with a preliminary or pioneering exploration) unpleasant facts should not appear alone, nor should they ever be used to characterize a whole unless they do. And this present study is offered as ripe, and so assumes the responsibility which flows from purporting to offer roundness and balance.

Which leads into the second matter to pin down, one which, again, many critics of the realists missed. To wit: that to see and pound home that things are as they are, even when they may at the moment be brutally unpleasant, and even to think and say that much of what grinds or crushes or resists immediate desire is flatly and inexorably *there* — that does not mean, imply, or suggest that nothing can be done about it, nor yet that nothing should be tried, nor, finally, that effort should be postponed. The implication or lesson is, instead, if the observation or opinion be solid, merely that fresh study and a fresh approach are called for; that the case calls for some new angle in. With our present problem, {338} for instance, it was unmistakable in the '20's and '30's that the rules of law, as such, were not getting the results then desired; nor are they, yet. It seemed highly probable that they never would achieve the results which were then desired; and that still seems so. But this meant then and means now no counsel of despair. Instead, a fresh look has shown "the results then desired," the old ideal of "certainty," to be a false ideal, a desire not only futile but unfortunate. A very different thing, "reasonable regularity," is what is really needed for the adjustment of needed continuity to needed change. It becomes a corrected and substituted ideal which is not only within man's capacities but closer to his nature and to his culture's needs. It is good if this kind of fresh look and corrected ideal can be managed in conjunction with and as a part of the first recording of facts which challenge to thought and to curative effort. But I want to insist that, though good, it is as unnecessary as it is uncommon. There is worthwhileness just in digging out intelligence and getting it to the commanding officer.

In the present instance, which involves a study published not on first inquiry, but after years of thought and further testing, more is properly to be demanded. The plucking and processing of such concepts as craft and craftsmanship, period-style, type-problem-situation, and the immanent law thereof thus offer a new angle in, new measures and tools for forecast by the bar, stimulus and measures also for conscious toolmaking and for redesigning of craft-procedures by the bench. Such concepts then join with the theory of rules (which has been struggling along in semidarkness) to provide a wherewithal both to criticize rules, one by one, in terms of how far the particular one in hand is doing its appointed task, and to reformulate any but a singing rule in terms which can move it closer to that ideal and satisfying form. As has been insisted throughout, such reforging is in constant process not only in the field of case law rule and principle, but to an almost equal extent in the judicial handling of statutory material; and in my view that is not only a judicial function grounded in the whole history of our polity, but one of the most vital and useful phases of appellate judicial work. — All of this is fortunate to have; yet again I wish to insist that it is unessential to the value of that good reporting of needed facts which is a precondition to either stimulus or foundation for curative study.

The third thing to pin down is correction of another current error which rests on blindness to the obvious. This time it is the misconception which flows from dividing a field of discussion into {339} some arbitrary pair of areas, a single limited pair being assumed to have exhausted the possibilities, and then imputing to any position taken a necessary negation of some other supposed but really irrelevant position. What calls here for such pinning down is a cluster of related points: for instance, to urge one measure or twenty does *not* mean that any or the lot is urged as exclusive, nor that it is urged as a cure-all. Each one urged is urged for consideration, as a thoughtfully ripened and formulated idea which merits real consideration, not cheaply made, not lightly put out for inspection, yet plainly, like any tool, a thing for which any reader may have neither taste nor use. Next, to urge for the consideration of the appellate courts at large some thought or measure does *not* mean to urge it on any particular appellate court. Procedures of craft-work are not single, each supplements and complements its neighbor, a procedure which will fit comfortably into one set of working ways will need severe adaptation before it will fit into another, and might even prove disruptive in a third; these lessons are as old as the contact of civilizations. Moreover, a particular court may already be using the same procedure the lack of which may be causing knocks in twenty-six other appellate courts. But the spreading out for *general* consideration of lines and leads which are in effective use only somewhere is as worthwhile as is the spreading out for possible *regular* use by an individual or court of some useful line or lead which that individual or court is already resorting to every once in a while, yet by no means every time it is in order. In such matters as in all other matters in this study, I preach neither revelation nor novelty, I preach the neglected beauty of the obvious. I have gathered horse sense where I could find it, and have tried to piece it together. There is so much of it, scattered here and there. It is so much needed, everywhere. So many busy men pass by so much of it, so often, without a glance.

The last of these four caveat-points should be nailed down with spike and sledge: the underpinning of observation and fact and testable truth which is developed in this study with reference to what our appellate courts have been and now are doing — that underpinning stands firm, independent of and incorruptible by anything I, Llewellyn, may like or wish or be urging about our legal system or about our appellate courts.

What I counsel does indeed root — I think, firmly and with health — in the tested facts. But what I have observed and tested about the facts is unconnected with, and in no way derives from, the positions here put forward about wisdom for the polity or {340} about possible measures to step up the value of appellate judicial output. Quite the contrary. The observational studies began, in a serious way, in 1927, and have been going on, off and on, ever since, as appears in Appendix B. The main lines of observational results were taking much their present shape long before first conception of the theoretical positions on what it would be good to do about it all.

Hence, let me repeat, and as the material presented makes plain, you may (though it would not be prudent) reject every opinion and every counsel of mine which is explicit or implicit in this study, and you would still be faced here with a solid picture of what our appellate courts have been and now are doing. Notably, this bedrock fact-material includes such matters as the range of legitimate leeways in regard to both case law and statutory materials; the decree and nature of the limitations on the actual use of those leeways; the existence, importance, and change of the craft and craftsmanship of appellate judging and of period-style therein; the current trends especially in regard to the conscious and overt recurrent canvass, in the ordinary case, of sense and equities for the type-situation as the relevant rules of law are shaped, reshaped, or made (not merely as they are selected or applied); and the net combination of continuity, movement, and reasonable regularity of result both in its presence, and in its (as yet) only partial development, and in its possibilities for further flowering.

A Fifth Caveat: Only the Outcome, Not the
Ground of the Impending Decision — As Yet

There is a further possible misunderstanding which deserves a word: the forecasting in regard to appeals, to which so much of this study is directed, is as yet a forecasting of the outcome between the parties, not one of the ground on which that outcome will be rested by the court.

Thus in the simplest and largest grouping of cases, those "foredoomed" to affirmance, an outsider has no means at all of knowing what futile grounds the appellant may set up, and have knocked down. Indeed, on occasion, even counsel who is handling the appeal may find his point or points sustained as error, but ruled nonprejudicial. By the same token, in those much less frequent cases which are substantially "foredoomed" to reversal, the judicial hatrack can be foreseen, but not the peg.

The most striking contrary exhibit is the test case. For the {341} test case, well chosen and rightly handled in terms of type-background, particular flavor, legal context, and an opinion-kernel phrased in winsome clarity — such a test case can drive powerfully and reckonably toward adoption of a particular rule. But such a case, with its gamble or its forecastability in regard to the *rule* of law to be achieved, such a case (which is the verge to which the present study can take us) is rather rare; and rather rare, as well, are the counsel who have either opportunity or skill to build such cases into rule-reckonability. Alongside those infrequent cases stand the somewhat more numerous promising appeals well handled by counsel who both know what it is all about and have the brains and guts to focus on a major issue. Here again, to forecast victory is to come close to forecasting the ground on which the victory will be rested.

On the whole, an outsider who has not seen the briefs seldom has the wherewithal even to guess intelligently at the ground of prospective decision; in contrast, a good appeal lawyer, contemplating his own appeal, can do about as well in forecast of the ground as he can in forecast of the outcome. Today's ordinary lawyer still has as his first task to learn to tell a promising appeal from one with little outlook, but the same insights which can accomplish that, if he acquires them, will help him materially toward choosing and centering on a ground whose substance is rather likely to carry, if he wins at all.

The Need for Order

17. Phrased Order

With these caveats lodged, let us recur to the matter of ill-drafted rules of law and what can be done about them. It is time we did. This study has talked so much of movement and change in our rules of law that the force of frame, form, and phrase may seem scanted. So it may be, but conditions have left no escape from the risk.

For the vicious illusion is still powerful and pervasive that legal doctrine is rigid (at least in the normal case), that "following" consists in standing, and that "standing" (at least in the normal case) involves no choice, no action, no independent responsibility. This — even in the normal case — is an illusion, a mirage; "repose is not the destiny of man," as man, much less that of *homo juridicus*. Yet *stare decisis* does still mean, to most, passivity, so that it is not true *stare decisis,* not responsible standing by and {342} work with the authorities; it is instead some lotus-eating inertness or push-button operation which floats before law's yearners as their dream-ideal. Even the Conference of Chief Justices, a year or so ago, issued a pondered official pronouncement which took as one of its foundations that any important degree of creative action by an appellate bench normally is, and rightly should be, limited to rather unusual classes of cases.[315]

Against such a background it has been needful to stress and stress again the fact of movement, daily movement, movement of necessity on every opinion-day, almost of necessity in every other case or so, as any appellate court works with and on those materials of doctrine which it has received. It has been needful to stress as well that avoidance of such movement is not only unusual, and rather difficult, but that it also, and of necessity, rests on and requires a choice, a choosing among various legitimate and inviting possibilities, possibilities which are great and small, which above all are manifold — a choosing for which an appellate court must account, case by case, to its conscience, and for which it should account, no less case by case, to its constituents. Nevertheless, our exorcism of these malignant phantasms of immobility must not lead to overlooking the body and detail of phrased doctrine which it is the office of all movement to improve and strengthen.

One could, if there were occasion, do with regard to the uses and nature of our rules of law an analysis as elaborate as that with which we approached the steadying factors which work on our appellate courts. Coupled with writing, coupled especially with printing, "the frail-seeming but sometimes steel-strong girders of doctrine" can bridge individual differences and space and generations, can heap up experience and experiment and the machinery for rather unified and standardized control-activity, can go far to shape, instruct, guide, and hold up the hands of the newcomer, to hold down and rein in and channel the wayward or the fool, to furnish to the wise the experience of his forebears for a richer wisdom. If the rules are right rules, moreover, both the guidance for decision and the guidance for prediction which they offer is direct, time-cheap, simple, and just about sufficient. With that kind of rule, operated by and for men raised in a whole system of that kind of rule, such a rough study as this present one would be either funny or false, and any cumbersome machinery of studying judges and benches and even situation-sense would {343} change from a general professional necessity to a pursuit confined to the higher reaches of the art.

But all of that is doctrine of *posse,* not of current *esse.* As has been seen, the first step in a realistic appraisal was, and it still is, to note that right rules of this character are rare. They are not, for the most part, on hand; they still need making. Are there, then, effective and communicable ways for bettering our rule-stock where it is, in contrast, bad or at its worst?

On the side of substance, there is not much to say. Our world is too complex for any one man's suggestion of substance to hold much interest for another unless a particular case is up which offers room for that suggestion. But surely the theory of rules has picked up a few obvious hints for inclusion in a judicial tool kit. The most obvious of all, I suppose, is that a "rule" never rises to the full level of a rule, at all, except insofar as its sphere and criteria of application achieve a moderate clarity. There is a quotation at pages 95-96, above, from *Disston Estate,* which will point the moral, though it does little to adorn the tale. "The rule is . . . that '. . . such a broad interpretation will not be given the request, unless it clearly appears from the context to have been the meaning of the testator, or unless the will would otherwise be inoperative.'" The question there went to "grandchildren then living, per *stirpes* and not per *capita,*" and a greatgrandchild was pushing in to share with her uncle, a grandchild. I get out of the alleged "rule" the barest trace of guidance: "Offhand, more probably No." The second "unless" gives no help for any ordinary case. When one starts "applying" the first "unless," the *Disston* case itself makes plain the rule's guidesome clarity: the auditing judge voted one way, his majority voted the other, and "On the application of that principle to the record before us, the six members of this court who heard argument are evenly divided."

We can start, indeed, with the proposition that "The principle (or rule) is clear, but there is difficulty in the application" is an untrue statement. Such an alleged "principle" may and doubtless will point an issue, it may also (though this is not so frequent) suggest a goal. These are things worth doing; but they are fore-stages of rule-making, they are not yet rules. Thus I suppose the "rule" that if an expression of agreement is accompanied by a suggested further term, its effect turns on whether the further term is or is not to be understood as a condition to closing, can be seen as an effort to serve the needs (1) for definite {344} expression of legal obligation, and (2) for reading expressions as a whole, and (3) for reasonable interpretation. But what this kind of alleged rule or principle does *not* do is the very thing a rule of law is for: to wit, to produce a workable, working *measure* for moving toward the desired goal or goals.

In this, as in all other things, desire remains but one ingredient in fulfillment; if wishes were answers, wisdom would go begging. But my belief is strong that one reason why such pseudo rules or principles persist is that they have not yet in common thinking been stripped of their disguise; a court can still in conscience say and think such a sham as: "The *rule* is clear," and so stop puzzling. Whereas to know the true principle:

> *A formula which does not guide its own application is not as yet a rule of law at all —*

that forces any judge to keep on thinking. The Restatement picked up, out of various prior shrewd opinions, one skillful interim device, and turned it into a standard procedure: "Factors to be considered, in reaching the decision, are . . ." One may compare the quotation from *Huffman Estate,* above at page 144, in regard to determining an attorney's fee.

Even more helpful is the sorting out of the factors into those which probably tell in the one direction and those which probably tell in the other; with such a listing, one is more than halfway along toward a full rule, and the decision in any instant case frames and fits itself in as soon as made, for sharper guidance. The goal to be sought in such a problem of classification is, I suppose, what I think of as a Horace Stern "Unless" — a form of rule-making which that great craftsman made into a personal habit that ought to bloom into a general institution. Thus:

> Notwithstanding the fact . . . that there is concurrent jurisdiction of law and equity in actions by partners against co-partners in connection with partnership affairs, repeated decisions have indicated that resort in such cases should be had to proceedings in equity unless the partnership was for a single transaction, or, at least, unless the accounting required was not complicated, or unless the business had been wound up, all partnership matters settled, and a balance determined to be due. It is obvious that in all other cases the flexible methods of equity are better adapted to accomplish the proper distribution of the assets and to determine the relative rights and obligations of the partners.

On that basis it was surely predictable that the Supreme Court of Pennsylvania would sustain an assumpsit for contribution based {345} on the sole partnership transaction which had been left open after all other matters had been settled.[315a]

Stern's machinery here, in charting a path through an either-or, is to provide not only a rationale which informs the "main" rule but also a sufficient list of instances to chart the *line* of the exceptions. His machinery in *Slonaker* and *Hand,* mentioned earlier (pp. 310 ff.) is somewhat different:

> It is established in the law of contracts that when an agreement pro-vides that one party shall render service to another, but does not specify a definite time or prescribe conditions which shall determine the dura-tion, the contract may be terminated by either party at will, unless the surrounding circumstances, the situation of the parties, the objects they apparently have in view, and the nature of the subject-matter of the agreement, call for a construction of the contract as providing for a rea-sonable time for the duration of the relationship which it creates, or some particular period inferred from the nature of the undertaking.

Here the reason for the main rule: a court cannot move when there is hold for neither hand nor foot, remains tacit; but almost every conceivable place to find a handhold is explored, and the rhetoric invites discovery even of an implicit "particular period." It is enough for us to note, when no clear rule is available, the technique of exploring possible factors and of recording the exploration, so as to set a rule a-burgeoning.

18. A Word About the Scholar

In our law the systematizing judges have been rare. We do associate a few bodies of doctrine with particular judicial names; but even then it has been frequently because of what seems to have been side-line interest and extrajudi-cial labor and writing, as it was with Blackstone or Kent, or Holmes editing Kent, in regard to the over-all picture: so Coke and the Constitution; Hale and the Criminal Law; Story and Conflict of Laws; Cooley and Constitutional Limita-tions. Here and there long service and relative specialization of the case material have left the imprint of a powerful mind on a whole area of which that individual is remembered as the "father" or the architect: Mansfield and Commercial Law; Stowell and Admiralty; Eldon (at shameful cost to {346} his litigants) and Equity. In this country such a picture has shown chiefly in the Constitutional field, with Marshall and Taney, and what otherwise seems to me overemphasis on most Chief Justices. And though one does think of Foley in all phases of testamentary law, and though I hear of the elder Sanborn as a builder and shaper of our Western law of water, the other judges whom one associates with particular areas of doctrine seem to appear in the capacity rather of great craftsmen and great performers than of vaster architects in the manner of the earthy Parsons, or Langdell, or Williston, and the clean-lined and solid Corbin, in Contracts, Thayer and Wigmore in Evidence, or Borchard in his singlehanded creation of our law of Declaratory Judgments. It is striking, as one picks up anniversary or commemoration issues ("Judge Smothers and Trusts," "Justice Smirk and the Law of Torts") to find even the paean of celebration limited to six or a dozen home runs which "made history" and at best an equivalent number of two-baggers, and then to gauge how little of the history *of the field* the one judge's total has managed to make or be.

I take it that this is pretty much inevitable. Consider the separatist character of our doctrine ("The law of conveyances is *not* the law of contracts," etc.,[315b]), the accidents of litigation before a court whose work can extend over a literal hundred of "fields," and the number of jurisdictions which have to be influenced before "*the* law of a field" can be effectively molded or remolded. The joint effect of such factors is to cut out from under even the judge of thirty years of service much chance of rivaling Mansfield's range of building or Eldon's of consolidation.

The lesson is plain. That it is plain is attested by today's opinions, by the gratifying rise in thoughtful periodical literature, and by the definite shift, these last decades, away from the scissors-and-pastepot and toward the evaluating type of legal text. Both in the structuring of whole fields and in the sweating of clarity out of tangled lumps of five or fifteen or fifty or a hundred and fifty cases, it is the scholar who must carry the load first of stump-pulling and then of dreaming or sweating up intelligible tentative {347} drafts of sound design. The scholar is at it. The periodical literature shows the job to be in detailed process all over the doctrinal map. Side by side with the teeming particular jobs stand such architectural undertakings as the Restatements, the Uniform Commercial Code, the Model Criminal Code, full-scale treatises also in "newer" areas such as Estate Planning, Taxation, and Administrative Law, integrated series of papers such as those which preceded Davis' treatise, or Currie's current sequence on Conflicts as he reworks approach and material in an "old" area in which the older doctrine needs an oxygen tent and the newer is still groping.

It is patent today that the scholarly branch has both power and will to come to grips with the wide as well as with the narrow, with problems of far vision as with those of delving and "the dirt." There can be no doubt that the courts can find constant help in the scholarly writings. The general level of those writings (what a contrast to the "desert with oases" scene of my legal initiate!) makes their addition to the judicial working kit a duty. And, again in contrast to a day I still remember, when to find a judicial opinion mentioning, much less relying on, a law review was an event, a few hours with the advance sheets will convince the hardiest skeptic that our appellate courts today recognize this asset and this duty, and have adjusted their work accordingly.

When that has been said, however, the problem of the scholarly writings has only opened. There *can* indeed occur in such a writing, by genius or by luck, some combination of insight, of reason seen and given, and of art in phrasing, which in one case or in seven wholly relieves an appellate court of its burden of creation. The chance of this resembles roughly that of three of a kind in a game of five-card stud. For the normal case, in contrast, the scholar's work provides information (commonly rather accurate, so far as it goes), suggestions as to some useful arrangement of material and as to some more useful posing of an issue, and further scattered suggestions as to wise solutions. All of such suggestions can range from the stupid or perverse through the purblind or mildly helpful up into sheer glory. No touchstone — not even that of known ability and achievement — can test the location on the scale of any particular suggestions in hand. Thus some of Wigmore's best stuff came hidden under the devil's mask of "autoptic proference"; again, some of the most vicious suggestion in the books was penned by that same Wigmore, in regard to some aspects of criminal law. Greatness, then, may hide in rags or tinsel; on the other hand, the mere name, even of our {348} greatest legal scholar, has been no guaranty that the proposition may not cave in as did the Chase National Bank's engagement in *Irmaos*.[316] Indeed, as some of Cardozo's opinions remind us,[317] the great have often enough the gift of occasional mistakes which sizzle. Yet I am persuaded, in regard to those bloopers which I have met from either Wigmore or Cardozo, that the judicial sense of the ordinary American appellate judge will, eight times out of nine, sniff out the fact that here is nothing to be trusted, much less followed —

and so pass on. It is not, for instance, the few Cardozo blobs which I have been finding, all over the country, cited with admiring mention of his name.

Much more troublesome is the mis-suggestion which does not come signaled by the stench of scorched good sense. Two phases which perhaps especially repay discussion are (1) when the suggestion presents itself as a seemingly necessary consequence of what is or looks like pretty solid general doctrine; and (2) when the suggestion turns up as an aberration in a paper which has opened well and has continued for a time quite persuasively, or is a "conclusion" grafted onto such a paper by slippery rhetoric. The two can be dealt with together. They are of one get.

As to the latter situation I hold that scholarly writings need to be subjected to principles of reading akin to those which give us that doctrine of dictum with which we can so effectively peel off less useful parts of a judicial opinion. As has been seen, we have never dreamed of standing on that doctrine when the language has been wise, or when it "illuminates the whole field of controversy." By the same token, scholarly pieces or chapters or treatises are also to be worked over with a flail: what we want is the wheat, winnowed; *per contra* (and this is no less vital), suggestion which is wheat is not, there, either, to be discarded merely because it runs beyond the evidence or beds in chaff.

As to the other situation, that in which what seems like otherwise solid doctrine is driven to a conclusion which for the situation-type in hand yields distress, the scholar in question is commonly putting forward a claim to serve one of law's eternal values, though one which any formal style of judging or thinking can press to an extreme. A law-governmental system does have need of order within itself; this stands as given. The very concepts of "rule of law" or "legal concept" or "legal principle" are tools for producing such order. Not only ordered administration but {349} even thinking is impossible without classification. Such classification, however, as men and matters go, is almost inevitably rough, and any rough classification is bound to pinch or distort or ignore much of the tenderer or most meaningful portions of human situations and relations. The necessities of operation, the coarseness of our legal tools, as well as the needs of evenhandedness, are there to exact some human suffering as the price of any order in the kind of society we know. "John Doe," Pound writes and repeats, in wisdom, "must sometimes suffer for the Commonwealth."

The scholar, moreover, as has been suggested, is today's appointed apostle of order in legal doctrine. He has time for that; he specializes, he digs, he ruminates, he dreams up design; that is part of his office. He properly seeks to bring clarity, which is order. He properly, also, endeavors to increase the scale of clarity. That is the Formal Style's utter ideal of order, and it must be one ideal for any style. Indeed, even an attack by today's scholar upon what he conceives as misbegotten premises will be found proposing as a substitute, along with different results, what the assailant claims to offer as at least an equal, and commonly a greater, range or quality of order.

Against any spiderwebby, clumsy, or stingray conclusion, of course, has always stood the common law tradition of revising the premise when a conclusion proves too tough to take. The problem presented by the scholar in our situation is in essence that proverbially familiar as the problem of the "hard case." But we meet it this time on a larger scale and in a materially more sophisticated form: it is the problem, rather, of the "hard rule." For our scholar is not, under pressure of time, disposing of a particular appeal. He is, instead, at work on bringing order into some whole garden patch of doctrine. In place of a rule which threatens hardship (or nonsense) in a particular case he is backing a supposed or proposed ordering principle for a whole area. And it is not quite so inescapable, under the necessities of any law, any classification, any administration at all, that the whole Doe tribe, in contrast to just John, should become the scapegoat for the Commonwealth. Moreover, whereas in the "hard case" the rule comes simply handed down, with all the burden of any change or challenge on the challenger, in our situation the same scholar is providing in the same inquiry a full discussion which makes clear how far his "principle" has really settled in, how far, on the other hand, that "principle" may still be carrying the affirmative burden. Finally, whether or not the "principle" in {350} question is already, so to speak, in possession, one main purpose of the scholarly inquiry is almost inevitably to deal with a number of cases in which the courts have behaved in a manner at odds with that principle; and when courts have repeatedly slid away from a principle, common law experience shows that the fault may frequently (not always) be discovered less in the courts than in a "principle" which has not been making sense.

An ancient and familiar illustration may point up the line of thought: When the "principle" that no "offer" can be accepted by one who does not know of it first rose in majesty and demanded to be applied to the case of a reward which had been "earned" in ignorance — what was there in the books or in policy to show "its" applicability? The "principle" still had its way to make. The books indicated indeed that the performer could recover, despite his ignorance of the public announcement. Folk-understanding and folk moral judgment still see that as right, they still see the contrary as somehow indecent. So far as long-range policy goes, that willingness to take on trouble or risk to the public benefit, for detection of crime or for salvage of person or property, which rewards seek to elicit, is commonly thought to be a rather useful attitude to have around; and general knowledge that success will also harvest any reward there may be cannot help but set an atmosphere generally favorable to the growth and spread of such an attitude among the more enterprising of the public. The other side marshals first a "principle" which is of general value in the general law of contracts, and second a drive for expansion of contract law so as to substitute clean, simple, absolute, and central dictatorship for the heterogeneous local jurisdiction of Vendor and Purchaser, Bailment, Agency, Sales, Insurance (in four or five varieties), construction deals, personal service, etc., etc. — and of course also for any such tiny enclave or Liechtenstein as "reward." Even if, at the time we are discussing, the "principle" in question had been established in general, its imperial power was exactly what ought to have been up for debate.[317a] I have always felt the sense of the situation to be strongly {351} against the scholars; indeed, if ever there was a spot where, with no cost at all, and with probable gain, doctrine could have indulged the healthy American hunger for romance, this is that spot. ("Son," says the sheriff to the wounded hero, "it's good to tell you there was a $5000 reward on 'em, dead or alive!") Meanwhile, the supposed fundament of inevitable universality on which the defendants' reward-case victories rested has proved so unsolid — what single one of our principles about the scope of contract law or its any part has managed, through the years, to stand up as really universal?

The merits of this individual matter have moment neither in themselves nor to our discussion. All that is wanted is to exemplify the difference between the hard *case* and the hard *rule*, and to raise a doubt about Napoleonic or Hitlerian fiat extirpation of doctrinal enclaves or exceptions, in the interest of "simplicity" and "order," with no inquiry at all into whether the grain of the fact-situations concerned may not be resisting the knife. If it does so resist, the result is more than the direct cost in hardship or friction or upset which is the normal product of cross-grained doctrine. That cost is in our particular illustration negligible in regard to the plaintiff; though it is not negligible in regard to the public, and I think the public is the whole reason for contract law. In any event, and in any situation, such costs are a matter capable of consideration at the time of choosing. And a natural part of the business of a court is to weigh such costs against the possibly greater value to government and people of a simpler and therefore less expensive body of legal doctrine. But more, much more plaguey is the question of whether the supposed gain may not prove fool's gold; for we must not forget how often, especially in our law, verbally simple rules which run across the grain of the felt situational rightnesses come to be avoided, doggedly but unpredictably, in the case results, so that under the surface of the {352} simple-seeming "system" things work out for decades in true uncertainty and in an obscure complexity of the *working* law. The law of Sales, from 1800 to the Uniform Commercial Code (c.i.f. transactions excepted), is a monument to this possibility of blind black hidden under a shining pseudo simplicity of concept and of rule. Simplicity is in very sooth a goal almost central for good doctrine, but for it to be a right goal, the simplicity must be one which runs *with* the grain of life, one which grows in quiet from the grass roots.

I come out of such meditations persuaded that the best judicial attack, when the scholar is urging "order" into an area where it feels uncomfortable, is a most careful re-examination of the "discrepant" cases, on facts and issues, in an effort to locate type-situations or type-aspects which may suggest wise modification of the scholar's proposed basic situation-classification, or else wise shift of the issue on which any broad discussion by the scholar has been rested. In a word, the presumption seems to me in such case normally against the scholar. Certainly the presumption is strongly against any scholar who is assuming to dismiss discrepant decisions simply as "inadequate analysis." For the persons in our polity who as a class are best equipped by office and experience to smell out when a given rule or principle or "analysis" grates against the immanent rightnesses of the situation-type presented in the case — those persons are *not* our legal scholars.

Let me not be mistaken. There have been and there are some scholars with God-given sensitivity of this sort in their areas of labor; such scholars make any man proud to be of their fraternity. I cannot, for instance, readily conceive of a judge who in matters of procedure (for lawyers-in-litigation are also a most significant situation-type with immanent rightnesses) could have surpassed Jerome Michael. But, such paragons apart, when a keen and orderly mind sets about finding, framing, and phrasing principles of order in any legal area, five or ten years of living with those principles begins to turn them not only into an increasingly rigid habit of mind, and into a set of canons of rightness with a flavor of divinely inspired morality, and, further, into things cherished and to be defended, like own children, and beyond reason — five or ten years are enough to turn those principles also into spectacles which for the most part sift out any incoming discrepant fact-material before it can even be perceived, and which dull sensitivity to such faint emanations of "wrongness" as do register. Much, then, as scholarly work is needed by the appellate courts, and much as I value the scholarly work which has been {353} appearing on all hands, I hold the caveat still vital: When a scholar is readying for the garbage can what he sees as discrepant decisions, it pays, before one follows him a foot, to study with special care *the facts and the issues* of those decisions.

219

With that out of the way, however, one is entitled to note with peculiar pleasure that the tremendous increase in the periodical publication over the last three decades has been accompanied not only by the already mentioned addition of critical evaluation to reporting, but by two other phenomena, each of which tends strongly to lessen the particular danger we have been discussing and to render the material more helpful as a court reaches for significant underlying situation-types and for the rules which fit them. The first is the growing tendency of the literature — still far, far from full fruition — to dig in under rule and holding and to canvass, recount, and account to the *facts of the cases.* Whether this tendency in scholarship can continue to thrive in the face of too many casebooks which whittle the facts out of their so-called "cases," and which insofar shape in that featureless image each prospective lawyer's picture of the legal world and of what has meaning in it — that I know not; but as of today the tendency in the literature is still as clear as it is welcome. The other and indeed companion phenomenon is the sustained effort, already assuming the rank of the expected, to fill out to some degree the background of any problem-situation by recourse to descriptive and analytical material other than judicial opinion, statute, or executive regulation — while always seeking to build a clearer and a wider order. In this the scholarly branch is both digging out and making new topsoil for the law with the unnoticed but life-giving assiduity of Darwin's beloved earthworm; and I, for one, should be proud if his encomium could be generally accorded to us other delvers and re-creators, the scholars of the law: "It may be doubted if there are many other animals which have played so important a part in the history of the world."

A WORD TO THE SCHOLAR

The scholarly branch ought to be lifting a much more considerable portion of the burden of legal-governmental creation; taken as a branch, their quality of brain seems to me as high as that of any group in the profession, not excluding, as a comparative group, the cream of the bar. I do not of course mean by the "scholarly branch" the law teachers. I mean those men of law who, as T. R. Powell put it some thirty years ago, let a little of it {354} come out through the fingers and the pen, not all of it through the mouth; his illustrations at the time reached only to "two slender volumes, one by a practitioner and one by a judge." Today the scholarly branch is indeed manned primarily, though far from exclusively, by teachers; but regardless of how the writers may be earning their keep, the opinion I am asserting is that if you require as an admission test a bit more than one published speech, two articles in twenty years, and three book reviews, then the original legal writers show a level of intellect which rates with any level in our legal world.

The next opinion I wish to voice is that, taken as a branch, the scholars are altogether unduly conscious of the truth of the opinion I have just stated. Making law review, in law school, may have laid a foundation for this.[318] So far as they teach, their experience-superiority over any student, and their dialectic superiority over all but the best, each as a constant diet, may be laying further courses of the unblest structure. Then, too, today the scholar is no longer required to fight for basic recognition at his every meeting with the bar or with any member thereof; that useful corrective of self-inflation is no longer with us. With the result that insofar as time to specialize and the other stimuli of a university or of broadened reading combine with native intelligence to open up for our scholar either wide perspectives or insights in depth, he is these days exposed to parlous pressure, from circumstance and from his fellows, toward snobbery, tacit or overt. The overt aspect is of little general import; that man in due course pays his own price by getting in his own way, and in due time he learns better. The former, however, the tacit snobbery, is of moment to us all. For snobbery blinds the eyes to things and to work which the legal scholar needs to see, and snobbery dulls sensitivity to needs and above all to processes which the legal scholar needs to feel. It will be a cause for grief, indeed it will be a cause for grievance, if our sources — save for the poet, the prophet, and the prodigy, our sole sources — of high or deep vision proceed to cut themselves off, and to cut off their vision, from those simple earthy problems of hands-and-feet, of ways-and-means, which demand intimate knowledge of and empathy with the many very ordinary persons with very ordinary minds and very ordinary ideas and ideals who make up most of the staff of law-government, and without whose active shoulders to the wheel the wain of vision settles gently but inexorably into an ever present mud. {355}

In particular, I resent a superciliousness too prevalent among my scholarly brethren in regard to our appellate courts and how they do their work and write their opinions. The resentment is not because I do not think that the appellate courts could write better opinions; God wot, they could. Neither — as surely this book shows — is it because I do not think that they could do better work. They can. They will. It is, instead, because the scholars too often forget that (as they arrange these matters into Order) they may still need to go to school to life, in order that they may put human flesh upon that skeleton of doctrine which almost any one of them knows how to build; in order, further, that they may check each abstraction against concrete case and *need* after *concrete* case and need; always with a view to guidance for wise *decisions* coming up. In order that they may wrestle, as a part of the price of any ordering doctrine, with the question of how it *works,* and of how it can be made to work.

Hence, when any scholar says in his heart: "Thank God that *I* am not as these mere other men are," I resent it because (to the disadvantage of the Common-wealth) he is cutting himself off from a curiously valuable, accessible, and time-cheap fountain of instruction about life. There is indeed no known way to muddy the message of such a document as a judicial opinion more effectually then by approaching it with scorn.

* * *

The truth is that we of the law are almost as blind to the instruction-power of our case reports as are the psychologists, the sociologists, the descriptive economists, the ethnologists, and even, in the main (the United States Supreme Court Reports excepted), the historians and the men of that other half of our own discipline: Government.

The "outsiders'" blindness is due mostly to the fact that we ourselves have made clear to them that until any one of them first has a thorough legal training, he cannot understand an opinion at all. *It does not mean what it may seem to say,* has been our teaching. So. What "outsider" wants either to stick his neck out or to expend three precious years in order to learn to read, without being publicly scourged, in scorn, by an initiate?[319]

Our own blindness is the correlative blindness of the insider. We insist, even among ourselves, on treating the cases primarily as repositories of doctrine. They are that, and of course we need {356} both to know it and to use our skills in the refining of that ore. But opinion by opinion, and peculiarly if the reporter deigns to give more than the opinion (as, e.g., an intelligible outline of the arguments), case by case, the reports offer vastly more than data about the prevailing rules of law. If *"case"* books had not over these later generations tended to pare opinions down first to the single "relevant" issue, and then to the "purely legal" discussion, I should feel embarrassed at reminding people supposedly reared on "cases" that each such case reflects a human crisis in a situation set by our society; a crisis seen, reported, and judged against the background both of the situation and of the people; and so perceived, judged, and reported only after professional but human advocacy and by a professional and human tribunal. "A priceless vignette from life," says Lloyd Garrison. Few are the men, today, whose intensity and range of living have alone been enough to fit them out with what they need to know of man, of men, and of society. Not only the philosopher but the statesman has found that he needs turn to biography, and to history, and to the drama and the novel, if he would round out his foundation for action as for thought. I like Bacon's phrasing (and he was neither cloistered nor what one might call unintellectual): "*Reading* maketh a *full* man." (My italics, of course.)

What Bacon thought about the reading of case reports, in this connection, I do not know; but I now propound an opinion cut as carefully as if I had been charged with the cutting of a gem: The more pungent essayists apart, and with particular reference to biography, the novel, the drama, and all but the cream of history, the case reports, rightly read, and hour for hour over the years, can for a law-trained man yield as high a return in understanding of man, men, and the ways of our society as any other material he will find in print. Save for the great book which happens to hit some one man's mind just when that man is ripe for that particular book, and save for the "outside" material needed to supplement any "law" books in reference to a particular pending matter, the return from rightly read law reports is both more accessible to a lawyer than other high-yield stuff, and hard to rival. I mean, on the "humanities" side, the psychology side, the sociology side, the side of general understanding, and the side of making any dream come true. And as a companion piece: except, as to any particular area of life, for some distinguished reportorial series or monograph or "survey," light on fact-situations, factual problems, on the ways in which this society of ours is going on — this supplement of and "substitute for {357} personal experience" derives for a law-trained man more readily and effectively from case reports, rightly read, than from any other printed source I have met. In each aspect, what is needed, and all that is needed, is first to read the reports for what they are: human histories about situations which have arisen in our society. And, second, to group together for instruction — in a way which other literature rarely, in equivalent time, permits — six or a dozen or forty significantly comparable histories, to be thought about together: whether in terms of situation, or in terms of process, or along any other line. But, if I may repeat, this last (indeed a real approach even to the first) is almost hopelessly handicapped if you approach the opinion not to reach its human meaning, or to garner its yield of fact, but instead are snooting because *you* think *you* could have done a neater or a wiser *doctrinal* job.

On the matter of information about conditions and problems, both the possible range and the possible poignancy are indicated by our short New York foreign exchange sequence, above at pages 208 ff. Those case reports, only eight in all — even the extracts presented here in a different context and for different purposes — give an amazingly enlightening picture of a metropolitan foreign-language "colony" with its home ties and its quick-adjusting, enterprising petty buccaneers (one remembers also imported "contract-labor") who exploit the home ties; set against, and contrasted with, the great international market for exchange; with, in between, the little private banker, with his problems, his needs — and his own service to the whole. I have met no such completeness of scene in any "economic" literature. Of course, as our case series ends, it becomes clear that detail on the dominant aspect, that of the international banker's operations, must be hunted out elsewhere; but when you turn to any economic or business treatise on the subject, I defy you to find a passage which will bite fact into your blood the way *Musco* will, or *Legniti,* or *Equitable v. Keene.* I am not of course suggesting that the current foreign exchange scene is even adumbrated by these scenes from the days of a free market; what I am trying to do is to illustrate the range and power with which reports prepared for other purposes can and do portray the conditions of their own day.

It will not do to waste space. For further illustrations of what a case sequence can show about how our economic life goes round, it is enough to suggest merely (1) that the *facts* in the case sequences on election in conditional sales cited and partly discussed {358} (above, pp. 124 f.), will give any economic historian a better picture of pre-Finance-Company installment buying in this country than I think he can locate in the same time anywhere else; and (2) that the *facts* in the New York consumer-warranty sequence (including, of course, the city water supply case, *Canavan,* above, p. 106), if studied *as facts,* are enough, in themselves, to raise (*as of, say, 1930*) a serious question as to why we have had to wait till the 1940's and 1950's for the Torts boys to really wake up to something called "strict liability," and for scholars who had for generations been shrugging "Sales" off into the dustbin to undertake (with a touch of surprise, it seems to me) "a new look at Warranties."[320]

Perhaps what the reports offer on the human side is less easy to see. But, really, it is not less plain, and it can be more lovely. The picture of a great judge, Horace Stern, baffled by the blindness of reporters, and with an almost unexampled joinder of doggedness, delicacy, and delight, putting his sweet song over, and for the benefit of at once the Commonwealth and the craftsman — this is not a thing you will match readily among belles lettres, certainly not in the same space, and it has a deal more of guts and bones than most of the stories from that genre. Or take our "incompleteness" cases on formation of contractual obligation. (This is entirely in addition to what the recurrent facts show about the business need for some kind of legal recognition of some kind of open-term arrangement.) My concern this time is with the problem presented to Cardozo when, a year after *Schlegel* (per McLaughlin) had decided that a dealer's promise to take "requirements" meant nothing, and after *Duff-Gordon,* the most carefully constructive of his prior opinions on incompleteness and "commercial" reading had thus been substantially erased, he had nevertheless persuaded the court back onto the right road in the reading of commercial writings.[320a] As has been noted above, at page 115, this judge who within the limits of possibility came close to making a fetish of judicial candor then did as technically pretty and as intellectually dishonest a job of face-saving for his brother McLaughlin as you can discover in the books; this judge who as a habit and practice (at least in his later work) cleaned up every prior adverse precedent, in this instance left *Schlegel* open and threatening behind. I think that, with burning conscience, he sacrificed the lesser value to the greater: a right way {359} of reading documents covered a thousand cases; so did harmony in the court; distortion of this precedent seemed to touch only one.

The raw facts sit on the record, for the reading. They open up, for wonder, any number of questions about the more intimate operations of a court. Above all, they force to any scholar's attention that there are, in defiance of any blunt generalizations, all kinds of very intimate operations of any court, and within one. This, for my money, is "the humanities," and is "belles lettres" deeper criticism.

* * *

What, cuts in the carper, you dare to put forward judicial opinions as reports on the *facts* of *life?* Have you forgotten your own decisive indication,[321] or Radin's demonstration,[322] of the many removes from the facts of life represented by any litigation, and above all by an appellate opinion? Surely it has long been established that, what with the screening through legal theory and through the rules of procedure and of evidence, what with the unavailability or unreliability of oral testimony, the facts of life show up even in the trial courtroom only as unrecognizable distortion, let alone then in an appellate judge's little selective essay built to put rouge and lipstick on his court's decision!

It does indeed pay to remember that an opinion is no photograph of nature. It pays to remember that even a sequence of correspondence which comes into court intact contains no direct showing of *why* any letter took the form it did; a reader is left, for instance, to his own feeling for situation and for language, if he wants to spot which is the first letter written by counsel for the client's signature. Radin, as mentioned, devoted half of a book to the unreality of such "truth" as appears in court, and Jerome Frank has been quite rough with me for urging that opinions could significantly reflect significant facts of life.[323]

I am quite impenitent. I have never been able to avoid Bishop Berkeley's views about my definite lack of *any real knowledge* that this manuscript I am working on, or a printer, or a reader, is really there at all, much less to avoid Kant's views about my absence of knowledge as to what (if they are there) any of them is *really* like. Nevertheless, like the rest of mankind, I get on with {360} a working substitute for that "true knowledge" which I do not have. And the case is not too dissimilar in regard to the judicial opinion and its "facts." I know, and I remember, that the appellate opinion is no photograph of what "was there." But I simply do not understand the pertinence of the standards about truth — *for working purposes* — which Radin on the one occasion and Frank as a practice set up in regard to either the trial courtroom or the appellate opinion. For Frank's own thinking, any anecdote from somebody somewhere (not subject even to cross-examination) was sufficient to buttress a clobbering of Langdell, for instance, as a cloistered neurotic (Langdell, whose investments survived the panic of '93, and who taught his cases from the front, as jobs in argument!).[324] But in regard to the standard by which the raw facts of a case are to be tested, Frank and Radin suddenly step up the standard, and refine the scale to micro-millimeters. I do not see why. *Of course,* there are distortions, sometimes (though rarely) distortions into unusable unrecognizability. But in the main, for any reader with any sense (it need not be that fine *horse* sense) the raw facts come through well enough for real instruction. Indeed, for those ignorant of the type-situation, even wrongly distorted "facts" can be instructive. As novels show.

I view most pictures of events found in appellate opinions as having a higher likelihood of significant accuracy than J. Frank's anecdotes (which I know, repeatedly, to be distorted amazingly by wrenching out of context of time or subject matter). But I see most of those anecdotes as also probably true enough, commonly significant, and certainly interesting. So with the pictures of life which emerge from the reports. They are typically incomplete; and what picture of life is not? They are screened {361} through lawyers' conceptions of the "legally relevant" and "legally admissible," and that frequently has involved severe distortion of what "was there"; yet enough often appears in the way of improperly admitted evidence or of properly rejected offers of evidence or the like to suggest a good deal of what is most needed to round the matter out. And as one gathers cases around a type-situation the divergence in the theories of the various trial counsel brings out whole series of converging and complementary aspects. As against the chronic accusation that the writing judge's summary of the facts is "merely" a prettification of the decision, I rely on three things: (1) those cases in which — especially as a teacher of argument — I have studied first the record and then the opinion; (2) my general feeling for the nature of a statement of facts (checked also against my background knowledge whenever I happen to be informed); and (3) my knowledge of the character of individual judges. The upshot I think quite clear:

First: the better written the opinion, the more likely the facts are to be organized in support of the judgment; and some uncomfortable facts may be omitted. Cardozo's *McPherson* opinion, discussed below (p. 430) is an admirable example.

Second: even then, willful omission of significant *bothersome* facts is not common. Though the outcome may color the writer's judgment on what is significant.

Third: most opinions lack the literary compression which would admit of severe distortion by way of advocate's omissions; *and few opinions represent a court on the defensive* or under pressure to avert criticism of *that particular* decision; so that most opinions, instead of being sharply slanted, tend rather to sprawl a little in their presentation of the facts, with the contra aspects which fill out the life-situation likely to peek out all over.

Finally, one observes that what is being urged is not that study of opinions is a substitute for study of life, when the study of life is accessible. What is being urged is that, if read with care and empathy for their facts, opinions offer an amazing range, at amazingly low time-cost, of amazingly significant and convenient broadening, deepening, and balancing of any scholar's own direct experience. This, I insist, is in any aspect and for any legal scholar hard to rival; and in many aspects and for many scholars there is no remotely competing source of needed knowledge.

* * *

The foregoing sums up in the proposition that the clan of legal scholars and the tribe of appellate judges are allies willy-nilly in {362} the Herculean labor of producing and expanding order in our legal doctrine, and that in this as in most alliances there is room for much meditation over ways and means.

Let us, then, on one concrete sequence, watch the interaction of case court and scholarly work over a very troubling area.

19. The Form or Boiler-Plate "Agreement"

I know of few "private" law problems which remotely rival the importance, economic, governmental, or "law"-legal, of the form-pad agreement; and I know of none which has been either more disturbing to life or more baffling to lawyers.

The impetus to the form-pad is clear, for any business unit: by standardizing terms, and by standardizing even the spot on the form where any individually dickered term appears, one saves all the time and skill otherwise needed to dig out and record the meaning of variant language; one makes check-up, totaling, follow-through, etc., into routine operations; one has duplicates (in many colors) available for the administration of a multidepartment business; and so on more. The content of the standardized terms accumulates experience, it avoids or reduces legal risks and also confers all kinds of operating leeways and advantages, all without need of either consulting counsel from instance to instance or of bargaining with the other parties. Not to be overlooked, either, is the tailoring of the crude misfitting hand-medown pattern of the "general law" "in the absence of agreement" to the particular detailed working needs of your own line of business — whether apartment rentals, stock brokerage, international grain trade, installment selling of appliances, flour milling, sugar beet raising, or insurance. It would be a heart-warming scene, a triumph of private attention to what is essentially private self-government in the lesser transactions of life or in those areas too specialized for the blunt, slow tools of the legislature — if only all businessmen and all their lawyers would be reasonable.

But power, like greed, if it does not always corrupt, goes easily to the head. So that the form-agreements tend either at once or over the years, and often by whole lines of trade, into a massive and almost terrifying jug-handled character; the one party lays his head into the mouth of a lion — either, and mostly, without reading the fine print, or occasionally in hope and expectation (not infrequently solid) that it will be a sweet and gentle lion. The more familiar instances, perhaps, are the United Realtors' Standard Lease, almost any bank's collateral note or agreement, {363} almost any installment sale form, an accident insurance policy, a steamship ticket, a beet sugar refinery contract with a farmer or a flour miller's with its customer; or, on a lesser scale, the standard nonwarranty given by seed companies or auto manufacturers. In regard to such, one notes four things: (1) sometimes language which seems at first sight horrifying may have good human and economic stimulus; thus, suits for loss of crop before a farmer jury are pretty terrible things to face for the price of a few bags of seed; and (2) there are crooked claims and there are irrationally unreasonable ones — each with its jury risk — as well as solid ones; and only a clause which in law bars the claim absolutely can free an outfit like an insurance company to deal fairly though "in its discretion" with the latter class. On the other hand, (3) boilerplate clauses can and often do run far beyond any such need or excuse, sometimes (thus, as early as our *Lake v. Columbus Ins. Co.,* Ohio, 1844, above, pp. 69 f., and distressingly today in, e.g., the cheap furniture business) involving flagrant trickery; and (4) not all "dominant" parties are nice lions, and even nice lions can make mistakes.

There is a fifth and no less vital thing to note: Where the form is drawn with a touch of Mr. Dooley's "gentlemanly restraint," or where, as with the overseas grain contracts or the Pacific Coast dried fruit contracts or the Worth Street Rules on textiles, two-fisted bargainers on either side have worked out in the form a balanced code to govern the particular line or trade or industry, there is every reason for a court to assume both fairness and wisdom in the terms, and to seek in first instance to learn, understand, and fit both its own thinking and its action into the whole design. Contracts of this kind (so long as reasonable in the net) are a road to better than official-legal regulation of our economic life; indeed, they tend to lead into the setting up of their own quick, cheap, expert tribunals.[325]

* * *

Such is the background of a phenomenon which has been gaining in importance for more than a century, its well-done pieces tending, as stated, to slide off out of court or "legal" notice because of dispute avoidance, ready adjustment, or arbitration. For the work of official law that has been unfortunate. It has tended {364} to keep out of the familiar law books, where they might stir imitation and imagination of other lawyers, the balanced type of boiler-plate. It has tended also to keep away from the appellate courts enough contact with the balanced type of form to let that type grow into a recognized pattern and a welcomed standard against which hog-drafting can be spotted, measured, and damned, so that the two different approaches and technique-lines of construction which are needed could be made articulate and reserved each to its appropriate sphere.[326] Instead, the material which has come into court and into the American books has been in the main the jug-handled, mess-making stuff. What, then, of that?

For the courts, the story is quick to tell, though the cases must run into the thousands, and with no reckonability anywhere in sight. Unpredictably, they read the document for what it says, drop a word about freedom of contract, or about opportunity to read or improvident use of the pen, or about powerlessness of the court to do more than regret, or the like, and proceed to spit the victim for the barbecue. With equal unpredictability, they see the lopsided document as indecent, and evade it:

> A court can "construe" language into patently not meaning what the language is patently trying to say. It can find inconsistencies between clauses and throw out the troublesome one. It can even reject a clause as counter to the whole purpose of the transaction. It can reject enforcement by one side for want of "mutuality," though allowing enforcement by the weaker side because "consideration" in some other sense is present. Indeed, the law of agreeing can be subjected to divers modes of employment, to make the whole bargain or a particular clause stick or not stick according to the status of the party claiming under it: as when, in the interest of the lesser party, the whole contract is conditioned on some presupposition which is held to have failed. The difficulty with these techniques of ours is threefold. First, since they all rest on the admission that the clauses in question are permissible in purpose and content, they invite the draftsman to recur to the attack. Give him time, and he will make the grade. Second, since they do not face the issue, they fail to accumulate either experience or authority in the needed direction: that of marking out for any given type of transaction what the *minimum decencies* are which a court will insist upon as essential to an enforceable {365} bargain of a given type, or as being inherent in a bargain of that type. Third, since they purport to construe, and do not really construe, nor are intended to, but are instead tools of intentional and creative misconstruction, they seriously embarrass later efforts at true construction, later efforts to get at the true meaning of those wholly legitimate contracts and clauses which call for their meaning to be got at instead of avoided. The net effect is unnecessary confusion and unpredictability, together with inadequate remedy, and evil persisting that calls for remedy. Covert tools are never reliable tools.[327]

It is plain that the effect of such work on "Words and Phrases" and the like can be pretty awful. Above all, the sound impulse for fairness — better, against outrage — fails to *cumulate* into any effective or standard techniques, except in a very few areas such as life and fire insurance. Moreover, such techniques as the above are, for the most part (the "repugnancy" idea is a striking exception), mere dodge or artifice, ready to prove embarrassing if taken seriously tomorrow in a case of a different flavor. Thus, knocking out an auto manufacturer's enforcement of a power-clause in an agency contract on the ground that the bargain lacks consideration or "mutuality" can lead (and has) to conferring at-will termination power on the same manufacturer, so to speak by operation of court.

What, now, have the scholars added? They began, so far as my reading goes, by making the matter worse. The Story passage on nominal consideration which was quoted at page 166 is typical of the all-or-nothing approach which was applied, as well, to contract formation; the "classical" law of offer and acceptance may have made it tricky to accept those offers which their "master" was supposed to shape with fiendish ingenuity to keep the deal from being closed, but once one was cleanly closed — as by an accepting signature on a form — the "classical" approach to what had been "assented to" was equally formal, rigid, and devoid of contact with the facts of life. Up until 1925 or 1930, except for a luggage check or so, the classrooms of the country honored the problem by ignoring it, by quiet assumption that signature means assent, and, should one of the tough cases cross the mind, then, whenever "consideration" could be technically established, pilloried the "inadequate analysis" of judges who were finding in absence of "mutuality" a way of protecting the signer-upper whose nose was firmly in the dirt. The matter paralleled the {366} harshness of the keen-eyed scholar on those more labored forms of misconstruction of "description" in a sales contract which courts have (irregularly) used to work out an undercover law of substantial compliance in cases where such a rule is needed.

There came then a trickle of scholarly effort at diagnosis: Isaacs pioneered it in 1917,[328] Wigmore and Kocourek got some of Demogue's thinking published in translation in 1921,[329] Wright's rather exciting paper came out in 1926.[330] By the time of Dawson's French-German study[331] and Prausnitz' English-Continental comparative treatment,[332] both in 1937, and my review of the latter,[333] worry over the general problem was spreading rather widely.[334]

But no one was able to come up with any practicable *general* line of remedy. The New York model lease-form was disregarded. Insurance was partly under legislative and/or administrative control — as in due course were, for instance, the agreements of bond issue trustees; and efforts were being made to slightly clean up the installment selling abuses by way of legislation — but no such attack had any general application. Everyone with sense did agree that the bargained-out form-contract was a device of value, of singular promise.

But even where the form moved into the shockingly outrageous, there was not too much general operating help to be had from going at the matter bluntly by way of reality of assent to the boiler-plate material, because among those terms which plainly are in fact assented to only one time in a thousand there are still many which are sound particularizations of the deal to the business, very useful and wholly within reason; and those ought to be sustained and applied. A workable guide for courts must offer some wherewithal to sort such out from the clauses of oppression or outrage, some wherewithal to sustain the one, reject the other. As suggested above, the court's own lines remained {367} almost equally blind on this; they tended (save in regard to the infrequent "repugnancy" concept) to strike down the whole deal in order to prevent enforcement of the obnoxious clause. The following passage of mine from 1939 was entirely abreast of the thought of the day. Note the almost complete absence of available *measures* and traditional support to allow an appellate court to justify to its own conscience that remodeling of the agreement which is so often called for:

> The crude but effective ax-work of centuries past on forfeit of security can serve as precedent and impetus, but the examination of the standardized contract of a particular modern line of trade to distinguish clauses serving the better functioning of the work from those inspired by the sole interest of the higher contracting party (to paraphrase

Demogue . . .) is not a task for which a common-law judge's equipment has peculiarly fitted him.

Nor do I think it will ever so fit him fully. But what it does fit him for is to see that there is such a distinction; to see that free contract pre-supposes free bargain, and that free bargain presupposes free bargain-ing; and that where bargaining is absent in fact, the conditions and clauses to be read into a bargain are not those which happen to be printed on the unread paper, but are those which a sane man might reasonably expect to find on that paper. The background of trade prac-tice gives a first indication; the line of authority rejecting unreasonable practice offers the needed corrective. The distinction involved, even when applied to the testing of a standardized printing, is a simple one, and one which responds rather readily to the trained intuition of a case-law judge for what is *too* unfair. Courts have taken distinctions much like it, as Prausnitz shows, for instance, in regard to what kind of policy an oral contract for insurance called for. It is a distinction, too, which makes sense in the reading of people's actions. It offers a wherewithal for striking out utterly unreasonable clauses, while yet leaving a due presumption in favor of an expert's knowledge of what the conditions of his trade may be calling for. Courts' business is not the making of de-tailed contracts for parties; but courts' business is eminently the mark-ing out of the limits of the permissible, and the reading of fair under-standing, and the adaptation to the modern form-pad bargain of older rules based on the individualized *writings* of an earlier day — and still applicable to such writings.[335]

What the story shows thus far is first, scholars persistently off-base while judges grope over well-nigh a century in irregular but dogged fashion for escape from a recurring discomfort of imbalance {368} that rests on what is in fact substantial nonagreement despite perfect semblance of agreement. We have then thirty-five years or so while scholars slowly wake up and launch a type of general inquiry, comparative study, diagnosis, and analysis which develops a depth and a perspective hard for judicial case-by-case experience to rival. Yet thus far the scholars are still sticking in the bark of the job: they cannot come to grips with effective *measures:* while the appellate judges, still irregularly, but somewhat less so, are slowly getting (as a class) a little clearer about the net ideals of avoiding indecency and preserving at least a color of balance, in form-pad deals.

In truth, judicial work had set up, here and there, the lines along which scholars might have builded a road out. There was first the heritage from Tudor days of *loan* as a transaction-type which had an iron essence that neither form nor formula could reach — so in regard to contracting away the equity of redemption; so in regard to masking usury. The same basic approach underlay the view of the contract for common carriage as one which did not admit of the carrier's contracting out of liability for negligence. The picture is one of this or that transaction-type as having, I say, an essence which contains a minimum of balance, a core without which the type fails of being: a "principal" or a "partner," for instance, must "take the burdens with the benefits." (1) The doctrine of "repugnancy" sees the type-transaction intended, and kills off the clause which will not square with the iron core; (2) the doctrine of illusory promise and the vaguish manipulation of "mutuality" see balance as of the essence, fail to find it, and so find no transaction achieved at all; (3) the Cardozo approach sees the arrangement as unmistakably intended, balance as of the essence, and so reads the balance in.[336] The first and third ways of work are effectively curative, and offer mutually complementary, and general, patterns.

Here, as I see it, was the scholar's proper field: the searching out and assembly of a battery of such techniques, perhaps with needed invention thrown in. That, as the first job. Second, the examination of half a dozen or a dozen major transaction-types, to {369} locate, describe, and test proper specifications for an iron core of each. I am not, mind you, speaking of such transaction-types as are set up by the Uniform Sales Act or Uniform Partnership Act with regard to most of their provisions, all effective only "unless otherwise agreed," but of basic unavoidables like the partnership gain-loss or the sales sell-buy combinations, or the delivery-on-shipment inherent aspect of a c.i.f. contract.

This open and inviting field is still substantially unoccupied. In regard to contracts for the sale of goods, one effort which may have some small promise has been made, in the Uniform Commercial Code. The lines of approach are three, in combination. First, "Every contract or duty . . . imposes an obligation of good faith in its performance or enforcement" (§1-203), and good faith, in regard to sales, includes "in the case of a merchant . . . the observance of reasonable commercial standards of fair dealing in the trade" (§2-103(1)(b)). Second, under Section 2-302

> (1) If the court as a matter of law finds the contract or any clause of the contract to have been unconscionable at the time it was made, the court may refuse to enforce the contract, or it may enforce the remainder of the contract without the unconscionable clause, or it may so limit the application of any unconscionable clause as to avoid any unconscionable result.
>
> (2) When it is claimed or appears to the court that the contract or any clause thereof may be unconscionable, the parties shall be afforded a reasonable opportunity to present evidence as to its commercial setting, purpose, and effect to aid the court in making the determination.

There seems to me to be some possibility that these provisions may lead appellate courts into a machinery for striking down where striking down is needed, without getting in the way of reasonable construction of the reasonable, and without need for wholly upsetting the deal in order to escape a particular obnoxious result. Especially would there seem to be hope of this because the Code itself provides without need of clause for the more usual type of protection which has needed in sales cases to be arranged by contract: thus, for example, for excuse (§§2-615, 2-616) or substituted performance (§2-614) on failure of presupposed conditions (shipping facilities, strikes, destruction of plant, etc.) or on impairment of expectation of performance (§2-609) (slow pay, successive deficient deliveries, etc.). And the Code provides without need of clause for such commercially needed good faith remedies as partial acceptance (§2-601(c)) or an informal {370} covering purchase (§2-712) or resale (§2-706). It is possible, it may even be likely, that the fairly drawn statutory coverage of such matters will set for a court a standard against which to judge when an unbalanced clause on the same subject, or on any other, moves out into what may shock conscience and good faith.

At best, however, in our system an approach by statute seems to me dubious, uncertain, and likely to be both awkward in manner and deficient or spotty in scope. And the true answer to the whole problem seems, amusingly, to be one which could occur to any court or any lawyer, at any time, as readily as to a scholar who had spent a lifetime on the subject — though I doubt if it could occur to anyone without the inquiry and analysis in depth which we owe to the scholarly work.

The answer, I suggest, is this: Instead of thinking about "assent" to boiler-plate clauses, we can recognize that so far as concerns the specific, there is no assent at all. What has in fact been assented to, specifically, are the few dickered terms, and the broad type of the transaction, and but one thing more. That one thing more is a blanket assent (not a specific assent) to any not unreasonable or indecent terms the seller may have on his form, which do not alter or eviscerate the reasonable meaning of the dickered terms. The fine print which has not been read has no business to cut under the reasonable meaning of those dickered terms which constitute the dominant and only real expression of agreement, but much of it commonly belongs in.

The queer thing is that where the transaction occurs without the fine print present, courts do not find this general line of approach too hard to understand: thus in the cases Prausnitz gathers, in regard to what kind of policy an oral contract for insurance contemplates;[337] nor can I see a court having trouble, where a short memo agrees in due course to sign "our standard contract," in rejecting an outrageous form as not being fairly within the reasonable meaning of the term. The clearest case to see is the handing over of a blank check: no court, judging as between the parties, would fail to reach for the circumstances, in determining whether the amount filled in had gone beyond the reasonable.

Why, then, can we not face the fact where boiler-plate is present? There has been an arm's-length deal, with dickered terms. There has been accompanying that basic deal another which, if not on any fiduciary basis, at least involves a plain expression {371} of confidence, asked and accepted, with a corresponding limit on the powers granted: the boiler-plate is assented to en bloc, "unsight, unseen," on the implicit assumption and to the full extent that (1) it does not alter or impair the fair meaning of the dickered terms when read alone, and (2) that its terms are neither in the particular nor in the net manifestly unreasonable and unfair. Such is the reality, and I see nothing in the way of a court's operating on that basis, to truly effectuate the only intention which can in reason be worked out as common to the two parties, granted good faith. And if the boiler-plate party is not playing in good faith, there is law enough to bar that fact from benefiting it.[338] We had a hundred years of sales law in which any sales transaction with explicit words resulted in two several contracts for the one consideration: that of sale, and the collateral one of warranty.[339] The idea is applicable here, for better reason: any contract with boiler-plate results in *two* several contracts: the *dickered* deal, and the collateral one of *supplementary* boiler-plate.

Rooted in sense, history, and simplicity, it is an answer which could occur to anyone.

20. In Regard to Statutes

This book is not, as a book, about how our State supreme courts do deal or ought to deal with statutes. Yet again and again, in order to avoid misinterpretation, I have had to insist that the *range* of techniques correctly available in dealing with statutes is roughly equivalent to the range correctly available in dealing with case law materials. For instance, in connection with a paper of mine ten years ago, Charles Driscoll prepared twenty-eight pairs of alternative explicit canons or rationales available to use at need, with complete correctness, in either direction.[340] I have also seen the MSS of a forthcoming paper in which Judge Breitel of the New York Appellate Division makes explicit the variety of current techniques in dealing with statutory materials, showing {372} in each instance a reason which on occasion presses for drawing on that particular technique. That paper reaches so far beyond anything in print as to fill me with healthy and altogether joyous envy; but it is not yet available for reference.[341] True, meanwhile anybody who is really interested can discover, without going beyond the covers of this book and in almost any cross section sequence presented, a handsome variation in techniques with statutes. I recall from here or there (1) restrictive construction, either (a) in fresh attack, or (b) as controlled by prior interpretation, or (c) under the slogan of derogation of the common law, or (d) because of the seeming purpose of the statute, or (e) because of the background of law and sense into which the statute was to fit. I recall (2) wide construction (including at times the insertion of provisions not written) fitting into each of (a), (b), (d), and (e), and also, as a substitute for (c), because the new statutory purpose was in plain abrogation rather than derogation. I recall prior judicial interpretation being treated as controlling per se, or being rested on the fact that the legislature had amended in other points but not in this — *or* being upset. I recall constant but not regular recourse to situation-sense as a guide or buttress. And so on more.

But these are gleanings from more than a single acre. And I suspect that folks again (as they have been doing) will just let such material roll along, unnoticed, certainly ungathered. Moreover, Breitel's paper is deficient in one aspect: he simply speaks the truth; he does not write a book to prove it to the deaf. And my own paper was deficient in two aspects: first, its citations work in sweep across the States, in the normal American "law text" manner, without settling cleanly on any single court, in regard to that court's work of a given day, or week, or month. Second, my paper does not touch the range of "legislative history" variations, "administrative interpretation" variations, etc., which have been developed in such fullness in the federal courts. This second is, to be sure, no direct part of our State court inquiry. Nevertheless, in Appendix C, I have included along with a reproduction of Driscoll's arrangement of canons a similar gathering of federal material, especially on this missing aspect. The difficulty of not gathering State material from a single jurisdiction is remedied immediately below.

Yet before turning to that I should like, if I may, to set out from {373} the earlier paper (with slight changes) something of the general conclusions there arrived at.[342] There is such a fog of traditional thought rolling around that the obvious is hard to see without some special lighting.

> All of this (the general ways of operation with case law materials) is paralleled, in regard to statutes, because of (1) the power of the legislature both to choose policy and to select measures; and (2) the necessity that the legislature shall, in so doing, use language — language fixed in particular words; and (3) the continuing duty of the courts to make sense, but to make sense under, with, and within the law.
>
> For just as prior courts can have been skillful or unskillful, clear or unclear, wise or unwise, so can legislatures. And just as prior courts have commonly been looking at only a single piece of our whole law at a time, so have legislatures.
>
> But a court must strive to make sense *as a whole* out of our law *as a whole*. It must, to use Frank's figure, take the music of any statute as written by the legislature; it must take the text of the play as written by the legislature. But there are many ways to play that music, to play that play, and a court's duty is to play it well, and to play it in harmony with the other music of the legal system.

Hence, in the field of statutory construction also, there are "correct," unchallengeable rules of "how to read" which lead in happily variant directions.

This must be so until courts recognize that here, as in case law, the real guide is Sense-for-All-of-Us. It must be so, so long as we and the courts pretend that there has been only one single correct answer possible. Until we give up that foolish pretense there must be a set of mutually contradictory or conflicting *correct* rules on How to Construe Statutes: either or any available as duty and sense may require.

Until then, also, the problem will recur in statutory construction as in the handling of case law: *Which* of the technically correct answers (1) *should* be given; (2) *will* be given — and Why?

And everything said above about the temper of the court, the temper of the court's tradition, the sense of the type-situation, and the sense of the particular case applies here as well.

Thus in the period of the Grand Style of case law statutes were construed "freely" to implement their purpose, the court commonly accepting the legislature's choice of policy and setting to work to implement it. (Criminal statutes and, to some extent, statutes on procedure were exceptions.) Whereas in the Formal {374} period statutes tended to be limited or even eviscerated by wooden and literal reading, in a sort of long-drawn battle between a balky, stiff-necked, wrongheaded court and a legislature which had only words with which to drive that court. Today the courts have regained, in the main, a cheerful acceptance of legislative choice of policy, but in carrying such policies forward they are still hampered to some extent by the Formal period's insistence on precise language.

One last thing is to be noted:

If a statute is to make sense, it must be read in the light of some assumed purpose. A statute merely declaring a rule, with no purpose or objective, is nonsense.

If a statute is to be merged into a going system of law, moreover, the court must do the merging, and must in so doing take account of the policy of the statute — or else substitute its own version of such policy. Creative reshaping of the net result is thus inevitable.

But the policy of a statute is of two wholly different kinds — each kind somewhat limited in effect by the statute's choice of measures, and by the statute's choice of fixed language. On the one hand there are the ideas consciously before the draftsmen, the committee, the legislature: a known evil to be cured, a known goal to be attained, a deliberate choice of one line of approach rather than another. Here talk of "intent" is reasonably realistic; committee reports, legislative debate, historical knowledge of contemporary thinking or campaigning which points up the evil or the goal can have significance.

But on the other hand — and increasingly as any statute gains in age — its language is called upon to deal with circumstances utterly uncontemplated at the time of its passage. Here the quest is not properly for the sense originally intended by the statute, for the sense sought originally to be *put into it,* but rather for the sense which *can be quarried out of it* in the light of the new situation. Broad purposes can indeed reach far beyond details known or knowable at the time of drafting. A "dangerous weapon" statute of 1840 can include Tommy guns, tear gas, or atomic bombs. "Vehicle," in a statute of 1840, can properly be read, when sense so suggests, to include an automobile, or a hydroplane that lacks wheels. But for all that, the sound quest does not run primarily in terms of historical intent. It runs in terms of what the words can be made to bear, in making sense in the new light of what was originally unforeseen.

When it comes to presenting a proposed construction in court, there is an accepted conventional vocabulary. As in argument over points of case law, the accepted convention still, unhappily, requires discussion as if only one single correct meaning could exist. Hence there are two opposing canons on almost every point. {375} An arranged selection is appended. Every lawyer must be familiar with them all: they are still needed tools of argument. At least as early as Fortescue the general picture was clear, on this, to any eye which would see.

Plainly, to make any canon take hold in a particular instance, the construction contended for must be sold, essentially, by means other than the use of the canon: The good sense of the situation and a *simple* construction of the available language to achieve that sense, *by tenable means; out of the statutory language.*

STATUTORY TECHNIQUES, OHIO, 1939

In preparing to work over the cases, in printed sequence, from one single jurisdiction, I happened onto my old study material from 135 Ohio St. 1-307 (1939). A man could hardly throw a better pair of snakes' eyes. The subject matter does not spread over our legal world, as with New York or Pennsylvania or Washington. In the three hundred pages one deals eternally with Workman's Compensation, mandamus dealing with little problems about classified civil service, some rather sharp but also sharply limited problems of administrative commissions, constitutional problems, problems of appeal procedure, although there is (with consequent excitement to me) an occasional negligence matter, and one dog bite. But the jurisdiction is closely held down. For instance, inside of three hundred pages, I noted no less than twenty "appeals as of right" which the court dismissed because "no debatable constitutional question is involved." The court was taking the jurisdiction matter seriously; for instance, at page 280, a problem involving the employment of a child under eighteen years in selling liquor was thrust off on the court's own motion on this ground; and the official reporter headnotes such cases with a detail of fact which the terse opinion has not mentioned. Now it is the range of such cases as these last (or as those which the local system kept an Ohio appellant from even trying out) which I should have thought most likely to develop, within a single three hundred pages, a really roving-roaming reach into the full resources of a judicial Hornblower against the sea, the statutes, or the enemy.

Nevertheless, I offer what I found:

First, and obvious, and routine, are what one may call the simple applications: the relevant statute is set out and its rather manifest meaning is applied. Examples are *Wapakoneta v. Helpling,* p. 99; *H. & K. Motor Transportation Inc. v. Public Utilities* {376} *Commission,* p. 145. Or else a reading (e.g., of "injury" in the W.C.A.) has been settled (and settled on the narrow side) by "a long line of decisions, consistently," as in *Goodman v. Industrial Commission,* p. 81 at 82. But in material contrast, such a phrase as "gambling device" can be construed with great breadth, and preventively, both with reference to a prior holding and also with strong reliance on the prior rationale, as in *Kraus v. Cleve-*

land, p. 43. Again, the construction of a statute may be rested on the circumstances and the general background (conditional sales act filing on furnace is no notice to persons interested in the realty), *Holland Furnace Co. v. Trumbull Savings etc. Co.,* p. 48, or can be rested on the intention of the Legislature as indicated by its journals, to which "the court *may* look" to give effect "to any *manifest* intent," as in *Toledo v. Public Utilities Commission,* p. 57 (my italics).

Yet again, a later statute, though in new language, may be held declaratory, not changing the prior law, as in *Central United National Bank v. Abbott,* p. 37, or the construction may be tackled with no reference to prior statutes, but rather by analogy to somewhat similar language in a federal statute and one from South Carolina — with a touch of overt policy discussion thrown in — as in *Squire v. Standen,* p. 1, or else there may be deliberate expansion (this time of Constitutional language) on the basis of plain need ("judgment" covers "final orders") which is then suddenly fenced in because the courts "have gone to the limit" — all as approved or decided in *Hoffman v. Knollman,* p. 170.

Some of the more sharply divergent procedures appear when one puts together *State ex rel. White v. Cleveland,* p. 13, where we learn (in regard not to statutes, but to a Commission's rules) that "Since the rule does not provide that a pension shall date from the application therefor ... this court cannot read that qualification into the rule by judicial fiat," and the court instead, by judicial fiat, reads in another and different unprovided qualification; and *Laudato v. Hunkin-Conkey Construction Co.,* p. 127, where the familiar phrasing "arising out of and in the course of" is astoundingly transformed by judicial fiatissimo, and in judicial italics, thus: "The injury did not have its cause *outside of* AND DISconnected with the employment." (p. 133; my caps.) Or again, let us look at *Dragonette v. Brandes,* p. 223, a dog-bite statute construed flatly and curtly, as imposing "an absolute liability upon the owner of a dog, and *scienter,* fault, negligence or contributory negligence are not involved." (Three simple cites, at 224.) But a little earlier one has found the court in *State {377} ex rel. White v. Cleveland,* already mentioned, first sizing up the situation and only then going along with the construction by prior cases (at 18): "Were this question here for initial consideration, we would reach the conclusion that," etc. "Substantially the same question having been determined in the cases of ... and ... we approve and follow those cases." Then one locates *Triff, Administratrix v. National Bronze etc. Co.,* p. 191, where history and reason are elaborately examined to work out the meaning of a statutory provision, *but* (and over a three-man dissent) two solid previous cases to the contrary are firmly overruled. To which one should really add *Northwestern Ohio Natural Gas Co. v. Public Utilities Commission,* p. 85, where a prior syllabus which did a net construction of various statutory provisions is interpreted not only, and explicitly, in the light of the opinion in that case, and of its rationale, but, in addition, thus (p. 87; my italics): "*Then, too, the court had in mind* that the statutes themselves disclose no legislative intent to deny rate-fixing powers to municipalities." (Truly, in Ohio, "*the syllabus states the law*"!)[343]

I have not attempted to exhaust these three hundred pages. It is already clear that both in initial approaches to the meaning of a statute and in the ways in which the court's own prior constructions are handled, this single sequence of cases, decided at a single term of court, displays a versatility of techniques which is strictly comparable to our familiar correct techniques with case law authority.[344] I think that one can fairly regard the sampling — it was, for the purpose, a disadvantaged sampling — as justifying an inference that Driscoll's range of contrarying techniques (techniques always with alternatives available, and

235

leading, *each at need,* in truly varying directions) — that these or their like are to be found at work not merely in extreme cases for which one has to scour the nation, but State by State, and in comforting frequency and profusion.

Neither — though this presentation has been directed much more largely to paralleling the precedent techniques — neither does there seem to be room for doubt that one sees at work, here as in all the other samplings presented, a sustained drive by the court to find sense in or to put sense into the relevant statutes and, more often than not, to draw in consequence on some one {378} of the technical devices which will serve the purposes of that sense.

This ought, I am urging, to become the procedure not merely "more often than not," but regularly. As argued above, the courts have duties of creation with regard to statutory rules quite as much as with regard to case law, and the way to perform them is by recognizing what they are. Let me again quote; this time from what I presented to the Chief Justices on this matter of statutes:

> Here the image of 1909 — "We must accept what is written, we have only to read the [mostly nonexistent] 'intent of the legislature,' we have no *power* to add" — modified only by the 1959 willingness to abdicate self-will and to try to make sense — here, I say, the image of 1909 stalks not only active (though most intermittently) but vicious.
>
> The simple basic principle which expresses both the Grand Manner and today's need is this: It is contrary to a Supreme Court's duty, and therefore to its legitimate power, to allow any statute to remain as an undigested and indigestible lump in the middle of Our Law.
>
> Even the most formal judges of the Formal Period recognized this principle. Their response was sound in terms of office-instinct: The Law does call for wholeness. Their response was not good, in terms of measure. They refused to participate in the intrusion. They excreted what they could, via unconstitutionality. They walled off the rest by literalistic construction.
>
> That is past, in general. But it is still with us at odd moments, and vigorously, whenever a court settles down to a sermon on its lack of power over the written word.
>
> But in my samplings
>
> (a) I have found no single court which, if it mouths the statute-image from 1909 today, cannot also be found *operating* in conflict with that image, and in an approach to the Grand Approach to statutes, on the same opinion-day or on the next.
>
> (b) Nor have I found any court which, *judged on a sequence of cases,* is not moving with regard to statutes about as freely in the average as it is in the case-law field. This holds also for the 1939-1940 and 1944 work examined from six courts. What you get in the statutory field is a jerkier movement: here more of a hitch, there a sudden jump, so to speak, under cover.
>
> That is not healthy judging.
>
> According to the Grand Style, it is the office of the Supreme Courts in these United States to do, with statutes, too, what you have over now a demonstrable two legal generations been doing {379} for the rules of our case-law: you must accept them, to start with: you are no independent agents. You must shape yourselves to what in essence, they give you to receive: you are no officers to move as *you* see fit; you must also accept policy and basic measure, if, as, and when the legislature gives

them to you. Indeed — and here begins the tough duty — your job is *also* the perplexing one of remaining true to such policy and measure and at the same time to the nature and spirit of the inherited rule-machinery — of somehow handling the individual case according to all of these at once, as you labor in the vineyard of the heritage. You accept today from the Legislature, as your forebears of 1889-1909 would not, the Legislature's essential declarations of policy, and its outlines of measures. But as you do it, and very queerly, you still proceed to pick up, proclaim, and sometimes even trip yourselves on, the very noises that the foot-draggers of 1909 used to use in order to keep legislative policy from receiving any real recognition. For "We have no power," when that slogan was first popularized in the Formal Period, meant "Thank God, we can whittle it down to frustration."

Briefly, then: (1) A piece of legislation, like any other rule of law, is, of course, meaningless without reason and purpose.

(2) Few are the legislatures, even when equipped with tops legislative reference bureaus, who also have had time to give this particular bill the visiting Queen Elizabeth treatment, or who, in passing any bill, pass it with any "intention," as to the special question which is now before the court.

(3) Even when legislators do have demonstrable intentions — as with an open grab-bill — there can be times when a court has a duty of restrictive construction.

In the net: as in the Grand Tradition, so it is largely in current practice, and even more in current need; but while the recapture of the Grand Tradition is almost there, it is irritatingly not yet there, quite. It needs to be fulfilled.[345]

* * *

There is one matter to add. The unevenness, the jerkiness, the consequent lessening of reckonability which attends statutory work as against work with case law authorities rests of course primarily on this persisting explicit, indeed loud-voiced, conceit that "We have no power," etc. Such an emblazoned tenet drives much of real operation underground. Work, however useful, which is forced underground is inherently both less reckonable {380} and less regularly efficient than the work of calm confidence in the open; doubly so, naturally, when pressure to go under cover is self-supported by an image of rightness largely accepted in the worker's own mind. We have noted this in the case law field;[346] it holds no less for work with the frozen word.

What we have in the field of statutory construction seems to be a sort of persistence of a judicial technique, attitude, and set of blinders closely akin to the case law thinking, working, and feeling of an earlier day, so well typified by Taft. It will be recalled that Cardozo found it difficult to believe that the statutory field would display any of the large-scale or even of the conscious creation with which he had often had to wrestle in case law areas. And a current example is presented by Cardozo's successor on the Supreme Court: Frankfurter writes, talks, thinks, and feels in the case law bailiwick or in that of such broader Constitutional provisions as "due process" in the Holmes tradition of conscious and responsible, although ordered and restrained, creation; but on a point of statutory construction he can write in a fog or phantasmagoria of fictional legislative intent and of a judicial powerlessness and consequent non- or irresponsibility that forfeits all intellectual contact with the Grand Tradition of case law. In this formal self-prostration before the legislative power Cardozo and Frankfurter seem to me rather typical than otherwise; Breitel's paper, viewed as the organ of a new dispensation, is as far ahead of today's current articulate ideology as Cardozo's *Nature* was of articulate case law ideology forty years ago.

This has three important consequences. The first, already mentioned, is a certain jerkiness in the handling of statutory material. It is much less easy than with pure case law to foresee whether, how, and how far situation-sense will break through; and the art of effectively accommodating needed sense-meaning to the given statutory material of authority is (as contrasted with the case law art) still a crude art, sometimes a rude one. It is indeed both sobering and saddening to match our boisterous ways with a statutory text against the watchmaker's delicacy and care of a theologian, or of a Continental legal crafts-man, or even of a good American lawyer when the language he is operating with is that not of a statute, but of a document.

The second consequence flows out of the first: *cumulative* shift seems in the statutory field to be harder to bring into order and relative forecastability than in the case law areas. I am not {381} sure of this. Levi's presentation of expansion of the Mann Act has, e.g., something of the awfulness of a most predictable Medusa, and there are other statutes which have developed rather clear "lines" of construction. Nevertheless, I suspect such to be relatively few and nontypical, and the mining-claims of specialists. And I suspect that the coarseness of our tools of statutory shaping is even more important than the fixity of statutory language in making most change-successions difficult to plot.

It is manifest that I see no reason — other than inertia, which is not a reason but a cause — for the continuance, much less for the deliberate continuation, of these two troubles. Nor, indeed, of the third, which bothers me the most: the tension, if this formal-style statutory manner insists on bunking with the maturing and expanding Grand Style generally, the tension which seems inevitably a growing one between a high court's conscious duty in their office and their craft on the one hand and, on the other, their image of how their work ought to be done, and must be publicly presented. Above, in dealing with Ideal and Symbol and Hypocrisy in regard to the ways of appellate judging and of appellate opinions, I urged that inner security and honor can stand firm so long as the symbol and ideal are taken for what they mean in essence, even though the letter of the official ideal be disregarded. And the astounding shift in opin-ion-writing style over the last three legal generations lets us see that so far as concerns case law that adjustment has been pretty well achieved. I cannot feel the same way on the side of statutory construction. I cannot see how some of the things done to statutes (though in good causes) by noncitation or by disregard of word, phrase, or clause can fail to rasp the gullet even of the prescribing physi-cian. If some horrendous result is treated as the letter seems to demand, that is a different matter: it leaves the high image of duty bravely but pitifully faced. But the duty of accounting which an appellate court owes to the given authorities cannot with either decency or wisdom be ignored; so that the responsibility for making situation-sense out of the statutes (an obligation which the appellate courts are insistently and with increasing regularity facing up to) carries with it a responsibility no less, both in the guild and in the individual craftsman, for developing the art of handling frozen language up toward a level comparable with the current art of handling case materials.

Once let the job be seen, however, for what it normally is: to quarry out of a legislative text the best sense which the text permits, and a flock of questions start to home. Should an opinion {382} quote the statutes in question? Of course, and not alone because the statutory text may not be readily available across the border or to the bar of ten years hence, but also and particularly because such quotation presses upon the court itself its duty to work with and from that text, and an appellate court has as much need for accounting and audit as does a trustee or a treasurer.[347] Should the crucial language be italicized in the opinion? Again and obviously, yes. In a regime in which the simple cite is, by practice, careful and accurate,[348] and in which distinctions have come to be taken only for good reason given,[349] minimum decency of craftsmanship with the frozen word requires that the key words be spotted and faced. Finally, I know no way to exorcise the omnipresent demonic fiction of "legislative intent" which can compare with attention to the language and basic design of any statute when set into the general context of life and the law. One time out of ten, to repeat, a legislative intent with some concrete reality can be uncovered in circumstance or legislative history. For the rest, the court's work is not to *find,* any more than it is with case law. It is to *do,* responsibly, fittingly, intelligently, with and within the given frame.

RECKONABILITY FOR OFFICE COUNSEL

The present study has paid little heed to the situation and needs of office-counsel. The very base line for judging of reckonability has been set carefully at the completion of the trial of a litigated cause. But the counselor can argue solidly that his advice must rest on footing more sure than any needed by an advocate, that what is a "good business risk" for the litigating lawyer can and normally does still contain the very kind of danger he, the counselor, is called on to avoid. What comfort, then, to him, in all these pages? Pound, too, from time to time, has rather apologized for than defended the law phase of our Law-Government in this respect: people who complain of its uncertainty, or yearn for building which can stand safe and lasting like that of the engineer, overlook, he has reminded us, that unlike the work of men who deal with things, the work of men who deal with conflicting interests of men is tested by litigation and shrewd lawyers out to {383} the very edge and limit. And so far as concerns efforts at legislative control of behavior, there is wisdom in the observation.

But I do not see that any of this bars the counselor off from the comfort which an accurate conception of the way in which appellate courts decide should carry to him. He is not like the person pressing for legislation, who must often push out to the limit of the feasible and risk pushing beyond; in that area you get what you can get while the legislative getting is good. In sharp contrast, office-counsel can in all but rare circumstances play well inside any penumbra of doubt; he can work, like an engineer, with a substantial margin of safety; he can chart a course which leaves to others the shoal waters and the treacherous channels. For unlike the ordinary advocate, the counselor need not take the situation as it comes, but can shape and shore it in advance; he can draft documents and set up lasting records against the accidents of memory, death, or disappearance of witnesses, even to some extent against the hazard of bad faith — doubly so if he keeps his protective drafting within those bounds of reason which make a court want to give effect to manifest intent; trebly so if he sets a picture of situation and purpose which can appeal even to an outsider as sensible, reasonable, and inherently probable — and it is comforting how much of this last can be gotten by careful counsel into documentary form. Besides (or perhaps first), office-counsel are in peculiarly good position to study and discriminate among rules and rulings with reference to how strong and solid any of them is, how much weight it will carry, how far the relevant type-situation is already at home in judicial understanding, or is of a character to find a ready welcome. After such discrimination, it is on the rocklike law-stuff that the sane counselor does his building.[349a] Finally, wherever advising counsel can rely on being able to control any relevant litigation, another vital contingency is set to dwindling.

I retreat not at all, in regard to a novel legal enterprise, from the sad scene conjured up on page 17, above, of unforeseen disastrous anticipation by a band of idiots; but that type of cataclysm is not only rarish at worst, but is confined to novel undertakings which the client must be warned may touch off the unforeseeable. Neither, even in regard to ordinary cases, do I wish to belittle that bogey of the counselor, the calamitous trial. Nevertheless, {384} J. Frank to the contrary notwithstanding, I claim that the tools of analysis here put forward afford the careful counselor a degree of solidity in forecast and an available safety which if his were a business enterprise would make it a preferred investment. I say: a careful counselor. I think I may have to add: one also moderately able and moderately imaginative. For the skills which can keep transactions reasonably proof against bad faith, catastrophe, and perjury are only beginning to be again (as in the days of apprenticeship training and circuit-riding) reduced to communicated knowhow; and the counselor's task, working as he does at so many more removes from the final testing, is much more complex than that of the appellate advocate. It thus calls, at least as yet, for materially more than average ability, if a satisfying measure of safe reckonability is to be introduced into other than a purely routine transaction.

That fact, however, in no way impugns either the theses of this study or their utility in counseling. The less skilled counselor can learn without delay to be more cautious in his advice, and somewhat more effective in his work — compare as simple a thing as the nominal consideration matter touched above at page 273. That very process tempts and presses him into better-based invention; while the knowhow and postgraduate phases of legal education and writing are slowly stockpiling a wider wherewithal both of tool and of stimulus.

No. This study has not been directed or addressed primarily to the counseling lawyer; but it is down his alley, too.

AND THE SUPREME COURT?

These recent years have seen a recurrence of that old storm of criticism of the Supreme Court which seems to renew itself in our history every twenty years or so. The main lines of the attack, whether by lawman or layman, have had a quiet consistency. The underlying beat is always: "*I* don't like these *results!*" And that underlying drumbeat is commonly, though not always, masked by noise about how the Supreme Court (or the members thereof) are abandoning their Constitutional function, usurping legislative power, disrupting our commonwealth, and this or that in addition. Marshall's court got this treatment; Taney, after a while of relative peace, came up with the *Dred Scott* opinion; *Gelpcke v. Dubuque* seems to have tizzied the bar into a nervous breakdown, and each *Legal Tender Case* must have done the same; one by one, the Roosevelts girded their loins, lifted Neanderthalic {385} clubs, and went to battle — not the proudest feat of either. And here we are again.

Now it is plain, it is manifest, that the stuff of this book has bearing on the problems of that unique — and to my mind glorious — institution, the Supreme Court of the United States. Back in the '30's, when I was still touching and missing as I groped and bored after understandable communicable ways and patterns in the flow of appellate judicial deciding, I used to tell colleagues that in regard to method the Supreme Court was only, and quite slowly, coming abreast of the courts of the country, and was being picked on for beginning to do what every respectable other supreme court had been doing long and wisely. All I ever got on that, even from friendly souls, was the kind of blank stare which sends you either to the nut-house or else to painful documentation, in print, and between board covers, and under the imprint of an "established" publisher.

So this book is not about the Supreme Court. On the contrary, as just suggested, I have felt long and deeply that a common law and case law Supreme Court can soundly be judged only against the background of the common law and case law system in which the judges have been raised; and I have therefore, in order to get that background built right, kept myself perhaps more than a citizen should away from the Supreme Court reports themselves. Nevertheless, or therefore — I cannot tell which — this background study seems to me to make a few very useful matters very clear, things which most experts on the Supreme Court seem to me to have been too close to that Court to get, or to keep, in focus.

I put on one side attacks which run to the substance of results. These will be with us always. So long as the Court stays within the issues presented, or within the issues which the times permit to be embraced in or under the issues presented, the results are the Court's business, and no citizen who has any conception of any "free" society can really doubt that the price he pays in disappointment or dismay is amazingly like the price for losing a national election on a landslide good for a second term. This is no hindsight or shift of position by a "converted" realist. I am in print on this one, from 1931, when I was hating a considerable number of the then Supreme Court results.

> Social science students have their attention so largely and so vigorously fixed upon the peculiarities of their own constitutional system that their reactions on isolated constitutional decisions {386} tend to set their picture of the work of the appellate bench entire. . . . Even on the constitutional side it may fairly be argued that the attention of social science students turns almost exclusively upon the sore thumbs of the law. But law is more than sore thumbs; it is a going whole. Yet see. If a desirable statute is upheld, that fact passes as a matter of course. Whatever wisdom the court exercises is taken for granted, sinks out of sight, is honored by burial, or oblivion. But to the court's mistakes the trumpets blare — and blare again. I do not quarrel with this. The court has need of it. Yet if a scientist is interested in his perspective he must look to the rest of the court's work as well. Excavations among the legal records will yield their buried treasure, and without stint. The somewhat astounding achievement of making a document a century and a half old meet the needs of a community which insists on retaining the document in substantially its ancient verbal form, despite a tenfold expansion of territory, despite a twenty-fold expansion of population, despite the shattering onset of an industrial order, seems by nonlegal critics to be taken almost without comment. A word for Marshall, who died before industrialism had begun. A word for Marshall — and then silence. And this although it may fairly be said that such a minor change in our judicial machinery as making declaration of unconstitutionality require a vote of seven judges would eliminate three-quarters of the current criticism, so few are the instances on which that criticism rests. Let me be clear. I share the criticism. I sputter scorn and dismay into the trumpet, as do you. But I would have you, as reasonable accountants, tot up the credit column before you judge the net worth of the judges' work.[350]

Those were the days when useful State statutes were being smacked down; and I find it difficult to remember who, among my States' Rights friends, was then being worried about the Supreme Court's trespassing. But that goes to substance. The lessons of this study go to manner and method.

For in regard to manner, the Supreme Court proceeded to suffer, and is only in process of coming out of, a sea-change. I am no student of that Court; but the delicacy with which Hughes leaves seven swinging doors in *Minnesota Moratorium;* the careful building by Stone of new, but reliable, tax *law* (I mean new, careful *rules);* Cardozo's infinite expenditure of time in order to clean up, and produce reliable *guidance* — such things, for a {387} while, waned on a court which was addressing itself more to getting case results, case by case, than to building and rebuilding and recorrecting clear, sharp *rules* to guide a country.

No single thing can hope to explain a most complex phenomenon. But this I do assert; I assert it on the basis of this study: there has been, on the Supreme Court of the United States, until quite recently, a loss of the doctrine-responsive, doctrine-responsible, doctrine-rebuilding tradition, as a *man-dominating power*. I am, I repeat, no careful and sustained student of that Court. But I find in my own reading and in the comments of sympathetic careful readers signs and patterns — recently lessening — that have troubled me far more than could any particular decisions. Frankfurter can want his own doctrine until it is to hell with the Court and with his duty as a team-player. Douglas can twist a case beyond all legal decency or honesty, and use it, straightfaced, as if it supported his conclusion. Black can whittle authorities into shavings, and who knows, from this, where he is at? Warren can put out a principle as broad as all outdoors, and then disregard it in the next case, as soon as one touch of the phrasing proves uncomfortable. This is not, I say again, a book about the Supreme Court, and I do not propose to document these observations about the work of particular Justices whom I admire both as men and as judges. I do instance some types of error of method because I feel strongly that all that the Court has to do is to free itself from such errors of method, and to recur cleanly to the Grand Tradition of method, and manner, in order once again, as always, to find itself sheltered from any storm.

Let me then comment, in the light of the present study, on a few comments on the Court. Re substance, and in particular in regard to segregation, I suggest that what we have is *Dred Scott* in reverse; the court has again bitten off more than it can chew. But not, this time, by running out to grab. The cases came, almost inescapably. Let there be no mistake: in net, on substance, I go with my Chicago brethren in seeing the net results of substance on *in personam* jurisdiction, on commerce, on security, and on criminal procedure, for instance, as better and wiser than their contraries.[351] I feel the same about the desegregation {388} cases.[352] Let me add that I think the Court's results are also better and wiser than one has a right to expect to see worked out in the same time, under the same pressure.

Yet I feel entitled to criticize a point of method. I note, e.g., the sequence of Per Curiams presented by Wechsler, with the Court ducking the conjoint implications of prior broad "principle" upon flat, presented issues.[353] Even in a pinch, I do not like this. I say, and I think I show, that our Supreme Appellate Courts have achieved the full prestige and standing which are needed for frankness in their work; and the Supreme Court of the United States can similarly, in its own right, climb down from any small or large mistake. What it cannot do, consistently with its duty and its conscience, is to leave things unclear, leave them messed up, and do this *deliberately*.

Griswold, also, is right, when he urges (my phrasing, not his) that the Doug-las-Black's sometimes unreasoning love for little men is out of place in Federal Employer's Liability Cases.[354] The Court simply has no time to take these cases, in the interest of what amounts to two Justices' private crusade.[355]

Per contra, it seems to me obvious that Griswold and various others of the Harvard contingent are wrong when they suggest[356] that the Court ought to refrain from putting cases on broad principles, especially Constitutional cases. They are (if possible) more wrong insofar as they purport in this to line up behind Frankfurter; Frankfurter has indeed often preached so, but as often or more often he has in his action disregarded his own {389} preachment. What our study shows — and this fits Great Constitutional Issues it does little matters — is (1) that a court ought always to be slow in *uncharted* territory, and, in such territory, ought to be narrow, again and again, in any ground for decision. Until the territory has been reasonably explored. But what our study shows is (2) that *once there is clearish light,* a court should make effort to state an ever broader line for guidance. And (3) so long as each such line is promptly and overtly checked up and checked on and at need rephrased on each subsequent occasion of new illumination, such informed questing after broader lines is of the essence of good appellate judging.

What the Griswolds are really complaining of, in this connection, is a War-renish type of broad generalization not built in care on and out of eight or eighteen prior cases but framed ad hoc to support the conclusion for the case in hand. That is of course out of line. Anybody can see that, who gets far enough away to use two eyes. There is nothing new about it: There *is* a Law of Leeways. There *is* a Law of Fitness and Flavor. There *is* a Duty to Account *honestly* to the authorities. And by the same token there is a duty, case by new case, to rework all language, ancient or recent, into newer, cleaner guidance, a Duty of On-going Judicial Review of Prior Judicial Decision.[356a]

Three more observations about the relations of this study and the Supreme Court are worth mention. First, the threat to balance which pulses in any "managed" series of cases (see above, pp. 262 ff.) is for other courts either a possibility or an occasional danger. For the Supreme Court it is a chronic ill. The mass of material available to be drawn on is not that of a State, but of a Nation. The government departments are organized enterprises, and the Administration commonly has policies. The power of the {390} Solicitor General's office to select, arrange, and shape for presentation, dictating not only the business of the Court, but much of its flavor, and above all the order in which inchwise exten-sions in some desired direction are made persuasive — this is almost frighten-ing.[356b] That power demands the correlative sense of responsibility for sound law, of severe restraint, of obligation to our Law-Government as a whole, which characterized a Jackson or a Fahey in the office. That the demand is not always met is cause for alarm. Moreover, organized groups outside of government have power, certainly in the Constitutional domain, to arrange the "chance" emer-gence of issues-insequence in equivalent fashion, and such groups can rarely be expected to be thinking for the whole. Our discussion above suggests strongly that preservation of a court's balance in such a campaign, a campaign organized on one side only and by consistently able and careful counsel, calls for work outside the issues and facts in actual litigation: for background building work to round out the picture before an un-thought-through bias gets so built into the picture as to twist vision and befog any needed efforts at reorientation.

But work means man-time; and it is hard to conceive of squeezing more of that out of this hard-driven court. One recurs then, in application to the Supreme Court, to the labor-saving device we have found in such common current use among the States: the adoption of an opinion below, in whole or in part. It seems queer that this handy tool should not already be in vogue. The last quarter century of the Court's life has seen a remarkable shift away from personal aloofness, a willingness of the Justices, when off the bench, not to rely upon position for prestige, in a word the growth of an attitude toward life and office and other persons which one would have expected to see reflect itself also in adoption of the "adoption" technique. Meantime, one can only call attention to the fact that the technique does set free man-hours that are badly needed; and one can remind that as a morale-builder for a subordinate judiciary its equal has not yet been invented.

The third observation works in reverse: This study draws in one matter with peculiar profit on our experience with the Supreme Court. Here is one court in regard to which, for half a century to my knowledge, many scholars, many of the bar, and many among the public have addressed attention to the Justices {391} one by one, as persons and as players on a team. How any man can doubt that that attention has proved its value is quite beyond me. It has raised the level of understanding of the office, the work, the processes of appellate deciding generally. It has opened to the counselor and to the advocate in areas of Federal law a tool for stepping up forecast which to the man who uses it seems if anything even less dispensable than current information on the actual decisions. It has led the skilled observer into that more refined and accurate understanding of the impact "of the times," or "of public opinion," or "of social need," or "of justice," the impact *by way of the eyes and knowledge and values and insight of the individual Justices individually* AND *of the Court corporate* which used to be reserved for such ideas as "prejudice," "pigheadedness," or broad, vague, and not too useful whole-outlook concepts such as "liberal" or "conservative." On this body of study and this way of observation the present book draws happily for confirmation. It was natural for the approach to be launched where issues were big, where a whole nation of observers could be tapped, all looking at a single body, where cases and judgments more readily showed the policy-elements and the effects of variant individual experience, where passions ran high in regard to the results, where, finally, the relative frequency of separate opinions gave wider and easier bases for comparative judgments. But the techniques thus developed are available for use with any court. It must have been in the early '20's that Herman Oliphant, as he prepared to knock out yellow-dog clauses before the New York Court of Appeals, began his preparation by examining each sitting judge's opinions and votes in every labor case that judge was recorded as ever having sat in. The instance is not typical; few practicing lawyers will get a case which warrants that quantity of preparation. But *no* practicing lawyer who either counsels or does appellate work can afford not to keep currently abreast of the flavor of the work and reactions of the individual sitting judges not only in his own particular areas of activity, but in general. Every time he reads a new Supreme Court opinion, or reads of one, this is one summons — or reminder — it should bring him.

Here endeth this message *from the work* of our State supreme courts to our Supreme Court.

That message reacheth not primarily to substance. Insofar as the Chief Justices, a year or so ago, conceived that it did, they are {392} shown, it seems to me, to be in error, and shown by the very memoranda from my brethren on which they were relying.[357] But as of the time of their pronouncement, the Chief Justices were very solid in their flair. Something was, something for some years had been, very wrong. And to me as a preacher of the Grand Tradition of that Common Law Tradition which is the taproot of our Supreme Court it was a lovely thing that the one group who could really feel themselves as the Voice of that Tradition were impelled to voice their Voice.

It is of course important that they, and we, as well as their addressees on that high Court, should see that — taken as a group — the Chief Justices are individuals and team-players who have been hard at their work (and doing it, within reason, well) but who have been doing it without much articulate communicability about *how* they do it. It is important, I say, that we — and they — and the Supreme Court — should realize this. In talking to the Chief Justices I found only about a third (including, and this gave me comfort, all but one out of the youngest third) who could recognize that I was telling truth about what they were doing, daily. There was even one who had been made to see that he "had been doing, all along, exactly what he didn't want to"; but who guessed, wryly, that he would go on doing it. I am talking the simple obvious, with evidence direct from the mouth of the horse. *And* I am writing in the thirty-ninth year after Cardozo's first challenging, hugely publicized, definitely ex sancto, and three-times-reinforced discussion. Yet my friend Weintraub, C.J. of N.J., a clean-thinking and hard-hitting successor in the Vanderbilt-Brennan tradition, still becomes just a little embarrassed when he talks to me about a speech in which he grappled in public with the real problems raised by that inevitable and precious thing: *judicial legislation.*[358]

As I sat in the workshop meetings of the Chief Justices, on the afternoon after my effort to make articulate, from the side lines, some of the nicer and cleaner moves which the good players have been making for years, and then stayed around, if anybody wanted to say "Hello," I also got a delayed reaction which I think it proper to report. Occasional judges who, as I felt it, had either resented or missed the substance of the talk, were finding that with a little cooking it took on some meaning; and there could be talk, sometimes for my information, sometimes for theirs.

That was, for me, a cross-check, so to speak from the inside. If {393} an occasional Chief Justice hunts you up to discuss his court's problems of deciding, you find assurance that you are not too far off the base line. And that base line holds solid for the Supreme Court of the United States as it does for any other supreme tribunal of the common law.

The new flurry of criticism seems to me therefore as passing as the older ones have been. The one bothersome thing, the loss for a while of the finer rule-building and rule-rebuilding tradition (with appropriate initial caution, but with appropriate dogged recurrence) — that seems to be already waning. And the most striking single factor in the discussions of the last few years seems to me to be the naivete with which so many "experts" from each side have juggled, fumbled, or completely muffed the nature of the supreme judicial job, of *any* supreme judicial job, in this system of law in which those experts have been reared.

No wonder that the less "expert" have drifted or been driven into a crisis of confidence and of faith.

POCKMARKS, PREJUDICE, POLITICS, AND PEEVE

Well! And well, again! Here is this man about to wind up a so-called "study" of that very ordinary, intensely human, daily process known as "the reaching by an American appellate court of its decision," and this supposed or self-alleged "studier" has not even discovered that a judge with a bounding flea or an inset chigger uses his priceless and crucial *attention* in a different fashion from a judge or other person who, for the moment, has no urge to scratch. And this, Heaven help us, puts itself forward as a "realist" being "realistic." Don't you remember when Dick had had three drinks too many, and he got to swapping stories: "And so, John," he said, "you said, 'Hell, let's reverse!' So we reversed!"

* * *

Do you, reader, want more of such? I can give so much more, as accurate in report as it would be misleading in implication. Not scuttlebutt about influence or the like (though I have never poured wax into my ears). I mean stuff authenticated by man, circumstance, and inherent probability, suggesting or showing decision after decision to have turned on what Hutcheson, trying in vain to find a pattern, dubbed "the little, small dice." Traynor, almost two legal generations later, is on a similar quest: How can you set up a *formula to* test what is *reversible* error? {394}

And — since no such formula is buildable during the next twenty or forty years — Traynor will join Hutcheson in sweating out votes he knows he cannot wholly account for *by opinion,* and registering those votes even though he knows that a legal *system,* a system of law-government, cannot allow mere reference to the official's conscience to be a sufficient guide. Each has, therefore, been thrust into a bothering search which is typical of the tribe. What is not at all typical is the stubborn insistence of each on putting into print results which, on this matter, express personal bafflement in the job thus undertaken. We need, in matters of law-government as elsewhere, much more work and meditation done with this Toledo steel integrity: indeed, only such work has likelihood of yielding real help in pinning the baffle-factors somewhat down to pattern. The lines of promising approach are illustrated by the little technical helps toward eliciting an emerging rule, dealt with above,[359] or by the Laws of Leeways, Lawful Discretion, and Fitness and Flavor.[360]

But what emerges from all of such material is fourfold. The first point is that however much these doggedly doubtful cases stick in the mind and memory of the judge, the doubt and its happenstance resolution come not in lieu of labor and tradition and the application of best judgment, but on top of these, and to supply an answer where these, all together, have proved not quite enough. The second point is that the cases which will put forth such doubts, the cases which are really chancy cases, are moderately well detectable in advance; and it adds materially to reckonability of a total scene to know which areas are the areas of heavy risk. The third point is that an observer who studies the men and their work can develop not unuseful capacities to intuit or forefeel the prospective net reactions which will ultimately control the deciding in many or most of such cases.

The fourth point reaches over to deal not only with the unarticulated or seemingly petty or irrelevant factors in crystallizing judgment, but to deal as well with blemishes or personal defects. Any realist is aware that some judges who sit on high appellate courts are stuffed full of shavings and others full of quirk or prejudice or petty vanity; that some are sometimes lazy or slipshod or bingy or sick or seekers of preferment or acclaim. And any case may be the occasion for the pimple to become a vicious boil. I know, too, that when the rules of law are both ill-designed and vague (as in my home domain of Sales, before the Code) {395} there can be areas in which the upshot seems, at least on the surface, sometimes to be wholly unreckonable chance.[361]

Against all this, a really realistic observer simply remains a realist: he makes his judgments *on the basis of the daily grist*. He looks at the whole man, the going man, functioning as an officer in office, not at one pimple or one fleabite or one pockmark, or even a Job's plague of boils. And when the idiosyncrasy grows suddenly and with a serpent's tooth, as can a stomach ulcer of the body or the soul, a realistic observer reckons in the presence of felt office, and also the votes of brethren who are not, at the moment, subject to the same distractions.

* * *

There is one judge who must not be forgotten, the man of care and conscience, the man of a candor to himself that in the silences can turn into caricature as he contemplates the blemishes that mar his own breast and his brethren. The goals stand out for him so sharp, so challenging, so unreachable; except for odd moments of inspiration, achievement seems always to limp, and little things which have stood in the way swell in the lonely night. He looks at such a book as mine and takes an acrid comfort in that *other* courts at least are answering the muster. — The only way of dealing with this man is in the manner of Carlyle: Go to, Brother of the Goodly Company! Not for thee censure nor burden of remorse! Neither the law nor the Lord makes requisition of more than honesty and industry can yield; and it is a tough-minded or a callous man indeed who does not need the constant spur of falling short.

* * *

Let me close this whole study on the same note on which it opened: in the teeth of all troubles with our rules and concepts of our law — ungainly, outaged, technically deficient — and despite the fact that (as our judicial heroes demonstrate) the appellate judge's task makes demand and gives scope for brains God has granted to few appellate judges, and notwithstanding the disappearance from general consciousness of the Grand Style, plus the eternal presence of petty frailty in the man — as if in conscious defiance of all such things the great tradition of office seems somehow to pick up these individual lawyers and their work and {396} turn out something much better than was in them, of themselves, to give. The "purity" which our great Learned Hand ascribed to Cardozo is hard to find among them; but what is easy to find, a firm sense of the obligations of the office — that seems to be one vital factor. Much beyond this I cannot get. My analysis has been painstaking, over many years, but I come up with results my "factors" are not sufficient to explain.

Two legal generations ago, after fifteen years in the law, I was trying to express this queerness; further analysis has left the same puzzle, merely sharpened up. I quote, without change, from what I published for law students in 1930, in that *Bramble Bush* which among the jurisprudes who do not read it has become through the years a byword for cynical and irresponsible denial of ideals and guidance in the law:[362]

> You come then to us. Whatever has gone, the law is yet left to you. Left to you as the fixed sure order of society. Left to you as that which controls the judges, which clothes the judge with a certain majesty even while and indeed because it does control him, which lifts him and his work to a level he could not attain alone. Left to you as the million of

sonorous sentences that in a million cases expound the inescapable logic under which the judgment is dictated by the law. And we? These fab-
rics we seize and tear as idle cobweb. These mirrors of old dear-held
truth we shatter. The law itself dissolves before our acids. Right and justice come to figure as pretty names for very human acts done on often
the less human of human motivations. I have said before that this tendency of our teaching has caused me worry, in its aspect as developing
the technician at the cost of the whole man. It gives me double pause in
this connection — in its effect on young men already disillusioned beyond the portion of young men.

In the first place, iconoclasm can be a sport as well as a condition;
even when not so viewed, the fact of smashing calls disproportionate
attention to the broken pieces; revolt is seldom characterized by balanced judgment. We of the teaching world are still as full of our discovery as once was tortured Galileo: move, move it *does,* the law. And if to
make you see the movement we must shout down the pious words with
which courts have pretended that no change occurred — then we must
shout, shout disbelief. We must blaspheme the legal oracles. Well, then,
we do. We strip the trappings, verbal and other, off the courts. We turn
the spotlight on the places where the tinsel gaps, where you see cheap
cotton, or see sweaty skin beneath. These are the crucial cases {397} for
the argument — but are they type or caricature of the run of legal work?
The tendency of the teaching has its worry. To get across a vital lesson
one must risk distortion.

The sight of falling tinsel, too, may seem to argue falling dignity. It is
a vicious seeming. It is as false as the ill superstition that the tinsel is
the measure of a man. Rather are measures and dignity of man and office to be found when folderol and claptrap are stripped off; when, free
of pomp, on the record and the naked fact, they stand four-square. So
must we strip the courts; so must we test them. The stripping is a tribute. An institution we could not honor naked we should not dare to
strip. You are to remember, too, the dignity and measure of a critic: they
lie in that he sees the record whole; in that his judgment and his tone of
judgment weigh the accomplishment against the difficulty, weigh partial flaws against the fullness of what has been done. Seen thus, judged
as you would judge a man upon his life, law and the courts stand up. It
may be that as your knowledge grows your disillusion will be tinged
with wonder, as has mine. The heaped-up cases through the centuries;
the heaped-up wisdom. As I watch the succession of the cases — moving, rising, taking form eternally — as I see the sweep of them entire, I
find old formulae of tribute rising to my tongue: "the full perfection of
right reason"! The closer I can come to seeing law whole, the more nearly do I, of the skeptic's clan, find myself bordering on mysticism. There
is such balance and such beauty and skill beyond the little powers of the
individual judges. It is the little powers you are watching in the individual cases. Loose logic, or even bad, lies open to your sight; the wisdom
of the holding when set in the rhythm of the pillaring years — to see that
is not so simple.

Single case after single case there is that irks me, that I would pluck
out. Yet take them: what is it that offends? Here is the case whose reasoning is wretched, grotesque. Yet how of the outcome, on the *facts* —
was it not rather sane? Systematizing conclusions is after all the busi-

ness of the second or the fourth case in a series, not of the first; our law has grown by trial, and then correction. This same court which has mangled the authorities; may it not when the need comes mangle this one, too — and reach another sane result? Here is another case; it seems outrageous. Yet stay — why so outrageous? Because it cuts across *my* opinions. But how many are there here beside the judges who do not square with my opinions? These judges may judge social values differently from me: no sign that they are fools; opinions differ. A third type of case: a technical problem; a crazy decision; the court has utterly failed to see the point. Look to the counsel: has a Root misled the court? Yet even so, that would be but an {398} excuse. But now the question rises of perspective. *How often does it happen, in the large?* How often, too, in the light of the maze of matters that in a year are brought before a court? Criticize such a decision, attack it — yes; attack it with all vigor that is in us, as we attack the others that we doubt. *The courts need such attacks.* The court requires attack on its *decision*, because the *court* is strong. The law requires detailed surgery, the law can stand up under major operations, because the law is strong to stand the shock. Foursquare it stands, upon its whole performance. He who helps cut out error gives it strength.

A few years later, I worked into a ballade the intellectual side of the puzzle: How, in view of the silly, etc., things we know they feel and do, can these supreme courts keep coming out with such relatively satisfying results?[363] It is not a particularly good ballade, even against the low standards of "legal" verse, so it may be left undisturbed; but I do want to mention that although it seems to me to have achieved its goal of tribute, it also was treated as an attack.[364]

I must, therefore, fear that this book, too, will be so treated. Against what was done to *Bramble Bush* (see Appendix B) there is of course no known defense. But there may perhaps be a shifting of the forum. "Let me write the songs of a bar, and I care not who writes its jurisprudence":

A COME-ALL-YE FOR LAWYERS
The Common Law Tradition

A Come-All-Ye for Lawyers
THE COMMON LAW TRADITION

Air: Pelagius   Arrangement: Jerry Green and Christopher Moore   Words: K. N. Llewellyn

Come ga-ther and sing to the Com-mon Law whose leaf and seed we are,
John Ad-ams who fought in — Li-ber-ty Hall when the Bell rang down a king
The names — we learned while the eye-balls burned put — life in-to the letter
So sing Bran-deis, Burch and — Swan and Doe, sing — Camp-bell, Coo-ley, Cowen,

Whe-ther we live by the wag-gling jaw or coun-sel, miles from the Bar. — The
Had risked his all on a law-yer's call, lest Eng-land's Pres-cott — swing. — It's
Names — of jud-ges who ne-ver turned From ma-king the mor-row — better: — Car-
Am-i-don, Lump-kin — up they go! The blind ones sing we — down! — Each

wood is good and the sap is strong that gave us Coke and Hale,
du-ty geared to a zest for deeds has made our Com-mon Law;
do-zo, Gib-son, Ruf-fin, Shaw, and Hough and Holmes and Hand,
man who wrought on the migh-ty bench our weal in peace and war

Right is a bat-tle to win from Wrong, in spite of con-tempt and jail. — It
The men she needs are the men she breeds, men with a fight-ing jaw. — No
To chang-ing need they they shaped the Law, and e-ver their way shall stand. — Some
Had served like us in the front-line trench: he fought at the Bar be-fore — It

calls   for brain and   it   calls for will, but an   a - corn knows his   mis - sion: __
Rule   was   e - ver   e - nough to halt cor -   rup - tion or   am - bi - tion __
say   our Law's in   a   sor - ry plight, and __   fol - ly   its   fru - i - tion. __
calls   for brain and   it   calls for will, but an   a - corn knows his   mis - sion: __

Law is   the Oak   of   Li - ber - ty still, in the Com-mon Law Tra - di - tion.
Till manned by law - yers who earn their salt in the Com-mon Law Tra - di - tion.
The an-swer to that   is   to set it right, in the Com-mon Law Tra - di - tion.
Law is   the Oak   of   Li - ber - ty still in the Com-mon Law Tra - di - tion.

Row - dy dow - dy doo-dle - ee - o   In the Com-mon Law Tra - di - tion.

Row - dy dow - dy doo-dle - ee - o   In the Com-mon Law Tra - di - tion.

Notes to Part I

{footnotes appeared on page number of original text location}

1 I shall indicate below, at pages 38, and 184 ff., that whereas the formula "of *laws* and not" is inherently false, the formula "*by the Law,*" rightly understood, can, when provided with the right rules, right techniques, and right officers, come close to being accurate.

2 The Nature of the Judicial Process (1921); The Growth of the Law (1924); The Paradoxes of Legal Science (1928); Jurisprudence, N.Y. St. Bar Assn. Rep. 263 (1932). All are found in Hall, Selected Writings of Benjamin Nathan Cardozo (1947).

3 The Theory of Judicial Decision, 36 Harv. L. Rev. 641, 802, 940 (1923); and there was earlier material in Justice According to Law, 13 Columb. L. Rev. 696 (1913), 14 ibid. 1; 103 (1914), and Pound's prior studies (e.g. The Decay of Equity, Mechanical Jurisprudence) therein cited.

4 The First American Labor Case, 41 Yale L.J. 165 (1931); A Strike and Its Legal Consequences — An Examination of the Receivership Precedent for the Labor Injunction, 40 ibid 507 (1931). Useful also, especially in regard to the growth and persistence of the idea and ideal of decision by the law, impersonally, is Nelles' more general study: Towards Legal Understanding, I, 34 Columb. L. Rev. 862 (1934), n, ibid 1041.

5 Legal Rules: Their Function in the Process of Decision, 79 U. Pa. L. Rev. 833 (1931), Their Application and Elaboration, ibid. 1052.

6 The Sales materials were in classroom use in 1928, the Leipzig lectures on American case law were delivered in 1929, with the materials already pretty well annotated. Bramble Bush and the elaborate case studies in the Sales materials both appeared in 1930; the detailed Warranty studies in 1936-1937: Courts, Quality of Goods, and a Credit Economy, a Study of Interaction Between Economic Background, Legal Ideology, Social Function, and Judicial Personality, from papers in 36 and 37 Columb. L. Rev. (1937).

7 4 Enc. Soc. Sci. 450 (1932). The particular studies are especially The Jurist's Art, 31 Columb. L. Rev. 1073 (1931) (on Brandeis); Cardozo the Craftsman, 6 U. Chi. L. Rev. 1 (1938); Preview of a Justice, 48 Yale L.J. 819 (1939) (on Frankfurter); and one should add 39 Columb. L. Rev. 724 (1939) (on Blackstone); and for background, also the striking article Institution, in 8 Enc. Soc. Sci. 84 (1932).

8 These are too many for convenient citation, and too familiar to warrant it. I will note only that Powell's steady flow of shrewd and often caustic comment on method has not become dated merely because the particular issues may have lost importance.

9 Two of Radin's papers, though later in date, and not directed primarily to process, are too incisive and illuminating to leave unmentioned in any gathering of the material which comes to grips with the problem. Like Hamilton's stuff, they have been ignored. Case Law and Stare Decisis: Concerning Präjudizienrecht in Amerika, 33 Columb. L. Rev. 159 (1933); The Trail of the Calf, 32 Cornell L.Q. 137 (1946). I omit Oliphant and Goodhart. Oliphant wholly misses the guidance in an appellate opinion; Goodhart exalts it into providing a Never-Never Single Answer. Both are hopelessly off target. Though both, amusingly, are far more cited than any of the others, they are little used. People have not been interested in the slow job: how and why it happens, but have wanted a quick, cheap answer: the right way, without inquiry. Or else they have wanted convenient material for a fight. — The test-studies I refer to were mostly law review notes or such papers as Wright's Opposition of Law to Business Usages, 26 Columb. L. Rev. 917 (1926); Eno's paper used below at page 123, note 158, my own Warranty studies, and the like. Or Tulin, The Role of Penalties in Criminal Law, 37 Yale L.J. 1048 (1928). — See also page 18, note 11a.

10 By me, too, until The Constitution as an Institution, 34 Columb. L. Rev. 1 n.l (1934).

11 This is developed in Appendix B.

11a In view of my many differences with J. Frank, let me here pay tribute to his insistence and persistence in severing problems of trial out for their due separate focus and emphasis, as against the muddy topic "the judicial process," or Pound's "'justice' under law." It is good to see the recent Chicago studies putting new vigor and skill — and, with the addition of arbitration, breadth — into the lines of inquiry charted by Sunderland, Leon Green, and Frank.

Let me also add to note 9 that Oliphant's 1925 paper must not be taken to indicate any doubt in the value of either doctrine or case law; it was instead a machinery for destroying *other* scholars' doctrine, so as to reformulate into the Gospel according to St. Herman; and that Goodhart's later writing has made very clear that he has long outgrown his indiscretion of 1930.

12 The "policy" discussion of this and the next cluster are combined for convenience with that on 3: Known Doctrinal Techniques.

13 Effort to locate these notebooks among the Taft MSS in the Library of Congress has been luckless; nor did a hasty search of the Yale-period unbound papers turn up anything in the way of notes for the Law School course.

14 It is hard to believe that there are not values in each of the foregoing three closely interrelated clusters. No legal system for a culture at all complex seems to be able to get on without them. Even the legally sure-footed Cheyenne (Llewellyn and Hoebel, The Cheyenne Way (1941)) must, it seems to me, have developed the professional lawman, had they either acquired a sedentary economic base or moved into trade as an occupation or seen their buds of capitalism push out into branches. Three or four of the lines of value are obvious, over and above service to so much of the justice-picture as roots in the drive for like treatment of like cases. The *rule* phase of law-stuff is peculiarly well adapted to getting moderately similar results across space, time, and divergency of personnel. It is both a training machinery, a machinery for accumulation of experience and wisdom, and a machinery for moving rather effectively toward readjustment where needed. The knowhow aspects, especially in the hands of trained professionals, are tools not only for building but for work to purpose: consider pleading techniques for a moment as devices not for manipulation but for getting quickly to a clean, sharp, significant issue; or consider the advantages of a flexible and cleanly guided approach to construction of language over one purely word-bound. Limitation on the range of the recognized techniques is in turn one device for keeping the professional personnel within bounds; some of them still seem to call for watching.

But when it comes to how much? or what kind of? in regard to law-conditioning of the men, or in regard to the doctrinal material or to the recognized techniques for handling the same — there my experience and reading indicate little hope of agreement, and no persuasive general principle except "such balance as may be suited to the time and place, and such machinery and control as are suited to the personnel." Overprofessionalization, whether by way of rigidity and costliness or by way of gain- or power-seeking or by way of venality, has always been a peril; but what we see used for preventive or for cure varies from simple hanging of the knaves to revolutionary reframing of the legal-governmental system, from simple reorganization of the profession and its recruitment to effort at abolition of both, with all kinds of other institutional or doctrinal changes in between. As significant a variation as any is in the type of device employed to hold down or counteract the effects of overprofessionalization: at one end appeal to or pardon by a nonprofessional ruler or other superior; at the other the entrustment of initial business to a purely lay officer, whether an American J.P. or an English lay bench with a professional as clerk and advisor or one of twenty types of administrative tribunal; in between, mixed tribunals in more styles than a historical fashion show: our judge-and-jury; the various German or Scandinavian mixed courts, with lawyers and laymen sitting together in one combination after another; the old English and New York top appeals court consisting of the highest legislative body augmented by all or invited judges. And so on more.

On what makes for better lines of concept and rule, and for better techniques in work thereof, however, on that a fair portion of my own views are scattered through this book. Each had better be met against its appropriate background.

15 There is no use in arguing with any man who does not see the drive for justice as a prime good in law. As Sumner remarked in another connection, the only thing you can do is knock him down — and, you hope, out. But if his trouble is that he sees as attributes of justice *only* what is deserved, or what is equal, or some compromise between those two,

then there is still hope for his salvation. A working introduction to my own views can be had from my On the Good, the True, the Beautiful, in Law, 9 U. Chi. L. Rev. 224 (1942), perhaps especially at 250 ff.; and in my Syllabus on Law in Our Society, Lectures V-VIII.

16 Cardozo, The Nature of the Judicial Process 164 (1921): "Of the cases that come before the court in which I sit, a majority, I think, could not, with semblance of reason, be decided in any way but one. The law and its application alike are plain. Such cases are predestined, so to speak, to affirmance without opinion." The Growth of the Law 60 (1924): "Nine-tenths, perhaps more, of the cases that come before a court are predetermined — predetermined in the sense that they are predestined — their fate preestablished by inevitable laws that follow them from birth to death." In 155 N.E. (1927) out of 137 N.Y. Court of Appeals cases, 88 (64 per cent) were affirmed without opinion, 8 (6 per cent) were reversed without opinion: 70 per cent, then, pretty well foredoomed. Llewellyn, *Präjudizienrecht* etc., 345 (1933). In discussing this with Loughran, who had read the 1942 MSS from my Storrs Lectures (and had sat in the cases from 281 N.Y. which had been their basic subject matter), I found him agreeing that the outcome was pretty certain about 8 times out of 10, as soon as the court got their minds around the case, but that there was no such certainty about the ground of the decision.

17 The "Single Right Answer" does have further unhappy effects, with appropriate but to my mind not counterbalancing happy ones. They are indicated moderately well in the discussion above, pages 21 ff., about doctrinal techniques insofar as they operate "almost without consciousness." The good effect is the preservation of self-confidence and good conscience in the law-personnel and of a quiet faith among almost all law-consumers who are neither too sophisticated nor too severely squeezed. The unhappy effect is that of driving readjustment and creation into the underground, which not only decreases reckonability but seriously hampers reasoned study and thought about the relative values and costs of any competing objectives and of the always various available or devisable measures. This threatens smugness on the one side, or regretful outrage; it threatens, on the other, a resort to trickery, conscious or unconscious, which cuts Law-Government off from its proper rooting in life and in general understandability. The Persian immutability of a king's official decree will serve as a horrible illustration: it forced the wisest statesman and essential prime minister of the realm into the lion's den, when no legal expedient could be turned up; on the other hand, Esther under Mordecai's counsel wangled a line of nonreversal which amounted to official advice that the law should be flouted by armed violent aggression, accompanied by an administrative pressure on officials to disregard the particular decree which must have been demoralizing to any confidence in the law at large, as well as to any administrative machine. Each of these results turned on "the law is the law, and there is only one right *legal* answer"; and the fact that the second one has led to a Hebrew Holy Day does not make it any better legal method for the Persians.

18 There are also available, especially to a court of last resort, certain thoroughly illegitimate leeways of action which can "buttress" or cover unreckonable deciding. Thus: the flat ignoring of authority in point which is technically controlling; the presentation of prior cases as if they held what they do not, or did not hold what they did; the ignoring or outright twisting of vital facts in the record in hand; and the like. The horrible thing here is that unwillingness to face up to responsibility for needed change in law or inability to discover and phrase a broadly solving rule can in a good cause lead even an upright and careful court to blacken the judicial shield by such procedures. See discussion below, pages 133 ff., 256 ff., 450 ff.

19 The matters suggested in the text patently reach in effect beyond the furtherance of reckonability; they lead, for instance, toward not merely continuance but cumulation and refinement or refreshment of wisdom. They add the individual's labor and pondered thought to his intuition and inspiration. They put well-nigh every opinioned deciding through something of a ripening process. Many an appellate judge agrees with Traynor, that he has found no test of a decision which has the rigor offered by having an opinion to compose. The opinion-system holds relatively steady, moreover, not merely the succession of upshots, but the body of doctrine, the ways of work, and (not to be forgotten) the men's training in their office. And despite the increasing complexity of legal doctrine, and despite, again, all that can be said about the power of skilled words to mask what has been

done, there is in the opinion a real pressure to account to lay and legal public, and a real wherewithal for semi-check-up on the work. At this point our institution of the dissent comes up with a value sadly overlooked: the recognized possibility of a published dissent is as useful a measure to insure against secret (and fitful) unconscionable action by a bench as ever has been devised. It has rarely been needed, but it is there for use, and, to repeat a figure to which I shall be recurring, its presence is as valuable as is the audit of an honest banker's books.

Let us not, however, forget that our ways in this are in no way the only ways, nor necessarily the best. Good law and a more sharply etched schooling of the men and tradition which has its values have both long been achieved in England by opinions normally delivered in spoken words at the immediate close of argument; and what J. Gillis Wetter in The Styles of Appellate Judicial Opinions (now in press with Sÿthoff, Leyden) shows of Swedish, German, and French work in comparison with English and American (Arkansas and California) demonstrates that different traditions not only weight various values differently, but may select and combine them differently, and instructively, as well.

20 One remembers that our system has also known the idea of a complete new trial, and the idea of free review of "the facts"; that appellate "judicial notice" can vastly enlarge the fact-picture; and that in many situations much could be said, given an uncrowded docket, for allowing an appellate court to arrange for needed clarification on one point or another in lieu of sending the case back. Also that the French, for example, seek systematically to avoid any undercover influence of fact-views other than those "found" below by limiting high appeals to "abstract" questions of law, somewhat in the manner of a question certified. Perhaps I like our standard system because I both grew up with it and understand its work. I like the saving of appellate time by way of the frozen record. I like the leeway left for the court to react to its feeling for net sound result by deciding errors to have been either material enough or not material enough to warrant reversal. But in this as in other matters I think the system does better when matters of public concern come into the open. For example, the Illinois practice in criminal cases of looking over the whole case to determine whether the error has caused or threatened a "miscarriage of justice," and of reviewing enough of the evidence to make a decision on that persuasive — that practice seems to me not only wise, but wise also as a pattern for civil appeals. We know that the court's "smell" for the "facts" beneath the officially given "facts" is frequently, not just semioccasionally, a factor in the deciding. Any frequently occurring phenomenon which is capable of isolation into a pattern or into an issue-focus repays bringing out into the open for conscious study, conscious and reckonable use, and possible conscious guidance or control; and this country ought to have learned by now that prohibition which persistently fails to prohibit is more than confusing and wasteful; it is dangerous. See also The Law of Lawful Discretion, below at pages 217 ff.

21 On this last, as appears below at page 325, I am strongly with the bar, but think opportunity for rehearing can cure that evil while leaving useful freedom to the bench. On the general value — for court, for counsel, for client, and for taxpayers and law-consumers — of *having issues reasonably but not rigidly clarified in advance,* no one who has suffered under any disparate practice can have doubt; issue-clarification is indeed as central and vital a law-job and law-skill as is advocacy. But as to method, the problem is the same as in note 13 above, re clusters 1 through 3; I get no further, for general statement, than the italics above.

22 Were the unevenness, and the plain incompetence of many, vastly greater than they are, I still would rate the party's free access to counsel as one of the most precious values of our system. Indeed one real bother, for me, has long been the difficulty, in city conditions, of making such access *informed,* for anybody, and available, for the economically disadvantaged; and such efforts in the unauthorized practice campaign as have barred out those lists of available, reliable counsel, anywhere, which the A.A.A. used to provide for member motorists, and as now attack similar operation by labor unions and the like, have distressed me both for the public and for the future of the bar. The Bar's Troubles, 5 Law & Contemp. Prob. 104 (1938).

I do remind, however, that there can be and has been purely written argument (as, often, in Continental history) or purely oral argument (as, still, in the English courts of appeal) or 3-hour or 3-day orals with *briefs* as maps (as in our earlier days), or half-hour orals with "briefs" doing the heavy work. Among these, as will appear below, I feel *some* oral argument to be functionally of superior value.

I remind also that in my view legal education is still lamentably deficient, all over the country (including the top schools) in the training of a third or more of the graduates; that training in advocacy, in school, is both feasible, vital, and neglected; and that some type *of responsible* apprenticeship akin to interneship (nowhere yet in operation) is also needed, before the ideal of adversary advocacy can begin to body forth its hope and promise in any reliable manner to the ordinary American appellant in the ordinary daily little case.

23 We commonly attribute to the multiman bench, in addition to steadiness, safety-factors against bias, effective corruption or improper influence, overhaste, slackness, etc., and increased likelihood perhaps of vision (which any member may provide), certainly of balance, so that safety may emerge even if vision be outvoted. The pattern has seemed to justify itself across nations and centuries; and non-judicial experience is in accord.

24 The values of an independent judiciary are so obvious that attention is needed rather to machinery for reducing the risks and costs. One risk, that of too great insulation of the court from the felt needs of the law-consumer, we have for the most part sought to prevent by popular election and to restrain or cure by short terms. I find the first machinery dubious, and feel the Missouri plan to be as good a general substitute model as has yet been devised. The second machinery, the short term, dates from the days of an evil now dead and most unlikely to revive. Into the foreseeable future I think it hampers rather than helps our courts in their very response to current need; and it leaves them more cautious than is healthy, in dealing with the bar. In addition, one important value, for me, is relatively long service, with the gains in experience, skill, and team-building which such service brings. I therefore lament any custom of rotation, welcome one of bipartisan renomination, and wonder whether, even where initial election follows the general pattern, a Missouri-type ballot could not be introduced in regard to any re-election. This, in a short-term State, would leave open the old safeguard, should the ills of 1900 ever recur, but would greatly cut the cost of the insurance. That, however, would in turn increase the cost and danger of the man in office who can no longer be relied on-whether because of unjudicial conduct, illness, drunkenness, senility, or just plain laziness or inattention. Only the first of these can really be reached by impeachment, and impeachment is so shot through with politics as to be almost impossible, always awkward, and not only bad for the system, and uncertain, but shamefully cumbersome and expensive in needed legislative time. Pound's facts on impeachment, Justice According to Law, II, 14 Columb. L. Rev. 1, 9-10 nn. (1914), are terrific-and uncited. Something of this material is in his Jurisprudence, Vol. 2, 400 ff. (1959). It seems to me plain that a removal tribunal staffed primarily by judges, who understand the problems both of the system and of the man, and who operate with professional skill but in an essentially judicial capacity, promises real help in these occasional embarrassments.

25 Moran v. Standard Oil, 211 N.Y. 187, 105 N.E. 217 (1914), decided shortly after Cardozo joined the Court of Appeals, is on the second cause of action more than an intelligent contract decision; it initiates in the court a whole new way of reading commercial documents. Within three years Cardozo has swung a majority all the way to Wood v. Duff-Gordon, 222 N.Y. 88, 118 N.E. 214 (1917), which reads into the written agreement an unexpressed fair understanding, even in favor of the side which prepared the language, and which when I was teaching at Harvard ten years ago was still viewed there as somehow not quite nice. The year before, Cardozo had built a majority in McPherson v. Buick, 217 N.Y. 382, 111 N.E. 1050 (1916).

26 Just because we happen to be used to both of these-as also to the privilege of public dissent, we must not forget how unusual any of the three is, among developed states. I have talked with serious Continental lawyers who felt strongly that anything but a unanimous front would destroy public respect for either court or law; and Rugg came close to putting an approach not too far different into operation in Massachusetts.

27 I incline to think that as the population of a State spreads more thinly, this lack is increasingly made up by personal acquaintance with the individual judges. In any event, such acquaintance is likely to grow among the senior bar and those located where the

court sits. Yet surely many who pursue such acquaintance do so less with an eye to study of the man than in a vaguish hope of developing some general benignity.

28 For the *interested* public, this "known bench" factor has value chiefly in heightening predictability. For the advocate in the case it has further value in focusing his argument. Compare below, pages 251 ff. For the *general* public, on the other hand, the values run in terms rather of the teamwork which develops out of the members' service together; a by-product of the semipermanent grouping.

29 When, as typically in the Code Napoléon, the pungency is lacking, there is a recurring danger that the verbal pseudosimplicity may mask distressing functional dissimilarities, as with "choses in action" or "bona fide purchase for value" in our law. I note that the utter praise of the simple style of that code derives from men of literature (Stendhal, e.g.) who were unaware of the occasional technical obscurity — though in style the Code is in truth a matchless job. I note also that in Cardozo's opinions, it is where he is off-base that the creaking ornament and oversubtle phrasing chiefly flourish.

30 Law, Its Origin, Growth and Function (1907).

31 I have not myself come across this in print, but Pound used to quote Parke roughly thus: A strong opinion was one in which by the employment of pure legal reasoning one arrived inescapably at a conclusion which no layman could possibly have foreseen.

32 Background and development in the labor field are superbly painted by Nelles, A Strike and Its Legal Consequences — An Examination of the Receivership Precedent for the Labor Injunction, 40 Yale L.J. 507 (1931). Observe especially the contrast between 1877 and 1894.

33 The Causes of Popular Dissatisfaction with the Administration of Justice, 40 Am. L. Rev. 729 (1906); 20 J. Am. Jud. Soc. 178 (1937).

It is extraordinary to contrast the tone of this with Pound's Justice According to Law, III, 14 Columb. L. Rev. 103 (1914) — culminating (at 115): "For a time there was need of propagandist agitation. It was necessary that the public, the legal profession and the courts be made to recognize that our legal system was to be reexamined, many of its fundamental principles recast, and the whole readjusted to proceed along new lines. *This task of awakening has been achieved.*" (My italics.)

34 Chief Justice Wilkins informs me that only in rare instances are these Opinions not drafted by the Chief.

35 On why, contrary to the fact, the Supreme Court acquired the reputation of being an innovating tribunal, indeed the innovating tribunal, in this matter, see page 141 below.

36 See more fully below, pages 371 ff. One can mention here the weird traditional rule that any appeal at all, especially with reference to a statutory remedy, must be provided for by statute *with explicit* detail. In contrast, insofar as the Uniform Sales Act changed the rules about implied use-warranties in sales and remedies therefor, a court ought, as of course, to make parallel changes in regard to use-bailment for hire; and thus, in Agar v. Orda, 264 N.Y. 248, 190 N.E. 479 (1934), where the same rule on suit for the price had previously applied both to physical goods and to choses in action, a change by the Uniform Sales Act in regard to goods (which "include all chattels personal *other than things in action*") was soundly held to change the old New York policy which underlay the old rule, and therefore to carry over to shares of stock as well.

37 This means in turn a steady general rise in predictability, as the rules, one by one, gain in excellence of form and substance. Cf. below, pages 183 f., 291 ff.

38 I spot relatively little direct influence of the Cardozo theoretical writings on other judges; and except as they may have contributed, generally, to making examination of appellate judicial work take on mien of the respectable rather than of the sacrilegious, and so to slacken the Formal Style's scissor-hold on the judicial imagination, I doubt that his specific theories have had much indirect effect. But among the modern reports my reading shows no other State judge cited and quoted nationally with anything like the frequency of Cardozo; and the passages quoted and joyously seized on are with regularity passages in which he was *doing* Grand Style very well indeed. I have to judge that the example tended to be catching.

39 Cf. note 15 above, page 24.

40 A prevailing style has great value in shaping recruits to the profession; a mixed style handicaps such shaping. The nature of the prevailing style tends also to sieve out leading figures so as to fit the style: the tidy-minded, patient, and safe accumulator, for example, as against the more adventurous, impatient, result-oriented creator. Desirable combinations of such qualities are found often enough in individuals, but almost never as traits of a dominant style. Apart from our early nineteenth century, I have come across the Grand Style only twice: in Cheyenne Indian law and in the classical Roman period.

41 There is neither magic nor any assumption of the absolute in this "fourteen." The number of sets of factors one may hit upon is either arbitrary or accidental. One might well, e.g., sever out our peculiar *separate*-opinion institution (concurring or dissenting) for special treatment; or divide off as a separate factor the *professional* aspect of the office which our appellate judges share with baseball umpires and standing committees of appeal in an arbitration-minded trade association such as the London Corn Trades Association. One could also, with profit, reach "fifteen" or "eighteen" by adding such significant lines of factor as secrecy of deliberation and the rapidly growing use of legally skilled judges' clerks. Or one could cut to twelve or ten by consolidating items here dealt with separately. The present selection is offered as significant and convenient; no more.

42 Current general role theory (most of which is rather solid) of course applies to the situation, and with illumination. But this role of appellate judge is so peculiarly established, so clearly felt, so implemented and documented not only in content but in panoply, not only in panoply but in behavior, that its careful study might well refine general role theory in the same manner (though hardly to the same degree) in which sustained study of appellate judicial deciding can certainly refine and advance the theory of problem-solution by small groups.

43 Can this be due partly to a kind of craft-shyness and self-consciousness in regard to the range of tenderer and more delicate qualities which appellate judges need and use but which a gruff or flip culture makes them blush to allow naked in public, or indeed in private?

44 It seems hard or harsh sometimes that, as old Sumner wryly observed, nobility is the one virtue which man can by direct effort neither sow nor reap.

44a In Justice According to Law, 13 Columb. L. Rev. 112n. (1913), Pound argues the popular impression of Jeffreys to be "quite unfounded." If so, read "Macaulay's Jeffreys."

45 Pound's most recent phrasing will serve: "If tradition sometimes holds too fast, yet it holds fast and so makes judicial justice reasonably uniform and predictable." (p. 452.) "It provides for certainty through the training of judges in logical development and systematic exposition of authoritative grounds for decision." (p. 456.) "In the case of appellate courts, all important decisions and the grounds thereof and reasons therefor are published in the law reports ... Moreover, a bench of judges sit to hear appeals and the traditional ethics of adjudication require each of them to act in person." (p. 457.) 2 Jurisprudence (1959).

46 The passages in Langbridge's Case, Y.B. 19 Edw. III. 375 (C.B. 1345), are priceless and eternal: Sharshulle, J.: "... no precedent is of such force as resoun ..." R. Thorpe: "... I think you will do as others have done in the same case, or else we do not know what the law is." Hillary, J.: "It is the will of the Justices." Stonore, C.J.: "Nanyl; ley est resoun." Beale, from whose Cases on Criminal Law (2d ed. 1907) I take this, renders "resoun" "that which is right"; I should render it "right sense," or even "principle." In any event, each of the blind men is right, so far as he goes, and wrong insofar as he is suggesting that his phrasing begins to grasp the whole elephant. Nelles' treatment of the case is interesting: Towards Legal Understanding, II, 34 Columb. L. Rev. 1041, 1045 ff. (1934).

47 Those odd teachers who do fall into such a practice have typically cast themselves as holding a different and "nobler" office: that of rebel-reformer of the whole regime, lion of justice, or protector of the poor.

48 See below, page 371, for a short general examination of this. Meanwhile, both the diverse ways in which the courts treat statutes technically and the relative reckonability of

their actual use of those techniques will be presented regularly from our case samples, along with the materials on case techniques.

49 American Legal Realism, 82 U. Pa. L. Rev. 429, 441 (1934).

50 The lead-off paper was Legal Education and Public Policy: Professional Training in the Public Interest, 42 Yale L.J. 203-295 (1943).

51 His Sense of Injustice (1949) has much stuff that fits a court's daily need.

52 Holmes' "I hate 'justice'" sprang from and expresses a normal appellate judge's revulsion at the too frequent ranting about justice which hopes to conceal either a weak case or a shoddy preparation.

52a The forthcoming results of the University of Chicago Law School Project on The Rule of Law in Commercial Groups promise real illumination on the operation of values and on workable classifications thereof with reference to study and practice of conflict-adjustment.

53 On "rules" of law, cf. my A Realistic Jurisprudence, 30 Columb. L. Rev. 431 (1930); on "custom," Llewellyn and Hoebel, The Cheyenne Way 275 ff. (1941).

54 The chapter is from his Lord Mansfield 198-229 (1936).

55 Ibid. at 228-229. I go further with Fifoot that when under attack Mansfield sheltered, sometimes with hypocrisy, behind the precedents; also that in his innovations "he strained a legitimate faith to the verge of heresy." But in his particular case I see almost none of this as deserving Fifoot's label: "unconscious." And I doubt whether Fifoot does, except in one final and uncharacteristically gentle sentence. Mansfield lived by a high duty of reformulation and broad reform, he drove at it with every technical tool at his command, he had as little innate judicial restraint as any honest judge who ever sat, and he learned "the law of leeways" only when revolt of the profession drove that law home to him *vi et armis*. — I differ also, and strongly, with Fifoot's suggestion that the English precedent system came "soon" after Mansfield into any heavy loss of resilience. The Exchequer of Parke's time apart, I find in the English cases (most notably, perhaps, in Best and Blackburn) up into the 1880's a strong component, often dominant, of that Grand Style which, by the time Fifoot was writing, had indeed almost passed from living memory, and which, even after Wright's work, is beginning to show again rather in Denning than in the British bench at large. On Wright, Julius Stone is excellent: The Province and Function of Law 166-204 (1946). Mansfield's varying use of precedent techniques is indicated (but much less satisfactorily presented and evaluated than by Fifoot) in Shientag, Lord Mansfield Revisited — A Modern Assessment, 10 Ford. L. Rev. 345, 382 ff. (1941).

55a He can be seen in detail in the discussion of Hartfield v. Roper, below at page 423.

55b Grain Elevators, 6 Am. L. Rev. 450 (1872) (unsigned). For its day the paper is an astoundingly ingenious manipulation of doctrine to a wise end. And in its day the ingenuity was a necessity. Neither fact affects the text.

56 In Cooley on Brief-Making (2d ed. 1909). Most of the case material used by Wambaugh in illustration of his points is indeed pre-1880 English or else American of the Grand period. Yet there is enough to show that Wambaugh's positions are not mere academic carryover; he matches with what little there is in Mr. Justice Miller's paper of 1889: The Use and Value of Authorities, 23 Am. L. Rev. 165; and he matches almost point for point with Henry Campbell Black's excellent chapter on Precedents in his Construction and Interpretation of the Laws 382-438 (1896). I locate no other contemporary American literature except a useless edition of Ram, and Lieber's Legal and Political Hermeneutics (1880), which last is theory, not a reflection at all of American practice; but Black's Law of Judicial Precedents (1912) digs up and uses a good deal of additional judicial material from the Formal period.

57 Study of Cases 76 (3d ed. 1909).

58 See Vanderbilt, 556 and 558, ex Wambaugh in Cooley on Brief-Making (2d ed. 1909).

59 Vanderbilt, ibid. 579.

60 See note 56 above.

61 When the entitlement is thus spread over *any* language or holding, the term *formally* is necessary. For the entitlement, as contrasted with the *power,* of a court of last resort, is of course subject to the Laws of Leeways and of Fitness and Flavor (below, pp. 219 ff.). A technique correct and available as such may yet, in decency, require to hang unused upon the wall in regard to particular authorities in a particular pending case.

62 In another aspect the technique says to the advocate: I am available to help you argue. But with regard to those of the techniques which are either relatively unfamiliar, or relatively subtle or complex, or not yet admitted to the more exclusive social clubs, the advocate must avoid indelicacy. It will not do to say: "This court being, as it is, in the habit of consecrating practically any old dictum as a rule of law without prior notice to anybody, I wish to submit what was written completely off the then point by Judge Smooch just last November." It is wiser to argue: "This court clearly announced the true principle in Wolff v. Lamm: . . ."

63 Scofield v. J. W. Jones Construction Co., 64 N.M. 319, 328 P.2d 389, 392 (1958) (an automobile collision case): "It is no longer open to question ip this state that a juror may not impeach his verdict by affidavit or testimony after verdict." So ruled, and judgment was affirmed.

64 Broughton v. City of Cleveland, 167 Ohio St. 29, 146 N.E.2d 301, 303 (1957), in regard to municipal tort liability when a governmental function — garbage collection — is being performed: "Perhaps we are behind the times, but, in the absence of legislation by the General Assembly, this court is not yet ready to abandon the position adopted and retained for so many years." (The dissent insists, however, [146 N.E.2d at 305 f.,] that the court's application of the rule to garbage is a change and extension. If so [and I think it is], then as against "the times," it is an extension backwards.)

65 I do not have a recent American decision ready at hand. In Household Fire etc. Ins. Co. v. Grant, 4 Ex. D. 216 (CA. 1879), a letter of allotment of shares in answer to an application had been posted but never received. The plaintiff had judgment for the balance due on the subscription. Dunlop v. Higgins, 1 H.L. Cas. 381 (1848), had ruled that a contract is closed when a letter of acceptance is posted, although in the case in hand — one of an unstable market — it had been delayed one day in arrival because of bad roads. Thesiger, L.J., at page 218 f.: "It is true that Lord Cottenham might have decided that case without deciding the point raised in this. But it appears to me equally true that he did not do so, and that he preferred to rest and did rest his judgment as to one of the matters of exception before him upon a principle which embraces and governs the present case. If so, the court is as much bound to apply that principle, constituting as it did a ratio decidendi, as it is to follow the exact decision itself." So held; judgment affirmed.

66 Forastiere v. Springfield Institution for Savings, 303 Mass. 101, 104, 20 N.E.2d 950, 952 (1939): "It has been held that where the debt from the depositor to the bank is a secured one, a contract is implied that the bank may resort to a set-off of a deposit only for any balance of the debt beyond the value of the security. [2 simple cites.] That is the settled law of this Commonwealth, even though it may seem inconsistent with the principle that a secured creditor may ordinarily pursue all his remedies until he receives satisfaction. [5 simple Mass. cites; 3 from outside.]" The defendant savings bank, which had foreclosed a mortgage against the depositor without showing the relation of the foreclosure to the debt, was therefore held to have established no right to set-off, even assuming the commercial banking set-off rule should apply.

67 Massachusetts had held its jurisdiction in equity not to extend to enforcement of a money judgment obtained by a wife against a husband in an annulment suit in another state. In Blumenthal v. Blumenthal, 303 Mass. 275, 21 N.E.2d 244 (1939), a curative statute on the matter was stated to be inapplicable because the defendant there was a resident of New York. The broad language of the uniform fraudulent conveyance act "must be construed in conjunction with all other pertinent statutes so as to form a consistent and harmonious statutory system . . ." and "cannot be construed to apply to those who, by established law . . . are prevented from being included . . ." (303 Mass. at 277). A prior often-repeated statement of principle "cannot be wrested from its context and stressed to support a proposition entirely foreign to what the court had in mind in employing the words in question. [2 cases cited.] Moreover, it is shown by the supporting authorities

cited when the principle was stated," etc. (My italics.) And the case stating the principle was later cited "to support the statement that . . . The matter was finally settled in Giles v. Giles, 279 Mass. 284, 181 N.E. 176, where, after quoting the above statements from the Gahm case, it was said that the wife was a creditor of her husband and could not maintain a bill for the collection of her claim." (303 Mass. at 279-280.) Decree dismissing the bill affirmed.

68 In re Hawkeye Oil Co., 19 F.2d 151 (D. Del. 1927); United States etc. Oil Co. v. Keystone Auto etc. Co., 19 F.2d 624 (W.D. Pa. 1924); and Massachusetts Gasoline etc. Co. v. Go-Gas Co., 259 Mass. 585, 156 N.E. 871 (1927), all dealt with hybrid or bastard corporate gas-station "securities" called Participating Operation Certificates. Whatever rights the holders sought, in each of the actions the document was held not to fit into the necessary conceptual frame.

69 Lewis v. National Shawmut Bank, 303 Mass. 187, 21 N.E.2d 254 (1939), involved an attack on awards to counsel and guardians *ad litem* as grossly excessive. "The principles to be followed by courts in allowing such costs are set forth in Frost v. Belmont, 6 Allen, 152, 164, 165, and in Boynton v. Tarbell, 272 Mass. 142, 145, 172 N.E. 340. They have been described as 'strictly conservative principles.' . . . We have no disposition to modify them." (303 Mass. at 191.) The court thought some of the allowances in the instant case to be probably excessive, but the matter had not been raised seasonably, by evidence below. Affirmed.

70 Matter of City of New York (Northern Blvd.), 281 N.Y. 48, 22 N.E.2d 157 (1939), ordered a condemnation award stricken because it covered damages still speculative. 281 N.Y. at 54: "By emphasizing the tentative nature of the proposed plans for the bridge, we do not mean to overrule our holding in Sauer v. City of New York, 180 N.Y. 27, 72 N.E. 579, 70 L.R.A. 717; affirmed 296 U.S. 536, where an owner of property abutting upon a street owned in fee by the city was denied relief in the absence of legislation." — a reservation emphasized by reciting another prior holding as dealing with a "private" condemnor.

71 Goodman v. Industrial Commission, 135 Ohio St. 81, 82, 19 N.E.2d 508 (1939), "Whatever the rule in other jurisdictions may be, the Supreme Court of Ohio, through a long line of decisions, has consistently defined the meaning of the term 'injury,' as used in the Constitution and statutes, to be physical or traumatic injuries accidental in their origin and cause; the result of a sudden happening at a particular time. [2 straight cites.]" Upsetting seeming departures by two Courts of Appeals, held: no "injury" when a baker simply collapsed while handling dough in the usual manner.

72 Eagles v. General Electric Co., 5 Wash. 2d 20, 26, 104 P.2d 912, 914 (1940): "As recently as November, 1939, this court in the case of White v. Gehrman . . . quoted, with approval, the following language used by this court as early as 1909 and which was quoted with like approval in . . . and . . . : 'Whatever the rule may be in other jurisdictions, it is firmly established in this state that a void tax deed may constitute a sufficient basis for the running of the statute of limitations.'

"The opinion in White v. Gehrman, supra, not only reaffirms that declaration, but goes on to hold that the rule applies even though the deed be void upon its face." Followed.

73 Fletcher v. Commissioners of Buncombe, 218 N.C. 1, 12, 9 S.E.2d 606, 613 (1940) (three-judge dissent): "State v. Dixon, 215 N.C. 161, 1 S.E.2d 521, 525, is directly in point. It is there said: 'Sound policy demands that when the General Assembly has adopted a general and uniform plan or policy to be applied consistently throughout the State, local measures which tend to disrupt or destroy that plan must yield to the more basic de-mands, State policy. The policy of the general "law of the land" prevails over that of a contrary, local act.' Therefore, the Act is unconstitutional under the principles in the Dixon case." Creation of a county school district was in question.

74 State v. Barton, 5 Wash. 2d 234, 242, 105 P.2d 63, 68 (1940): "No case has been cited in which this court has passed upon this precise question. State v. Lewis . . . upon which appellant relies, holds merely that . . . On the other hand, in State v. Whitehouse, 123 Wash. 461, 212 Pac. 1043, and State v. Taylor, 185 Wash. 198, 52 P.2d 1252, the right of the state to demur to a special plea of former acquittal, while not disputed, was tacitly recognized and approved." So held, in a case deciding that acquittal of first degree murder

while robbing did not bar later prosecution and conviction for the same robbery, simply as such.

75 Eagles v. General Electric Co., 5 Wash. 2d 20, 31, 104 P.2d 912, 916 (1940), called "particular attention" to an excerpt from an old English case and two American cases of 1878 and 1865, with an excerpt from the latter, all in emphasis of the reason for the rule that where the trustee's right against a third person is barred by delay, so is the cestui's. That rule is then applied, because its reason is thought to apply (although the reason ran to the cestui's right to proceed *if the trustee refused to act,* while in the case in hand the cestui had learned the facts only in 1938). For fuller presentation, see page 113.

76 In Canton Provision Co. v. Gauder, 130 Ohio St. 43, 196 N.E. 634 (1935), plaintiff had been suing the dealer and the manufacturer for injury due to meat bought in a sealed container by plaintiff's mother; the court had ruled out any possibility of recovery in implied warranty because "There was no privity of contract between the plaintiff and either of the defendants. . . ." (196 N.E. at 636.) In Wood v. General Electric Co., 159 Ohio St. 273, 112 N.E.2d 8 (1953), an action by a subpurchaser of an inherently dangerous article: ". . . Here, there was no . . . privity and hence no implied warranty. . . ." (112 N.E.2d at 12.) On the basis of these cases, the court in Welsh v. Ledyard, 167 Ohio St. 57, 146 N.E.2d 299 (1957), an action in warranty by a wife for injury due to an exploding electric cooker bought by her husband, sustained 4-2 a directed verdict for defendant. (But, 146 N.E.2d at 300, "we express no opinion" as to the result had there been allegations of purchase by the husband either as agent for or for the benefit of his wife; and the possibility is seemingly left open of proving an express warranty to the plaintiff herself.) For fuller presentation, see page 111.

77 Keljikian v. Star Brewing Co., 303 Mass. 53, 62, 20 N.E.2d 465, 471 (1939): After affirming an order sustaining a demurrer, judgment for the defendant has been ordered by this court in a number of cases. [4 cites to pages, plus a "see also."] That course will be adopted in the present case."

78 Germanow v. Standard Unbreakable Watch Crystals, Inc., 283 N.Y. 1, 27 N.E.2d 212, 217-218 (1940): "No precedent exists in the recorded decisions on unfair competition where under similar facts an injunction has been granted. Such a step would extend the doctrine of unfair competition much too far." So held. Gerdes v. Reynolds, 281 N.Y. 180, 185, 22 N.E.2d 331 (1939), a corporate action against directors for diversion of assets: "Nothing said or decided in any of those cases supports the action here." Held accordingly.

79 Comunale v. Traders & General Insurance Co., 50 Cal. 2d 654, 238 P.2d 198, 201 (1958): "Those cases are, of course, factually distinguishable from the present one since Traders never assumed control over the defense. However, the reason Traders was not in control of the litigation is that it wrongfully refused to defend Sloan, and the breach of its express obligation to defend did not release it from its implied duty to consider Sloan's interest in the settlement." So held. Cohn v. Taunton, 303 Mass. 182, 21 N.E.2d 281 (1939), action by b.f.p. to recover amount of coupons of bearer bonds stolen from city treasurer's vault. As against the prior case, in the instant one the treasurer had completed the issue of fully registered bonds of like amount. "In our opinion this difference in the facts does not lead to a different result . . ." (303 Mass. at 182); and the reason for negotiability of municipal bonds is explored.

80 Davis v. Starkenburg, 5 Wash. 2d 273, 282, 105 P.2d 54, 58 (1940): "We are clearly of the opinion that the decree entered in the foreclosure action is res adjudicata of the question now sought to be raised by the administratrix of the estate of Swan Finney in this action. See [three cases, from 181 to 196 Wash.]. While the cases last cited do not present factual situations such as appears in the instant case, we are of the opinion the cited cases announce rules applicable to the instant case, on the question of res adjudicata." So held.

81 Butler v. Carolina Power etc. Co., 218 N.C. 116, 121, 10 S.E.2d 603, 606 (1940): "[T]he recognition of a nuisance, sans negligence, does not mean that the conduct and conditions brought to our attention in the instant case must necessarily be so classed . . . [T]he nuisance, if it may be called such, was negligence-born, and must, in the legal sense, make obeisance to its parentage. Doctrinal distinctions may not be pressed too far." Judgment on verdict for defendant on a negligence submission affirmed.

82 Kimberley v. Ledbetter, 183 Kan. 641, 331 P.2d 309 (1958), repeats the essential reason of a prior case and applies its holding that an action lies for death caused by negligent abortion. "The defendant directs our attention to cases. . . . A review of these authorities will not here be made since they were carefully considered by this court in Joy v. Brown, supra, reference being made to that opinion. The simple import of the defendant's contention is that the Joy case be overruled. No sound reason has been advanced to overthrow that decision, and we adhere to its ruling" (331 P.2d at 309).

83 Williams v. Williams, 105 So.2d 676, 678 (Ala. 1958), quotes from a prior case a description of circumstances which *will* support a nullity suit, and then applies the description, without discussion, as a criterion for holding the bill in hand *in*sufficient. Detail sub Alabama, below, page 165.

84 Rozell v. Rozell, 281 N.Y. 106, 109, 22 N.E.2d 254, 255 (1939): "Persons who are not members of the family when injured through the tortious negligence of minors may recover damages against them by way of compensation for injuries suffered. The principle is not affected by the mere fact that the injuries are caused by the negligent operation of an automobile. No logical reason nor reported authority exists to indicate that the rule of liability should be changed when brothers and sisters are involved." As here; and so held.

85 Edgerton v. Johnson, 218 N.C. 300, 10 S.E.2d 918 (1940). Plaintiff, holding a judgment against defendant, alleges defendant to be insolvent and moves to have his judgment set off against an earlier judgment obtained by defendant against him. Denied, because defendant claims the judgment against plaintiff as his personal property exemption under the Constitution. "The procedure here adopted finds support in the case of Hogan v. Kirkland, 64 N.C. 250 [1870]. There a similar motion was made and allowed in the absence of a claim of exemption from sale under execution, such as the defendant is making here. This is the only essential difference between the two cases. It was intimated in the Hogan case, however, that this difference might be vital. And so it is, because the motion has the same effect as an execution" (10 S.E.2d at 919). Affirmed.

86 Jolly v. Martin Bros. Box Co., 158 Ohio St. 416, 109 N.E.2d 652, 657 (1952): "It would, therefore, be better practice, if not in fact necessary, that a motion for new trial be lodged to an order overruling a motion for judgment *non obstante* and be overruled before such order becomes an appealable one. The question becomes unimportant, however, in the instant case. . . ."

87 In Channel Master Corp. v. Aluminium Limited etc., 4 N.Y.2d 403, 151 N.E.2d 833, 835 (1958), the court in an action for fraudulent misrepresentation rested on "[t]he essential constitutents: . . . fixed as representation of a material existing fact, falsity, *scienter*, deception and injury" — as laid down in the precedent. The extension was to oral misrepresentations of capacity and intention to supply plaintiff with 400,000 pounds of aluminum monthly over five years, no closed contract and no signed writing being allegedl See Appendix A, New York, page 473.

88 Wenzler etc. Co. v. Sellen, 330 P.2d 1068, 1069 f. (Wash. 1958): "The controlling rule of law was summarized by the United States supreme court in Bigelow v. RKO Radio Pictures, Inc. . . . a private triple-damage action under the anti-trust laws:

"'The most elementary conceptions of justice and public policy require that the wrongdoer shall bear the risk of the uncertainty which his own wrong has created. . . .'

"Our cases are in accord. In one of them . . . a wrongful death action, the court quoted with approval from Bigelow v. RKO. . . . Other cases are collected in the margin. [Simple-citing 2 Wash. cases and 9 others.] In Sund v. Keating, 43 Wash. 2d 36, 259 Pac. 2d 1113, 1118, the court reviewed the situation in these words:

"'As to appellants' claim that damages here are speculative and conjectural, it seems sufficient to cite our recent decisions in . . . wherein we pointed out that while uncertainty as to the *fact of damage* is fatal; nevertheless, uncertainty as to *the amount* or *quantum* of damages is not to be regarded similarly. . . .'"

The startling but useful application in Wenzler was to a *breach of contract* where the damage established was the total for several subcontractors who had failed to furnish drawings of underground installations, and the share of damage due from the party in suit had to be estimated.

89 King Estate, 349 Pa. 27, 36 A.2d 504 (1944), involved a struggle between corpus and income with regard to new common stock in a merged corporation. The whole four-branch theory laid down in Buist's Estate is accepted, used to line up two later decisions, and one branch of it is applied. Quoted in full below at page 93. The four branches of possibility covered could hardly occur in a single case, and had not.

90 Matter of Divisich v. Marshall, 281 N.Y. 170, 173, 22 N.E.2d 327, 328 (1939): "If there be one public policy well-established in this State it is that public education shall be beyond control by municipalities and politics." This principle is applied; it is rested on quotation from, indication of the decision in, or mere citation of, five cases, none of which mentions any such principle, though they do touch administrative independence of Boards of Education.

91 Valera v. Reading Co., 349 Pa. 123, 127 f., 36 A.2d 644, 646 (1944): "In Anzinger v. Pa. R.R. Co. . . . we said, 'The tendency of our decisions is to hold a passenger responsible for his actual negligence in joining with the driver in testing a danger he knows exists and not for the result of mere inaction in failing to discover dangers of which he is ignorant, but might have discovered had he been giving attention to the roadway ahead of him.'" With the further help of a rationale from Rhode Island, against meddlesome interference by passengers, judgment against the passenger reversed, with a new trial. People v. Bellows, 281 N.Y. 67, 73-74, 22 N.E. 238 (1939): "It is a question of law whether . . . there was a question of fact regarding the defendant's guilt. . . . This point has not been squarely decided by this court, yet the cases lean to the conclusion, and some dicta indicate that we have considered such to be the law." So held. Compare use of "the attitude of our own Court on the subject," Carruthers v. Atlantic etc. Ry., 218 N.C. 49, 54, 9 S.E.2d 498, 501 (1940).

92 Opinion of the Justices, 303 Mass. 631, 641-643 (1939): "In the case of Lea v. Lynn . . . it was said . . . : 'Since it [the General Court] is a public agency directing the expenditure of money raised by taxation, it cannot make arbitrary discriminations and favor the employment of one class of citizens to the exclusion of others.' This statement was made in a case which sustained the validity of a statute providing that in the 'employment of mechanics and laborers' in the public service 'preference shall be given to citizens of the Commonwealth.' The further statement was made: 'But a preference of citizens over aliens in the public service is not favoritism among the subjects of the Commonwealth' . . . We think that the statements here quoted — one group of them by the court of which we are Justices and the other in conformity therewith by the highest court of a sister State — represent the law of this Commonwealth, and that *consequently* [my italics] the General Court cannot constitutionally enact a law, even with respect to employment in the public service, that arbitrarily distinguishes against any class of citizens by excluding it from such service."

93 Shaw v. Railroad Co., 101 U.S. 557 (1879), discussed below, pages 229, 231, involved a full-dress parade in favor of the original owner against any bona fide purchaser of a cotton bill of lading from a drawee who has improperly abstracted the bill of lading when the draft for the price is presented; but there had been a special verdict that the purchaser was not bona fide. There is no way of making the "main" ruling into a real holding; it is an excursion. But for decades the Shaw case was cited and used by courts for its unnecessary "principle."

94 New York Water Service Corp. v. Water, P. & C. Commission, 283 N.Y. 23, 31 f., 27 N.E.2d 221 (1940) (review of determination of commission denying application to operate additional wells in Brooklyn): In a prior case which was a liquidation proceeding conducted by the Superintendent of Insurance the court had "said we think it appropriate to suggest not only that the superintendent should disclose in first instance the fundamentals of the theory of his future action in fixing the losses of claimants, but that fair play requires also that an opportunity should be afforded to test by cross-examination the validity of any appraisal entering into the allowance of a claim.' (Cf. [two U.S. cases.].)" That is the whole *authority* foundation for the principle applied in the case. Proceeding remitted with instructions to make findings of fact, on evidence.

95 McPherson v. Buick, 217 N.Y. 382, 385, 111 N.E. 1050 (1916): "Thomas v. Winchester became quickly a landmark of the law. In the application of its principle there may at times have been uncertainty or even error. There has never in this state been doubt or disavowal of the principle itself." And compare, re a rule felt to be clear, Disston Estate, quoted at the end of *Pennsylvania, March 20, 1944,* at pages 95-96.

96 Town of Farmington v. Miller, 328 P.2d 589 (N.M. 1958), involved the liability of an itinerant salesman, an independent enterpriser selling suits to be tailored outside the State and shipped in, to pay a tax levied on "all occupations" at $1 per thousand of gross volume with a minimum of $5 per annum. After a review of the history and circumstances of the drummer taxes and the holdings against them: "These practical considerations, which presumably motivated the Robbins decision and those which followed in its wake, are in large measure absent in this case. And the particular facts of each case must control the decision."

97 The situation, though not in the exact language, is presented in Disston Estate, 349 Pa. 129, 135, 36 A.2d 457 (1944), where the "rule" of a prior case is adopted, with no reference to or help from the outcome of that case and no guidance to the court in the case in hand or in the future. Detail and discussion below, pages 95-96, 343 f.

98 Seattle v. King County, 3 Wash. 2d 26, 30, 99 P.2d 621, 622 (1940): "Without going into detail, the case of State ex rel. Spokane v. DeGraff, 143 Wash. 326, 255 P. 371, upon which the city relies in this regard, is clearly distinguishable." Held against the city, re retroactivity of a tax exemption statute. See also Mario Pandulf Co. v. Commonwealth, 303 Mass. 251, 256, 257, 21 N.E.2d 221 (1939).

99 Thus one sees this today peculiarly in Australian cases in which the High Court is evading the compulsion of the Privy Council; and home rule policies may justify what from the standpoint of a clean legal system is a dubious and costly tool. In St. Joseph's Hospital v. Bennett, 281 N.Y. 115, 22 N.E.2d 305 (1939), the two-judge dissent saw the majority taking just such a distinction. A bequest "to be held as an endowment fund and the income used for ordinary expenses of maintenance" was held unavailable to pay off a mortgage. A whole sequence of cases had held such bequests *"absolute gifts and not trusts."* (My italics.) The majority read these holdings as meaning "not trusts, but gifts," and as having been reached sometimes precisely because the law could (and in the instant case would) keep the corporation from diverting the fund from its expressed purpose. To the minority, gift meant gift, and absolute meant absolute.

100 Perhaps the most striking single instance is the series of charitable promise cases in New York, best known for Cardozo's opinion in the Allegheny College case, 246 N.Y. 369, 159 N.E. 173 (1927). From the Hamilton College case in 1 N.Y. to the Allegheny case and on beyond, the decisions have swung back and forth, neither side ever killing off the adversary cases, but merely "interpreting" them out of the way on ruling and on facts — only to have the rascals vote themselves back in.

101 The most notorious instance, because so long-continued, unmistakable, and hotly debated, is the Supreme Court's shameless and in my view shameful operation with two alternative series of precedents on the issue of Gelpcke v. Dubuque, 1 Wall. 175 (U.S. 1863), with the deliberate ignoring, in each sequence, of the existence of the other. Taft used to be eloquent on this. It did not fit his views of right judicial behavior. A modern parallel on a minor matter is presented from Illinois, below, pages 450 ff.

102 Paige, in Hargous v. Stone, 5 N.Y. 73, 88 (1851), utterly mangles the facts of Boorman v. Jenkins, 12 Wend. 566 (N.Y. S. Ct. 1834); see my On Warranty of Quality, and Society, II, 37 Columb. L. Rev. 341, 346 n.12 (1937). But Paige does not match the brazenness of Gibson's distortion of Borrekins v. Bevan, 3 Rawle 22 (Pa. 1831), in McFarland v. Newman, 9 Watts 55 (Pa. 1839); see Warranty, I, 36 Columb. L. Rev. 699, 733 if. (1937). The two instances may serve as another reminder that even the prevalence of a Grand Style is no cure-all. A modern instance is Cardozo in Cohen v. Lurie Woolen Co., 232 N.Y. 112, 114, 133 N.E. 370 (1921): "Schlegel Manufacturing Co. v. Cooper's Glue Factory (231 N.Y. 459) is not adverse to our conclusion. There the option stood alone; it was voluntary and revocable." In sooth, as appears below, at page 116, Cohen eviscerated the Schlegel approach to the reading of a document. Less troublesome, but related, is a citation supporting a proposition which it simply does not support: thus in Dayton v. Glidden, 303

Mass. 268, 270, 21 N.E.2d 229, 230 (1939), the citation of First National Bank v. Francis, 290 Mass. 49, 50, 194 N.E. 663 (1935).

103 King Estate, 349 Pa. 27, 31, 36 A.2d 504 (1944): "Reliance is also placed upon what we stated in re Daily's Estate . . . in connection with the respective rights of life tenant and remainderman in a merger and re-organization. But here again if the opinion of the lower court . . . be examined, it will be found" that the facts made the language inapposite. See also a wholesale slaughter of dicta in Keljikian v. Star Brewing Co., 303 Mass. 53, 55 ff., 20 N.E.2d 465 (1939).

104 There is no point in citation. But it is worth noting that certainly during the last twenty years this type of distinguishing comes close to drowning out all other types. The old-fashioned digging out of a distinction on a procedural issue is almost never met; and little play is made in today's opinions even with the fact that the ruling is found in a multiple-point decision. Compare page 103 below. I think it probable that the newer tone reflects at once a more rapid shifting in the facts of litigation, a decreased interest in procedural niceties, and a greater willingness to face up to needed shift of base. But exact reading has not gone out of fashion. Compare Duschaine v. City of Everett, 5 Wash. 2d 181, 188, 105 P.2d 18 (1940).

105 A prior decision is undercut with reference to its manner ("without written opinion") and its foundation ("solely on authority" of a case so set out as to appear perhaps, though barely, distinguishable on its facts): Broughton v. City of Cleveland, 167 Ohio St. 29, 146 N.E.2d 301, 304 (1957), re City of Cleveland v. Russo. Cf. the three-judge attack on the majority's text-authority in Long v. Melton, 218 N.C. 94, 101, 10 S.E.2d 699, 705 (1940); or the knocking out of a case in Kingston v. Anderson, 3 Wash. 2d 21, 24, 99 P.2d 630, 632 (1940), as resting on an undiscussed assumption.

106 Hoffman v. Knollman, 135 Ohio St. 170, 20 N.E.2d 221 (1939). The Constitution of 1912, in revising and limiting appellate jurisdiction, had taken from the legislature all power to review "judgments." Need, convenience, and established past practice had induced the Supreme Court to strong-arm an extension of "judgments" so as to include "final orders," and, down through 133 Ohio St., to further extend the final order idea to the granting of certain new trials. "In the opinion of the court, the courts of this state have gone to the limit in construing court orders as 'final' for the purpose of bringing them within the comprehension of the term 'judgment,' and the attempt to make the setting aside of a verdict and the granting of a new trial a final order not only goes beyond any reasonable limits and violates the Constitution, but, if approved, would by inference withdraw all limitation against future enlargement of the jurisdiction of the Court of Appeals by legislative enactment." (135 Ohio St. at 186.) Judgment dismissing the appeal affirmed.

Varney v. Ditmars, 217 N.Y. 223, 111 N.E. 822 (1916): "The opinion of this court in United Press v. N.Y. Press Co. (164 N.Y. 406) was not intended to assert that a contract of sale is unenforceable unless the price is expressly mentioned and determined." — which it had not only asserted, but had argued in the teeth of contrary authority.

107 Grain Dealers National Fire Ins. Co. v. Union Co., 159 Ohio St. 124, 111 N.E.2d 256, 261 (1953), presented below, page 153. The Pickering case, there "confined to its exact facts," had in the absence of higher declared valuation and charge therefor given validity to a §25 limitation of liability, unsigned, printed on the receipt, and not called to the depositor's attention.

108 Connor v. City of Haverhill, 303 Mass. 42, 46, 20 N.E.2d 424 (1939): "If we assume that the case of Friend v. Gilbert, 108 Mass. 408, cited by appellants, would be decided the same way today, it must be regarded as distinguishable on the ground stated in Whittaker v. Salem, supra, at page 485." So, in essence, re flat *sub silentio* overruling, State v. Endsley, note 110 below.

109 McPherson v. Buick, see note 95, above, disposes of a number of bothersome authorities thus. See discussion below, pages 431 ff.

110 Hughes v. State, 328 P.2d 397, 402 (Idaho 1958) (destruction of business access is a "taking" within eminent domain rules): "Crane v. City of Harrison, 40 Idaho 229, 232 P. 578, 38 A.L.R. 15, appears to be the only decision of this court expressing views divergent

to those stated herein. Insofar as that case is in conflict with the views announced herein, it is overruled." Broughton v. City of Cleveland, 167 Ohio St. 29, 146 N.E.2d 301 (1957), given with some fullness under Number 2, above at page 77, either overrules City of Cleveland v. Russo, 98 Ohio St. 465, 121 N.E. 901 (1918), or puts the stamp of approval on prior overruling of the Russo case. State v. Endsley, 331 P.2d 338, 341 (Ore. 1958), overrules a tacit ruling made in two prior cases, and at page 342 records a *sub silentio* overruling of two other cases which "has since been cited many times and followed in an unbroken line of cases. . . ."

There can be amusing prudery in the language: Williams v. City of New Bedford, 303 Mass. 213, 216, 21 N.E.2d 265 (1939): "In so far as Chase v. Lowell, 7 Gray 33, in its statements may be in conflict with this conclusion it is not followed." The Chase case had been contra not only in language but in holding. Or take this, from Weiner v. Pictorial etc. Corp., 303 Mass. 123, 126, 20 N.E.2d 458 (1939): "Any intimations in reported cases to the contrary, countenancing a right of appeal from a decision other than a 'final decision,' cannot be approved." The power of a particular court's currently accepted manner and style (here, still the Rugg manner) crops out when one realizes that the last phrasing stems from none other than Lummus, as that in Connor v. City of Haverhill (note 108 above) does from Qua. Neither was writing thus seven years later.

111 Burlington Grocery Co. v. Lines, 96 Vt. 405, 120 Atl. 169 (1923): The clause to be construed was: "Price, not over 26 cts. per lb." "By proper construction, it is a stipulation for a reasonable price, to be determined by market conditions existing at the time of delivery, but not, in any event, to be more than the maximum named. . . . See Parker v. Adams, 47 Vt. 139; Ames v. Quimby, 96 U.S. 324. . . ." Neither case does more than squint toward the result. And compare Memphis Furniture Manufacturing Co. v. Wemyss Furniture Co., 2 F.2d 428, 431 (6th Cir. 1924): "The ruling made in La Grange Grocery Co. v. Lamborn & Co., 283 F. 869, 872 (C.C.A. 5), is helpful." The facts and rulings then given in some fullness are nonpertinent, unless perhaps in showing that another court has interpreted a commercial document commercially.

112 Matter of Bums v. Wiltse, 303 N.Y. 319, 323, 102 N.E.2d 569 (1951): "We find no specific constitutional or statutory authority that prohibits or permits the nomination of the same person as a candidate for the office of District Attorney and County Judge at the same election. Nonetheless, we are convinced that the spirit and intent of the Election Law forbids such a dual nomination, particularly where, as here, the candidate may not, if elected, take and hold both offices." So held. Prior cases which had derived similar statements of policy from similar sources were presented in support. Wiltse, already irrevocably on the ballot as nominee of all three major parties for D.A., had on the death of the Republican candidate for County Judge obtained the County Committee's indorsement as substitute.

113 Persinger v. Rhay, 52 Wash. 2d 762, 329 P.2d 191 (1958), involved an information whose allegations were insufficient to support the judgment. The court, approving two tacit overrulings of a rule adhered to "as recently as 1945": "This is, we recognize, an extension of the holdings of the *Sorenson* case [judgment *ambiguous* as to offense] to an entirely different type of case, but we are satisfied that it is a desirable and proper extension."

114 Cardozo's work on this is discussed at pages 34, note 25, and 115 f. Moran v. Standard Oil Co., 211 N.Y. 187, 196, 197, 105 N.E. 217 (1914): "An intention to make so one-sided an argument is not to be readily inferred . . . The very word 'agreement' connotes a mutual obligation . . . The law, in construing the common speech of men, is not so nice . . ." and in Wood v. Duff-Gordon, 222 N.Y. 88, 91, 118 N.E. 214 (1917): "A promise may be lacking, and yet the whole writing may be 'instinct with an obligation,' imperfectly expressed . . . If that is so, there is a contract." Finally, Cohen v. Lurie Woolen Co., 232 N.Y. 112, 114, 133 N.E. 370 (1921): "Indefiniteness must reach the point where construction becomes futile."

115 Enlargement: Nelson v. West Coast Dairy Co., 5 Wash. 2d 284, 290, 105 P.2d 76, 79 (1940): "From the necessities of such situations, and in reason, the consumer's right of recovery is not limited to an action against his own immediate vendor, but reaches the retailer, wholesaler, producer, and all others who participate in the sale and distribution of such deleterious articles of food." The action was against the milk farmer, the general

dairy company, and the retailing distributor; judgment was sustained against the 2 last, and the court suggested that dismissal against the first, because the infected milk might have had another source, might be improper. The only prior Washington case had been one of a consumer against a meat packer. Implied warranty and negligence are seemingly merged. Compare the extraordinary extension of a statutory concept in Laudato v. Hunkin-Conkey Construction Co., 135 Ohio St. 127, 19 N.E.2d 898 (1939), discussed below, page 112. The *"compensated* surety" represented a subdivision of a concept, to produce enlargement of the obligation.

116 Background and process, in regard to one new concept, are rather well painted by Frederick, The Trust Receipt as Security, 22 Columb. L. Rev. 395, 546 (1922), in regard to both State and Federal courts; the introduction of the new concept into further jurisdictions continued into the '30's. Spread and rerecognition of what was in 1914 the substantially forgotten American banker's letter of credit as an independent contract and concept can be followed especially in Hershey, Letters of Credit, 32 Harv. L. Rev. 1 (1918), and Finkelstein, Legal Aspects of Commercial Letters of Credit (1930).

117 McPherson v. Buick, 217 N.Y. 382, 111 N.E. 1050 (1916), discussed below, page 430, is an excellent example; or any of the cases clearing up the joint tort feasor mess in regard to contribution.

118 Here I prefer to use old cases, whose subsequent history demonstrates the pseudo character of the innovating "solution" principle. Gaylord v. Allen, 53 N.Y. 515 (1873), introduced, to modify Day v. Pool, 52 N.Y. 416 (1873), a distinction in regard to remedy, after acceptance of goods under a contract for sale, for breach of warranty. The remedy turned on whether any words of warranty were part of the contract or were collateral; 37 years of chaos ensued, until the Uniform Sales Act. Elterman v. Hyman, 192 N.Y. 113, 84 N.E. 937 (1908), and the companion case, Davis v. Rosenzweig Realty Co., 192 N.Y. 128, 84 N.E. 943 (1908), made a vendee's lien for price-payments, after default by the vendor, turn on whether the buyer's actions had amounted to such a "rescission" of the contract as destroyed it; and for generations nobody in New York knew (if anybody does yet), before decree, what this would mean.

119 In Disston Estate, 349 Pa. 129, 135, 36 A.2d 457 (1944), the Supreme Court adopts a rule previously stated at first instance and then accepted by the Superior Court. In Broughton v. City of Cleveland, 167 Ohio St. 29, 146 N.E.2d 301 (1957) (also, above, p. 77, note 64), Court of Appeals cases appear to be accepted as overruling a prior Supreme Court decision. Atty. Gen.: Bradley, below, pages 172-173.

120 King Estate, 349 Pa. 27, 31, 36 A.2d 504 (1944), digs facts out of the lower court opinion to explain away language in the supreme court's own prior case. In Northwestern Ohio Natural Gas Co. V. Public Utilities Commission, 135 Ohio St. 85, 87, 19 N.E.2d 648, 649 (1939), the court explains a prior syllabus in the light of the opinion, and adds, "Then too, the court had in mind the fact that the statutes themselves disclose no legislative intent to deny rate-fixing powers to municipalities." Nothing in the prior report had revealed this.

121 Shawmut Corp. v. Bobrick Sales Corp., 260 N.Y. 499, 184 N.E. 68 (1933). The bank's customer had arranged debit of its account to prepay its obligation to indemnify the bank against a draft which under a credit had been accepted by the bank on the customer's behalf. The customer claimed preferential payment of that draft, even though the bank had become insolvent. (1) Cases holding that the customer remained liable, notwithstanding the letter of credit, and the rationale of a case which had refused the preference where no particular draft had been specified, were extended to sustain the customer's claim. (2) The case was also said to be indistinguishable on its essential facts from a prior case in which the court had treated as a trust fund in a bank's hands a check on itself which it had received as "pre-payment" of the customer's note, which the bank had, however, previously transferred. Whether the latter ground is joint with or independent of the former, I cannot make out.

122 Rozell v. Rozell, 281 N.Y. 106, 109, 22 N.E.2d 254 (1939) (auto accident): "No logical reason nor reported authority exists to indicate that the rule of liability should be changed when brothers and sisters are involved." At page 110: "'The modern tendency of decided

cases is to ignore fictions and deal with things as they are.'" At page 113: "Insurance as protection to the sufferer is now a matter of common knowledge." Recovery sustained.

123 Matter of Porges, 281 N.Y. 205, 210-211, 22 N.E.2d 341 (1939): "The question is open as to whether, assuming the illegality of an investment made by a prior Chamberlain, a direction to a Chamberlain in office to turn over moneys never received by him is proper, and the answer to that question is obvious, namely that such order is improper and must be reversed." This seems to me creation straight out of natural justice as seen by the court. Compare the "self-evident" in Hoffman v. Knollman, 135 Ohio St. 170, 181, 20 N.E.2d 221 (1939), and Lindberg v. Steele, 5 Wash. 2d 54, 60, 104 P.2d 940 (1940).

124 Gerburg v. Crosby, 329 P.2d 184 (Wash. 1958), presented below, page 174, by way of recourse to the critical literature materially extends the cases liberalizing the use of expert testimony. Cf. Fosdick's Trust, 4 N.Y.2d 646, 152 N.E.2d 229 (1958) (see below, pp. 477 f.) and Cunningham's Estate, 395 Pa. 1, 149 A.2d 72 (1959), in each of which the critical literature on stock dividends was able to shake only 2 of the judges off the limb of the old rule on division between corpus and income. Town of Farmington v. Miller, 328 P.2d 589 (N.M. 1958), presented above, page 84, note 96, rests almost entirely on discussions in the field by 4 named writers and 2 law review notes.

125 Harris v. Shorall, 230 N.Y. 343, 130 N.E. 572 (1921), quoted fully on this below, page 207. And compare note 85 above, page 82.

126 Examples below, pages 305 ff.

127 4 Coke 92b (Q.B. 1602).

128 248 N.Y. 339, 162 N.E. 99 (1928).

129 I had been invited to address the Brandeis Lawyers' Society in Philadelphia, had decided to talk on How Appellate Courts Decide Cases, and chose for study the then last available published volume of Pennsylvania reports, Vol. 349. (141 pages from the same opinion-day, in 348 Pa., are not here included.) The results of the study appear in the Society's publications and also in 16 Pa. Bar Assn. Q. 220-248, 17 id. 54 (1945).

130 The quote which follows is somewhat shortened and paraphrased from 16 Pa. Bar Assn. Q. 230-234 (1945).

131 The opinions run from April 23 to July 24, 1940. There were 5 or more opinions from all but Lewis (4), Rippey (3), Loughran (2), with 8 Per Curiams strewn in. It was unhappily not till years later that I noted that July 23-24 alone would have offered the prettier parallel: pages 244-550. Something of the range of precedent techniques in 292 N.Y. (1944) is suggested by Radin, The Trail of the Calf, 32 Cornell L.Q. 137, 158 (1946).

132 Report of the Cincinnati Conference on the Status of the Rule of Stare Decisis, 14 U. Cin. L. Rev. 203, 218, 284-285 (1940). I made a short sampling of then current Ohio material, and reported thereon in Impressions of the Conference, ibid. 343, 348 f., that the Ohio court seemed to be doing much what nonsyllabus courts did, with their prior opinions. This in turn led to picking Ohio for one of the 300-page samplings, where the picture was the same. Years later, in preparing to deliver Marx lectures at the University of Cincinnati in the late spring of 1953, I used the successive Ohio Supreme Court full opinions found in the advance sheets of January 14 through April 22 of that year (109-111 N.E.2d). Among the 19 treated in this study (cf. pp. 148 ff.), there were 3 or more opinions from 3 of the judges, 2 each from Weygandt, Hart, and Middleton, and one from Zimmerman, plus 7 Per Curiams.

133 October 22, 1958, 152 N.E.2d 827 ff.

134 Below, at page 287, there is further discussion of this rarity, today, of cases being distinguished on other bases than reason and the facts. Below, also, it will become clear that the infusion of the appellate court's reason and sense into its rulings on the law is so strong these days as to make entirely understandable this lifting of a "nonholding" but considered ruling out of second-class citizenship.

135 Frank gathers some printed expressions in Law and the Modern Mind (1st ed. 1930), e.g., Gmelin, at 280; Hutcheson, at 341. He is concerned with showing that the rules of law do not dictate outcome by way of formal logic. The gatherings make clear, I think, that they do not, *always*. Such gatherings cannot, of course, support a conclusion that they do

not, *ever*. And the real problem goes to neither proposition, but to when, and how much, the frame and relevant detail of accepted doctrine influences, presses, shapes, and often largely determines outcome by means vastly more subtle than conscious formal logic. See below, passim.

136 1 Principles of Psychology 260 (1890).

137 From time to time I have had occasion to comment on the unhappy result of mistranslation and misconception of some rich insight which happens to come to us in a foreign tongue: thus re *ius,* which means for jurisprudence not "law" but "right law," or re *expressio unius est exclusio alterius,* which is in point only in regard to excluding the other one of possibilities limited in advance to two. Similarly, *stare decisis et quieta non movere* is a counsel which in its first branch has never when rightly understood included any definite article; a good precedent-system is too wise for that. And in the second branch the only things we are told not to move are such as have truly "come to rest" — of which, in the law of a changing world, there are not too many.

138 Canavan v. City of Mechanicville, 190 App. Div. 252, 180 N.Y. Supp. 62 (3d Dept. 1920), 229 N.Y. 473, 128 N.E. 882, 884 (1920).

139 Compare Fuller, American Legal Realism, 82 U. Pa. L. Rev. 429, 437 (1934), on the animal too tightly penned.

140 Bryant v. Isburgh, 13 Gray 607, 611 (Mass. 1860). The full story is presented in my Cases and Materials on Sales 217-221 (1930).

141 "More than forty years" is three legal generations. It has rarely been noted, and perhaps never printed, that in our system a legal generation runs fifteen years or less.

142 283 N.Y. 33, 38-39, 27 N.E.2d 225 (1940).

143 349 Pa. 123, 36 A.2d 644 (1944).

144 E.g., Pound, The Theory of Judicial Decision, III, 36 Harv. L. Rev. 940, 941 (1923): "In a very great proportion of the causes that come before the judge on the crowded judicial calendars of today this additional duty [providing a basis of analogical reasoning in the future] is relatively negligible. Happily, the bulk of these cases repeat or ring insignificant changes upon familiar states of fact." Compare Cardozo, The Nature of the Judicial Process 163 ff. (1921), reprinted in Hall, Selected Writings of Benjamin Nathan Cardozo 176 ff. (1947), re the cases where the controversy "turns not upon the rule of law, but upon its application to the facts: ... But they leave jurisprudence where it stood before."

145 I am a believer in the importance of the hero; but I also go with Holmes in his thought that one major aspect of a great man's greatness is that he happens to be *there* at the telling moment. For a case which would have been "leading," had it found a following, see Laudato v. Hunkin-Conkey Construction Co., 135 Ohio St. 127, 19 N.E.2d 898 (1939), below, pages 112 f.

146 Compare and contrast the modern vogue of *"out of and,"* noted below, page 246; which courts are only beginning to break away from.

147 An Introduction to Legal Reasoning 6-19 (1949). The Mann Act material runs 19-40.

148 Skinner v. Stone, 144 Ark. 353, 222 S.W. 360 (1920); Kingston v. Anderson, 3 Wash. 2d 21, 24, 99 P.2d 630 (1940).

149 Dissent in Sun Printing etc. v. Remington Paper etc., 235 N.Y. 338, 139 N.E. 470 (1923).

150 Cohen v. Lurie Woolen Co., 232 N.Y. 112, 133 N.E. 370, 371 (1921).

151 Jurisprudence, N.Y. St. Bar Assn. Rep. 278, 293 (1932), reprinted in Hall, Selected Writings of Benjamin Nathan Cardozo 20, 33 (1947).

152 N.Y. St. Bar Assn. Rep. at 275, Hall at 17.

153 N.Y. St. Bar Assn. Rep. at 278, Hall at 19. Note the "even."

154 Hutcheson on "the little small dice" can be read only by a moron as suggesting gambling probabilities. His insistence is on the frequent determinative character of factors not as yet reduced to formula or to any other diagnosis which is communicable by more

than such terms as "hunch," or "insight," or "something" — all used in terms of responsible conscience and tradition. The Judgment Intuitive (1938).

155 Preface to Kritik des Entwurfs eines Handelsgesetzbuchs, Krit. Zeitschr. f.d. ges. Rechtswissenschaft, Vol. 4, No. 4.

156 159 N.Y. 188, 53 N.E. 810, 811 (1899).

157 Thus whereas in the Littlejohn case the waiver simply made it unnecessary for the seller, in his action for price less proceeds, to prove compliance in any particulars not mentioned on the rejection, in Ginn v. Clark Coal Co., 143 Mich. 84, 106 N.W. 867 (1906), an action for nonacceptance, assignment of the ground "Not Pine Grove coal" was actually held to bar defendant from introducing his own affirmative evidence of nonmerchantability to justify rejection, or even to lessen damages.

158 The cases are gathered and well discussed in Eno, Price Movement and Unstated Objections, etc., 44 Yale L.J. 782 (1935). I find nothing in Kennedy's lively recanvass of the same material, Realism, What Next? II, 8 Ford. L. Rev. 45, 48-71 (1939), to alter my own interpretation of the data, which squares well enough with Eno's. Kennedy exposes nonconclusiveness, not nonpersuasiveness, in the material. Kennedy's distaste for recognition that situation-type equities influence the work of appellate courts is at interesting variance with the observations of the courts themselves. (The matter is of course not limited to the "waiver" rule.) Compare Rose, C.J. in National Bank of Commerce v. Lamborn, 2 F.2d 23, 29 (4th Cir. 1924): "From much which was said by the tribunals which have heretofore passed upon the obligation of buyers to accept sugar from the West Cheswald, it would seem that it is at least possible that their conclusions were influenced not a little by their natural desire to prevent purchasers on a rapidly falling market from escaping from a bad bargain, by taking advantage of a variation from the terms for which they in fact cared nothing."

159 Well treated by Honnold, Buyer's Right of Rejection, 97 U. Pa. L. Rev. 457 (1949).

160 The matter is developed in two careful and illuminating Notes: 29 Columb. L. Rev. 960 (1929) (Massachusetts), ibid. 1123 (California). Holmes, in White v. Solomon, 164 Mass. 516, 42 N.E. 104 (1895) (full price recovered, despite rejection), carried a majority into a crashing exception by a wooden and needless application of the doctrine of independent promises. Queer, for Holmes, in Contracts.

161 Haynes v. Temple, 198 Mass. 372, 84 N.E. 467, 468 (1908).

162 Frisch v. Wells, 200 Mass. 429, 86 N.E. 775, 776 (1909).

163 Muncy v. Brain, 158 Cal. 300, 110 Pac. 945 (1910).

164 An Introduction to Legal Reasoning 6-19 (1949) on McPherson, ibid. 19-40 on the Mann Act. See also page 430 below.

165 The detail is in my On Warranty of Quality, and Society, I, 36 Columb. L. Rev. 699, 737-744 (1936), II, 37 ibid. 341-357 (1937).

166 Ibid., for the whole story. On Paige's methods, 37 Columb. L. Rev. 346 n.12.

167 It pays, with these or any other more concrete fact-situations in mind, to reread the beautiful Goldschmidt passage on page 122 above.

168 For illustration, among the New York incompleteness cases, the record was innocent of utterly necessary evidence on the price-practice of the relevant market in the leading anticommercial decision, United Press v. New York Press, 164 N.Y. 406, 58 N.E. 527 (1900), and the complaint even in Sun Printing etc. v. Remington Paper etc., 235 N.Y. 338, 139 N.E. 470 (1923), which came at the end of a long series of decisions, was allowed to remain so bare of similar material that a highly favorable court felt itself unable to do more than give the plaintiff's counsel instruction on how to handle the cause in pleading over.

168a In print, on this, cf. Simmons, Better Opinions — How? 27 A.B.A.J. 109 (1941). Some appellate judges insist, almost with indignation, that they simply hew out a sound opinion on facts, issues, and the law, and watch never a chip; and may be reporting accurately. That has nothing to do with the life-fact that they have grown into advocates as an acorn grows into an oak. Cf. re Taft, pages 21-22, and re Cardozo, pages 115-116, above.

168b See also The Curse upon Illegitimate Authority Techniques, pages 256 ff. below; and the "court's witness" cases, pages 450 ff. below.

169 By the same token, I resent the portait-painter's painting out the pockmarks; the face is more powerful with them in. And I think the Washington command of objurgation would do better to be in by anthology, as against mere and inconclusive description.

169a On this, two notes. (1) As appears below — see note 168b — a thing may be both understandable and pure in heart, and yet be wretched practice. (2) "Commonly" does not mean "always," and until a long sequence like the "court's witness" one, what outside mark is there to assure of the purity? Sometimes, as in the Per Curiam device for ducking responsibility to doctrine (past *and* for the future), one gets unpleasant suspicion of evasion or lack of candor by the court. Note, Per Curiam Decisions of the Supreme Court: 1957 Term, 26 U. Chi. L. Rev. 279 (1959).

170 See, e.g., from this same July 11, Matter of Spector v. Allen, 281 N.Y. 251, 253, 258, 259, 22 N.E.2d 360; or the whole opinion in the American Molasses Case, 281 N.Y. 269, 22 N.E.2d 369; or Matter of Vanderbilt, 281 N.Y. 297, 314, 316, 317, 22 N.E.2d 379.

171 The latter is quoted below, pages 143 f. Contrast that blurred presentation with those of New York, above, or Ohio or Washington, below.

172 Above, pages 92 ff.

173 From 16 Pa. Bar Assn. Q. 228-229 (1945).

174 This case is further discussed below, pages 275 f.

175 Compare the quotation from Disston Estate, 349 Pa. 129, 36 A.2d 457 (1944), above, pages 95-96, with pages 178 ff. below, and especially with pages 343 f.

176 It is as good as certain that this language — a standard "canon" — can be matched from the Pennsylvania books. It represents and matches what the Pennsylvania court did in the rather parallel Merchants' Warehouse v. Gelder, 36 A.2d 444 (1944). See page 144 above. But observe what it would have meant if applied not in the Salvation Army Case, 36 A.2d 479 (1944), but in the hospital case which had preceded. See pages 146 f. above.

177 Above, pages 64 ff. Enlightening material from England and early Pennsylvania, and New York is presented in detail, with an eye particularly to its effect on adjustment of doctrine to conditions, and of the effect of the dominant personnel, in my On Warranty of Quality, and Society, I, 36 Columb. L. Rev. 699 (1936), II, 37 ibid. 341 (1937).

178 Compare Beutel, Some Potentialities of Experimental Jurisprudence (1957), on the bad-check situation.

179 One must here distinguish between what one hears from two quite different classes of consummate artist: the articulate artist (John W. Davis, Charles Evans Hughes, and, I suspect, Proskauer) as against the doer-artist who does not, even to himself, do much verbal accounting for most of his technique. Here belong Cardozo as an advocate, and Griswold, and Frankfurter.

180 Fuller, American Legal Realism, 82 U. Pa. L. Rev. 429, 437 (1934).

181 Levi's sequences are superb illustrations, especially re the Mann Act.

182 Confusion in the old days bulked in the "Value" controversy, with some slopping over into "Good Faith." The N.I.L. attempted to dispose of both aspects by substantially removing the need for either, even in transactions wholly out of current course. The courts' groping after sense continued, however. Hence, the "legal" issue of the lasting controversy just moved over into the area of "notice" (neatly escaping the statute's planing off of "value" and "good faith"), where the same sense-urges remain busy, and where the annotations have come in consequence to drown the investigator. Compare sub Miller v. Race, 1 Burr. 452 (K.B. 1758), below, page 410. The blinder and less informed of the New York City bar, the bankers in general, and history-ignorance, duly forced a rather simple clarification of the matter to be deleted from the Uniform Commercial Code.

183 Matter of City of New York (Elm St.), 246 N.Y. 72, 76, 158 N.E. 24 (1927).

184 See the subsequent history.

185 Uniform Commercial Code §2-306(1).

186 Above, page 180. It is fascinating to observe the detailed worries of the New York Law Revision Commission, whose whole history and practice have been built in terms of exact and detailed minor reforms, with each imaginable contingency given accurate advance coverage, as they wrestled with the completely variant drafting philosophy of the Uniform Commercial Code in the 1952 draft. There open-ended drafting, with room for courts to move in and readjust over the decades, had been a basic piece of the planning. Some of this is suggested in N.Y.L.R.C. Report Relating to the Uniform Commercial Code, 1956, pp. 15-20; but to get the picture one must explore the full two volumes of Studies (1955).

187 Above, pages 124 f.

188 See Pound, most recently, in 2 Jurisprudence 349 ff. (1959).

189 On this Pound has written excitingly. See my On Reading and Using the Newer Jurisprudence, 40 Columb. L. Rev. 581, 585, 589, 594, etc. (1940).

190 I have tried to express this in Law and the Modern Mind, 31 Columb. L. Rev. 82, 87-90 (1931). Nelles, Towards Legal Understanding, I, 34 Columb. L. Rev. 862 (1934), II, ibid. 1041, builds a beautiful background on the growth and success of this tradition of seeing and thinking in our legal history.

190a 194 U.S. 120, 24 S. Ct. 581 (1904).

190b Pp. 300, 303, 337 (1881).

190c 244 U.S. 12, 37 S. Ct. 490 (1917).

190d 191 U.S. 379, 24 S. Ct. 107 (1903).

190e 179 Mass. 114, 60 N.E. 397 (1901).

190f 167 Mass. 92, 44 N.E. 1077 (1896).

190g 155 Mass. 523, 30 N.E. 364 (1892).

190h Commonwealth v. Peaslee, 177 Mass. 267, 59 N.E. 55 (1901).

190i Commonwealth v. Kennedy, 170 Mass. 18, 48 N.E. 770 (1897).

190j Globe Refining Co. v. Landa Cotton Oil Co., 190 U.S. 540, 23 S. Ct. 754 (1903).

190k White v. Solomon, 164 Mass. 516, 42 N.E. 104 (1895), above, page 124, note 160.

191 The Path of the Law, 10 Harv. L. Rev. 457 (1897), especially at 467. But that paper suggested no "pattern" of this kind as a normality.

192 Above, pages 13 f.

193 There is in some of the larger "acre-office" firms a recognizable effort to carry on knowhow, in some of the departments or in general. But what I have been able to observe is spotty. Except for the pioneering machinery of Kurt Pantzer of Indianapolis, I have met almost nothing that builds the rounded man-of-law. Thus even the careful and articulate Bromley ex Stimson ex Root on Preparing for Trial — in Llewellyn, Materials on Argument (mimeo.) — gives no suggestion of any other Root tradition as having been standard teaching even in Root's office, nor of Bromley as having come into contact with any of Root's transcendent other-than-trial knowhow. Something of this unevenness of trans-mission holds even in the more rounded offices of the smaller city. We turn, for hope, to the newer drive toward a *recorded* tradition — in Postgraduate Legal Education and what one may call "clinical" literature. — Let me add at once, to avoid misconception, that I see sound study of any of the practical arts of law-government as a discipline of necessity built around deep theory, and as a branch of the humanities. Rules of thumb are small change, necessary but minor.

194 The mere existence of the Conference of Chief Justices offers both a wherewithal and a stimulus for renewal. Meantime we have an emerging body of publication which is patently at work to cut from the general to the particular. The immediate post-Cardozo articles (Hutcheson apart) tended to offer an almost carefully vague wave of a wand toward change which once in a blue moon might be necessary. No gears meshed. More recently the judicial speaker has tended much more to get down to how, in particular. Judge Wilson (An Outlet for My Soul, 37 J. Am. Jud. Soc. 109 (1953)) was talking to a bar convention, but he went into the intangibles of his office. Later papers move, if anything, even more into the down-to-earth, hardheaded wrestling with daily problems: Justice

Schaefer (then Chief), Precedent and Policy (1955), Ernst Freund Lecture, University of Chicago Law School; Judge Breitel, Judicial Legislation, N.Y.L.J., Dec. 8-12, 1958; Chief Justice Weintraub, Judicial Legislation, ibid., Mar. 19, 1959; and the forthcoming paper of Judge Breitel on statutes, In Regard to Statutes, noted below, page 372. Judge Traynor (Some Open Questions on the Work of State Appellate Courts, 24 U. Chi. L. Rev. 211 (1957)) got down further, and in a stubborn, lovely fashion, more closely to tomorrow's cases than did Cardozo at any point, if you read in terms of exactly how to do tomorrow's job. Let me say that I think my brother Traynor's major worry, the finding of a *pattern* to tell reversible from nonreversible error, is probably a full generation ahead of him and me. But he is *at it,* and being at it is what pushes the job along. E.g., without Traynor's worrying, how would I ever have picked up, to throw into the pool, the Illinois Supreme Court's explicit practice, in criminal cases, of offering as a criterion "whether there has been a miscarriage of justice"? That Criterion is plainly inadequate; but it is no less obviously an admirable *first* step into the problem. It poses the major issue clearly. (Compare below, p. 455.)

The striking thing, may I repeat, as contrasted with the tenuous Cardozo-echoes of two generations back, is *bite* in the current approach from the judiciary. Their interest is in *how* to handle *tomorrow's* case. Characteristic is the advice by Kenison, C.J. (N.H.), to appellate advocates on how to "reach" the court they address: Some Aspects of Appellate Arguments, 1 N.H.B.J. 5 (1959).

Useful, very, from outside, is such a study as Merryman's The Authority of Authority, 6 Stan. L. Rev. 613 (1954). I wish Merryman might have centered his study on the guts-conclusion from page 627: "Actually the application of authorities to cases to arrive at decisions is not nearly as simple or mechanical a process as the layman thinks it should be."

Merryman's concentration on purported "authority" makes his net result as much out-of-line as it is useful; there are other factors which need meditation. Nevertheless, this is the kind of basic job, in research, which breaks down smugness and which opens up, for the sensitive: an entering wedge.

195 For a guess, this is the most controversial single unprovable judgment expressed in this book. But it is a careful one. And it is one which I should take aesthetic and even sadistic pleasure in debating. Pound was arguing the same, with much less current basis, as early as his conciliatory papers of 1914, Justice According to Law, I, 13 Columb. L. Rev. 696 (1913), II, 14 ibid. 1 (1914), III, ibid. 103.

196 Law in Our Society, Syllabus, Lecture XIII (mimeo. 1949).

197 A by-product might be to uncover leads for sounder methods of conditioning our judges; for we need more of it. But the tools must be good: the effort to use rules of law alone or chiefly, *and without regard to form or content of the rule,* we have seen to defeat its own purpose. Moreover, the conditioning must for wise results be held well within bounds: we want no brainwashing, no Kipling's "man who was," no puppet-court. Yet we are horribly deficient in breaking our trial judges in to any kind of *practice* of the trial bench. We do not even *consider* having a new trial judge sit as an associate, for a month at a time, with each of three of his established brethren.

198 They *are* wonderful legs.

199 Again the short term plus absence of "accepted" re-election cuts down on the phenomenon; in my view, most unwisely. Ct. Illinois' sad loss of Davis, 1960.

200 239 N.Y. 264, 146 N.E. 374 (1925).

201 The Paradoxes of Legal Science 70-71 (1928).

202 230 N.Y. 343, 130 N.E. 572 (1921).

203 Cammack v. Slattery, 241 N.Y. 39, 148 N.E, 781 (1925).

204 This aspect of this series of cases is unique in my limited reading. What astounds is that it is unique even in the reading of such an encyclopedic scholar as my brother Rheinstein.

204a Equitable Trust Co. v. Keene, 232 N.Y. 290, 292, 133 N.E. 894 (1921).

205 Compare Whiting v. Hudson Trust, below, pages 436-440.

205a The statute covers "a *contract to sell* or a sale of *any* goods or *choses in action.*" To limit this to an *existing* credit flouts the meaning of "goods"; future *goods* ("goods to he manufactured or acquired after the making of the contract") are included. It also flouts the policy re shares of stock or receivables. A more comfortable argument could run: (1) Foreign exchange deals fall outside the statute's purpose and policy; oral deals not only work but are necessary. (2) Foreign exchange is a significant unit-type of situation, whether the form by the bank's draft (not *sold,* but issued), or a payment (no *sale,* but a service), or a credit. Any distinction based on form would be arbitrary. Hence *for this purpose,* establishing a credit will also be treated as a service, and so outside the statute.

206 Square roots shook me out of this, with the ± answer. I can still suffer those weeks of distress while my heart rebelled against the outrage that there *could* be *two* right answers. Then came the awful clarity that *selection* depended on the circumstances. Jurisprudes need to remember their elementary algebra.

207 The job of again making clear and communicable the ways of work in each of the crafts of our law has begun, and is progressing, slowly. The interesting thing is: that the practicing lawyer has slid so far into just-not-knowing, simply doing, that conscious efforts have to be made to wake him up. Meanwhile, the great Law Schools are in this a legal generation behind the Bar, which is itself at least two legal generations behind simple need. Exception: N.Y.U. re judging.

208 This also, I may add, is what German-speakers *ought* to be meaning with *Rechtssicherheit.*

209 Such an issue can, e.g., with a gold decree, blow up in a counselor's face. That does not mean that he has to be less careful.

210 Mentioned above, page 107, note 139.

211 His Legal Foundations of Capitalism (1924) and his subsequent more detailed study have received little attention from the theorists of abstract economics. Yet I should have thought it impossible to play with any sequence of price figures without reckoning, as an inherent and changing base, with whatever legal allocations of risk underlie the prices.

212 From my Remarks on the Theory of Appellate Decision and on the Rules or Canons About How Statutes Are to Be Construed, 3 Vand. L. Rev. 395, 398 (1950). Pound gathers, in Justice According to Law, I, 13 Columb. L. Rev. 696 (1913), II, 14 ibid. 1 (1914), an almost terrifying succession of views which run in terms of *either* it is "by rule" *or* it is "arbitrary." I find the same idiotic misposing of "the" issue still rampant among my students in 1959. The cleanliness and pressure of felt office are hard for the impatient to take in.

213 Pound is grand in that piece of Contemporary Juristic Theory (1940) where (p. 31) he deals with "the upright man" as reliable. "Upright" gathers 30 intangibles into a meaningful net.

213a See Professional Judicial Office, above at pages 46 f.

214 Cardozo moves rather rarely into "Children, This Is Simply So." But you can feel that come through in his Jurisprudence lecture, N.Y. St. Bar Assn. Rep. 263 (1932). Some of the children seemed to him to have missed the whole implicit base of restraint and of method. The anomaly about J. Frank is his deliberate obtuseness to this in his jurisprudential writing, even while, as a governmental officer (counsel for A.A.A., chairman of S.E.C., circuit judge), he was working, day by day, in the most careful and responsible response to the things which, via intangibles, make a man's own conscience seek the regular. *Sit terra ei levis.* It was a troubled man and almost great.

215 From 3 Vand. L. Rev. 395, 398 (1950). The bracketed passage is added.

216 Ibid. Judge Ethridge, of the Mississippi Supreme Court, came across the Vanderbilt paper, and wrote me. He saw nothing new in it; and why should he? He did think it, however, a clarifying statement of how judges have been going about their work with statutes. I am not clear that without the encouragement of Judge Ethridge I should have undertaken the backbreaking analysis of pages upon pages of reports which has made this book possible.

217 Fuller, American Legal Realism, 82 U. Pa. L. Rev. 429 (1934). The most familiar example goes back to everybody's first-year contracts. Cook v. Oxley, 3 Term R. 653 (K.B. 1790), lacked the "conceptual bridge" of "continuing offer."

218 Compare the Illinois "court's witness" cases discussed below, pages 451 ff.

219 Schlegel, presentd above, pages 115 f.

220 Assume a variation of requirements which remained within reason and a defendant-manufacturer who felt it was too much, or who was seeking escape, and the issue centers on whether "requirements" does not imply an agreement to purchase exclusively from the supplier, plus good faith in handling the article on the market. The answer to that, in the then court, would turn on the presence or absence of Cardozo.

221 Compare pages 251 ff. — One can go wholly with Traynor in regard to the "expert" in the college: "What knowledge he has he can share with his colleagues, who are competent to understand him if they are competent to sit on a court." Some Open Questions on the Work of State Appellate Courts, 24 U. Chi. L. Rev. 211, 217 (1957). But a busy man who is *not* sitting does not so readily come to share his relevant knowledge, nor can he be argued to or educated.

222 Effective Appellate Advocacy, c. 2 (1950). An excellent book in a neglected field. On the particular point Traynor's full description of the California Supreme Court is especially instructive. See note 221 above.

223 Pages 251 ff., especially 252, 254.

224 Cf. Peart v. Jones, 159 Ohio St. 137, 111 N.E.2d 16 (1953), above, page 153; and Smith v. State, 39 Ala. App. 501 (1958), above, pages 166 f.

225 Jenkins v. Moyse, 254 N.Y. 319, 172 N.E. 521 (1930). Proskauer had come into the case for the lender in the final appeal. His work shows. The opinion was by Lehman, who understood both real estate and business finance.

226 101 U.S. 557 (1879). On the case for the pledgee, see Bank v. Shaw, Fed. Cas. No. 843 (C.C.E.D. Pa. 1876).

227 Stollenwerck v. Thacher, 115 Mass. 224 (1874); Farmers' Bank v. Logan, 74 N.Y. 568 (1878). Tiedeman v. Knox, 53 Md. 612 (1880), is no exception to this; quite the contrary. It does freely uphold the relevant Maryland statute of 1876, but that statute had been enacted, in language extending into kindergarten detail, with the special purpose of upsetting the same court's prior refusal, in perfect seaboard-center fashion, to find any negotiability at all in bills of lading.

228 Vanderpool v. Burkitt, 113 Ore. 656, 234 Pac. 289 (1925).

229 Schumann v. Bank of California, 114 Ore. 336, 233 Pac. 860 (1925). There is no cross-mention, let alone synthesis, of the two cases. See below, page 458n.

230 Commercial Finance Corp. v. Burke, 173 Ore. 341, 145 P.2d 473 (1944).

231 Perhaps not for the court. In Plummer v. Kingsley, 190 Ore. 378, 381, 226 P.2d 297 (1951), the Burke case "appears to be directly in point"; but it had been cited by *neither* party.

232 Is it so very hard to see common investment in the same crook with regard to the same thing as a common venture and so to apply the principles of general average or of grain elevators?

232a I suppose one should add as a further one of the ABC's of appellate advocacy which derive directly from the conclusions of this study (presented below, page 237): 7-A, *Early Stage-Setting:* The time to introduce background facts or evidence which interpret documents, statutes, or case law principle is as early as technical imagination and ingenuity will permit. Such material is better there for any tribunal to see *with* than introduced later in an effort to correct a possible false impression. Sun Printing etc. v. Remington Paper etc., 235 N.Y. 338, 139 N.E. 470 (1923) (above, page 128, note 168), is an admirable illustration.

233 It is in this connection that I find myself irritated at preachments on trial tactics which urge that pleadings (and opening statements) must "avoid argument and be

confined to facts" — as if facts rightly arranged and rightly presented did not in themselves constitute the most powerful of arguments.

234 Compare also, from 1842, Alexander v. Greene (N.Y.), above, page 67, and from 1844, Miami Exporting Co. v. Clark, pages 68 f., and the 1844 Ohio cases generally. — Yet in quantity or intensity of use Brandeis did strike a new note.

235 In England, Holt, Mansfield, and Scrutton made themselves a tradition on this, matched among us by Cowen, Hough, and Learned Hand — praised be the name of each! "Scrutton," said Kilmuir to me, "was not harsh on younger counsel, *but you knew you had to know your stuff."*

236 Slightly paraphrased and shortened from my The Modern Approach to Counselling and Advocacy, 46 Columb. L. Rev. 167, 182 ff. (1946). The present footnotes to the quotation do not appear in the original.

237 There is no room among such ABC's for consideration of such technically — and ethically — more delicate approaches as an appellee's careful complication and obfuscation of the facts, say to resist a certiorari, or to muffle and smother the force of an appeal, nor yet to discuss the suicidal character of such tactics if the court eludes the snare.

237a Further ABC's touched on in this study would include the most basic of all: *The Target Is the Particular Tribunal,* which underlies item Twelfth, below; and item 7-A from note 232a, above, page 232.

238 On the oral argument this puts respondent up against a problem of footwork. He cannot rest on any properly done statement of the facts by the appellant. Neither can he allow the court to settle back with a bored sigh: "Do we have to listen to all this again!" Standard and useful entrances are, e.g., by way of a desire to clear up some "misconception possibly left by one's friend," or by asking the court's particular attention to one aspect of the facts "which the appellant did not perhaps develop as fully as the case deserves." Sometimes, but I think rarely, it pays respondent to crash in with the true and very different story.

239 I am not dealing here with the special problem of the brief to avoid review by permission, with its peculiar techniques. On those Wiener is all I have met in print, and he is good. Effective Appellate Advocacy, §33 and c. 11 (1950). Compare also note 237 above.

240 Reliance on the chief need not be conscious. But many judges in many courts, over many decades, especially where the chief's office is permanent, have fallen into an almost-habit of voting with the chief unless moved enough to stir into independent action. Cardozo (who in some matters remained childlike) was almost shocked when he discovered that as chief he had suddenly acquired a "persuasiveness" in conference which he had never enjoyed before. And like many another chief, he liked it, and he pressed the possibility a bit. Lehman (then Chief) told me: "He was always fair, but he did *not* like to be unable to line up his court, and you knew it. — But who does?"

240a Far the best single job on this is Whitman Knapp, Why Argue an Appeal, and If So, How? 14 Record 415 (Assn. of Bar, City of N.Y. 1959). Excellent complementary but more general papers are Pollack, Some Practical Aspects of Appellate Advocacy, 31 N.Y. St. B. Bull. 81 (1959), and of course Kenison's superb job cited note 241, below.

241 I first heard this phrased, as a principle, by J. Carlisle Pryor, of Burlington. I was delighted then, and have been since, that this beauty derives — at least for me — not from Wall Street or similar acres, but from the open spaces. It gives great satisfaction to find it becoming a standard procedure; thus Kenison's proposal to give it status and a heading in any brief: "A Rationale for This Case." Some Aspects of Appellate Arguments, 1 N.H.B.J. 5, 10 (1959).

242 Above, page 34; especially pages 115 f., page 86, note 102.

243 See above, page 116, note 149. On the merits of the situation, there still is trouble. Liberal contracts scholars of 1923 (including, I regret to state, me) saw Cardozo's opinion as a bothering backward step. Nor did the master himself know quite where he was at. The essence, after the years, comes to this: If an explicit agreement has to be implemented by material from outside the explicit language, the person who relies on the implementation has the burden of getting that material into court. — Only the sillinesses of prior years

could have made this simple issue so hard for any of us to see; but bad pleadings can deflect the eyes of other men than judges.

244 Compare above, pages 210 f.

245 Clemens Horst Co. v. Biddell Bros., [1912] A.C. 18 (H.L.).

246 I have not often met a more majestically and gracefully misleading brief.

247 Matthew Smith Tea etc. Co. v. Lamborn, 10 F.2d 697 (2d Cir. 1926).

248 One also observes the extraordinary statement that insertion of the original condition that a copy of the ocean bill of lading be tendered to evidence the Java to Philadelphia shipment "must be regarded as inadvertent." It was in fact waived as impracticable simply because the seller had on the one vessel sugar for too many contracts for his bill of lading "parts" to go round.

249 The best discussion of this in legal literature is Arnold's treatment of the tramps in the old Central Park reservoir. Symbols of Government 47 f. (1935).

250 It has been noted, in contrast, that Laudato, if buttressed by following decisions, could have become a Leading Case. But even today *"out-of"* constricts.

251 *Per contra,* note the awkward hazard if the case should come into bankruptcy, with the more ill-begotten spawn of Erie v. Tompkins dug into ambush.

252 Whether seller's sight draft is drawn to his own order and indorsed or is drawn to the bank's order direct, it still contains no obligation that can be sold or purchased, much less one which any bank dealing directly with seller can take as a holder in due course. The bill of lading can indeed be "purchased" by a bank-pledgee, but in an honest transaction there are no equities of any kind to be wiped out, except conceivably the buyer's beneficial interest — and of that the seller's bank has the best of notice: for without assurance that the shipment represents a real contract it is bad banking to make the discount. And once the draft is paid, the bill of lading drops out of the picture, the controversy going to the proceeds *of the draft.*

253 The argument is by connotation and flavor, not direct. Against "bona fide *purchase for value"* is set "mere *agency.*" Agency there is, which "must" mean "no purchase," and therefore no rights at all. The fact is, on the other hand, that there has been a loan, with security in the bill of lading and authorization to collect and apply the proceeds of the draft. The solid answer to buyer's "agency" argument is another side step: agency indeed, and the duties of collection agency; but in the form of a power coupled with a 100 per cent interest.

254 Compare Precedent Technique Number 21, above, page 81.

255 Beginning with Strohmeyer, above, pages 209 ff.

256 Further discussion with particular reference to inconsistent lines of court's witness evidence, below at pages 450 ff.

257 E.g., State v. Endsley, 331 P.2d 338 (Ore. 1958), Appendix A, page 498. Compare People v. Toomer, 14 Ill. 2d 385, 152 N.E.2d 845, 847 (1958): ". . . defendant relies upon People v. Nicholson . . . and People v. Camy. [Both in 404 Ill.] The Nicholson case was expressly overruled by the Ferguson decision; and the holding in the Camy case, to the extent that it is inconsistent herewith, is hereby overruled."

258 E.g., Persinger v. Rhay, 52 Wash. 2d 762, 329 P.2d 191 (1958), above, page 175.

259 Below, page 450: People v. Hundley, 4 Ill. 2d 244, 122 N.E.2d 568 (1954), and People v. Siciliano, 4 Ill. 2d 570, 123 N.E.2d 731 (1955).

260 Better Opinions — How? 27 A.B.A.J. 109 (1941).

261 Sometimes the court, though dealing with the point, fails to cite the authority it is disposing of. This makes for inconvenience, but not for lack of confidence. — Two able students checked briefs against opinions, looking for trouble, and brought me five instances for my personal examination.

261a Jenkins v. Moyse, 254 N.Y. 319, 172 N.E. 521 (1930), above, page 228 and note 225.

261b Thus in the Whiting case, below, page 437, what made the advocated rule seem to be wise was a *surface* appearance of "speeding transactions," which could have been countered by a description of how accounts of the kind are actually handled; and counsel's effective job in the Lamborn case, above, page 243, drew its power from a hands-and-feet discussion of a *buyer's* interest, and depended wholly on keeping the court from seeing in equivalent terms the operating problems of the defendant *bank.*

261c Compare the report from Rutledge, below, pages 447 ff.

262 Jurisprudence, N.Y. St. Bar Assn. Rep. 298 (1932), reprinted in Hall, Selected Writings of Benjamin Nathan Cardozo 37 (1947). In talking with the Chief Justices about this, at their 1959 meeting, I found roughly a third of them both reflective and somewhat articulate about these problems of method and knowhow of their craft, and about a third still somewhat disinclined to open such inquiries even to themselves. The former group, taken as a percentage of skilled, active *doers* in the work of a practicing craft of intellectual work over *human* problems (as contrasted with the manipulation of *things),* seems to me amazingly high. The group of the disinclined, on the other hand, seems to me to represent a much higher percentage than would be found in any purely "lay" calling; they reflect not only the tradition but the fact that some phases or touches of appellate judging do have and should retain a touch of the mystic. But the two groups differed strikingly in average age.

263 Stone, The "Equitable Mortgage" in New York, 20 Columb. L. Rev. 519 (1920).

264 I cannot escape the feeling that we have here not parallel but convergent sense-estimates of the "snow-covered sidewalk" situation. What in Massachusetts, New Jersey, and Illinois has the aspect of engineering the sound way through a mean but regularly recurrent problem has in Oregon almost the flavor of allocating the risks attendant upon a visitation. The case is further noted App. A, p. 498.

265 Legniti v. Mechanics and Metals National Bank, 186 App. Div. 105, 173 N.Y. Supp. 814 (1st Dept. 1919), above, page 210.

266 Allendorf v. Elgin, J. & E. Ry., 8 Ill. 2d 164, 133 N.E.2d 288 (1956), below, page 282 f.

267 Above, page 210.

268 Clarke v. McGinn, 105 S.2d 668 (Ala. 1958). See pages 165 f. above.

269 People v. Clair, 221 N.Y. 108, 116 N.E. 868, 869 (1917).

270 Temple v. Keeler, 238 N.Y. 344, 144 N.E. 635 (1924).

271 In my youth I fell into this same error. Comment, Tort and Contract in the Marketing of Food, 27 Yale L.J. 1068 (1918). Cases and Materials on Sales 340-343 (1930) presents a fairly mature analysis: On Warranty of Quality, and Society, II, 37 Columb. L. Rev. 341, 405-406 (1937), gives interesting historical material.

272 This appears fully, e.g., in Dickerson, Products Liability and the Food Consumer (1951).

273 [1920] 1 K.B. 668.

274 Hoisting Engine Sales Co. v. Hart, 237 N.Y. 30, 142 N.E. 342, 31 A.L.R. 536 (1923).

275 Aron v. Sills, 240 N.Y. 588, 148 N.E. 717 (1925). It is interesting to find the "merchantability" idea proceeding to weaken the "fitness for consumption" idea. In 1936, when McSpedon v. Kunz, 271 N.Y. 131, 2 N.E.2d 513, brought trichinae again before the court, with a wholesale butcher and the original packer impleaded, 3 votes were for barring action against the packer because with fresh pork it was not the practice to freeze low enough and long enough to kill the trichinae, and because raw pork was not sold for raw eating.

276 Ryan v. Progressive Grocery Stores, 255 N.Y. 388, 175 N.E. 105 (1931).

277 Canavan v. City of Mechanicville, 190 App. Div. 252, 180 N.Y. Supp. 62 (3d Dept. 1920), 229 N.Y. 473, 128 N.E. 882 (1920), above, page 106.

278 Chysky v. Drake Bros. Co., 235 N.Y. 468, 139 N.E. 576 (1923).

279 Redmond v. Borden's Farm Products Co., 245 N.Y. 512, 157 N.E. 838 (1927).

280 Vaccaro v. Prudential Condensed Milk Co., 133 Misc. 556, 232 N.Y. Supp. 299 (1927). This I take to be overruled.

281 It is interesting to turn up in our small 1957 Ohio sampling two exhibits in which two phases of these same developments enter the home stretch. Broughton v. City of Cleveland, 167 Ohio St. 29, 146 N.E.2d 301 (1957), below, page 300, and Appendix A, page 486, fits with Canavan, above, note 277, for of course tort and warranty are but two alternate means for getting at a single policy-problem. Welsh v. Ledyard, 167 Ohio St. 57, 146 N.E.2d 299 (1957), discussed above, page 111, shows Ohio trembling on the verge of wiping out the strict privity requirement in the consumer cases.

282 See also below, pages 310 f., 345.

283 181 U.S. 155, 21 S. Ct. 544 (1901).

284 Cleveland Crime Survey (1919). The many criminal cases in my current samplings are on the whole very gratifying in their combination of interest in the whole case, care in regard to essential procedural fairness, and refusal to be confounded by technicality that does not reach to substance.

284a The best single piece in print on opinion-writing — though unhappily misguided on the matter of precedents — is Smith, The Current Opinions of the Arkansas Supreme Court — A Study in Craftsmanship, 1 Ark. L. Rev. 89 (1947).

284b The lawyers one talks to may often feel that there is in fact no rule controlling the courts, but that idea is set in a frame that says rules should and can control them. Among the scholars of today I find but a single current suggestion, and that indirect, that rule-and-principle are not right legal tools. Northrup, The Complexity of Legal and Ethical Experience 24 (1959): ". . . [F]or Professor Sturges it ["the application of the empirical method to the study of statutes and cases"] results in the conclusion that legal science contains no principles, either new or old, and that the search for principles is merely an emotive hang-over from the past which one should get rid of as quickly as possible." Sturges still talks this way, apparently, and he may even, somewhat dated, still feel this way. But Northrup exhibits unworthy naïveté when he continues: "Professor Sturges' work in the field of arbitration [citing *merely* the Cases on Arbitration Law] and the late Professor Shulman's recommendation of arbitration rather than litigation *under legislative statutes and legal* principles in the field of labor law *support this existentialist philosophy of law* [my italics] — the philosophy which affirms that it is of the very nature of any concrete case of ethical or legal judgment that it is particular and unique, and that, hence, one falsifies the very nature of any dispute if one attempts to resolve it by recourse to *universal* [what a convenient dialectic exaggeration!] principles, *thereby* [note the shift from "universally exact" to "substantially similar" as if they were the same] treating it as if it were *like* other disputes." (Again my italics.) One notes first that no good philosopher has any business talking of the art or craft of judging as if it could be a "legal science." One notes second that it is not possible to operate *under* a rule or principle without finding *likeness,* among cases. One notes third that despite Sturges' pleasure in shocking by language, his *work* (even re arbitration) was built rule-wise, and skilfully so; and also that Shulman was about as predictable a labor arbitrator as we have had: he moved with considerable consistency on his own implicit, occasionally explicit, principles. One notes, fourth, on the face of the document, such an incomprehension not only of legal matters but of logic and of sense that one must yearn for the return of Walton Hamilton.

285 Sattelmacher, Bericht, Gutachten und Urteil (21st ed., Luttig and Beyer, 1955).

286 On which I hold pronounced views. Compare my On the Good, the True, the Beautiful, in Law, 9 U. Chi. L. Rev. 224 (1942), especially 254 ff.; Law in Our Society, Syllabus (mimeo. 1949), especially Lectures VI-VIII.

287 I remind again of the remarkable Platonic character of our case law rules, which can be felt and even known as "the same" despite divergent phrasings which in a statute or a contract would drive lawyers and judges into hours of meticulous verbal comparisons.

288 I have been checking up on alleged "weights of authority," off and on, for now forty-three years, and I do not believe there has been one instance out of five in which the "weight" could not be shifted by a re-examination of the facts and issues in the cases. And

I doubt whether I have met as many as one instance in three where material re-examination was not rather badly needed, in order to make sense.

289 See above, page 97.

290 64 N.C. 250 (1870). See sub Precedent Technique Number 23, above, page 82, note 85.

291 167 Ohio St. 29, 146 N.E.2d 301, 305 (1957). The case is also mentioned sub Precedent Technique Number 2, above, page 77, note 64, and App. A, p. 486.

292 Jurisprudence, N.Y. St. Bar Assn. Rep. 296-297 (1932), reprinted in Hall, Selected Writings of Benjamin Cardozo 36-37 (1947).

293 287 U.S. 358, 53 S. Ct. 145, 85 A.L.R. 254 (1932).

294 My work on the Uniform Commercial Code and the resultant hassle with the more ignorant among the highly placed "commercial and banking" counsel of the Wall Street area has left me a little weary of critics who condemn for "uncertainty" legal proposals which would reduce existing uncertainty by a half or nine tenths. Existing uncertainty is much like mist just too thin to be fog; one sees a little and forgets how infinitely more is hidden.

295 The Juice in the Orthodox Ideology, above at pages 184 ff.

296 The material is well enough gathered in Black, Law of Judicial Precedents (1912); Freeman, The Protection Afforded Against the Retroactive Operation of an Overruling Decision, 18 Columb. L. Rev. 230 (1918); the passionate attack (in the name of all theory and all expediency) on Gelpcke v. Dubuque, 1 Wall. 175 (U.S. 1863), and all its progeny, in 9 Am. L. Rev. 381 (1875); and the recent Decennial Digests.

296a The exceptions among our samplings have been almost entirely cases where the ruling now upset has been inadvertent. An exception to this statement is probably Gould v. Stelter, above pages 295, 300, which I think saw the old rule as having been bad from the beginning. But the typical picture is that presented by Cardozo re "fixtures" in the modern apartment. The Nature of the Judicial Process 295 f. (1921), reprinted in Hall, Selected Writings of Benjamin Nathan Cardozo 35-36 (1947).

297 Again the question goes to method, not to substance. Experience shows, I think conclusively, that the court was thoroughly sound on the point of an adequate face-of-the-record, but could hardly find a rule to raise more human trouble than the insistence that natural parents must know the identity of adopting parents. A general consent to an *approved* screening agency, but revocable for a due cooling period, is sound legal engineering.

298 Vaughan v. Harp, 49 Ark. 160, 4 S.W. 751 (1887). In general see Radin's excellent paper, The Requirement of Judicial Opinions, 18 Calif. L. Rev. 486 (1930).

298a Citations to a number of recent, worried studies, and a full discussion of a whole term's work, in an excellent Comment, Per Curiam Decisions of the Supreme Court: 1957 Term, 26 U. Chi. L. Rev. 279 (1959).

299 Slonaker V. P. & G. Publishing Co., 338 Pa. 292, 13 A.2d 48 (1940), discussed above, pages 310 f.; Allendorf v. Elgin, J. & E. Ry., 8 Ill. 2d 164, 133 N.E.2d 288 (1956), discussed above, page 282. The late and great Hiram Thomas of New York met this problem by keeping his own notebook of unkeynumbered points of interest found in his research or current reading. His "Little Black Book" became the first port of call for any brief in the office on a commercial point.

300 Clemens Horst Co. v. Biddell Bros., [1912] A.C. 18 (H.L.). Goldschmidt is quoted above at page 122.

300a Holt founds the tradition, but on the commercial side is not fully up to it. The Dutch Wars were over, the Mayor's Court in London had long been showing understanding of commercial need, a Holt of true commercial genius could have done something much like a Mansfield's work under William and Mary, and Anne.

301 Compare Hough, Concerning Lawyers, 5 Ohio St. L.J. 1 (1938).

301a On the matter of the burden, we finally have a clean study: Hart, The Supreme Court, 1958 Term, Foreword: The Time Chart of the Justices, 73 Harv. L. Rev. 84 (1959). First-water opinions have continued to go neglected. Thus Learned Hand's classic work in Aluminum was redone a few levels down in American Tobacco: and Magruder's luminous working out of the conflicts problem on burden of proof of contributory negligence, in Sampson v. Channel, 110 F.2d 754 (1st Cir. 1940), was disregarded on appeal as if he had been Hough.

302 Matter of Ciminera v. Sahm, 4 N.Y.2d 400, 151 N.E.2d 832 (1958).

303 105 So.2d 668, 671 (Ala. 1958).

304 5 N.Y.2d 1, 152 N.E.2d 241, 243 (1958).

305 167 Ohio St. 38, 146 N.E.2d 293, 297 (1957).

306 Compare pages 241 ff.

306a For more than thirty years there have been two divergent lines of change in case-books or course books. The more prevalent one is to edit facts out, and simplify issues, saving little treatises on doctrine; and to footnote with doctrinal quotations. The opposing trend is to build up the individual case into a richer picture, use text to "cover ground," and footnote rather to fact-background and other fact-situations. I think the latter trend destined — slowly — to victory.

307 Described in Zeisel-Kalven-Buchholz, Delay in the Court 217 ff. (1959).

308 It is as well to remember that neither secrecy of the court's deliberation or later secrecy about what went on during that deliberation rests in the nature of things or in any ordinance of God. The roots of each are either practical or accidental, and it is only either ignorance or tradition which makes us feel that we have here something untouchable, a semiholy arcanum. We tend to forget that in common law history the centuries of the Year Books rest on a practice of conference, consultation, and decision going on in open court before ears and eyes of counsel, the bar at large, and the apprentices; and most of us do not know that the Supreme Court of our first neighbor to the South still works out its conferences in this same solid common law fashion. I personally suspect that our own secrecy practice began when decision began to be postponed beyond the close of argument, with an eye to avoiding misapprehension and disappointment, and then to avoiding financial speculation. And I suspect the carryover into later secrecy about past deliberations to represent partly a closing of ranks to protect the court from criticism or attack, and in later years a similar closing to allow free discussion with no possible repercussions in a re-election campaign. Thus the storied sanctity of the conference room represents to me as pragmatic and nonmystic a phase of appellate judicial work as the handling of the docket. Our modern fetish of secrecy reminds me of the shock German lawyers displayed at the notion of such dangerous things as published dissenting opinions. 1 *Präjudizienrecht* etc. 6in. (1933).

309 I find troubling the absence of conscious large-scale tradition of a parallel kind covering the deliberations of administrative agencies. Pound speaks in another context of a needed administrative "ethos." 2 Jurisprudence 443 (1959). — Re the judiciary: even the irrepressible T. R. could have Holmes to family dinner while Northern Securities was pending, and act as if the case did not exist.

309a Compare, e.g., Reason via the Law, above at page 201.

310 Dixon, Irmaos & Cia, Ltda. v. Chase National Bank, 144 F.2d 759 (2d Cir. 1944).

310b The British bankers, before the First World War and after, had a charming variation which shows how little "full set" can mean "full set." A credit expressed for honor in London "when accompanied by a full set of bills of lading" would simultaneously require that the set be broken by sending one bill of lading (with a copy of all other documents) direct to the branch which had advised the credit to the exporter.

311 Swan writing, L. Hand and Frank with him.

312 Among law teachers this has moved, in substance, into an aspect of office.

313 An indication of the range of interest in this problem can be had in Kalven's review of Green, Traffic Victims: Tort Law and Insurance (1958), in 26 U. Chi. L. Rev. 679 (1959);

and in James, The Columbia Study of Compensation for Automobile Accidents, etc., 59 Columb. L. Rev. 408 (1959).

314 Some Open Questions on the Work of State Appellate Courts, 24 U. Chi. L. Rev. 211, 217 (1957).

314a One can really include here, also, the carefully balanced work of Dickinson, Nelles, Hamilton, of Pound himself on the constructive side, and of Cardozo's capstone job: Jurisprudence. All of these — cited above, pages 13 f., notes 2-7 — were shrugged out of the attention-catching controversial literature and have remained in deep-freeze practically ever since.

315 Report on Federal-State Relationships as Affected by Judicial Decisions, Conference of Chief Justices, August, 1958.

315a Stern's rule is from Donatelli v. Carino, 384 Pa. 582, 585, 122 A.2d 36, 38 (1956). The application is in Taylor v. Richman, 149 A.2d 69 (Pa. 1959). For a more elaborated illustration of the possibilities of this general approach to rule-making, see page 419, note 39.

315b One recalls also from the Legal Apocrypha: "And the Lord said: Let there be contracts and let there be torts. And it was so. And He divided contracts from torts. And darkness, etc." How apocryphal this notion of the nature of things is, our small samplings show: Washington, 1940, shows tort and contract merging in regard to bad food; Washington, 1958, builds a principle of proof of damages which covers contract and tort alike; Ohio, 1957, is breaking the warranty action loose from "privity" in regard to an electric cooker; New York, 1958, is spreading actionable misrepresentation over into the field of contract formation — not with respect to out-of-pocket "reliance" damages, but with respect to lost-bargain damages, as well. — Yet the Legal Apocrypha still wield vicious power.

316 Above, pages 328 ff.

317 Whiting, below at pages 441 f., is an example; or the hopeless technical confusion of Glass v. Misroch, 239 N.Y. 475, 147 N.E. 71 (1925).

317a The first American case to raise the issue whether the plaintiff requires to have knowledge of the reward before performance appears to be Lee v. The Trustees of Flemingsburg, 7 Dana 28 (Ky. 1838). It held allegation of knowledge of the offer necessary to making the plaintiff a party to the agreement: and without an agreement there was no obligation. No authorities were cited or mentioned. None of the three prior American cases had called for any such "straight contract" theory. In Symmes v. Frazier, 6 Mass. 344 (1810), the defendant had lost a large number of bills, etc., and offered §200 to any person who should "find and restore the same." The plaintiff found and returned part, but recovered seemingly *pro rata*. The court found the "legal effect" of the promise to be so, rewriting the words on grounds of policy. That is surely no straight general contract law, any more than was the familiar Williams v. Carwardine, 4 B. & Ad. 621 (K.B. 1833), where lack of knowledge of the offer had been flatly held no bar. In that same year Deslondes v. Wilson, 5 La. 397, presented a loss of $3000 plus promissory notes and the like in the amount of §15,000, with an offer of §500 for their recovery. The facts strongly suggest that the plaintiff knew nothing of the reward when he took §2500 of the money from the corpse of the thief, deposited it in a bank, and turned over a "check" therefor not to the owner, but to the Mayor. The court, "doing complete justice," allowed the plaintiff *half* the offered reward. Again reward is treated as a special category. The only other case I find possibly in point is neutral: in City Bank v. Bangs, 2 Ed. Ch. 95 (N.Y. 1833), the offeror paid into court, and the facts are blind on whether the successful claimant did or did not know of the reward at the time he instituted the successful search.

318 Riesman is cogent on the sometimes effect of law review. E.g., Law and Social Science, 50 Yale L.J. 636 (1941); Individualism Reconsidered, c. 27 (1954).

319 When the outsider is willing to go through the initiate, the result can be glorious: consider Walton Hamilton's work. And the reports on the Yale Law and Behavioral Science Program promise well. 12 J. Legal Ed. 83-106 (1959).

320 Another round table on the subject was scheduled for the 1959 meeting of the Association of American Law Schools.

320a Cohen & Sons v. Lurie Woolen Co., 232 N.Y. 112, 133 N.E. 370 (1921).

321 The Conditions for and the Aims and Methods of Legal Research, Handbook of Association of American Law Schools 25 (1929); Bramble Bush, c. 2 (Oceana ed. 1951).

322 Law as Logic and Experience (1940).

323 Courts on Trial, e.g., 75-77 (1949).

324 Ibid. 225. Frank was almost impervious to facts, once his view had set. Vanderbilt had in my hearing rubbed in the first of these facts; any reading at all on the original case system shows the second; Frank ignores both. There was indeed a world-remoteness which afflicted our law teaching along with and in the wake of "the" case system's victory. But it had different causes, and I prefer my survey on the causal sequences to either Frank's or McWhinney's more recent job. See The Place of Skills in Legal Education, 1944 Report of Committee on Curriculum, Association of American Law Schools, 45 Columb. L. Rev. 345 (1945). There was also in Langdell's theory of contracts a disregard of the facts of life which I have cartooned with a touch of malice earlier herein (at pp. 38 f.). But that is nothing peculiar to Langdell. He felt the drive for order earlier than most, and did a cleaner job than almost any, and over an area singularly wide. This meant of necessity doctrine stripped rather clean of fact — which would have meant particularity. That made Langdell a prophet of the Formal Style and of its era; but what is there of the neurotic in an effort to bring order into the chaotic law and wildly turbulent economy of our later nineteenth century?

325 See especially the various forthcoming studies from the University of Chicago Law School Project on the Rule of Law in Commercial Groups. Also Testimony of Soia Mentschikoff on the Uniform Commercial Code, 2 New York Law Revision Commission, Report and Hearings on the U.C.C. (1955), especially 1391 ff.

326 Such a development is a possibility only. Thus in England, even though balanced form-contracts have been frequent in the courts because of the practice of appeal from the arbitration tribunals of the trades, the courts have been very slow to develop the two different conscious manners of construction which are required for health.

327 From my review in 52 Harv. L. Rev. 700, 702-703 (1939), of Prausnitz, The Standardization of Commercial Contracts in English and Continental Law (1937).

328 The Standardizing of Contracts, 27 Yale L.J. 34 (1917).

329 Modern French Legal Philosophy (1921), in Continental Legal Philosophy Series.

330 Opposition of the Law to Business Usages, 26 Columb. L. Rev. 917 (1926).

331 Economic Duress and the Fair Exchange in French and German Law, 11 Tulane L. Rev. 345 (1937), 12 ibid. 42.

332 The Standardization of Commercial Contracts in English and Continental Law (1937).

333 52 Harv. L. Rev. 700-705 (1939).

334 Symptomatic and characteristic, from two strikingly different sources: the "fair" model apartment-lease form prepared in New York in the '30's by a committee of the Association of the Bar and the attention given the problem in Kessler and Sharp, Contracts: Cases and Materials (1953).

335 Review of Prausnitz, cited above, note 327, at 704.

336 Moran v. Standard Oil Co., 211 N.Y. 187, 105 N.E. 217 (1914), opened the ball, reading in a promise to employ for five years to balance the agent's promise to work. Wood v. Duff-Gordon, 222 N.Y. 88, 118 N.E. 214 (1917), applied the same method to what appears to have otherwise been a fair contract, in favor of the contract-drafter, who had left out his own promise — which he then later needed, to serve as consideration. The first agreement was tailor-made, the second may have been. But the approach is perfect for the handling of one phase of boiler-plate.

337 See especially his pages 53 ff.

338 The one case in a thousand where the dirty clauses have been read and truly agreed to can, for my money, be discarded both as *de minimis* and to keep that issue from disturbing all the litigation to which it is in fact irrelevant. The common law technique, when the facts run so profusely in a single direction, would be a simple "conclusive presumption" — that boiler-plate has *not* been read.

339 Discussed above, page 107.

340 Driscoll's alternatives are reproduced in Appendix C, together with a note by John A. Spanogle, Jr., on alternate official rationales current in the Federal courts.

341 This has now appeared as The Courts and Lawmaking, in Legal Institutions Today and Tomorrow 1 (Paulsen, ed. 1959). No lawyer concerned with statutes can afford to miss it.

342 Remarks on the Theory of Appellate Decision, etc., 3 Vanderbilt L. Rev. 395, 399-401 (1950).

343 Discussed above, pages 97 ff.

344 See Appendix C. I feel reasonably certain that a week's work could turn up as varied an exhibit as our Selection of Available Impeccable Precedent Techniques, above at pages 77 ff.

345 Address on the Current Recapture of the Grand Tradition, to the Conference of Chief Justices, Miami Beach, Florida, August 18-22, 1959. 9 U. Chi. Law School Record, 6 (1960).

346 The Juice in the Orthodox Ideology, page 184 ff.; and cf. pages 21 ff.

347 I have mourned for thirty years a failure to save an advance sheet where one opinion closed with a sole citation: "This is the manifest intention of the Legislature. Uniform Sales Act, Secs. 1-76."

348 Above, page 101.

349 Above, pages 103, 287. — Compare in regard to a statute page 212, note 205a.

349a Compare, along with any good text on, for example, Estate Planning, the base lines discussed in my The Modern Approach to Counselling and Advocacy, 46 Columb. L. Rev. 167, especially 167-178 (1946); and compare especially Pantzer's Materials, in use at the University of Indiana Law School.

350 Brookings Institution, Essays on Research in the Social Sciences, Legal Tradition and Social Science Method 89, 117-119 (1931). There is in that same paper, at pages 106 ff., some text and a footnote about judicial method which ought to brick-redden faces of various critics of "Neo-Realism," especially such as used to abuse Bramble Bush without bothering to read it.

351 The initial papers submitted to the Chief Justices are all found in 8 U. Chi. L.S. Record, Special Supp. (Autumn, 1958). Revised versions have been published: Cramton, The Supreme Court and State Power to Deal with Subversion and Loyalty, 43 Minn. L. Rev. 1025 (1959); Kurland, The Supreme Court, the Due Process Clause and in Personam Jurisdiction of State Courts from Pennoyer to Denckla: A Review, 25 U. Chi. L. Rev. 569 (1958); Meltzer, The Supreme Court, Congress, and State Jurisdiction over Labor Relations, 59 Columb. L. Rev. 6, 269 (1959); Allen, The Supreme Court, Federalism, and State Systems of Criminal Justice, 8 De Paul L. Rev. 213 (1959).

352 Though, as I have indicated elsewhere, I think the Court pressed there on too broad an initial front. What Law Cannot Do for Inter-Racial Peace, 3 Villanova L. Rev. 30 (1957).

353 Wechsler, Toward Neutral Principles of Constitutional Law, 73 Harv. L. Rev. 1, e.g., 20 ff. (1959). On the Per Curiam problem generally, see Sieving the Cases, above at page 312, especially at end.

354 Griswold, Morrison Lecture, 43 Mass. L.Q. 97 (Oct. 1958).

355 On how private the crusade is I have formed my opinion on the say-so of various expert observers plus my own judgment on the ways of a bench. — Since the foregoing was galley-proofed, I have met Arnold, Professor Hart's Theology, 73 Harv. L. Rev. 1298 (1960). Arnold points to Douglas' opinion in Harris v. Pennsylvania R.R., 361 U.S. 15, 17

(1959), stating that in 10 years only 12 FELA cases have been fully dealt with, and only 32 certiorari's granted in such cases. On Douglas' facts, my text is unjustified, and calls for apology (though I conceive three certiorari's a year to be too many); for I wholly go with Douglas and Arnold (as against some of Frank's suggestions) that an *occasional* review and statement of a rule can have real effect on trial courts and trials.

356 Griswold, Morrison Lecture, 43 Mass. L.Q. 97 (Oct. 1958); Freund, The Supreme Court Crisis, 31 N.Y.S.B. Bull. 66 (1959).

356a Compare the thoughtful suggestions of Kenneth Davis in the Preface to his Administrative Law Treatise, v (1958):

"... [O]ne chapter after another of this treatise, each on a separate subject, seems to provide solid support for five constructive suggestions: (1) The Court probably should write fewer general essays in its opinions and it should give more meticulous care to the ones it does write. (2) The Court should take greater advantage of the values of case-to-case development of law. (3) The Court should make further effort to reduce the frequency of contradictory holdings, and it should check its apparently growing tendency to indulge in easy generalizations that are misleading if read literally. (4) The Court should have greater respect for its own holdings and for its own opinions; without restricting its freedom to overrule, it should restrict its freedom to violate its own doctrine. (5) The Court should inquire whether it is often too light-hearted about the manipulation of technical doctrine in order to produce desired substantive results in particular cases."

356b For an illustration, see Freund, Toward Understanding the Supreme Court, c. 3 (1949).

357 See page 387 above, note 351.

358 See page 197 above, note 194.

359 E.g., pages 343 ff. above.

360 Pages 217 ff. above.

361 This does not of course mean that reanalysis and reformulation of criteria may not sometimes turn up a rather solid predictability — as in regard to "notice" and bona fide purchase since the N.I.L., or, indeed, in Sales.

362 From 1951 printing (Oceana Ed.), pages 124-126.

363 Ballade of the Oracle's Priests' Miracle, 1 Nat. Lawyers Guild Q. 30 (1937).

364 Pound, Fifty Years of Jurisprudence, 51 Harv. L. Rev. 777, 794 (1938), thought the Ballade could only be called a violent outburst to the contrary of the idea of a systematic legal order and rational judicial process, and of any desire only to understand and improve. Compare also White, "defending" the judges against me: Whistle Up a Complex, Judge, 2 Nat. Lawyers Guild Q. 17 (1939).

PART II

The Style of Reason at Work

IT IS SO HARD TO SAY

It is hard to take things which are unconventional or otherwise unfamiliar to the addressee and to get them said so that they come through as intended. We all know this. Within the home, or with a friend, we approach a delicate problem of communication alert to "baby it in," to avoid triggering some known or suspected response which will make our words suddenly appear to say what they not only do not want to say, but simply do not say at all. I say we all know this, and we all try to canvass and prepare, to choose words well and to arrange them better, so that they may become true messengers.

But on a job like the one in hand, things happen which scare me. Part I, Deciding Appeals, was being finished, and its subject matter, with some of the preliminary studies, had made up maybe half of the quarter's work of my Jurisprudence class, when one student, moderately sympathetic, reasonably industrious, and quite reasonably able, turned in a report. He had taken Pennsylvania for his comparative period-style reading, and had met Gibson no longer merely by reputation, but firsthand. He was impressed; who isn't? Then came the snapper: "These cases indicate that at least in Pennsylvania there is something to Llewellyn's thesis about an early style. *Gibson C.J. decided as he wanted to, whether the precedents were in his way or not.*" (My italics.)

Now I have tried hard here — as I had in class — *not* to say that I admire as our Grand or classic Style of Reason any way of deciding that leaves even a Gibson or a Marshall free to decide "as he wants to." What I see around me, at work, and what I take pride in, is a way of deciding in which the materials and structure of doctrine (case law and statute, each) contain, as part of themselves, along with words of command to courts, elements of reason and of purpose which vest in the appellate courts power and duty, within the flexible leeways, not only to work toward wisdom with the materials, but, again within flexible leeways, to reword the materials themselves into wiser and better tools for tomorrow's judging and better guides for tomorrow's counselor {402} and law-consumer. In the execution of this duty I have tried to make clear that three properly controlling factors tower each alone, and geometrically in their product, above the will or individual urges even of a Gibson or a Mansfield — than whom I know no more powerful or restive stallions of the law. Those three factors: (bridle, breaking to harness, and guiding hand on the reins) — are the doctrinal structure, the craftsmanship of the law and of the office, and the immanent rightnesses, largely to be felt and found, which are embodied in the significant type of situation up for judging. These three handle man and court; they set man and court free by turning them, in first instance, into officers and voices.

It is my position that in the Grand Style of Reason which dominated our appellate deciding a century back and which we have for twenty and more years been ever closer to recapturing, the juice lies first of all in the application of reason and sense to spotting the significant type-situation and diagnosing the sound and fair answer to the type-problem. This leads to *rules* of law, not to mere just or right *decisions,* much less to decisions merely according to any personal equities in individual cases. But it leads toward *good* rules of law and in the main toward flexible ones, so that most cases of a given type can come to be

289

handled not only well but easily, and so that the odd case can normally come in also for a smidgeon of relief. The whole setup leads above all — a recognition of imperfection in language and in officer — to *on-going and unceasing judicial review of prior judicial decision* on the side of rule, tool, and technique. That, plus freedom and duty to do justice *with* the rules but *within* both them and their whole temper, that is the freedom, the leeway for own-contribution, the scope for the person, which the system offers.

No such short phrasing can be accurate in detail; but at least the argument for the inevitability (like it or not) and the duty (like it or not) of *constant* choice and of *constant* change in the authoritative doctrine can by some such phrasing be set into perspective.

I add three final points:

First: The necessity and duty of constant creative choice demands open accounting to the authorities, to the situation, and to reason; with an eye always on the basic need for wiser and for clearer guidance for tomorrow.

Second: A conscious recognition of the foregoing and a conscious effort to mobilize the best tested resources can very materially {403} step up marksmanship and reduce off-target shots. Insight and inspiration flourish best in the black earth of schooled craftsmanship. The great stroke, the fortunate stroke, that can clarify a whole area, is most likely when the years of neat smaller jobs have gone before.

Third: There are no panaceas.

* * *

With these things as background and as theme, I should like now to wander with you for a bit in a more leisurely fashion than the packed problems of Deciding Appeals permitted, and smoke a pipe or two among some phases of our Style of Reason at Work.

MANSFIELD'S METHODS, REASON INTO
SAND, AND REASON RESURGENT

Two examples from Mansfield will make clear, especially along with certain virtues of the style of life-reason, first, the degree to which those virtues call for consistent use by the bench as a whole craft, over the years, if the gains are to be accumulated or consolidated by the less-than-Mansfields; second, the problem of blur even in the writings of the great, and the way in which reclarification depends then upon successors; third, the way in which vexation can flourish when the reason of a situation fades, or sinks beneath the surface of the channel; fourth, the stubbornness with which a good reason can run underground for decades, and yet manage, in whole or in part, in health or in mutilation, to re-emerge and bring life.

Due Diligence Against the Drawer

Let me take him first in *Heylyn v. Adamson.*[1] That case was an action by an indorsee against an indorser, after dishonor by the acceptor of an inland bill of exchange, due diligence having been used as against the defendant indorser. The precise issue was whether the indorsee was required also to show notice to and demand on the drawer of the bill. It was held, no. The holding is still law. But the richer meaning of the opinion does not lie in the holding. It lies in the general manner of explicit attack on the problem, and it lies especially in certain recurrent phrasings of the reason of the general situation which were early allowed to drop from attention.

Mansfield was faced — as appellate courts so often are — with a body of prior cases whose language was muddy, though each of them seems to have been soundly decided. He therefore goes after the situation as a whole. What is the essential position of an indorser? An indorser is — as against his indorsee — a "new {405} drawer." Mansfield shows the inconvenience if one should require a mere indorsee to locate that original drawer with whom he has not dealt; he carries over this rationale as Holt had laid it down for foreign bills. Then: "Every inconvenience here suggested holds to a great degree, and every other argument holds equally, in the case of inland bills of exchange." (2 Burr, at 676.) He proceeds to take up certain confused language from the prior cases on promissory notes; he spots the confusion as resting on the use of the word "drawer" to describe the man who makes a note as well as the man who draws a bill; he shows the note to correspond to the three-party bill of exchange only when the note comes to be indorsed. "But *the same law must be applied to the same reason;* to the *substantial resemblance* between promissory notes, and bills of exchange; *and not to the same sound,* which is equally used to describe the makers of both." (ibid. 677; my italics.)

Now one would have hoped that such an exposition and clarification of the whole situation, with the rationale of decision explicitly extended beyond the immediate issue so as to require due diligence against the indorser of a note, too — one would have hoped that this might lead not only to careful noting of such wider range of the rationale (as did happen), but that it might lead to no less careful noting of what Mansfield had had to say, as a further portion of the same rationale, about the *consequences* when there was default in the "required" diligence. What was said about that was technically dictum, but it was also inherently a part of the *reason of the situation,* both as Mansfield laid out that reason, *and* as it makes commercial sense.

Quoting Holt, once, and three further several times in his own language, discharge for lack of due diligence is made to depend not upon absence of due diligence alone, but no less upon an interesting additional condition: "if the acceptor . . . happens to break"; "and the drawee becomes insolvent . . ."; "if . . . the maker becomes insolvent . . ."

The opinion is in the ripe perfection of the Grand Manner, when the court is conscious of clean grasp of the full situation. But the subsequent history is not. Mansfield himself hit the matter again in *Blesard v. Hirst.*[2] "This is an inland bill made payable to one man, and indorsed by him to a third man. This third man tenders it for acceptance and it is refused. He keeps it for three weeks without giving any notice of such refusal to {406} accept. [On the nineteenth day, the drawee then ceased to be "in credit."] He ought to have given notice of this refusal, and not to have concealed it; and *by not giving notice, he has taken the risk upon himself.* [My italics; now watch the blur: the shift from "taken the risk" to "*must* suffer."] The indorser of the bill is imposed upon. The person who neglected to give the notice *must suffer for it.*" (5 Burr, at 2671-2672.) Willes and Ashhurst concurred. "They held that the holder of a bill *ought to suffer for having neglected to give notice. . . .*" (ibid. 2672; all italics mine.)

Here is the adder's egg, waiting to hatch. It is plain that the junior judges have no feeling for the immanent condition needed to determine whether the "risk" becomes a loss: if the drawee becomes insolvent. The general picture in Mansfield's mind — which no case forced into detailed drawing — is that of effects left by a drawer in his drawee's hands, over a course of dealing, in justified reliance on bills being honored when drawn. Notice of dishonor is a needed warning to go about inquiry and salvage, before insolvency can make the latter hopeless. But unless the "risk" actually becomes a loss the discharge *by operation of law* is — if you understand the situation — a brutal penalty inflicted for a harmless neglect. Mansfield does understand it, his language shows it, and "ought to suffer" is used in the context of the case: the loss has there become actual. Ashhurst does not understand at all. When he picks up "suffer" (with no modifying qualifier) he means *suffer.* He "added that it was understood (upon inquiry) to be the practice of merchants, as well as agreeable to the reason of the thing, that notice should be given." (ibid.) Thus, then: an earnest judge, seeking light, but without the background to take in the meaning of what is shown him. We have met the problem before.[3] If Mansfield had been on his toes, he would have noticed, spoken again, and touched up the "risk" aspect in scarlet. But Mansfield was assuming that the obvious was obvious, and both using language and hearing it against that assumption. When wise men do this, they find themselves misunderstood; and their teachings, bereft of implicit delicacy, reason, and balance, are twisted or coarsened into unintended, venerated forgeries. For philosopher or teacher the choice is hard: to reiterate the obvious is to drive away those really worth-while listeners to whom it is already obvious; to leave it unstressed is to mislead all but the elect. But the choice {407} is not hard for counsel or for court. Each of them can learn from Mansfield's inattention here. Each of them needs to make sure that any implicit life-reason shall stand forth and be recognized.

Our instance is peculiarly instructive because the life-reason proved so hardy. Supervening insolvency of the party primarily expected to pay as an important, nay necessary, further precondition to discharge — that did indeed proceed at once to get completely lost. By 1800, Lord Kenyon at Nisi Prius is flatly refusing evidence to show that failure of notice caused no prejudice.[4] In these United States, during the very period of the Style of Reason during which one might have hoped the contrary, and despite Chitty's neat discussion in 1807,[5] despite, finally, a refusal by Cowen himself in 1837 to allow discharge of an indorser who was shown to have suffered no loss by the nonpresentment,[6] "due diligence" crystallizes into a wooden essential, regardless of consequence[7] — which shows, I hope, first, that a style is not necessarily a universal, merely because it is prevalent; and second, that no "style" can ever lift off any court's shoulders its unceasing job of being awake and at work in recanvass of underlying reasons as well as of overlying rules. Courts nodded, and "due diligence, or else discharge" became a *formal, external* rule; its reason lost; its reason no longer interesting, its reason no longer inquired into, its reason, if inquired into, denied. Such is the state of the Negotiable Instruments Law today,[8] and of American thinking on the subject.[9]

But the reason did not die, simply because it had been lost. A reason with right roots is hard to kill. There is fascination in the discomfort, perplexity, complexity, which ensued on the loss of this one. Manifestly the rule as we have it is not right, and it never has been; and when the drawer or indorser has in honest fact received his full value for the bill, and is then discharged for a slip in "diligence" which has hurt him not one whit, the rule feels wrong, indeed. Many businessmen so feel it wrong, and say, then, that of course they will make good, anyhow; courts feel it wrong, and seize on such a businessman's statement, even {408} though he may have later changed his mind, so that "waiver" acquires a peculiar extension: a drawer or indorser, notwithstanding that he has been utterly discharged, can yet reacquire his obligation in full, with no slightest new consideration.[10] A double "anomaly" was thus built during the later nineteenth century, to semicure the earlier nineteenth-century blob: an "anomaly" first, in the creation of contractual obligation without consideration; and a true anomaly, in allowing suit "on a negotiable instrument" based on expressions, even oral expressions, not found on the paper, not found even in the transactions of creation and transfer — thus, a *jury* gamble catapulted into the very citadel of *commercial* "certainty."[11] Such a semicure is not, of course, a full cure: something amounting to a "waiver" is needed, before the cure can take hold. On the other hand, the semicure sometimes goes too far: if there *has* been supervening insolvency of the expected "primary" party, it is the holder should stand the actual loss; so that the semicure is not limited, in its turn, to *its* reason.[12]

Nor is that all. For when American deposit banking began, and the essential situation which had been in Mansfield's mind faced our courts again in this new institution, with checks displacing notes as payment instruments, then Mansfield's lost reason struggled partly out of hibernation (the "effects" left in the hands of the drawee deposit banker are peculiarly salvageable: they are demand deposits). It was hard to miss; so the drawer of a check was discharged for delay in presentment "only to the extent of his loss"; only, therefore, if the drawee bank "happens to break," and only to the degree of the breakage. This was fresh building, and it was good building, so far as it went. But it got built for the new and special situation alone; it neither extended over to the other types of instrument, nor did it fully capitalize the prior recorded insight, and work even its own self into clean functional form, so as, for instance, to cover explicitly delay of notice in the same way as delay in presentment. And it left on the wrong party both the burden of establishing the extent of the loss and the burden of waiting for that extent to become clear as the insolvent bank was wound up. It would be {409} much handier to let the drawer turn over to the holder all the drawer's right to the effects, leaving on the faulty holder, then, the trouble and delay incident to discovering what the "extent of the loss" may prove to be.[13] But this new rule-building was not done by a Mansfield, nor did it cumulate upon his doing, nor upon Chitty. Instead, as an *ad hoc* creation limited to checks, *it* became yet another "anomaly," yet again complicating the rules of law.[14] And when a note made payable at a bank is then made to constitute an order to pay, or when, later, deposit insurance appears on the scene, we find further rich, ripe fields of uncertainty and litigation.[15] All because, in the reading and use of an opinion built transcendently in the Style of Reason, the Style of Reason, and so the reason, had come themselves to be overlooked.

Do I mean by this instance that I want mere Dictum — the dicta of *Heylyn v. Adamson* range far — or sweeping Rationale, to be made Authority, and so to blast out every safety-gate built by our techniques of doctrine? I trow not. What I mean is that I want the reason of a situation, when that reason has been made explicit, to be looked over carefully — this though it be dictum unalloyed — for whatever light it may have to offer, later; and if on such looking over it proves to offer light, then I want that light used as present-day appellate courts show in their current work that they know how to use it, and so often think it good to use. Use it as "Authority" which just controls? Never. Use it as illumination, adopt it as a guide if it seems wise and helpful? Yes, and always. That procedure leaves no safety-gate unguarded. Nor does it hurt to capitalize that other feature of our system, the signed opinion, which lets us know from what lips the dictum has fallen. A wise man can be wrong; still, it pays to ponder a bit before you so decide.

Meantime, and as against such approaches as Wambaugh's contrasts of "imperative," "persuasive," and "quasi-" authority,[16] or the mildly disgusting modern English efforts to live in intellectual decency with the Impossible Dogma of Infallibility of Each Highest Court, Mentschikoff's operational approach is outdoors and healthy: "What they cannot take away from you, without plain overruling, is the clean holding on the narrow issue. Anything else, everything else, is a matter of their judgment, and of {410} your persuasion. But you need a solid reason even for your bedrock." Surely what we have examined in modern American case law leaves us wondering, even where "It is well settled," whether if the well-settled had seemed strikingly to be unwise for All-of-Us, the court might not have made it a springboard for distinction, or for a more than ordinary scrutiny of These Facts — or for a rephrasing that would move the rule inches or feet over into needed territory.

Let me, on this, ask a question appropriate only to an addressee who has really worked through the text and the Appendix A samplings of current supreme court work, or through their equivalents: How often is the "well-settled" basis appealed to, *today*, when the court has found that answer to be actively unjust?

Again, a point made above, how curiously often, when the court does talk thus these days, does it rest on a recent and careful reexamination of this so simply "settled" rule!

CURRENT COURSE OF TRADE, AND SWIFT V. TYSON

Miller v. Race, another famous opinion from the same man and date,[17] is not less clear in its reason, and is even more unhappy in its sequel. Again the trouble is that a clean phrasing of the life-reason of the situation, though it recurred, was still not so focused as to become the unmistakable nub, unmistakable even to the ignorant. But this time the trouble comes not from ignoring one consequence of an implicit basic reason, but by disregard of the basic reason itself. This time, too, the issue remains in doubt for half a century, as the reason keeps struggling up. This time the final skewing of the matter is due not to an accidental error of an Ashhurst, but to High Policy on a Broad National Matter, as manipulated by a certain Joseph Story.[18]

The action in *Miller* was trover to recover the value of a bearer bank note from a taker "for a full and valuable consideration, and in the usual course and way of his business, and without any notice or knowledge" that it had been stolen before it came to him. The opinion recurs over and over to "the general course of business," "the ordinary course and transaction of business," under which bank notes are treated as money. "It cannot be recovered after it has passed in currency." Holt is quoted that {411} this is "by reason of the course of trade; which creates a property in the assignee or bearer." "Here, an inn-keeper took it, bona fide, in his business, from a person who made the appearance of a gentleman."

Taking "in the usual course of business" or "in the course of currency, and in the way of his business" (the rationale repeated by Mansfield *upwards of eight times in the one opinion),* is, however, (1) coupled *once* with "for a full and valuable consideration"; and (2) *once* the phrase "for valuable consideration" appears in a clause of its own, with "passed in currency" separated by a colon; and (3) *once,* even (thus three times in all) "for valuable consideration" appears in a sentence by itself, and at the end of a paragraph, and the explanatory following paragraph mentions only twice the taking "in the course of currency."

There can be no question which is the dominant aspect, to Mansfield, of the taking. Indeed a quarter century later, in *Peacock v. Rhodes,*[19] a case of a stolen blank indorsed bill of exchange, the real rationale appears twice as the *sole* rationale, clean-drawn and free of blur: "coming fairly by a bill or note"; "it was received in the course of trade; and, therefore, the case is clear." I do not see this as any effort to forestall or correct misreading of the prior case; it is simply that, second time over, the Master's pencil draws the line with simple sharpness.

But in *Miller v. Race,* the first and "leading" case, Mansfield had nowhere explicitly said that "in current course of business" must commonly *involve* not only bona fides but a normal quantum of value given, though these were to be sure but incidents or marks, not the essential. And there is high probability that "taking in currency," since that phrasing was being applied to a bank note, may have carried to later readers a flavor of taking "*as* currency," rather than of taking "in the current course." There is, moreover, one passage which shows signs of having misled the unwary by sad gratuitous negative inference:

> But Ld. Ch. J. Holt could never say "that an action would lie against the person who, for a valuable consideration, had received a banknote which had been stolen, or lost, and bona fide paid to him:" even though the action was brought by the true owner: because he had determined otherwise, two years before: and because bank notes are not like lottery-tickets, but money.

That, may I insist, is what Holt had been accused of saying, but what Holt "could *never*" have said. But I do suspect that phrasing {412} to have contributed to deflecting emphasis. It is certain that Burrow's headnote mentions nothing of the "course of trade" or "currency" ("paid" is his only word), and that his note to one Holt case, which itself rests explicitly upon the "course of trade," reads that "the case turned upon his having gotten it for a valuable consideration." And Bayley's purblind little volume, in 1789, three times gives the formula "take bona fide, and give a valuable consideration for it."[20] All of this may have been aided by the fact that losing counsel in the original case had said much of the course of trade, while winning counsel's first point was phrased in terms of valuable consideration.

Chitty, writing in 1807, remains ambiguous, with the Mansfield idea barely dominant. On page 124 of his *Bills of Exchange,* he speaks of a lost or stolen bill or check, transferable by mere delivery, getting "into the hands of a person who was not aware of the loss, for a good consideration, previously to its being due." But on page 113 the matter of transfer after a bill is due is put on its being "out of the common course of dealing"; and on page 118 the lost bill is spoken of as "getting into the hands of a *bona fide* holder"; while on page 122 the "assignee" who acquires "all the rights, privileges and advantages that can in any case be acquired under it" is one who takes "fairly and bona fide."

And Kent was not misled. The famous case of *Bay v. Coddington,*[21] as decided by him, has no bearing on "value" as the vital factor, at all. Rather does Kent hit the "course of trade" as his main reason (again eight times or more!) and finds a transfer, on the known eve of bankruptcy, of a note which did not belong to the impending bankrupt, to be clean out of that *course of trade* which is the reason of any commercial bona fide purchase doctrine. Marcy, in the senatorial Court of Errors and Appeals, does draw the "antecedent value" issue; but there were other views expressed, as well, aplenty.[22] Thus, although Kent failed to get completely clarified, for others, what Mansfield had left slightly blurred, at least we have one major master of equity who managed to see and deal with commercial bona fide purchase in terms of the commercial reason which informs it, and who was not sidetracked by "the same sound" to apply to it doctrines developed in chancery to deal with noncommercial trusts in land; nor yet to let the issue of "value" in land cases draw his eye off the commercial issues in a commercial cause. {413}

A series of New York cases from 1858 to 1840 worsens doctrinal confusion. In 1838, McCoun, V.C., holds a misappropriated note recoverable from one who has by express agreement forborne on the basis of it, and who has also given up a third party's note on receiving this new "collateral security" for an antecedent debt.[23] His rationale does run in terms of receiving "in the course of trade or business for valuable consideration"; but the weight of his stress lies on the "value" aspect. His conception that giving up the third party's note does not make out "value" (at least to the extent of that note) is ludicrous. But his feel for the case is sound: a transaction more flagrantly out of current course could hardly be conceived; the misappropriator was being *pressed to make good a check which he had given in payment of a current purchase,* but which had bounced. This parallels the squeeze which Kent refused to hallow as giving the blackjacker more than the blackjacked had to give.

In 1839, Nelson, C. J., protects a banker who has discounted and credited the avails of a misappropriated note and then charged against the account two overdue notes (one of them with a sound indorser) which were lying at the bank and apparently held by it.[24] The reasoning again runs partly in terms of parting with value; but what makes the case is the "usage of the bank" in handling a running account with persons of extensive dealings, and at a distance. That usage ran to discounting notes as received, and to paying off notes in hand whenever the balance permitted. Under modern conditions of communication, it would be loose usage; but I think Nelson right in feeling it to be a sound enough current course, as of the time. Nelson on another occasion holds the taking of a note, without recourse, in satisfaction of a debt, to protect the taker "receiving it for value within mercantile usage."[25] Bronson holds similarly, in 1840, with regard to a usurious note improperly transferred by a "broker" without indorsement, the avails of the plaintiff bank's discount thereof going to pay the broker's own debt to the bank; but Bronson's issue is: "whether they paid a valuable consideration."[26]

Be it noted that at this point "the current course of trade" feeling, and even idea, is far from lost. Kent's "known impending bankruptcy" case had been out of that current course, and so {414} had McCoun's case; and in neither was the taker protected. Two of the three Nelson and Bronson decisions which protect the taker are cleanly within the current course, as that course stood in that day. Taking notes of third parties in "payment" of a debt still was or ran close to the lines of standard practice. Indeed, since the last case has to do with a "broker" whose business was not placing paper for a principal, but was instead discounting and selling, the indorsement "without recourse" fits into a course of trade which remained current at least for another hundred years. So long as the *feel* of the situation can be thus kept live, there remains hope of surviving the mistwist which has been corrupting the language. And the express reasoning of each "application" was still displaying and keeping live a real portion of that feel. E.g., even from Bronson: "It is the same thing, substantially, as though Ward had first received the money, and then paid it over to the plaintiffs." The plaintiffs were bankers, and the observation is true. Bronson goes on, however: ". . . or, indeed to any other creditor." That becomes dubious.

Into this marches a case whose marks are still on the law: Story's *Swift v. Tyson*.[27] It was a case of an acceptance procured by fraud, and taken then by the plaintiff in "payment" of a prior 'debt due from the transferor-indorser. The exact transaction (which did not interest Story) was in modern terms a renewal by substitution, and with the surrender of the old paper rights against an indorser thereon had been foregone. On the facts, this makes a real case for the holder. It is regular, especially as of the day; and it is real.

Story has been so kicked around for some of his work in that case that one feels hesitance about jumping on a man when he is not only dead but down. Yet there are things that do need saying about the bills and notes side of the opinion. First, Story sets the rule up as one of "bona fide purchase for value" — like that — so well established that "*it requires no reasoning* to be brought in its support." (16 Peters at 15-16; my italics.) This is Story's overextension of a search for purely verbal order, done at the shallowest level. For Mansfield knew his bills and notes; and if he did, then this new formulation of the question by Story called for very considerable reasoning in its support. Second, Story poses the issue in full overbreadth (and that is a normal and evil outgrowth of any man's accepting any rule for development as such, without re-examination of its reason). "Does a pre-existing {415} debt constitute a valuable consideration?" That is Story's posing of the issue. That posing gathers into one catchall basket any kind at all of "payment" of such a debt, together with any way at all of giving security therefor, both utterly irrespective of that commercial course or circumstance which is the sole warrant in wisdom for ever giving any taker more than his transferor had, or for departing from the equity views on "value." "*The opposite conclusion*" becomes then in Story's dialectic consequence: "that negotiable paper *cannot* be applied *in payment* of *or* as security for pre-existing debts." (ibid. 20; my italics.) To knock out this whole overswollen negative "opposite" conclusion, it will of course seem necessary only to knock out any weakest part. You set up the false issue as broad and high as a barn door, and shoot at it from three feet away. Story rests on the need for recognizing and protecting renewals and substitutions — which of course do not touch the difficult questions of security, nor yet do they touch Kent's problem of clubbing "payment" out of tomorrow's bankrupt, nor McCoun's of hammering to have a bad check cured. Here, then, Story "gives reason," with a flip of the hand. It is also bad reason, and it shows its badness on its face. Without extending the discussion, one may further note that the use he makes of the English cases pays no attention to the English financial practices (e.g., of arranged overdrafts in current account) on which those cases rested.

Catron's partial dissent has been little noted. We need to note it. It demonstrates that the commercial reason of the situation was still live, still explicit, in our legal tradition of the time and at the place. It strongly suggests that the sudden wine of carrying the court into a great new field of Federal action had gone more than a bit to Story's head. Catron strongly disapproves this pronouncement, "*aside from the case made by the record or argued by counsel,* assuming to maintain that a negotiable note or bill, pledged as collateral security for a previous debt, is taken by the creditor *in the due course of trade.*" "*I never heard this question spoken of as belonging to the case, until the principal opinion was presented* LAST EVENING." (ibid. 23; my emphasis.)

Now a style of work is a thing of value, and a good style is a pearl of price; but a style can bear only the load which can be lifted by a style. Not even an ingrained style of reason can hold judgment level when hot jurisdictional conflict, pride of office, and clash of personality come to shape an issue for which the particular point of law becomes merely a symbol and occasion. Story and the Court, on "general commercial jurisprudence," {416} chose to challenge New York, the proudly new commercial center, with a new Federal doctrine (and with that, certainly as of 1840, I have no personal quarrel). But Story chose also to rest his challenge on the quicksand of a "principle" at once horrendous as law, unnecessary to the case, and badly argued. That was bad judging. And it was lawyering so bad that a right lawyer would have mourned it through sleepless nights. It made no atmosphere to produce a thoughtful clarification. It made no atmosphere, and it laid no foundation, to produce persuasion and success in what had been an enlightened and statesmanlike ambition: to wit, to produce one dominant forum to unify the commercial doctrine of the growing, legally sprawling, Nation; to do a Marshall in commercial law.[28]

Meanwhile, where doctrine shows a crack, counsel will be at it with a crowbar. Counsel attempted to carry Story's rule and the new Federal Authority into the New York Court of Errors.[29] The results were happy neither for counsel nor for us. Impatience and wrath speak from the opinion of the Chancellor. Walworth flatly, unnecessarily, almost with exaltation, joins on the full issue, as already overdrawn by Story, draws it still more broadly, and then smacks down Story's view, inside New York, on the absolute whole of it. All the case involved was transfer of a misappropriated note, by a factoring house, a transfer only as security for an old note which the factoring house had persuaded the holder to withdraw from the bank, lest it go openly to protest. Nothing could be less current in its course. Nor was any ruling on "payment" required; no evisceration was required of the recent still salvageable New York cases above. But while Walworth was at it, he took the full fateful step: "This principle, of protecting the *bona fide* holder of negotiable paper who has paid value for it, or who has relinquished some available security or valuable right on the credit thereof, *is derived from the doctrines of the courts of equity in other cases* where a purchaser has obtained {417} the legal title without notice of the equitable right of a third person to the property." (My italics.)

The passion of the conflict thus drowned out all sense on *both* sides; the false issue had crystallized.[30]

Indeed, the fate of this opinion of Story's seems to be to stir heat that burns and blacks. A hundred years later, in *Erie v. Tompkins*,[31] it has not been enough to whittle off the excrescences engrafted later on Story's attempted *commercial* doctrine; in the very period when the commerce power was being otherwise restored,[32] *Swift*, despite its contribution to commercial law *possibilities,* is exhumed, convicted of Constitutional heresy, and has its moldering bones burnt at the stake. Nor was that sufficient. The Walworth of a century back had not been content to parry Story's thrust; he had to go further, he had to explore all history to show up nonsense, he had to beat down not the thrust alone, but Story. And Story's successors have seemed now for a generation disposed not only to wipe out a ruling they found "unconstitutional" but to swing on into the building of a worse one in its place. That movement of decision is not even yet clearly reversed, which made a single clear expression, by even "any jackleg judge" of an inferior State court, control the Federal court absolutely, control without regard to the sense of the ruling or to its possible or probable reversal or rejection above.[33] It makes hard understanding how a court itself engaged vigorously, consciously, and conscientiously upon the re-examination of its *own* case law doctrines (as, in *Erie* itself) could (on the basis of that same *Erie*) approach the problem of what the case law *of a State* is as if sound reason and steady search for {418} righter rephrasing of rules to fit such reason could be, or could be made by fiat, a Federal monopoly to be jealously confined to use on such particular Federal questions as do not happen to embrace special and most particular inquiry into *uncertain* areas of State law.[34] One hopes, here, that a certain new application of "the rule of reason" which seems to be at work in silence may go undisturbed. But why the silence?

The effect of the older controversy on the law of commercial bona fide taking has of course been sad. It has been touched on already.[35] Turn the question from the working query "taking in current course" onto a mere formula: "What constitutes 'value'?" — worse: "What *has been held* to constitute 'value'?" leaving out of account the whole *reason* for letting either taking or "value" have any peculiar commercial importance, anyhow, and you degenerate into the type of logomachy whose peak is presented below, in *Whiting v. Hudson Trust Co.,* with Cardozo himself misled into the peddling of nonsense.[36]

Yet the uniformity in verbal rule thus sought could not be achieved. From the Negotiable Instruments Law of 1897 on through the Trust Receipts Act of 1934, the uniform commercial statutes rejected the equity concept of "value"; each, in one way or another, went after some separate "commercial" rule.[37] It is an irony of intellectual history that to escape Walworth's uncommercial rule, men should have taken refuge in Story's — which, under today's financial conditions, is worse than Walworth's, if one has to choose.[38] {419}

As has been noted above, the Negotiable Instruments Law did indeed almost break back into full sense and reason. It invented and created the concept of a "holder *in due course*"; it needed only to fill out the phrase with sap, only to see a due *course* and an *occurrence* within it, instead of an arid status; it needed only to look for a holder "taking" in due course of trade. Given that, and the acceptance of any form of antecedent debt as "value," whenever the taking did happen to be in due course of trade, would have been the obvious, wise choice. But when the draftsmen then listed, in Section 52, the conditions of taking which create the status, they left out that very "in current course of trade" which "holder *in due course,*" if the phrase had been taken seriously, would have required to be added as the governing purpose and essence. "In due course" has consequently lain unnoticed, save as a status-title, ever since.[39]

Meantime, the approach by way of the "sound" has become so familiar that, offhand, most lawyers will find the notions and reasoning of the above discussion to be somewhat freakish, and the policy-judgments expressed to be both idiosyncratic and arbitrary.[40] Indeed, my own effort, successful for a while, to reintroduce {420} the "current course" idea into the Uniform Commercial Code article on commercial paper stirred up a witch hunt almost like that of Brandeis against *Swift v. Tyson.* About all that is left is that receipt of goods in fulfillment of a preexisting contract to deliver is expressly recognized as "ordinary course," and that the "payment" idea is cut down to current course in regard to documents of title. But it is plain that I could not be less convinced of error. In addition to Mansfield (for whose lasting commercial judgment I have learned respect) let me therefore adduce as evidence of the utility of the distinctions and the policy-judgments: first, the Factors Acts of the 1830's (passed before this issue had got itself misdrawn) — those reformatory Acts of documented commercial origin, in which the proper current course of trade is the clean thread through the careful distinctions laid down about transfer in security for debts antecedent and other.[41] And secondly, let me instance the partial recapture, in the Uniform Trust Receipts Act and in the inventory provisions of the Code, of Mansfield's same clean thread of discrimination: current course of trade.[42]

Again, as with *Heylyn v. Adamson,* the story is one of the reason of a situation, guidesome and grasped; but in the case of *Miller v. Race* that reason was not *worded* in unambiguous adequacy. (Phrasing is *also* a major job of juristic craftsmanship.) Again the story is one of needed *further* work, by further courts, throughout the years, along the line marked out, in terms of reason; work this time, and by Kent (there, by Chitty and Cowen), partly performed. Again the story is one of confusion, welter, and error, as soon as the *reason* came to be lost; doubly, when it came no longer to be even looked for, when it came to have substituted for it a *mere* rule, a word-form. Again, when the situation comes to be re-examined for its reason — this time, in the preparation of statutes — the mere rule proves to need remaking, and reveals that, bereft of its reason, it has been causing complexity, {421} uncertainty, injustice, and unnecessary litigation, across the country and across the years.

It does not seem to me too much to suggest that if in either of these lines of doctrine the query had been constant: What is the sense of this rule, in terms of what goes on? Where does the rule stop making sense, so that it should not be applied? Where does it need modification or qualification or reformulation, so as to clarify its proper application — then Mansfield's vision and expression could have been made to profit us, throughout. First in greater justice and wisdom; second, in greater certainty and clarity, for new conditions as for old; third, in greater simplicity of law and of statement, on the matter of indorser's or drawer's discharge. (All of this, as to the drawer's discharge, the Uniform Commercial Code does achieve.) In the matter of purchase in current course of trade, the Walworth and Ames approach sought exactly this greater simplicity of statement, but the category selected was inept. So, first, we suffered under it; and had "conflict" or "confusion." Later, we took on complexity by dividing off "commercial" transactions, but we did that poorly. And, third, we find recorrection for commercial wisdom's sake coming back only stepwise, and spasmodically, with still further interstitial complexity. With "current course of trade" the test throughout the commercial field from the beginning, the simplicity of statement would have equaled that of Ames, but would have added both the de facto guidesomeness and the wisdom which the bald bona fide purchase for value formula was predestined never to achieve*because it did not fit the situation.*

OUR EARLY STYLE OF REASON AGAIN

At the cost of interruption, let me again lodge a caveat here. Some reader may be tempted by these instances in each of which the style of reason, even in its last high period, lost itself in sand, to come to the belief that the high period itself is but a figment of one man's imagination. My samplings may have been unpersuasive. That would be regrettable. The easy test is, of course, as suggested above, to pick up a volume from the period and to read a couple of hundred consecutive pages, beginning anywhere. Several skeptics have tried that; each reports conversion. But those who prefer expert judgment to their own may be referred to Pound,[43] or to Fuller,[44] or even to Nelles.[45] All of {422} these find the work of the period characterized by "Natural Law" thinking, all find it creative, all find it skillful in the building of rules, all find it wholly admirable. To me (and I think to them) the feature which they treat as "Natural Law" thinking has as its essence a conscious and sustained quest for and accounting to the best reason a court can find, and not in any particular assumed "Natural Law" premises or source of premises; still less in any aberrant assumption that an appellate judge should guide himself by his own sole head without careful and conscious responsibility to the going legal heritage of the society around him, and to its reckonable future ordering. It is the practice of careful questing for, and of answering to, reason, as best a judge-in-action knows how, and of doing so consistently, recurrently, and not only in deciding but in working out grounds for tomorrow as well as today, which Pound and Fuller are speaking of as characteristic of the period; that practice is one part of what I am speaking of. It is a technique, plus an attitude; and it is quite independent, I repeat, of any philosophy as to the proper sources of "Right Reason" which may be held by any "Natural Law" philosopher.[46] In our case law scheme of things, this has only rarely been either an armchair technique or an arrogant one, nor does it work comfortably as a subjective one.[47] It answers instead to current {423} life, and it answers to the craft. Meantime, Pound, who was centering his attention on the rules, "the law," of the time, and Fuller, whose interest was in rules and reasoning equally, presupposed as of course the same constant concern of the courts of the time with those rules, the constant responsibility to them, on which my focus on process has forced me to insist.

To me, the creative aspect of the judging of that era is wholly normal to a civilization in movement. The queer thing is that, later, middle in the very age of industrialization, it should have bogged down for a while.[48] To me, the admirable aspect derives therefore not from the times or the circumstances, but rather simply from the nature of case law judges and their office, given an open technique of reason at work on the authorities, and given reasonable consistence and craftsmanship in the use of that technique. To me, that makes out a craftstyle, and a great one. But on the point of fact, apart from evaluation, to wit: Was there such a clearly marked period of the use or style of life-reason? — on that, if it has been observed independently and in differing contexts by Pound and by Nelles and by Fuller and by Llewellyn, with the disposition of those four persons to avoid agreement where honor will permit — that ought to be enough to settle anybody's doubts.[49]

COWEN: HARTFIELD V. ROPER

Yet a right way of attack means not any automatic wisdom of result, but only a much greater likelihood of such wisdom. So with the style of reason. But what that style (in contrast to {424} many good lines of method in many other areas of human effort) offers also, so long as the style maintains itself, is that it brings out and exposes to view, for easy later correction or judicial review, each error of judgment that may have crept in. I choose an instance of what I think to be outdated reason, from another hero of our law in our high period. It may be, indeed, that this craft-style, just as such, can be seen best when the particular product is meanly unwelcome, but when no factor of passion or politics is available to offer seeming explanation. One can then perhaps see that his admiration is not dependent on pleasure at the outcome, but is directed to the pure *manner* of the work. And to Cowen, even when I fight him in result, I bow. As I bow to Scrutton or to Learned Hand.

So the opinion will be that of Cowen in *Hartfield v. Roper* (1839).[50] This is the same Cowen whom we watched in 2 Hill, above,[51] and whom we have come upon as late as 1837 still seeing and ruling soundly in regard to nondischarge of an indorser who was shown to have suffered nothing by the holder's failure of due diligence.[52] He was an amazing judge. In only eight years on the bench he managed to stamp his mark on the law not of New York alone, but of the nation, and this although he never sat as Chief.[53]One puzzle I have not solved is how Pound and Wigmore, both, when canvassing the earlier days for notable judges, have been able to prefer for mention from New York of this day a Bronson, as he sits in the shadow of his so much greater junior. Visit Cowen with me, at home in *Hartfield v. Roper,* and you will not be seduced into that slip of judgment even by the conjoint expressions of our two greatest legal scholars.

The action was case, "by" a two-year-old who had been in a snow path and had been run over by the horses pulling a sleigh, "trotting, but not at great speed." The sleigh, first descending a hill to a bridge, came upon the child a hundred feet or so beyond the bridge.

The tone of the opinion is set by the opening: "The injury to this child was doubtless a very serious misfortune for him. But I have been utterly unable to collect, from the evidence, anything by which the jury were authorized to impute such carelessness as rendered these defendants responsible. It is true, they might have seen the child from the turn of the road in descending, had {425} they looked so far ahead: but something must be allowed for their attention to the management of the horses and their own safety in descending the hill to a bridge."

How far Cowen was disturbed by testimony given (without objection) that one of the defendants was "esteemed to be worth ten thousand dollars," one cannot tell; somewhat, yes; and liability insurance was not yet in the picture. But what he sees chiefly is a significant type of situation, in two aspects. Dominant (the railroad era lies still in the future) is the highway, its purposes, its values. There are the normalities and needs of travelers not "in a populous village or city," but in the country, "where was a solitary house; a child belonging to it happening to be in the road, a thing most imprudently allowed by its parents, and what [*sic*] could have been easily prevented by ordinary care. Travelers are not prepared for such things. They, therefore, trot their horses. . . . To keep a constant look out, would be more than a driver could do, even if he were continually standing and driving on a walk. . . . The roads would thus become of very little use in the line for which they were principally intended." (21 Wend, at 618.) We need highways; highways need use: hence, no negligence shown. This same situation-picture seems to me also to be one underlying drive for the imputation of negligence to the plaintiff which follows as the other leg of the opinion. "A snow-path in the public highway is among the last places in this country to which such a small child should be allowed to resort, unattended by any one of suitable age and discretion." (ibid.) "Lawfully in the highway . . . can scarcely be said of a toppling infant, suffered by his guardians to be there, either as a traveler or for the purpose of pursuing his sports. The application may be harsh . . ." (ibid. 619.)

Cowen plainly feels it harsh. He tests the conclusion, he tests it again, and tests it again. "An infant is not *sui juris*. He belongs to another, to whom discretion in the care of his person is exclusively confined . . . Suppose a hopeless lunatic suffered to stray by his committee . . . An infant or lunatic is liable personally for wrongs which he commits against the person and property of others. And when he complains of wrongs to himself, the defendant has a right to insist that he should not have been the heedless instrument of his own injury." (ibid.) "More fit that he should look for redress to that guardian." (ibid. 620.)[54] And there is testing by precedents in trespass and trover {426} and in land cases: "If that suit depends upon a condition on his side, he must show that it was performed." (ibid. 621.) Take an infant landowner failing to keep up his share of the partition fence; can he sue for trespass of his neighbor's cattle? If animals "are allowed to run at large for the purpose of grazing, or for any other purpose, entirely unattended, and yet travelers are to be made accountable in all cases of collision, such a doctrine might supersede the use of the road, so for as comfort or expedition is concerned." (ibid. 622.) A nonsuit should have been granted, and the new trial asked is ordered.

You can love this or leave it; what you cannot do is mistake it. You cannot miss the why of the rules laid down for these significant phases of a type-situation of importance. My own guess is that the country was not yet ready for a different point of view; human wastage from fights, accidents, winter, and starvation, Americans were still leaving largely where they fell, and highways and their use still had an importance they were to wait another century to regain. But that is neither here nor there. If you are a later court, you meet *here* rules resting on and limited by their reasons. If you do not find those reasons to have been good, or to remain good, and no other adequate reasons occur to you, then manifestly you have no business going along with these two rules. And in truth, that process described, but not loved, by Cardozo, whereby the reason often drops from notice, while the rule persists or even expands blindly without answering to any reason, that is no process for a case law court to take pride in. Or to take part in.

THE SCOPE OF THE SIGNIFICANT TYPE-SITUATION

I hope also that this case from Cowen may help again to illustrate both what I do mean, and what I do not mean, by dealing with "the type of situation." *Heylyn v. Adamson,* faced with an inland bill, "ruled" also on notes; and my complaint was not about that but about the later disregard of what was said there about what consequences a failure of diligence would entail; said, though there had been no such failure in the case. In the present case, contributory negligence was dealt with, with much closer approach to necessity, because a new trial was ordered, which might show greater evidence of initial negligence by the defendant. But in *Swift v. Tyson* I complained (in surface contrast) of the completely unnecessary expansion of the ruling to cover "security" for "an antecedent debt"; and of Walworth I complained because {427} in a case involving only security he unnecessarily extended his treatment to cover "payments" of an antecedent debt. Once again, then, what is this "*the* problem-situation" I am speaking of? How wide is it to be staked? How far is the staking to extend beyond the issue?

Clearly it is not a matter of urging, in mockery of all the wisdom of the common law, that courts should set out happily to make rulings over all outdoors. The case from Cowen serves well enough to point the discussion. He had the matter of negligence before him, or else the matter of travel on the highway, or else that of travel in the country, or perhaps only the matter of taking a team-drawn sleigh down the snow path of a country hill road to a bridge. He had before him, again, the matter of a two-year-old at play, or else that of any living person or thing without discretion of its own, improperly left unattended in a highway snow path just beyond a hill and a bridge, or left unattended on a lonely country highway, or on a highway, or left unattended at all. No rule or principle can ever, in such a choice, tell any court, in concretely definitive terms, what scope "the" problem-situation before it has, or, more accurately, is best made to have. There is a line of guidance, but it speaks only to conscience plus judgment. That line is: "the" problem-situation extends as far as you are *perfectly* clear, in your own mind, that you have grasped the picture fully and completely *in life-essence and in its detailed variants,* and therefore *know* it to present a *significantly single* whole, *and one over which your knowledge and judgment have command.* That far, it is wise to deal with it, and right to deal with it, because small things take on fuller meaning in the context of greater ones. And also because the law does well to trend into ever larger unities, *so long as they remain meaningful as they grow.* But those unities must be and remain meaningful, over their whole scope, in terms of life and sense, not merely in terms of formula and "sound," else they do harm. That is why a court is doing its duty when, contrary to the sense *you* see and desire, but with clear consciousness that it understands what it is doing and why, *and with clear statement of both,* it goes to bat on the whole of a broad situation.

But that is also why any doubt about whether the court has the whole situation in sure grasp is to be resolved *by the court always in favor of a narrower* rather than a wider scope. When felt mastery is present, wide scope is indeed not only sound; it verges on duty. Precedents are always needing synthesis into rules which make better sense for a whole situation-type, for a whole {428} set of really or seemingly variant decisions. Rules, too, are always needing to be re-grouped and rephrased around principles which can guide through still wider situations in terms of surer sense. But, just as truly, facts are constantly emerging which call for subdivision and distinction even within those older, wider rules and categories which heretofore have been able to give satisfaction. Which way to do the growing, or whether in any instance to resist either line of growth, that is a question of sense, a question which only sense can answer wisely. Again, "knowledge is necessary to understanding, as understanding is to sound judging."

Thus, if Story was really conscious of sure grasp of the meaning and import of his inept wide rule as he drew his issue in its terms, then that choice of wide ground was in itself good judging, and what is to be criticized is his folly in not knowing that he knew not, when he did not know. Save for this: that a strong doubt from a brother ought to cause not necessarily a narrowing of scope, but surely a due extra heart-searching on whether one's broader "grasp" is in truth sure and solid (for which Catron testifies that Story took no time). And save for this further matter: hasty work, work not fully consulted on, work with no time for second thought, is never safe; and as the stake rises, so rises also the risk that haste may spell irresponsibility. Rarely does judicial emergency demand both breadth and speed; and rarely has any court left record of a more lighthearted high-stake gamble than *Swift v. Tyson.*

As contrast, Mansfield, in *Heylyn v. Adamson,* will serve, or Kennedy (with the House of Lords follow-up) in *Clemens Horst v. Biddle,* above at 317, 243, or Cardozo, below, in *McPherson v. Buick.* Wide-ranging mastery of this sort is rare on any bench. But when man and occasion meet, "the" problem-situation rightly expands to suit.

The normal run of things is clear enough, and is documented in all parts by the tradition. The great opinion of great scope and prophetic content can illumine the future, and find honor. It can also, as has been shown, be misread — or forgotten. The blob-opinion of great scope is, unhappily, not so often forgotten, and can badly hamper the game. It does, however, commonly reveal its blobbishness to successors, and so, for the most part, becomes a source of shame and rapid whittling. Strong-minded, tough-minded men, peculiarly those also gifted with a certain clarity of line and structure in their work, do tend to deal with bigger situation-chunks than most. Cautious-minded men play situations in the main closer to their chests. The contrast may {429} engender a touch of safety for us all. There may be another such in the tendency, when the nonexpert or the muddy-minded attempt a situation which is beyond their grasp, for that fact to show up in fogginess or nonpersuasiveness of diagnosis, and in unclarity or worrisomeness of the rule achieved. It seems to me that the reader (the subsequent reviewing judge included) does not commonly have to be himself an expert, in order to tell the difference between murk and light — though, as the simple-seeming rules about the passing of title to chattels remind us, or that extraordinary legal category "choses in action," forms of words which have a surface-simplicity can delude wise men by the thousands, over the generations, into overlooking a hundred sins and a thousand unreckonable uncertainties.

In the main, however, the safeguard lies in craft-tradition. In the main, the courts show no great desire to spread their work too wide. In the main, they show some skill in widening, when they do undertake it. For most courts the danger lies on the other side — in an unwillingness to tackle the broader picture, even when the materials are at hand, and even when the scholars have been breaking ground. What is sure, however, is that borrowing, like building, needs to be with reason, and for reason given, and falls comfortably within that great institutional device which I should like again to call "judicial review of prior judicial decision," coupled with the institution of the signed opinion and any judge's just desire not to be publicly made a fool of by that future for which, willy-nilly, he must write. Our judges do sign their opinions, and that makes a difference. When not fully conscious of command of the sense of the situation, the appellate judge will be the more cautious not only for his conscious sense of duty toward guidance in that situation, but for his consciousness that his opinion bears his name. He will remember that such caution looks above all to cumulation and to on-going correction. But meantime, and daily, *some* guidance, though it be tentative, is called for in each case. *Some* diagnosis of *some* type-situation remains the essence of case law appellate judging.

THREE PHASES OF CARDOZO

{430}
The whole matter comes into striking focus if we put together three jobs of Cardozo's. His work was almost always sharp-drawn and deep-graven, each job very much itself, its character as plain as the pure peal of a trumpet. Our specimens consist of a masterpiece, a decision and opinion in the clean Style of Reason about whose wisdom men can differ, and a blooper.

1. *McPherson v. Buick*

The sharp difference between a deliberate attack on a wide situation presented, and effort primarily at fair disposition on the case in hand, could hardly be better presented than in the familiar *McPherson v. Buick*,[55] Indeed, especially when the illuminating dissent of Willard Bartlett is studied along with the Cardozo opinion, that case lights up half a dozen of the points of theory raised by the present study, and provides as well a classic example of how a troubling sequence of cases can be handled in argument. Thus the case will again illustrate how the outcome, both on rule-for-future-guidance and on case-in-hand, may well differ according to the shift in lighting produced by inquiry addressed first to the type of situation with its equities and immanent sense, or, on the other hand, addressed first the particular narrow facts and the individual equities. The case further illustrates again how a solution for the situation-type can (four times out of five, it does) carry with it a satisfying solution on the immediate "equities of the case" — partly because those equities themselves tend to line up more significantly and more incisively, when viewed against the larger situation. The case illustrates, yet again, the drive which an attack on the situation-type can bring forth for a reformulation of a rule or principle of law which frees it of the accidental or historical sequence of prior language, and freshly tailors the words to what has now come to be perceived as the true sense in life of the situation-type. This malleability of {431} language, we recall, is a major by-value of our manner of case law rule, notwithstanding all the "technical deficiency" which, for a more tight-minded lawyer of the Continental type, appears to characterize our rules.

Equally important, *McPherson v. Buick* shows the "style of reason" at its best, in full recrudescence, indeed in full recapture, both in the deciding and in the opinion-writing, and more than two generations ago. It displays, in addition, an identifiable manner and technique of opinion-writing peculiarly adapted to the present-day task of getting back to the reasoned creative method of the early nineteenth century, while both capitalizing on and reckoning with the insight and authority embodied in the intervening cases — while also disposing of such of them as may prove too remote from life because either the Formal Style or some other aberration has in the interim lost contact with life-needs or even made conscious rapprochement therewith seem immaterial.

For the prevailing opinion in the *Buick* case is cast in a characteristic and wholly communicable Cardozo pattern, one of his best patterns. A situation of breadth and significance is diagnosed and sense in it and for it is discovered.

This I suspect to be the first vital step. An authority, preferably from before the Formal period, is examined and a principle, or the germ of a principle, is extracted from it which fits and serves the needed current sense. That principle is then *re*formulated to fit the modern need, to solve the case in hand, and to guide the future, its reason being made as explicit as itself. The intervening authorities are then dealt with, practically all of them. They are dealt with in time-perspective, and as if they had been a series of efforts along the line which has been thus redrawn; they are in consequence re-examined, exploited, distinguished, recast, or discarded, *and*, above all, *cleaned up*. It will be observed that this pattern of opinion not only has as obvious goals an accounting to the given authorities and then the provision of a fresh and fertile start, behind which there is no need to go back; but a start which utilizes all the prior experience. The pattern presents also a *method* for utilizing such experience, for profiting by past insights, for discarding past blobs, and for the forward-pointing of the central *re*formulation.

In this aspect, the *Buick* case becomes peculiarly instructive when placed side by side with the second branch of the same great judge's opinion in the *Whiting* case, below.[56] That a single {432} man could achieve the one and commit the other, and could carry the court in both, and never be conscious that both in essential manner and in essential effect the two jobs are utterly irreconcilable — this I hope may help make the point that so long as a "style" or manner of work in the craft of appellate judging fails to become *conscious and clear* and *therefore* readily consistent in application, so long reckonability of outcome must remain in jeopardy, and wisdom both of rule and of decision must rest quite unduly on the chance that peculiar inspiration may descend upon counsel or upon court.

The *Buick* case, as we all remember, involved a defective automobile wheel made by a reputable manufacturer and built into the car in good faith but without inspection. The plaintiff had bought not from the defendant, but from a dealer who had so bought; the plaintiff had been injured when the wheel suddenly collapsed. The case turned on whether it fell within the "general rule" limiting claims to persons who had contracted directly with the defendant; "privity" was still an idol of might. Cardozo finds the scope of the situation which is directly presented to lie in an automobile "designed to go fifty miles an hour." To see the question thus is to open up the whole field of the "dangerous instrument" exception to the "general rule of no liability to third parties," so far as concerns any *new* device which raises a *new* worry — both novelty and worry being measured in terms of *purposes* of use: as, "a defective engine for a railroad." "Precedents drawn from the days of travel by stage coach do not fit the conditions of travel to-day." (217 N.Y. at 391.) A question seen thus widens out; and, as is familiar, the resulting rule or principle must therefore also widen out, to fit the now perceived sense and need which only such a viewing of the question could have opened. Clearly felt, moreover, and repeatedly almost phrased, is the growing dependence of the modern consumer on the manufacturer of complex products which must be used, if at all, on faith. "A scaffold (*Devlin v. Smith, supra*) is not inherently a destructive instrument. A large coffee urn (*Statler v. Ray Mfg. Co., supra*) may have within itself, if negligently made, the potency of danger, yet no one thinks of it as an implement whose normal function is destruction." What is true of the coffee urn is equally true of bottles of aerated water. (ibid. 387.) "The defendant knew the danger. It knew also that the car would be used by persons other than the buyer. ... [T]he things subject to the principle do change. They are whatever the needs of life in a developing civilization require them to be." (ibid. 391.) {433}

Willard Bartlett, C.J., however, who dissented, did not at all envisage an automobile "designed to go fifty miles an hour." He saw before him an automobile which *at the time of the accident* "was moving at a speed of only eight miles an hour [ibid. 395] . . . not any more dangerous *to the occupants of the car* than a similarly defective wheel would be to the occupants of a carriage drawn by a horse at the same speed" (ibid. 400; my italics) — in regard to which latter a leading English decision and leading New York language were clear and strong against the plaintiff. The Chief Judge thus saw, and he was accurate in seeing, that the theory of the situation laid down in the language of the prior cases made recovery very difficult to allow in this case. And if one were to insist on the particular phase that "carriage" equals passenger vehicle moving at carriage speed, then one of the prior cases was flat against recovery. The flavor of Bartlett's opinion, moreover, suggests strongly that he felt recovery unjust: the defendant had bought of the same manufacturer "eighty thousand wheels, none of which had proved to be made of defective wood prior to the accident in this case." (ibid. 395.) If that does not weight the fireside equities for the defendant, what can? And certainly Bartlett did not like *judicial* widening of the rule; one's feeling is that he also did not approve any widening (see ibid. 399-401).

Across Bartlett's path, and in Cardozo's favor, was that bottle of aerated water which had exploded and injured the purchaser's servant, where the opinion had allowed recovery "under the doctrine of *Thomas v. Winchester (supra),* and similar cases based upon the duty of the vendor of an article *dangerous in its nature, or likely to become so in the course of use to be contemplated* by the vendor" to give warning or to take reasonable care to prevent danger. (The italics are Bartlett's, at page 398.) "Reasonable care" might of course be found, in the *Buick* case, in the record of experience with those prior eighty thousand wheels; still, the language was bothersome. But Bartlett's phrasing, to hold that language down, is master advocacy: "The character *of the exception* to the general rule limiting liability for negligence to the original parties to the contract of sale, *was still more clearly stated by Judge Hiscock,* writing for the court . . . [three volumes later, in allowing recovery for injury from an exploding coffee urn] where he said that in the case of an article *of an inherently dangerous nature,* a manufacturer may become liable for a negligent construction which, when *added* to the *inherent character* of the appliance, makes it *imminently* dangerous . . ." (ibid. 398-399; all above italics mine). Hiscock, thus flatteringly {434} quoted (thus, therefore, to be pinned to his own language?) was also sitting in *Buick.*

How anyone can argue that Bartlett is not here presenting "good law," I do not see. It is not only technically sound; it is closer to the "feel" of both the authorities and the case in hand than is its opposite. Nor can I doubt the immediate fairness of protecting the Buick Company, if reasonable ways of doing business and reliance on real and long experience are to safeguard any outfit against liability. And "fifty miles an hour" is not before the court.

What, then, is wrong with this "correct" opinion by Willard Bartlett? Nothing, if the appellate court's function in our polity is to leave all work of legal readjustment to the legislature, and is merely to decide individual cases on the authorities as they happen to read, allowing nothing for differential wisdom, treating them as if they had all been decided on a single day, with no history, no growth, no errors, no insights better one time than another, and attending within that frame only to such immediate justice as may prove feasible without the ruffling of a hair. Nothing, either, if closely holding the "exception" down fits our modern need. Nothing, again, if "inherently" or "imminently" dangerous, covering a scaffold and a bottle of aerated water and a coffee urn, but excluding a defective automobile, lets any future court or lawyer know where he is at. Bartlett's opinion is solid on law and fact, and is both shrewd and stirring argument. The only thing wrong is that it would leave the meaning of this phase of law, in life, hopelessly tangled; that looks, in first instance, to the future. And that his opinion is out of line with needs which recurrent cases in his court and elsewhere have been forcing to attention: that looks again, in first instance, to the future.

Cardozo, as indicated, sees the case as presenting the purposed use of the car. In the context of precedent, this raises the question of "dangerous instruments" in modern conditions. The original "landmark" of *Thomas v. Winchester,* 6 N.Y. 397 (1852) — belladonna, mislabeled — Cardozo pins, by quotation: "The defendant's negligence put human life in imminent danger." (p. 385; watch here the immense covert expansion from "drugs" to "things.") That ruling is then explained: "Because the danger is to be foreseen, there is a duty to avoid the injury."

Now the point of method begins to develop. When precedents are to be straightened out, and some are to be avoided in favor of others, and language which has gotten too tangled to guide is to be recast, the appropriate common law tool is *principle.* That is {435} one point. The second is, that if *principle* is to be *sound* principle with a life-basis, a sense-basis, and a solid guidesomeness into emerging conditions, then it must have an explicit *reason* which both displays its wisdom and helps to clarify its application.

The opinion in *Thomas v. Winchester* itself had spoken freely of cases where its rule on drugs did *not* apply; and among the instances was that of the carriage-builder. To this, Cardozo: "Some of the illustrations might be rejected today. The *principle* of the distinction is for present purposes the important thing." (His italics.)

"*Thomas v. Winchester* became quickly a landmark of the law. In the application of its principle there may at times have been uncertainty or even error. There has never in this state been doubt or disavowal of the principle itself." (p. 385.)

It will be remembered that what *Thomas v. Winchester* had in fact had to say is here in process of being radically extended. Its "principle" is not being found in its language, qualified by its other language: it is a something larger, to be newly phrased. The cases are then lined up on the time-dimension — an extremely serviceable means of spanning over any embarrassing work of the most Formal period, and a no less serviceable means for charting a *direction.* "These early cases suggest a narrow construction of the rule. Later cases, however, evince a more liberal spirit." (p. 386.) "It may be that *Devlin v. Smith* [defective scaffold] and *Statler v. Ray Mfg. Co.* [exploding coffee urn] have extended the rule of *Thomas v. Winchester.* If so, this court is committed to the extension." (p. 387.) (Note that the *Winchester* "principle" has thus been here all along. The "rule," as we go back and pick it up, *may* have been a little small for the foot, at first; that is all.)

Cardozo now approaches the embarrassing language from Hiscock, quoted against him so tellingly by the Chief Judge. An almost unnoticeable shift of phrasing, from "dangerous" to "destructive," coupled with a stressing of fact and situation, and of the language *not* of Hiscock in a prior authoritative opinion for the court, but of the *defendant's* misguided counsel in the case in hand, bridges into the new principle which the Court approves. "The *defendant* argues that things imminently dangerous to life are poison, explosives, deadly weapons — things whose normal function is to injure or destroy. But whatever the rule of *Thomas v. Winchester* may once have been, it has no longer that restricted meaning. A scaffold (*Devlin v. Smith, supra*) is not inherently a *destructive* instrument. It becomes destructive only {436} if imperfectly constructed." (ibid.) "*Subtle* distinctions are drawn *by the defendant* between things inherently dangerous and things imminently dangerous, but the case does not turn upon these verbal niceties." (p. 394; my italics; but Hiscock, reviewing *his own* past judicial decision, concurred.)

With this, the course of handling the authorities becomes clear. What remains is to state the principle in its new form, cleanly for *guidance,* and with its life-reason clear. That statement, on pages 389 and 390, is too long to quote. I note merely its method: It runs wholly free of all prior language, with a "We hold, then, that . . ." Even in its expansion, it is expressly confined within the field of discussion forced by the initial posing of the issue. Its limitations and conditions are pointed in terms which not only guide, but persuade. The prose reflects the clean line of the thought. The application which follows, moreover, is not formal. The application is indeed made to illuminate the future by being an elucidation of the full-running *reason* of that application. "It was as much a thing of danger as a defective engine for a railroad. The defendant knew the danger. It knew also that the car would be used by other persons than the buyer. This was apparent from its size; there were seats for three persons. It was apparent also from the fact that the buyer was a dealer in cars, who bought to resell. . . . The dealer was indeed the one person of whom it might be said with some approach to certainty that by him the car would not be used . . ." (p. 391).

The law of the country, and legal analogues, are then explored. This tests, checks up, lines up, and rounds out — as Cowen did with lunatics and strays. In one type of schoolman's theory of dogmatic strictness, such portions can be regarded as strays in the opinion. But *given the mastery of the whole area,* this type of semiconsolidation breaks out discrepant and troubling thought-tight bulkheads, and makes for comfortable and efficient work and planning.

One semi-stray there is in the otherwise superb performance; a familiar stray, but one which I regret. "The principle that the danger must be imminent does not change, but the things subject to the principle do change. They are whatever the needs of life in a developing civilization require them to be." (ibid.) This is comforting; and its perception that principle, in terms of "the needs of life," must be recurred to constantly, so as to correct and to readjust precedent — that is vital. But so far as it suggests that principles themselves do not change, the suggestion is legal convention and not legal fact. Principles are born in travail, and {437} some of them die, and sometimes, like the one here, they take new shape in mid-career.

2. *Whiting v. Hudson Trust, I*

What illustration sketches, contrast colors. I turn to Cardozo's opinion in *Whiting v. Hudson Trust Co.,* 234 N.Y. 394 (1923). That case involved the suit of a surviving executor of the Denham estate to recover from the remains of the Snyder estate, and from a bank, an amount plundered by his late co-executor, one Eckerson, who had been "serving" both estates. Eckerson had embezzled handsomely from the Snyder estate, and had in part met a court order for distribution out of it by using and paying over Denham funds.

Case and opinion have two main branches. The first concerns the bank. Eckerson, holding a power of attorney from the then still living Denham, had deposited with the bank to open an account a check signed "Denham, by Ecker-son" to order of "Eckerson, *Trustee.*" But the account he arranged to have kept in the name of "Eckerson, *Special.*" This bothered the bank officer, who raised questions, but became satisfied. (I am interested in the fact that he was both-ered; I am interested in the fact that his sound banker's judgment led him to raise questions. The opinion shows no such interest.) Denham proceeded later to die; and Eckerson became co-executor, had securities of the estate sold, and deposited in this same account labeled "Eckerson, Special" various checks drawn by the brokers to order of "Eckerson, Special" or of "Eckerson, Executor." That was the account on which Eckerson, the double-trustee, proceeded to draw to avoid audit or detection, when he was faced with an order to pay out what he had already secretly defalcated from the Snyder estate. And he drew to the order *of the Snyder estate.* These substitutional and newly defalcating checks "were placed to the credit of 'Eckerson, Executor.'" "He distributed *the moneys thus obtained* among the Snyder legatees." (p. 401; my italics.) In fuller and more accurate statement, he used checks on the "Eckerson, Executor" account to pay off judgment creditors of assignees of the Snyder legatees.

That is the case, complex and dirty enough. As to the bank, a judgment of the Appellate Division holding it liable because of constructive notice of the breach of trust is reversed. The *reason* which leads to judgment and to rule is explicit. It will be noted that counsel had been at work hard and skillfully to show and {438} sell the court the nature of a significant type-situation, of its working needs or necessities, and of its consequent immanent law. "The transactions of banking in a great financial center are not to be clogged, and their pace slack-ened, by over-burdensome restrictions." (p. 406.) Now to the technique: "The argument is that the trust company made itself a participant in the wrong when it placed the description 'special' rather than 'trustee' in the title of an account. *Rights and wrongs are not built upon distinctions so inconsequent.* If the word 'trustee' had been added, Eckerson would have been equally free to draw the money out and use it as he pleased (*Gray v. Johnston,* L.R. 3 Eng. & Ir. App. 1). [And this is true.] *The style of the account, the term of description attached to it, had no bearing on the result, no relation to the consequences.* [This, however, as we shall see, is not true.] A different question would be here if the trust company had received the check to its own use [citations]. . . . [T]he defendant is to be held liable, if at all, only upon a showing that by the form of the account it has facilitated a conversion *and made itself, in so doing, a party* to the tort [cita-tions]. The fact that the check described the payee as trustee, though suggestive of a trust, was not conclusive [two cases]. Whether a trust did in truth exist, the defendant could not be sure. [Exactly!] What it could be sure of was *that the style of the account would neither change the quality of the ownership nor work injury to any one.*" (pp. 402-403; my italics.)

Here is, again, a reason of and for a situation of a general type, and despite the multiple citations, the reason neither purports nor attempts to be *merely* legal. It runs in terms of law and sense at once; and it proceeds to offer also the reason of its application to the case. Utterly characteristic is the Cardozo ap-proach to any subtle distinction, whether of rule or of application, when he has achieved a clear view of sense for the situation, and knows that he has ("The transactions of banking in a great commercial center . . ."): "Rights and wrongs are not built upon distinctions so inconsequent." Compare the dismissal of "these verbal niceties," in *Buick.* Or turn back to the preceding opinion in 234 N.Y., *McGovern v. City of New York,* at 390, 392: "The underlying realities of plan and purpose and effect must prevail over the form or the disguise which may encumber or belie them. . . . We cheat ourselves with words and forms when we speak of this surrender as the dominant inducement moving the defendant to the assumption of its added burdens. Here was no genuine balancing of values, no estimate of *quid pro quo* {439} as even approximate equivalents. . . . We are not to 'shut our minds' as judges to truths that 'all others can see and understand.'" Characteristic, I say, of Cardozo is this brushing off of the subtlety built on yesterday, whenever he sees that that subtlety does not make sense for today and tomorrow; characteristic is the substitution of a related but bolder and simpler rule and phrase which builds on and drives toward any reason of and for the situation which he feels to be well in hand — *and which he always then makes explicit.* Our study of July 11, 1939, and our 1958 sampling as well make clear that this characteristic "of Cardozo" is not that of one individual person who sat upon a particular bench and whom first it and now we have lost, but that the same drive is in significant degree a lasting characteristic and established tradition of that bench — of a *way* of work that has done much to mold new judges as they appear.

But when that has been said, of method, not all has been said. Under the method of *explicit* life-reason given, it must never be forgotten that there is *left behind the wherewithal to test the value* of that reason and its consequent rule. I happen to be a banking lawyer, with some understanding of the needs and ways of "banking in a great commercial center"; therefore I know how much operating trouble the rule here laid down does save. But, if you will excuse me, I *am* a banking lawyer; and so I know also that an account once safely labeled "Eckerson, Special" drops almost by necessity out of further notice, unless attachment papers are served; or unless the bank (by accident) is making sure that payment made of a debt owing to itself is a payment which is safe to rely on. *Whereas an account initially and continuously labeled "Eckerson, Trustee" can hardly escape remaining an account for officers to watch.* Such watching is uncomfortable, but it does not clog the transactions of a great commercial center. What it does is to risk estranging an honest — and especially a dishonest — trustee who wishes his word to be the bank's bond.

The bank officer who handled the opening of the account in the case was a man who knew this, too, and that is why he was worried. Indeed, Cardozo's own distinction, making a difference if the bank should have itself received in payment of an Eckerson debt to the bank a check on this "special" account, that check then later proving to have been delivered in misappropriation — that distinction itself must lead to trouble and uncharted danger in unwatched metropolitan bank operation. For "Eckerson, Special," once established as an account, with the circumstances of its opening forgotten, is, I repeat, an account label which {440} no longer gives notice even that checks from it *are not to be relied on in payment of personal Eckerson debts.* A man holds plenty funds of his own in "special" accounts for "special" reasons. But funds which he wants, for whatever reason, to control without question, he did *not* in the '20's deposit (even when he should have) as "trustee." That is one side of the situation. The other side is that on which Surrogate Foley used rightly to be eloquent: bank men not only have facilities, but have a training, which makes them excellent holders-down of lawyers' and executors' and trustees' opportunities for misappropriation; *and nobody else occupies an equal key position* for that useful purpose. Take away from bank men the responsibility for doing reasonable guard duty, and leave them only a desire for deposits, and you throw into reverse their impact on such opportunity. One can add that banks have rather better facilities than have the run of beneficiaries for spreading any losses, and for using insurance to further spread them, quite as well as for reducing the losses to be spread.

The sense of the situation, as the court here sees it, thus deserves severe re-examination.[57] Indeed, the case itself shows that. For the checks of misappropriation ran to the *order of the Snyder estate*. What we have is another instance in which shrewd appellate advocacy has sold a pup to one of the best of our judges. Such checks, signed by "Eckerson, Special" look right; *signed by "Eckerson, Trustee," they would have challenged inquiry*. It is indeed true that a skilled and painstaking defalcator could still have managed to defalcate without arousing notice; but one important lessener of either tyranny or defalcation is complication of the processes and an increase of the outlay in time, care, and skill necessary to succeed. Cardozo and the Court, *though wholly right in method and manner,* are thus here plain wrong in rule and reason. And in the true manner of the Grand Style, both facts appear. {441}

3. *Whiting v. Hudson Trust, II*

It is when one turns to the second branch of the same opinion that one meets true contrast to the style of reason. Sense for any situation at all as a type of life-problem does not seem to me, there, to have been remained in grasp at all.

This phase of the case was argued on the basis of bona fide purchase for value, and, by the plaintiff, also on a basis on constructive equitable assignment to, or subrogation of, the Denham estate to the judgment claims which had been wrongfully paid off out of Denham funds. I should have thought this last a rather appealing line for decision, even though some rather silly New York authorities (which needed cure) stood partly in the way. As a line of principle, its sense is clear, its limits needfully elastic, its remedial power welcome, and its range of use very wide indeed.

The court chose a different line. The drive and urge of the reasoning seem to me to rest on a direct feeling for the equities of the individual controversy. For if you take as your base line the condition as it stood just before Eckerson's last misappropriation, you will have difficulty in not feeling that the Snyder estate has had judgments against its legatees' assignees satisfied by plainly traceable Denham funds, that this is an arbitrary benefit to the Snyders out of Denham assets, and that it therefore ought to be made good. Such is the court's result.

Standing in the way is one phase of doctrine which has grown up around "equity" formulas about "bona fide purchase for value without notice." While "notice to an agent" is commonly treated as "notice to his principal," often by way of a fiction either of identification or of "presumed disclosure," yet where the information or notice is the kind of thing that a sane, though dishonest, agent would hide from his principal, this "imputation of notice or knowledge" does not hold — the fiction being for that moment taken seriously. Now if we divide one Eckerson into two with a metaphysical cleaver, we find Denham-Eckerson "paying" to his other self, to wit, Snyder-Eckerson, "money" by an "act of transfer and acceptance." (234 N.Y. at 406-407). There are nice points of "value" hidden here, too, which the court finds immaterial; the spiderwebby question could easily be whether Snyder-Eckerson did not further pay over into "the Snyder estate," or to the representatives of the legatees, and thus pay off that much of his debt to "it" (or them) for his prior Snyder-defalcation, as to render their taking of some "legal title," without notice of trouble, {442} a taking for "value." But the suit is not against those who ultimately benefited. The court cuts in earlier. A metaphysical "payment" by one phase of Eckerson *to* the other Eckerson it accepts; but simultaneously the single actual person, J. C. R.

Eckerson, is seen to have "actual" "notice" that his left hand has stolen what it is "transferring" into the "acceptance" of his right hand. And the Snyder "estate" cannot be severed off as "a principal" — as it could under the "agency" rule above mentioned, if the fiduciary Eckerson had been only an "agent." "Eckerson, trustee under the Snyder will, was not an agent identified with some one else, a principal, as the result of legal fiction. He was the principal himself. It is only a form of words when we speak of him as the representative of an 'estate.' *The 'estate' had no separate existence.* It was not a legal person. The only person was the trustee. His acceptance with guilty knowledge charged him as trustee with a duty to restore" (p. 407; my italics) — which duty passes to his successor-trustee, the defendant.

Now if one has any sense, one will not on this basis soothsay that fiduciaries will hereafter for the purpose in hand be divided as between "agents" and "trustees," and that if the defalcator be only "agent" for A but happens to be "trustee" for B, there will be a difference in result according to which fund he last plunders to cover prior defalcation in the other. But what one can safely state is that short of clarification in a further litigation or several such, a new and high uncertainty has been created; and also that the distinction taken has no life-sense in it, when it is applied to a *single* embezzler who is dipping into *two* funds. "Rights and wrongs," the same opinion reads five pages earlier in unintended irony, "are not built upon distinctions so inconsequent." When two *different* fiduciaries are concerned, the distinction may at least claim color. But was there ever legal fiction balder, less self-consistent, or less serviceable than this "act of transfer and acceptance" between Eckerson₁ and Eckerson₂ "paying" and "accepting" as two persons, while "knowing" all the while as one? When such a fantasy is indulged in a passage which frowns on fiction and on "form of words," then certainty is in trouble.

The next step of the opinion pours equally fanciful metaphysics into a different channel. "The stolen money" has been paid over, and is gone. "The equitable lien is destroyed by the dissipation of the fund." But "The defendant's enrichment is a direct and immediate, not an indirect or collateral, consequence of the act of the trustee. It is an enrichment independent of the volition of the defrauded plaintiff or of those for whom he acts. The fruits {443} of the tort are *profits in the coffers of the estate*. We cannot characterize enrichment so procured as other than unjust [citing Stone and Scott]. *The trust is still augmented* by assets unconscionably retained." (p. 409; my italics.) Earlier, and as I read it, most significantly: "Money accepted by a trustee with knowledge that its acceptance is a theft never becomes of right a part of the estate." I read this to mean that it does become "a part of the estate" (else how could a successor trustee who has not received it become obligated?) but not "of right." What interests me is: where and what is this "estate" of which the "money" "accepted" has become "a part." Above, Eckerson was the only "person," and "the estate" had no separate existence. The specific avails of the specific final defalcation have been paid over not by an estate, but by a certain Eckerson out of "Special" into "Executor" and thence to the good faith judgment creditors, all as has been noted. But in between, those avails were somehow so "accepted" as to become "a part" of something which they "enriched," leaving the fruits ("profits") in "the *coffers*" of "the estate," the same estate which, above, "had no separate existence." Thus opens a second puzzle for the future. When and under what circumstances will "the estate" be denied separate existence, and the trustee be seen as the only legal person? When, on the other hand, will the estate bob up without identification as a thing or fund of which things become a part, with ensuing consequences to successor trustees? How will one determine whether a thing thus gets into "an estate's" "coffers"?

It is a fair comment on Cardozo's opinions that if you do not see real and rather clear guidance for the future in them, then neither did he. It is a fair comment, also, that no judge has ever had a stronger urge to leave an opinion in clean harmony with the authorities — duly explained; in such harmony that on the point in hand it supersedes them. It is a fair comment, finally, that his mind was inherently on the oversubtle side, and at the same time sensitive to the immediate equities of the controversy to a degree rarely rivaled. What in the ordinary course, and transcendently in his best work, controlled all this was his drive to give clear and reasoned guidance for a whole type-situation and his wisdom in judging where sound guidance lay. Then sensitivity to equities sharpened his wisdom, then subtlety of craftsmanship became a tool to clean up the messes left by anybody's oversubtleties of yesterday. But even when the feeling for situation and for guidance failed him, the craftsman's urge for the cleanly surfaced result remained; it is the same artistry in advocacy {444} which in *Buick* substituted "destructive" for "dangerous" and "defendant" for "Hiscock" that here conjures forth this unholy mystic two-in-one of Eckersons, along with a third something, "the estate" which is not, or else is, according to whether you have turned a page.

The point for us is, once more, that for reasonable reckonability plus relative ease in later correction of any miss, it is not enough that judge or court have even the greatness of a Cardozo. We need, in addition, a conscious mold of *technique:* the Grand Tradition, with awareness of it added. Had Cardozo had not only an urge and intuition of the steady need for future guidance, not only, in addition, a skill and joy in its provision; had he had also on the Court of Appeals the full conviction that came to him, before the end, on another court, that *no* opinion which did not accomplish clear guidance *in life,* for like situations, was soundly written — then the second branch of this *Whiting* case could not have had the shape it has. Whatever it might have done or might not have done about either result or rule, it *could* not have opened up two deep general perplexities in order to get a single controversy settled.

For the situation was not one in which there was no sense to be had. It can be viewed as of the moment before the last defalcation, with unjust enrichment dominant; and then a clean clarification and, if necessary, an extension of the principle of subrogation — argued by counsel — would have made thoroughly acceptable sense. Or the situation could be viewed much more broadly, as that of a common fiduciary plundering two or more funds entrusted to him; and one first gain in clarification would lie then in showing the ineptness of playing tiddlywinks with bona fide purchase rules between the same person's right hand and his left; and that would open up a really seagoing problem on the legal effects to be given to accounting entries which are all in the control of a single *dishonest* hand. Or, if one wanted to avoid that, one could still, without important countervailing authority, treat a common fiduciary shown to be plundering with fine impartiality two entrusted funds as constituting a common hazard to both, whose whim of choice has no business to have definitive effects on the desirable prorating of the loss. There is no "trusting most" in this picture. If specific assets had been really traceable "into" anything, or if one body of specific assets had happened to remain untouched, the case law would make such an angle harder; though it makes equal sense if negotiable securities come to be switched back and forth between two safe-deposit {445} boxes to meet annual audits. But here we have the happy case of no traceability, both "funds" tapped, and a consequent easy chance at a fresh start back to sanity. What line of sense for the future a court might choose to seek is not, however, the important point. It is enough that more than one line was open, that none was taken, and that the contrast, even to the first branch of the same opinion, let alone to *McPherson v. Buick,* displays out of a single judge's work both the need and the value of the Grand Tradition as a phase of conscious craftsmanship.

METHOD IN THE MODERN STYLE
OF REASON

{446}

Let us see now whether out of all the foregoing we can gather a set of ordered suggestions about general approach which are definite enough to have meaning and which, if put to regular use, would give some assurance of infusing into appellate decision and opinion something of the virtues of the Grand Style of Reason.

1. THE OBVIOUS CASE

It has been urged above that even as to the most obvious of cases there are several useful leads. (1) Given a case in point, cleanly enough in point to justify a memorandum opinion, still there is value in resting the instant holding on the *Reason* of that case in point.[58] That stirs a useful line of thought. (2) Again, even when there is both an obvious answer and an obvious case proper to control, there is always the question, if there be a few related cases, whether it may not be time to tidy up by putting them together into a fresh start for this little corner of the law — perhaps with a re-examination of the reasons. This is the procedure constantly turning up in the current advance sheets: "This whole matter was thoroughly gone into in our recent case of Hammer v. Nails, where we said. . . . See the cases there cited." It is a valuable procedure not only as a stock-taking but also as a rearrangement and modernization of the rule-stock. The *McPherson v. Buick* procedure is good in the little as in the large. The question is one of time-allocation.[59] (3) While, if the obvious "legal" result flows from a formula or a concept (e.g., "no privity, no recovery," as in the New York consumer cases; or "sale, therefore warranty," as in Cuthbert Pound's approach to *Canavan,* above, p. 106) or the obvious result on the facts is seeking to shelter under the nearest available concept (e.g., "the payment has {447} to be recovered; call it a 'trust,'" as with *Legniti* in the Appellate Division, above, p. 210), it plainly pays to stop and think three times: First: Does the purpose of the formula or of the application of the concept fit the situation of this case? Second: Will borrowing the formula or concept in this case entail or strongly urge unhappy further consequences in related cases? (as to which the general books can stimulate the imagination). Third, if on either question a discomfortable answer emerges, is there not some alternative technical road to the same or to a sounder outcome? and is that not a problem worth sleeping on? Cf. *Whiting II.*

2. "LAW" AND SITUATION-SENSE AT ODDS: RUTLEDGE

The second situation (and in the present semiadjusted state of our legal doctrine this one is far from infrequent) is that in which the factually sensible outcome is clear, but the pertinent law seems equally clear to the contrary. In view of my reiterated views about the need, in *any* case, to reach first for the significant type of situation and only then for the equities between the parties, it hardly needs reminder that by "factually sensible outcome" I mean the outcome sensible in the situation-*type.* If no significant type is as yet apparent, so that all that is available is a gutreaction that "This ain't right," it is not the Grand Style of Reason to go at once in search of an appropriate rule of law to cover the case. Such procedure would spell the hard case busy at making bad law, and that is neither grand nor reason — though if regular it could, I suppose, become an abominable style.[60] The first quest is, instead, for some significant classification of life-facts into which the instant litigation fits, and which, as has been suggested almost *ad nauseam,* may be hoped either to temper a gutreaction which is maudlin or to underpin with reason one which is within fair *legal* cognizance.

On the procedure appropriate to the Grand Style in this dilemma, the best I have encountered is a story from Rutledge — given in partial stead of the journal notes he did not make. While on the District of Columbia Court of Appeals he met a case of the description in hand. His conservative colleague plumped for "the law," argued for it, and wrote a simple, formal, cogent opinion. His liberal colleague plumped for the factually sensible result, argued for it, ignored "the law," and wrote a sociological essay. Neither was operating in the Grand Manner. Rutledge was {448} — not that he said so. He could stomach neither the answer of the one proposal nor the literal law-lessness of the other. Again and again, however, he found himself stymied in his efforts to build a solid technical arch up to the only decent capstone. He put it away, and came back after a couple of months of that subconscious brewing or stewing which is sometimes necessary. The technical answer, he said, he then found open on the page; "the law" had somehow taken on new lighting.

Very plain, as useful method, are the stubborn refusal to acquiesce in the apparent dilemma, the stubborn struggle for an out, the intensive initial thinking, the commitment then of the unsolved problem to the files, for a while, to stew. If some suddenly obvious answer does not cook out in time to serve, my own view of the Grand Style calls either for frank fresh creation, at least for the case in hand[61] (which was not available in Rutledge's case; he was faced with statutes) or for following "the law." Under no circumstance can one honor as Grand Manner the deciding of any case without either a *rule* or an effort to work toward one.

The aftermath of the story has its lessons, too. Rutledge's little opinion (a typical job of Rutledge craftsmanship, but untypically brief) was sent to his brethren.[62] For all its beauty, it failed to shake the conservative. *He had frozen on the case.* He could no longer take in a different view of the meaning of the text. Also, by that time he was becoming entirely comfortable with a result which had at the outset been unpleasant necessity. Both phenomena are typical of human beings, lawyers, and appellate judges. We see the latter of them in any lawyer as he hatches within himself a deepening conviction of the righteousness and the terrific importance of his cause. We see the former in the same lawyer's view of the law: the only true view, which the court will be distorting if it should decide against him. Inside an appellate court this freezing on the case takes the form especially of the view the court has come to *of the facts* and the issue; by the time an opinion has been handed down, the facts have normally shaped up to the court in a way which makes the outcome seem *right,* and which makes any other shaping of those facts seem wrong and false. It seems to me that rehearings must be relatively rare which bring change in the upshot of the {449} appeal (as contrasted with change in some ground on which the first opinion may have placed the result, or change in regard to some minor matter overlooked, such as an interest allowance). I have made no study of this; and such a study wants making; but if I am anywhere near the bull's-eye in my guess, then there is a huge saving of court time to be had, without cost to justice, by forcing a petition for rehearing to really make a case.

The second piece of aftermath is more on the amusing side, but has its lesson, too. The liberal colleague did not substitute the good opinion for his poor one. He simply and with pleasure pasted Rutledge's technical job on behind his own essay, saving personal vanity and pride of authorship, absorbing (without giving credit) the work and imagination of his brother, a master craftsman; indeed, laying a reputation-foundation to sustain his own possible next flutter without the benefit of "law." Not all appellate judges see duty the same way, nor do they all play team in preference to grandstand, nor are they, even, all nice people.

3. THE ELUSIVE PROBLEM

The next matter of method goes to the more frequent type of puzzlement: where the facts and the "law" do not shape up with clarity as they are met; where, therefore, under the style of reason the first and most important problem is to locate and semi-define the significant type of situation which is up and to diagnose the significant type of problem of which the litigation in hand presents an example. Part of the job here is focus. The problem goes to direction and to scope; but it goes also to sharpening line, to reducing blur.

As to scope, we have seen that the counsel of the grand manner is clear: as wide as conscious complete mastery *and time* permit; with every reasonable doubt resolved in favor of limitation; with any untried step accompanied if possible by technical machinery for a second and corrective step; and, finally, with exploratory hints where careful pondering has opened up any likely possibilities.[63]

As to direction, I find no general guidance in the records or in observation. A man either has some sensitivity to the world around him and to the feel and structure of the going body of the doctrine of his time, and to the interplay of these, or else he has none. If none, that is one thing he can get neither by taking {450} thought nor by climbing onto a bench. If any, of any, he will use what nose he has. Since the question here is only of direction, there is no direct question of self-restraint, save in this: that insofar as the chosen direction may be unconventional or otherwise unfamiliar the case for small and tentative steps grows stronger.

When it comes to the matter of reducing blur, however, a bit of analysis can push method perceptibly into communication. One can usefully distinguish, though the two are interrelated, (1) the effort to diagnose the significant problem involved, and (2) the effort to mark out the life-situation which gives rise to the problem. Distinct from either is (3) the effort to determine an, or the most, appropriate *line* of solution or treatment, and then (4) the specific prescription which may be called for. Blur can of course occur anywhere along the line. Only when there is clarity, at each step, in both line and reason, does the whole resultant rule become the clean working tool the style demands and labors to produce.

4. AND WHAT WHEN THE COURT IS BAFFLED?
THE ILLINOIS "COURT'S WITNESS"

Let me close with discussion of one case sequence in which a court with a reputation among our best has, in these aspects of method, failed to adhere to the principles of the Manner of Reason. The manifest result has been to mislead the law-men, to throw many criminal trials into embarrassment and uncertainty, to produce a body of appellate litigation half or more of which has been unnecessary, and at the end (I think) to seduce the court itself into a ruling which calls for reconsideration. The illustrative court this time is Illinois.

My brother Meltzer, reading a large piece of this MSS, challenged my feeling that our supreme courts had yet become in all particulars as candid as they have become in general. He led me to an exhibit on which his challenge is hard to duck, and which in addition serves as a study on these points of method. The matter centers, *as a question of the rule of law,* on a witness whom the prosecution has dug up and gotten statements from, when that witness proceeds to become prosecution-unreliable at or before trial; and the question is: when can such a witness properly be made a *court's* witness, and so be cross-examined by the prosecution, with the prior statements moving, in panoply {451} (and whether or not they are technically "evidence"), into impact on the jury.

Illinois still suffers from the queer rule that one side "cannot impeach its own witness." The Illinois Supreme Court has been endeavoring for half a century[64] to work out some wherewithal to avoid that rule in criminal cases where avoidance is necessary, and yet to keep available in such cases various protections which American procedure takes as fundamentals. This effort has led between 1903 and 1955 to more than twenty appeals to the Illinois Supreme Court; but nobody can yet tell from that court's language where he is at. The Style of Reason, in this, has *not* been at work. True, over the fifty years, it seems to me, all but a possible one or two of these cases have been well decided. But no man knows how many needless worries or unappealed blobs have briared below because of what I repeat is, on this one point (and uncharacteristically for the court), just plain bad method.

The climax is reached with *People v. Siciliano,* 4 Ill. 2d 570, 123 N.E.2d 731 (1955), which was decided originally on September 23, 1954. It involved what had become the old, old question of whether, to be made a *court's* witness, the witness had to be an *eye*witness. On September 23 the court held: no. It was a little witness, in *Siciliano;* and it was a little prosecution — merely for bribery of an officer inspecting a meat-processing plant; and the evidence of the witness had not amounted to much. But there was before the court at the same time one which was big: a murder charge where the evidence, absent the testimony of one particular court's witness, would probably be too inconclusive to avoid the Illinois court's deep bother over "miscarriage of justice."

The court knew that these two cases were in a snarl. They had reason to. Only a year or so before, two cases on the same matter had been before them. The opinions there had sought a simple verbal formulation by brushing off the entire complicated body of prior decision. The twice-announced rule had rehearsed the original eyewitness requirement, with the simple {452} notation that "we later announced that this rule should be confined within narrow limits, being adopted only where it is shown that otherwise there would be material injustice"[65] or "a miscarriage of justice."[66] Such oversimplification did not remove a complex, unresolved problem. It could not. "The effort to diagnose the significant problem involved" and "to mark out the life-situation which gives rise to the problem" — this was diverted into an effort to find a simple formula. But a simple formula which is to work and guide can come only by inspiration or else after an analysis which lays bare the very taproot of the trouble. Here the earlier cases had made it very clear that there was more to the problem-situation than avoiding material injustice by having the court call a needed witness; there was an intertwined problem of avoiding a different kind of no less material injustice that might come from abuse by court or prosecutor after such calling had occurred. A troubling body of cases had signaled that an untangling of the snarl was long overdue. Instead of effort to "diagnose" and "mark out," the aching tooth was capped, not cleaned. The problem therefore turned up again, and promptly; and by coincidence again in a pair of cases, looking again in opposite directions.

On November 15, 1954, the court made a new move toward possible light. With the opinion in the murder case about to come down, they granted a rehearing in the bribery case, *Siciliano,* in which you remember that a non-eyewitness had been called by the court. Then, on November 18, they handed down the opinion in the murder case, *People v. Hundley,* 4 Ill. 2d 244, 122 N.E.2d 568 (1954). *Hundley,* as we shall see, again pressed the idea that a court's witness should be an eyewitness: Thus, with regard to the "well-established" law that on proper {453} showing the State's Attorney may have an untrustworthy witness made a court's witness, and so cross-examine him: "The purpose of this rule is to prevent a miscarriage of justice *by having an eyewitness to the crime,* for whose veracity neither party will vouch, fail to testify. (*People v. Cardinelli,* 297 Ill. 116.) But *such witness should be an eyewitness* to the crime, (*Carle v. People,* 200 Ill. 494; *People v. Boulahanis,* 394 Ill. 255) . . ." (my italics). In *Hundley* the controversial witness had indeed been an eyewitness, but her postevent statements about what the accused had said were nevertheless ruled improper for the State's Attorney to bring in by way of cross-examination. I pass at this point the wisdom of that ruling. I am concerned here with the fact that the language quoted was handed down only three days after *Siciliano* had been granted rehearing. I am concerned with the fact that *Hundley* cited or mentioned neither *Siciliano* nor a single case cited in *Siciliano.* Patently, clarification of the puzzlement was left for the redoing of *Siciliano.* That seems to me a sound way to join speed in the important case with taking time to work the difficulty out; doubly so because work was needed; the *Hundley* authorities remained to be dealt with.

Then, two months later, that original *Siciliano* opinion of September 23 was "reaffirmed and readopted" (4 Ill. 2d at 592). "*The power of the court to call witnesses is not limited to the calling of eyewitnesses.* (*People v. Gibson,* 385 Ill. 371, 381; *People v. Tuohy,* 361 Ill. 332, 349-350). The court may call a witness for whom the State's Attorney cannot vouch where it is shown that otherwise there might be a miscarriage of justice. (*People v. Bennett,* 413 Ill. 601; *People v. Laster,* 413 Ill. 224.)" (p. 590; my italics.) The testimony of a noneyewitness to minor corroborative *action* (he had, for defendant-briber, delivered adulterated meat) was then held properly admissible by way of the "court's witness" procedure. In sum, the power "is not limited to the calling of eyewitnesses," but "the purpose of this rule" deals with eyewitnesses, and "such witness should be an eyewitness" — and what should poor Robin do now?

Effort to "diagnose" and "mark out" had obviously been made. It had no less obviously failed; determination of "a line of solution" could thus not even be begun.

The problem of method becomes then a different one. It changes to: what is the sound approach of a thoroughly baffled court? First, decide each case according to the best light it has. That the court did. Second, wrestle with the authorities. That the court did not do. Each case did line up one group of authorities; {454} but lining selected cases up on one side alone involves no wrestling with recalcitrant material. Third, be frank about the difficulty. On this the court deliberately committed serious judicial sin. This has been discussed at length above. Here let me add only that in addition to what is there said about the effects of this type of sin on the court's prestige and on the bar's morale, there speaks from the present series of cases an embarrassment and disturbance of operation in trial courts and in prosecutors' offices which sketches in purple how far the evils of sinful method can reach.

In the above, as in the following, I follow the court in its view of the problem as one which turns on cross-examination and impeachment in criminal trials. It is not my office here to complicate the matter — and perhaps ultimately more deeply clarify it — by Meltzer's reminder that leading questions which lug in prior statements (not only contradictory but perhaps supplementary) may rest on solid theories which are independent of impeachment, such as that of refreshing or probing a recollection which appears to be exhausted, or testing the accuracy of a recollection which comes as a surprise.

Meanwhile, when one goes through the whole body of cases, some guidesomeness does emerge from their facts and issues and decisions, even though the court has been so queerly reluctant to call all of these into a single mass meeting and try to elicit some sense of the house.

As stated above, the story began in Illinois in 1903; the situation was remotely similar to *Hundley*.[67] A question about a killing in a bar turned on murder-or-self-defense, one of the eyewitnesses was a reluctant witness, his testimony was important; we do not know whether, as seemingly in *Hundley*, that testimony was an almost necessary link; indeed we do not know the testimony given. The ruling (it was one of five, and the one most briefly treated) was simply that the court might make a dubious witness its own; it was stated in terms of both "killing" and "person present." (200 Ill. at 504.)

From here on in it pays to put out of the way that set of cases in which either eyewitnesses or noneyewitnesses whom the State's Attorney showed to be dubious witnesses have been made court's witnesses on points deemed by the reviewing Supreme Court to be only incidental to the prosecution's case. These cases have language, sometimes, which has led prosecutors into overenthusiasm. {455} But their juice is really absorbed by the Illinois doctrine that error has to look really prejudicial in terms of the net case before it can mean reversal of a conviction which seems otherwise solidly founded. The phrasing is in terms of a "miscarriage of justice" or of "the case is clear." Of these cases the strongest is *Cleminson*[68] (a sound decision, but one which in my opinion might not be repeated in the court today). A doctor accused of murdering his wife, faking a robbery to explain the corpse, was faced by one noneyewitness who was duly made a court's witness and who was then cross-examined in regard to unusual intimacy with the defendant, and in regard to statements about having had abortions managed by the defendant, and the like. This was seen by all the court as palpable error; but four judges thought guilt so clear as not to warrant reversal. In the next year *Baskin*[69] sustained a conviction for receiving stolen goods, notwithstanding that one "eyewitness to the sale" had been a court's witness. The other evidence was powerful, and the court brushed off the point. Again, in *Curran*,[70] when in a well-constructed labor racket prosecution (plate glass windows) two union business agents were made court's witnesses, the court did not even bother to indicate what, if any, was the importance of their particular testimony. My strong guess is that except for *Cleminson* these cases fit roughly with *Tuohy*,[71] the Factor kidnaping case, in which the noneyewitness court's witness testimony has almost the weight of a housefly's foot, and with our present *Siciliano,* in which the court says "little or no information was obtained" from the relevant witness. (4 Ill. 2d at 590.)

The total pattern which derives from the cases is a bit complex, but it offers ample guidance to either any prosecutor or any trial court not addicted to brinkmanship. Thus:

(1) If the prosecution's case is solid without the out-of-court statement which comes in by way of impeaching the court's witness, then error in regard to nonnecessity for the court to call that witness will in itself normally be held harmless.[72] As to collateral {456} buttressing material this is almost certain;[73] and it seems to hold also for such buttressing as a second or third eyewitness account of some portion of the vital events. But what the court feels to be not only prejudicial but willfully unfair handling of the prosecution's cross-examination becomes risky in the measure of the weight of the penalty at stake and of the supposed effect on the jury; and if these are severe enough to bother, the degree of the unfairness or seeming effort to evade the defendant's due legal protections also goes into the scales.[74]

(2) If the out-of-court postevent statement to be elicited in impeachment is a crucial nail in regard to a crucial element in the prosecution case, the chances are powerfully in favor of reversal.[75] The chances for reversal decrease somewhat, however, if the witness (a) was an eyewitness; (b) was seemingly sober and otherwise in control of self when making the statement; (c) made the statement almost immediately after the event; but especially, as indicated above, (d) if other evidence can carry all or most of {457} the prosecution's case.[76] The chances for reversal increase, on the other hand, as under (1), if (a) the penalty is severe, or (b) the cross-examination hammers the inadmissible. On this last the Illinois court is sensitive. (See also page 461, *Addendum*.)

The court's reiteration that the trial court should make the witness its own only when furtherance of justice so demands, and that in such cases cross-examination should be severely confined, and that the prosecution will not be permitted to use the device for the primary purpose of introducing by way of impeachment out-of-court unsworn statements — especially statements in the nature of confessions which are vital to the People's case — these principles have proved, in the decisions, to have teeth. And the opinions have over decades been written with passion.[77] There {458} have been very few dissents. But since *Cleminson* in 1911, and especially since *Dascola* in 1926, there comes through the opinions a strong flavor of presence on the bench of judges with strongly divergent basic philosophies on the conflicting policies which plague the situation: the civil libertarian versus the law enforcer. The more striking opinions have tended to fall each to a judge whose basic philosophy it fitted, and I find myself wondering whether the growth of these two lines of authority which so snidely ignore each other may not have been furthered by the adherents of each approach trying to make any welcome decision an occasion for strengthening the general case each for his preferred policy.

But I have been moved, and impressed, as I have worked through the sequence. Personnel has changed. Times have changed. What has not changed is the steady feel of the court for the sense of the type-situation and its no less steady feel for the sound net decision. If one should ask for evidence of the values inherent in a groping legal system like our own, I am ready to argue that this to me strange body of material (thrust upon me, and at my age I do not enjoy such thickets of utterly unfamiliar doctrine and policy) — I am ready to argue that we have here at its best what my brother Katz dubs the {459} Nose of the Judicial Heart. But I am ready to urge, and equally, that we have here a peculiarly interesting example of the need for *method* in the Grand Manner.

To begin with, the cases presented should be enough to persuade of a court's rather clean smell for sound result. And the cases as a body have run the full gamut. That is the first aspect. But the second aspect is that the cases have *had* to run the full gamut. The true Grand Manner, it must be repeated, seeks for Reason and Guidance in Words which are clear enough to keep from happening any such thing as twin cases before a single court twice within a couple of years.

Now what have we been observing here? It starts on the basis of an ancient in-built rule, rooted somehow in the responsibilities of parties in our particular adversary scheme of procedure. I suspect that this rule against "impeaching your own witness" rests on an effort to reduce the trickeries so easily generated by an adversary scheme if such a scheme ever begins to let the combat submerge its purpose. I suspect that "the rule" has then in turn rigidified far beyond its own utility. But regardless of such speculations, it is clear that our Illinois Supreme Court early became clear that in criminal cases "the rule" needed correction.

It is good to watch their working. A killing; a doubt on a vital fact; an eyewitness; and he is wiggle-waggle. The "court's witness" concept can evade the rule and let in vital testimony, subject to all the otherwise proper protective *and investigative* court procedures. The next case turns up a hanging trial judge cooperating with a shrewd prosecutor; they find the device a joyous road around the normal protections. The fact that the witnesses had not been eyewitnesses is mentioned by the Supreme Court. That fact forthwith obscures the basic issue. For "eyewitness" is in truth only one normally strong indication of the value, perhaps even of the need, for the testimony. *Per contra,* the later heavy discussion of need for "strict confinement of the cross-examination to the issues" is only a single aspect of not interfering with the whole body of fundamental procedural guaranties. But with the "eyewitness" talk curtained before the court, the basic conflict between the two equally valid, though opposing, policies fails to work into clarity and into appropriate arbitration of their border-controversy. Each in turn, however, is felt and responded to as need arises. Still, failure to canvass the whole body of experience on each occasion leads to wobble of language and of rationale. *Much worse, the court falls into judicial sin: divergent lines of deciding which deliberately ignore {460} each other.* And this continues even after the fact has become fully conscious, and after conscious effort has been made to find a better way.

What, now, could have been done by judges on whom particular inspiration had not descended; by judges who found the knot too Gordian? The Method of Reason urges something very simple. First: a frank statement of what was bothering the court, so far as the court can get that into clarity. The Method of Reason does not require that men shall do what they lack time to do, or lack experience to do, or, for that matter, lack brains to do. I get impatient with the scholarly critic who sets up as the first step of the Method of Reason a clean and searching analysis of the problem; I get impatient not because that is not a good first step (after the information has been gathered) but because it is no part of the Method of Reason to demand such analysis of men to whom the problem is stubbornly refusing to open for analysis. No, what I mean is something much simpler, something within the compass of any court faced — as this court twice has been — with companion cases at war with each other, or with a single case equivalently baffling. Something, say, like this:

"We have cases which seem to look two ways on this matter. In *Carle* we held ... and yet we later announced that this rule should be confined within narrow limits, being adopted only where it is shown that otherwise there would be material injustice. On the other hand, there are cases in which we have extended the rule so as to allow a noneyewitness to be made a court's witness. It is not as yet clear to us what the exact line of discrimination is, but there is no doubt as to which side of the line to place the present case. Here" etc.

Such an approach — with, as the next aspect, the facts and holdings of the bothering cases *on each side* set forth — such an approach sets anybody thinking. (1) It will cook, inside the court. That may prove enough. (2) In a situation like ours, it gives this much direct guidance: it will make any prosecutor or lower court pause long before he presses happily into abuse of the procedure. (3) It will bugle to any law review staff that here is one to get after, enlisting such aid as the scholarly branch can yield.

In a word: in these latter days, when foiled, the Style of Reason at Work must summon, not duck or seek cover from, what I like to think of as the *posse comitatus* of the scholars. Thus summoned, in the present instance, there is a possibility that the scholars might even enlarge the field, deepen the inquiry, and work out a rationale which would clear up, along with this impeachment {461} problem itself, its relation to the use of prior statements for refreshment or for probing on the civil side as well. I cannot judge that. If it should happen, however, it would be pure gravy; simple bread and meat can always be had.

* * *

But the vital question is not one of occasional blob, nor of occasional sin. The vital question is: *in general,* do we have the Style of Reason at Work in our appellate courts today? Not necessarily with consistency, but more frequently than not? Even as the dominant practice? Not necessarily in conscious purpose or program, but in palpable effect? Sometimes in awkward groping, maybe, but in a groping which moves toward the goal?

Look back over the text and over the illustrations and the samplings in the text. Look forward into the samplings in Appendix A. And judge.

EFFECTS: DISSENT; STYLE OF WRITING

WILL THE STYLE OF REASON DESTROY COURT TEAMWORK?

{462}

The first of the "current" samplings for this volume was that from Ohio. It became most uncomfortably plain that dissenting opinions had been increasing, as the Style of Reason had also been increasing, not only from 1939 to 1953, but again from 1953 to 1958. This was to me a troubling idea. Roughly, out of fifty Ohio decisions on the merits in 1939, recorded dissenting votes occurred in about one tenth, and there were only three dissenting opinions. But a comparable count in 1959 showed dissent in one quarter of the cases, with nine dissenting and three specially concurring opinions. So: Does regrowth of the Style of Reason threaten the court? More specifically: is it the regrowth of that style which kills court teamwork?

Let me answer these questions first, and come to analysis later:

Is it the regrowth of the Style of Reason which threatens court unity? No. North Carolina is a persuasive exhibit. In our 1940 sample, with the Style of Reason at work, but so to speak still downy-yellow from the egg, we had out of fifty cases nine dissenting opinions and three special concurrences. The Style of Reason has flourished, since, in North Carolina. But the dissents have amazingly decreased. And the nasty tone of the 1940 dissents has entirely disappeared.

Second question: Does regrowth of the Style of Reason kill court teamwork? No.

I note first that the current Ohio dissents have none of the edge and rancor which characterized North Carolina in 1940. This suggests that differences of opinion within a court can rest on other things than difference of judicial method or style.

As a second point, I turn to the other jurisdictions we have sampled in sequence. In neither Washington nor Massachusetts has twenty years of patent regrowth of the Style of Reason meant any increase in dissenting opinions. In Pennsylvania (after fifteen years) the increase in dissenting opinions remains minor. {463} Nor, in the other jurisdictions in which our current sampling has found the Style of Reason at work, have we found the court plagued greatly by dissent.

New York appears at first glance to be an exception. Out of thirty-five fully opinioned cases in 5 N.Y. 2d (1959) I turn up seventeen with dissenting opinions, and (as I read my notes) twenty-six nonmajority opinions. This would make one out of four (as in current Ohio or 1940 North Carolina) look pretty sickly. But one must remember that in the New York Court of Appeals, five sevenths of the decisions on the merits go off without full opinion; one has therefore about one developed dissent not out of two cases, but out of seven.

At least in New York, it seems to me that we can trace this practice of dissent directly to the Style of Reason. In 1913, before Cardozo joined the Court of Appeals, dissenting votes were not infrequent (maybe once out of five or six), but dissenting opinions were freakish. By 1916 (Cardozo on for two years) one finds things stirring. By 1927, there is a dissenting opinion about one time out of seven. I do not see how one can doubt the impact of that great man and great exponent of the Style of Reason: Benjamin Nathan Cardozo.

But I note that now, thirty-two years later, and twenty-seven after his baleful influence departed, dissents are still running only at about this one out of seven rate.

This seems to me what is to be expected. Not only our examination but the careful studies of Mentschikoff and Haggard make clear that men seeking right and justice both perceive the facts and turn for standards to the body of met and organized experience with which they are equipped. These "experience-spectacles" must of necessity yield differing results both of intake and of applicable standard, must yield results which differ increasingly as our modern variegated world dilutes community of experience among the individual members of the bench and multiplies and differentiates the situations out of which conflicts emerge to be adjudicated.

So that the Style of Reason which once could he hoped — even despite the conflict of Federalist and Republican, or of the Jacksonian and the Solid Citizen — to yield some relatively single way of seeing, and then of judging, for addition to the brew of "the authorities and justice" — that style, today, must give a wider range of result. Queer, and lovely, I should argue, that after the years it yields dissenting opinions only one time in seven, or at most in four. {464}

STYLE IN DOING AND STYLE IN WRITING

One has only to skim through an advance sheet to perceive that the Style of Reason, which is a high style, in our law an earthy style, and above all a living style, can be and commonly is found in opinions whose style of writing is neither high nor earthy and can at times be dull, almost dead. The bulk of current American opinions pass a reasonable muster in structure and in clarity; but despite all the many, the gratifying, exceptions, they are likely to lack grace, compression, and incisiveness. Responsibility to the facts, for instance, is much more likely to show by way of an extended and even sprawling rehearsal than in the manner of the pencil artist whose seven lines depict a man's whole character. The words are: adequate, mostly undistinguished, sometimes dull, often verbose. But as against this last common complaint of the bar, I find a good number of short opinions, and where as so often length turns up it turns up commonly in a good cause, to wit, in a laudable pursuit of reason either in application or in the shaping of the rule.

Such observations of course reinforce what has been plain throughout: that "style" for this book refers to style of work, of craftsmanship, of doing, not to individual or period literary style. But the observations do more: they raise a most interesting query. Period-"style," difficult though the concept is to define, carries the flavor of being some outgrowth and aspect of a going whole; and if so, the various manifestations of that whole would be expected to be driving toward a harmony. How come, then, that a high style of reason-in-the-doing locks arms so often with a definitely nonhigh style of using language?

One might begin by challenge to the general assumption that we should expect harmony in manner and tone among the many manifestations of a culture, or even of a major institution. Just as a period-style, though pervasive and unmistakable, means no close-order drill of uniformity among persons — else a style once established would go on forever — so, at least in any mobile culture or major institution, we should expect a substantial portion of *dis*harmony among the aspects. Thus, for example, the neoclassical tone and feeling of literature in the polite society of Queen Anne's day would seem to be characteristic of the age, and, in letters, definitely marks a style. That style rimes rather well with the lovely proportions of the furniture, with its ornament, with its simplicity; I should indeed argue that the delicacy of the {465} furniture, though I know of no ancient furniture to match, fits and expresses a feeling of restraint, moderation, quiet dignity, and elegance which was felt and sought as a classic ideal. But I find neither in women's clothing nor in ruffles on men's shirts anything but a jarring note: elegance may harmonize, daintiness does not, with the heroic couplet.

If all of that be granted, however, one is still left uncomfortable. One or another and yet another aspect of the culture or of a great-institution like Law-Government may well run at odds with the pervading style of the whole, yes. But to have a clash between the manner of work in a particular craft and the direct product of that same work, between the doing and the very form which is its monument — that still seems queer. Phases of the same small job, recurrent and inseparable, these ought to sound in chord. And certainly in the days of our Grand Style, to a large extent they did: the opinion which represented a decision in the Grand Style had something of the Grand Style in its own composition. Indeed until that harmony is more fully recaptured we shall use terms more aptly if we speak of today's appellate judging merely as being again in the Style of Reason, reserving "Grand" to designate a going unity of the craft-work and its evidence. Meantime, a unity of that sort is as unmistakable in the characteristic opinion of our Formal Style and period as in the Grand. Which seems to me to be altogether natural.

Recent exciting evidence of such normality is found in J. Gillis Wetter's remarkable forthcoming book, *The Styles of Appellate Judicial Opinions*.[78] Gatherings of opinions, sometimes in series, from Sweden, Germany, and France are presented with introductions and running annotations which leave no doubt that the ways of judging and the ways of writing interlock characteristically in each instance with ways of work and thought which form a style of judging of which the style of opinion is a clear and appropriate product and monument. Three opinions from England suggest a similar phenomenon there. A less tight and schooled manner of writing is presented from Nova Scotia, from Arkansas, and, at fifty-year intervals, from three periods of judging in California — with further penetrating comment.

What is thus patent (once displayed as a good museum director can display his paintings for heightened effectiveness by contrast, accompanied by a lecture shrewdly pointing up detail) — what is thus patent from three distinct legal cultures, what is {466} unmistakable no less in the best, and I should argue also the most, of American work in either the Grand or the Formal Style, and what, in this light, becomes also the strong impression given by the modern English cases one remembers: this we ought to be able to take rather more than tentatively as a normal and natural something to expect. Why then do we not find it in our own current advance sheets?

There are two answers to that. The first is that in each of Wetter's trans-Atlantic systems both bar and bench go through a much more extended, much more uniform, and much more tightly channeled training than is the case with us. "Taught law makes tough law," said Maitland. "Taught style makes tight style" is our picture here. Yet with a difference: Maitland meant law taught explicitly. I mean that, too; but I mean even more the absorbed and ingrained ways of doing and feel for what is and what is not done which a lawyer or judge grows into by way of a long apprenticeship and work in association with seniors, or, as in England, by way of continued work in a single center full of personal contacts, orally mobilized "public" opinion, and shop-gossip. We have almost none of this, affecting our courts. One of our metropolitan bars, so far as group-conscious, is not a bar, but many bars. Our rural or small-town bar scatters over the State. Nationally, our bars have for these purposes of style-production the training and conditioning unity of mixed seeds spilled on a waxed floor. Neither do the benches go through any apprenticeship, save as a new judge breaks in *after* he mounts the bench. Contact between benches is an innovation, limited largely to Chief Justices in annual short conference and to the New York University seminars.

In the early days this was not nearly so true. Our lawyers and so our judges were trained largely by apprenticeship, and group-conditioned by riding circuit and constant observation of their seniors. Moreover, despite all differences of ability, temperament, or background, the culture was so much simpler a culture as to nudge and thrust men in their ways of work and *craft-thinking* into rather closer likeness than is the case today — for of course *craft*-ways and *craft*-thinking can be common to a Jefferson and a John Adams, to a Webster and a Calhoun. Less clear to me is the convergence of manner that marked the Formal Style at its height, and the accompanying coincidence, there, too, of style-of-doing and the writing style. I make a guess that the pattern — essentially the simple syllogism — was so simple to teach and learn, and fitted so well with all other branches of learning and with our elementary education on separation of powers, that it {467} took hold easily; while urges to break the mold in the interest of what seemed fair would run up against that streak of Puritanical self-flagellation which among our finer citizens for a century or more ran in team with sentimentality. As against these, we are today still in the last lap or two of style-transition. During a transition the pressures of what Bechtel calls the *Lebensform*, the shape of living, run in varying directions. Only as a style establishes itself does it integrate itself into a frame that tends to condition work, thought, value-judgment, even imagination and so to produce and set up boundaries within which the creative impulse is to find its outlet. Furthermore, the addition to an old-fashioned opinion of an inquiry into situation-reason not only increases the material to be handled, but complicates the task of composition — doubly so if the new material be imported less by plan than by intuition. Until new patterns develop, this is likely to blur structure and to cost space, except among those peculiarly skilled.

The other answer is to me a much more interesting answer. That is: that we *do* find in our advance sheets a stylistic consistency between opinion-writing and the style of actual deciding, that we are finding more and more of it, and — this is best — that where it happens the page sings that it is giving satisfaction to the author. This is a phenomenon, moreover, which is waxing, and which is country-wide. And there is every indication that this manifests itself more strongly as the Style of Reason settles in and makes itself at home. One must not rely too strongly on the evidence from great judges; but Burch and Mason, pacemakers in the modern movement, not only judged but wrote in the Grand Manner, while the relative lag of their court today in Style-of-Reason judging parallels a style of opinion which is adequate, but not much more. Again, the Court of Appeals in the decade or so before Cardozo was moderately muddled or dull in writing as in judging; the level of opinion-writing rose steadily, throughout the court, as the Style of Reason took firmer root; today, long after three such notables as Cardozo, Pound, and Lehman are no more (and though their mark is missed) the level and manner of opinion-writing twines still with judging in the Style of Reason. In Oregon the level of the writing has climbed along with the rise of situation-reason in the deciding steadily from the beginning to the middle of the century; I regard it as almost certain that the next development will be toward compression. In Washington, North Carolina, in Ohio (where the personnel have held so steady), Pennsylvania, and most strikingly of all in Massachusetts, a comparison of our earlier {468} samplings with our current ones yields a single answer: the puzzle with which we opened this last inquiry, seen in historical perspective, is as false a puzzle as the one about whether appeals are decided by "the law" or by "the men." Inside craft-work, style *does* tend to unify. Our opinions show indeed nothing of the relatively tight lines which characterize the unsigned corporate opinions of the Continental courts, nor even that relative homogeneity of tone and manner which an American eye seems to find among the English appellate judges. What our opinions do show is a drive to fit the style of reason in judging into a type of opinion which is appropriate, and which has structure, form, and life. The ways are manifold, and the path is long, but the work is in process, and the literary level of our opinions is rising as a necessary consequence.

In literary form, then, as in the full reconquest of situation-reason and the on-going rebuilding of doctrine toward and into singing rules, our appellate courts are not only on their way, but well along. The Grand Tradition waits, indeed — and not too far ahead.

Notes to Part II

{*footnotes appeared on page number of original text location*}

1 2 Burr. 669 (K.B. 1758).

2 5 Burr. 2670 (K.B. 1770).

3 Above, pages 241 ff.

4 Dennis v. Morrice, 3 Esp. 158 (N.P.).

5 Bills of Exchange 88-89, and cf. 85-86. But cf. 101.

6 Commercial Bank of Albany v. Hughes, 17 Wend. 94 (N.Y.S. Ct. 1837).

7 Compare Story, Bills of Exchange §112 (2d ed. 1846). He cites Bayley and Heineccius. He already recognizes waiver.

8 Sections 70, 89, 143(1), 152. All of the N.I.L. sections cited reproduce, on this matter, the later nineteenth-century case law.

9 Thus Williston, when the idea was first presented to him of recurring to the classic view, found it "almost too great an innovation to discuss."

10 N.I.L. §§109, 111, 82(3); Britton, Bills and Notes 919 (1943).

11 This is no longer a conscious disturbance to bankers because their note forms carry an indorser's waiver on the face, and their customer's drafts are handled under a signed charge-back agreement. But it still bites in odd cases.

12 It is interesting that in Blesard v. Hirst, 5 Burr. 2670 (K.B. 1770), there had been an unambiguous promise to take up the bill. But since the failure of notice had led to the loss, no one even thought that that promise could not be retracted.

13 Compare Uniform Commercial Code §3-502(l)(b). But the Code discharges indorsers for delay in presentment or notice, and drawers for delay of a necessary protest. §3-502(l)(a) and (2).

14 N.I.L. §186.

15 Compare annotations in Beutel's Brannan's N.I.L. to §§87 and 120(4).

16 Discussed above, pages 73 ff.

17 1 Burr. 452 (K.B. 1758).

18 I think Pound's admiration for Story excessive. Except for flashes of brilliance, I find

Story's work as shallow as it is broad; and I resent his debasing of the law curriculum into purely trade-style cheapness, cut devastatingly loose from the overall vision insisted upon by such thinkers as Franklin, Jefferson, and Kent.

19 2 Doug. 633 (K.B. 1781).

20 Bills of Exchange 64, 69 and (in a digest) 74.

21 5 Johns. Ch. 54 (N.Y. Ch. 1821).

22 Coddington v. Bay, 20 Johns. 637 (Ct. Err. 1822).

23 Francia v. Joseph, 3 Edwards Ch. 182 (N.Y. 1838).

24 Bank of Salina v. Babcock, 21 Wend. 499 (N.Y.S. Ct. 1839).

25 Bank of St. Albans v. Gilliland, 23 Wend. 311 (N.Y.S. Ct. 1840).

26 Bank of Sandusky v. Scoville, 24 Wend. 115 (N.Y.S. Ct. 1840).

27 14 Curtis 166, 16 Peters 1 (U.S. 1842).

28 I should of course have preferred to see the court start with a transaction from Boston or Baltimore or Philadelphia, with a "necessary" point of law, and with decent analysis and reasoning thereon. A craftsman squirms in undeserved sympathy as Walworth puts the boots to Story. But if the innovation had been engineered with a touch of lawyer- and statesmanlike persuasiveness, and if Story's successors had had the wit to keep the doctrine within Story's own suggested bounds: "jurisprudence" which would be both "commercial" and "general," then I think the virtues of Swift v. Tyson would have far outweighed its vices. Query also, under those circumstances, whether Brandeis' bitter campaign against it would ever have been launched.

29 Stalker v. McDonald, 6 Hill 93 (N.Y. Ct. Err. 1848).

30 Compare this from Ames, from whose careful collection of cases I derive most of these references: Re "paper taken in conditional payment of a debt," and "the suspension of the creditor's right of action on the debt": "The conflict of authority on this question would have been avoided if the courts had adopted the view of merchants[!!] that a creditor who takes a bill or note in payment of his debt merges the debt in the paper." 2 Ames, Cases on Bills and Notes 867 (1894).

31 304 U.S. 64, 58 S. Ct. 817 (1938).

32 On the original broad intention as to the commerce power I find Crosskey entirely persuasive. Politics and the Constitution cc. 3-7 (1953). But if you do not like to depart from traditional views of our Constitutional history (whatever the evidence), then read "expanded" for "restored." Either view of history is of course immaterial to my view on the sound construction of a doctrinal text that is old: soundly you do with it as much of what need demands as the wording can be made to yield; "intention" is to be seen not as a basic guide, but as argument-ammunition.

33 Hutcheson, at the Cincinnati Conference on the Status of the Rule of *Stare Decisis,* 14 U. Cin. L. Rev. 245, 246 (1940).

34 On this matter nothing in the books can compare with Corbin, The Laws of the Several States, 50 Yale L.J. 762 (1941).

35 Above, page 181.

36 Below, pages 441 ff.

37 N.I.L. §25; but with the "equity" qualification of Section 54. Sales Act §76(1), Warehouse Receipts Act §58(1), Bills of Lading Act §53(1), Stock Transfer Act §22(1), all omit the qualification, so that antecedent or pre-existing obligation, *whether for money or not,* and regardless of whether the taking be in satisfaction or as security, sits not only firm but seemingly complete. Hence: enter "Notice."

38 The complexity of the problem can be suggested briefly: (1) an obligation to deliver goods (one therefore not "for money") is rightly satisfied in current course by transfer of documents of title which represent appropriate goods; this, without reference to such other transactions as the giving of security for such current obligations as a new construction job, is enough to justify expanding the "value" idea out beyond "money" obligations.

(2) On the other hand, the satisfaction of a money-debt by transfer of goods, documents of title, or shares of stock is not in any current course that ever was, whereas the giving of shares in security (as with call loans) is, and the question whether further security for an "antecedent" debt is or is not in current course of trade depends on circumstances. The thing to remember is that the guillotining of defenses or prior owner rights has as its prime justification not the protection of particular bankers who have slipped in credit judgment but the building of a *market* in which those thousands of *current* transactions which are entirely honest in character are enabled to move fast and freely. The only other relevant policy is that of spreading losses by centering them on the professional; and that one, these days, works entirely against the banker.

39 One can hook up here with our prior discussion of a "singing rule" and move a bit further into implementation than the "factors to be considered" when the rule is not yet clear. Consider such an approach as this:

"(1) A holder in due course is a person who has taken the instrument regularly and in current course of trade.

"(2) Such taking normally includes as attributes

(a) that the instrument be regular on its face;

(b) that it be taken for value;

(c) that it be taken without notice of defects.

"(3) Value may include . . .

"(4) Notice of defects is given by . . .

"(5) Notice of defects is not given by . . .

"(6) In otherwise judging of notice of defects (or currency of course of trade) the following factors may be considered: pro . . . ; con. . . ."

My argument is that such drafting, by centering the basic question, adding the normal keys to answering and the available clear experience, and suggesting lines of useful further inquiry, would provide something much more certain (as well as much more easily usable) than the hundreds of pages of labyrinthine annotations to the N.I.L. which hide the law today.

40 An interesting and radically different discussion of the loss of the "course of trade" idea is Fagan, Commercial Bad Faith in the Law of Negotiable Instruments, 25 Ford. L. Rev. 449 (1956). His concern is not with overnegotiability when the transaction is not fresh, but with undernegotiability in fresh discount transactions if a purely subjective standard of good faith and notice be not seen as inherent in the factual course of trade. His argument stirs the always troublesome query of when a line of established practice may need rejection or qualification as being bad practice: as when a particular discounter takes all the paper of a dealer whose unreliable lines of operation it has ample reason to know of, though it knows nothing of particular transactions.

41 This is discussed in some detail in my First Struggle to Unhorse Sales, 52 Harv. L. Rev. 873, 890 ff. (1939). The "Factors Acts" concerned are those of the 1830's, not those which on the later New York model build a type of inventory lien for "factors" who are not selling-and-buying agents, but bankers.

42 Compare, e.g., Trust Receipts Act §9.2(a) on sales in ordinary course of trade, §9.2(c) on liberty of sale, §11 on liens in course of business; Uniform Commercial Code §2-403 on power to transfer goods, §7-501(3) on due negotiation of documents of title, and even §3-302(3), excluding certain odd transactions from producing a holder in due course.

43 Most fully, in The Formative Era of American Law (1938). His phrasing about the "classic" period is from the 1914 articles cited above, page 13, note 3. And Pound and Plucknett, Readings on the History and System of the Common Law (1927), with reference to judicial decision as a "source of law" (pp. 272-295) gather a multitude of suggestive quotations from the period.

44 Most fully in The Law in Quest of Itself (1940).

45 Towards Legal Understanding, I, 34 Columb. L. Rev. 862, 874-889 (1934). Nelles differs from the others in taking the formal opinions of the period as the type or standard,

and elaborating then on the astounding degree to which it was "departed" from by "non-mechanical" opinions.

46 I have elsewhere indicated my objection to the cold-shouldering of the great Gény by Holmes (in his paper on Natural Law, begun as a review of Gény) because, as I see it, Holmes did not read far enough into or past the limping semiphilosophical introductory stuff to meet, at work, over the volumes, the sweet craftsmanship as Gény uses an ancient text to handle the most modern of cases. Had Holmes gone into the meat, it would have been psychologically impossible for his own superb craftsmanship to miss this. Patterson also once dismissed my praise of Gény: "after all, a second-rate Natural Law writer." But one does not find Cardozo lacking in appreciation of Gény's "brilliant book." The Nature of the Judicial Process 138 and passim (1921). And there was Kantorowicz. As a legal historian, he rates at least with Holmes. As a logician and technician, he rates only one notch under Jerome Michael himself. As an embodiment of vanity, he rates above any but one I have known. But Kantorowicz said to me with fervor, and at the height of his career: "I would give everything I have done, and more, to have written Gény's Méthode." And Kantorowicz was not a Natural Law man.

47 An excellent and extended presentation of what is in effect work in the style of reason and a critique thereof from the angle of the Formal Style, also a demonstration at once that any "prevailing style" on any court may be marbled by contrast and that the time-incidence of a style within a country may vary hugely, appears in Reid's study of Doe and Carpenter in New Hampshire, The Reformer and the Precisionist: A Study in Judicial Attitudes, 12 J. Legal Ed. 157 (1959). Doe mounted the bench in 1859, already a fully formed and powerful exemplar of the Grand Style. He sat, with a 2-year intermission, till 1896. "Remembered as one of the great reformers" — but in essence until the latter years (when he sometimes did not bother to wrestle with authority he was overturning or remodeling) less a reformer than a follower of the Grand Tradition who combined vision, drive, and craftsmanship and who was granted 35 years of working time, 2 decades of it as Chief. Carpenter, appointed in 1881, had already long embodied the attitudes and manner which outside of New Hampshire typified his time of service, and in his opinions, especially in dissent against Doe, gave them classic expression.

48 Some effort at reaching an explanation for this change, which by 1900 seems to have occurred throughout the industrial countries, in my On the Good, the True, the Beautiful, in Law, 9 U. Chi. L. Rev. 224, 239 ff. (1942).

49 I am not suggesting that a "Natural Law," or "Right Reason" "method" cannot gallop off gaily in all directions or be bigotedly smug about goals and results. We have Constitutional decisions to remind all of us, and for the specialist there are weird things written in the "family" field, the "labor" field, even in "torts" or "courts." But excesses and errors do not test the value of a core, nor a fool that of a tool.

50 21 Wend. 614 (N.Y.S. Ct. 1839).

51 Above, page 64.

52 Above, page 407, note 6.

53 See my On Warranty of Quality, and Society, I, 36 Columb. L. Rev. 699, 737-744 (1936), II, 37 ibid, 341 ff. (1937). Compare Cardozo on the Supreme Court.

54 This seems a slip. The guardian will normally be the father, or the mother. What "redress" would Cowen then propose? But it is an interesting bud, and it is characteristic of his drive for thinking through.

55 217 N.Y. 382, 111 N.E. 1050 (1916).

56 Page 441.

57 It is true that over the last forty years or so successive uniform statutes with careful and skillful organized backing have built into our law in this area lines of exemption from responsibility of banks handling accounts, of transfer agents, etc., which might seem to settle policy permanently against the considerations urged in the text. But I think good policies still worth discussion. Good situation-reasons can emerge from seeming graves long after men think them wholly turned to earth. On the side of practice, I can recall when all men knew that an indenture-trustee could never be expected to be ever held to

any responsibility at all. On the side of law, consider the two negotiable instruments sequences examined at the outset of this paper: in each instance an idea so long dead that its serious discussion was ridiculous has not only revived, but shown teeth. Or consider the tide of "simple validation" law in assignment of accounts receivable, which then suddenly reversed itself.

58 See page 312 above.

59 Compare pages 294 ff. above.

60 Compare pages 274 ff. above.

61 Such fresh creation does not require a complete new concept. It is enough to recognize explicitly that the problem is a new one, and to use the case for a fresh start.

62 From here on, though the events are from Rutledge, their interpretation is mine.

63 Compare pages 426 ff., 305 ff. above.

64 The matter opens with Carle v. People, 200 Ill. 494, 66 N.E. 32 (1903), which involved mixed evidence on whether a saloon killing was murder. An eyewitness was held properly made a court's witness. The limitations on the procedure begin with People v. Bernstein, 250 Ill. 63, 95 N.E. 50 (1911), a sufficient but not overwhelming case, largely circumstantial, of arson. The record showed "no overwhelming need" of the evidence in order to avoid a miscarriage of justice, and no reason for examination of two witnesses by the court or for allowing the state's attorney to cross-examine. It was noted that they had not been eyewitnesses. Reversed.

65 People v. Laster, 413 Ill. 224, 232, 108 N.E.2d 596 (1952). The record showed no objection to the witness' being called as a court's witness, or to the admission of the prior written statement, nor was an instruction asked to limit the purpose of the evidence. All of the cases cited by defendant are, says the court, without naming them, "patently distinguishable." The court found defendant's story of the involved transaction "fantastic and illogical," noted that the jury had fixed the minimum penalty for the killing, and affirmed.

66 People v. Bennett, 413 Ill. 601, 604, 110 N.E.2d 175 (1953). In a trial for burglary and larceny, a witness who had been separately indicted for the same burglary was, although he had claimed his immunity, called as a court's witness and so pressed by questioning as to let the renewed claim of immunity be used by innuendo and insinuation against the defendant. Nor was any showing made that a miscarriage of justice threatened, without this witness; nor was much material evidence added. The court notes that the foundation is peculiarly needed where the witness is under indictment for the same crime. Various further items of prejudicial evidence had also been received. Reversed.

67 Carle v. People, see page 451, note 64; for Hundley, see p. 457, note 77.

68 250 Ill. 135, 95 N.E. 157 (1911).

69 254 Ill. 509, 98 N.E. 957 (1912).

70 286 Ill. 302, 121 N.E. 637 (1919).

71 361 Ill. 332, 197 N.E. 849 (1935).

72 People v. Curran, 286 Ill. 302, 121 N.E. 637 (1919), a plate glass labor-union racket case; two of the many witnesses were business agents of the alleged racketeer's. People v. Daniels, 354 Ill, 600, 188 N.E. 886 (1934), a holdup of a book-making joint, with ample eyewitness evidence apart from the court's witnesses. People v. Tuohy, above, note 71, the Factor kidnaping case, in which the evidence of the court's witness hardly touched the vital issues. People v. Rotello, 339 Ill. 448, 171 N.E. 540 (1930), may seem at variance. It involved a back-seat rape; the testimony and cross-examination of the court's witness (an eyewitness), complainant's girl friend, seems to me to be upheld in part because it was inconclusive, looking both ways. But "in furtherance of justice" no more pertinent witness can be imagined.

73 Siciliano, discussed above, page 451, is an instance; or Tuohy, above, note 72; or Cleminson, above, note 68, below, note 76.

74 These last judgments rest on the whole body of the cases: results, plus flavor. But Hundley can serve as a quick indication. Compare also People v. Boulahanis, 394 Ill. 255,

68 N.E.2d 467 (1946). That was a murder case where identification turned almost solely on the testimony of the "26" girl in a bar where 20 other customers had been. The cross-examination, which strongly suggested that this witness had been tampered with, seems to me to be the basic ground for reversal. Moreover, had badly improper cross-examination not botched the case, I do not believe that the court would have insisted that a further witness, who had not been an eyewitness, had been improperly made a court's witness.

75 Examples are People v. Dascola, 322 Ill. 473, 153 N.E. 710 (1926), a murder case which may have involved manslaughter or self-defense by a father who believed his daughter had been seduced, and which rested (in my opinion) partly on a seriously accusing alleged statement by deceased which, although of most dubious admissibility, had not been properly objected to. The girl, made a court's witness, had been examined exhaustively and prejudicially as to matters occurring long before the shooting. Reversed. People v. Krejewski, 332 Ill. 120, 163 N.E. 438 (1928), a conviction for robbery with a gun, where identification was far from clear, alibi evidence was strong, cross-examination *by the court in* regard to the out-of-court statements was unduly searching. People v. Johnson, 333 Ill. 469, 165 N.E. 235 (1929), a burglary conviction, reversed because (among other errors in a case which was not convincing) a woman was made a court's witness in order to be impeached by her prior statement that defendant had sold her a radio (a radio had been part of the stuff stolen). People v. Barragan, 337 Ill. 531, 169 N.E, 180 (1929), again robbery with a gun; the very identification turned on the unsworn out-of-court statements of another defendant who had pleaded guilty to the same robbery, made out of defendant's presence; their admission was held prejudicial error. People v. Quevreaux, 407 Ill. 176, 95 N.E.2d 62 (1950).

76 People v. Cleminson, 250 Ill. 135, 95 N.E. 157 (1911), was a wife-murder case very fully established. Improper and prejudicial cross-examination of the two noneyewitnesses made court's witnesses was held not enough for reversal. Even so, three judges dissented; and Johnson, above, note 75 (where the opinion was written by one of them), and Hundley, below, n. 77, show that their views are still important. In sharp contrast to Cleminson stands People v. Grigsby, 357 Ill. 141, 191 N.E. 264 (1934), a murder conviction involving dubious identification in which the People's case rested essentially on a woman's statement that defendant had told her that he had just shot a couple of guys — evidence brought out by a long impeachment examination. Reversed — almost of as course.

77 Hundley marks the spot where hiding from the cross-purposed policy-problem finally misleads the court itself. What was involved was a barroom killing which no witness saw happen; when the witnesses looked up, after three shots, each man was holding a gun. The court's witness had made statements that night that, as she was driving defendant to the bar, he had told her he intended to kill deceased "and if I said anything, he was going to kill me, too." To resolve the murder-or-self-defense issue this witness' testimony was the sole relevant testimony, which surely goes to avoiding a "miscarriage of justice." It was not that unsworn pseudo confession after the event, by some other person "for" the defendant, which the court has been careful to pillory. It was direct evidence of a state of mind existing immediately before the decedent was shot, evidence as close as human affairs normally permit. And the opinion shows nothing of that improper innuendo or overpounding which has marked other cases, such as Boulahanis, above, note 74. The girl's actual testimony in court, indeed, was that she "thought" he told her he was going to kill the deceased, so that the prior statement was less impeaching than clarifying. But the conviction was reversed. The case is singularly close to the juice (though not to the rationale) of Gibson, 385 Ill. 371, 52 N.E.2d 1008 (1944), where two women had had a bloody fight, one left but got back into the room, and the other was then found dead. Testimony was there properly admitted — as being "clearly within the rule of *res gestae*," statements "immediately prior to the affray" (385 Ill. at 380-381) — that the witness was awakened by pounding on the door, recognized the defendant's voice, and heard the door open and the defendant rush in saying, "Come on here, bitch, I'm going to kill you." (ibid. 375.) But the court likens Hundley to Grigsby, reported at note 76, above, where the alleged remarks of the defendant went not to the operative state of mind at the time of the act, with its probable implication of who had been the aggressor, but to a sort of casual postevent confession to the witness, who then, on the stand, proved "unsatisfactory" to the prosecution. Such a slip in analysis is a normal fruit of having kept the issue not in the

sun, but in the cellar, to ferment.

Another example of the same type of intellectual trouble, cleanly before the court, unresolved, and then committed to silence (the particular cases being quite reasonably decided), has crossed my path from Oregon. There was no great emotional flavor present, nor was there in 1925 a recognized and available scholarly fraternity to call on; but the intellectual problem is exactly parallel, and there must be many other instances. The Oregon cases had to do with bona fide purchases for value. One, Vanderpool v. Burkitt, 113 Ore. 658, 234 Pac. 289 (1925), involved an estoppel against a moronic conditional seller of an automobile which, on resetting original quarterly payments to monthly payments, had turned over the first papers marked "Paid." That case came to the court January 27, and went to the same judge who wrote the opinion in the second case. It was affirmed en banc on March 17. The other case, Schumann v. Bank of California, 114 Ore. 336, 233 Pac. 860 (1925), had been argued January 13, was decided February 24, and was denied a rehearing April 21. It also was en banc. It involved a batch of conditional sale contracts assigned "absolutely" for security, with the assignor collecting on them, and the papers coming home monthly for check-up and substitution. The assignor detached the assignment slips and reassigned. The court thought a first assignment with delivery to prevail, notwithstanding an assignor's intervening criminal act, but ducked the consequence by treating the first transaction as a pledge, so that redelivery sacrificed the security. Here were two "estoppel"-type situations, complicated by a "chose-in-action-assignment" idea half thought through and by the "intervening criminal act" evasion of the estoppel idea. It is manifest that the court was seeking a guidesome whole-situation answer, and did not find one. But to have the court en banc, within these dates, approve two opinions (by a single judge) neither of which refers either to its companion or to the problem which bothered the court: this is both to exhibit a conscious embarrassment, and to illusstrate one wrong poultice to apply. — On these cases see also pages 230 f., above.

Addendum to pages 455-457, the "guidance-pattern": Two earlier cases deserve mention. In People v. Rardin, 255 Ill. 9, 99 N.E. 59 (1912), "the court was very careful" to safeguard the defendant's rights on cross. Affirmed. People v. Bote, 379 Ill. 245, 40 N.E.2d 55 (1942), involved an eyewitness who on the second trial repudiated his evidence on the first. Insofar as the three-judge dissent argues that the conviction could not stand without the former testimony introduced on cross, and that "matters thus proven by way of impeachment" merely nullify and do not provide positive evidence, it is the dissent rather than the holding which is in line with the general and currently dominant pattern. Of the more recent cases, People v. Banks, 7 Ill. 2d 119, 129 N.E.2d 759 (1955) (murder) raised no real problem (sole eyewitness gave surprise new self-defense testimony and there was no abuse of the cross). Affirmed. The unresolved dilemma appears again, however, in the two last decisions, both by a single justice and within a year of each other. People v. Robinson, 14 Ill. 2d 325, 153 N.E.2d 65 (1958), involved sale of heroin to three men, the only eyewitnesses, who were all made court's witnesses. "We may consider, too, that justice would demand corroboration of an accuser where such corroboration is known to be available and that a defendant, who may cross-examine such witnesses freely, has the added advantage of discrepancies or contradictions that would not appear if the practice were limited to the calling of but one court's witness." (p. 335.) Affirmed. People v. Tunstall, 17 Ill. 2d 167, 161 N.E.2d 300 (1959) (armed robbery), though not a court's witness case, cites Hundley, page 457, note 77, and Barragan, page 456, note 75. There, although identification evidence was powerful and the alibi evidence blew up, conviction was reversed because of improper hammering on and reading of an out-of-court accusation of defendant by the man who had been indicted with him, but who was now testifying that he had done the robbery alone. How far a restrictive instruction as to the use to be made of the statement would have saved the conviction is not clear. I doubt that it would. "If, from the competent evidence already admitted, the jury entertained any doubts that defendant was guilty, it would be difficult, if not impossible, to remove the impression of guilt which would follow from such a statement." (N.E.2d at 303.) — In the net, both the pattern of outcome and that of leaving guidance as between the basic policies to the implicit thus remain consistent, but there is one advance: Robinson, by citing Hundley even while affirming, breaks the bulkhead between the two lines of authority.

78 Sitjoff Leyden (1960).

APPENDIX A

FURTHER CURRENT SAMPLINGS

{469}
It is of the essence of this book to test and report on whether we find in current American appellate judging a trend or drive toward recapture of the manner and virtue of the earlier Grand Tradition. See the discussion above, under The Contemporary Scene, Nationally, page 158. Such a test is best dealt with in time perspective. I therefore append here in first instance and with most fullness current samplings from the work of courts previously visited as of 1939-1940 (New York, Massachusetts, North Carolina, Ohio, Washington) or as of 1944 (Pennsylvania), 1951 (New York), or 1953 (Ohio). Trends show in time depth.

On the other hand, it is no less of the essence of this book to test and report whether the drive or movement toward recapture of the Grand Style spreads over our Nation, or is merely local. To this end I have done further, scattered, sampling. The detailed reports on this are, in the text above, from Mississippi and Alabama, and here from Kansas, Oregon, and Illinois. The two first I chose because at this moment I wanted to have the deep South well represented. Kansas was chosen because I wanted to see what had come, as a possible tradition, out of the great work of Burch and Mason. Oregon is, from a sampling viewpoint, either accident or intrusion: the material was in the same advance sheets I was using for Washington, and I have sentimental attachments to the State. Illinois was selected not only because it is my home, but to provide background for the occasional detailed Illinois material in the text.

Neither is there any "systematic" reason for choosing for summary rather than for full presentation Missouri, California, New Mexico, and Indiana. The more detailed stories must surely make clear to any person how I read and how I judge, and, indeed, how I report. So the ones which happened to get written up last are written up most briefly. I want the book to go to press.

Of my current samplings I should regard only Alabama's supreme court as inconsistent with my basic thesis on constant overt use of sense to shape the rule (see text, above, p. 162); I should regard Indiana, Missouri, and even Kansas as off-line for major persuasiveness. Each of these last is, nevertheless, entirely consistent, even mildly favorable. And there are eleven samples out of the fifteen which are striking and {470} conclusive. Something is present, at work, and significant, in the appellate judging of our country.

On the ranging of the authority techniques, there is no exception.

* * *

The reports follow in this order:

1. The "time-depth" jurisdictions: Massachusetts, New York, North Carolina, Ohio and Pennsylvania.

2. Further full current reports: Kansas, Oregon and Illinois.

3. Brief reports: California, Indiana, Missouri and New Mexico.

MASSACHUSETTS, 1959

The current Massachusetts sample is from 155 N.E.2d 158-193, the issue of February 11, 1959. The twelve cases were all decided January 6-15. It will be recalled that the 300-page sample from 1939 (noted above, p. 97, and drawn on twelve times in the Selection of Impeccable Precedent Techniques) caught the court at the moment of transition from a Formal Style of opinion-writing to the modern recapture of overt recourse to reason. That transition has long been completed. There does remain an occasional touch of magisterial austerity, and elaborate discussion of situation-reason as such is not yet as frequent in Massachusetts as in most other courts; but the facts of case and situation are regularly presented with patent intention of making the reason appear on the face of the opinion. The first, second, sixth, and ninth of the twelve cases (three tort, one contract) gave no seeming occasion to reexamine rules, but — even the two which were rescripts — show care for sense in application. The same can be said for *Margolis v. Margolis*, p. 177, where a finding below that "the adoption of false surnames is not in the best interests of the children" led to an injunction in favor of a divorced father; and for *Graves v. Fairhaven*, p. 179, where a "long line of cases" upholding "the traditional supremacy of the school committee in the field of education" were applied with vigor but with discrimination.

The remaining cases (six out of twelve, and from five different judges) show the court at work in the use of situation-sense to shape the rule.

Juchno v. Toton, p. 162, involved efforts by a housekeeper to enforce a judgment for services and loans against land of a decedent which had been conveyed to the latter's sons. The question went to whether the sons had assented to the conveyance. Prior cases on the effect of a mortgage later given by the grantees were distinguished on their facts and the reason of the situation, and the rule was carefully reformulated. (I think, unhappily, with "knowledge" the sole criterion, instead, in proper cases, of "reason to know"; and so what?)

In *Brush Hill Development, Inc. v. Commonwealth*, p. 170, an eminent {471} domain proceeding, the court goes through point after point of exclusion of testimony which would have favored the owner, upholding each ruling as within the court's discretion or as justified by inadequate foundation for the offered evidence. But, at the end, the consistent exercise of discretion in a single direction was found prejudicial. I see this as constituting a subrule full of situation-sense. A similarly procedural but useful rule was developed in *Turner v. Oxford*, p. 182. The town was in possession of a dump under a contract without fixed term. It was held that even if it were not liable for damages resulting from operation of the dump, "still it has a tenancy in land sufficient to justify enjoining the town from permitting a nuisance to be conducted upon the land"; this, in favor of an adjacent owner; but the decree below was rephrased to keep the town from having "to determine what is a 'nuisance' at its peril." (p. 184.)

The next two cases to be noted go more fully into rationale. *Cavarnos v. Kokkinak*, p. 185, was slander by a teacher in an Orthodox Theological School in regard to a false accusation of attempting to introduce Communistic literature into the school. "Much which was stated in a recent decision of this court is here pertinent. . . . 'Neither the school committee nor the court exists in a vacuum. Neither can profess ignorance of the currents of opinion which sway great masses of the people. It cannot be doubted that multitudes of people in this community regard with abhorrence the Communist Party and communism as that term is generally understood. It is not for this court to say why this is so or whether this feeling has gone too far or not far enough. It is sufficient for us that the feeling exists. . . . It is apparent that a school teacher has extensive and peculiar opportunity to impress his attitude and views upon pupils in his charge.'" (p. 186.) The court refused to distinguish a theological school, and sent the case to the jury. In *Commonwealth v. Goldberg,* p. 187, the rule-making was narrower, more technical, and addressed in first instance to the language of a statute; but it was no less a deliberate shaping to fit what the court saw as sense. An abortionist, after administration of a drug, had prescribed and procured intercourse as a further measure; the girl remained conscious and was able to dress. The statutory language "by force and against her will" was ruled (notwithstanding prior dicta and in reliance on outside authorities) not to justify a conviction for rape. "Fraud cannot be allowed to supply the place of the force which the statute makes mandatory." (p. 192.) {472}

But the most impressive case of the sample is *Kirby v. Kirby,* p. 165, a proceeding under the Runaway-Pappy statute, where the court surveys the whole proceeding, with a careful insistence on essentials coupled with firm dismissal of technical objections. "The purpose of the uniform reciprocal enforcement of support act is to obtain support for dependents, and not to provide a procedural field day for defaulting husbands and fathers." (pp. 168-169.)

Use of authorities. We meet distinction and reformulation (*Juchno,* above), quotation and use of a full rationale (*Cavarnos,* above), the usual plentitude of simple cites, the long line of cases to which "the challenge comes much too late" (*Graves v. Fairhaven,* above), rejection of prior dicta and borrowing of a rule from other jurisdictions (*Goldberg,* above), "see's" and "cf.'s," deliberate extension of a concededly distinguishable precedent. Statutes are sometimes merely referred to, sometimes quoted in part, sometimes quoted in full, sometimes examined in terms of exact particular phrasing, once with reference to the material difference between the current statute and its predecessor; always the flavor is one of situation-sense as being one gratifying element in the application or interpretation which results from the statute. An unusual feature of this sample, as against most others, is the frequency with which the court expressly reserves a point about which "we make no intimation" or on which it is "unnecessary to pass."

NEW YORK, 1958

The sampling started with 152 N.E.2d for September 17, 1958. This yielded five cases, all of which were addressed to situation-sense, only one of them indirectly and by way of a prior controlling case. But four of the cases had to do with the more intricate phases of modern economic life, and only two of the judges were represented, and New York is the oldest friend among the courts studied. The sample was therefore pressed back to September 10, with a fine widening of subject matter and, skipping further opinions by the judges already sampled, with two opinions apiece by three more. The opening cases of September 3 (151 N.E.2d) tested out as two Per Curiams and one more judge, making a total of sixteen cases and six judges. New York's old tradition of open and independent thought is still in flower; only seven of the cases were unanimous; and in seven dissenters wrote opinions. No "group" lines of voting appeared; one judge did dissent five times, but each time in different company.

Twice the argument makes a technical case and stops. Thus *Matter of Ciminera,* 4 N.Y.2d 400, 151 N.E.2d 832, simply Per Curiam, holds good a petition to command enforcement by town officials of an ordinance about topsoil, where "specific instances of their . . . failure to enforce it" are recited. The three-judge dissent deals, however, with policy: "If anything be clear, it is, as Presiding Justice Nolan wrote in dissent in the Appellate Division, that 'a proceeding in the nature of mandamus [will not] lie to compel a general course of official conduct, as it is impossible for a court to oversee the performance of such duties . . .' [T]o permit a taxpayer to mandate those officials to enforce such a law as the town ordinance here involved would truly open up a Pandora's box of controversy and litigation." (151 N.E.2d at 832-833.) {473}

Again, in *Channel Master Corp. v. Aluminium Sales, Inc.*, 4 N.Y.2d 403, 151 N.E.2d 833, although in the process of opening up vast tort liability out of mere contract negotiations, the opinion unfolds in dominantly technical terms. The complaint alleged a false representation of uncommitted capacity to furnish the plaintiff 400,000 pounds of aluminum per month, made with the successful purpose of inducing the plaintiff not to close contracts with other suppliers — with damages through *injury to plaintiff's business* when supplies ran short; and a second count alleged false representation of intention to make available to the plaintiff that monthly quantity over five years. The court finds allegations of fact and reliance sufficient to make a case in fraud, finds the cause to be entirely independent of contractual relations, and finds the statute of frauds to be inapposite in law and, on the basis of an inconclusive passage from Prosser, in policy. The three-judge dissent this time accepts, seemingly, each of these doctrinal premises; it attacks solely the application: the representations were not of facts susceptible of knowledge. For such a court, on such an issue, this is truly extraordinary. The situation is one in which the torts theorists (Restatement, Harper and James, Prosser, all gathered and cited) have launched as unconsidered a jamboree as ever has been suggested in the books: in the instant "application" of the idea, word-of-mouth negotiations for a contract which have led to no acceptance, which need not have led even to an offer, and which would in an action on an actually completed contract be incapable of submission to the jury for lack of a signed writing — these become admissible in the teeth of the statute against frauds and perjuries, admissible, moreover, in such fashion as to allow damages of a range and extent which would be dubious of procurement in any action based on an agreement fully closed, formally authenticated, and unambiguously relied on. All of this by virtue of merely adjusting the pleadings and the evidence to run down an alley which is rather easier to travel with persuasiveness than is the alley of contract-closing — and one in which any perjury or mistake is harder to pinpoint for pillory. For these are not the type of "conversations" which (like a true-blue offer or acceptance for a five-year deal) are hard to believe in unless "confirmed" in writing on the same day; instead, they run loose, without confirmation, or exactness, or top limit, or any other check-up. And these adventures into space are undertaken on the policy say-so not of thoughtful commercial scholars who are for instance somewhat bothered about a bit of untoward tightness and overtechnicality in the contract rules of damages, or about an unwise and unbusinesslike precisionism in requiring a mere "note or memorandum" under the Statute of Frauds to recite accurately every agreed term. No, these adventures are undertaken instead on somewhat loose general language about misrepresentation put out by scholars whose delight is to see the law of torts inherit the earth. Extraordinary indeed; and happily most uncharacteristic. {474}

Before conning the ten contrasting cases, we may briefly note four in which the discussion is addressed to the application of the rule concerned, each time with cogency. All are insurance cases if, as I assume, *Sellas v. Smith*, 4 N.Y.2d 412, 151 N.E.2d 838, was brought in essence against an insurer; a guest was there suing a host for an accident caused by the reckless driving of the guest's wife. The court thought, "Leave her alone. She knows what she's doing," in answer to the plaintiff-husband's remonstrances, "reflects participation in her negligence." In *Nobile v. Travelers Indemnity Co.*, 4 N.Y.2d 536, 152 N.E.2d 33, the insured wanted a cancellation as soon as he could get it, got it, according to the policy's terms and his own request, a few days before the accident, and — upsetting both courts below — was held to his cancellation. In *Concoff v. Occidental Life Ins. Co.*, 4 N.Y.2d 630, 152 N.E.2d 85, credit for extra premiums paid for residence in China, but unearned because of return to this country, was needed in order for a $50,000 life policy to be kept alive till the death; the court sustained a verdict, despite a merger clause, by locating an ambiguity in the policy which made evidence of highly credible agreements admissible. *General Accident etc. Assurance Corp. v. Piazza*, 4 N.Y.2d 659, 152 N.E.2d 236, a game of musical chairs between two insurers in regard to an accident in the loading of a truck, finds simple trucking from a Yonkers plant to a Brooklyn pier to involve no "common arrangement" for transportation via ocean to the Western interior.

Now the opinions (from six of the judges, and Per Curiam) in which *overt situation-sense is used to shape a rule of law*: *Pieper v. Renke*, 4 N.Y.2d 410, 151 N.E.2d 837, was a suit for an accounting by mother against daughter; the trial court found over $12,000 to have been misappropriated. "[T]he fact that an accounting is not needed to ascertain the amount of the misappropriation will not deprive the plaintiff of the sort of judgment which entitles her to enforce it by contempt proceedings. . . . The judgment herein should be modified by including a recital that the defendant wilfully breached her fiduciary duty," etc. (Per Curiam, 151 N.E.2d at 838.)

Two cases dealt with attacks by taxpayers on the making and financing of improvements, each dealing with the legitimacy of the legislature's approval of a situation which involved both local and state benefits and concern. In *Grimm v. County of Rensselaer*, 4 N.Y.2d 416, 151 N.E.2d 841, the challenge was to the county's financing its share of a technical institute attended 1956-1957 about 2 to 1 by nonresidents of the county. "The problems suggested . . . relate rather to the propriety of specific applications of article 126 than to the validity of the statute itself. In our view, the only question for decision is whether a county-established college may be regarded as an institution operated for a proper 'county purpose' within the sense of section 2 of Article VIII of the Constitution." (151 N.E.2d at 843.) "Education has long been regarded as serving a public and governmental purpose {475} . . . The ownership and operation of public facilities serving the welfare of a municipality are not deprived of their municipal character because they may serve a larger interest as well . . . The constitutional provision that no county shall contract any indebtedness except for county purposes, is aimed at prohibiting local indebtedness for expenditures which serve no local purpose . . . and the courts do not insist upon precise measurement of the respective interests." (ibid. 843844.) The project rested on county initiative and was under county management. "In addition, as the court at Special Term observed, the residents of Rensselaer County are eligible for entrance to community colleges in other counties, in which counties the residents may also be less than 50% of the student body. And, quite apart from this, the expenditure of Rensselaer County here involved is for an important county facility having a lasting value obtained by the county at one half of its full cost . . . [C]ertainly, no statute will be held invalid merely because some unauthorized action might be attempted under it." (All ibid. 844.) The essential problem and outlook did not change when, in *Whalen v. Wagner*, 4 N.Y.2d 575, 152 N.E.2d 54, the other face of the coin turned up. There the statutes under attack had authorized construction of metropolitan bridges in an interstate pattern. The question went to whether the legislation was required to go through the complex procedures prescribed by the Home Rule amendment. Cardozo was twice quoted: "The test is rather this: That, if the subject matter be in a substantial degree a matter of State concern, the Legislature may act, though intermingled with it are concerns of the locality." (152 N.E.2d at 57.) "If all these acts are in truth invalid, we must submit to the inconvenience that would result from such a holding. It is not one to be invited." (ibid. 56.) The history of the Port Authority, of the cases which "bear upon various aspects of this topic" and of the particular projects, all combined to defeat the attack; situation-sense and "the law" shone forth in happy indistinguishable amalgam.

A brewery sold to out-of-state distributors, making final delivery at its own plant to each buyer's trucks. It was taxed by the city on the "gross 'receipts' for 'the privilege of carrying on . . . business' within the city." *Schaeffer Brewing Co. v. Gerosa*, 4 N.Y.2d 423, 151 N.E.2d 845, upheld the tax. "A sale of goods in which delivery is taken within the seller's state is a local transaction which is taxable; 'neither the Commerce Clause nor the Fourteenth Amendment,' the Supreme Court has said, 'prevents the imposition of the tax on receipts from an intrastate transaction even though the total activities from which the local transaction derives may have incidental interstate attributes.'" (151 N.E.2d at 846.) "The petitioner's contention that the Wood and Harvester cases are not applicable because they deal with a different type of tax is without merit. In purpose and in language, the similarity between the Indiana tax there involved and the New York City tax {476} with which we are concerned could hardly be more complete . . . That the [New York City] measure is further described as a tax on 'the privilege of carrying on . . . business' — the sole prop for the petitioner's point — is neither meaningful nor consequential. As a matter of fact, both the Supreme Court of the United States and the Indiana Supreme Court have also denominated the Indiana tax 'a privilege tax' . . . a clear indication that the validity of a tax, or of the statute imposing one, depends on substance, not labels." (ibid. 847.) The frame of the discussion is here given, and the outcome is both indicated and urged, by the authorities; yet no man can doubt that the reason of the situation has been retested and found good, nor yet that, had reason pressed strongly the other way, the other door of decision stood open: "This is a privilege tax *and not*," etc.

Loeb v. Loeb, 4 N.Y.2d 542, 152 N.E.2d 36, roots in the national divorce situation. The New York Law Revision Commission had recommended a statute "to protect *a New York wife* whose right to support . . . may now be completely cut off by an *ex parte* foreign divorce decree." The statute made no mention of New York wives; "the court *may*, [my italics] nevertheless, render in the same action such judgment as justice may require for the maintenance of the wife." The wife in question, a Vermont girl with a Vermont matrimonial domicil, had been barred from remedy by the Vermont court's ruling that it was powerless, and had, pending a Vermont appeal (which she duly lost), sought to acquire a New York residence, living at first in New York with her mother-in-law, then buying a house. "Recognizing the social problems created by the frequent inequality of mobility and financial means as between husband and wife, the Legislature aimed to aid those wives who were unable to pursue their itinerant spouses and obtain support rights in foreign jurisdictions. However, such a policy is not furthered by allowing emigrant wives to journey to this State to avail themselves of this remedy. The interest of this State is the protection of the families located here, not the attraction of out-of-State spouses . . ." (152 N.E.2d at 39). The two-judge dissent protests the ruling that the New York courts are without power. It argues that "she moved here by agreement with defendant and at his request. She did not shop around and pick the State most advantageous to her and most inconvenient and expensive for her former husband." (ibid 41.) "Some point is made that because of the use in section 1170-b of the word 'may' the granting or refusal of relief is discretionary. Possibly that is so, at least as to the amount of support money, but the Appellate Division apparently granted leave to appeal so that we might pass on a question of law and that law question must be as to whether there is in this case any legal bar to relief. I think there is none." (ibid. 42.) — See further, ex the *Loeb* case, Precedent Technique Number 13.

Harbison v. City of Buffalo, 4 N.Y.2d 553, 152 N.E.2d 42, is the zoning fight in its modern dress. In *People v. Miller,* 304 N.Y. 105, {477} 106 N.E.2d 34, the whole New York situation had been worked over in the finer style and, it was hoped, cleaned up. In the main existing uses had been seen as constitutionally protected, with parking lots an exception and deprivation of projected uses permissible if they involved only a "relatively slight and insubstantial loss." The *Harbison* case now involved the city's power to "amortize" without compensation a long-existing use, a plant for reconditioning steel drums, with outdoor storage, no nuisance aspect being claimed. Two judges, examining history and need, joined the modern trend as to the city's power, if reasonably exercised, but sent the case back for full development of the facts, with strong suggestion that the commonly used indiscriminate blanket type of provision may run into trouble in New York, certainly on the period necessary for a particular enterprise, perhaps on whether any particular use is open to elimination at all. The *Miller* case was the legal foundation. Two further judges concurred in the result "on the principles stated in People v. Miller." To three judges, on a careful and skillful though slightly unfair canvass of the opposing line of the situation-reason, "The decision . . . marks . . . the beginning of the end of the constitutional protection of property rights in this State in pre-existing nonconforming uses under zoning ordinances." (106 N.E.2d 48.) Especially embarrassing is the attack on the concept "relatively unsubstantial": "It is arbitrary, in my view, to draw the line at buildings or structures valued at $500 or less. That sum is negligible in the case of large stores or factories, whereas it may represent the savings of years to small proprietors." (ibid. 49.)

The three cases next to be presented are alike in that in each the opinion-writing judge plainly felt forced by the authorities to reach the decision; they are alike in that in each one situation-sense is also drawn on; they are interestingly unlike in the net of the interplay of these two major factor-clusters. *Aetna Casualty etc. Co. v. United States,* 4 N.Y.2d 639, 152 N.E.2d 225, sustained a contractor's surety in its claim to the earned price as against the government's claim to a tax lien against the contractor. A particular case was "dispositive of this question." The facts were given and the rationale quoted. "The law of the Triborough case, followed in other cases, is well-settled law." See half a dozen cases. The technical rationale, to wit that the defaulting contractor never acquired, as against its surety, any rights to which a tax lien could attach, is satisfying enough as a sensible road through an intricate interplay of interests. The result — squaring with neither of the two decisions below — was unanimous. *Fosdick's Trust,* 4 N.Y.2d 646, 152 N.E.2d 228, required construction of a trust deed of 1918 under which the residuary legatee came into "any and all stock dividends." General Electric stock in the trust had benefited by a distribution which under the New York decisional law was a "stock dividend," but under the current views of the market and the writers was at least dominantly a "stock split." "The term 'stock dividends' has {478} been frequently the subject of litigation and has acquired a fixed judicial meaning which clearly includes the corporate action in question. *Since before the execution of the subject deed in 1918* it has been held and understood, etc." (152 N.E.2d at 232, my italics.) "It is the almost exceptionless holding of the later cases ... [citing 5 Misc. cases] ... Respondent correctly points out that the only inconsistencies in these recent decisions pertain to questions not here involved." (ibid.) "Having ascertained the meaning of 'stock dividends' as existent *at the time of its selection by the settler we are obliged to apply it here.* What appellants argue, in effect, is that we should now alter the traditional meaning of the term to comport with the definitions used today by the New York Stock Exchange and some accountants ... What appellants suggest actually presumes — without warrant — an intention on the part of the settlor [to avoid depletion of the fund] and then seeks to effect it by applying to the language he used a new definition...." (ibid. 233, my italics.) I can personally follow this, thus far, with much sympathy. But note the unnecessary conclusion: "Perhaps the definitions suggested by appellants and the *amici curiae* more nearly comport with the meaning of stock dividends and stock splits as understood in the modern communities of economics and finance and should be altered. *However, that function is properly for the Legislature alone.* A judicial change in these definitions now, changing the frustration of the intent of many settlors and testators who no doubt have relied upon what has heretofore been held to their meaning, seems to us unwarranted." (ibid., my italics.) This, though any such reliance in the *future* drafting of such instruments could have been made impossible by a dozen words. And what has the legislature to do with changing the meaning of language in private instruments? One judge limited concurrence to the result. One dissented with particular reference to modern financing of corporative expansion out of earnings. — The third of the cases, *Birnbaum v. New York State Teachers etc.*, 5 N.Y.2d 1, 152 N.E.2d 241, is one in which the court felt a constitutional amendment of 1938 to have been "designed to overcome" a dictum of its own from 1935 which had denied contractual protection to pension funds; therefore, even though the Education Law had from the beginning envisaged keeping the annuity fund actuarially sound, it felt obligated to knock out reductions in pension threatened if a new actuarial table were applied to persons already in the system. "Defendant argues that if this court holds that new mortality tables adopted by the Retirement System are applicable only to those persons who joined the system subsequent to the date of such adoption, the system will be plunged into bankruptcy. The answer to that argument must be that if the people intended to decree, by the constitutional amendment, that mortality tables adopted by the system after one has become a member are not to be applied in the computation of the annuity of such person, {479} we are not at liberty to hold otherwise simply because the system may become bankrupt as a result." (152 N.E.2d at 247.) The system, instead of acting within the year and a half leeway granted it, had delayed for over five and a half years after the amendment became effective. It was remitted to the legislature for aid. The lone dissent argued a different conclusion from "the whole sense of the statutory scheme."

Finally we have *Ferrara v. Galluchio*, 5 N.Y.2d 16, 152 N.E.2d 249, a suit for malpractice in X-ray therapy. The sole question was whether an award of $15,000 out of $25,000 for mental anguish flowing from cancerophobia was proper. After two years of unhealed burns the plaintiff had been sent by her attorney to a doctor who advised a check-up every six months because cancer might develop. "This case is somewhat novel, of course, in that it appears to be the first case in which recovery has been allowed against the original wrongdoer for purely mental suffering arising from information the plaintiff received from a doctor to whom she went for treatment of the original injury." The recovery was sustained. *"The problem is one of adequate proof,* and it is not necessary to deny a remedy in all cases because some claims may be false." (152 N.E.2d at 252, my italics.) "It is common knowledge among laymen and even more widely among laywomen that wounds which do not heal over long periods of time frequently become cancerous." (ibid.) The three-judge dissent stressed that the cancer-fear was linked only with a "statement *plaintiff claims* to have been made by a dermatologist . . . which statement he did not acknowledge having made." (ibid. 253.) But the dissent goes also to the rule: "The decision of the majority introduces into the law a new field of damages for cultivation by plaintiffs and affording countless opportunities for fraudulent unverifiable claims." (ibid. 254.)

Overt sense-discussion in fourteen out of the sixteen cases, and going in ten of them to the shaping of the rule; dissenting opinions in seven cases; the recurrence of problems raised by the intricacies of modern economic and governmental organization — these characteristics have been noted. The last case serves to point up two other features. Twice in this small group of cases (*Ferrara* and *Channel Master*) we meet the law of torts in sharp expansion; thrice we meet three-judge dissents (comprising, in cumulation, six of the judges) which worry about proliferation of unforeseeable and troublesome litigation ("Pandora's box"): "a new field of damages . . . countless . . . unverifiable" (*Ferrara*), supervision of enforcement of ordinances on topsoil, etc. (*Ciminera*), admeasurement for countless individual cases of "amortization" of an existing use (*Harbison*). Against this background there can be no doubt that one cofactor in producing the "Our courts are powerless" decision on support for non-New York divorcees (*Loeb v. Loeb*) was a desire to keep at least that nestful from hatching. But {480} open sense-discussion, growth, worry, free dissent without factionwise dissent — these are the attributes of healthy method on an appellate bench, if two features are added; a respect for and craftsmanlike treatment of authorities, and sustained effort at finding explicit lines to guide the future, with on-going openness to self-correction. Each of these features shows in the:

Precedent techniques. The frame of authorities and the duty to them is unmistakably felt in these cases. Of course I do not suggest that the authorities are not also used as means. Thus in the *Loeb* case the Law Revision Commission Report is quite as welcome as it is persuasive, and it might have been dispensable if not at hand. But it is duty and high office of an appellate court to use as well as to follow; a line officer must deal with the conditions on the line. In another instance, the almost violent creation in *Channel Master,* the court finds comfort, guidance, *and safety* in a formula with a long New York history: "The essential constituents of the action *are fixed* [my italics] as representation of a material existing fact, falsity, scienter, deception and injury." (151 N.E.2d at 835.) It is out of and with that sure solidity that the pioneering venture moves. And throughout, the authorities come in for candid treatment; if anything, they are underplayed in presentation. Thus, as in *Channel Master,* whole lists of clean holdings can appear as "see." Quoted language which is only language appears as such, and mere squints or suggestions can indeed be used to found propositions of law, but are duly noted as "cf." As usual, the simple citation dominates in the laying of any foundation or disposition of a minor point. On the major point, any controlling case appears typically complete with facts and quoted rationale. The "net effect" of a body of decisions can be controlling, or the necessary implication of one prior holding. Distinctions, where needed, almost always show their reason. Typically, again, but not always, a fresh direction or extension in the application of a rule or principle is signaled as such. The court is interested in the consolidation of court opinion when dissenters come around later (*Whalen v. Wagner re Adler v. Deegan,* at 152 N.E.2d 57); and twice it notes that the instant holding will square even with the dissents in controlling cases (152 N.E.2d 36 and 239). It sometimes stresses its exact prior language; and in its current opinions it repeatedly looks forward to similar stress; "we do not say . . ."; or "Material triable issues of fact thus remain . . . — in each instance proceeding to detail points *not* disposed of by the holding.

Two further matters of method in writing need special note: there is occasional indication of *who* wrote in a prior opinion (Cardozo, Cooley, etc.), one of the characteristic features of the Grand Style; and there is a striking, repeated practice of relying in argument or quotation on an effective opinion below. Compare the illustrations at pages371 ff, above. {481}

NORTH CAROLINA, 1959

The material hit upon was the advance sheet for October 22, 1959, 110 S.E.2d 278-328. The first four cases, involving a suit to quiet title against a receiver's deed, arose out of a single set of facts and on pleadings identical save as to parties defendant and parcels of land concerned, were disposed of under a single reasoned opinion, and are here reckoned as a single case. So reckoned, we have ten full opinions (four judges represented) and four Per Curiams. The tone of reason runs throughout, even through two of the Per Curiams, sometimes in the application of a rule whose language shows its reason on its face (whether or not the rule be new to North Carolina), sometimes in the recital of evidence or findings which make the application reasonable, sometimes in a discussion or in a quotation (from North Carolina or from elsewhere) which briefly indicates or explores the reason of the type-situation.

Two of the Per Curiams are flat and formal: it is "too well settled . . . to require citation" that a referee's findings, approved by the trial judge, and supported by competent evidence, are conclusive on appeal, *Clay Hyder Trucking Lines v. General Realty & Ins. Corp.,* p. 293, 250 N.C. 732; and there is no appeal from an interlocutory order, *Green v. Western & So. Life Ins. Co.,* p. 321, 250 N.C. 730 — but the dismissal is carefully without prejudice. The other two P.C.'s are characteristic of the whole sample: *State v. Banks,* p. 322, 250 N.C. 728, sets out elaborately the reasons why a patrolman became convinced that a car had been illegally loaded with liquor, and then rules (with a simple cite) that a radio message by that patrolman to a colleague at headquarters was sufficient "information" to authorize a search warrant.

Johnson v. Lamar, p. 323, 250 N.C. 731, dismisses an appeal from a nonsuit because the accident was in South Carolina, the substantive law of that State determines the cause, and no argument addressed to that law is presented; but "attention is directed to the provisions of C.S. §1-25" — which allows a new action if commenced within a year.

Reason in the application of the rule is illustrated in *Waters v. Harris,* p. 283, 250 N.C. 701. The defendant, who sold used refrigerating machinery, conducted plaintiff, his prospective customer, into an unlit portion of a warehouse with a rough and trash-strewn floor, where plaintiff slipped in a greasy puddle and broke his hip. A "combination of circumstances" took the case out of a prior rule and precedent which had required the plaintiff to prove that notice of any unsafe condition had been brought home to defendant. So in *Everette v. D. O. Briggs Lumber Co.,* p. 288, 250 N.C. 688, not only is the situation-reason developed for the rule admitting telephone conversations, but the evidence is rehearsed which made plaintiff's identification of "the anti-phonal party" practically conclusive. Similarly, in *State v. Bryant,* {482} p. 319, 250 N.C. 720, an involuntary manslaughter conviction, in applying the North Carolina rule that "any person of ordinary intelligence, who has had an opportunity for observation, is competent to testify as to the rate of speed of . . . an automobile," (110 S.E.2d at 320-321) the court does so on the basis of a statement of facts which shows not only unusual opportunity in the witnesses, but use thereof. Much less explicit or indeed implicit is the reason which appears in *Johnson v. Wayne Thompson, Inc.,* p. 306, 250 N.C. 665, for holding it not contributory negligence as a matter of law to become a passenger, in hilly country, in a car the plaintiff had herself discovered to have somewhat defective brakes. But the court develops an elaborate and thoroughly persuasive parallel with a prior case. I should guess that the reason in the application which is really at work is that contributory negligence as a matter of law is today in North Carolina a concept that is losing sex appeal. Finally, in this group, we should include *Skinner v. Jernigan,* p. 301, 250 N.C. 657, where an affirmative defense of contributory negligence was not available for lack of pleading, but the court went on to see plaintiff's riding, standing and holding on, in the back of a truck that overturned, as neither dangerous conduct nor a contributory factor in the injury; and we should include also *MacGray v. Bennett,* p. 324, 250 N.C. 707, a malicious prosecution case in which a nonsuit was reversed. There the court for more than two pages digests evidence of tricky and nasty persecution culminating in prosecution (for embezzlement) of an ex-Marine laundry route man by his employer, remarks that even if an employer-employee relationship had existed, there was a case on want of probable cause, and then, via an almost identical Washington case, fully presented, and via a cite from Am. Jur. which uses as its example a laundry agent working like the plaintiff on commissions, and charged like the plaintiff with the full amounts due the laundry, proceeds to find a pure debtor-creditor relationship and hence no color of embezzlement.

The court's readiness to *shape* the rule to fit the situation-reason shows plainly at least three times. In *Whiteside v. McCarson,* p. 295, 250 N.C. 673, the court notes that under a statute upsetting an earlier decision "the pendulum swung from one extreme to the other" (110 S.E.2d at 299); hence, with the statute carrying the question of the operator's agency to the jury on mere proof that the defendant owned the car, the defendant-owner is held entitled, even in the absence of special request, "to an instruction *related directly to the evidence in the particular case*" on when it is the jury's duty to answer the agency issue "No" — as, when the operator is using the car purely on his own, on a date. "Fairness requires" this. (ibid., court's italics.) Again, in *Moore v. WOOW, Inc.,* p. 311, 250 N.C. 695, a ruling about when a default divorce decree can be vacated on a second application, by a second judge, after a first application has failed, is made general for all defaults that fit the reason of the situation-type. Yet again, in *Everette,* {483} p. 288, already mentioned, a defendant corporation's claim that the acts of its substantial owner were *ultra vires* is met by quoting the statute which limits that defense. "In view of the foregoing, it is unnecessary to call attention to the fact that D. O. Briggs owned 90% of the capital stock of the D. O. Briggs Corporation and that said corporation received benefits from the transactions with plaintiff." (110 S.E.2d at 293.) Finally, in *Whiteside,* mentioned just above, we find reason working in the other direction; it can constrict: a partial new trial is confined to a single issue out of five, explicitly departing, because reason so demands, from the "somewhat different course" followed in a prior case. (110 S.E.2d at 300.) These opinions are from three different members of the court.

But perhaps the most interesting pattern in this sample, in its bearing on the court's drive for a situation-reason, is the court's effort to find, in *addition to a precedent* in point, an authoritative phrasing which either shows a reason on the face of the rule or adds a reason in discussion. When this can be found in a North Carolina case, the single precedent does the work. Thus, *Waters v. Harris,* pp. 283, 287, 250 N.C. 701, quotes from a prior North Carolina opinion: "Unless obviously dangerous, the conduct of a plaintiff which otherwise might be pronounced contributory negligence as a matter of law would be deprived of its character as such, if done at the direction of the defendant or its agent. [Citing authorities.] Here, the plaintiff and her companions were directed by defendant's agent to go to the balcony for seats. In following this direction, plaintiff was injured. The case is one for the jury." And such, substantially, is the approach in *Everette,* pp. 288, 291; *Skinner,* pp. 301, 303; *State v. Bryant,* pp. 319, 320. Twice there seems to have been no North Carolina precedent on the point; each time the resort is directly to an outside case and to an encyclopedia to reach an appropriate rule plus reason. *Skinner,* pp. 301, 305; *MacGray,* pp. 324, 327. But three times the pattern of *further* questing turns up unmistakably: A rule of law is announced on the basis of simple North Carolina cites; the substance has thus been decided; but the court goes on to an encyclopedia or to outside case material, or both, to find a satisfactory reason made clear, too. Thus in *East Carolina Lumber,* pp. 278, 280, 250 N.C. 681: "Upon his appointment, the property of the East Carolina Lumber Company vested in the Receiver subject to all liens then outstanding thereon. *National Surety Co. v. Sharpe,* 236 N.C. 35, 50, 72 S.E.2d 109. As stated in 45 Am. Jur., Receivers §407: 'Where an order of sale is made without notice to lien holders and they are in no way parties thereto, a sale made thereunder will not impair their liens, but the purchaser at the sale will take the property subject to their liens. If the order of sale makes no mention of such prior lien, or of encumbrances of any kind, the sale passes the title in the property as it is in the receiver, and subject to whatever encumbrances exist.'" Much fuller further statements {484} of the situation-reason are hunted up in *Moore,* pp. 311, 314, and *Lampley v. Bell,* pp. 316, 317.

It should be noted, in conclusion, that twice "all the remaining exceptions and assignments of error" are disposed of in bloc (pp. 306, 321) and in the plural. One hopes that this indicates their being viewed in their cumulative effect. Certainly this is the meaning in *Everette,* pp. 288, 292, of "a reading of the entire record" to determine whether many leading questions by the trial judge at crucial points led to clarification or to unfairness.

Use of authorities. Precedents were for the most part simple-cited, singly or in batches. Sometimes the rule to be applied was quoted. Occasionally the facts of similar cases were presented to justify analogical application, or a closely parallel case was given with some fullness. Infrequently there was a plain extension of prior holdings, rather frequently an overt distinction — each time, I think, for reason carefully shown. Once, to hedge in an overenthusiastic statute, there is frank new creation. Several times there are rulings which approach the. character of subrules, with no authority given; and twice authority *and* reason are borrowed from outside.

In the main the treatment of statutes is obscure, on the face, because their text is not given. Once a statute is quoted; it fits, it is applied. Once, as indicated above, a statute is provided with a brake.

The net, as compared with 1940 (218 N.C.) is gratifying. The unhappy internal feud of those days is no more, and the unity of the court has almost certainly freed time and energy for more craftsman-like work. Style and composition are easier and cleaner. But the striking thing is that, throughout, Reason sits as the eighth member of the court.

OHIO, 1957-1958

The first current sample studied was that from Ohio, 146 N.E.2d 287-308, the issue of January 8, 1958. This netted five single-paragraph formal dismissals on the ground that no debatable constitutional question was involved; these will be disregarded. It included one unanimous Per Curiam, *In re Bates*, p. 307, 167 Ohio St. 46, quoting from a prior opinion that "this court has often held that reports and records, concerning an accident in which a party is involved, which reports and records, according to the custom of such party, are turned over to and remain in the possession of such party's attorney, are privileged communications. . . ." (146 N.E.2d at 308.) The rule was applied according to its implicit reason to protect from contempt proceedings a physician who on behalf of a traction company had examined a person injured in a bus accident and had turned the records over to the traction company's attorney. There remain four full cases with a total of *nine* full opinions. Four different judges are recorded as authors; one {485} three-judge P.C. is almost certainly from the pen of a fifth. All of these opinions draw as of course on the sense of the situation as they wrestle with the shaping of the rule, and I thought them enough to demonstrate the continuance into November, 1957, of the manner which has been fully documented above, in our text, for 1953. But as work on the MSS progressed it became both more unmistakable and more significant that overt recourse to situation-reason has been on the increase in Ohio, both in degree and in regularity, not only from 1939 to 1953 but from 1953 to 1957. I have therefore added the Ohio material from the February 11, 1959, issue which contains the Massachusetts sample: four more full cases, including two long P.C.'s and one elaborate dissent, from a writer new to the sample, all from December 24, 1958. This material leaves no doubt that the progress in method between 1953 and 1957 is not an illusion but is characteristic of the court's current work.

State ex rel. Commissioners of Sinking Fund v. Brown, 146 N.E.2d 287, 167 Ohio St. 71, which opens the ball, was mandamus to the Secretary of State to require execution of a million-dollar note incident to a hundred-and-fifty-million-dollar bond issue authorized by constitutional amendment. The legality of the issue was challenged on the ground that the short text on the ballot had been misleading. A three-judge P.C., in the light of the purposes of the statute ("condensed text that will properly describe") and the necessities of balloting, distinguishes one adverse case, for reason given, capitalizes an excerpt from another, and rules the amendment valid. As a second ground: a syllabus paragraph and the opinion in a prior case show an election contest to be the specific and exclusive remedy here, and any such contest should have been undertaken two years ago. A three-judge concurrence has "grave doubt whether this court could reasonably have sustained" the amendment under proper challenge; and the P.C.'s own cases are cited to buttress this doubt. "However, it would be intolerable if there were no limitation on the right to question . . ." (146 N.E.2d at 290); and one batch of cases is gathered to support election contest as the proper and limited remedy, while another batch is distinguished for reason. The seventh judge examines italicized specific language in statute and in ballot, deals with the purpose of both and the nature of voters, distinguishes in regard to liberality of construction between indication of candidates and misrepresentations about bond issues, and would excuse the two-year delay because the matter of issuing the bonds has only just become actual.

Against that background, which is characteristic of the whole double-sample, other cases can be presented more briefly. *State v. Miclau*, 146 N.E.2d 293, 167 Ohio St. 38, involved a conviction for contributing to the delinquency of a child (the statute goes on: *"or* act in a way *tending to cause delinquency"* — my italics). A teen-ager who had been buying too many hard drinks was taken back to one of the restaurants {486} by a reporter, under police cover, and a drink was served her on the reporter's order. The drink was then seized as evidence, and the prosecution instituted. The majority held a conviction by the juvenile court improper because no delinquency of the teen-ager had been shown to which the proved actions of the defendant had contributed. Language in a prior case used there to facilitate conviction was turned to the aid of rigid requirements for conviction on "a criminal charge," and sloppy drafting of the charge (omitting reference to the language italicized above) proved fatal. The three-judge dissent uses the spirit, intent, and italicized exact language of the statute to reach a contrary result. *Welsh v. Ledyard*, 146 N.E.2d 299, 167 Ohio St. 57, expanded prior privity doctrine as if by compulsion to bar a wife's suit in warranty for injury from an electric cooker bought by her husband; but as appears above at note 76, page 80, and in the text at page 111, situation-sense was both felt and patently at work, in regard to shaping the rules for the situation. In *Broughton v. Cleveland*, 146 N.E.2d 301, 167 Ohio St. 29, outside general criticism of the rule against liability of a municipality for torts in performance of a governmental function is recognized and rejected, and the general Ohio position against liability is affirmed and extended to municipal garbage collection even though this involves overruling or abandoning a decision to the contrary. The scene discussed is wide, including, for instance, sewer maintenance and construction. The two-judge dissent goes only to doctrinal consistency, seeing prior Ohio decisions which have recognized liability in regard to sewer maintenance as, in reason, covering garbage collection *a fortiori*. Details from *Broughton* appear above at note 64, page 77; note 105, page 86; note 110, page 87; and in the text at page 300.

Of the more recent cases in question the simplest is *State ex rel. Gullett v. Klapp*, 155 N.E.2d 200, 168 Ohio St. 374, an action in prohibition to keep the Industrial Commission from trying certain charges of misconduct in practice before it. The relator failed for alleged reasons of health to comply with a subpoena to force his deposition. The court, P.C., applied the statute permitting dismissal of an action without prejudice for disobedience by the plaintiff "of an order concerning the proceedings." A precedent allowing such dismissal for refusal of a personal-injury plaintiff to submit to a reasonable physical examination was extended to make this plaintiff's refusal to submit to the statutory duty of cross-examination, where request was properly made, constitute "in effect, disobedience' of an 'order,'" etc. (155 N.E.2d at 202.) Situation-reason is implicit and obvious. The other P.C., *Zanesville Rapid Transit, Inc. v. Bailey*, 155 N.E.2d 202, 168 Ohio St. 351, turned on a question of lockout, with reference to unemployment compensation. The company, in distressed financial condition, had given some six weeks' notice of cancellation of its contract with the union, after which the union filed a notice of dispute. The company {487} had attempted in vain to get relief from the city, and finally *gave* notice of a wage reduction, the old wage to be restored if relief should be procured. The men did not report to work. The statute barred unemployment benefits for lack of employment "by reason of a labor dispute other than a lockout." The court reached for authority partly (Kentucky) expanding, partly (Connecticut) in a long quote of rationale limiting the lockout concept. It relied on two and a half months' notice of the company's difficulties and on the company, as a public utility, having no independent power to raise prices; and found the announcement of wage cut therefore not so unreasonable as to constitute a lockout.

The two remaining cases, both in domestic relations, though amazingly unlike in net attitude and technical flexibility, are nonetheless of one piece when it comes to using situation-sense to shape the rule. *In re Fore,* 155 N.E.2d 194,168 Ohio St. 363, was a guardianship struggle between a paternal grandmother from Louisiana and a maternal aunt in actual custody of a three-year-old orphan boy. The father, native and resident of Louisiana, went into the armed services, and sixteen years later was killed with his wife in a motor accident in France. The boy, after an investigation by the Red Cross, was turned over to the mother's sister, of Ohio, who had gone abroad for her sister's funeral. An Ohio Probate Court then granted her letters of guardianship, now challenged in habeas corpus by the petitioner on the basis of letters of tutorship later granted in Louisiana. The court sets forth the "rules" (court's quotes) of domicile which would give Louisiana exclusive jurisdiction to award custody, finds a closely parallel Alabama case protecting an aunt in actual and legal custody as having power to choose a domicile for the infant, and relies on Cook to avoid too broad conclusions from domicile. Then, however, it turns to the welfare of the child, to a long quote from Stumberg, and works out the power and duty of the court where the child is, as against any sole jurisdiction of the domicile. The Ohio enabling statute in favor of a "resident" is then held not limited in this context to domicile. Finally, the full faith and credit clause is briefly held to be inapplicable in favor of the Louisiana decree because of lack of jurisdiction over the person of the child. The grasp of situation, sense and law, are refreshing. *Mazzolini v. Mazzolini,* 155 N.E.2d 206, 168 Ohio St. 357, presents a tougher technical problem, plus a situation which the court finds opaque. An Ohio widower of fifty-eight went to Massachusetts and there had a Church marriage with his first cousin, a long-time Massachusetts resident of fifty-one. The relationship was disclosed; the Archdiocese gave permission. The union did not work and the wife returned home. Before she did the husband sued in Ohio for annulment on the ground that the marriage was void *ab initio.* Dismissed. On appeal the Court of Appeal had found the marriage to be founded on a "fraudulent contract" under Massachusetts law, so that the divorce laws of Ohio provide an exclusive {488} remedy for dissolution. The majority start with the general policy in favor of marriage, note that first-cousin marriage is legal in Massachusetts, but come then to that statute which makes "*null and* void" a marriage in that state by a party residing and continuing to reside elsewhere if the marriage would be "*void*" under the law of the home jurisdiction. "It is, therefore, apparent that we are squarely confronted with the question of whether a marriage between first cousins is *void* in Ohio" (155 N.E.2d at 208). (This, I suggest, is the same type of verbalism rejected on the same day in *Fore;* and I suggest that while the Massachusetts statute is patently intended merely to protect that Commonwealth from being a haven for evasion of other States' serious policies of marriage-control, yet an elastic construction of the Massachusetts statute by the Ohio court would cost Ohio no forseeeable price.) Taking the whole situation — common law marriage recognition in Ohio, first cousins marriageable at common law, first-cousin intercourse not incest, the enabling statute about persons "not nearer of kin than second cousins" being capable of construction as contemplating only ceremonial marriage, and voidity of marriage requiring by the trend of the more modern cases an express statutory declaration — the court held that the marriage here would not have been void *ab initio* in Ohio and that therefore a suit for annulment" did not lie. Edward Mazzolini got, in the process, no advice as to "what course, if any [he] might pursue under the divorce laws of Ohio" (ibid. 209). The three-judge minority see the Ohio statutory policy as necessarily affecting the capacity of first cousins to enter into a common law marriage, which they find to exist only as an alternative *form* of marrying; see the majority as holding a common law first-cousin marriage merely voidable, with the consequence that mere one-sided disavowal will void it. "[S]uch a situation would make a mockery of the marriage statute ..." (ibid. 210). — I do not myself see why the lone word "void" in the Massachusetts statute, when contrasted with "null and void" three lines away in the same sentence, does not invite giving it such a meaning as "without full legal effect and contrary to declared policy"; nor can I see why a decision explicitly and in italics announced as *"in the instant case"* (ibid. 208) should not be tailored so far as reasonably possible to the needs of that instant case — always assuming that Ohio annulment permits proper alimony allowance and declaration of legitimacy of any children.

Authority techniques. Sufficient illustration appears above of expansion, restriction (overruling included), selection and redirection, borrowing from other courts and from the literature, building with either syllabus or opinion or both, and varying ways with statutes. One adds: a full supply of simple cites and "see's." {489}

PENNSYLVANIA, 1959

The sample is from the issue of April 11, 1959, 149 A.2d 28-128, twenty cases, with six of the court writing and four opinions from below adopted as either the whole or the substantial basis for the decision. The sample is spectacular. Thus the first five cases offer more than five rules tested and worked over in terms of explicit situation-reason, the opinions coming from four of the judges, with one four-and-a-half-page adoption from below. This is more than enough to make the case, and is all I shall here present in full; but enthusiasm took me into a thorough canvass of the other fifteen opinions. Some of the results appear above in the text of the book. Thus, re use of the opinion below, at page 317, re the expansion of a doctrine by sloughing off a makeweight factor, at pages 305 ff. It should also be noted that *In re Cunningham's Estate*, p. 72, 395 Pa. 1, deals, at great length like *Fosdick's Trust* in the New York sample, with the impact of changed economic conditions and practices on allocations as between life tenant and remainderman, resilient awareness and adjustment appearing in the opinion on each side. In tone and method the whole body of these twenty cases runs along the same lines. Careful reason in application also appears throughout. The advance in the fifteen years since 1944 is amazing; the Grand Tradition has been fully recaptured. In six cases there were dissenting votes and in one a special concurrence; but only in two companion cases did this lead to special opinions.

Schechter v. Zoning Board, p. 28, 395 Pa. 310, had to do with an application for a zoning variance, with points of procedure, and with an unsuccessful effort by the applicant to bring himself within a rule of expenditures incurred in good faith reliance on a validly issued permit. The municipality had moved in to contest. "Municipalities and boards of adjustment, unlike private litigants, have a duty to protect the public interest and preserve the character of the community." (149 A.2d at 32.) "The recent statement of this court in ... where the

Township was substituted for the board *after an appeal had been taken to this Court,* [court's italics] is most appropriate: ... although the present appeal has been taken nominally by the board of adjustment, we find that as a matter of substance the real party there is the ... Township." (ibid. 34.) Substitution allowed; remanded for hearing *de novo* in the light of newly discovered evidence. "However, in remanding the matter for this purpose, the attention of the court below is directed to the firmly established principle that variances are to be granted only where *a finding of unnecessary hardship is adequately supported by competent evidence,* and that a general rezoning of an area of land cannot be accomplished under the guise of a variance ..." (ibid.; court's italics).

Craig v. Thiele, p. 35, 395 Pa. 129, was a question of venue in a contract {490} action against a corporation. The Rule is set out fully and its language carefully examined, especially "(4) a county where a *transaction or occurrence* took place out of which the cause of action arose." (My italics.) In contrast to the Illinois Code of Civil Practice which had been the model, "we deleted that part of the rule which authorized venue in any county wherein a 'part of the transaction' occurred." (149 A.2d at 37.) Here the averment was that plaintiff had "placed an order with the defendant" in the county. Held insufficient: "It would lead only to confusion and to a practice which we have heretofore referred to as 'forum shopping' if the law were to permit suit to be commenced against a corporation where any facet of a complex transaction occurred." (ibid. 37.) "Occurrence" is ruled inapplicable — somewhat surprisingly — not because it patently does not refer to transacting, but "on familiar principles of *eiusdem generis.*" (ibid.) "Substantial justice will be accomplished" by reference back with leave to amend. (ibid.)

In re Adoption of Maisels, p. 38, 395 Pa. 329, is another of those nasty adoption cases in which a real parent is attempting to assert rights after the foster parents and the child have become a working family. A mother, after divorce from a drug addict and after her three-year-old daughter had gone to live with the ex-husband's married sister, spent her time with a lover, paying no attention to the child over periods longer than the six months required by the statute for effective abandonment. The statute is quoted, there is the usual holding about strict compliance, and the evidence is fully examined and held to support the Orphan's Court's finding of abandonment. "The language of this Court in ... is most appropriate. 'Abandonment is not an ambulatory thing the legal affects of which a delinquent parent may dissipate at will by the expression of a desire for the return of a discarded child. We do not mean to say that the natural parental right to a child, which has been nullified by abandonment, may not be later retrieved. It may be. But ... once abandonment has been proven with the required legal sufficiency, the welfare of the abandoned child is the primary and paramount concern of the court...." (149 A.2d at 42.) Decree of adoption affirmed.

In *McAvoy Vitrified Brick Co. v. North American Life Assurance Co.,* p. 42, 295 Pa. 75, a company beneficiary had recovered a §240,000 judgment on a contract to insure the life of its president. After examination, physical acceptance, and application, the full first-year premium was paid, a receipt and interim assurance certificate were handed over by the insurer's authorized branch manager, and the application forwarded to the home office. The decedent died of a coronary before the home office had acted. The premium receipt denied any liability before delivery of a policy "unless an interim insurance certificate has been issued." The matter was of first impression in the court. The court below (whose opinion is quoted at length and made the basis of {491} affirmance) examined the situation as a type, the particular documents, a Yale L.J. comment, and an extensively quoted California case, and ruled the certificate's condition that the applicant be found by the company's officers to be "an insurable risk on the date of the medical examination" to refer primarily to physical condition, and so ruled that the deceased had died insured, notwithstanding that the insurer's practice might be to refuse to issue a policy of the size in question on a person of the deceased's age and income.

The final case here presented, *Chestnut Corporation v. Bankers Bond and Mortgage Co.,* p. 48, 395 Pa. 155, is not only seemingly a case of first impression, but is decided without reference to any authority of any kind. A $300,000 bond issue had provided a right to prepayment on thirty days' written notice against a premium of 2 per cent. After a year the property was completely destroyed by fire, and the mortgage paid out of the insurance. The question went to whether the 2 per cent premium was also due. 4-2, the court held No. ". . . [A]t least in theory, defendant would be put to some cost and expense to make a new mortgage loan. On the other hand, plaintiff, while it has received the full net amount of the fire insurance, has lost its building, and if it desired to rebuild it would have to obtain a new mortgage loan, and in the meantime it would be without a building and would lose whatever contracts and/or leases it had made. In such a situation both parties suffer, but the owner suffers most."

Authority techniques. These range from no citation at all (*Chestnut,* above) through use of a law review or the Restatement and of outside cases, of "we said," on through a case where the "see's" and "cfs." far outnumber the points that rest on a simple cite (*Schechter,* above), to the quotation and adoption of a rule, a rationale, or both, and to the use of a case out far beyond its holding or language. There are simple cites and cites accompanied by facts and holding. There is deliberate severe restriction, distinction for cause, overt discussion of overruling. The pure simple cite is materially less frequent than in the other courts examined. Statutes (or court rules) are dealt with by meticulous attention to the full language, by use of their history, by quotation of excerpts, by use of canons, by using a quoted statutory foundation to knock out the force of outside decisions, etc. One statute has its policy applied to a situation completely outside the scope of its language.

KANSAS, 1958

The advance sheets explored were those already used for Oregon, to wit, Pacific 2d for September 5 and December 5, 1958. The first yielded only a pair of companion cases and one further case; the second was read (under the basic sampling procedure of this study) until four cases were found which showed some application of sense to the testing or {492} formulation of a rule of law. This required fourteen cases, the writing of which ranged over all seven of the judges; but the overt applications of sense to rule-shaping, even when one dissent and one special concurrence were added, came from the pens of only three. Ten of the cases involve little but technically accurate disposition of a matter on the settled law: in *Dawkins v. Dawkins,* 328 P.2d 355, the foregone application of the rule of the first *Dawkins* case; four matters of procedural housekeeping, handled in the main with some attention to producing a serviceable result; four applications of the rules which leave decision on facts to the lower court or to a commission. One further case on appeal procedure is handled, and the relevant statute and cases applied, as if the matter had been purely technical, although the dissent persuades me that application of sense was called for. In four cases, as already indicated, overt situation-sense enters into the rule announced, but less openly, much less freely and fully, and (to my feeling) rather less sensitively than in most of the other courts examined. The "syllabus by the court" is uneven and varies greatly in method and in guidesomeness, and shows no signs of being shaped under any clear theory for making the syllabus serve its own peculiar values. This is not owing merely to variation in who prepares the opinion; thus the most serviceable of the fourteen and one of the blinder ones are both opinions by the same judge.

The precedent techniques also being in this sample unusually wooden (e.g. distinctions being taken by merely saying that the case is distinguishable, statutes typically paraphrased in substance rather than examined in text, quotations including rationale being rare), I ran through the rest of the cases in December 5 (eight) to see if any different flavor would show. The additional cases moved both re precedent technique and re use of situation-sense noticeably, but not greatly, toward the manner and tone generally current today.

The second *Dawkins* case has already been mentioned.

The procedural cases need not detain us long. *Richey v. Darling,* 331 P.2d 281, simply applies the sensible rules, announced earlier, "that in order to constitute an abandonment of his right to appeal from an adverse ruling on a demurrer when a defendant answers his attitude in the answer must be inconsistent with that which he maintained in support of his demurrer" (p. 281); and "that where a petitioner sufficiently alleges a cause of action on any theory, a general demurrer thereto cannot be sustained." (p. 282.) In *Acme Foundry etc. Co. v. Brennan,* ibid. 282, similarly: ". . . suffice it to say that we have carefully examined each of them . . . they are all trial errors for which redress could be obtained only by filing a timely motion for a new trial pursuant to G.S. 1949, 60-3003." (p. 283.) This case is nevertheless to be classed as involving situation-sense in regard to the rule, because the opinion concludes with an obvious willingness to adjust the rule to shown need: "On the hearing of the motion for a new trial no evidence {493} was presented which indicated, or tended to indicate, unavoidable casualty or misfortune preventing the appellant from filing the motion for a new trial in time." (p. 284.) *Grigsby v. Jenkins,* ibid. 285, is a short review, summarized in four singing paragraphs of syllabus, of ancient Kansas lore on the effect of a general verdict, the duty of a trial court to set an unsatisfactory verdict aside, and the difference between the motion for a new trial and that for n.o.v. In *Philipps v. Hand,* ibid. 291, "Under our state constitution as explained in the Jewett case, a district court has no jurisdiction in habeas corpus over persons outside of its own district." (p. 292.) And dismissal of the writ is affirmed. The court notes that the applicant had had counsel appointed by the State, and that he had previously been before both the proper county court and the supreme court with petitions for habeas corpus. Finally, in *Farmers State Bank v. Irsik,* ibid. 292, we meet various shenanigans attempting to beat the law on venue. "[I]t is quite apparent the court was well aware of the maneuver by which it was attempted to convert the action by the bank into one by Irsik, as plaintiff, against Bugner," (p. 296), so the appropriate rulings below are sustained.

The cases which apply rules leaving questions of fact to a trial tribunal range from a workman's compensation matter, *House v. Greer,* ibid. 289 ("A very comprehensive and detailed discussion of this court's appellate jurisdiction in workmen's compensation cases is set forth in *LaRue v. Sierra Petroleum Co. . . .*" — p. 291), to the trial court on a matter of raising a trust in lands, *Estate of Meyers,* ibid. 287, and on the allotment of property on divorce, *Long v. Long,* ibid. Each time enough of the evidence is given to persuade that the trial tribunal had a reasonable basis for its decision. *City of Wichita v. Bumm,* ibid. 301, is in this aspect a somewhat different case. "Where it is possible this court strives to uphold the ruling of the trial court. In our opinion the trial court properly construed the petition." (p. 304.) The petition had been to enjoin a highly litigious recalcitrant from interfering with an easement for a water-transmission line on the matter of its installation and perhaps generally. Installation having been accomplished, the trial court had dismissed the petition as moot. The petition was readily capable of wider interpretation and the scene as depicted in the opinion suggests that trouble might have been saved by allowing an injunction against interference with maintenance. It seems to me probable, therefore, that the court was using its own sense (as per the second sentence quoted) as to application of the rules to the facts, rather than merely sustaining the trial court as having remained within the scope of the possible legitimate readings of the petition.

Situation-sense and the rule or principle (three of the judges represented). In any event, the *Wichita* case presents two further matters of interest. On page 304, the court deals with an "In all other cases" clause of a statute and subjects it to heavy restriction because of limitations implicit in situation-sense: "If this statute is all inclusive of a {494} party's right to dismissal of an action, obviously neither the trial court nor this court could dismiss any action that has become moot if the plaintiff objected to a dismissal." The next three columns sweep away four successive piddling difficulties ("Technicalities cannot be stretched to the point where they become absurd") — and raise a doubt as to whether it may have been such misargument which killed off the city's chance at a more favorable interpretation of its petition. *Temple v. Continental Oil Co.,* 328 P.2d 358, likewise brings situation-sense to bear, this time for the purpose of bringing life and punch into an established case law formula. What we have is a second opinion which with spirit defends the decision and prior opinion against an arbitrary misreading. Oil lessees are being held liable for unreasonable delay. "The term 'Prudent,' with reference to an *Operator* of an oil or gas lease, is sufficiently broad to ensnare any ingenious device or scheme conceived to circumvent the plain meaning of the Prudent Operator Rule." (p. 360, court's italics.) — The court disregards "a generous supply of proration data" in the brief because "the record is barren of any stipulations or evidence ... concerning restrictions or regulations of the State Corporation Commission relative to the Geneseo Pool ..." (p. 361); but I read this as addressed to the particular case, not as involving any unwillingness to look at established technical information when the question goes to formulation of a rule for the problem-situation.

The first *Dawkins v. Dawkins,* ibid. 346, had to do with the split-up of a marriage and of an evangelizing church completely dominated in its finances by the husband-pastor. The court used history, law, and horse sense to find a necessary trusteeship in the pastor and a forfeiture of property interests by the departing schismatics, so that the parsonage could not be awarded to the divorcing wife as if it had been her husband's individual property. The case is unique in my reading in that the same Justice who writes for the court with careful restraint also, in a much more vigorous opinion, concurs specially with himself.

Kimberly v. Ledbetter, 331 P.2d 307, is the second of two cases in the sample which involve injury by grossly negligent illegal abortion. The policy issue was fully argued. "This question was disposed of ... in *Joy v. Brown,* 173 Kan. 833, 252 P.2d 889, where, in the course of the opinion, it was said: '... We are of the opinion that no person may lawfully and validly consent to any act the very purpose of which is to destroy human life.'" The court continues: "The wrongful death statute (G.S. 1949, 60-3203) was enacted to inure to the exclusive benefit of the surviving spouse and children, if any . . . and is for their protection when wronged by a proximate negligent act killing their decedent. Their right of action against the defendant should not be denied because the decedent unlawfully consented to the abortion. (*Joy v. Brown,* supra, 173 Kan. at pages 839, 840, 252 P.2d at page 893.)" (p. 309.) {495}

In this group of decisions, at least because of the dissents, belongs also *Estate of Allgire,* 331 P.2d 296, where a husband was seeking to contest his wife's will. His notice of appeal was served on the attorneys who were shown by the record to be serving as attorneys for all the adverse parties, but the acceptance of service and waiver of proof of service were signed by them only as attorneys for the executor. "In our recent case of In re Estate of Freshour, 177 Kan. 492, 280 P.2d 642, we had occasion to again review our decisions and construe G.S. 1949, 59-2405 providing for appeals from the probate court to the district court on the questions similarly involved herein. What was said there is applicable here." (p. 299.) The court adhered to the construction that for the district court to gain jurisdiction to "do any other act necessary to perfect the appeal" the appellant must first have given "due notice of appeal," and held the appeal properly dismissed for a "*concededly* defective and insufficient notice of appeal." (My italics.) But the dissent argued that notice had been actually given and received by the statutory "counsel of record," that the defect had gone only to acceptance of service and waiver of proof, and that all the authorities cited involved omissions in the notice or actual service or filing of proper bond; and so wished to apply sense to both the statute and the case.

Precedent techniques. The range has really appeared in the foregoing: along with the ever-present simple citation of a single case or a series, there is the "many times" announced rule, or that which "we have long adhered to"; there is the quotation and rediscussion of rationale or the mere reference to a recent opinion which fully considered the matter; there is heavy redirection or extension in the process of "mere" following (e.g. *Allgire*); cases are moved out of the way by simple pronouncement that they are "clearly distinguishable"; there is the quiet suggestion, even in sharp rulings, that a reasonable exception will be made at need; there is obvious use of such leeways as even strict rules of practice allow to get a sensible result in the case in hand. The sample suggests the court to be unduly plagued by sloppy work at the bar. Twice, on points of simple practice, the court notes sadly how old and repeated the lesson is, once the syllabus sets out the proper procedures in the situation in words of one syllable, once the abstract is sadly noted as "very confused," and again "550 pages of abstract and counter abstract" turn up, *neither one including the pleadings.*

OREGON, 1958

The advance sheets (chosen for fatness) hit upon for the sampling were September 5, 1958, 328 P.2d, and December 5, 330 P.2d. This yielded six cases, one a half-column Per Curiam citing one case to show a pleading point "well-established," one an interpretation of a Federal {496} statute which might (though it did not) involve noncharacteristic procedures, and one a strong-arming of a sensible result in the particular case by maiming a special statute, one other case which used overt sense in application of the rule, and two which resorted to such sense in the choice and shaping of the rule or rules to be applied. Three judges were represented. A fourth judge appeared in the same issue, in the 331 P.2d material; the first two of his opinions are companion cases which make a significant addition, or corrective, and are therefore added here. The ninth and last case in December 5 fits the general pattern in all aspects including the use of situation-sense in the shaping of the rule; e.g. its quotation, in dealing with a matter of statutory regulation: "But meanings, though not explicitly stated in words, may be imbedded in a statutory scheme." The quotations needed to fully present that case, *Morgan v. Portland Traction Co.*, 331 P.2d 344, however, would consume undue space. It needs mention that whether in the quest for sense or as a precedent technique or (which is my view) as both together, each of the six full opinions turns to other states, in addition to the Oregon material, for light on legal wisdom; and that the four cases in which situation-sense shaped the rule come from four different members of the court.

Wright v. Blue Mt. Hospital District, 328 P.2d 314, deals in essence rather with application than with rule. It was an action to challenge the validity of a 1949 election establishing the district, *which had been operating since 1950-1951*. The applicable law read that "No person may vote ... unless he is an elector of this state *and has resided in the district*" for 90 days. "That the legislature cannot add to the constitutional qualifications of voters, unless expressly provided therein, is too well established to admit of contradiction." (p. 317.) The Constitution entitled every citizen who had resided in the State during the six months immediately preceding. The only relevant Oregon decisions upheld regulation against fraud and abuses by way of registration laws. The opinion does not mention delay in the challenge to the election, nor does it rest upon the requirement as a mild effort toward keeping pure transients from determining a local matter, which I would read the prior Oregon authorities, as seen by the court, to validate. Instead, "unavoidably," the 90-day period "... is coincidental with and becomes an integral part of the six-months constitutional period" (ibid.). This seems to me to make the statute meaningless. The court's language about "a mild restraint on newcomers," etc. (ibid.) I also find no sense in. Purpose and juice center for me in the result: "We find ... that the election of 1949 was regular" (p. 320). The opinion shows nothing as to whether any action had been taken to disqualify any would-be voter under the statute. As against a challenge purely on the constitutionality of the statute the hospital district is ruled to have been validly created.

Phil Grossmayer Co. v. Campbell, 328 P.2d 320 (Dept. I), involved {497} the "adverse claims" statute which protects a bank, in the absence of restraining order or acceptable indemnity, against need to recognize notice of adverse claim to a deposit "standing on its books to the credit of any person." After the defendant had sold out everything but the form of a corporation, he used false corporate "resolutions" to open and run an account in the corporate name. The governor included that corporation the next January in his proclamation of dissolutions (a matter stated but not discussed in the opinion). Two months later garnishment papers were served on the bank claiming assets of the defendant "in his name or in the name of" the corporation. The bank had received credible information that the sole asset it held, the "corporate" account, was no concern of the defendant's, and had honored a "corporate" check closing it out. The court read the purpose of the statute as being "to relieve the bank of the financial responsibility attendant upon deciding" on any claim in the absence of protection (p. 325), and on a review of the facts saw no notice to the bank that the "corporate" account was not bona fide; and the court below had failed to make any finding of notice to the bank, as contrasted with trickiness in the garnishment debtor. Reversed and bank discharged.

In *Allen v. Oceanside Lumber Co.*, 328 P.2d 320 (Dept. I), the court examined in the light of the authorities and of sense an assistant engineer's claim under the Federal Employers Liability Act for injury sustained by jumping in the dark aboard a vessel with moorings lengthened to adjust to the tide. Various questions were held to be for the jury. The Oregon statutes on business and government records were held, partly on their language, partly in view of sense and Wigmore, not to permit introduction in evidence of an "abstract of clinical record" purportedly signed by a medical officer deputy over the seal of the United States Public Health Service. "There is no reason to believe that the officer who prepared the abstract had personal knowledge of the facts recorded, nor does it appear that he had the duty of ascertaining their truth" (p. 338); and "we do not believe that in the present case the abstract is admissible as a copy. It is more accurately described as a summary." (ibid.) Remanded for new trial.

The next two cases move out of mere application into open remodeling of the rule according to what seems sense. *Druck v. Plastic Sheeting Co.* (in Banc), 328 P.2d 339, held a foreclosing mortgage of fixtures and equipment entitled to take free of a county's claimed lien for taxes. "It was established in Owens v. Oregon Livestock Loan Co. . . . that a tax lien attaches only to the specific property assessed and that with respect to other property of the taxpayer a lien does not arise unless distraint is made on such property. . . ." (p. 341), which had not occurred here. "In the Owens case it was said: '. . . To hold that a tax assessed against specific personal property is a lien not only upon that property, but also upon all of the rest of the tax debtor's property, and that a distraint may be enforced long after the property has {498} passed, through successive sales, into new ownerships could certainly occasionally result in injustice. . . .' Injustice could result as well where the new 'ownership' is the limited ownership of a security interest." (ibid. 341f.) After examining certain possible presumptions which might result in a lien for some proportion of the tax claimed: "We are aware of the frequently stated policy in favor of simple, unimpeded, and sometimes even summary methods of collecting taxes. But there is a limit to which this court can go in excusing a tax collecting unit from following the rules of pleading and proof. . . ." (p. 343.) The statute which makes mortgaged personalty, for tax purposes, "the property of the person in possession" simply designates the taxpayer who is to be responsible for paying the tax, and does not increase the right of the county in regard to property retained for a while by the mortgagor under a recorded mortgage. (p. 344.)

Again, *Kelley v. Park View Apartments, Inc.* (en banc), 330 P.2d 1057, presented a verdict for injury due to slipping at 8:30 a.m. on a small patch of ice on the public sidewalk, formed overnight from the meltings of snow cleared off steps onto the side bank. An earlier case, in sustaining recovery for a fall by slipping on the drippings from window washings onto a sloping sidewalk, had phrased the rule in terms of creating a hazard by placing, or not removing, "any matter that would cause a slippery or dangerous condition." ". . . [A]n imposition of liability in this case would virtually demand that the court employ a rule of strict liability." (p. 1061.) The court canvasses the departure from such a rule in New Jersey, and relies on Massachusetts and Illinois cases which favor citizens' reasonable efforts after snowfall. "In our view, the likelihood of any increased danger from removing the snow from the steps and casting it beside them on the grass is so remote that it could not have been foreseen by a reasonable man. To the contrary the natural and probable consequence of such action, according to our belief, would be a lessening of danger, for if the snow had been allowed to remain on the steps," etc. (p. 1064.) The cause of the ice was the non-negligent act of the defendant. There was a general lack of any duty to clear the public sidewalk. To pile the snow along the curb might have increased the danger from melting, and presents an unreasonable burden in regard to an apartment complex of four city blocks. The landlord-tenant relation did not increase the duty. Reversed for directed verdict.

State v. Endsley (en banc), 331 P.2d, 338, moves on severely technical lines. The legislature has twice laid down ("the *only* mode of reviewing"; "in the cases prescribed in this chapter, *and not otherwise*") that appeal in a criminal case needs an explicit statutory base. "An appeal is not a matter of absolute right, but of statutory privilege . . . We have repeatedly said that it is unnecessary to cite authorities for a rule so well established and familiar." A person serving penitentiary sentence for second degree murder filed a "petition of a writ of error {499} Coram Nobis" attacking his conviction on the ground that his plea of guilty had been induced by a coerced confession. The court, after a hearing, denied the petition. The Supreme Court found no appeal provided in the statutory scheme. It pointed out that it had explicitly avoided the question in a prior case. "Since State v. Huffman, supra, two coram nobis cases have come to this court in which we passed on the merits . . . In none of these cases was appealability of the order challenged, and this court failed to raise the question on its own motion. If this assumption of jurisdiction was error, as we think it was, the error should not be perpetuated." (pp. 341-342.) A similar result in New York had been followed by a curative statute. "The question whether a similar change in the law of Oregon is desirable is one which should be addressed to the legislature, not to the courts." (p. 342.) The case seems to me one in which the court's proper use of sense was clearly limited to the course it took, and one in which language of the statutes forced the result. The court meant what it said: in the companion case, *State v. Brooks,* 331 P.2d 343, the circuit court had denied the defendant's motion: "the motion for relief in the nature of a Writ of Error Coram Nobis on the grounds of newly discovered evidence does not lie for the purpose of extending the time within which to file a motion for a new trial based on newly discovered evidence." The State had not moved to dismiss the appeal. The court therefore did so on its own motion.

Precedent techniques. In the *Endsley* case, above, "We have repeatedly said that it is unnecessary to cite authorities for a rule so well established and familiar"; but there is an explicit overruling of a rule necessarily contained in two prior cases, and there is a recital of two cases being overruled *sub silentio* by a third decision which has, however, been "followed in an unbroken line of cases and has been the law of Oregon ever since it was rendered." In addition, in the other cases, we meet redirection in "following" a rule or principle, both by expansion and by qualification; we meet factual distinction; narrow and wide construction of statutes according to purpose; the quotation and application of the rationale or policy of prior decisions; application in terms of rationale not quoted but phrased by the instant court; the use, for the base line, of a single decision as well as of a series; the imposition of limits on a policy conceded to be wise in general; the adducing of a pair of decisions for their suggestion, flavor, or analogy, rather than their strict holdings on the crucial point in hand. There are of course the frequent simple citations. And as mentioned above, there is regular use, criticism, or capitalization of outside authority in addition.

ILLINOIS, 1958

The Illinois sample is from the issue of October 22, 1958, 152 N.E.2d 825-873. To find four cases which used situation-sense to shape a controlling {500} rule or subrule it was necessary to read only four cases. But that sampled only three writing judges. The next case fitted in manner, and added one more judge. But in pushing on from there one ran into cases in which all that was needed was sense in application, or one got the same judges again, or else it was another criminal case. The tone does not change, but we have to move four cases further in order to pick up a fifth judge at work on rule-shaping. I add the eleventh case because of its inherent interest. The four cases first found are numbered, in support of the statement above.

(1) *People v. Greeley*, p. 825, 14 Ill. 2d 428, was statutory rape, with "insinuating matters which the prosecution was legally obligated to prove. . . . A jury is quick to recognize evidence of defendant's other acts of indiscretion, and even though a portion of such testimony may be stricken, as a practical matter it cannot be said that by so doing it is entirely removed from jury deliberation. The gravity of mistake must be considered in relation to the facts of each individual case to determine whether reversible error has occurred." (152 N.E.2d at 827.) As indicated above, re the Court's Witness, the Illinois court takes this test very seriously. Reversed and remanded.

(2) *Durchslag v. Smith*, p. 828, 14 Ill. 2d 549, the auditor's refusal to license a new currency exchange. The statute is quoted and its parts drawn together, in consonance with a prior construction. Both the fact of hearing and the finding at hearing are stressed. "Obviously the legislative intent to limit the number of currency exchanges to the needs of the community they are to serve would be thwarted if each license applicant was permitted to carve out his own proposed community. . . . One of its purposes was to prevent saturation of an area with currency exchanges with possible instability for all." (152 N.E.2d at 830.)

(3) *People v. Hinton*, p. 830, 14 Ill. 2d 424, was another sex case, this time indecent liberties with an eight-year-old boy whose testimony ran so many ways as to leave a complete blank on, say, whether a low-intelligence eight-year-old child has been abused or two such low-intelligence children were being used to convict. The court, noting alibi evidence from the defendant's prospective wife and her two children, reversed a conviction. They worried: "It is not supposed that an eight-year-old child will remember with the accuracy normally expected of his elders. But this does not warrant a relaxation of the requirement that the guilt of an accused person be proved beyond a reasonable doubt. As we have pointed out on more than one occasion: 'An indecent liberties case is similar in character to that of rape, because it is an accusation easily made, hard to be proved, and harder to be defended by the party accused, though ever so innocent.'" Reversed and remanded. I see this opinion (though under pressure of *this*-case "equities,") as nevertheless very carefully reexamining the situation-reason for a rule deeply rooted in our culture, and very carefully {501} deciding, on the net, whether and how to apply that *rule*. The court was unanimous.

(4) *Getzelman v. Koehler*, p. 833, 14 Ill. 2d 396, was a complex partition suit among heirs. After a first purely technical but careful (and, I think, sound) ruling on a point of appellate procedure, the court moves into sense not only in application but for a rule that is buttressed by no authority: "A lease, wherever possible, should be construed reasonably and in such a manner as will be most equitable to the parties and give neither party an unfair advantage over the other." (152 N.E.2d at 837.) (Why this rule should be limited to either "a lease," or "wherever possible," is beyond me; but who — except West's headnoters — can duck the court's deliberate setting up of a standard rule for dealing with a type of situation?) The judgment was sense in application, the court showing the facts on which it moved.

* * *

A few of the next following cases will be dealt with as a group. *People v. Flowers,* p. 838, 14 Ill. 2d 406, involved a robbery and a defendant who was found to have on him a specially thought-out cash-register batch of marked two-dollar bills. In relation to a lie-detector test, defendant had made *and signed* certain statements. And the statements were used "for impeachment purposes" (152 N.E.2d at 843; my quotes). "A review of the entire record fails to sustain defendant's general allegation that the court exhibited an adverse attitude. . . ." (ibid.) The court is careful, in explicit language, to suggest that "trick" is no part of the base of its decision. That goes to method, and to the court's understanding of the situation, and (for my money) is solid. But I find myself surprised about the court's seeing of the situation. *What has* SIGNING *statements to do with a lie-detector test?* To me, this smells of "trick." — This remark is addressed to doctrine. In the particular case, I think the court, quietly, makes a case hard to object to. So also as to the minor matter of *People v. Toomer,* p. 845, 14 Ill. 2d 385, where a *pro se,* using the liberties and facilities provided in some (and only some) of our penal institutions, found that the case he relied on had been expressly overruled, and that the court felt that overruling to be wise. In *Toomer* there is no explicit discussion of policy, on what is essentially a question of whether technical language shall be construed to purpose, but simply a clean decision that one can't duck solid law by tiddlywinks.

In contrast, *People v. Aldridge,* p. 847, 14 Ill. 2d 320, moves with the under-lying and explicit premise that too many occasions of exercise in one direction can cumulate. "In this case, however, it appears from the abstract that all of the 12 instructions tendered by the defendant were refused and all of the 27 instructions proffered by the prosecution were given. This circumstance has prompted us to depart from the usual rule . . ." To me, this is a subrule. The evidence is set {502} forth, however, and I think conclusively, to sustain the conviction. Similarly, *In re Eaton,* p. 850, 14 Ill. 2d 338, a disbarment proceeding, takes the total reason not only of the man's conduct but of the situation as a basis for regarding a plea of "nolo contendere" as equivalent, re conviction on a moral turpitude charge, to one of "not guilty." The next case, *Lux v. Lelija,* p. 853, 14 Ill. 2d 540, a family land mix-up, involves no point of law, but uses sense in application.

Gould v. Stelter, p. 869, 14 Ill. 2d 376, was a suit for specific performance of a contract to sell land. The transaction went by way of customary strawmen and nominees in a degree unnecessary to detail, but which appears to be the manner of some phases of the business. (Compare *Crowley v. Lewis,* above, p. 207, from New York.) Questions of undisclosed principal and of the exact extent of powers of attorney, as they might bear on Fry's rule of the need for mutuality *ab initio,* were brushed aside by the court, and Fry's rule was flatly rejected. "We hold that want of mutuality at the inception of a contract is not a bar to specific performance." (152 N.E.2d at 872.) (To me it seems that the New York and the Illinois courts were dealing with single angles of a nominee situation which goes not only to effective enterprise operation but no less to tax evasion and to avoidance of liability from slum operation. But I suspect this Illinois decision, as contrasted with the New York one, to be peeling off one small layer of the onion. On the dissent, see above, page 295.

The final case for discussion is *James v. Grand Trunk Western R.R. Co.,* p. 858, 14 Ill. 2d 356, as nasty a mess as the books have recently brewed. The essential question, never mentioned, is whether employee-plaintiffs against railroads can get their cases to Chicago for high verdicts. The jurisprudentially exciting aspect is that here, for once, it is the defending side which has spotted and almost won a favorable test case. A Michigan widow brought an action in Chicago against the Grand Trunk under the Michigan Wrongful Death Act. The action came under attack by a veritable legal Pooh-Bah. As attorney for the railroad he enjoined the woman from pressing her Chicago action; when she was persuaded to resist (against threat of imprisonment for contempt), Pooh-Bah, "as prosecuting attorney" for the local county, had her removed as administratrix. Whereupon (even the Greeks and Gilbert had no name for this one) Pooh-Bah himself made "all the arrangements" for a new lawyer to "represent the claim *against*" the railroad. (My italics.) Original plaintiff's counsel did not miss the opportunity, and, by 4-3, got a counterinjunction sustained. My concern here is not with the merits. It is with two facts. First, in a very sticky situation, each side shapes the authorities to what is seen as the vital situation-sense. "In applying these principles to the instant case, we cannot close our eyes to the fact that the intended effect of the Michigan injunction, though directed at the parties and not at this court, is to prevent the Illinois court," etc. (152 N.E.2d at 865.) {503} Against which: "The place to stop this unseemly kind of judicial disorder is where it begins." (ibid. 868.) Second: Neither majority nor minority face up cleanly to the basic factual problem. The real question is not about "transitory causes of action," whatever the Supreme Court may say. The real question is about shopping for big-verdict centers, *even though the shopping may clog all other legal business in those centers*. And a little explicitness on that in State courts might produce a little more explicit sense upstairs.

Authority techniques. "We have said . . ." "This jurisdiction has followed . . ." (using lower court authorities). A case we have ourselves relied on has rejected that case. That case has since its decision been shown up as not solidly based. We distinguish for cause stated. We rely on the quoted reasoning. We quote Cardozo, and use the quote. We recognize one overruling and announce another. We simple-cite and simple-cite and simple-cite again. "We pointed out . . ." in regard to a statute. "We stated . . ." "In accordance with the views expressed in . . . we hold . . ." "The rule is established . . ." "We have pointed out on more than one occasion . . ." "We have consistently . . ." — But we also "see . . ." And we solve cases of first impression. We borrow from outside. We "cf." We refuse to distinguish — also for reason. — But this is the same body of material noted above, in which the simple cites outweigh all other forms of authority, two and a half to one.

CALIFORNIA, 1958

The first of our California cases, from the issue of September 5, 1958, 328 P.2d, involves a matter as sticky as this last Illinois job. This time the struggle has its technical center not in the power of a State, *"our"* State, but in some queer quirk of California language which makes one kind of marital arrangement, as the parties part, a something not wholly subject to the sense-rule of supervening impossibility, but enough subject to the concept of "debt" to make "an integrated adjustment" bar out contempt-imprisonment as against a delinquent husband. Never did an opinion display more clearly the shaping of authorities to fit sense as the court saw sense. I suspect, too, that there must be a rather largish background of un-thought-through doctrine which has been built to protect courts from the need of reviewing every alimony decree every time a movie star changed status, or fell. (Nevertheless, it is a little awful to find *child support* explicitly and carefully put into the category of an obligation *not* subject to contempt proceedings, just because a *mother* may have made a contractual adjustment.) Carter, a chronic dissenter, objects in general, not seeing the end.

Traynor, who troublesomely insists on trying to make sense, tries to go along, but can't quite make it. *Plumer v. Superior Court*, p. 193. {504}

This began to show the judges' situation-sense at work in rule-shaping, in California. The next case runs through many rules, still shaping. "Those cases are, of course, factually distinguishable. . . . However," etc. (p. 201.) That is all from September 5. And September 12 offers only one case. It, again, goes cleanly, indeed even more explicitly, into situation-sense to shape the rule. *Deshotel v. Atchison, Topeka & S.F. Ry.*, p. 449, 50 Cal. 2d 664. "The Legislature has not seen fit to alter the common law rule that the wife cannot recover for loss of consortium. . . ." 328 P.2d at 452.) A careful, exploring job; Carter dissenting.

My next number at hand is September 26. The first case (Carter writing this time for the court) again goes to bat on situation-reason as shaping the rule. The two following cases read statutes in the same fashion. The tone of the court is clear, with opinions now sampled from five of the Justices.

Authority techniques. Simple cites; quotes of language; "factually distinguishable" cases built on; "see"; "cf."; "well settled." On the other hand, "we do not agree"; we distinguish for cause; we leave it to the legislature, even on a case of first impression; we read particular statutory language with italics; we hit for "the purpose" of the amendment of 1914; we use "the rule, supported by reason and by authority."

INDIANA, 1957-1958

The first sampling was from the issue of January 8, 1958, 146 N.E.2d 239-258. This yielded eight cases, two of them (*Theede*, p. 246, and *Davenport*, p. 247) simple P.C. rulings that since the public defender was available to produce a record, a *pro se* could not cut corners in regard to not having one. I do not count these two.

The first merits case, *Meier v. Social Security Administration*, p. 239, 237 Ind. 421, presents only a defect in technical appeal procedure. The second, *Penn v. State*, p. 240, 237 Ind. 374, is a rape case in which situation-sense is firmly used to shape the rule. See the text above at page 276. "Ordinarily reasonable men know that a wife will not knowingly and willingly share the sex life of her husband. Experience teaches . . ." etc. (146 N.E.2d at 248.) The third, *Gaddie v. Holloway*, p. 247, 237 Ind. 382, briefly and carefully knocks out an ultra-technical objection to an appeal. The fourth, *Public Service Commissioner v. Indiana Tel. Co.*, p. 248, 237 Ind. 352, looks situation-sense in the eye, but yields to more immediate pressures for what the court sees as justice: "Although we recognize by a recent rule made by this court, not yet effective, that a special finding in proceedings of this sort is helpful and an aid in considering a review on appeal, we must under the present holdings of this court," etc. (146 N.E.2d at 251.) The court goes on (p. 255) to use situation-sense both in application and in the shaping of the deciding rule. In *Cowherd v. State*, {505} p. 257, 237 Ind. 370, "Under the record as presented to us, we could, with propriety, hold that the evidence which implicated the appellant was excluded from consideration by the initial ruling of the court and that therefore there was no evidence to support the conviction. However . . ." (146 N.E.2d at 258). So the question of hearsay in a burglary trial is considered in more detail, and the conviction is reversed.

These cases do not in any striking way support my theses about the rather regular use of situation-sense in the shaping of the rule. Yet they are more than consistent, they even urge, in that direction.

Three more cases from a chance-picked 1959 issue, 155 N.E.2d 125 ff. add a fourth writing judge (out of five) and two more instances which urge the conclusion rather unmistakably in the same direction.

Authority techniques. Straight cites, of course, and in profusion. "It is well settled in this state . . ." "This court gave careful consideration to this issue in the recent case of . . ." (with a column and a half of quotation). "See . . ." "Both those cases concerned the fixing of rates. This is not a rate case." "There may be rare instances, as urged by appellee . . . but this . . ." "When confronted with this issue the United States Circuit Court of Appeals, Eight Circuit, stated: . . ."

MISSOURI, 1958

The Missouri sample is from the January 13, 1959, issue: 318 S.W.2d 163-234.

Explicit and implicit reason in application of the relevant rule run through the sample. The second and third cases show situation-reason directly but not explicitly at work: "In . . . this court said, 'The acts of the plaintiff tending to enhance the injury are admissible in evidence to reduce the amount of the damages under the general issue, whether considered as in mitigation or as a rule of limitation of damages. . . .' And we find no statute in Missouri which has changed the common-law rule. . . ." *Stipp v. Tsutomi Karasawa,* pp. 172, 175-176. "Defendant had objected to the admission of the records and the objection should have been sustained. The objection, however, was overruled and plaintiff's counsel then read to the jury only such portions of the exhibit which he deemed to be most favorable to plaintiff. In that situation defendant's counsel could read other portions of the exhibit without waiving his prior objection." *Lockhart v. St. Louis P.S. Co.,* pp. 177, 180. Both the reticence of the opinions and the complicated Missouri Division, Commissioner, and Court setup required extended reading. The cases, chiefly in Division 1 but also in Division 2 and en banc, run in much the above fashion until the fourteenth, *St. Louis Southwestern Ry. v. Loeb,* p. 246, where a row between preferred and common stock produces a most explicit attention to situation-reason. (See especially p. 261.) {506}

In the net, the manner of this Missouri sample is closish to the 1939 sample from Massachusetts. I take this to mean that Missouri has almost worked up to the jumping-off point. But there is in these cases neither such direct evidence of this as was offered in 1939 Massachusetts from the Opinions of the Justices nor such indirect evidence as is offered in Alabama by the reports from Alabama Appeals. *In terms of pinnable data the Missouri sample offers relatively little to my theses.* The data are indeed consistent therewith. *St. Louis and Southwestern is* even ready to get off and push. But I can see only a single instance out of fourteen or so as "showing" anything. And it might be *the* exception.

On the other hand, I have some claim to be a careful student. My judgment, I repeat, is that the Missouri Supreme Court, in this matter, is about where Massachusetts was in our 1939 sampling. A court can either consciously or unconsciously tremble on the verge of using, as a regular matter, situation-sense in the shaping not only of the application, but of the rule itself. Take a single case: ". . . the basis of his liability is his superior knowledge." *Harbourn v. Katz Drug Co.,* pp. 226, 229. Nonetheless, for the general theses of this book the Missouri sample remains, as evidence, close to neutral, if one omits (as for purposes of *proof* one must) the pervading, persistent flavor.

Authority techniques. The range is all that I hope, by now, you would expect. A feature not commonly found is recurrent specific reference, in regard to an opinion, to the West number, closing in on exactly what is being cited. Sometimes statutes are handled with gratifying careful attention to their language.

NEW MEXICO, 1958

The New Mexico sample started with 328 P.2d of September 5, 1958, which I was using for Washington and Oregon, and led into the next issue, which, for a change, was rich in New Mexico material. It was necessary to read only five cases in order to find four in which situation-sense was patently at work to shape not merely the application but the phrasing of the rule. But devils dog the path of the inquirer. The opinions began to be from not the supreme court, but from conscripted district judges. They were nice; but were they characteristic? The next issue at hand in my house was September 26, with an opinion by a judge who had been in my prior material, but who this time had found no need to go beyond the use of reason in mere application. I hope you feel with me the relief when the next further case turned up a third supreme court judge, who not only saw but stated a reviewing court's duty to the whole of the case: "Candidly, the appellants are not entitled to a hearing on this question because not having been raised properly below. . . . But it is not likely appellants were prejudiced. . . ." (p. 1095.) {507}

I pick up then two cases from the next issue at hand (December 5) both using situation-reason to shape the controlling rule, and one of which yields a dissent by the major writer of the earlier opinions. This seems to me to settle down into a picture of situation-reason at constant work in this court, in the shaping of the rule.

Authority techniques. An overruling is recognized. But "We believe it is implicit in . . ." and "It is no longer open to question in this state . . ." "We are well satisfied with that decision . . ." "Otherwise almost every judgment would . . ." "This is obviously a borderline case . . ." "For a case almost in point . . ." Why continue? The range is as evident as its use is sure.

REALISM, THE GENESIS OF THIS BOOK, THE TREASURE OF THE LAW REPORTS FOR BEHAVIORAL SCIENCE, THINGS THIS BOOK DOES NOT DO AND SOME POINTS OF METHOD

{508}

This Appendix wants to develop into a book in itself, but will not.

I must at least point out, however, that the present volume is a direct product of sustained study of appellate judging, attempting to use that child's-eye approach advocated by the realistic realists of the late '20's and the early '30's, using the persistent and careful follow-up without which no "approach" can amount to more than a dream, and with, I hope, something of the roundedness which ought to result from patient effort to work around the whole, and to keep judging it as a whole. One thing is clear: This job is no "fighting" or "program" job; this one cannot be excused for deficiencies of underpinning or of insight or of emphasis because of any lack of time or because of any temper of particular times. It has been more than thirty years in the making, with the surrounding "temper" shifting through half a dozen phases. The book has undertaken to combine solidity and roundedness and balance, and must be prepared to meet the reader or critic on those terms.

That is a particular reason why, as I come to the slow finish of the task, I want to write a word about a movement in thought which was vibrant and vocal when the study began, was violently misunderstood and misrepresented, and today, even where partly understood and recognized, is tending in modern American jurisprudential writing to be treated as an episode to be relegated to history. I refer to what has come to be known as American Legal Realism. It was a surprise and a sadness to find the doughty and penetrating Thurman Arnold announcing that of course realism had had but a temporary virtue or to find McWhinney regretting a supposed disappearance of the fervor realists once possessed.[1] For there is no lack of fervor. There is no {509} lack of current need for realism. There is indeed no lack of need to stop painting goblins. All that has shifted is the field of operation: after the need to do combat comes the need to do work. And I put this book forward both in its plan and on its descriptive side as a solid and unmistakable product and embodiment of American Legal Realism. I should indeed like to use the book to shame either old critics of the movement or later ones.

The situation is astoundingly simple, and the amount of print wasted on it is equally astounding.

Realism was never a philosophy,[2] nor did any group of realists as {510} such ever attempt to present any rounded view, or *whole* approach. One or two — perhaps for instance Underhill Moore — may (though without companion or adherent) have conceived and even put forward his thinking as sufficiently complete to deserve description as a philosophy, as expressing views on those phases of the institution of law which reach beyond description and the techniques of operation. I know of no other such, however, unless Jerome Frank's faith in the unreachability of fact be deemed of this nature.[3] No. What realism was, and is, is a method, nothing more, and the only tenet involved is that the method is a good one. "See it fresh," "See it as it works" — that was to be the foundation of any solid work, to *any* end. From there, one goes on into inquiry about e.g. What-it-is-for (function or goal), or e.g. to build a judgment on how far the measure fits the purpose, or e.g. on how far the particular purpose harmonizes with the Good Life, or e.g. on whether we do not then have to reexamine the original data about "How it has been working" — a matter which often answers very differently to different questions.

Of all of these things, only "see it fresh," "see it clean" and "come back to make sure" are of the essence. They go to method. *That method is eternal.* That is point 1. The method may have come into first discussion among lawyers in relation to rules and judicial decision, but it is no more limited to that area than it is to matters legal. It applies to anything. That is point 2. But *the method* includes nothing at all about whither to go. That is point 3. *Realism* is *not* a philosophy, but a *technology.* That is why it is eternal. The fresh look is always the fresh hope. The fresh inquiry into results is always the needed check-up.

If any person caught up in the enthusiasms of the moment paraded a banner that suggested more than this, he was a parader, not a thinker, no *real* realist, certainly not one who had status to speak for any "movement," much less for any "school." It is true that there were a few misguided souls who, having observed with accuracy that often neither the established and accepted generalizations ("rules" of law) nor the ones a court in trouble was swinging around at the moment would fit into any comfortable simple pattern of prediction or of guidance, arrived at the strange conclusion that no generalizations in {511} the law got anywhere or meant anything. Except for supposed flavor, there is little of this in print; the last I have come across is Northrop's recent echo of a class lecture by Sturges.[4] And any such noise is of course made nonsense for Sturges, as for Frank, by his interest and labor over putting effective legal guidance into words. Sturges' work and writing on arbitration procedure, and the effective running of an arbitration *institution,* give the lie to any lectures about nonexistence or impossibility of rules. Frank as he drafts briefs or regulations for the A.A.A., or builds opinions to guide the securities industry, or fights with L. Hand over how to guide lower courts on points of criminal procedure — that is the Frank to watch and read on this matter. In my own case, a single sentence from page 3 of the original *Bramble Bush:* "What these officials do about disputes is, to my mind, the law itself" — became, without anybody's reading either the context or the rest of *Bramble Bush,* and in august disregard of 1081 pages published the same year which centered on the rules of Sales law and the proper construction of the governing statute — this lone lorn sentence became, internationally, *the* cited goblin-painting of realism.[4a] But the crowning example is the treatment of Thurman Arnold. One of his major descriptive theses in *Symbols of Government* was that when courts and administrative agencies did substantially similar things in substantially similar ways, the courts were trusted and approved, the administrators distrusted and decried. He then became head of the Antitrust Division. He put his realistic observation into immediate practice, putting on the most resourceful, smooth, effective, and fair administration that Division has ever known. He was as vigorous as any other New Deal agency, and uniformly successful. But his Antitrust Division, and it alone among the New Deal agencies, went unattacked and unvilified: he was working through the courts. Here was the classic *experimentum crucis.* He even called attention to his policies and their reasons in *The Bottlenecks of Business*. What was the effect on the anti-realists, or indeed on jurisprudential writing in general? Zero. Patterson, a very friendly critic, in general, of realism, mentions the semantics of Arnold's "satirical works" as faulty (*Jurisprudence — Men and Ideas of the Law* 546). Period. The manner of such general neglect of what is not on the immediate page reminds me of the general treatment of Jerome Michael. His work in *course books* in the fields of crime and procedure establish his standing as perhaps the most powerful and original American thinker of his time in *jurisprudence*. Books on jurisprudence do not even mention him. Truly {512} jurisprudence-in-English is still bound by the labels put not only on "schools" but on book covers.

In any event, I claim to have introduced the term "Realistic Jurisprudence" into the modern literature;[5] I claim to have made moderately clear, as soon as the wilder type of controversy started, what was really up[6] as well as to have followed the matter up, after a decade of controversy and of pudding-proof by many hands, with a rather careful survey.[7] I therefore claim to know what it was about, and what it is about. I now put forward, explicitly as a proper product and exhibit of *real* realism, this book.

Here you can meet not the goblin, but the horse.

* * *

This volume gathers together, in matured and tested form, the substance of four earlier sets of lectures. These are the Storrs Lectures of 1940, at Yale, two lectures in 1945 before the Brandeis Lawyers Society in Philadelphia, the Mitchell Lectures at the University of Buffalo in 1951, and the Marx Lectures at the University of Cincinnati in 1953. In each case a recent body of local case material formed the working basis, and the results have been incorporated in this text, save that the specific 1951 New York case material has not been fully treated; New York is already too heavily tapped to make that justifiable. Of these lectures only those in Philadelphia have appeared in print.[8] It would be pleasant if Yale, Buffalo, and Cincinnati would regard the book as filling out, in a sort of postgraduate form, the series of their respective lectures. The only discussion omitted is that from the Storrs group about the common law tradition in relation to administrative officers, which would require, these days, to develop into a book in itself. In contrast, the ideas and treatment have become riper and sharper, and I have added to the material of the various lectures so much on the theory of courts and rules and on that of appellate argument, and so much especially on the theory and art of appellate decision, that the book must be regarded as in essence a new product standing on its own.

* * *

The whole job became possible when an invitation to lecture in Leipzig about American case law happened to coincide with labor over an unusually extensive and intensive book of cases and materials on Sales.[9] The need for explaining to lawyers of completely different background and training not *what* our case results were, but *how* we {513} got them, threw the judicial opinions into a completely different lighting; and the cases being handled in and for the Sales book suddenly came in for detailed examination of *exactly what they had been doing to the materials* which they had used to work with and from, and of how far their new version of what the earlier authorities had stood for amounted to a reshaping of those prior authorities. This gave me new eyes. It opened up not only a new way of reading opinions but a new world of thought and light.

Then, a few years later, the law of the Cheyenne Indians made clear to me what I had never before dreamed: to wit, that law and justice had no need at all to be in conflict or even in too much tension, but could instead represent a daily working harmony.[10] For in common with most lawyers, and indeed with most jurisprudes, I had mostly taken for granted a sort of perpetual struggle between the needs of regularity and form and of the precedent-phase of justice on the one side and, on the other, any dynamic readjustment of a going system to what just needed to be done. Pound had rightly stressed shifting tides in the struggle, and that I had seen. But I had to get to the Cheyennes in order to wake up to the fact that tension between form, or precedent, or other tradition and perceived need requires, in nature, to be a tension *only for the single crisis*. It does not have to be a continuing tension in the legal system as a whole, because an adequately resilient legal system can on occasion, or even almost regularly, absorb the particular trouble and resolve it each time into a new, usefully guiding, forward-looking felt standard-for-action or even rule-of-law.[11] To think of such steady readjustment — what Mentschikoff calls the legal artist's job of producing a new technical guiding form which can supply both needs at once — this was to get a further new pair of eyes. And it was on this foundation of experience with Cheyenne law that I became able to spot and understand the Grand Style as I met it in the early work of our own courts.[12] These, along with a deep interest in {514} Gothic, were so far as I can reach back, the two big intellectual jolts which opened up for me the material of this book. But I see no reason why any other person should be in need of similar disruptive or volcanic jolts. The door is open; anybody can go through. The obvious is obvious: the judicial opinion is a human document and a fascinating record, there, for anybody's use. From the standpoint of behavioral study these are data in which so many factors are held equal as to outrun the results of an ordinary ten- or even hundred-thousand-dollar grant. All there. All waiting. Already gathered. Merely neglected.

There is little use in preaching, and less in indignation. But when I find an economic historian leaping like a tomcat in May upon some colonial court record of 1758, while neither he nor his sociological confrere nor his colleagues in psychology nor even his brothers in government are willing to save foundation money and their own time by exploring from the behavioral side the amazing *gathered* treasure of the law reports — then I feel I ought at least to point the fact that these ready records, *with all kinds of factors "held equal,"* are there waiting for exploitation. And they are rich. On "small-group behavior" — in decision or otherwise, three or five hundred of the opinions from a single court, in sequence, and really studied, will make the results available from any normal *large* research grant look sick. The number of factors "held equal," I repeat, is unbelievable, if measured in terms of any known experimental techniques. Furthermore, in the same series of reports, one can simply move five or six years, and then commonly find a "control group" in which again oodles of identifiable factors are held more equal than they are on any large scale in today's normal (and expensive) testing methods.

This goes obviously to decision-making, and, as the text above makes dear, it goes to much nicer lines of discrimination in this area than current socio-psychological "design" has as yet preached: certainly to nicer lines than have been open to any but those gifted — gifted both by God and by Foundations. But that is not all. For instance, the lines of interacting person-and-personality within a working group not only have not been but are not soon likely to be recorded with the fullness and clarity which the law reports reveal. *And the Supreme Court is not the best focus of such study.* It is too much in the public eye. Its documents are too much consciously built for public view. Its issues are too likely to distract the student of human behavior by their general importance and by his own desires, and indeed to obscure, among the judges themselves, the normal interactions of a less intense environment. But the reports from New York, or Ohio, or North Carolina, or Pennsylvania, or California, studied in this light: these are gifts to behavioral research as valuable, let me repeat, as tens of thousands {515} from foundations. The type of thing I have in mind is quick to suggest; in this one study various probable effects of Cardozo on his court are suggested:

(1) By repeated discussions of one small series of cases on indefiniteness in business agreements; this is a qualitative examination, in sequence, on a single theme, with particular personnel particularly regarded. What is wanted is the spotting and tracing of a dozen more of such sequences, with their similarities and dissimilarities. Things unmentioned in the present text (such as the arrival of new judges, the exact line-ups of votes, case by case, individual studies of the individual judges concerned) would be of the essence. If such studies were then pursued until three or five of them were in hand for comparison, I submit the results would be as striking and informative as anything in print.

(2) By the rough but exciting purely quantitative checks on the growth and nature of dissent in the Court of Appeals. (Here, indeed, I think the whole relation of shift in style of decision to dissent to be a further valuable and feasible project.)

(3) By the detailed case studies, one of which suggests the power of a great judge's persuasiveness by way of substance, the other his power, in spite of absence of substance, to mislead by prestige and manner.

Such lines of approach, and more, would be needed in combination, and suggest that a behavioral science man would do well to team up with a law man, to throw variant techniques and combined insights into the needed smelter. And they will find that they talk at crosspurposes for longer than they will enjoy. But what a product they can bring out!

Note that I am talking thus far of the law reports almost pure. If one can add to them the type of letters which enrich Taft's biography,[13] or Stone's,[14] or the working papers which Cardozo bequeathed to Columbia University, or any other material with similar supplementary value, the volume and range of the law report evidence still stands ready as the base material, waiting to be deepened, widened, and intensified.

* * *

There are three remaining things I feel need to say. I do not like, in case analysis, to leave out the person and the variation. But in dealing with a multitude of courts upon a multitude of themes, as in our cross-section samples, individuals are not met with sufficient contact to justify risking judgments, and time is lacking to extend the acquaintance by study outside the samples. Moreover, the study is directed at courts *and not* at individuals, and the "average" appellate judge displays himself better in the blurred but real corporate person of the {516} court and in the corporate behavior than he can by any analysis of individuals and averaging of their attributes. I therefore make no apology for adding my own piece of depersonizing to the depersonizing sought and somewhat accomplished by our general institutional machinery.

The second matter I like even less. I do not like coarse analysis and coarse results when more refined analysis and results are available. To come out of a study merely with a picture of a process dominated by the authorities on the one hand, the judge's best judgment about sense and justice on the other, the interaction being played upon by counsel, by the craft tradition, and by one's colleagues, but in differential fashion case by case, and the whole — both intake perception, organization for meditation, and standards against which to set the case for judgment — being conditioned by what are for law-governmental purposes accidents, the accidents somewhat of temperament and endowment, but more of individual experience — this is in itself an almost disgustingly crude and loose result in terms of crude and loose factors in what sounds almost like free association. And better, very much better, can be done, as, e.g., the forthcoming results of Mentschikoff and Haggard make quite clear. Each of the factors mentioned can be broken down, the statement of interactions can be materially clarified and tightened and (I am convinced) shown to differ in perceptible fashion in reasonably identifiable type-situations. Being fully persuaded of such things, it irks me to leave the analytical results in the shape they are. Yet once again I have no intention of making any apology:

A job is the job it is, and it is not any other. The tools to use and the results to get are those which fit that job. My task here has not been to push social or behavioral science techniques and results as far along as I was able. My task has been to wrestle with an unjustified crisis of lawyers' confidence in appellate courts, and with worries among the courts themselves which slow and hamper their work. To do that I must come up with tools of analysis which any thinking man of law can understand both in their nature and in their use, and I must come out with results in words which he can not only understand but put to work. Refinement, therefore, must go not into analysis for professional students of behavior, but into communicable knowhow for practical application by the men of law. That, if I may recur to the opening of this Appendix, is what realism calls for. That, to the best of my ability, is what I have done.

The third matter which needs mention is the difference in treatment of the same material as between such a study as the present and one directed to the growth-processes and growth-results of case law, whether in our own system, or generally. This latter field is an old sweetheart of mine. It also uses cases as the primary raw materials; it also involves the reading of the opinion as a human document. {517} Not only that, but it also requires attention to the process of deciding and to the nature of facts, situation, and general background in their impact on the court. It may have some value for general method, therefore, to indicate briefly some of the ways in which the two lines of inquiry diverge.

The first and most striking difference is of course that for case law study *every* decision requires to be placed in its own time sequence of doctrine, and requires to have its own doctrinal background fully explored, so that the state of relevant doctrine as it came to bear becomes concrete, clear, and close to complete.[15] That is the body of doctrine about to be affected, and must be so known in order to determine either what its effect ought, doctrinally, to be, or what effect the actual decision has upon it. The manner of such exploration is suggested in the New York consumer warranty series here, and, with respect to the two culminating cases, in the sequence on the Illinois court's witness, and in less complete but more elaborate form in the New York indefiniteness sequence. It is illustrated in model form only once in this volume, and that only because one particular short sequence, so treated, happened also to make a couple of points vital to our own study; this was in the foreign remittance series.

The next difference, which hardly needs mention, is that whereas for us the way of use or reshaping or discard or neglect of each prior pressing authority has been a question merely of what *kind of treatment* it got, for the case law student the question is also: what happened to it in *substance?* What did the change or nonchange result in? (set in the whole time-sequence of the particular line of doctrine, past and prospective)

But common to the two lines of inquiry is the question of *why* any of this occurred; there I see little difference in the lines of interest or of work. Save in this: that the intense concern of the student of case law with the impact of the particular judge or combination of judges (the kind of thing we have touched on in the indefiniteness cases) belongs, for a study of appellate deciding, not on the elementary level of the present job, but to more advanced and refined inquiry. Common again is the interest in style and manner of the court, its sensitivity to or knowledge of the situation, and the like, and in whether the court does a craftsmanlike job either on the facts, or on situation-sense, or on the framing of the measure, or on tidying up behind, or all of these. But the minute the particular decision has been {518} handed down, interest forks again: the effects we have sought to follow, if we could, are the effects on bar, on public, and inside the court itself, of the manner and general cumulation of the work; the effects which interest our case law inquirer are the effects of each single case and of the particular succession of cases on his pet body of doctrine and on *its* effects outside. Deciding is, for him, the moving chisel of doctrine. Doctrine has been for us, on the other hand, one major force in the shaping of decision.

In similar fashion, the use of case materials for the study of case law opens out into the whole doctrinal structure and the *system's* methods for readjustment thereof, whereas the use of those materials for the study of deciding heads rather into the particular craft of the appellate judge and into the system's organization of courts and appellate procedure. Like us, the student of case law finds himself welcoming the earthiness of the case law approach to rule-making and rule-revision, but he is forced to canvass also prices which are no part of our problem in the present study: What does it cost a polity in delay and uncertainty and in legal discomfort or injustice to have the making or review of a rule wait upon the chance raising and appeal of issues one by one by dragging one? Consider, in contrast, what a Uniform Commercial Act or a Uniform Commercial Code does in making available in a jurisdiction where rulings are sparse the experience and wisdom of the whole country — all at a single stroke. Or consider the problem of accessibility of doctrine, as it bears on the man-hours of talented labor (if there is to be accuracy based on knowledge), and so on the expense, needed for advice. Such things are not our worry here. We note rather that one contributing factor, perhaps a major one, to that rigidification we call the Formal Style may well have been the relative inaccessibility of authorities and stimulus from the other States; and that the all-State finding-apparatus which began to be available in 1896 may well have been one important factor in that re-entry of overt sense and reason which has come to mark the modern style.

Thus it is much as if the study of deciding were the study of the point in flux, and that of case law rather the study of the resulting curve: though they both use and focus on the same basic stuff.

The two different approaches stand out most strongly, perhaps, if one considers 218 N.C. and its negligence cases: three of the judges could only see and judge with a defendant's eyes, three only with a plaintiff's. The seventh judge (a) did all the deciding in, and (b) made all the law of the field. Or take the story of Musmanno in Pennsylvania. For years his effects on the deciding seem to have been negligible; and so on the case law. Even as he so very slowly broke himself into teamwork, and also began to affect the team, his impact on substantive case law reached not much beyond some occasional "liberalization"; but on the *manner* of deciding *any type of case at all*, I see Musmanno as rivaling in effect

Horace Stern himself: it is the conjoint, {519} balanced influence of the two which I see as primarily responsible for Pennsylvania's full and general recapture of the Manner of Reason.

* * *

There is little need to spend time on acknowledgments. As always, I take the state of the art for granted. As always, what I have to offer is the neglected obvious. But in this instance there is one idea, and a most valuable one, which when the basic picture first began to shape itself up twenty years ago was rather novel: the idea of period-style in application to the work of law. I do not want the recent social science stirrings toward a "style" concept to lead to any idea that I am just joining what promises to become the next fad.[16] The seed and impetus {520} in my case lie almost thirty years back, though, as indicated above, nothing germinated until after meeting the Cheyennes. That seed and impetus was Bechtel's brilliant *Wirtschaftstil des deutschen Spätmittelalters* (1930); my copy shows it in my hands by 1932.

The degree to which my book rests on the American pioneer in the field, Cardozo, speaks again and again; what does not so speak is the debt to Walton Hamilton, who over decades worked beside me in mutually illuminating and cooperative rivalry and brotherhood. My brethren Levi and Meltzer read much MSS and pointed out many obscure or dubious passages; Kurland checked, generally, my layman's observations on the Supreme Court, and led me to material I should certainly otherwise have missed. Soia Mentschikoff's patience, vision, and inspiration inform every page.

Still, mostly, the material has always been there to see; acknowledgments go to help in managing to get it noticed.

If noticed, if taken to heart, it may help to bring back into blossom and fruit Lemuel Shaw's noble dream of American law and decision made plain, made warm and near, made proud, to the men and women from whom and for whom they are.

Notes to Appendix B

{footnotes appeared on page number of original text location}

1 "Realistic jurisprudence is a good medicine for a sick and troubled society. The America of the early 1930's was such a society. But realism, despite its liberating virtues, is not a sustaining food for a stable civilization." Arnold, Jerome Frank, 24 U. Chi. L. Rev. 633, 635 (1957). McWhinney concurring: Methodology and Values in American Legal Education, etc., 4 Natural L.F. 119, 128, n.39 (1959). The McWhinney reference to waning fervor I paraphrase from memory; it is also recent. Compare also Gilmore's review of Bramble Bush, 2d ed., 60 Yale L.J. 1251 (1951), or the elegiac flavor of Patterson's rather sympathetic discussion in 1953: Jurisprudence — Men and Ideas of the Law 537-556. Note also that those friendly souls who have sought to make sense out of the picture have operated each independently, with no cumulation at all. My own Some Realism About Realism, 44 Harv. L. Rev. 1222 (1931), is the only piece which finds recurrent use. Cardozo's admirable study of 1932, Jurisprudence, N.Y. St. Bar Assn. Rep. 263, has been discussed, so far as I have noticed, only by Patterson (at his pages 536-537), who completely misunderstands both its content and its purpose. Goodrich's interpretation in the Harvard Tercentennial, The Future of the Common Law (1937), I have never seen cited. Fuller's caustic but not unsympathetic full critique, American Legal Realism, 82 U. Pa. L. Rev. 429 (1934), does not mention the Cardozo paper, rejects my effort in Some Realism, and despite its own title, accessibility, and insight, has been little used. It is also most unusual to find anyone

using my own later and broader paper, On Reading and Using the Newer Jurisprudence, 40 Columb. L. Rev. 581 (1940); and I have run across no reference to either Paton's discussions in the two editions of his Text-book of Jurisprudence (1946 and 1951) nor even to Julius Stone's critical but really perceptive discussion in his striking work The Province and Function of Law (1946) (but that whole large volume is shamefully neglected). On the other hand, Paton and especially Stone make effective use not only of their own realistic thinking but of American theoretical realistic writing. The truth is, of course, that realism has been good method since man began to think. — Since the above went to press, Arnold has joyously demonstrated (a) that he is still as tough a realist as he ever was, and (b) that realism is still "a sustaining food." Professor Hart's Theology, 73 Harv. L. Rev. 1298 (1960).

2 It is persistently treated as such. So, e.g. Patterson, cited above, note 1, at 556. But realism is a method which can serve any goal at all. A main trouble with treating either the descriptive or the technological branch of a discipline as a philosophy is that any preliminary or partial work is likely to be viewed as if it were trying to be a whole, with negative implications read in, indeed read in even though they be denied. A very mild example is in front of me at the moment: at his page 448 Fuller, cited above, note 1, read "I make no effort *here* to indicate either the proper rule, or the proper action on any legal subject" (italics added) as a *disclaimer* that my "own *approach* involves any distinctive ethical bias." (Italics added.) I am reminded of Sombart's mournful introduction to the great work in which he wove together the strands of many single-factor investigations: each of the latter, when published, had been viciously reviewed as a hopelessly misguided single-factor explanation. Der moderne Kapitalismus (1928). I have expressed myself fully on my own position, so far as concerns what the positive law is (rules, organization, how things go round, tendencies, and all the rest) in The Normative, the Legal, and the Law-Jobs: The Problem of Juristic Method, 49 Yale L.J. 1355, 1370-1372 (1940).

3 I have never been able to make out whether it was. But even in his 1954 paper, A Conflict with Oblivion: Some Observations on the Founders of Legal Pragmatism, 9 Rutgers L. Rev. 425, his effort at a more mature and restrained phrasing of the certainty problem: "whether, before suits commenced, lawyers *usually* could, with *some* high degree of accuracy, foretell the *specific* decisions of the trial courts" (my italics, his p. 447) — even this effort finds the qualifiers dropped at once, and carries "specific" (equals "what the amounts of the judgments would be") in its belly as a self-destroyer.

4 See page 289, n. 284b.

4a "It is easy to paint a goblin. It is hard to paint a horse." The book was my Cases and Materials on Sales (1930). I had then already been serving for four years as Commissioner on Uniform State Laws for the Conference, and had been the draftsman for them of the Uniform Chattel Mortgage Act. But the passage "shows" me to deny both the existence and the function of rules of law. The goblin passage is quoted by A. W. Hummel from Yen Yuan, 28 Bull. Am. U. Prof. 358, 366 (1942).

5 A Realistic Jurisprudence — The Next Step, 30 Columb. L. Rev. 431 (1930).

6 Some Realism About Realism, 44 Harv. L. Rev. 1222 (1931).

7 On Reading and Using the Newer Jurisprudence, 40 Columb. L. Rev. 581 (1940).

8 How Appellate Courts Decide Cases (Brandeis Lawyers Society Series).

9 Cited above, note 4.

10 See Llewellyn and Hoebel, The Cheyenne Way (1941), especially c. 12.

11 In a developed system, this is the singing rule.

12 This is the kind of contribution by anthropology to Jurisprudence for which I have always hoped. You suddenly hit upon beauty and vision in a strange culture, and you may be the person in whom a seed takes root, so that light is shed at home. The values of comparative law and comparative politics are not different, except that the chances of deep illumination may be less.

    I am fortunate in having persuasive record of the process. The warranty material in the Sales book was historically dealt with and took me into a good deal of the judging of the Grand Style, especially in New York and Massachusetts. What I found was law and the theory of case law; and both were exciting. Courts, Quality of Goods, and a Credit Economy (1937) (corrected reprints from 36 Columb. L. Rev. 699 and 37 ibid. 341) contains another and deeper historical study in the same field. But it was done after Cheyenne results had been cooking for two years, and were jelling. So there turned up not only law, theory of case law, and enriched understanding of judging generally, but clear recognition of the Grand Style and its meaning — which became vocal in the Storrs lectures and in The American Common Law Tradition and American Democracy, 1 J. Legal & Pol. Soc. 14 (1942).

13 Pringle, The Life and Times of William Howard Taft (1939).

14 Mason, Harlan Fiske Stone, Pillar of the Law (1956).

15 Beginnings of this can be found in my Präjudizienrecht u. Rechtsprechung in Amerika (1932) and the Sales book, cited above, note 4a, the work on which was done at about the same time: the emphasis was chiefly on the doctrinal background of the main holding and on the shape of the materials used in the opinion before the opinion itself took hold of them. Courts, Quality, etc., cited above, note 12, adds the full historical sequence in the single jurisdiction, with similar sequences on the same topic in other jurisdictions developed for comparison. By part II the method is beginning to assume rather satisfactory form.

16 Overstress on the meticulous and quantitative has been in vogue long enough to be working toward some reaction in terms of synthesis and large sweeps. For some years now the Social Science Research Council has been looking into procedures for new-type studies of government in terms of the going whole, an approach which leads not necessarily but very readily into "style." In two recent publications which I have happened on, the idea is already conscripted for use in the analysis of *activities*, and given the label: Spiro, Government by Constitution (1959); Peairs, Essay on the Teaching of Law, 12 J. Legal Ed. 323 (1960). The present volume of course takes style as a central if not the central analytical tool. Wetter puts it into his title and makes it his whole theme.

If a fad should develop, there are hazards to be warned against. "Style," in analysis of great-institutions, is tricky. It needs vigilance lest it move into vague and sloppy word-slinging. Consider what has been done with "Volksgeist" and "ethos," the "spirit of the age," or, in medicine some decades back, with "constitution" (which *de facto* meant most of the time "everything about him I don't know," treated as if that were an entity). Yet it is plain that goingness is goingness, and has a way of its own, that wholeness is wholeness and has a character not to be reached merely by way of the parts, and that going wholeness is the essential ultimate subject of study. And I do think the "style" idea an effective road in. I would simply remind that the places where we have done best with this most undefined of thought-tools are music, literature, architecture, and the graphic arts, or furniture or silversmithing and the like, where a *tangible monument* results and holds still for examination, for cross-check, for comparison, for recurrence; *and* where each single monument is, as compared with say "law" or "government" (or, better than either, "Law-Government") small and readily compassable as well as concrete. Where pure behavior is concerned — Bernhardt's acting as against her author, Nijinski's dancing as against his choreographer, Toscanini's conducting as against his composer, the delivery phase of oratory — there we have done best with "style" where the behavior is repetitive either in itself or on closely similar occasions; and again the unit is small enough to be grasped cleanly as a whole, again the wherewithal is given to return for further observation. In the field of the law-crafts "style" is thus well enough at home. Appellate judging, the drafting of documents, the drafting of pleadings, the writing of briefs, the drafting of legislation — these leave monuments. Negotiation (contrast an Oriental dicker with an old New England horse trade with a current settlement of a negligence suit with an international diplomatic negotiation of the old school) or the handling of a trial, or the oral argument of an appeal, or the handling of the chair — any such acts-of-a-craft recur in sufficient patterning to admit of study that has teeth. But as soon as the focus widens the difficulties must be watched. Bechtel's heaped-up careful detail is then the kind of buttressing which a style-hypothesis or style-attribution needs.

CANONS ON STATUTES

{521}

Although, as has been insisted, statutes and their meaning are not the focus of this book, there may be value in reproducing here some material gathered and arranged for me ten years back by Charles Driscoll, on the State courts' handling of statutes, and adding some material on the Federal courts' approaches gathered for this volume by J. A. Spanogle, Jr. In neither case does it seem needful, since this is not a focus of the study, to demonstrate the use made in each case cited of the general canon there announced. The purpose is indicated clearly enough by Driscoll's language: "Statutory interpretation still speaks a diplomatic tongue. *Here is some of the technical framework for maneuver.*"[1] (My italics.) I reproduce here from my article, Remarks on the Theory of Appellate Decision and the Rules or Canons About How Statutes Are to Be Construed,[2] Driscoll's collection of canons and my own immediately introductory paragraphs:

When it comes to presenting a proposed statutory construction in court, there is an accepted conventional vocabulary. As in argument over points of case-law, the accepted convention still, unhappily, requires discussion as if only one single correct meaning could exist. Hence there are two opposing canons on almost every point. An arranged selection is appended. Every lawyer must be familiar with them all: they are still needed tools of argument. At least as early as Fortescue the general picture was clear, on this, to any eye which would see.

Plainly, to make any canon take hold in a particular instance, the construction contended for must be sold, essentially, by means other than the use of the canon: The good sense of the situation and a *simple* construction of the available language to achieve that sense, *by tenable means, out of the statutory language.*

CANONS OF CONSTRUCTION {522}

THRUST	BUT	PARRY
1. A statute cannot go beyond its text.[3]		1. To effect its purpose a statute may be implemented beyond its text.[4]
2. Statutes in derogation of the common law will not be extended by construction.[5]		2. Such acts will be liberally construed if their nature is remedial.[6]
3. Statutes are to be read in the light of the common law and a statute affirming a common law rule is to be construed in accordance with the common law.[7]		3. The common law gives way to a statute which is inconsistent with it and when a statute is designed as a revision of a whole body of law applicable to a given subject it supersedes the common law.[8]

377

4. Where a foreign statute which has received construction has been adopted, previous construction is adopted too.[9]

4. It may be rejected where there is conflict with the obvious meaning of the statute or where the foreign decisions are unsatisfactory in reasoning or where the foreign interpretation is not in harmony with the spirit or policy of the laws of the adopting state.[10]

{523} 5. Where various states have already adopted the statute, the parent state is followed.[11]

5. Where interpretations of other states are inharmonious, there is no such restraint.[12]

6. Statutes *in pari materia* must be construed together.[13]

6. A statute is not *in pari materia* if its scope and aim are distinct or where a legislative design to depart from the general purpose or policy of previous enactments may be apparent.[14]

7. A statute imposing a new penalty or forfeiture, or a new liability or disability, or creating a new right of action will not be construed as having a retroactive effect.[15]

7. Remedial statutes are to be liberally construed and if a retroactive interpretation will promote the ends of justice, they should receive such construction.[16]

8. Where design has been distinctly stated no place is left for construction.[17]

8. Courts have the power to inquire into real — as distinct from ostensible — purpose.[18]

9. Definitions and rules of construction contained in an interpretation clause are part of the law and binding.[19]

9. Definitions and rules of construction in a statute will not be extended beyond their necessary import nor allowed to defeat intention otherwise manifested.[20]

{524} 10. A statutory provision requiring liberal construction does not mean disregard of unequivocal requirements of the statute.[21]

10. Where a rule of construction is provided within the statute itself the rule should be applied.[22]

11. Titles do not control meaning; preambles do not expand scope; section headings do not change language.[23]

11. The title may be consulted as a guide when there is doubt or obscurity in the body; preambles may be consulted to determine rationale, and thus the true construction of terms; section headings may be looked upon as part of the statute itself.[24]

12. If language is plain and unambiguous it must be given effect.[25]

12. Not when literal interpretation would lead to absurd or mischievous consequences or thwart manifest purpose.[26]

13. Words and phrases which have received judicial construction before enactment are to be understood according to that construction.[27]

13. Not if the statute clearly requires them to have a different meaning.[28]

{525} 14. After enactment, judicial decision upon interpretation of

14. Practical construction by executive officers is strong evidence of true mean-

particular terms and phrases controls.[29]

ing.[30]

15. Words are to be taken in their ordinary meaning unless they are technical terms or words of art.[31]

15. Popular words may bear a technical meaning and technical words may have a popular signification and they should be so construed as to agree with evident intention or to make the statute operative.[32]

16. Every word and clause must be given effect.[33]

16. If inadvertently inserted or if repugnant to the rest of the statute, they may be rejected as surplusage.[34]

17. The same language used repeatedly in the same connection is presumed to bear the same meaning throughout the statute.[35]

17. This presumption will be disregarded where it is necessary to assign different meanings to make the statute consistent.[36]

{526} 18. Words are to be interpreted according to the proper grammatical effect of their arrangement within the statute.[37]

18. Rules of grammar will be disregarded where strict adherence would defeat purpose.[38]

19. Exceptions not made cannot be read in.[39]

19. The letter is only the "bark." Whatever is within the reason of the law is within the law itself.[40]

20. Expression of one thing excludes another.[41]

[Quite typically: not "*the* other." Cf. page 106, note 137.]

20. The language may fairly comprehend many different cases where some only are expressly mentioned by way of example.[42]

21. General terms are to receive a general construction.[43]

21. They may be limited by specific terms with which they are associated or by the scope and purpose of the statute.[44]

22. It is a general rule of construction that where general words follow an enumeration they are to be held as applying only to persons and things of the same general kind or class specifically mentioned (*ejusdem generis*).[45]

22. General words must operate on something. Further, *ejusdem generis* is only an aid in getting the meaning and does not warrant confining the operations of a statute within narrower limits than were intended.[46]

{527} 23. Qualifying or limiting words or clauses are to be referred to the next preceding antecedent.[47]

23. Not when evident sense and meaning require a different construction.[48]

24. Punctuation will govern when a statute is open to two constructions.[49]

24. Punctuation marks will not control the plain and evident meaning of language.[50]

25. It must be assumed that language has been chosen with due regard to grammatical propriety and is not interchangeable on mere conjec-

25. "And" and "or" may be read interchangeably whenever the change is necessary to give the statute sense and effect.[52]

ture.[51]

26. There is a distinction between words of permission and mandatory words.[53]	26. Words imparting permission may be read as mandatory and words imparting command may be read as permissive when such construction is made necessary by evident intention or by the rights of the public.[54]
{528} 27. A proviso qualifies the provision immediately preceding.[55]	27. It may clearly be intended to have a wider scope.[56]
28. When the enacting clause is general, a proviso is construed strictly.[57]	28. Not when it is necessary to extend the proviso to persons or cases which some come within its equity.[58]

Spanogle has gathered in items 1-7, below, a few indications that the Federal courts talk in happy parallel to the kind of stuff set forth above. That I suppose needs no proof. The following material, however, items 8-19, has some value. In this day of much noise, particularly in regard to Federal statutes, about legislative history, this day in which such real or supposed history is not infrequently dealt with by otherwise intelligent judges as if there were some overpowering magic in one or another aspect of such history or in one or another canon about use thereof, it really pays to collect and arrange a few official remarks which show that legal "compulsion" in the matter points in any or all directions at once, so that the matter necessarily becomes one of judgment in the particular case, and of consequent responsibility *resting on the court* for choosing one "lead" rather than another. There may even be a slender hope that putting such material out baldly, boldly, and in its unmistakable and shameless cross-"guidance" may lead an occasional court to cease driveling about some compelling "legislative intent" which flatly controls the court, even in cases where no such intent existed or can be found, and to settle {529} down instead to a court's own real and responsible business of trying to make sense out of the legislation, so far as text and context may allow.

Let me not be misunderstood. I think any aspect of legislative history may be useful, and should be looked at, for what it is worth; thus, the contrived "friendly colloquy" deserves attention, frequently, as evidence of what was *carefully left out* of the bill. But I feel utility, no less, in background which is not capable of being canonized as legislative history. And, above all, I view "legislative intent" as being in eight litigated cases out of ten pure will-o'-the-wisp. In addition, I think it a false guide as a statute ages.

THRUST AND COUNTERTHRUST

1. "[I]f extreme hardship will result from a literal application of the words, this may be taken as evidence that the legislature did not use them literally." Ballon v. Kemp, 92 F.2d 556, 558 (D.C. Cir. 1937).	"It is not enough merely that hard and objectionable or absurd consequences, which probably were not within the contemplation of the framers, are produced by an act of legislation.... [I]n such case the remedy lies with the law-making authority, and not with the courts." Crooks v. Harrelson, 282 U.S. 55, 60 (1930).

2. "[T]he two [statutes] are in pari materia and must be construed together." Sanford's Estate v. Commissioner, 308 U.S. 39, 44 (1939).

"[T]he rule of in pari materia is resorted to only in cases where the meaning of a statute is ambiguous or doubtful." Northern Pac. Ry. Co. v. United States, 156 F.2d 346, 350 (7th Cir. 1946).

3. "[T]he meaning of a word may be ascertained by reference to the meaning of words associated with it." International Rice Milling Co. v. NLRB, 183 F.2d 21, 25 (5th Cir. 1950).

A "word may have a character of its own not to be submerged by its association." Russell Motor Car Co. v. United States, 261 U.S. 514, 519 (1923).

4. "[W]here words of a particular or specific meaning are followed by general words, the general words are construed to apply only to persons or conditions of the same general kind as those specifically mentioned . . ." Lyman v. Commissioner, 83 F.2d 811 (1st Cir. 1936).

"[The rule] gives no warrant for narrowing alternative provisions which the Legislature has adopted with the purpose of affording added safeguards." United States v. Gilliland, 312 U.S. 86, 93 (1941).

{530} 5. "[W]hen a statute is adopted from another jurisdiction, in substantially the same language, the provisions so adopted are to be construed in the sense in which they were understood at the time in the jurisdiction from which they were taken." Fiske v. Buder, 125 F.2d 841, 844 (8th Cir. 1942).

"When a statute is adopted from one jurisdiction into the jurisprudence of another, it will be construed so as to harmonize it with its new environment in preference to a rigid adherence to the interpretation given it in its original home. . . ." United States v. Farrett, 87 F.2d 957, 963 (8th Cir. 1937).

6. "The heading of a statute, or a section thereof, may not be used to . . . restrict the language of the statute itself." Bersio v. United States, 124 F.2d 310, 314 (4th Cir. 1941).

"The heading here considered is part of the context of the statute" (and unambiguous words were in consequence limited). Carter v. Liquid Carbonic Pacific Corp., 97 F.2d 4 (9th Cir. 1938).

7. "[T]he presumption [is] that a proviso 'refers only to the provision to which it is attached.'" United States v. McClure, 305 U.S. 472, 478 (1939), quoting United States v. Morrow, 266 U.S. 531, 535 (1925).

"[A] proviso is not always limited in its effect to the part of the enactment with which it is immediately associated; it may apply generally to all cases within the meaning of the language used." McDonald v. United States, 279 U.S. 12, 21 (1929); U.S. v. Collier and Son Corp., 208 F.2d 936, 939 (7th Cir. 1953).

8. "[T]here is no need to refer to the legislative history where the statutory language is clear." Ex Parte Collett, 337 U.S. 55, 61 (1949); and see Nicholas v. Denver & R.G.W. Ry. Co., 195 F.2d 428, 431 (10th Cir. 1952).

"But words are inexact tools at best, and for that reason there is wisely no rule of law forbidding resort to explanatory legislative history no matter how clear the words may appear on superficial examination." Harrison v. Northern Trust Co., 317 U.S. 476, 479 (1942).

{531} 9. [LEFT] "Such general remarks . . . were obviously not made with this narrow issue in mind and they cannot be said to illustrate a Congressional de-

[MIDDLE] "While [the legislative] history provides no conclusive answer, it is consistent with the view taken . . . by the Courts of Appeal . . ." Mastro Plastics

sire. . . ." Jewel Ridge Corp. v. Local, 325 U.S. 161, 168-169 (1944).[59]

Corp. v. Board, 350 U.S. 270, 287 (1956).

[RIGHT] "Legislative materials may be without probative value, or contradictory, or ambiguous, it is true, and in such case will not be permitted to control the customary meaning of words . . . they can scarcely be deemed to be incompetent or irrelevant . . . The meaning to be ascribed to an Act of Congress can only be derived from a considered weighing of every relevant aid to construction." United States v. Dickerson, 310 U.S. 554, 562 (1940).

10. [LEFT] "[The statute's] meaning ought justly to be gathered from its words as promulgated to the public rather than from the expressions of legislators or even of their committees pending its passage." Marchese v. United States, 126 F.2d 671, 674 (5th Cir. 1942).

[MIDDLE] "Whatever is said in the debates on the bill or in the reports concerning it . . . must give way to its language; or, rather, all the reasons that induced its enactment must be supposed to be satisfied and expressed by its words." Mackensie v. Hare, 239 U.S. 299, 308 (1915).

[MID-RIGHT] "[R]eports of committees in either or both branches of Congress, and reports of conference committees are parts of legislative history which may be taken into consideration in ascertaining the meaning of a doubtful statute passed by that body." Nicholas v. Denver & R.G.W.R., 195 F.2d 428, 431 (10th Cir. (1952).

[FAR RIGHT] "[G]reat weight must be accorded . . . to opinions expressed [in the Congressional Record] by members of committees having the legislation in charge. . . ." United States Federal Power Commission, 191 F.2d 796, 802 (4th Cir. 1951).

11. "[I]ndividual expressions are without weight in the interpretation of a statute." McCaughn v. Hershey Chocolate Co., 283 U.S. 488, 494 (1931).

"But statements made by the chairman of the committee in charge of the bill stand upon a different footing, and may be resorted to under proper qualifications." Nicholas v. Denver & R.G.W.R. Co., 194 F.2d 428, 431 (10th Cir. 1952); United States v. St. Paul, M. & M. Ry. Co., 247 U.S. 310, 318 (1918).

12. [LEFT] [D]ebates in Congress are not appropriate sources of information from which to discover the meaning of the language of a statute . . ." United States v. Freight Assn., 166 U.S. 290, 318 (1897);

{533} [MIDDLE] "[B]ut where, as in this instance the congressional debates are in harmony with a fair construction of the act, they are highly persuasive in arriving at the legislative intention."

cited with approval in McCaughn v. Hershey Chocolate Co., 273 U.S. 488, 494 (1931).

Maxwell v. Brayshaw, 258 Fed. 957, 961 (D.C. Cir. 1919).

[RIGHT] "In order to ascertain the *intent* of Congress in passing this provision, we have made an exhaustive search of the Congressional Record containing the debates on the [bill]." Kaline v. United States, 235 F.2d 54, 63 (9th Cir. 1956).

13. "[W]e think that the interpretation given to the bill before the Committees . . . is a persuasive indication of the legislative intent." Switchmen's Union v. NLRB, 135 F.2d 785, 796 (D.C. Cir. 1943).

"While [Committee hearings] may be related to the enactment of the provision, we feel certain that it should not be resorted to for the purpose of showing the intent of the legislature." Boston Brokerage Co. v. United States, 22 C.C.P.A. 452, 460 (1934).

14. "The amendment was put to a vote and rejected . . . [That is] a circumstance to be weighed along with others when choice is nicely balanced." Fox v. Standard Oil Co., 294 U.S. 87, 96 (1934).

"[T]he courts have never given the introduction of an amendment by a legislator the force of evidence tending to prove legislative intent. . . ." Stone and Downer Co. v. United States, 12 Ct. Cust. App. 62, 69 (1923).

15. "[N]o aid could possibly be derived from the legal history of another act passed nearly six years after the one in question." Pennsylvania Mutual Life Ins. Co. v. Lederer, 252 U.S. 523, 538 (1920).

"[Subsequent legislation may be considered to assist in the interpretation of prior legislation on the same subject." Tiger v. Western Investment Co., 221 U.S. 286, 309 (1911); Great Northern Ry. Co. v. United States, 315 U.S. 39, 44 (1939).

{534} 16. "The Court is not bound by an administrative construction. . . ." Burnet v. Chicago Portrait Co., 285 U.S. 1, 16 (1932).

"The construction given to a statute by those charged with the duty of executing it . . . ought not to be overruled without cogent reasons . . . and the administrative interpretation is of controlling weight unless plainly erroneous. . . ." Bowles v. Mannie & Co., 155 F.2d 129, 133 (7th Cir. 1946), citing United States v. Moore, 95 U.S. 760, 763 (1877), and Bowles v. Seminole Rock and Sand Co., 325 U.S. 410, 414 (1945).

17. "The regulations and rules promulgated by a Commission pursuant to the statutory authority have the force and effect of Federal law." Skelly Oil Co. v. Phillips Petroleum Co., 174 F.2d 89, 97 (10th Cir. 1949).

"[A] regulation . . . has the force and effect of law if it be not in conflict with express statutory provision . . . [including] rules and regulations of department of a state government." Maryland Casualty Co. v. United States, 251 U.S. 342, 349 (1919).

18. "The meaning of a word may be ascertained with perfect propriety . . . by

"While Dictionary definitions are helpful, they do not . . . forbid an inquiry examining the lexicographical and technical authorities. . . ." Absorbo Beer Pad Co., Inc. v. United States, 30 C.C.P.A., Cust. 24, 30 (1942).

19. "Although the tax years involved in the cases before us are 1948 and 1950, and a 1954 re-enactment of course cannot conclusively demonstrate the propriety of an administrative {535} and judicial interpretation application as made to transactions occurring before the re-enactment, the 1954 action of Congress is significant as indicating satisfaction with the interpretation consistently given the statute by the Regulations here at issue and in demonstrating its prior intent." Cammarano v. Commissioner, 358 U.S. 498, 510 (1959).

into administrative interpretation as an aid in construction . . ." Ramsey v. Commissioner, 66 F.2d 316, 318 (10th Cir. 1933).

"Re-enactment — particularly without the slightest affirmative indication that Congress ever had [a prior] decision before it — is an unreliable indicum at best." Commissioner v. Glenshaw Glass Co., 348 U.S. 426 (1955).

Notes to Appendix C

{footnotes appeared on page number of original text location}

1 3 Vand. L. Rev. 395, 401 (1950).

2 Ibid. 401-406.

3 First National Bank v. DeBerriz, 87 W. Va. 477, 105 S.E. 900 (1921); Sutherland, Statutory Construction §388 (2d ed. 1904); 59 C.J., Statutes §575 (1932).

4 Dooley v. Penn. R.R., 250 Fed. 142 (D. Minn. 1918); 59 C.J., Statutes §575 (1932).

5 Devers v. City of Scranton, 308 Pa. 13, 161 Atl. 540 (1932); Black, Construction and Interpretation of Laws §113 (2d ed. 1911); Sutherland, Statutory Construction §573 (2d ed. 1904); 25 R.C.L., Statutes §281 (1919).

6 Becker v. Brown, 65 Neb. 264, 91 N.W. 178 (1902); Black, Construction and Interpretation of Laws §113 (2d ed. 1911); Sutherland, Statutory Construction §§573-75 (2d ed. 1904); 59 C.J., Statutes §657 (1932).

7 Bandfield v. Bandfield, 117 Mich. 80, 75 N.W. 287 (1898); 25 R.C.L., Statutes §280 (1919).

8 Hamilton v. Rathbone, 175 U.S. 414, 20 Sup. Ct. 155, 44 L. Ed. 219 (1899); State v. Lewis, 142 N.C. 626, 55 S.E. 600 (1906); 25 R.C.L., Statutes §§280, 289 (1919).

9 Freese v. Tripp, 70 Ill. 496 (1873); Black, Construction and Interpretation of Laws §176 (2d ed. 1911); 59 C.J., Statutes §§614, 627 (1932); 25 R.C.L., Statutes §294 (1919).

10 Bowers v. Smith, Ill Mo. 45, 20 S.W. 101 (1892); Black, Construction and Interpretation of Laws §176 (2d ed. 1911); Sutherland, Statutory Construction §404 (2d ed. 1904); 59 C.J., Statutes §628 (1932).

11 Burnside v. Wand, 170 Mo. 531, 71 S.W. 337 (1902).

12 State v. Campbell, 73 Kan. 688, 85 Pac. 784 (1906).

13 Milner v. Gibson, 249 Ky. 594, 61 S.W.2d 273 (1933); Black, Construction and Interpretation of Laws §104 (2d ed. 1911); Sutherland, Statutory Construction §§443-48 (2d ed. 1904); 25 R.C.L., Statutes §285 (1919).

14 Wheelock v. Myers, 64 Kan. 47, 67 Pac. 632 (1902); Black, Construction and Interpretation of Laws §104 (2d ed. 1911); Sutherland, Statutory Construction §449 (2d ed. 1904); 59 C.J., Statutes §620 (1932).

15 Keeley v. Great Northern Ry., 139 Wis. 448, 121 N.W. 167 (1909); Black, Construction and Interpretation of Laws §119 (2d ed. 1911).

16 Falls v. Key, 278 S.W. 893 (Tex. Civ. App. 1925); Black, Construction and Interpretation of Laws §120 (2d ed. 1911).

17 Federoff v. Birks Bros., 75 Cal. App. 345, 242 Pac. 885 (1925); Sutherland, Statutory Construction §358 (2d ed. 1904); 59 C.J., Statutes §570 (1932).

18 Coulter v. Pool, 187 Cal. 181, 201 Pac. 120 (1921); 59 C.J., Statutes §570 (1932).

19 Smith v. State, 28 Ind. 321 (1867); Black, Construction and Interpretation of Laws §89 (2d ed. 1911); 59 C.J., Statutes §567 (1932).

20 In re Bissell, 245 App. Div. 395, 282 N.Y. Supp. 983 (4th Dep't 1935); Black, Construction and Interpretation of Laws §89 (2d ed. 1911); 59 C.J., Statutes §566 (1932).

21 Los Angeles County v. Payne, 82 Cal. App. 210, 255 Pac. 281 (1927); Sutherland, Statutory Construction §360 (2d ed. 1904); 59 C.J., Statutes §567 (1932).

22 State ex rel. Triay v. Burr, 79 Fla. 290, 84 So. 61 (1920); Sutherland, Statutory Construction §360 (2d ed. 1904); 59 C.J., Statutes §567 (1932).

23 Westbrook v. McDonald, 184 Ark. 740, 44 S.W.2d 331 (1931); Huntworth v. Tanner, 87 Wash. 670, 152 Pac. 523 (1915); Black, Construction and Interpretation of Laws §§83-85 (2d ed. 1911); Sutherland, Statutory Construction §§339-42 (2d ed. 1904); 59 C.J., Statutes §599 (1932); 25 R.C.L., Statutes §§266-267 (1919).

24 Brown v. Robinson, 275 Mass. 55, 175 N.E. 269 (1931); Gulley v. Jackson, 165 Miss. 103, 145 So. 905 (1933); Black, Construction and Interpretation of Laws §§83-85 (2d ed. 1911); Sutherland, Statutory Construction §§339-42 (2d ed. 1904); 59 C.J., Statutes §§598-99 (1932); 25 R.C.L., Statutes §§266, 267 (1919).

25 Newhall v. Sanger, 92 U.S. 761, 23 L. Ed. 769 (1875); Black, Construction and Interpretation of Laws §51 (2d ed. 1911); 59 C.J., Statutes §569 (1932); 25 R.C.L., Statutes §§213, 225 (1919).

26 Clark v. Murray, 141 Kan. 533, 41 P.2d 1042 (1935); Sutherland, Statutory Construction §363 (2d ed. 1904); 59 C.J., Statutes §573 (1932); 25 R.C.L., Statutes §§214, 257 (1919).

27 Scholze v. Scholze, 2 Tenn. App. 80 (M.S. 1925); Black, Construction and Interpretation of Laws §65 (2d ed. 1911); Sutherland, Statutory Construction §363 (2d ed. 1904).

28 Dixon v. Robbins, 246 N.Y. 169, 158 N.E. 63 (1927); Black, Construction and Interpretation of Laws §65 (2d ed. 1911); Sutherland, Statutory Construction §363 (2d ed. 1904).

29 Eau Claire National Bank v. Benson, 106 Wis. 624, 82 N.W. 604 (1900); Black, Construction and Interpretation of Laws §93 (2d ed. 1911).

30 State ex rel. Bashford v. Frear, 138 Wis. 536, 120 N.W. 216 (1909); Black, Construction and Interpretation of Laws §94 (2d ed. 1911); 25 R.C.L., Statutes §274 (1919).

31 Hawley Coal Co. v. Bruce, 252 Ky. 455, 67 S.W.2d 703 (1934); Black, Construction and Interpretation of Laws §63 (2d ed. 1911); Sutherland, Statutory Construction §§390, 393 (2d ed. 1904); 59 C.J., Statutes §§577, 578 (1932).

32 Robinson v. Varnell, 16 Tex. 382 (1856); Black, Construction and Interpretation of Laws §63 (2d ed. 1911); Sutherland, Statutory Construction §395 (2d. ed. 1904); 59 C.J., Statutes §§577, 578 (1932).

33 In re Terry's Estate, 218 N.Y. 218, 112 N.E. 931 (1916); Black, Construction and Interpretation of Laws §60 (2d ed. 1911); Sutherland, Statutory Construction §380 (2d ed. 1904).

34 United States v. York, 131 Fed. 323 (C.C.S.D.N.Y. 1904); Black, Construction and Interpretation of Laws §60 (2d ed. 1911); Sutherland, Statutory Construction §384 (2d ed. 1904).

35 Spring Canyon Coal Co. v. Industrial Comm'n, 74 Utah 103, 277 Pac. 206 (1929); Black, Construction and Interpretation of Laws §53 (2d ed. 1911).

36 State v. Knowles, 90 Md. 646, 45 Atl. 877 (1900); Black, Construction and Interpretation of Laws §53 (2d ed. 1911).

37 Harris v. Commonwealth, 142 Va. 620, 128 S.E. 578 (1925); Black, Construction and Interpretation of Laws §55 (2d ed. 1911); Sutherland, Statutory Construction §408 (2d ed. 1904).

38 Fisher v. Connard, 100 Pa. 63 (1882); Black, Construction and Interpretation of Laws §55 (2d ed. 1911); Sutherland, Statutory Construction §409 (2d ed. 1904).

39 Lima v. Cemetery Ass'n, 42 Ohio St. 128 (1884); 25 R.C.L., Statutes §230 (1919).

40 Flynn v. Prudential Ins. Co., 207 N.Y. 315, 100 N.E. 794 (1913); 59 C.J., Statutes §573 (1932).

41 Detroit v. Redford Twp., 253 Mich. 453, 235 N.W. 217 (1931); Black, Construction and Interpretation of Laws §72 (2d ed. 1911); Sutherland, Statutory Construction §§491-94 (2d ed. 1904).

42 Springer v. Philippine Islands, 277 U.S. 189, 48 Sup. Ct. 480, 72 L. Ed. 845 (1928); Black, Construction and Interpretation of Laws §72 (2d ed. 1911); Sutherland, Statutory Construction §495 (2d ed. 1904).

43 De Witt v. San Francisco, 2 Cal. 289 (1852); Black, Construction and Interpretation of Laws §68 (2d ed. 1911); 59 C.J., Statutes §580 (1932).

44 People ex rel. Krause v. Harrison, 191 Ill. 257, 61 N.E. 99 (1901); Black, Construction and Interpretation of Laws §69 (1911); Sutherland, Statutory Construction §347 (2d ed. 1904).

45 Hull Hospital v. Wheeler, 216 Iowa 1394, 250 N.W. 637 (1933); Black, Construction and Interpretation of Laws §71 (2d ed. 1911); Sutherland, Statutory Construction §§422-34 (2d ed. 1904); 59 C.J., Statutes §581 (1932); 25 R.C.L., Statutes §240 (1919).

46 Texas v. United States, 292 U.S. 522, 54 Sup. Ct. 819, 78 L. Ed. 1402 (1934); Grosjean v. American Paint Works, 160 So. 449 (La. App. 1935); Black, Construction and Interpretation of Laws §71 (2d ed. 1911); Sutherland, Statutory Construction §§437-41 (2d ed. 1904); 59 C.J., Statutes §581 (1932); 25 R.C.L., Statutes §240 (1919).

47 Dunn v. Bryan, 77 Utah 604, 299 Pac. 253 (1931); Black, Construction and Interpretation of Laws §73 (2d ed. 1911); Sutherland, Statutory Construction §§420, 421 (2d ed. 1904); 59 C.J., Statutes §583 (1932).

48 Myer v. Ada County, 50 Idaho 39, 293 Pac. 322 (1930); Black, Construction and Interpretation of Laws §73 (2d ed. 1911); Sutherland, Statutory Construction §§420, 421 (2d ed. 1904); 59 C.J., Statutes §583 (1932).

49 United States v. Marshall Field & Co., 18 C.C.P.A. 228 (1930); Black, Construction and Interpretation of Laws §88 (2d ed. 1911); Sutherland, Statutory Construction §361 (2d ed. 1904); 59 C.J., Statutes §590 (1932).

50 State v. Baird, 36 Ariz. 531, 288 Pac. 1 (1930); Black, Construction and Interpretation of Laws §87 (2d ed. 1911); Sutherland, Statutory Construction §361 (2d ed. 1904); 59 C.J., Statutes §590 (1932).

51 Hines v. Mills, 187 Ark. 465, 60 S.W.2d 181 (1933); Black, Construction and Interpretation of Laws §75 (2d ed. 1911).

52 Fulghum v. Bleakley, 177 S.C. 286, 181 S.E. 30 (1935); Sutherland, Statutory Construction §397 (2d ed. 1904); 25 R.C.L., Statutes §226 (1919).

53 Koch & Dryfus v. Bridges, 45 Miss. 247 (1871); Black, Construction and Interpretation of Laws §150 (2d ed. 1911).

54 Jennings v. Suggs, 180 Ga. 141, 178 S.E. 282 (1935); Ewing v. Union Central Bank, 254 Ky. 623, 72 S.W.2d 4 (1934); Black, Construction and Interpretation of Laws §151 (2d ed. 1911); 59 C.J., Statutes §631 (1932).

55 State ex rel. Higgs v. Summers, 118 Neb. 189, 223 N.W. 957 (1929); Black, Construction and Interpretation of Laws §130 (2d ed. 1911); Sutherland, Statutory Construction §352 (2d ed. 1904); 59 C.J., Statutes §640 (1932).

56 Reuter v. San Mateo County, 220 Cal. 314, 30 P.2d 417 (1934); Black, Construction and Interpretation of Laws §130 (2d ed. 1911).

57 Montgomery v. Martin, 294 Pa. 25, 143 Atl. 505 (1928); Black, Construction and Interpretation of Laws §131 (2d ed. 1911); Sutherland, Statutory Construction §322 (2d ed. 1904).

58 Forscht v. Green, 53 Pa. 138 (1866); Black, Construction and Interpretation of Laws §131 (2d ed. 1911).

59 For divergencies as to what the "controlling" leads in Numbers 9 through 13 may mean, compare the discussions in Paulsen (ed.), Legal Institutions Today and Tomorrow (1959), especially Hart and Douglas, and more especially compare Moorehead, Planned Colloquy and Its Effect in the Interpretation of Statutes, 45 A.B.A.J. 1314 (1959).

TABLE OF CASES

[Page numbers reference the original pagination of the previous printed editions. This pagination is found embedded into the text by the use of brackets.]

INDEX

[Page numbers reference the original pagination of the previous printed editions. This pagination is found embedded into the text by the use of brackets.]

Visit us at *www.quidprobooks.com.*